Ismail Kac

The Writer and the Dictat

Ismail Kadare

The Writer and the Dictatorship 1957-1990

Peter Morgan

THE CENTRE FOR ALBANIAN STUDIES

VIA EGNATIA, TIRANA

Published in 2013 by The Centre For Albanian Studies
100 Pall Mall, London SW1Y 5NQ

In association with Via Egnetia, Tirana

Cover design by Westrow Cooper

ISBN: 978-0-9546-041-1-0

Printed and bound in the UK by Biddles, part of the MPG Books Group,
Bodmin and King's Lynn

ACKNOWLEDGEMENTS

The Centre for Albanian Studies would like to thank Noel Malcolm, Vullnet Muharremi, Sergio Bitici, Lewis Gjelaj, Fadil Maqedonci, Abdul Gula, Vjosa Muharremi and Azem Kovaqi for their financial support regarding publication of this book.

CONTENTS

TO DIMITRY MORAITIS

ACKNOWLEDGEMENTS

I am indebted to many friends, colleagues, and associates who have helped me over the past five years. This is a chance to put my thanks into words.

Ismail Kadare generously gave his time to me on various occasions in Paris and Tirana. Jean-Paul Champseix and Ilir Yzeiri have contributed greatly to my understanding of Kadare, sharing their knowledge of the great writer and his country over years of friendship.

Professor Em. Leslie Bodi and Marian Bodi have provided decades of wise insight into the workings of socialism and into European literature and history. Dr Kati Tonkin, a valued colleague, read and commented on various draft chapters. The copy-editor, Nigel Hope, made many helpful suggestions. Mr Dimitry Moraitis edited and proofread the manuscript.

In Albania, many have helped me either directly or indirectly in amassing a large amount of information. First, I am indebted to those friends and colleagues of Kadare whom I met and interviewed at the beginning of my researches in 2004: Altin Raxhimi, Piro Misha, Remzi Lani, Fatos Lubonja, Artan Puto, Stefan Çapaliku, and Aurel Plasari. Lisena Gjebrea adopted me on the plane to Tirana and provided a great deal of help in a new environment as well as valuable advice regarding Albanian usage. Mr Piro Misha in Tirana provided help in checking historical and biographical details regarding Kadare's life and work.

In France, I have been helped by the organizers of the June 2008 'Colloque Kadaré' in Paris, in particular Véronique Gély, Arianne Eissen, and Jean-Paul Champseix. The assistance of Mr Daniel Henrot-Dias in preparing photographs for publication, and Ms Dominique Fusco of Fayard publishers for helpful advice regarding access and copyright.

In the UK, I thank Dr Anne White, Professor Tim Unwin, Dr Kay Chadwick, Professor Lyndal Roper and Professor Nick Stargardt for valuable discussions.

In the United States, Professors David Clark and Daniel Simon, editors of *World Literature Today*, and Professors Ernst Fischer, John Cox, and David Bellos helped with information at various points. The indefatigable Robert Elsie's translations and studies of Albanian literature and culture have been invaluable to researchers throughout the world. Dr Elsie's assistance on matters of Albanian usage and culture is acknowledged with thanks.

In Australia, Mr Eric Lloga provided advice about Albania; my UWA colleagues, Professors Srilata Ravi, Andrew Hunwick, and Hélène Jaccomard helped with French translations, and Dr Mark Edele with Russian. Dr Trevor and Mrs Vi ApSimon offered their country house as a writing retreat for a wonderfully productive month. Lastly, my thanks go to Dr Graham Nelson, Managing Editor of Legenda, for his interest in Kadare and support of this publication.

Needless to say, responsibility for any faults or mistakes lies with me.

The project was supported very generously by the Camargo Foundation. Thanks to the Foundation and its director, Dr Michael Pretina, and to my colleagues in Cassis in 2004, above all Professor Pamela Genova, for hours of fascinating inter-disciplinary discussions.

Research support from the Alexander von Humboldt Foundation of the Federal Republic of Germany, from the Australian Research Council, and from the University of Western Australia is gratefully acknowledged.

Part of Chapter 4 appeared in different form in my 'Between Albanian Identity and Imperial Politics: Ismail Kadare's *The Palace of Dreams*', *The Modern Language Review*, 97 (2002), 365–79; 'Ancient Names . . . Marked by Fate: Ethnicity and the "Man without Qualities" in Ismail Kadare's *Palace of Dreams*', *The European Legacy*, 7 (2002), 45–60; and 'Ismail Kadare's *The Shadow*: Literature, Dissidence and Albanian Identity', *East European Politics and Society*, 22 (2008), 402–24. I thank the editors of these journals for permission to republish this material.

P. M., September 2009

NOTE ON TITLES AND PLACE NAMES

Owing to the particular nature of publishing under the Albanian regime, Kadare's works appeared in various versions and translations, over which the author did not have complete control. Kadare also often revised his work for republication and the *Œuvres* edition contains many changes, additions, and deletions. Since I am working with the texts in their historical context, I have matched the edition cited as closely as possible to its time of production. All quotations have been compared to the *Œuvres* text (Ismail Kadaré, *Œuvres*, ed. Eric Faye, 12 vols; Paris: Fayard, 1993–2004) and notes have been made in cases where there are significant variations. In order to avoid confusion, given that many works appeared under different titles, I provide a listing of the main works in the table overleaf. References to editions and translations will be made in endnotes. Titles are translated in the text and page numbers are given in brackets after quotations, with an abbreviated title where necessary. Translations from Kadare's works are my own unless a published English translation exists, as indicated in the endnotes. I have noted amendments in those cases where I have felt it necessary to improve the published translations.

Note on Albanian place names: Albanian nouns, including proper nouns have both a definite and an indefinite form. The indefinite form makes use of the 'ë' (Gjirokastër, Vlorë) which will be unfamiliar to most English readers. I have chosen to use the definite form in English (Gjirokastra, Vlora) throughout the text. I have retained the form 'Kosovo' rather than the more accurate 'Kosova' in deference to English and international usage.

Autobiographical Works, Interviews, Documentations

French Title	Modified/Alternative Title
Dialogue avec Alain Bosquet	—
Entretiens avec Eric Faye en lisant en écrivant	—
Invitation à l'atelier de l'écrivain	—
Le Poids de la Croix	—
Printemps albanais: Chronique, lettres, réflexions	—
La Disparition des 'Pachas rouges' d'Ismail Kadaré (Maks Velo)	—
La Vérité des souterrains	—
Le Dossier Kadare (Shaban Sinani)	—

Fictional and other work

French Title	Modified/Alternative Title
A quoi pensent ces hautes montagnes?	—
A minuit le Bureau Politique s'est réuni	Les pashas rouges
Avril brisé	—
Chronique de la ville de pierre	—
Concert en fin de saison	Le Sang froid, Le Concert, Concert à la fin de l'hiver
Eschyle ou le grand perdant	Eschyle ou l'éternel perdant
Froides fleurs d'avril	—
Jours de beuverie	—
L'Année noire	—
L'Hiver de la grande solitude	Le grand hiver (2nd version)
L'Ombre	—
La Niche de la honte	—
La Peau de tambour	La noce, La noce étrange
La Pyramide	—
La Vie, jeu et mort de Lul Mazrek	—
La Ville sans enseignes	Le Tour des cafés (excerpts)
Le Cortège de la noce s'est figé dans la glace	—
Le Crépuscule des dieux de la steppe	—
Le Dossier H.	—
Le Général de l'armée morte	—
Le Monstre	—
Le Palais des rêves	—
Le Pont aux troix arches	—
Le Successeur	—
Les Tambours de la pluie	—
Mauvaise saison sur l'Olympe	—
Novembre d'une capitale	—
Qui a ramené Doruntine?	—

Autobiographical Works, Interviews, Documentations

English Publication Title	Literal Translation of Title
—	Conversations with Alain Bosquet
—	Interview with Eric Faye
—	Invitation to the Writer's Studio
—	The Weight of the Cross
Albanian Spring: Anatomy of Tyranny	Albanian Spring: Chronicle, Letters, Reflections
—	The Disappearance of the 'Red Pashas' of Ismail Kadare
—	The Truth of the Tunnels
—	The File on Kadare

Fictional and other work

English Publication Title	Literal Translation of Title
What are these mountains thinking about?	What are these high mountains thinking about?
The Red Pashas	At midnight the Politburo met ...
Broken April	—
Chronicle in Stone	Chronicle of the Town of Stone
The Concert	Cold Blood, The Concert at the end of the Season / Winter
—	Aeschylus or the Great Loser
Spring Flowers, Spring Frost	Cold Flowers of April
—	Days of Drink
—	The Black Year
—	Winter of Great Solitude, The Great Winter
—	The Shadow
—	The Niche of Shame
—	The Wedding, The Strange Wedding, The Drum-Skin
—	The Pyramid
—	The Life, Game and Death of Lul Mazrek
—	The City without Signs
—	The Wedding Procession Turned to Ice
—	The Twilight of the Steppe-Gods
The File on H.	—
The General of the Dead Army	—
—	The Monster
The Palace of Dreams	The Employee / Official of the Palace of Dreams
The Three-Arched Bridge	The Bridge with Three Arches
The Successor	—
The Castle, The Siege	The Castle, The Siege, The Drumming of the Rain (French)
—	Bad Season on Olympus
—	November of a Capital
Doruntine	Who Brought Doruntine back?

FOREWORD

In some quarters nostalgia has been felt, in the aftermath of post-communism, for Cold War stability and for the moments of private happiness in the 'niche societies' of post-war Eastern Europe. In retrospect, the surveillance, fear, bitterness, and misery of life in the socialist dictatorships can fade from memory. Ismail Kadare does not allow us to forget so easily. His works preserve the memory of the bizarre life-world of tiny Stalinist Albania. Perhaps that very absurdity — the sense of nightmare in a doll's house — makes these works a fitting final statement for the century whose literary beginnings were marked by the terror to which Kafka gave his name. For those coming after, Brecht's *Nachgeborene*, the question arises of the value of these works written under a defunct ideology. Are they obsolete as literature, and of historical interest only in so far as they reflect life under a past regime in a closed Stalinist state on the periphery of Europe? Or do they continue to tell us something important about ourselves?

A decade ago I discovered Kadare's novel, *The Palace of Dreams*. This work reminded me that Stalinism had survived in Europe until quite recently. I recognized in Kadare a great writer, who, like many writers from small nations and little-known languages, seemed not to have achieved the recognition he deserves. A subsequent research project, begun in 2003, led to Kadare's other works, to journeys to Albania and to the writer himself in Paris and Tirana. In the course of writing this book I have come to view Kadare as a man whose experience of writing, politics, and ethnicity was exceptional even in twentieth-century socialist Europe. The context of the Albanian dictatorship, the writer's education in Moscow and early recognition of the complexities of writing in the newly formed communist society of the post-war period, and his refusal during the 1970s and 1980s to leave his country or to compromise his writing, render Kadare unique as a writer in the socialist environment.

The inaugural award of the International Man-Booker Prize for Literature in 2005 marked an important milestone in the global recognition of Kadare. In awarding the prize, Professor John Carey hailed Kadare as a guardian of Albanian identity, 'a writer who maps a whole culture [. . .] a universal writer in a tradition of storytelling that goes back to Homer'.[1] Kadare certainly brings a powerful sense of ethnic identity to his writing, introducing for the first time on the international stage the customs of his native land. However, he does not dwell on local colour for its own sake and the bardic quality of his work must be read in its contemporary context. Ethnicity exists alongside something much more modern, relevant, and unsettling to a contemporary audience. Kadare is also the last great chronicler of life under Stalinism. His novels, while determined by the history of the dictatorship, transcend the immediate history of their genesis to communicate to a wider audience.

In November 2004 I first met Ismail Kadare. I found a man preoccupied with Albania, its recent history, and his own role, and, not surprisingly, sceptical of the ability of an outsider to penetrate its secrets. I began this study with the intention of discovering the answer to the contradictions in Kadare's life and work. I have presented Kadare's journey from the young man enjoying the first fruits of communist modernization to the wily, defiant, and self-doubting writer of the end of the dictatorship. The historical and literary analyses reveal Kadare's works to represent a single-minded and coherent defiance of the dictatorship from *The City without Signs* in 1959 to *The Shadow* and *The Pyramid* at the end of the 1980s. Over the past four years I have discovered that the truth of Kadare's existence lies in the contradictions. He is the voice of Albania's modernity *and* the singer of its ancient identity. He is the alter ego *and* the nemesis of the dictator. In this ambiguity lies the key to his life, his reputation, and his works.

Note

1. Quoted from *The Guardian*, Friday, 3 June 2005, (http://www.guardian.co.uk/uk/2005/jun/03/world.books). Carey's speech was widely cited in the press and appears to have taken its cue from the early French studies by Faye and others, which focused on Kadare's use of mythological and legendary motifs. Cf. Anne-Marie Mitchell, *Ismail Kadaré: le rhapsode albanais* (Marseilles: Le temps parallèle, 1990); Eric Faye, *Ismail Kadaré: Prométhée porte-feu* (Paris: Jose Corti, 1991); Mariam M'raihi, *Ismaïl Kadaré: ou l'inspiration prométhéenne* (Paris: L'Harmattan, 2004), 56.

INTRODUCTION

Ismail Kadare has experienced a life of controversy. In his own country and internationally he has been both acclaimed as a writer and condemned as a lackey of the Albanian dictatorship.

Context is all-important to an understanding of Kadare's work. The Albanian experience differed in important ways from that of the other Eastern European socialist dictatorships.[1] Albania remained Stalinist until the death of Enver Hoxha in 1985 and arguably until the fall of the socialist regime five years later. The country was sealed off from Europe and the West, and even from world communism by 1978, after the successive breaks with Yugoslavia, Moscow, and China. Comparison with Eastern European dissidents such as Havel or Solzhenitsyn is misleading. Internal opposition or dissent was not possible in Hoxha's Albania.

It would be a mistake to represent Kadare as a silenced figure under the dictatorship. In a land where writers were routinely harassed, imprisoned, tortured, and killed, Kadare produced some of the most brilliant and subversive works to emerge from socialist Eastern Europe. His work was published selectively and he was a well-known member of the Albanian Union of Writers and the Party. He was made a Deputy of the People's Assembly, and he was able to travel abroad. He managed to avoid prison, the labour camps, or the other forms of punishment meted out to those who stepped out of line.[2] There were indeed privileges. But it is important to understand that Kadare was not at liberty to reject travel opportunities or refuse to join government bodies. And the privileges he did enjoy came with a price. Like every other aspect of his life in Albania his works were subjected to control from above. Kadare also suffered tremendously from the strain, the threats, and the terror arising from the dictator's unpredictable moves. Hoxha retained a level of respect for France and he was wily enough to protect Kadare as a valuable figure to display in the international arena. However, Kadare did not give his imprimatur to the regime in this role as ambassador.[3] On the contrary, he used whatever opportunities arose to disseminate the literary works which spoke so eloquently of his country's plight. His literary record remains impeccable. In order to survive he had to acquiesce to the regime and use his privileges to further the cause of his writing.

Kadare is the only Albanian writer known widely outside his country. As the voice of an alternative, better Albania, he offered his countrymen one of their few sources of hope for change. He was committed to Albanian language, culture, and national identity, he believed in European humanist ideals and was attracted, to begin with, by the communist model of modernization in his socially and economically backward land. At the same time he built an influential base in

France, his chosen intellectual home in the West. Deeply aware of the need of Albanians to participate in European modernity, he nevertheless came to object profoundly to the ideal of the Albanian 'new man' propagated by the regime, and his works represent powerfully the positive force of ethnic identification.

As the memory of the Eastern European dictatorships fades, we must try to recreate in our minds the specific environments of the dissenting voice. Kadare voiced his opposition through literature, not doctrine or ideology. He expressed defiance through his representation of the grimness of everyday life under socialism and through his powerful evocations of an Albania more ancient and more durable than the new Albania of Enver Hoxha. He steadfastly refused to surrender his language and identity or to be forced into exile. But he paid dearly for this refusal. As a writer working in this Stalinist environment, Kadare represents the endpoint of a history of twentieth-century European socialist literature.

The aim of this study is to bring Kadare's works to a wider audience by explaining how he lived and wrote in the Albanian Stalinist environment, and by charting his development as the voice of an Albania suppressed in the course of socialist modernization. Chapter 1 provides an introduction to aspects of Albanian history and culture, material which is little known outside the country, and which is important to understanding Kadare's writing. The following chapters present Kadare's work in the context of Albanian socialism. Reference is made to the autobiographical works of the 1990s, in particular *The Weight of the Cross*, in order to provide a detailed reading of the socio-political and intellectual context in which Kadare wrote, and which determined the nuances of his Aesopian language.[4] Literary analyses are made of a range of Kadare's works written under the socialist regime, in order to demonstrate the depth, complexity, and value of the individual works for an international audience.

One of the criticisms of Kadare is that he wrote to accommodate the mercurial policy changes of the regime. The present study aims to show that this was not the case. Kadare's writing over the forty-five years of the dictatorship was extraordinarily coherent in terms of its themes and its focus on aspects of Albanian life. Emphasis is laid on tracing the thematic development of Kadare's works over the period of the dictatorship, with the intention of justifying his claim to have 'told the truth to power' consistently over the decades of his writing life. The focus is on the period from 1959 until 1985, the years of power of Kadare's nemesis, the dictator Enver Hoxha.

This focus on the writer and the dictatorship has determined the choice of works for study. Many of the short stories, some of which are masterpieces in themselves, and some of which rehearse themes which re-emerge in later full-length works, and the works from the post-communist period, fall outside the range of analysis. The works primarily dealing with, or owing their genesis to, the events in Kosovo and dealing with Kosovar identity (such as *The Marriage Procession Turned to Ice*, *The File on H.*, and the *Three Elegies for Kosovo*), with the exception of *The Palace of Dreams*, have been excluded as beyond the scope of the present study. A large body of novels, essays, stories, and other works remains, from which I have selected those exemplifying characteristic and significant aspects of the writer's genius.

Some, such as *The Concert*, while well known, are not covered in detail. Other, early and less well-known works, such as *The City without Signs* or *The Monster*, are given considerable attention since they introduce themes which will be developed over the following three decades. *The General of the Dead Army*, and the semi-autobiographical novels, *Chronicle in Stone* and *The Twilight of the Steppe-Gods*, represent important stages in the writer's understanding of self, culture, and society, leading through the historical allegories of the late 1970s such as *The Three-Arched Bridge* to Kadare's masterpiece, *The Palace of Dreams*. *The Shadow* represents one of Kadare's most soul-searching and private analyses of the writer himself. In the essay, *Aeschylus or the Great Loser*, Kadare brings together the themes of a lifetime of writing into a study of literature, history, and the nation.

Kadare's works were published in the communist environment in various forms and formats; different works were drafted as short stories, censored, revised, confiscated, reworked, and passed through the filters of comment, feedback, and revision, and were both translated and published inside and outside Albania. Transmission was by no means assured. The controversy over the poem 'The Red Pashas' reveals the extent to which texts were vulnerable in an environment of secrecy, seizure, and confiscation. In a country where photocopies and indeed all forms of mechanical reproduction were guarded, Kadare could not always keep copies of his works. He claimed that the manuscripts of 'The Red Pashas' had disappeared. Others asked whether it had ever existed. It was discovered in the vaults of the National Archive of Albania by the (ex-)director Shaban Sinani in 2002.[5] Other works, such as the novel *The Shadow*, were smuggled out of the country for safety.[6] Moreover, Kadare has retained the artistic right to revise and change his texts, refusing to allow them to be determined by the category of the political alone. Some of his works have been altered for publication in the post-communist environment in accordance with the author's desire for artistic control. Some have been returned to their original forms now that the controls of state censorship are no longer relevant.

Given the nature of the regime and the complexity of the assessment and publication process, the progress of works towards publication could take months or years and could involve substantial revisions. While Kadare offers a detailed, coherent, and convincing chronology of his writing in his interviews and in *Invitation to the Writer's Studio* and *The Weight of the Cross*, it is sometimes difficult to identify exactly when he was working on any given manuscript, especially during the period from the mid-1960s until the late 1970s. Much remains to be done by way of detailed documentation of the development, revision, and finalization of his works and of their relationship to immediate political events.

Kadare's work is known outside Albania primarily through its French, and more recently, its German and English translations. Relatively few writers enjoy a world readership versed in their native tongue. Even great figures such as Sophocles, Dante, Shakespeare, and Dostoevsky are read primarily in translation throughout the world. Less well-known writers, or those from minor languages, are more or less dependent on translations for access to a global audience. Hesse, Pasternak, Andrić, Kazantzakis, Mishima, and more recently Gao Xinjian, Kiš, Grass, Kundera, and Nádas, to name a few, have reached a world readership through translation. In an era of increasing dominance of English as the language of global communication and in Anglo-American environments in which the study of foreign languages is decreasing, translations have become crucial in bringing the voices of small cultural and linguistic groups to the world. Over the past five years translation has returned to the focus of comparative literary studies in recognition of its new importance in current global environments.[7] As an Albanian writer, it is hardly surprising that Ismail Kadare was conscious of the question of language. He knew that non-Albanian readers would come to his work via translation and has taken an active role in working with his French translators.

Albanians have become a presence in European consciousness since 1990, yet little is known about Albania, its people, and its past. Kadare continues to write, to speak as a witness of socialist dictatorship, and to represent his country at home, in Europe, and the world. He is regularly anthologized in his nation's educational texts and is generally recognized to be a master stylist in his native tongue. Kadare's novels bring the battle between the writer and the dictator, of freedom and oppression, to readers beyond the borders of Albania and Eastern Europe and across the decades which separate us from the era of Eastern European socialism. These works, which document the past, will help those coming after to safeguard the future.

Notes to the Introduction

1. Following János Kornai, I have adopted the term 'socialism' rather than 'communism' for the Eastern European post-war regimes, since this was the term they used themselves, in distinction to communism which in Marxism-Leninism refers to the achievement of a system in which 'all will share in social production according to their needs'. János Kornai, *The Socialist System: The Political Economy of Communism* (Princeton: Princeton University Press, 1992), p. 10.

2. Cf. Maks Velo, *La Disparition des 'Pachas rouges' d'Ismail Kadaré: Enquête sur un 'crime littéraire'*, trans. by Tedi Papavrami (Paris: Fayard, 2004), pp. 7–9 and passim; Visa Zhiti, 'Le Livre et la dictature', Preface to *Le Dossier Kadaré suivi de La Vérité des souterrains*, ed. by Shaban Sinani, trans. by Tedi Papavrami (Paris: Odile Jacob, 2006), p. 12.

3. 'À l'époque, j'ai accordé des dizaines de ces interviews, ici, en Occident; s'il vous était donné de les relire aujourd'hui, vous constateriez que, malgré ma situation, jamais je n'ai eu un mot d'approbation ou d'éloge pour le régime albanais. Jamais je n'ai raconté que, là-bas, vivait un peuple heureux, que régnait là-bas la liberté, que c'était un pays sans prisons ni détenus politiques.' 'During that era I gave dozens of interviews, here in the West; if you were to read them today, you would see for yourself that in spite of my situation, I never gave a word of approbation or of praise to the Albanian regime. I never said that people were happy there, that liberty reigned there, or that it was a country without prisons or political detainees.' Ismail Kadaré, *Dialogue avec Alain Bosquet*, trans. by Jusuf Vrioni (Paris: Fayard, 1995), p. 212.

4. Ismail Kadaré, *Le Poids de la croix*, in *Invitation à l'atelier de l'écrivain suivi de Le Poids de la croix*, trans. by Jusuf Vrioni (Paris: Fayard, 1991), pp. 279–558. The term 'Aesopian language' is used broadly for the language of indirect defiance or dissent in absolutist, authoritarian, or dictatorial environments, particularly in the context of Eastern European socialism. The term was introduced in Russia in the 1860s for forms of literary communication which deliberately evaded censorship. Cf. Lev Loseff, *On the Beneficence of Censorship: Aesopian Language in Modern Russian Literature*, Arbeiten und Texte zur Slavistik, (Schuylkill Haven, PA: Hermitage, 1985), pp. x, 1–2 and *passim*.

5. Velo, p. 201.

6. Kadaré/Bosquet, p.162.

7. Cf. Susan Bassnett, *Translation Studies* (London: Routledge, 2002); Emily Apter, *The Translation Zone: A New Comparative Literature* (Princeton: Princeton University Press, 2006); David Damrosch, 'Comparative Literature?', *PMLA*, 118 (2003), 326–30.

CHAPTER 1

Kadare's Albania

Albanian History, Culture, and Religion

Until the end of the nineteenth century the Albanian lands were provinces of the Ottoman Empire, cut off from the European Renaissance and Enlightenment, on the periphery of both the Western and the Eastern Christian churches. Albania lay largely outside the sphere of European consciousness from the late Middle Ages until the nineteenth century. If at all, it occupied the European imagination as a place of adventure, romance, and exoticism. Given that many readers of Kadare's novels and stories will have little more than a passing knowledge of Albanian history and culture, some background to and contextualization of his work is called for.

On the basis of archaeological finds and historical studies, Kadare posits an Illyrian–Albanian culture reaching back to a common Graeco-Illyrian pre-history of the Balkan peninsula before the Slav migrations. Informed debate on the origins of Balkan history is still skewed by ethnic and political biases and specialist historians and archaeologists are far from united. However, some consensus is identifiable regarding a 'common Illyrian language and culture' which can be traced back to the seventh century BC.[1] On the basis of the archaeological remnants of classical civilization in places such as Butrint and along the Adriatic coast of Albania, and through comparative study of themes identified in the Albanian epic songs, Kadare envisions a joint Greek and Illyrian civilization in the Balkans as a shared cultural environment which, at the point of emergence from pre-historical matriarchal clan-based societies to historical patriarchal early state formations, began to split and follow separate paths. In this early period Kadare imagines the relationship as a neighbouring and shared one. However, Greece in the fifth century BC experienced a cultural florescence that became the basis of European civilization. Illyria, by contrast, suffered as the Roman and then Byzantine and Ottoman empires relegated it to the badlands, situated between East and West, on what became the fault-line between Europe and Asia, one of the major fault-lines of global civilization over the following millennia.

Mountainous, especially in the north, Albania has few of the navigable rivers which facilitated communication in Western and Eastern Europe, and relatively small plains for agriculture. Its demographics have always been determined by its geography. The population is made up of two main ethno-linguistic groups, the southern Tosks who, until the mid twentieth century were primarily Muslim and Orthodox, and the northern Ghegs who were mainly Muslim and Catholic and who also extend into Kosovo. The Skumbi river valley is the main dividing line between the two linguistic groups. The northern mountain people preserved their clan identities and structures throughout the Ottoman period and were compared by early British travellers, such as Lord Byron, to the Scots Highlanders.[2] Ethnic Greek minorities existed in the south and Macedonians in the east.[3] Under the Gjirokastran Enver Hoxha, the southern Tosks became more powerful, and their dialect became the basis for the modern standard Albanian, which was a creation of the communist dictatorship.[4] Before that, bilingualism was common at the boundaries, in particular the south, where Greek and Albanian were spoken. In other areas to the north and east, spoken Albanian existed alongside more or less passive knowledge of Slav languages and dialects.

Albanian is a little-known language on the world stage. Indo-European, but occupying a place to itself with no close linguistic neighbours, it is considered the descendant of ancient Illyrian.[5] It is not a Slavic language and evidently pre-dates the Slav migrations into the Balkan peninsula which took place from the sixth century AD; neither is it related to Greek, its immediate and equally ancient neighbour. While many languages and empires have come and gone through Albania, the language has remained intact and early became the primary identity marker of Albanian ethnicity in the absence of state identity or religious unity.[6]

> In the belief of some etymologists the name Albania is related to the old Celtic form Alb or Alp, which means mountain. [. . .] The Albanians, however, do not call themselves by this name. They designate themselves as Skipetars or rockmen, and apply this appellation indiscriminately to all the inhabitants of Upper and Lower Albania who do not use Greek, Serbian or Rumanian as a vernacular.[7]

The language was written in Roman, Cyrillic, and Arabic scripts until well into the nineteenth century. According to Edith M. Durham, who travelled extensively in Albania at the beginning of the twentieth century, a uniform method of writing had yet to be developed:

> There is a tradition of an old Albanian alphabet both at Elbasan and at Skodra, but no successful attempt to find an alphabet in which the language could be printed was made till 1879. A special alphabet was then arbitrarily constructed, a sadly mongrel affair compounded of Greek, Latin, and Cyrillic characters and some specially invented letters. With modifications it is still used by the press at Sofia, which publishes the *Drita*, a paper in the Tosk dialect, and various books; also by the British and Foreign Bible Society for the translation of the Gospels. But it is hopelessly unpractical and very expensive, requiring special type and typesetter, and will soon be superseded. Many attempts have been made to use the Latin alphabet, and the extremely practical system invented by Mgr. Premi Dochi, the Abbot of the Mirdites, has overcome most of the difficulties, and, owing to its great simplicity, is making rapid way.[8]

From early times educated Albanians spoke various imperial and world languages in order to communicate with the rest of the world. Latin and Greek, Italian, Turkish, and Russian reflected the vicinity and the power of their neighbours and imperial masters. Turkish was an important administrative and bureaucratic language during the Ottoman period, and Russian the first foreign language of the intelligentsia in the immediate post-war era.

The early inhabitants of Illyria and Epirus participated in 'that ancient civilization which is wholly attributed to the Greeks of the classical epoch', and were even influential in the development of Greek culture.[9] After the third century BC Latin civilization superseded Greek influence. Situated between Rome and Constantinople, the provinces of Illyricum and Epirus were an important part of the Roman Empire, especially along the Adriatic coastline.[10] However Albania did not become a geo-political identity under the Romans. While the Via Egnatia passed from Rome to Dyrrachium and Apollonia and then crossed Illyricum to north of Lake Ochrid into Macedonia, mountainous northeast Albania remained untouched by Roman imperialism.[11] During the Roman period Christianity was introduced, and after the fall of Rome, in AD 395 the Albanian lands were subsumed into the Byzantine Empire, divided between the provinces of Dyrrachium (Durazzo) and Nicopolis. As at the end of the Greek period, this part of the Balkan peninsula remained in tumult for centuries after the end of the Roman Empire as various groups including the Goths in the sixth century, the Bulgarians in the tenth century, and the Normans in the twelfth century, occupied parts of the country. During the period of the Slav migrations into the Balkan peninsula, as various greater and lesser kingdoms were formed among the Serbs and the Bulgarians, the Albanians remained a people of clans and networks with few towns or proto-national networks. In the south, feudal structures took greater form than in the north where a pre-feudal clan structure predominated.

In the years following the Battle of Kosovo (1389) powerful feudal clans especially in the south capitulated to the Turkish forces and many became more or less assimilated into the Ottoman ruling classes over the following centuries. The Ottoman sultans Mehmed II, Bayezid II, and Süleyman I were responsible for the creation of the 'European core provinces of the Ottoman Empire', finishing off the process begun by Bayezid I and Mehmed I of inclusion of the European lands as Ottoman provinces rather than as vassal or allied states.[12] Under the Ottomans Albania was split into *vilayets*, *pashaliks*, and other imperial administrative units, and the ruling class was inducted into the Ottoman administrative structure.

The country experienced a brief moment of national liberation under Scanderbeg in the mid-fifteenth century and enjoyed a short period of protection by the Venetians and of connection with the West. As the son of a vassal chieftain, George Kastriote (Scanderbeg) proved himself in the Ottoman army and was sent as governor of the Albanian region of Dibra in 1436. He used the opportunity of the conflict between the sultan and the Hungarian leader John Hunyadi in 1443 to start an Albanian uprising and establish the League of Lezha (Alessio) in 1444, laying the basis for an Albanian state. In 1460 Scanderbeg signed an armistice with Mehmed II. After Scanderbeg's death in January 1468, the nascent Albanian state continued until 1479 when it was fully subjected to Ottoman rule.[13] While the memory of Scanderbeg as a national hero was maintained throughout the intervening centuries by the Italo-Albanians of Calabria and Sicily who had emigrated after his death, he re-emerged in the late nineteenth century in Albania as a national figure possessing 'the attributes which satisfied the religiously divided people of Albania', and representing 'a glorious past', of united Albanians.[14]

The mixed Greek–Albanian area of Chameria (Albania) or Northern Epirus (Greece) developed on the basis of the trading links among the towns of Janina, Berat, Gjirokastra, and Prevesa. This area became the core of the semi-autonomous state created in the late eighteenth century by Ali Pasha. The Greeks in this area were more clearly divided from those of the east by the Pindaric ranges than they were from their neighbouring Albanians. Likewise the Albanians of the north-east were separated from their ethnic brethren in Kosovo by the Accursed Mountains, while those in Kosovo itself lived side by side with the Serbs for centuries.

Unlike the Greeks, Croatians, Montenegrins, Serbs, and Macedonians, the Albanians converted in large numbers to Islam during the Ottoman period.[15] The Islamization of the Catholic north and the Orthodox south took place over centuries, beginning with the Turkish conquests in the fifteenth century. The process was slow and uneven. In the north, geography precluded the breaking up of the pastoral clans, and inaccessible parts, such as in the Mirdita, were never penetrated by the Ottomans and hence remained Catholic. In the south a socio-economic model developed in which a small number of landowning Muslim beys held power over a largely Christian Orthodox peasantry. Some clans and tribes retained their Christian beliefs, particularly the Catholics of the Mirdita in the north. Hall quotes Stavro Skendi's 1967 study, *The Albanian National Awakening*, to the effect that by 1610 there were still ten Roman Catholics for every Muslim in Gheg lands. Conversion increased during the seventeenth and eighteenth centuries as a result of financial and employment advantages for Muslims. Orthodoxy remained the majority religion in the south until the time of the Russo-Turkish war in 1768 when it was considered an indication of allegiance to the Russians and forced conversions took place.[16]

During the early period of relative religious tolerance, the Albanian language was suppressed, indicating that language represented a greater threat to unity than religion, which was not generally doctrinaire, dogmatic, or charged with proto-national significance. Even before the Ottoman occupation, Catholicism and Orthodoxy were flexibly adhered to. In the late Middle Ages, when the country was the battlefield between the Catholic West and the Orthodox East, the Albanian feudal lords — often followed by their populations — espoused Catholicism when the West was in the ascendant. Whenever Byzantium was predominant, they embraced Orthodoxy. 'They lived, one might say, a religiously amphibious life'.[17]

While the Ottomans introduced Sunni orthodoxy, particularly in central and eastern Albania,[18] the more popular form of Islam was a moderate Bektashism and a Sufi-like mysticism. The attraction of Bektashi Sufism lay in its syncretic nature in these areas of mixed religions on the borderlines between Europe and Asia. It provided a point of transition between ancient folk beliefs, the increasingly problematic Christian heritage on the fault-line between East and West, and the Muslim faith of the conquerors. Bektashism is believed to have originated in the Anatolian frontier regions in the thirteenth century where Islam, Christianity, and pantheism mixed, and is thought to have been introduced into Albania in the fifteenth century by the Janissaries.[19] Pagan rites of fertility and other folk beliefs basic to primitive rural life had remained beneath the acceptance of Christianity from the earliest times and they similarly permeated Balkan Islam.[20] The Bektashi dervish orders, which were responsible for conversions in Albania in the later sixteenth century, established their *tekkes* or monastic houses and communities and their code or *tarikat*, building on a tradition of Sufism that stressed the 'independent search for the right life'.[21] The *babas*, or wandering holy men, and one or two subordinate dervishes operated as small wandering cells and were instrumental in creating the syncretism of Christianity, Islam, and folk beliefs which came to characterize Albanian religion, particularly Islam. The result was a variety of European, or rather Balkan, 'folk-Islam', which included icons, baptism, and many other non-Muslim features. 'It was not difficult for Christians whose faith was of the superstitious folk variety to pass over to a similar but more secure folk version of Islam'.[22] Compared to the rigid prescriptiveness of Ottoman Sunni faith the Bektashism of the *babas* was flexible while still identifiably Muslim. However, the relationship was fraught with conflict. While the Albanians were referred to with contempt as 'Turks' by the Slav Christians, and were included as 'Turks', meaning 'Muslims', by the Ottoman authorities, the Bektashi Islam of the Albanians was, for the Sunni Porte, a heresy, and was dealt with harshly at various points in Albanian history.[23]

Drawing on the work of Speros Vryonis, Peter Sugar cites economic and legal advantages as the main influences on the conversion of Balkan Christians to Islam, along with the influences of the *medreses* and other Muslim institutions, fear of the authorities, and folk religion. In contrast to his predecessor, however, Sugar considers the adaptability of folk religion to have been a major factor in determining the type of Islam that came about in Albania. The specialist on Balkan Sufism, H. T. Norris, suggests that Albanian Sufism in particular represented a form of resistance to Ottoman domination while remaining Islamic in name. The implications of this aspect of Albanian Islam are important as a counter to the allegations, often aired in the Balkan context, that Albanians (and Bosnians) converted to Islam primarily for non-spiritual and mercenary reasons.

While religion itself did not play a role as a core value of Albanianness, the sect of the Bektashi dervishes, according to Hall, became associated with Albanian linguistic nationalism towards the end of the Ottoman period.[24] Bektashi leaders identified strongly as Albanian nationalists on the basis of language and literary tradition and 'Bektashi groups were often instrumental in smuggling into Albania works of literature printed in Albanian outside of the country'. Norris, too, notes the subversive role of the *tekkes* in the later Ottoman period: 'The *tekkes* were not free from Ottoman interference and, on occasions, destruction, if the Sultan suspected the incumbents of working for nationalist or subversive interests'.[25] Vickers also emphasizes the role of the Bektashis from the beginning of the nineteenth century, in particular after the conversion of Ali Pasha, in opposing Sunni Ottoman power.[26] (In his earliest novel, *The City without Signs*, Kadare locates a counterfeited early Albanian manuscript in a provincial southern *tekke*, and questions of religious and national identity are raised throughout his works.) John Norton quotes Philip Ward's assessment that 'the Bektashi movement [. . .] included so many Albanian nationalists that it can fairly be described as the most representative nationalist movement in Albania'.[27] Despite publishing positive comments about Islam, the post-war communist leader, Enver Hoxha, harassed the clerics, laid waste the *tekkes*, and finally banned Albanian Islam altogether, declaring his land to be officially atheist in 1968.[28]

In addition to the various folk beliefs, the customary laws of the Kanun remained influential, especially in mountainous northern Albania, until the communist takeover. The Kanun or *Doke* dates from the medieval period and was a set of tribal customs rooted in the pre-feudal clan-based society of northern Albania. According to legend it was formulated by Lekë Dukagjin (1410–81) and disseminated as a code of conduct and constitution of laws as a means of bringing order to the feuding clans. It exists as a written traditional legal code only since 1933 when it was written down and published by a Franciscan monk, Shtjefën Gjeçovi.[29] Blood feud, the honour of the individual male and of the clan, the accepted forms of compensation and revenge, and the conditions of truce or *besa* are central to this proto-legal code. The code shows similarities with the Old Testament and 'with early Teutonic, Slav, Greek and Roman codes' and evolved over a long period, developing regional characteristics and differences.[30] The Kanun provided a 'complete moral and legal framework for social interaction, covering every area of life from dispute settlement procedure to rules for marriage, division of property, blood feud, and rights of way'. It represented a popular and reliable 'dispute settlement system' in a largely illiterate environment, and its key element was 'the inviolate nature of private property'.[31] Communist modernization put an end to this pre-feudal system of laws, although it continued as a force well into the twentieth century in parts of Albania. Clarissa de Waal, a contemporary anthropologist working in the Mirdita, refers to the contemporary relevance of the codes: that these codes are more than ancient relics is clear from one of a series of textbooks [on Civic Education] currently (2000) used in the sixth grade of Albanian eight-year schools by twelve-year old pupils. [. . .] Pupils are required to collect information on customary rights in the area where they live, as well as to collect data relating to whichever Kanun once operated in their region. In the course of teaching in the town of Rrëshen, the capital of the Mirdita, at the end of the 1990s, writes De Waal, 'many of the final year pupils in the classes [. . .] argued for continuing use of the Kanun of Lek Dukagjin'. After the establishment of democratic government in 1991, 'many Kanun procedures were reinstituted, while religious practice [. . .] remained dormant'. In contrast to religion, the Kanun was both a practical legal code and 'source of moral authority', which survived in a way that formal religion did not.[32] Kadare's 1978 novel, *Broken April*, and his late essays such as *Aeschylus or the Great Loser* explore the significance of the Kanun for Albanian identity into the twentieth century. For Kadare, too, this pre-feudal, clan-based honour system retains its power as an expression of Albanian identity in the absence of other unifying factors.

The Albanian National Uprising

The Albanian secessionist movements which took place under Scanderbeg and Ali Pasha aroused the vigilance and mistrust of the Porte, the Istanbul seat of Ottoman imperial administration. Miranda Vickers points out that while the Albanians were among the most assimilated Balkan members of the Ottoman Empire, they were, for this reason, the most savagely punished at times of crisis.[33] When war broke out with Russia in 1829, Sultan Mahmoud II moved quickly to reassert imperial power in an environment of Greek, Serb, and other Balkan insurrections. In southern Albania in 1830 a massacre of the beys, or local landowners, took place and the ongoing tightening of control by the Porte both increased conversion to Islam and paved the way for 'the tentative beginnings of an Albanian national Movement'.[34]

Despite its attempts at modernization and re-organization, the Ottoman Empire was weakening in the second half of the 19th century. War broke out again in 1875 and in 1878 the victorious Russians imposed the Treaty of San Stefano on the Ottomans, assigning Albanian-inhabited territory to (Orthodox) Serbia, Montenegro and the Bulgarian provinces, and inciting Albanian nationalism.[35]

The Ottomans were seen as having failed to protect the interests of their still subject Albanian Muslims. The redoubtable early Albanologist, Edith Durham, wrote in 1917:

> After the Russo-Turkish war of 1877, when Turkish territory was being divided among the Balkan peoples, the Albanians saw with dismay, much of their best land torn from them and given to the Greeks, Serbs and Montenegrins. They resisted fiercely, saved some of it, and formed the Albanian League.[36]

In summer 1878 a conference of Albanian nationalists was held and permanent headquarters established in Prizren. The embattled Ottoman government was willing to support this organization as long as the representatives identified as Ottomans and Muslims, rather than Albanians and ethnic nationalists regardless of religion. Power in the organization oscillated between hard-line nationalists seeking Albanian unification and autonomy and the use of Albanian language in education and government, and those willing to accept limited autonomy from central Ottoman government. The Ottomans continued to regard the Albanians as closely linked to them on the basis of religion and tradition, in comparison to the Serbs, Croats, and other Balkan Christian national and ethnic groups. In early 1881 the Porte, sensing trouble, sent in its armies to wipe out the nationalist resistance and restore centralized authority. Nevertheless, the seeds of Albanian political nationalism had been sown.[37]

While Albanians played an important role in the Young Turk coup against the Sultan in 1908, the aims of the two groups were deeply different. The Young Turks wanted to consolidate and revitalize the Ottoman state and promised measures of autonomy to the Albanians which were not honoured. Disagreements over Albanian cultural and linguistic issues were the flashpoint for a deterioration of relations, and in 1910 and 1911 armed conflicts occurred. In the context of the upheavals that would result in world war, military conflicts broke out between Balkan nations and the Ottomans, in which the Albanians fought for the Turks against their Balkan neighbours. However, with the Ottoman Empire on the verge of collapse, and with the Serbs, Greeks, and others set to carve up the Ottoman Balkans, the Albanians also claimed national sovereignty in December 1912, a move ratified by the Conference of Ambassadors of the Great Powers in London in

1913. The borders of the new Albanian state were such that much of the Albanian population was excluded; however, German Chancellor Otto von Bismarck's famous statement of 1878 that 'there is no Albanian nationality' was proven wrong with the establishment of the first modern Albanian state.[38] The Albanian separatist movement was thus partially motivated by the desire to secede from the Ottoman Empire and partly by the need to establish the national borders in the face of Greek, Serb, and Bulgarian territorial claims and annexations. Albania was not a political unity before 1913, and the borders of Albania would change by the time the state was established. Even then, the borders with Yugoslav Kosovo and Macedonia remained flashpoints for ethno-national conflicts which would re-emerge during and after the fall of the socialist dictatorships.

For the Hungarian historian István Bibò, Albania represented a particular version of the 'misère' of the Eastern European state-structures. While the purported history of the Illyrians could be used as a powerful foundational myth for the new nation, the potential formation of the Albanian state was undermined by the imperial Ottoman administration in the fourteenth century, a time of proto-national movements in the Balkans. In Albania, in the absence as yet of a stronger sense of collectivity or of other strong binding structures (such as allegiance to a dynastic figure), the Ottomans imposed an administration, but created no internal structure. The land was separated into *vilayets* or provinces of the Empire, exacerbating the north–south divisions of Gheg and Tosk, and the partial assimilation to Islam created deep-seated divisions. When the Ottomans left, the European powers entered the scene. Having no history of European colonial contact, and little understanding of, or interest in, the history and culture of the Albanians, they offered no coherent solutions. In the absence of the Ottomans and surrounded by Greek and the Slav languages, Tosks and Ghegs in Albania, Kosovo, and parts of Montenegro and Macedonia retained their sense of ethno-linguistic connection, despite the differences of dialect. Threatened by Serb and Greek inroads, especially after the excision of Kosovo, the liberation movement was determined to maintain a sense of the historical Albania. But as a result of the political urgencies of the years 1912 and 1913 (for example the Austro-Hungarian interest in denying Adriatic access to Serbia[39]), the Albanian state constituted only a truncated version of the Albanian nation, a situation which continued to fester throughout the twentieth century.[40]

In the thirty years between 1913 and the coming of the communist government in 1944, political parties did not establish deep roots. The monarchy of Wied, the German prince appointed by the Great Powers, was a short-lived affair, and the First World War plunged the fledgling country into chaos as the armies of Austria-Hungary, France, Italy, Greece, Montenegro, and Serbia moved through it. National integrity was maintained after the Paris Peace conference (a British, French, and Italian plan to partition the country was defeated) and in the early 1920s a liberal-democratic and progressive movement gained momentum, leading to the short-lived left-wing government of Fan Noli, and opposed by a powerful, if fragmented, body of conservative landowning beys and tribal heads or *bajraktars* still strongly linked to the Ottoman and feudal past. The failure of the Noli government to deliver reforms in the impoverished state led to an armed coup led by the Muslim tribal leader, Ahmed Bey Zogu, who ruled from 1925 until 1939, renaming himself King Zog I in 1928. While some modernization occurred under Zog, political openness was hardly encouraged.[41] Zog used Italian finance in order to stabilize the economy but also opened the way for the Italian fascist regime to use Albania as a bridgehead for military expansion into the Balkans. On the night of 6–7 April 1940 the Italians occupied Albania in preparation for the October 1940 attack on Greece. Zog fled first to Greece and later to Egypt and France.

During the Italian and, later, the German occupations, with the Greeks and the Serbs threatening national sovereignty on either side of the tiny state, Albania could not develop a stable, let alone democratic, political system. In 1941 the scattered communist resistance in Albania came together, assisted by Yugoslav Communist Party delegates. Enver Hoxha participated in establishing the Albanian communist party. (Contrary to communist historiography, Hoxha was not elected to head the first Central Committee, but was coordinator, in his role as secretary of Tirana and head of the Party.) By 1942 the Albanian communist party, purged of factional elements, took a leading role in the formation of a Supreme Committee for National Liberation, hosting its first national conference in 1943 with Enver Hoxha in charge of political affairs and Mehmet Shehu of military and strategic affairs.

After the fall of Mussolini in July and the Italian capitulation in September, Hoxha met with the Balli Kombëtar or National Front, to form a national accord. (The Balli Kombëtar had arrived late on the scene, and was weak, fragmented along ideological lines, factionalized, corrupt, and superannuated. It had damaging links to the monarchy and the Italians, and was supported by the Germans, who invaded Albania after the collapse of Italian fascism.[42]) The national accord was opposed by the pro-Soviet Yugoslav communists both on ideological grounds and because they had a strong interest in keeping Kosovo as part of Yugoslavia. Hoxha was forced to renege on his agreement (by the pro-Yugoslav Koçi Xoxe), leading to civil conflict between communist and non-communist partisans. But he retained his position as leader of the communists and by the time of the German withdrawal from Tirana in November 1944, Hoxha at thirty-six was commander-in-chief of the National Liberation Army and designated President and Minister of Defence and Foreign Affairs. In spring 1945 the communists took charge throughout Albania. In September 1945 the Yugoslav leader, Marshal Tito, recognized Kosovo as an 'autonomous region' within Yugoslavia. Albanian was recognized as an official language alongside Serbo-Croatian and Kosovars were allowed to open Albanian-language elementary schools. Higher schooling was conducted in Serbo-Croatian.[43]

Albanian Communism

There had been neither a labour movement nor a history of Marxism in Albania before 1945. Even during the period of the Third International, or Comintern after 1919 there was little communist influence. 'It was only when, in the thirties, Moscow abandoned all squeamishness concerning the social structure and the doctrinal basis of national communist parties that Albania became suitable ground for communist action'.[44] As a result of the communist partisan leadership's machinations and the susceptibility of the British agents in Albania during the early 1940s, the non-communist partisan groups such as the Balli Kombëtar were effectively liquidated by the time of the communist takeover. For István Bibò, communism in 1944, rather than national liberation in 1913, brought the Albanian nation, ethnicity, and state into relation with each other, for the first time, with the exception of Kosovo, but at the cost of dictatorship.)[45] In the novel *Chronicle in Stone*, Kadare shows both the destruction of traditional life in the provincial town of Gjirokastra by occupation and war, and the role of the partisans in turning the national war against the occupiers into a class war in which the communists would be victorious.[46]

Kenneth Jowitt identifies three stages in the revolutionary seizure and consolidation of power. The first, 'transformation', is identified with the Leninist period and is the opening stage in which 'the new revolutionary party wrests political and military control from a pre-existing regime in order to transform the old society'.[47] The Albanian communists did not face the Leninist challenge of revolutionary 'breaking through' to eliminate established structures, since the Italian occupation ended the monarchy and the Second World War destroyed what little pre-existing order remained.[48] After their victorious emergence in the major towns from 1944 onwards, the communist partisans faced Jowitt's second, Stalinist, phase of 'consolidation', in which 'the new revolutionary regime seeks to insulate itself from the political, economic, and cultural threats of a society that still cannot be trusted'.[49]

By the end of the war the European powers had no established plans to impose on Albania. After the failure of their undercover operations to establish a non-communist political organization (due partly to the activities of communist agents), and in the absence of a Soviet military presence, Enver Hoxha's well-organized 'Provisional Democratic Government' took power unopposed in November 1944.[50] Collaborators with the Balli Kombëtar took to the mountains or fled to Greece or Italy. In the spring and summer of 1945 suspected 'war criminals' and 'collaborators' were rounded up and killed or sent to labour camps in a general liquidation of figures suspect or questionable to the regime. Target groups included upper-class families and intellectuals, the clergy, business figures and landowners, and tribal chiefs.[51] Hoxha moved quickly to introduce land reform in the late 1940s, although the first stage of redistribution was gradually rescinded through a programme of enforced co-operation during the 1950s, resulting in complete nationalization of property by 1967. Of course, Hoxha's communist programme also was determined by the need to break the traditional structures of Albanian society that had proved so durable over the centuries. Hence, while paying lip service to some aspects of tradition, the regime used the elementary education of children to break the clan structure and to change the role of women, which was so much a part of patriarchal power-structures.[52] The death of the clan, writes Jean-Paul Champseix, enabled the consolidation of absolute power and created the conditions for a new 'national feeling'.[53] Ironically, the party itself took on many of the features of traditional patriarchal clan-based culture while destroying the bases of this culture in the broader population.[54]

FIG. 1 (above). Enver Hoxha in uniform and Mehmet Shehu (to his right in civilian clothing) leading the members of the Anti-Fascist National Liberation Council in October 1944 in Berat. (Source: *40 Years of Socialist Albania*, Tirana: 8 Nëntori Publishing House, 1984.)

FIG. 2 (below). Nexhmije and Enver Hoxha at the time of the establishment of the communist regime

Enver Hoxha understood the implications of the 'charismatic impersonalism' of Leninist party organization. For Lenin, the Party commanded obedience as powerfully as had 'traditional charismatic, religious-type reference frameworks in times of deep moral and cultural crisis'.[55] Lenin's party structure combined 'an emphasis on individual revolutionary heroism with an emphasis on the superordinate impersonal authority of the Party, itself the central heroic actor and focus of emotional commitment'.[56] The outcome of this sacralization of the Party, was, as Stalin recognized, the tacit and implicit elevation of the leader or 'General Secretary'. This was not a personality-based charismatic relationship. It was based in the impersonalism of the Party. Nevertheless, the position involved a huge investiture of power in the individual leader, a power which Stalin turned into a personality cult, retrospectively in the battle with Trotsky for supremacy after 1924.[57]

The power-struggles within the new communist government dominated the period 1945 to 1948.[58] According to Champseix, the Albanian communist party split into two opposed factions after taking power, the one dedicated to Stalin's wish for Albanian integration with Tito's Yugoslavia, and the other, taking a more independent, and national course, influenced by the Western-educated intellectual and 'secret disciple of Mustafa Kemal', Enver Hoxha.[59] The Plenary Meeting of the Central Committee of the Albanian Communist Party in February 1948 marked the culmination of the plans of the pro-Yugoslav faction led by Koçi Xoxe and Pandi Kristo to bring together Albania along with Bulgaria as a Balkan federation under Yugoslav leadership.[60] Stalin, suspicious of Hoxha's nationalism, approved Tito's role as tutor to the Albanian leadership and protector of communist Albania. In the hope of strengthening its ties with the Soviet Union he encouraged Yugoslavia to 'swallow' Albania.[61] At this point Enver Hoxha and Mehmet Shehu were in danger of losing their positions to Koçi Xoxe and the pro-Yugoslav faction. Hoxha was humiliated and criticized for 'infraction of the Party line and for prejudicing relations with Yugoslavia' and Shehu for anti-Yugoslav activity.[62] Hoxha retained his position as General Secretary of the Party, but Shehu, who clashed with Xoxe over the issue of integration of the Albanian and Yugoslav armies, was excluded from the Central Committee.[63] Later in 1948, however, Stalin, suspicious now of Yugoslav intentions in the Balkans, accused Tito of nationalism and revisionism. Hoxha used the break between Stalin and Tito to undermine Koçi Xoxe and denounced the pro-Yugoslav faction at the 11th Plenum of the Central Committee. Mehmet Shehu was reinstated and in the following year Koçi Xoxe was executed. Hoxha reigned supreme. Neither the death of Stalin nor the transition to Khrushchevism several years later weakened his grip on power, which would remain firm until his death in 1985.

In November 1948 the First Congress of the Communist Party of Albania took place, and a new constitution was adopted along with a new name for the Party, which would henceforth be called the Party of Labour of Albania (PLA). Hoxha's ambitious programme for the industrialization of the country was officially launched in 1953, the year of Stalin's death, with the First Five-Year Plan (1951–55). Stalinism remained in full force. In April 1952 the Second Congress of the Party of Labour put literacy and educational infrastructure high on the agenda. The first radio station was set up, the Union of Writers adopted the new standardized national language (based on Tosk rather than Gheg Albanian), and universal elementary education was made compulsory up to grade 8. By 1954 the structure of the ruling elite was set for the post-war period as Mehmet Shehu replaced Hoxha as premier, leaving Hoxha a single, overarching role as head of the Party. The President of the Presidium of the People's Assembly Haxhi Lleshi was a titular figure of no power.

Leninism involved the acceptance of the party's claim to valid understanding of the laws of history as well as its messianic role. The Leninist principle of 'party mindedness' resulted in the infallible image bestowed on the General Secretary.[64] Hoxha understood that the softening of the boundaries between the Party and the people, identified by Jowitt in Khrushchevism as the third, 'inclusionist', phase of Soviet-style communism, represented a danger to the stability of his regime.[65] In this phase 'the party seeks to integrate itself with unofficial, non-party sectors of society without yielding its authoritative claims to the "correct line."' It signalled, for Hoxha, the end of the Leninist-Stalinist model in which the Party was sacrosanct.[66] Hoxha was a leader whose intellectual grasp of Marxism-Leninism was secondary to his political cunning. Like Mao Tse-tung he recognized that Khrushchev's revisionism would be poison to his regime. Khrushchev's critique of Stalin marked the end of the era of infallibility of the General Secretary in the Soviet Union. 'The magic evaporated once the historically anointed leader ceased to be the custodian of absolute truth'.[67] In 1956 Hoxha visited Budapest on the return trip from China and North Korea, and witnessed the first major popular demonstration for change after the death of Stalin: the 1956 insurrection.[68] He viewed the uprising as a direct result of Khrushchev's policies of liberalization. According to an editorial article in the Albanian daily newspaper and ideological organ of the regime, *Zëri i Popullit*, Khrushchev's de-Stalinization policy had 'provided grist for the reactionary and revisionist elements and facilitated conditions for them to carry out their hostile activity'.[69] Hoxha moved quickly to identify and eliminate opposition in the Party leadership.[70]

From this point onward, post-war socialist Albania remained closed to the world in a way that the rest of Eastern Europe was not. The Ottoman links were broken after the Young Turk rebellion and the collapse of the Empire. The democracy of Fan Noli was oriented towards the West but was short-lived. The Zog monarchy looked towards Italy but the financial crises of the inter-war period and the Italian fascist undermining of the nation's autonomy in the 1930s ruined relations with Italy. The links to Greece were destroyed by the ethnic tensions in Chameria/ Northern Epirus and likewise the border with Macedonia was fraught with strife. Tensions resulting from Titoite interference and the problem of Kosovo led to the early and decisive break with Yugoslavia.

Only two countries showed an interest in Albania during the post-war period: for the Soviet Union Albania promised an Adriatic harbour for naval and military purposes; and for China after the break with the Soviet Union, Enver Hoxha's regime was the sole remaining link with European communism. During the communist era, Albanian language and culture were little understood even in comparison to the country's South-Eastern European neighbours. World attention was first directed towards the Albanians in the context of the break-up of

Yugoslavia and the hostilities directed towards the Albanian Kosovar majority by Slobodan Milosevic and Serb nationalists in 1988. The images of desperate refugees on overcrowded boats crossing the Adriatic hit the world's news programmes in 1991 and the spectacular collapse of the pyramid schemes several years later came to typify the naivety of post-communist peoples in encountering capitalism. Against these images of the country, its people, rulers, and culture, the works of Ismail Kadare provide depth and complexity.

Albanian Society under Communism

Socio-political analysts since the 1970s have drawn attention to the dynamics of socialist nation-building, in which communist dogma and ideology, the processes of social transformation, consolidation, and inclusion, and the determining forces of socialist economic planning come into contact with each other. Janos Kornai demonstrates the internal consistency of socialist ideology, economics, and society, concluding that:

> Certain conditions are necessary and sufficient for the system to emerge and consolidate. The seed of this 'genetic program' is a particular political structure and related ideology: the undivided power of the Communist party and the prevalence of an official ideology whose cardinal precepts include the establishment of hegemony, and then dominance for public ownership. [. . .] This 'genetic program' fashions society in its own image; it creates a coherent system whose various elements connect, and assume and reinforce each other.[71]

Ideology played a special role. 'It is common knowledge that ideology plays a decisive role in Soviet social systems', write Féher and Heller,[72] and, as Kolakowski explains, ideology was an integral part of the Stalinist socialism, since it provided the basis of legality for the doctrine of communism. It is the 'sole raison d'être for the existing apparatus of power', justifying state policy at any given moment.[73] Soviet-style communism was not answerable to the people; the Party by definition represents the interests of the proletariat. Precisely because of this it is 'extremely sensitive to ideological criticism'. The intelligentsia is of central importance in protecting the ideological purity of the system, but it is also its weak point, inasmuch as the intelligentsia has the capacity to undermine the ideology that underpins the whole structure.

New social structures or 'class' formations took shape within this integrated system, focused on and determined by the central role of the Party.[74] The nomenklatura is the list of the positions of power and of the individuals authorized to occupy them, which make up the total administrative class of the socialist states.[75] The term was coined by Milovan Djilas for the political bureaucracy of the Eastern European socialist systems, in particular of the Soviet Union. This class of bureaucrats and administrators, the intelligentsia of Marxism-Leninism in Stalin's Soviet state model from 1936 onwards, was recruited — ideally — from the classes of the peasants and the workers and enjoyed a set of privileges denied to the administered mass of the people.[76] Real-existing socialism, for the GDR dissident Rudolf Bahro, became a class society of the administrators and the administered.[77] Mikhail Voslensky traces the critique of the socialist ruling class back through Milovan Djilas's first systematic work of socio-political analysis, *The New Class* (1957), to foreign commentators such as Orwell in Britain in the 1940s, and to internal figures, such as Trotsky, who had already criticized the bureaucratization of the Soviet state in the 1920s.[78] According to Djilas, Lenin believed that the dictatorship of the proletariat was a transitory phase in the creation of the new socialist society and the new socialist human being. It would last only until the state would 'die away', but in 1918 he provided the impetus for the creation of the nomenklatura with his argument that Party activists should be given extra food rations.[79] The point made by Djilas, Bahro, and others is that the dictatorship of the proletariat, far from being a transitory grouping of vanguard intellectuals, had become a class, following the classic structures of class empowerment, and introducing a new antagonism into post-revolutionary society. The communist state, that is, was not a classless society, but a state defined by the antagonism between the bureaucratic and the working classes, a political structure unforeseen in the writings of Marx and Engels. Voslensky refers to bureaucratic state-feudalism, implying that Lenin created a modernized feudalism, rather than a communism in Marx's sense.[80] For Voslensky, Stalin in particular created and controlled the nomenklatura. He maintained the balance in favour of the dictator until his death in 1953, after which the nomenklatura gained power and autonomy in the Soviet Union.[81]

Hoxha's Albania was no exception to the Eastern European states in experiencing the specific internal dynamics of socialism. The new communist government built up an administrative corps to help consolidate the regime, modernize the infrastructure and maintain ideological control. The Albanian administrative class remained small, confined mainly to Tirana and under the close scrutiny of the dictator at all times. Hoxha carried out purges of the administration from early in the regime. The work of writers and artists was taken extremely seriously and this creative intelligentsia was incorporated into the structure of the regime. The main difference between the Albanian nomenklatura and that of the Soviets was Albania's underlying clan and regional basis, which had its origins in the partisan era and became consolidated over the duration of the regime. The Tirana government was dominated by twenty-odd clans, primarily of Tosk origin. The Hoxha family, for example, came from Kadare's home town of Gjirokastra. Intermarriage among these groups during the communist period only strengthened this originally clan-based power-structure. More than half of the fifty-three members of the Central Committee were related, writes Jean-Paul Champseix. Power was shared, above all, by four interrelated couples: Enver and Nexhmije Hoxha; Mehmet and Fiqret Shehu; Hysni and Vito Kapo; Josif Pashko and his wife Heleni Terezi. Kadri Hazbiu, Minister of Internal Affairs, was married to the sister of Mehmet Shehu. Later the niece of Ramiz Alia would marry Ilir, son of Enver and Nexhmije Hoxha.[82]

The eventual socialist pyramid consisted of a top 4 per cent of Party members including, in descending order, the Party elite (Politburo), the members of the Central Committee, the Party and government bureaucrats, professionals, intellectuals, and managers of the state industrial and agricultural enterprises, and the rank-and-file Communist Party members. This group's leadership role was written into the constitution. Beneath them were the 96 per cent of the population who did not hold party membership.[83] Like Stalin, Hoxha knew that the nomenklatura must be kept in a state of insecurity and intimidation. The purges and the politics of isolation from Yugoslavia and the Soviet Union after Khrushchev were the result of Hoxha's recognition that absolute power was best maintained by clearing any domestic or foreign environments in which an opposition could arise. The Chinese connection was much safer in this respect: China, culturally as well as geographically so distant from Albania, was a much less likely source of, or ally, in any conspiracy against his leadership, but even the Chinese friendship waned after Mao too became a 'revisionist' in his dealings with the United States. Albania did not enter its 'post-Stalinist' phase until 1985, only four years before the collapse of Soviet-style communism throughout Eastern Europe.

Socialism, Literature, and Identity in the Soviet Union and Albania

The situation of the intellectuals in the socialist environments differed from that of the West in terms of their structural relationship to power. In those societies in which the history of the intelligentsia was typified by specialization and differentiation of roles, as was typically the case in the West, the possibility was greater for 'the development of relatively autonomous intellectual activities and institutions and of [. . .] critical stances, especially in relation to political authorities'.[84] This type of movement away from the centres of power to create alternative sites of critique, which has been identified as one of the core values of Western European identity, was not, of course, part of the historical experience of Albania or of those Central and Eastern European environments which had experienced modernization from above in the various forms of enlightened absolutism.

Russian writing before and after the Revolution belonged to the avant-garde of European Modernism and for a period, at least, envisaged no necessary conflict between freedom of thought and revolutionary fervour. However, as Stalin gained power in the late 1920s, he took control of literature and cultural production.[85] The modernism of figures such as Akhmatova was castigated as subjectivism or bourgeois formalism and replaced with an increasingly doctrinaire socialist realism.[86] In the period of disorientation after the death of Stalin various unorthodox and critical works were allowed publication. Pomerantsev criticized socialist realism and raised the issue of ideological stagnation in his article 'On Sincerity in Literature', published in *Novy Mir* (*New World*) in December 1953. Proscribed writers were rehabilitated in 1954 and 1955 at the Second Writers' Congress in December 1954. The new mood would be enshrined in the title of Ilya Ehrenburg's novel, *The Thaw*.[87] In 1955 the popular monthly journal *Foreign Literature* was founded and along with *Novy Mir* and a variety of youth-oriented publications made Western writers and themes accessible and popularized aspects of Russian folk culture previously frowned upon as the product of corrupt class relationships.

In February 1956, the new First Secretary, Nikita Khrushchev, signalled major change with his denunciation of Stalinism and the cult of personality at the Twentieth Congress of the Communist Party of the Soviet Union (CPSU). Under

Khrushchev the Party was to be re-established as 'the dominant institution vis-à-vis the secret police, army, and the ministries, and it established its control over the economy, and all cultural and social institutions'.[88] Khrushchev's intervention set into motion a complex series of responses and counter-responses in cultural circles which created periods of thaw and frost over the years from 1956 to 1964. The writers regarded the changes as an invitation to greater freedom of expression. Allusion was made to the crimes of the Stalin period. In his poem 'Stalin's Heirs', the young and outspoken Russian poet Yevgeny Yevtushenko made specific reference to Enver Hoxha as one of the Stalinist criminals still alive and thriving.[89] The bureaucrats who were instrumental to the process of regulation of literary expression lost control since there were no clear lines of demarcation. Some were also sympathetic to change.

The international repercussions of Khrushchev's speech were enormous. The memories of the crimes of Stalin were strong and the official denunciation created the environment for the upheavals in Poland, Romania, Bulgaria, Hungary, Czechoslovakia, and East Germany, all of whose leaders were disciples of Stalin. China gave notice that Khrushchev would no longer be accepted as the leader of international communism.[90] By late 1956, the literary dispute became caught up in the political crises in Eastern Europe. 'Both were the direct result of the de-Stalinization campaign, and both were solved by reversions to harsh repression'.[91] Khrushchev and his colleagues realized that liberalization could threaten the power of the Party and that they must regain control of 'the party's right [. . .] to lay down the truth, in whatever sphere'.[92] Khrushchev's 'frost', the necessary reassertion of control, began in October 1956. Vladimir Dudintsev's novel *Not by Bread Alone* was labelled 'anti-Soviet' and in 1957 Khrushchev attacked literary circles for 'piling together negative facts and commenting on them tendentiously, from a standpoint hostile to us'.[93] Already in June 1956 a resolution was passed giving credit to 'Stalin's services to the Party, the nation, and the international revolutionary movement' and characterizing his crimes 'merely as misguided abuses of power'.[94] At the end of 1956 the thaw appeared to be over. In fact, however, the regime followed an uneven line of policy over the next seven years. Without a single hard line, policy-making became ad-hoc, unpredictable, 'erratic and arbitrary'.[95] Despite the clampdown on Dudintsev and after the harassment of the ageing and frail Boris Pasternak in 1958, Solzhenitsyn, with the help of *Novy Mir*'s editor, Aleksandr Tvardovsky (whom Kadare met at the Gorki Institute and who plays a role in the novel *The Twilight of the Steppe-Gods*), and Khrushchev's friend V. S. Lebedev, managed to publish his novel of the Stalinist camp system, *One Day in the Life of Ivan Denisovich*. Likewise in the following year Lebedev introduced the Soviet Leader to Tvardovsky's satiric poem *Terkin in Paradise*, which Khrushchev reportedly enjoyed immensely and allowed to be published.[96]

In October 1961, however, the new party programme was announced at the 22nd CPSU Congress. In a restatement of orthodoxy entitled 'The Enhancement of the Educational Role of Literature and Art', the Communist Party was given the task of establishing 'the correct tendency in the development of literature and art'.[97] The tide had turned. At a special plenary meeting of the Party Central Committee in June 1963 liberal tendencies in art were banned and orthodox socialist realism reinstated, and Khrushchev warned the Soviet intellectuals against overstepping the Party's line.[98] However, the Khrushchev experiment was almost over. In the following year he was forced to step down. The trial and imprisonment in February 1966 of the satirists Sinyavsky (Tertz) and Daniel (Arzhak) for anti-Soviet agitation and propaganda marked the renunciation of Khrushchevite openness under his successor, Leonid Brezhnev, who became First Secretary (General Secretary after 1966).[99] The Soviet Union began the era of military and armaments expansion, economic decline, official cronyism and corruption, and disguised repression that would become synonymous with the name of its leader.

Under the Ottomans Albania remained divorced from European cultural movements such as modernism. The ancient oral epics handed down by illiterate singers provided the basis for the 'Albanian cultural renaissance' of the late nineteenth century, Zef Jubani and Thimi Mitko were instrumental in collecting and popularizing the oral folk-literature, the poet Migjeni (d. 1938) established a modern Albanian idiom, and the statesman and cleric Fan Noli was an important writer and translator.[100] However, the post-war socialist regime carried out much of the groundwork for the establishment of a national literary culture, such as the raising of literacy levels, the creation of an intelligentsia, and the standardization of the national language. Figures such as Ismail Kadare, Dritëro Agolli, Fatos Arapi, and others made major contributions to the creation of a national language and literature in this 'belated' national-cultural environment.[101] This historical-cultural role provides one of the keys to Kadare's identity and self-perception as a voice of Albania and the adversary of the dictatorship. The Albanian journals *Drita* (*Light*), *Nëntori* (*November*), and *Zëri i rinisë* (*Voice of Youth*) were modelled on the Soviet ones, with *Nëntori*, the official organ of the Union of Writers, copying the name of the Soviet *October* (*Oktyabr*), and *Zëri i rinisë* catering for a young readership based on *Yunost* (*Youth*). However these journals did not share the Soviet history of thaw (and frost) of the decade of Khrushchev's reforms; on the contrary, this was the period of the building and consolidation of post-war communism under Hoxha's dictatorship.

While Khrushchev was personally involved in decisions regarding literature and literary policy in the Soviet Union, he was neither a sophisticated reader nor deeply interested in literary affairs. Enver Hoxha was cut from a different cloth. The only one of the Eastern European leaders to be educated in the West, he was widely read, understood profoundly the importance of literature, and took a personal interest in and control of Albanian letters, considering himself the nation's first writer as well as its supreme leader. While he made frequent reference to European literature and culture in speeches and writings throughout his life, his closing address, at the 15th Plenum of the Central Committee of the PLA on 26 October 1965, 'Literature and the Arts Should Serve to Temper People with Class Consciousness for the Construction of Socialism', was particularly important. Here, at the height of his power in the decade leading into the Albanian cultural revolution, he laid out the Albanian communist doctrine of national literature.[102] This document, which coincided with Kadare's coming to maturity as a writer in the mid-1960s, proved immensely influential on the young writer, as a statement of everything that Albanian literature should not be.

Hoxha oversaw the establishment of the first Albanian Union of Writers on 7 October 1945. At that time it included non-communists. Sejfulla Malëshova, Minister of Culture and Propaganda, was elected president.[103] In December 1953, the writer Kasëm Trebeshina expressed open dissent in a letter to Enver Hoxha, criticizing the nepotism and bureaucracy of the Union of Writers:

> The Union of Writers in Tirana is organized like an order of mediaeval monks. At the head of the order is a Grand Master and all are obliged to hearken as he carries out his functions as such. Are you aware that the distribution of 'functions' and 'privileges' in this manner is mediaeval? [. . .] The oppression of opinions, even within the Party ranks, is becoming systematic.[104]

However, this overstepped the boundaries. Trebeshina, a committed communist, was arrested and given a seventeen-year prison sentence, a lenient punishment by later standards. In 1957 the Union was dissolved and was reconstituted together with the Union of Artists as a single League of Albanian Writers and Artists, with a set membership of 150 along clearer ideological and party lines. Writers were given better pay and conditions and were kept under closer scrutiny. Veteran communist Dhimitri Shuteriqi would remain president until July 1973 when, as part of the cultural revolution, he was denounced along with other bourgeois, revisionists, and decadents, purged from the party and sent to work in industry and agriculture alongside the people.[105]

It would be a mistake to underestimate the levels of coercion even in the post-totalitarian environment of the 1970s and 1980s in Eastern Bloc countries such as Czechoslovakia, the GDR, Hungary, and Poland. However, as Heller, Fehér, Joas, and others have shown, the situation after Stalin's death with the Khrushchevite reforms, and particularly after 1968 in Eastern Europe, can be termed 'post-totalitarian', meaning that the unquestionable authority of the Party had been undermined, and that mechanisms of control and punishment had changed as a result.[106] Albania did not experience this era of relative openness. This was not a 'post-totalitarian' environment in which dissident voices could begin to 'speak truth to power'.[107] The softening which took place after Khrushchev's reforms did not take place under Hoxha. Punishments for any sign of 'counter-revolutionary activity', such as the writing or publication of dissident opinion, were extremely harsh, including very long jail sentences, torture, and even assassination or execution. Moreover, the country had little to call on in terms of intellectual and political traditions. While a national intelligentsia and political class had begun to develop during the years from the 1880s until the 1930s, their roots were too shallow to survive the occupations and upheavals of the first half of the century, culminating in the imposition of partisan communism in 1945. Kadare has repeatedly pointed to the 'Ungleichzeitigkeit' ('non-contemporaneity') of the Albanian situation, in which the Stalinist environment of 1938 existed at least until the time of Hoxha's death in 1985. Kadare's attitudes towards the dictatorship changed, but the focus remained the same: to deny the dictatorship the sole custody of the voice of Albania.

Socialist Realism

While the underlying theory of socialist realism is to be found in Lenin's essays 'What is to be done' (1902) and 'Party Organization and Party Literature' (1905), the term, 'socialist realism' was not coined until 1932 at a meeting of the newly formed Soviet Union of Writers, and the theory itself was formulated over the following years and given canonical status at the First Writers' Congress in 1934.[108] Katerina Clark has shown how Lenin reformulated the role of the 'vanguard' and translated Marx's dialectic of 'nature' and 'freedom' into the conceptual opposition of 'spontaneity' and 'consciousness', thereby adapting the materialist dialectic to the vocabulary and the interests of the Russian intelligentsia at the turn of the century.[109] The doctrine of socialist realism was adopted under Stalinism as a means of bridging the gap between theory and praxis, communist dogma and real-existing socialist everyday life (*Alltagsleben*) on an aesthetic and ritualistic level, becoming a sort of 'iconostasis', an interface between ideology and experience. It mediated historical truth and everyday reality for a populace in which the state had not withered away, and the Party had not become congruent with the people. The problem of the discrepancy between communist dogma and reality became the basis for the aesthetic doctrine of socialist realism. Clark shows how socialist realism bridged the gap between communist dogma and communist reality in the lands of real-existing socialism. Socialist realism provided a 'master plot' rehearsing and showing the way forward for a people which had not yet fully internalized socialism. It rehearsed the transformation from spontaneous (i.e. non-historical, selfish, and anarchic) action to conscious (historical, revolutionary) action on the level of the individual 'positive' hero. The socialist realist novel enacted transformations in which 'the subject of the ritual goes from one state to another'.[110] For Clark the ritual transformation did not consist in transition from class society to the classless communist state but rather from the state of spontaneity to that of consciousness. The focal point is not the resolution of class conflict, but rather the individual's recognition of the necessity of historically conscious action (as opposed to selfish or anarchic behaviour). This model emulates at the level of the individual the historical pattern of the overcoming of spontaneous action by conscious action. For the 'positive hero' of socialist realism, individual, subjective responses and the best interests of the collective are one and the same.

Writers and dissidents throughout Central and Eastern Europe after the Stalinist period played more or less dangerous games, stretching the boundaries between conformism and dissidence within this literary paradigm. In doing so their relationships to the ruling parties became less and less clear as they occupied 'grey zones' between the regime and the people, as both instrumental and critical members of an intelligentsia playing a double game in which they were by no means in control.[111] Under the rubric of 'subjective authenticity', writers such as Christa Wolf in the German Democratic Republic sought a compromise position between individual and subjective perceptions of truth and socialist responsibility for the totality without falling into historically obsolete and discredited forms of 'bourgeois subjectivism', 'formalism', or 'decadence'. Even Alexander Solzhenitsyn's works, in particular *A Day in the Life of Ivan Denisovich*, were brought under the mantle of 'socialist realism' in Georg Lukács's late appraisal of the Russian author.[112] If the language of socialist realism was a 'ritualized one', in which abstract meanings are personalized and turned into 'comprehensible narrations', in such a way as to 'make specific meanings that would otherwise be general',[113] these writers subverted this language, showing the emptiness of the ritual and the perversion of relationships inherent in socialist realism.

While socialist realism was never officially instituted in Albania as the only acceptable writing style, there were strong expectations of the style and nature of literature which were modelled on the Soviet form approved by Stalin. Ismail Kadare openly defied these expectations even as early as 1959. *The City without Signs* takes as its protagonist Gjon Kurti, the 'hero of his time' as a weak and immoral character, whose forgery raises him to the heights of success as an Albanian intellectual and philologist. Moreover, Kurti is not an outsider; on the contrary, he is a model of the post-war generation. Even in *The Wedding*, considered Kadare's most orthodox piece of writing, the relationship of history to progress, and between tradition and modernization, is by no means unambiguous. In the novel *Winter of Great Solitude*, Kadare presented Enver Hoxha as a 'positive hero', but located him in an environment where everyday life collapses into tragedy, misery, and poverty.

The question of Kadare's readership in socialist Albania is a vexed one. The writer himself maintains that he was read broadly across the country, and that his works sold out in relatively large numbers whenever they were published. Libraries stocked those works which were acceptable to the regime and privately owned copies were circulated widely among networks of friends. Others point out that print runs were relatively small, that distribution was limited, especially outside Tirana, and that Kadare's style was difficult and inaccessible for this still barely literate people.[114] Socialist realism was not Kadare's style. His writing subverted the language of the dictatorship. It seems likely that Kadare's work was read primarily by the nomenklatura and the educated administrative class. However, we must not underestimate the sophistication of reading practices in Albania as in other socialist states. While the Albanian population did not have the educational resources and literary traditions of the East Germans, the Czechs, the Hungarians, the Poles or even the Russians, the desire to read and understand was powerful in this closed society.[115]

Albanian Language, Ethnicity, and Literary Identity

'I am an Albanian', answers 'the man of this country' to John C. Hobhouse, Lord Byron's travelling companion in the early 1800s, before any of the pre-national nation-building activity had occurred which Hobsbawm views as the pre-condition for the expression of national identity.[116] The term 'Albanian' had acquired a strong significance as a marker of group identity on the basis of shared language, which was the dominant core value prior to political, social, cultural, or religious identity. While language is not a simple factor in ethnic identity, it came to function in the particular circumstances of the Ottoman conquest of the Albanians as a powerful marker of group belonging and historical memory. The core lands of the Albanians had remained linguistically stable for centuries, even millennia, and were conscious of their linguistic identity despite the difference in dialect between Tosk and Gheg. According to Arshi Pipa, Ghegs and Tosks easily understand each other's speech.[117]

It is not surprising that the Albanian uprising followed the pattern of Herderian nationalism, basing itself on language in the first instance. Under the Ottomans the Albanian language was not accepted as a medium of teaching or literary publication and the alphabet was not standardized. The Albanians were educated either in Greek (for Orthodox communities) or in Turkish or Arabic (for Muslims). This masked 'the true nature and delineation of an Albanian nation' for this most integrated of Ottoman peoples, and contrasted them with the other nationalities, which were allowed to use their own languages.[118] Albanian was written in a variety of scripts, including Roman and Greek. At the turn of the twentieth century, Edith Durham found the origins of the new literacy in growing national awareness and resentment at increasing Ottoman suppression of the language:

> Latterly [the Sultan] has made very active efforts to suppress the tongue altogether. In the South many people have been imprisoned for possessing books or papers printed in it, and all schools teaching it are forbidden. But North Albania is a circumstance over which the Sultan has little control; it possesses a printing-press and several schools. [. . .] The knowledge of reading and writing the language is spreading rapidly. You find it in very unexpected quarters, and as a common bond of sympathy it is knitting together all classes of the people. Papers printed in London, in Rome, in Sofia, and Bukarest are smuggled in and read by Moslem and Christian alike all over the land. A literary language shows signs of development.[119]

Language acted as 'a common element and as a distinctive cultural and national trait separating Albanians from Turks, Greeks and Slavs'.[120] At the Monastir Congress of 1908 the Roman script was adopted, and the Shkodra Literary Committee sought ways of merging the two dialects in 1916–17. It was only in the late nineteenth century that Albanian philologists collected, selected, and moulded folk material in line with national aspirations. Collections of Albanian heroic songs were published in order to propagate the idea that what bound the Albanians together was 'common blood, language, customs, and common aspirations', which led Albanians to love their country and countrymen, 'even if they belonged to other religions'.[121] This latter point is important, since it indicates a shift towards ethnic identification in terms of 'Albanianness' understood as a link with Albania through 'blood', language, and culture, and away from allegiances in terms of religion and/ or Ottoman identity.

Despite these beginnings, the educational infrastructure remained undeveloped after 1913. Even under Zog, few secondary colleges were established and no university.[122] The French lycée at Korça was a training ground for the communist leaders, but it was unique. The University of Tirana was only established in 1957 by the communists. For the still small population, the communist regime trained a post-war generation of administrators and party members, a nomenklatura who, like Kadare, had little knowledge of the pre-war situation. The task of creating a standard language was also completed only under the communists. In 1952 the first meeting took place of the committee appointed for the task of standardizing the language and in 1972 the Congress of Orthography 'adopted uniform phonetic rules of spelling and declared that the Albanian people now possessed a unified literary language, incorporating the common elements of the two major dialects, Gheg and Tosk'.[123] However, this process proved controversial. According to the émigré linguist and philologist Arshi Pipa, the new post-war standard was based on the southern, Tosk variant, which was spoken by the majority of the members of the regime. For them Gheg signified anti-communism, royalism, collaboration with the fascists and Nazis, Catholicism, northern tribalism, and intellectualism. The standardized language, officially referred to as Unified Literary Albanian (ULA), is for Pipa 'an elaborate Tosk variant as to phonology and grammar, while its vocabulary incorporates the greater part of the richer Gheg vocabulary and phraseology, white-washed with Tosk phono-morphology so as to leave no indication of their true provenance'.[124] The result of language standardization, writes Pipa, has been 'the institutionalization of the language inferiority of Ghegs with respect to Tosks'.[125] More recently the Albanian linguist Xhevat Lloshi has provided a less polemical view of the development of standard Albanian, pointing out that authors such as Kadare and Agolli (both, admittedly, of Muslim Tosk background), along with linguists, have defended the literary language as 'an ordinary standard language and not a product of the convergence of two dialects'. Lloshi points out that national literary standards are rarely the product of dialectal evolution and that the concept of a standard language involves an element of choice and cultural politics. While critical of Pipa's polemical line, Lloshi admits that aspects of the communist language policy require revision along non-partisan lines, taking into account the political history of the standardization process. These issues include: 'the theoretical interpretation, the suppression of the free discussion, the extreme politicization, the expressive insistence on normativeness, the banishment of the Northern variant in new literature, and the means for future improvements in orthography'.[126]

In the dogma of socialism ethnicity was a suspect category which began in romantic nationalism and ended in fascism. In the literature of socialist realism, all forms of national identity were to be subsumed into the ideology of international socialism. In reality, ethnicity was long recognized by Eastern European regimes to be powerful and potentially subversive, and populist nationalism was manipulated and instrumentalized in many of the Soviet states and particularly in the Balkans. Enver Hoxha differed from most of his counterparts in his national separatism. Albania, for Hoxha, was an enclosed political space in which to continue the ideology of Stalinism after it had been corrupted in the heartlands of the Soviet Union and China. While calling for the creation of a new Albania, Hoxha instituted a cultural revolution in which the heritage of Albanian tradition and culture was largely sacrificed. His new Albania was not so much a call to Albanian identity as a complete makeover in his own image, although he couched his policies in terms of patriotism and nationalism, especially after the break with Chinese Maoism in the 1970s. Ismail Kadare's exploration of ethnic consciousness goes much deeper than the communist nation-state separatism of Enver Hoxha. For Jean-Paul Champseix Kadare tried to rescue the national identity that the Stalinist Hoxha destroyed in the process of remaking Albania in his own image.[127] In poems such as 'What are these mountains thinking about?' and in his frequent references to the power of the Albanian songs and epics, Kadare identifies the soul of his nation in its language. His defence of Albanianness has its origins in Herderian conceptions of language and culture, which aim to conserve, maintain, and consolidate identity.[128] 'Herder's theory of language binds the inventive individual, the original talent, to the tradition that he renews', writes Nicholas Boyle.[129] In Kadare's national identity, culture is transmitted through language in ways which are linguistically unique and ultimately incapable of translation. The long slow rhythm of Herderian accretion of identity lies at the core of Kadare's argument for Albanianness, against a history of incursions of imperial, cultural, and economic powers from all sides over long periods. Kadare defends the language, customs, and culture of his people against oppressive external forces, whether Ottoman, Soviet, or Serb, and his patriotism is closer in spirit to that of the nineteenth century ethno-cultural movements of Central Europe than to twentieth-century national chauvinism.[130]

Kadare's Translators and Translations

While communist Albania had isolated itself from East and West by the late 1960s, the regime continued to train large numbers of interpreters and translators, and foreign-language broadcasts were made to the rest of the world in a wide variety of languages. Albanian works were translated into French, English, and other languages as part of the regime's propaganda effort. It is not surprising that Ismail Kadare was conscious of the question of language. While devoted to the task of maintaining and renewing his native language, Kadare recognized by the time *The General of the Dead Army* was published in France that a reputation abroad, particularly in the West, would be of great value to him, both for his reputation as a writer and as a form of protection from the regime. His first and most prominent translator, Jusuf Vrioni, was an educated and urbane aristocrat who was raised and educated bilingually in France. He returned to Albania after the war, was imprisoned and subsequently stranded there. Unable to re-educate himself or find work in certain areas because of his descent from one of Albania's wealthy aristocratic dynasties and his record of imprisonment and labour camps, he found that his ability in French provided an anonymous, well-paid, and fulfilling career, as well as access to a great deal of otherwise inaccessible literature. (As an official translator he had access to the works of Sartre, Joyce, Faulkner, Beckett, Aron, Duras, and Barthes, among others.[131]) Vrioni discovered Kadare's work in the early 1960s after his release from detention, and was introduced to the young author in 1963. He was working at that time as a translator for the publishing house Naim Frashëri (later renamed '8th November' in commemoration of the foundation of the Albanian Communist Party) and would become the translator of the new journal *Lettres albanaises* which was edited by Kadare from 1978. He sensed the linguistic richness and value of Kadare's work and devoted his talents to it, becoming a friend of the author in the process. Two works were officially translated by him (*The Great Winter* and *The Three-Arched Bridge*); he worked on the rest as a labour of love during his leisure hours. Vrioni was given the task of translating the works of

Enver Hoxha, a position of prestige which aroused hostility among his peers and members of the nomenklatura, especially given his class and background. (Kadare made a point of being seen with and inviting Vrioni to official functions despite his peers' disapproval of the latter's 'political' record.) As translator Vrioni remained anonymous (owing to official policy and the jealousy of his superiors) until late in his career.[132] Vrioni's translations are considered by bilingual commentators to be extremely close to the originals in content, if not always in style, and generated acclaim in France.[133] Since Vrioni's death in 2002, Tedi Papavrami and others have taken over this task. To this day, many of the translations available in English are from the French rather than the Albanian. (An important exception is John Hodgson's translation of *The Three-Arched Bridge*.) Recent translators from French into English, such as David Bellos, have begun working closely with Kadare. While Kadare has now provided authorized versions of most of his work in both Albanian and French in the bilingual *Œuvres* (*Works*) published by Fayard under Claude Durand, earlier translations, particularly into English from the Albanian, were of dubious authenticity. A questionable version of *The Castle* was published without a named translator in the United States in 1974. This has recently been retranslated from the French under the title of *The Siege* by David Bellos, along with *Spring Flowers, Spring Frost, The Successor*, and *Agamemnon's Daughter*.

Notes to Chapter 1

1. Miranda Vickers, *The Albanians: A Modern History* (London: I. B. Tauris, 1999), p. 1.
2. Cf. Lord Byron [George Gordon], *The Major Works*, ed. by Jerome J. McGann (Oxford: Oxford University Press, 2000), p. 87 (quoting Hobhouse).
3. Leon Dominian, *The Language Frontiers of Europe* (n.p.: Henry Holt and Company, 1917), p. 193.
4. Arshi Pipa, *The Politics of Language in Socialist Albania* (Boulder: East European Monographs, dist. by Columbia University Press, 1989), pp. xii–xv.
5. Benjamin W. Fortson, *Indo-European Language and Culture: An Introduction* (Oxford: Blackwell, 2004), pp. 390–400.
6. In foreign languages, the medieval names survived, but the Albanians themselves substituted the words *shqiptarë*, *Shqipëri* and *shqipe*. The primary root is the adverb *shqip*, meaning 'clearly, intelligibly'. [. . .] The change [from usage of '*alban-*' to '*shqip-*' as the root-identifying particle, PM] happened after the Ottoman conquest. [. . .] A new and more generalised ethnic and linguistic consciousness of all these people responded to this, distinguished against the foreigners as a community of men (*shqiptarë*) clearly understanding each other, that is understanding each other '*shqip*'. [. . .] There is nothing scientific in explaining *Shqipëri* as 'the country of the eagle' and *shqiptarë* as 'the sons of the eagle'. Xhevat Lloshi, 'Albanian'', in *Handbuch der Südosteuropa-Linguistik*, ed. by Uwe Hinrichs (Wiesbaden: Harrassowitz Verlag, 1991), pp. 277–78; my translation.
7. Dominian, pp. 192–93.
8. M. Edith Durham, *The Burden of the Balkans* (London: Thomas Nelson and Sons, n.d.), pp. 232–33.
9. Joseph Swire, *Albania: The Rise of a Kingdom* (London: Williams & Norgate, 1929), pp. 4–5.
10. On the ancient history of Albania, cf. Swire, pp. 3–9; *Perspectives on Albania*, ed. by Tom Winnifrith (London: Macmillan, 1992), pp. 14–40; *The Transition to Late Antiquity: On the Danube and Beyond*, ed. by A. G. Poulter (Oxford: Oxford University Press, 2007), pp. 135–61.
11. Nicholas Hammond, 'The Relations of Illyrian Albania with the Greeks and the Romans', in Winnifrith, *Perspectives*, pp. 38–39; cf. also Swire, pp. 6–7.

12. Peter F. Sugar, *Southeastern Europe under Ottoman Rule, 1354–1804* (Seattle: University of Washington Press, 1977), pp. 64–65.
13. Sugar, p. 67.
14. Stavro Skendi, *Skenderbeg and Albanian National Consciousness*, Südost-Forschungen 27 (Munich: Oldenbourg, 1968), p. 88.
15. Albert Doja, 'A Political History of Bektashism in Albania', *Totalitarian Movements and Political Religions*, 7 (2006), 83–107 (pp. 85–86); Harry Thirwall Norris, *Islam in the Balkans: Religion and Society between Europe and the Arab World* (London: Hurst & Company, 1993), *Popular Sufism in Eastern Europe: Sufi Brotherhoods and the Dialogue with Christianity and 'Heterodoxy'* (London: Routledge, 2006); John Norton, 'The Bektashis in the Balkans', in *Religious Quest and National Identity in the Balkans*, ed. by Celia Hawksworth, Muriel Heppell, and Harry Norris (Basingstoke: Palgrave, 2001), pp. 168–99.
16. Derek Hall, *Albania and the Albanians* (London: Pinter Reference, 1994), p. 43.
17. Skendi, *Skenderbeg and Albanian National Consciousness*, p. 86.
18. Doja, p. 87.
19. Hall, p. 43.
20. Sugar, pp. 52–53.
21. Sugar, p. 53.
22. Sugar p. 54; Vickers, *The Albanians*, p. 22; Doja, pp. 85–86; Bernhard Tönnes, *Sonderfall Albanien: Enver Hoxhas 'eigener Weg' und die historischen Ursprünge seiner Ideologie* (Munich: Oldenbourg, 1980), pp. 33–34, 164–66.
23. Vickers, *The Albanians*, p. 22.
24. Hall, p. 43.
25. Norris, *Islam in the Balkans*, p. 125.
26. Vickers, *The Albanians*, p. 22.
27. Norton, p. 190.
28. Muriel Heppell, and Harry Norris, 'Introduction', in *Religious Quest and National Identity in the Balkans*, ed. by Celia Hawksworth, Muriel Heppell, and Harry Norris (Basingstoke: Palgrave, 2001), pp. 10–11.
29. Ismaïl Kadaré, and Gilles de Rapper, *L'Albanie entre la légende et l'histoire* (Arles: Actes Sud, 2004), pp. 103–04.
30. Clarissa De Waal, *Albania Today: A Portrait of Post-Communist Turbulence* (London: I. B. Tauris, 2007), p. 71.
31. De Waal, pp. 72–73.
32. De Waal, pp. 73–74. See chapter 6, 'The Kanun in the 1990s' for case-studies of the ongoing influence and usage of this ancient legal code (De Waal, pp. 83–94).
33. Vickers, *The Albanians*, p. 21.
34. Vickers, *The Albanians*, p. 25.
35. Barbara Jelavich, *The Ottoman Empire, the Great Powers, and the Straits Question 1870–1887* (Bloomingon: Indiana University Press, 1973), pp. 111–16; Barbara Jelavich, *History of the Balkans*, I: *Eighteenth and Nineteenth Centuries*; II: *Twentieth Century* (Cambridge: Cambridge University Press, 1983), I, 361–63; Stavro Skendi, *The Albanian National Awakening, 1878–1912* (Princeton, NJ: Princeton University Press, 1967), pp. 31–110.
36. Mary Edith Durham, 'The Albanian Question', *Albania and the Albanians: Selected Articles and Letters 1903–1944*, ed. by Bejtullah Destani (London: I. B. Tauris, 2004), p. 86, quoted in Norris, *Popular Sufism*, p. 90.
37. Jelavich, *History of the Balkans*, I, 365, II, 84–89; Skendi, *The Albanian National Awakening*, pp. 31–110.
38. Vickers, *The Albanians*, p. 34.
39. John R. Lampe, 'Introduction: Reconnecting the Twentieth-Century Histories of Southeastern Europe', in *Ideologies and National Identities: the Case of Twentieth-Century Southeastern Europe*, ed. by John R. Lampe and Mark Mazower (Budapest: CEU Press, 2004), pp. 1–14 (8).
40. István Bibò, *Die Misere der osteuropäischen Kleinstaaterei*, trans. by Béla Rásky (Frankfurt a.M.: Verlag neue Kritik, 1992), p. 49.
41. On King Zog's life and accomplishments in creating a modern Albania, see Bernd Jürgen

Fischer, *King Zog and the Struggle for Stability in Albania* (Boulder: East European Monographs, dist. by Columbia University Press, New York), pp. 62, 304–06.

42. Arshi Pipa, 'Subversion vs Conformism: The Kadare Phenomenon', *Telos* 73 (1987), 47–77 (p. 50).

43. Edwin E. Jacques, *The Albanians: An Ethnic History from Prehistoric Times to the Present* (Jefferson, NC: McFarland & Co., 1995), p. 466.

44. Franz Borkenau, *European Communism* (London: Faber & Faber, 1953), p. 396.

45. István Bibò, *Misère des Petits Etats D'Europe de L'Est* (Paris: Albin Michel, 1993), p. 47.

46. Pipa, 'Subversion vs. Conformism', p. 50.

47. Rudra Sil, and Marc Morjé Howard, 'Introduction: Ken Jowitt's Universe', in *World Order after Leninism: Essays in Honour of Ken Jowitt*, ed. by Vladimir Tismaneanu, Marc Morjé Howard, and Rudra Sil (Seattle: University of Washington Press, 2006), pp. 3–18 (4).

48. Kenneth Jowitt defines 'breaking through' as 'the decisive alteration or destruction of values, structures and behaviours which are perceived by a revolutionary elite as comprising or contributing to the actual or potential existence of alternative centres of political power'. *Revolutionary Breakthroughs and National Development: The Case of Romania, 1944–1965* (Berkeley: University of California Press, 1971), p. 8.

49. Sil and Howard, p. 4; cf. Ken Jowitt, *New World Disorder: The Leninist Extinction* (Berkeley: University of California Press, 1992), pp. 88–91, 96–97.

50. The Albanian Communist Party was founded on 8 November 1941 with Enver Hoxha as its elected leader. In September the following year the National Liberation Front and in mid-1943 the National Liberation Army were formed. After liberation of the country from German troops by November 1943, a provisional government was established and at national elections held in December 1945 the Democratic Front, the successor party to the National Liberation Front, won office with a landslide majority. In early 1946 the Constitution of the People's Republic of Albania was promulgated by the Presidium of the Constituent Assembly. Owen Pearson, *Albania in the 20th Century*, III: *Albania in Dictatorship and Democracy: 1945–1999* (London: I. B. Tauris/ Centre for Albanian Studies, 2006), p. 21.

51. Jacques, p. 432.

52. Ivaylo Ditchev, 'D'Oncle Enver à Oncle Sam: les ruines de l'utopie', in *Albanie Utopie: Huis clos dans les Balkans*, ed. by Sonia Combe and Ivalyo Ditchev (Paris: Éditions Autrement, 1996), pp. 28–39 (pp. 37–38).

53. Jean-Paul Champseix, 'Communisme et tradition: un syncrétisme dévastateur' in *Albanie Utopie: Huis clos dans les Balkans*, ed. by Sonia Combe and Ivalyo Ditchev (Paris: Éditions Autrement, 1996), pp. 53–61 (p. 57).

54. Champseix, 'Communisme et tradition', p. 56.

55. Vladimir, Tismaneanu, 'Lenin's Century: Bolshevism, Marxism, and the Russian Tradition', in *World Order after Leninism: Essays in Honour of Ken Jowitt*, ed. by Vladimir Tismaneanu, Marc Morjé Howard, and Rudra Sil (Seattle: University of Washington Press, 2006), pp. 19–33 (p. 20).

56. Jowitt, *New World Disorder*, p. 3.

57. Tismaneanu, 'Lenin's Century', pp. 19–20, 22.

58. Thomas Schreiber, *Enver Hodja: Le sultan rouge* (Paris: J.-C. Lattès, 1994), pp. 95–120.

59. Champseix, 'Communisme et tradition', pp. 54–55.

60. Pearson, III, 267.

61. According to Milovan Djilas, 12 January 1948, quoted in Pearson, III, 256–57.

62. Schreiber, p. 114.

63. Pearson, III, 267; Schreiber, p. 114.

64. Leszek Kolakowski, *Main Currents of Marxism: Its Origins, Growth and Dissolution*, III: *The Breakdown* (Oxford: Oxford University Press, 1978), pp. 77–78.

65. Jowitt, *New World Disorder*, pp. 88–120.

66. Sil and Howard, p. 4.

67. Tismaneanu, 'Lenin's Century', p. 22.

68. Roy A. Medvedev and Zhores A. Medvedev, *Khrushchev: The Years in Power* (Oxford: Oxford University Press, 1977), p. 70.

69. William Griffith, *Albania and the Sino-Soviet Rift* (Cambridge, Mass.: MIT Press, 1963), p. 136.

The complete text of the 9 January 1962 article is reprinted in Griffith, pp. 303–18.

70. Griffith, p. 26.

71. János Kornai, *The Socialist System: The Political Economy of Communism* (Princeton: Princeton University Press 1992), pp. 374–75.

72. *Dictatorship over Needs*, ed. by Ferenc Fehér, Agnes Heller, and György Márkus (Oxford: Basil Blackwell, 1983), pp. 187–204.

73. Kolakowski, p. 90.

74. Theories of the 'new class' of the intellectuals or the bureaucracy have been traced back to Bakunin in 1870: Lawrence P. King, and Iván Szelényi, *Theories of the New Class: Intellectuals and Power* (Minneapolis: University of Minnesota Press, 2004), p. xvii; Milovan Djilas, *The New Class* (London: Unwin Books, 1957), passim; György Konrad and Ivan Szelenyi, *The Intellectuals on the Road to Class Power*, trans. by Andrew Arato and Richard E. Allen (Brighton: Harvester Press, 1979), passim; Rudolf Bahro, *Die Alternative: Zur Kritik des real existierenden Sozialismus* (Köln: Europaische Verlagsanstalt, 1977), pp. 135–206; Michael S. Voslensky, *Nomenklatura: Die herrschende Klasse der Sowjetunion in Geschichte und Gegenwart* (München: Nymphenburger, 1987), passim.

75. Jowitt, *New World Disorder*, p. 64. 'The nomenklatura is a list of the most important positions; the candidates for these positions are tested, recommended and confirmed by the respective Party committee [. . .]. The persons belonging to the nomenklatura of the Party committees can also only be relieved of their posts with the agreement of the respective committee. Persons are accepted into the nomenklatura who occupy key positions.' Voslensky, p. 21, quoting the section 'Party Structure', from the 'Teachers' Aid for Party Functionaries, and for Listeners at the Party Universities and the Universities of Marxism-Leninism' of the Soviet Union; my translation.

76. Voslensky, p. 27. Foreword by Milovan Djilas, quoting Stalin, *Werke*, XIV, 61–64.

77. Bahro, p. 257.

78. Voslensky, pp. 34–35. Djilas's *The New Class* was based largely on the Yugoslav situation.

79. Voslensky, p. 14.

80. Voslensky, p. 643.

81. Voslensky, pp. 89–90.

82. Champseix, 'Communisme et tradition', p. 55.

83. Jacques, pp. 436–37.

84. S. N. Eisenstadt, 'Intellectuals and Tradition', *Daedalus*, 2 (1972), 1–20 (p. 13).

85. Orlando Figes, *Natasha's Dance: A Cultural History of Russia* (London: Penguin Books, 2003), pp. 445–521.

86. Victor Terras, 'The Twentieth Century: The Era of Socialist Realism, 1925–1953', in *The Cambridge History of Russian Literature*, ed. by Charles A. Moser, rev. edn (Cambridge: Cambridge University Press, 1992), pp. 458–519 (pp. 514–16).

87. Robert Conquest, ed., *The Politics of Ideas in the USSR* (London: The Bodley Head, 1967), pp. 127–28.

88. Mary McCauley, *Soviet Politics 1917–1991* (Oxford: Oxford University Press, 1992), pp. 63–65.

89. Medvedev and Medvedev, p. 130.

90. Medvedev and Medvedev, pp. 70–72.

91. Harold Swayze, *Political Control of Literature in the USSR, 1946–1959* (Cambridge, Mass.: Harvard University Press, 1962), p. 131.

92. Medvedev and Medvedev, p. 147.

93. Terras, p. 531.

94. Medvedev and Medvedev, p. 71; Swayze, p. 187.

95. McCauley, p. 73.

96. Swayze, p. 201; Medvedev and Medvedev, pp. 138–39. Neither Solzhenitsyn's *Ivan Denisovich* nor Pasternak's *Dr Zhivago* was translated or published in Albania.

97. Conquest, p. 134.

98. Conquest, p. 148.

99. Conquest, p. 145.

100. Skendi, *The Albanian National Awakening*, pp. 121–22.

101. For usage of the term 'belated', in the sense of comparative national development, see Helmuth Plessner, *Die verspätete Nation: Über die politische Verführbarkeit bürgerlichen Geistes* (Stuttgart: Kohlhammer, 1969).

102. Enver Hoxha, *Selected Works*, III, 1960–65 (Tirana: Nëntori Publishing House, 1980), pp. 832–59.

103. Malëshova was expelled from the Party the following year for 'bourgeois deviationist and opportunist tendencies', Luan Rama, *Le long chemin sous le tunnel de Platon* (Paris: Edition du Petit Véhicule, 1999), p. 19; Jacques, p. 465.

104. Pearson, III, i 560. Pearson's entry is dated 5 October 1959 and derives from the *Albanian Catholic Bulletin* of 1994. The reference is retrospective, but gives no further details. Luan Rama, pp. 23–27, cites the letter and discusses the affair in detail. For his troubles Trebeshina was imprisoned for twenty years and then incarcerated in psychiatric institutions.

105. Jacques, p. 495.

106. Agnes Heller, *Das Alltagsleben: Versuch einer Erklärung der individuellen Reproduktion*, ed. and intro. by Hans Joas (Frankfurt a.M.: Suhrkamp, 1978), pp. 7–23, 24–31.

107. Kadare uses the term 'post-dictatorial' to express the difference between Albanian Stalinism and the environment of dissidents such as Havel and Solzhenitsyn, *Printemps albanais: Chronique, lettres, réflexions*, trans. by Michel Métais (Paris: Fayard, 1991), pp. 62–63; *Albanian Spring: The Anatomy of Tyranny*, trans. by Emile Capouya (London: Saqi Books, 1995), p. 64. All further references are indicated in brackets after the text. Structural changes and developments within Eastern European totalitarian states especially after the death of Stalin are analysed by Hannah Arendt, *The Origins of Totalitarianism*, rev. edn (San Diego: Harvest/HBJ, 1973), pp. 305–40, and Vaclav Havel, 'The Power of the Powerless', in *Open Letters: Selected Prose 1965–1990*, ed. by Paul Wilson (London: Faber and Faber, 1991), pp. 125–214. The concept of post-totalitarianism is discussed by Ágnes Heller, *Der Affe auf dem Fahrrad: Eine Lebensgeschichte*, bearbeitet von János Köbányai (Berlin: Philo, 1999), p. 402, and *Das Alltagsleben*, pp. 55–65, and passim.

108. Katerina Clark, *The Soviet Novel: History as Ritual*, 3rd edn (Bloomington: Indiana University Press, 2000), p. 27.

109. Clark, pp. 20–24.

110. Clark, p. 15.

111. Šiklová, Jiřina, 'The "Gray Zone" and the Future of Dissent in Czechoslovakia', *Social Research*, 57.2 (1990), 347–63; repr. in *Good-bye, Samizdat: Twenty Years of Czechoslovak Underground Writing*, ed. by Marketa Goetz-Stankiewicz (Evanston, Il.: Northwestern University Press, 1992), pp. 181–93. The author traces the expression 'grey zone intellectuals' in the article 'Czech historiography past, present and future' [Ceské dejepisectví včera, dnes a zítra] in the samizdat journal *Historické Studie* 1 by authors writing under the pseudonyms R. Prokop, L. Sádecký, and K. Bína. (My thanks to Libora Oates-Indruchová for the Czech references.) The term was used by Albanian dissidents and post-communist intellectuals in their critique of members of the intelligentsia, such as Kadare, Agolli, and others. Fatos T. Lubonja, 'Albanian Culture and Pilot Fish, editorial' (1996), *Përpjekja/Endeavour: Writing from Albania's Critical Quarterly*, ed. by Fatos T. Lubonja, and John Hodgson, trans. by John Hodgson (Tirana: Botime Përpjekja, 1997), pp. 33–40 (p. 36).

112. George Lukács, *Solzhenitsyn*, trans. by William David Graf (London: Merlin Press, 1970), pp. 10ff.

113. Clark, p. 9.

114. Élisabeth Champseix and Jean-Paul Champseix, *L'Albanie ou la logique du désespoir* (Paris: Éditions la Découverte, 1992), p. 195.

115. Geoffrey Hosking, 'The Twentieth Century: In Search of New Ways, 1953–80', in *The Cambridge History of Russian Literature*, rev. ed. by Charles A. Moser (Cambridge: Cambridge University Press, 1992), pp. 520–94 (p. 522).

116. John C. Hobhouse, Lord Broughton, *Travels in Albania and other Provinces of Turkey in 1809 and 1810*, 2 vols (London: John Murray, 1855), I, 138.

117. Pipa, *The Politics of Language*, p. xii, 97–99.

118. Hall, p. 30.

119. Durham, *The Burden of the Balkans*, pp. 233–34.

120. Hall, p. 29.

121. Skendi, *The Albanian National Awakening*, pp. 121–22; cf. Tönnes, pp. 47–83, on the development of linguistic consciousness and nationalism.

122. According to Lampe (p. 9), Zog closed the Greek- and Italian-sponsored schools as a part of the project of nationalization of primary education in 1933–34, but failed to open enough new state schools to take their place. Fischer, *King Zog*, pp. 168–70, notes that the level of education in the Greek-influenced south and in the Catholic north was relatively high before the nationalization project was undertaken.

123. Hall, p. 29.

124. Pipa, *The Politics of Language*, pp. xii–xiii.

125. Pipa, *The Politics of Language*, p. 99.

126. Lloshi, pp. 296–97.

127. Champseix, interviewed in *Ismail Kadaré:* Un film de Jacques Audoir et David Teboul, Coproduction France 3, Tanguera films, Klan TV. 1999.

128. The German writer Johann Gottfried Herder formulated the philosophical foundations for the legitimation of culture against politics for the nations of Central Europe and thereby laid the basis for the concepts of ethnicity and of ethnic nationalism in political and socio-cultural analysis. In Central and Eastern Europe, the link between national and/or ethno-cultural identity and literature is well established. Ever since the mid-nineteenth-century revolutions against Habsburg power in Central Europe, intellectuals and writers have been in the forefront of 'imagining the nation', moulding a distinctive identity from the *mythomoteurs* and ethno-genetic elements of their respective cultures, giving them a voice and articulating an identifiable profile.

129. Nicholas Boyle, *Goethe: The Poet and the Age*, I: *The Poetry of Desire* (Oxford: Oxford University Press, 1992), p. 116.

130. Kadaré/Bosquet, pp. 111–15.

131. Jusuf Vrioni, *Mondes effacés: Souvenirs d'un Européen* (Paris: Jean-Claude Lattès, 2001), p. 239.

132. Vrioni, pp. 221–72.

133. Vrioni, always modest, cites the approval of Alain Bosquet, Gilles Lapouge, and others of his anonymous translations, pp. 230ff.

CHAPTER 2

The Young Writer and the Regime

Beneficiary of Communism

Beginnings in Gjirokastra, 1936–1957

Ismail Kadare was nine years old at the end of the Second World War. In *Chronicle in Stone* he documents a childhood of occupation, civil decay, and war as Italian, Greek, and German forces fight for his town of Gjirokastra near the Greek border. He remembers the environment of war and occupation, but was too young to have been involved in fighting or to have participated in or share responsibility for the establishment of communism. *Chronicle in Stone* ends with the partisan reprisals against nationalists and fascists as the Germans arrive in the final years of the war.

Born in January 1936, Kadare grew up in privileged circumstances in the provincial Ottoman town of Gjirokastra.[1] His maternal grandfather was an Istanbul-educated magistrate, who in addition to his professional income, owned property and shops in Gjirokastra. His father came from simpler stock and worked throughout his life as a court-bailiff, a fairly lowly occupation half-way between clerk and courier. (Kadare refers to him as a 'porter' and 'modest functionary'[2] and as 'a court messenger, the man who delivered the tribunal's letters'.[3]) In the political context of the late 1930s, as documented in *Chronicle in Stone*, the rich tended to identify with the fascists and the poor with the communists. Kadare's family politics, however, were complicated by the fact that his wealthy mother's side supported the communists, while the father was more traditional in his social and political attitudes and was strongly suspicious of communism but did not support fascism.[4] In one of the family disputes about politics a deaf uncle tells the boy that he left the communists because 'in the meetings it was risky to hear poorly'. Kadare was warned early to keep an ear to the ground.[5]

Gjirokastra with its mixed Muslim and Orthodox population was also the birthplace of Enver Hoxha. Born in 1908 to a family of Muslim — Bektashi Shiite — landowners, Hoxha was educated at the French lycée in Korça and at the University of Montpellier in France. His house in Gjirokastra was only a short distance from that of the Kadare family and the closeness of their origins goes some way to explain the curiously intimate relationship that would develop between the writer and the dictator, although they only met once in private.[6] Hoxha was a clever, handsome, and ruthless leader. During the early 1930s when he was in France, he was also rumoured to have been something of a playboy, willing to share his favours with both sexes.

FIG. 3 (left): The young Enver Hoxha.
(Source: *40 Years of Socialist Albania*, Tirana:
8 Nëntori Publishing House, 1984.)

FIG. 4 (below): Enver Hoxha opening the
'New Albania' film studio in 1952.
(Source: *40 Years of Socialist Albania*, Tirana:
8 Nëntori Publishing House, 1984.)

Coming of age after the war, and with little memory of his country before the Italian occupation of 1939, Ismail Kadare thus belonged to the first generation of new Albanians. He was among the beneficiaries of his country's early years of post-war modernization. He left Gjirokastra to attend university at the time that the teaching college in Tirana was upgraded to become the country's first university in 1957. Like many of his generation, he had high hopes for communism during his late teens.[7] In his memories of late adolescence the sense of the freshness of life and the euphoria of national liberation merge with the expectation of social moderni-zation. For the young Kadare the regime represented power and the possibility of change within his own lifetime. Radical modernization would transform society, liberate women, lift standards of literacy and education, open Albania up to the cosmopolitan influences of Moscow and Eastern Europe. As a member of the young intelligentsia of the 1950s he identified strongly with the more or less brutal cutting of links with the past. He was not nostalgic for the world of the 1930s and 1940s, or for the politics of the royalists, monarchist nationalists, or Ballists.

He was fortunate, too, in coming of age just as writing was allowed to recover after the wartime upheavals and when Enver Hoxha began to nurture a new literary culture. The immediate consequence of the communist takeover for writing after November 1944 had been the annihilation of the nascent liberal public sphere and the execution or imprisonment of those writers who did not have the foresight to escape. Only in the mid-1950s, as Kadare was beginning to publish, did a literary culture emerge again with the establishment in 1954 of the official monthly periodical *Nëntori* (*November*), and in 1961 of *Drita* the weekly magazine of the Union of Artists and Writers.[8] Gifted and precocious, he published his first book of poems, *Youthful Inspiration: Lyrics* as a seventeen-year-old in 1953.[9] The story 'Lost Memories' was written in 1955. A second volume of poetry, *Dreams*, appeared in 1957 when he was a student in the faculty of philology and history of the University of Tirana.[10] *My Age: Poems* was published in 1961, and *Solar Motifs: Poems* in 1968. A volume of poems, *Lyrika*, appeared in Russian translation in the series, 'Contemporary Foreign Poetry', edited by David Samoïlov in Moscow in 1961, after Kadare had left the country.

One of Kadare's earliest pieces, *The Princess Argjiro*, takes as its theme the origins of the town of Gjirokastra. The work was denounced and an official reader's report was commissioned. In a document dated 30 May 1958, Lefter Dilo, teacher and author of a monograph on Kadare's home town, points out the historical and ideological errors.[11] The young poet is taken to task for not having consulted the appropriate sources and is criticized implicitly for disregarding socialist literary principles. The town of Gjirokastra traces its origins back to AD 568 and the name derives from the early Christian 'Angelocastro', not, as Kadare suggests, from the name of an early warrior princess. The Turks had already arrived in Gjirokastra by the fifteenth century and it is unthinkable that they would have allowed the town to be named after such a figure. Dilo's report was addressed to Liri Belishova, who had heard of the gifted young poet from a friend, and who would bring him to the attention of Nexhmije Hoxha. Belishova was at that time a high-ranking member of the Politburo, secretary of the Central Committee, responsible for ideological matters, and closely linked with Moscow. This particular instance of government control is interesting, as Kadare had at this time been selected for higher education in the Soviet Union. Belishova noted that the criticisms should be raised gently with the poet, so as not to hurt him, 'since he is still young', and the document was initialled by Nexhmije Hoxha, wife of the dictator and herself an immensely powerful figure in the regime.[12] Neither Belishova nor Hoxha raised the question of the young poet's eligibility to travel to the Soviet Union, given the problems of ideology identified in his work. Such lenience would scarcely be likely even a decade later.

Lessons in Moscow: The Gorki Institute, 1958–1960

In 1958 Kadare, like many of his generation, was sent to the Soviet Union for his professional education. At the famous Gorki Institute for World Literature in Moscow he would learn to become a socialist writer and member of the nomenklatura, trained as a writer and 'engineer of human souls' to construct the new Albania alongside economists, technologists, and administrators.[13] He was able to read some of the latest Western literature, such as the works of Sartre, Camus, and Hemingway, which were beginning to be translated into Russian.[14] Influenced by Russian and European modernism, he experimented with language and was criticized for writing poetry imbued with morbid decadence and bourgeois formalism.[15] Mixing with émigrés, fallen functionaries, and intellectuals undergoing re-education, and observing the intricate links between politics and literature in the socialist state, the young Kadare began to draw his own conclusions.

This was still the period of the Khrushchev thaw. In Moscow he witnessed the workings of a sophisticated and established communist regime in cultural affairs. Under Khrushchev, Stalinist repression was replaced by a new model, characterized by cycles of thaw and frost in which periods of relative openness would be followed by periods of closure and reassertion of control. The workings of this model were by no means transparent, but it generated new, more subtle forms of control. In periods of thaw degrees of dissidence would be tolerated; however, at the same time the sources of dissidence would be able to be identified and, if necessary, silenced.[16] In a spare room at the Gorki Institute dormitory Kadare discovered a wad of pages from a novel about a doctor at the time of the Revolution. It was 1958 and, after the openness of the early Khrushchev years, the Pasternak affair was about to take place. The Russian original of Pasternak's Dr Zhivago was published in Italy by the left-wing publisher Feltrinelli in 1957 and it appeared in Italian and English in the following year. In 1958 Pasternak was awarded the Nobel Prize for Literature partly on the basis of the novel. Khrushchev used the alibi of Western interference to initiate the first major freeze since the introduction of his reforms. Pasternak was censured and mercilessly harassed. At the Gorki Institute and throughout the Soviet Union writers and intellectuals showed their true colours in orchestrated public denunciations of the novel and its author.[17] Kadare would remember these experiences in his second autobiographical novel, The Twilight of the Steppe-Gods, written in 1976 when his life in Albania had taken a very different turn.

Enver Hoxha viewed the uprisings throughout Eastern Europe after Stalin's death as the direct result of the softening of Soviet central control. He opposed Khrushchev's revisionism and rejected Soviet involvement in Albanian internal affairs. Tensions between Hoxha and Khrushchev came to a head at the end of the decade. The year 1960 began with a worsening of relations between Albania and the Soviet Union. Enver Hoxha had found an ally in Communist China to oppose Khrushchev's attempt to de-Stalinize world communism, accept peaceful co-existence with the capitalist world and improve relations with Yugoslavia. However, Hoxha's interest was driven less by ideological and world-political motives than by his fear that Khrushchev would sacrifice Albania to Yugoslavian interests. In 1959 Khrushchev visited Albania in order to re-establish relations between the two Balkan nations and to put an end to Albania's rapidly strengthening alliance with China. Despite the growing tensions with the Soviet Union, Khrushchev promised further aid, including the building of the Palace of Culture in central Tirana. At the end of his trip Khrushchev advised the Albanians to turn their country into an orchard and 'flowering garden' to supply fruit and vegetables to the Soviet Union, rather than cultivating wheat or industrializing the countryside. The Soviet Union, he said, 'has such an abundance of grain that the mice eat more than you can produce here'.[18] Despite the rhetoric of friendliness, Hoxha remained suspicious of Soviet designs on his country: of the dependence that being a supplier of fresh produce would bring, rather than the independence that would be gained through industrialization, and of the naval base at Vlora, which would provide Soviet submarines with permanent accommodation and access to the Mediterranean. While further top-level meetings occurred in the following year, Hoxha had decided that China would be a less intrusive and possibly more generous ally. In mid-year the Soviets changed the conditions of the student exchange agreements to Albania's detriment in a clear warning to the regime to begin cooperating. Hoxha moved against the pro-Soviet faction in the Central Committee. The Secretary of the Central Committee, Liri Belishova, who appears unnamed in Kadare's novel, *Winter of Great Solitude*, was denounced for her strongly pro-Soviet dealings by third-in-command Hysni Kapo. A pro-Soviet plot was discovered and Belishova and others were condemned to long periods of internment in labour camps.

In the summer of 1960 there were food shortages in Eastern Europe and famine in China. With Khrushchev's comment about the mice of Russia still ringing in his ears, Hoxha approached the Chinese who, in the midst of their own devastating famine, purchased wheat from France for Albania.[19] Khrushchev's perfidy was remembered and becomes a leitmotif in Kadare's epic novel of the era, *Winter of Great Solitude*. Hoxha refused to attend the gathering of East European leaders in Bucharest in June 1960 to discuss the ideological and political differences that had arisen between Russia and China. The Albanian delegation was led by Hysni Kapo, the third leading member of the Politburo.[20] Kapo supported the Chinese attack on Khrushchevism and refused to endorse the Soviet condemnation of the Chinese Communist Party's 'mistakes'. At the Moscow meeting of the eighty-one Communist Parties which opened on 10 November, Hoxha defended Stalin's heritage against the revisionists, bitterly attacked Khrushchev's anti-Stalinism, and criticized the Soviet Union for meddling in Albanian affairs, for bullying the world communists to condemn the Chinese, for trying to blackmail Albania into submission and for failing to support the country in its hour of need during the famine. Khrushchev was incensed, as were many members of the world communist parties, who lined up to condemn Hoxha and the Albanian delegation. Hoxha and Shehu left the meeting early, preferring to take a train rather than risk flying. In December Albania broke off diplomatic relations with the Soviet Union and strengthened relations with China. While Yuri Andropov headed a delegation to the meeting of the Fourth Congress of the Albanian Party of Labour in a last-ditch attempt to smooth things over in February 1961, and official communiqués continued until late in the year to refer to the 'unbreakable Albanian–Soviet friendship', the Soviets withdrew their specialists in the early months and cancelled all aid in April 1961. However, it was only at the end of September that Hoxha openly attacked the Soviet regime. In October 1961 when Khrushchev refused to invite the Albanians to the 22nd Congress of the Soviet Communist Party, the break was made publicly and acrimoniously. In the context of the crisis of world communism brought about by the conflict between the Soviet Union and China, the Soviet Union broke off relations with Albania.

Soviet influence was at an end. The controversial Soviet naval presence at the base in the Pasha Limani inlet on Albania's Adriatic coast near Vlora was terminated. This important strategic outlet into the Mediterranean was the main reason for Soviet interest in and perseverance with the unruly Albanians. Later in the year a conspiracy to overthrow the regime was uncovered in the Navy and the pro-Soviet Commander-in-Chief of the Albanian Navy, Admiral Teme Sejko, was arrested and executed along with other conspirators. Liri Belishova, the prominent Central Committee member and widow of anti-Titoist Naku Spiru, was arrested. (On the basis of Khrushchev's memoirs she was believed dead, but she emerged from the labour camps in the 1990s at the end of the dictatorship.)[21] This marked the end of the powerful Soviet faction, although pockets of pro-Soviet feeling remained in the Party. In an important speech on November 1961, almost a year after the Moscow meeting, Hoxha attributed the split to 'entirely ideological and political causes'.[22]

However, the Hoxha regime had made a fatal, if necessary, mistake in sending off the post-war generation of 'new men' (and women) to universities in the Soviet Union, Czechoslovakia, and elsewhere. On 1 September the Soviet government for its part terminated a Soviet–Albanian cultural agreement from 1952, depriving Albanian students of the right to continue their studies free of charge at Russian universities and higher educational establishments. In fact, most had already been recalled the previous year by their own government.[23] The abrupt recall of Albanian students was too late for one, at least, who had seen the consequences of Khrushchev's reforms. Kadare arrived at the Gorki Institute in the wake of Khrushchev's 'secret speech' of 1956: 'Je connaissais les crimes de Staline, les désillusions des Russes vis-à-vis du socialisme, le désespoir et l'ennui' ('I knew of Stalin's crimes, the disillusionment of the Russian with communism, their despair and boredom').[24] By the time he was recalled he had been exposed to the post-war new wave of youth literature and ideas, and observed the operation of ideology and writing at the centre of world communism.

FIG. 5: Ismail Kadare at the Gorki Institute (Moscow) at the age of 22 in 1958.
(Photo: Private collection of Ismail Kadare.)

Youth and Disillusionment in *The City without Signs*, 1959–1961

Generational Change

For Agnes Heller existentialism is the first of three stages in the post-war consciousness representing a *'revolt of subjectivity'* against the ossified forms of life of the past. 'Sartre's message', writes Heller, 'caught the minds of the young' in Central as well as Western Europe:

> What mattered now was doing things in our own way, practising our own freedom. Young men and women, intoxicated by the atmosphere of unlimited possibilities, began to dance existentially, love existentially, talk existentially, etc. In other words, they were intent on breaking free.[25]

Kadare emerged from a childhood of occupation, war, and anarchy, and experienced the early years of the post-war order as a freeing up of opportunities for self-development and even self-fulfilment. He came of age in the environment of post-war hope for national self-determination and socio-economic progress, and his early works were born of and operate in the new world order of the 1950s. They concern themselves with youth culture, social modernization, and cultural modernism, not with the ritual functions of socialist realism or the competing doctrines of socialism. In the late 1950s selections from the works of Salinger, Hemingway, and others were available in the Soviet Union as a result of the freeing-up of constraints on foreign literature.[26] Existentialism, identified in the popular imagination with the message 'to break free', influenced young people throughout Europe, even in the Soviet Union and post-war communist Albania. Kadare and his generation heard the message of European existentialism filtered through Italian films, French and American novels, and Soviet youth culture, and interpreted it in terms of their own concerns. With its focus on the uniqueness of individual existence and relegation of social considerations, existentialism proved powerful in encouraging the post-war generations of Europe to disengage from the problems and history of their parents' generation, and to focus on self-realization and the future. Kadare was alert to these movements of post-war youth culture and literature in Russia and in Albania, which, in the 1950s and early 1960s remained culturally relatively open.[27] Hosking refers to the upsurge of youth prose in the years 1960 to 1962 as the 'third and deepest' phase of the Khrushchev thaw.[28]

Kadare's earliest stories express the interests and concerns of a new generation in conflict with the old. In the short story 'The Nude', a family is split over the son's painting of a female figure which has scandalized neighbours and threatens his sister's engagement.[29] The conflict between father and son has political overtones in the communist environment where, after the egalitarianism of the partisan years, the liberation of women was a high priority in the program of modernization. Neither the dictator nor the regime is mentioned, but the presence of the centralized and modernizing government is implied in the state-run art-school which has created the conditions for the family conflict. As so often in the literature of early communism, politics and traditional values are expressed through the oedipal imagery of rebellious sons and daughters. The hodja, or Muslim teacher and cleric, who advocates a reactionary sexual morality in this story prefigures the hodja who blinds himself rather than witness the arrival of the communists in *Chronicle in Stone*. However, in 'The Nude', a compromise solution is found to the conflict between youthful sexual rebellion and traditional parental and religious authority. A curtain is conveniently placed so that both sides can keep face in the stand-off between modern art and traditional morality.

The modernization of the socialist regime was achieved at the cost of extensive limitations on personal freedom. This was not the modernity which lay at the heart of existentialism, and it was not long before the young Kadare began to stand out. In his photographs from the 1960s Kadare exudes a youthful rebelliousness. The photographs reproduced in the *Dialogue with Alain Bosquet* show a well-groomed young man cultivating a 'teddy boy' and a 'James Dean' image in prudish Albania where men's hair was cut uniformly short on government orders.[30] He mentions the humiliation and the resentment of having to cut his hair in accordance with government regulations.[31] His early pictures show him sporting a look modelled on French fashions of the 1950s and early 1960s. There is even a certain dandyism, which reminds the viewer of Kadare's frequent reference to that other famous dandy, Enver Hoxha.[32] While he penned some instrumental early odes to Stalin, which presumably brought him to the attention of the Party authorities, he also cultivated a stance of distanced contempt for the party hacks and the nomenklatura, an attitude which, he writes, was the product of youthful arrogance rather than of considered political opposition. His early writings are also marked by resentment at the exclusion from the Western culture which he and his friends had managed to glean from Italian radio, television, and cinema, and from modernist and contemporary literature. In his early stories he describes characters whose poetry is the product of their frustration and is provocative in the new state. In *The City without Signs* the decadent young poet Eugjen produces a poem in which taxis are likened to stars in the skies of the provincial town, and in the later autobiographical work, *The Twilight of the Steppe-Gods*, Kadare is sanctioned at the Gorki Institute for writing a poem in which 'The heavens are without form, like the brain of an idiot'.[33]

City without Signs

Kadare began *The City without Signs* in Tirana, and worked on it at the Gorki Institute in 1959 where he tried composing directly onto audio tape as an experiment in modern composition, before finishing it in writing after returning to Albania in late 1960.[34] The text was later revised and an excerpt was published in the literary review *Drita* in Tirana in 1961. The related story, 'Days of Drink', was published in a youth magazine in 1962 and, not surprisingly, contributed to the young author's reputation for decadence. The stories share themes of modernism, alienated youth, disillusionment, and cynicism influenced by post-war existentialism.

Both stories are about ambitious and unscrupulous young men in the provinces who are willing to go to criminal lengths to further their careers. However, there are important differences. 'Days of Drink' is negative and condemnatory. The youths are drunken failures whose plans come to nothing as a result of state invigilation and family intervention. In the longer novel *City without Signs*, told in the third person, themes of artistic creativity, careerism, and cynicism are brought together in a similar plot. However, the hoax succeeds and seems only likely to be unmasked at the end as a result of the self-incrimination of the one whose life does not improve as a result of the crime.

The protagonist of *The City*, Gjon Kurti, is sent out as a newly trained teacher to the provincial town of N. . . (identifiable by its architecture as Kadare's home town of Gjirokastra) for his first teaching position. He is unwilling to leave the capital, his girlfriend, his friends, his philological research and hopes of an academic career, in order to face the daily grind of a class of unruly and provincial children suspicious of his citified ways and clothes. Gjon soon falls in with the local bohemian intellectuals, the poet Eugjen Peri and the chemistry teacher Mentor Rada, both of whom had also studied in Tirana and, like Gjon, miss its urbanity and student life. In Tirana they can discuss art and formalism, subjectivism and history, and can recite poems such as Eugjen's 'A Sunday in the Country' ('Un dimanche en province') with its suggestive modernist metaphors of escape. Gjon feels an irrational anger towards the 'maître de maison',

> Un homme trapu, grisonnant, vêtu d'un complet à la mode des années 20, avec un noeud papillon. Un des respectables citoyens de N. . ., spécimen de cette précieuse réserve d'autochtones grâce auxquels la ville préservait avec rigueur la dignité de ses us et traditions.[35]

> A squat, greying man in a bow tie, whose suit had a twenties cut. One of the respectable citizens of N. . ., a specimen of that precious stock of locals thanks to whom the city rigidly maintained the dignity of its mores and traditions.

Early in the novel Gjon has already let himself go and is imagined as the survivor of a shipwreck, only just clinging to life. At twenty-three he sees himself as a failure, and regards with envy the gifted young poet of the town, alter ego of Kadare, who has gained 'a certain notoriety' in the capital, Tirana, and repudiates his provincial origins. He is faced with two possibilities: either to accept his role in modern Albanian life and set about contributing to the provincial environment as a teacher and Party member, like his friend Mercure; or he can become an embittered exile from the cosmopolitanism of the national capital, sinking into drinking and depression with an unsavoury group of friends. However, a third option occurs to him as a result of a chance comment by one of his pupils — a criminal careerism which will enable him to become professor of Albanian philology at the Academy in Tirana. Teaching his class about the importance of the earliest Albanian texts Gjon realizes that it would not be difficult to falsify such a document, and he sets about doing so with the help of Eugjen, a poet, and Mentor, a chemist.

It is 1959 and Albania is still a part of pro-Soviet Eastern Europe. The main threat to the country is from capitalist Greece, whose bombers regularly fly over the town on reconnaissance missions. However, Kadare's point of departure is not ideological dissidence. The themes of these early stories are post-war generational identity, the inflexibility and restrictiveness of the government, dominated by figures from Gjon's father's generation, and ideological and bureaucratic rigidity and corruption. The young people Gjon meets up with are clichés of disaffected youth, influenced by

Western popular culture. Gjon wants to escape provincial mediocrity, not Albania or communism. The socialist-realist world of work, optimism, and productiveness is barely perceptible in this environment of parties, alcohol, jazz, and sex:

> 'Tout le monde fait ça. En Europe, c'est chose courante. Tu sais bien que la population en France n'augmente plus . . . Tu ne t'es pas demandé pourquoi?'
> 'D'après notre prof de géo, à cause des conditions de vie difficiles en régime capitalist'.
> 'Ton prof est un âne. Moi, je vais te dire la vraie raison: c'est à cause des avortements. Oui, des avortements!' (*La Ville* 47)

> 'The whole world does that. In Europe it's the done thing. You know that the population of France is not increasing any more . . . Haven't you asked yourself why?'
> 'According to our geography teacher, it's because of the difficulties of life under capitalism'.
> 'Your teacher is an ass. I'll tell you the real reason: it's because of abortions. Yes, abortions'.

The depth of the cynicism with which the young protagonists face their futures is striking. Careerism lies at the heart of *The City without Signs*. Gjon succeeds because he can work the system. He is not a natural talent like the local poet who has won acclaim at an early age. Unlike his friend Mercure, the devoted Party-member and committed intellectual, he does not accept communism as an ethical-political system or as a nationalist-modernizing ideology.

Gjon suggests to Mentor and Eugjen that they collaborate — the philologist, the poet, and the chemist — on the falsification of an ancient document. The argument is insidious, as Gjon deliberately blurs the distinctions between ideology and historical fact in order to sway his friends:

> 'Nous devons être les fils loyaux de ce siècle, rejeter les préjugés, les attitudes idéalistes, la pseudo-morale et tout le bataclan, [. . .] et devenir d'authentiques matérialistes. . . [. . .] Avons nous le droit, nous, de chercher à faire carrière au bon sense du term? Bien sûr que oui, n'est-ce pas?'
> 'Oui, oui, naturellement. Un poète sovietique, Evtouchenko, a même écrit là-dedans un poème qu'il a justement intitulé *La Carrière* . . .'. [. . .]
> 'Écoutez-moi, les gars', fit posément Gjon, 'je vous demande simplement d'essayer de me comprendre. De comprendre qu'à notre époque, on ne peut plus se contenter d'être idéalistes et de penser selon les schémas des siècles passés. Au fond, quelle différence y a-t-il entre la découverte d'un manuscrit authentique et celle d'un faux?' (*La Ville* 86–88)

> 'We must be the loyal sons of the age, we must reject prejudices, idealist attitudes, pseudo-morality and all that stuff [. . .] and become authentic materialists . . . [. . .] Don't we too have the right to try to find a career in the good sense of the term? Of course we do. Don't we?'
> 'Yes, yes, of course. A Soviet poet, Yevtushenko, has even written a poem called *The Career* . . .' [. . .]
> 'Listen, boys', Gjon said with deliberation, 'I'm just asking you to try to understand me. To understand that in our age, we can no longer be content to be idealists and to think in terms of past times. When all is said and done, what difference is there between the discovery of an authentic manuscript or of a false one?'

Having convinced Mentor, the two of them set to work on Eugjen, who is shocked at the thought of taking the history of their country so lightly:

> 'Et puis,' renchérit Gjon, 'mettons que nous parvenions à démontrer que l'albanais, en tant que langue écrite, a été employé avant le XVe siècle: à qui cela causerait-il le moindre préjudice? Nous serions coupables au regard de la Vérité abstraite, mais tout à fait innocents vis-à-vis de notre Patrie'. (*La Ville* 90)

> 'Let's say that we show Albanian to have been used in written form before the fifteenth century. Who would be harmed in the least by that? We would be guilty with regard to Truth in the abstract, but completely innocent as regards our Homeland'.

Gjon's plan is to write in Tosk, thus giving primacy to the southern dialect spoken by the majority of the upper-level Party members, drawn from various primarily southern and Gjirokastran clans. The decision to forge a non-religious text would give a strongly secular cast to the origins of written Albanian, given that the earliest extant document in written Albanian is a baptismal prayer, and the earliest printed book, the fragmentary *Missal* (1555) of the northern Albanian Catholic priest Gjon Buzuku, is a liturgical piece associated with the northern Ghegs and Catholicism. Through the agency of the monk, the forged letter will plead the cause of the impoverished peasants to a bishop and feudal landholder, implying the early existence of a national identity brought about through class struggle. The lowly monk would be the only literate figure in this environment. The date will be 1387, several years before the earliest extant document in written Albanian, and just two years before the Battle of Kosovo. The Albanian nation thus will be shown to pre-date the Ottoman occupation. This letter is the work of the philologist, Gjon; a second document, a ten-line fragment from the lost work, *Songs and Tears from the Great War* by the Albanian poet and patriot, Andon Çajupi (1866–1930), will be fabricated by Eugjen, reinforcing the message of the letter, that it is the exploitative classes, not foreigners, against whom the Albanians should wage war. Both documents will be transcribed using paper and inks prepared by the chemist, Mentor.

The boys agree to collaborate on a line which will be welcome to the powers-that-be in the Academy of Sciences, namely that the beginnings of a class-consciousness can be demonstrated among the southern Tosk peasants rather than the northern Ghegs. This document will support the work of the current president of the Academy. Gjon has clearly learned the lessons of 'speaking lies to power' in order to become powerful himself.

> 'Et nous traînerons dans la boue le professeur O.B. . . . à propos de certaines formes du participe en albanais ancien', reprit Gjon. 'Nous insérerons dans le texte quelques formes qui infirmeront sa propre thèse . . .'.
>   'Non, non, surtout pas de règlements de comptes! intervint Mentor. Je crois me souvenir qu'il t'a recalé par trois fois à un oral, et . . .'. (*La Ville* 102)

> 'And we'll drag Professor O.B. through the mud . . . on the subject of certain forms of the participle in ancient Albanian', Gjon replied. 'We'll insert those forms into the text that will disprove his argument . . .'
>   'No, no. Above all no settling of accounts!' Mentor broke in. 'If I remember rightly, he failed you three times in the oral exams'.

Gjon has learned the language of party-line altruism, giving the discussion something of the flavour of a sitting of the Union of Writers:

> 'Pas du tout, réfuta Gjon. Pour moi, le destin de la langue albanaise prime toute considération personelle!' Eugjen émit un petit ricanement. (*La Ville* 102–03)

> Not at all, Gjon replied. For me the fate of the Albanian language takes precedence over all personal considerations'. Eugjen sniggered momentarily.

The three young men judge the mood of the regime and project their forgery skilfully into the ideological debates in such a way as to reinforce the orthodoxy:

> Au cours d'une conférence organisée à cette occasion à l'Académie, le président en personne prononça le discours attendu sur le premier des deux textes. Il évoqua les fausses interprétations émises antérieurement par de nombreux philologues, soulignant que le nouveau texte condamnait sans appel toutes les hypothèses déjà critiquées. Dans un intéressant commentaire, le vice-président analysa le caractère de classe dudit texte. (*La Ville* 145)

> In the course of a conference organized for the occasion by the Academy, the president himself delivered the anticipated speech on the first of the two texts. He mentioned the incorrect interpretations given previously by numerous philologists, emphasizing that the new text would put an end to the hypotheses which he had just criticized. In an interesting commentary, the vice-president analysed the class character of the said text.

Under the influence of his pupil and lover, Stella, symbol of well-meaning ordinariness and communist innocence, Gjon momentarily reneges, conscious of the damage done to history and his nation. However, his doubts are quickly dispersed after he is attacked by a couple of thugs at the behest of his ex-girlfriend, Luiza, from whom he contracted syphilis and whom he was obliged to identify as his partner in order to gain medical treatment at the local clinic. After the death of Mercure in an industrial accident, Gjon returns to his cynical and ambitious plan, rejoining Mentor and Eugjen to visit the monastery of St Trinity where they plant their forged documents. Kadare makes Gjon's motivation absolutely clear at this point: he is intelligent and ambitious, but uncommitted to the socialist project and frustrated and lonely in the provincial town, where he finds no-one other than the naive Stella, and where the one 'positive hero' and believer, Mercure, has died midway through the novel.

> Un misérable, voilà ce que je suis. Mais pourquoi? Parce que j'aime la capitale et que je ne me sens pas de renoncer à la vie de là-bas. [. . .] Je n'aime pas la province. Je n'aime que ma capitale. Peut-être me battrais-je si j'avais ici un ami. Mais Mercure est mort et je suis resté seul. Je finirai ivrogne. Il faut que je quitte N. . . (*La Ville* 137)

> Look what a wretch I am. Why? Because I love the capital and don't feel like renouncing it for life down there. [. . .] I don't like the provinces. I only like my capital. Perhaps if I had a friend here I could fight this. But Mercure is dead and I'm all alone. I'll finish up a drunk. I've got to get out of N. . .

The discovery shoots the three young men to fame as the party journals and newspapers, in particular the youth magazine, stress the social and political import of the discoveries, and the President of the Academy of Sciences and the professors follow suit in exploring the indications of democratic-revolutionary and anti-fascist tendencies in this earliest piece of Albanian writing. Çajupi becomes an Albanian precursor of Lenin and his plea, 'Ô humbles et pauvres gens | De Serbie et de Russie, | Tournez vos armes contres vos gouvernants' ('O lowly and poor peoples | Of Serbia and Russia, | Turn your arms against your rulers', *La Ville* 145), is interpreted as an ancient call with contemporary relevance, to transform imperialist war-making into civil uprising against class oppressors. Careers are ruined and political mileage is made as the discovery becomes a cause of local and national celebration. Gjon is offered a professorship at the Academy in Tirana but is tortured by fears of exposure. He dreams that his dead friend, the true believing socialist Mercure, has sent him a telegram of congratulations from beyond the grave. Gjon leaves the one person he loves, Stella, and boards the bus for the capital. The story finishes with an epilogue in which Eugjen, plagued by guilt, hesitates in front of the post office with a letter of confession in his hand. The final image is of the wet, cold, and grey communist everyday, the world that Gjon wants to escape, and that Kadare would return to in 1960.

> Autour de lui, la pluie fine ne cesse de tomber. Il souffle un vent glacé. Tout paraît osciller dans les ténèbres. Oscillent les arbres, les lumières, les silhouettes des gens. (*La Ville* 153)

> All around him the fine rain continues to fall. An icy wind blows. Everything seems to be flickering in the shadows. The trees, the light, the silhouettes of the people.

Careerism and Authenticity

Gjon Kurti is ambitious and frustrated. Careerism is his only way out. The means he chooses are criminal, and hence extreme even in the Albanian context. However, Kadare's point is that the structure which ordained Gjon's fate as a provincial teacher creates its own contradictions. Total control and determination of individual lives leads to careerist manipulation, fraud, and criminality.[36] The centralized, bureaucratic structure which has decreed Gjon's fate is the force behind the action. Gjon Kurti, like most heroes of Soviet socialist realism, goes through a process of discovery of self and the world. But unlike them, he does not come to find harmony between his own desires and the demands of his nation and the ruling party, thereby fulfilling the demands of the genre. Far from accepting his iconic role as a cog in the machinery of communist modernization, he becomes a careerist, whose success is based on personal weakness, ideological cynicism, and criminal forgery. In this sense the novel is a critique of a corrupt political system, rather than of generational conflict, as in Russia.

When Gjon first discusses his plan, Eugjen cites Yevgeny Yevtushenko's 1957 poem, 'A Career'. However, Yevtushenko's poem pits careerism against truth, criticizing the structures of power, and the opportunists who exploit them:

> In Galileo's day, a fellow scientist
> was no more stupid than Galileo.

He was well aware the earth revolved,
But he also had a large family to feed.
Stepping into a carriage with his wife,
after effecting his betrayal,
he believed he was launched on a career,
though he was undermining it in reality.[37]

The dualism of this poem, its opposition of ideology and truth, strikes at the heart of communist ideology by positing a scientific truth beyond class-consciousness. However, the moral of Yevtushenko's poem is lost on Gjon, who proceeds to argue the opposite, namely that the forgery is an existential act free of obsolete morality. Gjon makes the decision to pursue a life of inauthenticity to its conclusion. This is the life of the careerist who will vote with the party against Galileo. He will reappear in various forms in Kadare's novels as the opportunist, the weakling or coward, the power-hungry bureaucrat or the humiliated yes-man (for example, Mark-Alem in *The Palace of Dreams*, or the failed screenwriter in *The Shadow*).

Kadare's novel reflects aspects of the Soviet youth literature in its most radical phase. Geoffrey Hosking notes the surprising level of cynicism in these works. '"There's no such thing as love, that's an old-fashioned fairy tale. There's only the satisfaction of sexual need", declares one of the blasé young men in Aksënov's *Ticket to the Stars* (1961)'.[38] These young rebels travel not 'to the virgin lands or the great industrial sites of Siberia, but west, to the "decadent" Baltic coast, as near to the longed-for outside world as a Soviet citizen can get without an exit visa'.[39] Yet this rebelliousness did not (or was not allowed to) reflect disillusionment with Soviet society. While the heroes appear 'cynical, sophisticated and world-weary', rejecting their parents' values, having found themselves in rebellion, they return stronger and invigorated to the socialist project. 'They finish up at a Siberian hydroelectric power station after all, having restored some "revolutionary romanticism" to the prospect of constructing it and dedicating it to the future'.[40] The episode in *The City* in which the boys discuss brothels and masturbate over pictures of Bardot and Lollobrigida reflects the tone of this Soviet literature. However, Kadare does not redeem his disillusioned young men. The renewal implicit in the rediscovery of socialist ethics, which Hosking sees as central to the socialist realist novels of the younger generation of Soviet authors, is absent from *The City without Signs*. In its place is a nihilism and moral and ethical emptiness which explicitly refers to the romantic despair of Byron and Lermontov and to the decadence of Wilde, but which lacks the sense of individual authenticity of the former, or the social provocativeness of the latter. The revolutionary romanticism is missing and the stories of alcoholic binges, sex, venereal disease, and prostitution are sordid. The redemption of the young people does not take place. They remain deeply compromised by a youthful rebelliousness which becomes criminal in the socialist environment and all too easily uses nationalist-communist dogma to achieve its ends. Even the good young communist, Mercure, is tainted. He participates as an intellectual and a worker, and advocates openness in the spirit of the 20th Congress of the CPSU in which debate and discussion take the place of doctrine from above (*La Ville* 55–56). But he criticizes Eugjen's poem as reactionary and identifies the spirit of capitalism in his peers' attitudes and behaviour. In response to Luiza's appreciation of Eugjen's modernist metaphors, Mercure replies: '"tu veux peut-être dire qu'il aurait bien fait de mentionner aussi la marque des véhicules?"' ('"Are you trying to say that it would have been good to mention the brand of the cars as well?"', *La Ville* 56). He, too, is ultimately an inflexible ideologue who places socialist doctrine above individual freedom.

Written partly in Moscow under the influence of Dudintsev's critique of Soviet bureaucracy and corruption in *Not by Bread Alone* (1956), *The City* uses the current forms of youth literature to launch a powerful critique of socialist careerism and hence of Albanian socialism. Even at this first stage of his adult writing career Kadare refuses to make the reconciliatory gestures to socialist realism and the Marxist-Leninist view of history that could render this work acceptable to the regime. There is little romanticism and less naivety in Gjon's youthful rebellion, and while he finds the possibility of redemption in Stella, the naive, provincial girl who believes in communism, he abandons her for his life of inauthenticity as a professor and Academy member in the national capital. The theme of careerism and inauthenticity inverts the central tenet of socialist realism, namely that the link between existence and activity be meaningful, bringing together ideology and praxis in authentic, *lived* individual life.

Kadare's early stories draw on images from post-war film and popular culture still accessible in Albania at this time. Françoise Sagan's *Bonjour Tristesse* appeared in 1954, initiating the sexual revolution in post-war France, and Roger Vadim's pre-New Wave film, *Et dieu . . . créa la femme*, appeared in 1956, introducing Brigitte Bardot into a world of gilded youth, sexual innuendo, and glamorous Cote d'Azur settings. Gina Lollobrigida's first film, *La Città si difende*, released in 1951, also popularized youthful criminals and *femmes fatales* in an Italian version of Hollywood *noir*. In Kadare's story 'Days of Drink', Marilyn (Monroe) and Arthur (Miller), Simone (Signoret) and Yves (Montand) are topics of discussion. Gjon and his friends in *The City* refer to Gina Lollobrigida in *Arriverderci Roma*, and to the popular Italian hit of 1958, 'Volare' (by Domenico Modugno and Franco Migliacci) rather than to Sholokhov or Yevtushenko. The world of bars, cafes, and Westernized youth in these early stories is Kadare's response to the positive heroes and heroines of socialist realism. While the story remains focused on the youthful protagonist's frustration, the target of the novel remains the environment 'without signs' after which the novel is named. For unlike the Soviet environment, in which a generation moulded by Stalin was rejected by the young intellectuals of the 1950s, in Albania there was no possibility of such rebellion. Not only was the generation of the Stalinist fathers still in the process of consolidating its power under the patronage of Enver Hoxha, but the sons were without any signposts for their rebellion other than those of Western European existentialism.

In 'Days of Drink' the first-person narrator and his friend arrive in the provincial town of N. . . where they hope to find a lost manuscript by the Albanian writer and patriot Çajupi. Amid bouts of drinking they formulate a plan to falsify documents which will relocate the Albanian and the Balkan class struggle to the late Middle Ages, thereby rewriting the history of the Albanian nation. They are thwarted by the friend's uncle who sends them packing back to Tirana. In the showdown with his nephew the uncle calls on traditional values of family honour, honesty, and respect for the church and the institutions in which the falsified documents were to be located. No reference is made to socialism. Indeed the implication in both stories is that the dogma of Marxism-Leninism renders the regime open to fraudulent careerism. The post-war generation appears cynical and immoral in both stories, alienated equally from the traditional values of their parents and grandparents and from the new value-system of communism, and living out sordid fantasies of Westernized life. 'Days of Drink' ends with the protagonists looking back from a departing bus to the church-tower and the minaret and forward to a wintry road ahead.

> Nous aperçûmes pour la toute dernière fois à travers la brume, le clocher de l'église et la tour du minaret qui semblaient nous adresser de la main une sorte d'au revoir, à l'instar de deux connaissances décrépites et radoteuses. Ni moi ni mon copain n'esquissâmes le moindre signe de la main, ni n'adressâmes d'autre forme de salutation à la vieille ville de N. Nous fixions en silence, devant nous, la chaussée hivernale et en ressentions une espèce de soulagement. ('Jours' 205)[41]

> For the very last time made out through the fog the bell-tower and the minaret which seemed to be waving their hands to us in a sort of farewell, like two feeble and decrepit old friends. Neither I nor my pal made the least sign, nor gave any other gesture of acknowledgement to the ancient city of N. We looked ahead in silence, at the wintry road and felt a sort of relief.

The church and the mosque are decrepit relics of the past, and the road ahead, although wintry, offers a sense of relief. This final paragraph suggests that a life of hardened cynicism lies ahead for the two young men, detached from the traditional bases of identity in the past and facing with equanimity a future painted in grey. Relief in this context can only be read as defeated acceptance of the unmitigated mediocrity of everyday life under the regime, hardly a tribute to the successes of communism.

The City without Signs and 'Days of Drink' establish three important early themes in Kadare's work. The first is the theme of authentic versus inauthentic life. The cynicism, fatalism, and sense of loss and wasted opportunities of the young people evokes questions of what an authentic life is under socialism. Gjon, Eugjen, and Mentor reflect the frustration of youthful hopes of achievement and advancement. Between the traditional world of family and honour and the communist world of productivity and unquestioning belief there is little to appeal to them. The egoism which renders them such modern figures finds no outlet. The good communists, Mercure and Stella, are, as their names suggest, distant from the reality of Albanian everyday life. The second theme, of the rebel without a cause, which underwrites so much of the post-war youth literature and film, expresses the lack of direction which resulted from the disintegration of belief systems over the previous century throughout Europe and America. The borrowed Westernisms of Kadare's young people are an empty response to disillusionment at the new communist state. In Kadare's southern Albanian environment traditional life and values had depended on structures of Ottoman civilization. The communism which was imposed after

1945 offered little in the way of cultural depth. It was, from the beginning, a crude dogma relying on jingoistic nationalism and fear, and masquerading as a pure ideology in a corrupted world. There were few realistic identificatory structures for young people. Those who entered the bureaucracy and the nomenklatura did so in the understanding that this was a powerful new class entirely in the service of the regime. The themes of careerism and rebellion are associated with Kadare's third theme, Albanian identity and the function of literature. The betrayal of Albania, which lies at the centre of the hoax in *The City*, contrasts strongly with the redemptive rediscovery of the Soviet motherland by the younger generation of socialist realist writers. This theme will become more prominent as Kadare comes to see himself competing with the dictatorship for the soul of his nation.

Kadare's critique of careerism and modernization in *The City* does not indicate opposition to socialism as such. 'Il y a une époque où, comme tout le monde là-bas, j'ai cru au socialisme, au communisme; parce que je ne connaissais pas d'autre monde que la dictature socialiste' ('There was an era when, like everyone else there, I believed in socialism, in communism, because I didn't know any other world than that of the socialist dictatorship').[42] At this time he was a young man who had benefited from the new education policies, who had not yet experienced the dark side of the regime, and who could scarcely foresee how pernicious the regime would become. The disillusionment of Gjon Kurti in *The City* suggests an autobiographical component as Kadare struggled to adjust to life in the narrow home environment after his time in Moscow. Kadare had returned impressed with the city, the cosmopolitanism, and the scale of Soviet life. He was aware of the backwardness of Albanian culture and civilization and to some extent he identified with the young disillusioned and disabused figures of *The City*. However, *The City* is at its most interesting in the divided loyalties that it evinces. The writer's disapproval of the young people in the novel is palpable and is not merely a product of the inner censor. Western culture is genuinely unpalatable in this novel, but socialism offers nothing either. In 'Days of Drink' it is the traditional patriarch, not the communist father figures, who is represented most positively. In Kadare's later works, beginning with *The General of the Dead Army*, figures and images of Albania will take the place of those of the dissolute West vis-à-vis the corrupted vision of communism.

Home Again: The Early 1960s

Kadare returned home in October 1960 on Albanian orders, before the Soviet ultimatum in late 1961.[43] The young man missed the cosmopolitanism of the Soviet capital, the intellectual exchange with his friends at the Gorki Institute and the access to a relatively wide range of contemporary and classical literature. He had been taken with the sophistication of society in the capital but was unimpressed with his teachers and writers at the Institute. He felt contempt for the ageing Russian hacks worn out by Stalinism, as well as for the youthful apparatchiks from the Soviet satellite states. During this period he discovered in himself a powerful sense of ethnicity which would become his mainstay in isolated socialist Albania.

Russian nationalism in the form of Soviet hegemony proved to be an insidious force throughout Eastern Europe, generating a backlash of ethno-nationalist feeling and resentment.

> J'étais content de la rupture entre l'Albanie et l'U.R.S.S., car, comme la majorité des jeunes du camp socialist, l'omniprésence soviétique commençait à me taper sur le système (les inventeurs russes, la littérature russe, les hymnes sur l'amitié éternelle, etc.). (*Printemps albanais* 160)

> I was pleased with the break between Albania and the Soviet Union, since the omnipresent USSR (Russian inventors, Russian literature, hymns to eternal friendship, etc.) had begun to get on my nerves, as it had for most young people in the socialist camp. (*Albanian Spring* 154)

At this time, after the purges of the late 1940s, the atmosphere in Albania was still relatively free in cultural matters in particular.[44] The years from 1958 to 1961, when Kadare returned from Moscow, were memorable for their openness, and the situation remained relatively liberal until midway through the decade.[45] Soviet aid had provided a relatively high standard of living and pockets of the Westernized culture of the Zog years remained until the summer of 1960:

> Le pays traversait une période de très relative libéralisation. L'effet Khrouchtchev devait durer jusqu'à la rupture avec Moscou, vers 1961–1962. Pour l'instant, nous étions au summum de son succès sur la scène internationale. Les magasins publics étaient bien fournis; on voyait les premiers téléviseurs importés d'Union Soviétique, et même des scooters. [. . .] Je me souviens des boutiques et des pâtisseries de la rue de Dibra. . . Des adversaires farouches de régime ont été eux aussi fort surpris lorsqu'ils ont recouvré la liberté à cette période-là. Ils étaient bien obligés de constater le niveau de vie relativement acceptable de l'époque, dû à l'importance de l'aide que les Soviétiques [. . .] fournissaient à l'Albanie.[46]

> The country was passing through a period of relative liberalization. The Khrushchev effect would last until the break with Moscow, until about 1961–62. For the moment, we were at the peak of success on the international scene. The public shops were well stocked; we could watch the first televisions imported from the Soviet Union, and there were even motor-scooters. [. . .] I remember the shops and the patisseries of the Dibra Road . . . Fierce critics of the regime were most surprised when they recovered their freedom during that period. They had to admit the relatively acceptable standard of life of the era, due to the aid [. . .] which the Soviets provided to Albania.

In 1958 and 1959 as a result of the competition between the Soviet bloc and China, foreign capital was pouring into the country, supporting rapid economic growth and increases in the standard of living. As a result of the cooling of relations with the Soviet Union this influx of aid was dramatically interrupted when the break occurred in the early 1960s. While China continued for some time to support Albania, the boom of the late 1950s did not last. Albania was in the full swing of its modernization programme, ready for the entry into the next stage of 'complete socialist construction' with the Third Five-Year Plan of 1961–1965 when Soviet aid stopped.[47] The withdrawal of Soviet and Eastern European economic aid would bring about a drop in the standard of living unless the regime found ways of supplementing the national income. Despite the magnanimous gesture of the Chinese who, while dealing with their own financial and agricultural difficulties at that time, bought wheat from France to cover the shortfall in the disastrous drought year, overall Chinese aid turned out to be substantially lower than that which the Albanians had come to expect from the Soviet bloc.[48]

During this period Enver Hoxha was sending out multiple signals to the communist and non-communist world. Until 1961 he continued to support the Soviet Union while at the same time stressing the ideological alliance with China in the battle for correct Marxism-Leninism and against revisionism. He also concluded an agreement on reparations and approached the Italian government regarding the expansion of trade between the two countries, while *Zëri i Popullit* was referring to the Italians as neo-fascist imperialists in daily denunciations of Yugoslav-Italian rapprochement.[49] 'Considering the large unfavourable Albanian trade balance with Italy', notes Griffith, the Albanian trade proposal 'could only mean in effect Italian economic aid'.[50] Hoxha's move also signalled the possibility of limited opening up towards the West. In his report to the Fourth Congress of the PLA, published in *Zëri i Popullit* on February 14 1961, Hoxha wrote of current Albanian relations with Italy in the light of the presence of the American Sixth Fleet in the Mediterranean, the plot by 'certain Albanian traitors' with the support of Greece and Yugoslavia to attack the regime, and the stationing of rockets on Italian soil. 'We cannot stand by', he writes, 'with our hands folded'.

> We think that trade, cultural relations, and communications between our two countries can be developed successfully and to our mutual advantage if the ruling circles of Italy show a more realistic understanding of these problems. We think that it would be in the interest of friendly relations between our two neighbouring countries and in the interest of peace in this area if Italy should give up her role as a den for Albanian war criminals, for this does not conform to normal relations between the two countries.[51]

In this speech and in articles in *Zëri i Popullit* during 1960 and 1961 Albanian support is advertised for various peoples and regimes, presumably as a means of preparing for further negotiations with those, such as some Arab regimes, which may have been tempted to provide economic assistance in the future. In Hoxha's speech, France rates positive mention among the Western European nations. For many Albanian intellectuals who had their education in France, Italy, or elsewhere in the West, such a fervently hoped for move seemed not incompatible with Hoxha's politics of non-alignment. These were still early days for the regime and Hoxha had not yet openly demonstrated his ruthlessness. Kadare has elsewhere referred to the hopes of members of the intelligentsia for rapprochement with the West in the early 1960s.[52] They could not foresee the level of ideological and political isolationism the Albanian regime would embrace during the following decades.

According to Jusuf Vrioni, Hoxha and Shehu as well as Ramiz Alia and Manush Myftiu, the 'top four' of the Politburo, were prodigious readers of contemporary literature and had built up substantial personal libraries ordered from French bookshops.[53] Enver Hoxha in particular was impressed by France, remained in thrall to ideas of French culture and civilization, and longed to be read in France.

Speaking to Alain Bosquet, Kadare refers to Hoxha's 'obsession' with France as 'sans doute le seul sentiment humain qui lui fût resté de son séjour dans votre pays' ('without doubt the sole human sentiment that remained with him from his time in your country).[54] Soviet functionary Vyacheslav Molotov remembered Hoxha in 1946 as 'un bel homme cultivé, qui laisse une bonne impression mais on sent les influences occidentales dans son éducation' ('a cultivated man, who left a good impression, but it was possible to sense the Western influences in his education').[55] Hoxha came from the urbanized middle class of Gjirokastra and unlike his political comrades throughout Eastern and South-Eastern Europe appears to have harboured intellectual ambitions during his period as a student in France and Belgium.[56] He made use of Jusuf Vrioni on the basis of the latter's translation of Kadare and success with French readers, and later (unsuccessfully) approached Kadare's French publishers for his own autobiographical works. Literature was important to the dictatorship and the Albanian leaders, Hoxha in particular, unlike their Eastern European colleagues, could recognize good writing. Dritëro Agolli, also a gifted writer, became something of a protégé of Enver Hoxha as well. He was made President of the Union of Writers in 1972 in the wake of the purges of the intelligentsia and retained this position until the end of the regime.[57]

In May 1956 the literary periodical *Nëntori* carried an article by the leading critic, Riza Brahimi, entitled 'Some Problems in our Literature', quoting the Soviet writer Konstantin Paustovsky, and suggesting a revisionist, typically post-1956 platform for Albanian communist literature. And in May 1957, the critic Koço Bihiku advocated 'the necessity of controversy and tolerance as opposed to keeping quiet about the negative aspects of Albanian life'.[58] However, change was in the air. Hoxha had signalled his displeasure at the level of dissent at the Tirana City party conference in April 1957. He had learned during the early leadership crises that the maintenance of power depended on a successful strategy of prevention of the formation of any fronts which could generate an oppositional power base. The strategy of thaw allowed him to entice potential oppositional figures to reveal themselves. A frost would follow in which signs of dissent were ruthlessly persecuted. In the wake of his consolidation of his position by the late 1950s, Hoxha initiated a period of thaw in the early 1960s after the break with Moscow, presumably in order to identify those areas of potential disaffection or challenge in the context of the new isolationism in Europe and the rapprochement with China as a non-revisionist, Marxist-Leninist state. It was in this context that he divided and ruled the old guard of the nomenklatura at an important point of generational change.

Nation or Exile

By the early 1960s Kadare was already well-known for his poetry collections, *Youthful Inspiration* (1953), *Dreams* (1957), and particularly *My Age* (1961). Young people, in particular, loved his work. Helena Kadare was still a schoolgirl in Fieri when she wrote the fan letter to the writer in Moscow that would lead to their marriage. Jusuf Vrioni vividly remembers his girlfriend's admiration for the young poet in 1963. For the post-war youth of Albania, Kadare was a poet with something new to say.[59] He came to the attention of literary circles early and was on close terms with editors and literary figures such as Llazër Siliqi, Todi Lubonja, and others after publishing his first poems in the early 1950s. Kadare's political profile was raised in 1961 when Enver Hoxha intervened in a literary dispute between the wartime writers and the post-war generation, who were now coming of age. Kadare had just returned from Moscow. Along with Dritëro Agolli, Fatos Arapi, and others, he was accused of anti-national attitudes, cosmopolitanism, and decadence.[60] Enver Hoxha unexpectedly took the side of the younger generation against the old guard who were critical of liberal attitudes and writing styles. His intention appears to have been not merely to disabuse his old companions of any notions they might have regarding their ongoing authority as ex-partisans. In driving a wedge between the generations, empowering the younger, 'liberal' post-war writers against the older 'conservative' Stalinists, he purchased their allegiance at a time of change and potential ideological isolation. The leader requested a response from the young writers, in particular Kadare, who at one point during one of the savage attacks dared to get up and leave a meeting. During the lunch break Kadare drafted a response, accusing his accusers of monarchist leanings. He had learned how to defend himself in the environment of party meetings and denunciations. Hoxha may have already known of the young writer's existence; he certainly became aware of Kadare during the meeting and quickly surmised that he was someone who could be of use. No one, writes Kadare, expected that Hoxha would take their side. But in preferring this young man, Hoxha both made him untouchable and rendered him a figure of envy to the rest of the creative intelligentsia. In retrospect Kadare recognizes Hoxha's cunning move as 'un de ces gestes dont il était coutumier, qui désorientaient périodiquement la société albanaise' ('one of those gestures for which he was known, which regularly disoriented Albanian society').[61] From this time onward Kadare had powerful enemies among the hard-core Stalinist left wing of the regime as well as a powerful protector in Enver Hoxha.[62] In siding with the 'young Turks' on literary questions at a crucial turning point, Hoxha unsettled the cultural dogmatists of the partisan generation in the lead-up to the Albanian cultural revolution of the second half of the decade, and gave the younger generation of the creative intelligentsia a taste of power which would prepare them for inculcation into the upper echelons of the ruling class.

Working as a journalist and writer and as editor of the foreign literature section of the long-standing Albanian literary review *Drita* after his return, Kadare continued to have access to contemporary work from the wider world as well as to newspapers such as *Le Monde*.[63] Hemingway was popular, recent American and Western European literature was available, and Western culture was accessible via radio and television from Italy and Yugoslavia.[64] Kadare experimented with voice-recording and other forms of composition and was interested in film. A film industry had been founded with strong Soviet support in Albania in the late 1950s and even small towns such as Fieri in the Myzeqe (where Kadare would be later sent as a punishment for his over-intellectualized writings) had a cinema.[65]

> Pour la première fois,
> Sur ce morceau d'écran,
> Nous avons vu un morceau du vaste monde,

Sur six mètres carrés.
De limites, le monde n'en avait pas . . .

On that bit of screen
We saw a bit of the whole world,
For the first time.
On six square metres
The world had no limits . . .[66]

However, the cinema was more closely guarded by the regime than writing and his natural talent for writing and poetry reasserted itself.

Je me rapprochai à nouveau de la littérature, mais la crise eut au moins un effet fondamental: elle grava dans ma tête la décision de ne jamais rassembler en rien aux écrivains soviétiques du moment, à commencer (bien évidemment!) par leur apparence extérieur.[67]

I took up literature again, but the crisis had at least one lasting effect: it inscribed in my head the decision never to resemble in any way the Soviet writers of the time, beginning (of course!) with their outward appearance.

Of his early works, 'A Tour of the Cafés' (excerpted from *The City without Signs*) and various short stories (subsequently collected in *Stories across Time* and *Eleven Short Stories*) were published in periodicals such *Drita*, *Zëri i Rinisë*, and *Nëntori*. At this stage Todi Lubonja was responsible for youth affairs in the regime and was instrumental in having Kadare's work published in the youth journal, although it was banned immediately on appearance. (Lubonja would be a major source of support for Kadare in the inner sanctum of the regime until his fall and imprisonment for liberalism in 1973 as a result of the scandal surrounding *The Great Winter*.) Themes, motifs, and episodes from Kadare's early works and unpublished stories and poems re-emerge later as the author makes connections and explores the permutations of life under communism. Early sketches of the Italian occupation, the story of his home town's first brothel and other material would appear in 'The Great Aeroplane' and 'The City of the South' before finding its final form in *The General* and *Chronicle in Stone*.[68] The poems 'Laocoon' and 'The Trojan Horse' rehearse themes which re-emerge in *The Monster* in 1965 and in his late essay *Aeschylus or the Great Loser* in 1985. The novel, *The Great Winter* takes up themes from the poem 'The Sixties'. And the 1988 political allegory *The Pyramid* has its origins not in the newly planned and built mausoleum for Enver Hoxha in central Tirana, but in the poem 'The Pyramid of Kheops' from 1967. *City without Signs* would wait a further forty years, hidden in Kadare's flat, before being published in its complete form. *The General of the Dead Army* appeared in instalments in *Zëri i Rinisë* in 1962, before its publication in book form the following year and in a revised version in 1967.

After the successes of his youth, with his popularity among young people and his Gorki Institute qualifications, and in the wake of the unexpected victory over the old guard, Kadare sensed that he was being offered the role of national writer-in-the-making during the honeymoon years of the early 1960s: 'Je sentais quelque chose de nouveau et de dangereux s'approcher de ma vie. C'était le frôlement du manteau de l'écrivain national. Le lourd manteau de l'écrivain national sous une dictature' (*Le Poids* 298, 'I felt something new and dangerous coming towards me.

The mantle of the national writer brushed my shoulders. The heavy mantle of the national writer under a dictatorship').

In 'On a Lost Train in the Winter Night' (1964) Kadare revisits themes of nationalism and rejection of Soviet hegemony which he experienced at the time of his repatriation.[69] The young writer sleeps fitfully through the night-time train journey through the frozen countryside from Moscow to Yalta in the Crimea. The rhythmic beat of the engine evokes the name of the Yugoslav major-general, Svetozar Vukmanović-Tempo, who had recently visited Moscow. For Albanians, Vukmanović-Tempo was associated with the Titoist plot to 'swallow' Albania.[70] He had sought to bring Albania into the Yugoslav federation in the late 1940s, and was linked in Albanian memory with the Titoist ex-Minister for the Interior, Koçi Xoxe, who was executed as a traitor in 1949 after the first round of purges in Albania. Vukmanović-Tempo was present in Moscow in July 1955 when Khrushchev, having invited Enver and Nexhmije Hoxha to the Soviet Union 'for a holiday', brought about an enforced rapprochement between Albania and Yugoslavia. Of course Hoxha reneged on this agreement as soon as he left the Soviet Union, and in the following year thumbed his nose at the Soviet Union by executing the alleged Titoist spies and former associates of Koçi Xoxe, General Dali Ndreu and his wife, Liri Gega.[71] In Kadare's short story a Russian-speaking stranger enters the train compartment and mysteriously disappears, leaving the Albanian disorientated and suspicious. We experience the mounting hostility of the young writer to the Soviets as he travels through the arid plains, reflecting a patriotism that would become more and more apparent in his writing, feeding off rejection of the hegemony of Soviet culture, just as Herder's new nationalism rejected the dominant culture of the French two centuries before.

However, the problems of writing in Albania are also evident in this story. It reflects the official hostility towards the Soviet Union and Yugoslavia and was, no doubt, acceptable on this account to the Ministry of Culture and the Union of Writers. Here, as in the later stories, 'Winter Season at the Cafe Riviera' and *The Wedding*, we can identify signs of the young writer's attempts to find compromises and can imagine the directions in which his writing could have developed should he have become the 'national writer' of the regime.[72] At this early stage he was still seeking points of orientation in the post-war socialist environment. In the works from the early 1960s we sense a welter of directions as the young writer imagines his options. On the one hand he is flattered by the attentions of the leader and the unspoken sense that he could become the officially sanctioned 'national writer'. But on the other hand he is aware of the limitations of life in Albania. Where 'The Nude' and even *The City without Signs* reveal a certain callowness in terms of their social realism, in other works from the early 1960s a scepticism has begun to express itself. The theme of exile emerges. In the 1960 short story 'On the Edge of the Airport', set in Moscow, two young lovers talk as Russian Tupolevs and French Caravelles arrive and depart. The young writer is about to leave. But for where? West or east? Into exile or to return home? Kadare had secretly discussed exile with his friend Dhori Qiriazi.[73] In Prague, on the way home from Finland in 1962, he briefly took a hotel room off Wenceslas Square, intending to seek exile because of the intolerable situation in Albania. Faced with the grim reality of life in an unknown Eastern European country, he thought better of relinquishing his language and his homeland for a situation which was hardly better.[74] Looking back in the 1990s, he reflects on the perversity of seeking exile in the East rather than the West (he was on his way home from his first visit to a Western country, Finland).[75] However, it is a measure of the extent to which he was a product of socialism that the West did not yet appear on his political radar. He had been brought up in communism and the East remained his natural point of orientation. His decision to return to Albania, rather than remain in the 'steppes' of the East, was made in response to a deeper need. He recognized that his creativity, dependent on his native language, would wither and die in exile:

> A cette extinction silencieuse dans les steppes, je préférais l'arène remplie de hurlements et le manteau qui me ferait ployer les épaules. Et comme le pêcheur qui ne résiste pas à la tentation, je retournai à bord de l'appareil du vol Prague-Tirana accepter la couronne maudite. (*Le Poids* 300–01)

> To that silent death in the steppes I preferred the arena filled with howling and the mantle which would force my shoulders into a stoop. And like the sinner who does not resist temptation, I returned on board the machine from Prague to Tirana to accept the cursed crown.

Ethnicity, Patriotism, and Politics

While ethnic identity was an accepted part of Soviet literature, it was considered a phenomenon of transitional socialism and hence secondary to the greater goal of history, namely the achievement of the classless society. The inclusion of ethnic themes in socialist realism was considered one of the ills of transitional society, and yet it was implicitly accepted and exploited as a powerful motivating agent in real-existing socialism. Enver Hoxha was hailed from early on as a national hero for his wartime activities and his subsequent championing of Albanian independence against Yugoslav, Soviet, and even Chinese influence, even if the cost and the political motivations were clearly discernible behind the nationalist rhetoric. Hoxha would increasingly use Albanian nationalism and his own credentials as a freedom fighter to underpin his particular brand of Stalinism. From the mid-1960s national folklore was included in official cultural policy and dogma: 'The folk character of a literature or art is linked with the reflection of the national consciousness of a people. [. . .] The content in its historical moment deals with the ideas as well as the reality of life, and this includes the socialist along with the folk aspect'.[76] Bernhard Tönnes has argued that Hoxha's leadership was Marxist-Stalinist in name only, and that 'it had its roots in the nationalist ideas of the Albanian independence struggles of the nineteenth century and articulated itself only superficially as Marxist-Leninist-Stalinist'.[77] However, Tönnies underestimates the importance of the economic aspects of socialist planning and modernization in Albania, which was based on Stalinist principles, and the extent to which Hoxha's Stalinism derived from the practice rather than the texts of his hero.[78] Nor does he consider Hoxha's demolition of Albanian customs, environments, and traditional values from the mid-1960s onward in the name of revolutionary nationalism. The Albanian regime cynically manipulated its nationalism to strengthen the Stalinist model of modernization, to further the interests of the Party, and to strengthen the political power of the dictator. While Hoxha was certainly a patriot and partisan fighter in the national cause, questions must be asked about the nature of the patriotism of a man who set out to remake his country in his own image. Many of Hoxha's policies and behaviours suggest hatred, not love, of his country, its people and traditions.

As we have seen, Kadare's return to Albania was fuelled by a strong sense of ethnicity and of his role as an Albanian writer. In Moscow Kadare's intense nostalgia for his native land expressed itself in some exquisite poems:

> Elle m'a saisi la nostalgie de notre Albanie
> Ce soir alors que je rentrais par le trolleybus
> La fumée d'une cigarette 'Partizan' que fumait un Russe
> Se tordait, bleuissiat, faisait des spirales
> Comme pour me parler en secret dans la langue des Albanais
> Mes compatriotes à moi.[79]

> I was filled with longing for Albania
> Tonight as I returned home on the trolley,
> The smoke of a *Partizani* cigarette in the hand of a Russian
> Curled bluish, twirled upwards
> As if whispering to me, its compatriot,
> In the language of the Albanians.[80]

Kadare was deeply influenced by the two major Albanian writers of the century, Migjeni and Lasgush Poradeci, both of whom drew on earlier national traditions.[81] Bernard Tönnes has demonstrated how Bektashi and other earlier Islamic traditions influenced the creation of powerfully evocative poetry of the Albanian country and the nation. These influences extended from the nationalist movements of the late nineteenth century into the wartime works of Qemal Stafa and other partisans of the communist and national movements.[82] A powerful ethno-national component thus was transmitted through Albanian literature into the post-war period, despite the regime's effective silencing of their greatest poet, Poradeci, after the war.

Kadare expressed his burgeoning and powerful romantic nationalism in the long poem 'What are these mountains thinking about', dated Tirana 1962–64. In this work, which aims to plumb a deeper sense of national history than the communist present, the peasant's rifle becomes the measure of the country and its culture. The negative associations of the night-time journey to avoid death by vendetta are a metaphor of the country's *longue durée*.

> Un montagnard marche a l'orée de la nuit.
> Son long fusil
> Jette une ombre démesurée sur le sol.[83]

> A mountaineer sets out at the fall of night,
> His long rifle
> Casting a hundred-mile-long shadow on the ground.[84]

The highlander's journey reflects the hardness of the country, and the custom of the feud is an ancient legal system which has turned self-destructive, like Saturn devouring his children. The Latin Catholic rite has been unable to change it.

> Le tintement des cloches
> Agitées par la nuit
> Faisait écho sur les versants montagneux.
> Que disaient les cloches,
> Que marmonnaient les prêtres,
> En des langues étrangères
> Dans de hautes églises?
> La logique latine en de longues phrases
> S'efforçait de faire plier le long fusil. ('Montagnes' 71)

> The pealing of bells
> Rung by night
> Resounded over the mountain slopes.
> What were the bells saying,
> What were the priests murmuring
> To their high churches
> In their foreign tongues?
> Latin logic, in long sentences,
> Strove to bend the long rifle. ('Mountains' 88)

Despite the depredations of vendetta and the Kanun, Albanian culture exists in language and song, the mythological existence which pre-dates all invaders and which exists at the deepest levels of the collective unconscious.

> Et l'Albanie retournait se blottir dans une hutte,
> Dans ses obscures nuits mythologiques;
> Sur quelques cordes de lahute elle essayait de parler un peu
> De son âme incompréhensible,
> De ses voix intérieurs
> Qui avaient des résonances profondes et sourdes dans la terre épique.
> ('Montagnes' 73)

> And once again Albania cowered in a hut
> In her dark mythological nights
> And on the strings of a lute strove to express something
> Of her incomprehensible soul,
> Of the inner voices
> That echoed mutely from the depths of the epic earth. ('Mountains' 90)

With the beginnings of modernity, Western-educated Albanians begin to return to their homeland full of hope, national liberation occurs, and the Zog-regime dashes the hopes for progress:

> Les fils que tu as envoyés dans les villes d'Europe,
> Qui connurent des joies étrangères,
> Revinrent
> L'un après l'autre,
> Trouver dans la patrie tristesse,
> Nuages chargés de pluie jaune.
> La monarchie comme un carrier brisait leurs rêves.
> Ils revinrent

Avec des valises bourrés d'illusions
A l'ombre des minarets, des monastères,
Ils firent un petit tour du côté de vieux espoirs perdus
Jusqu'à ce que la terre les reprenne en son sein
Et les pourrisse sous le chant monotone des pluies. ('Montagnes' 75)

The sons you sent to the cities of Europe,
Who knew foreign pleasures,
Returned
One by one,
To find a sorrowful land,
Clouds laden with yellow rain.
The monarchy, like a quarryman, smashed their dreams.
They arrived
With suitcases full of illusions
Under the shadow of minarets, of monasteries,
And rambled in autumnal delusions
Until the earth returned them to her bosom
And they rotted under the monotonous song of the rain. ('Mountains' 91–92)

As a young man Kadare, like many of his compatriots, admired Hoxha's nationalism, his willingness to fight for Albanian identity and for independence from Yugoslav and Soviet influence, interference, and intervention. There is perhaps a political allusion to Hoxha as the mountains of Kadare's poem, prefiguring the appeal to the leader and the implication that all is not well in Albania that caused such trouble in the later poem, 'The Red Pashas'. Mehmet Shehu, the second-in-command and long-time comrade of the Supreme Leader, had celebrated Hoxha's fiftieth birthday on 16 October 1958 with a piece in *Zëri i Popullit*, entitled, 'May he live as long as the mountains'.[85] Be that as it may, 'What are these mountains thinking about?' also makes explicit obeissance to communism and the supreme leader. The mountains wait for someone who will guide them 'vers le monde modern. | [. . .] L'albanie attendait | Le Parti Communiste' ('Montagnes' 78, 'to a new world [. . .] | Albania was waiting | For the Communist Party', 95). Yet Kadare sets up an opposition between ephemeral history and eternal myth, in which the communist present must belong with the former, not the latter. It is the poets and the people, not the leaders, priests or hodjas, who represent the spirit of Albania in this work, despite the ritual praise of the leader and socialism. The flatness of the invocation of socialism in 'What are these mountains thinking about?' did not prevent this work being included in the canon of socialist patriotic works in the official history of Albanian literature published by the Albanian Academy of Sciences in the late 1970s. Koço Bihiku, one of the most eminent literary historians under the regime wrote of it:

> Kadaré exprima sous une forme interessante sa conviction que malgré les complots et les attaques farouches des ennemis, le peuple albanais ne voudra jamais se soumettre et que l'édification du socialisme continuera avec un plus grand entrain encore et avec plus de fermeté.[86]

> In this interesting form Kadare expresses his conviction that in spite of the plotting and the fierce attacks of its enemies, the Albanian people never wanted

to yield, and that the building of socialism will continue with an even greater spirit and with greater strength and constancy.

'What are these mountains thinking about?' fulfilled the requirements of Hoxha's new nationalism, even though its homage to communism was minimal. Kadare was criticized for the absence of enthusiasm.[87] During the second half of the decade Kadare became more critical of Hoxha's instrumentalization of nationalism and the Albanian 'new man' to strengthen the inner cohesion and the political hold of the regime. However, Kadare's poetic power could not be ignored by a socialist regime seeking to bolster its national credentials. Publication of the poem led to the poet's first personal contact with the dictator. Hoxha telephoned to congratulate Kadare. This was not just a courtesy call. The telephone call marked a milestone in the writer's development, the point at which the dictator let him know personally that he had come to his attention. It is unlikely that the young writer could realize at this stage the extent to which the dictator's regard would change his life. Hoxha was already known in the Party for his obsessive control and his ruthlessness in any matter where his power was concerned. He was obsessed with leaving his mark on literature as well as politics and in the later stages of the dictatorship would devote himself to writing his memoirs.[88] His telephone call to the young writer was a warning that from now on every word would be weighed up and judged.

The works of the first half of the 1960s are dominated by the young writer's commitment to his homeland after the break with the Soviet Union and increasing awareness of the problems of the dictatorship: generational conflict and friction between traditional and modern lifestyles, problems of corruption and nepotism in the regime, sterility in cultural and social matters, young people 'dropping out' through frustration and boredom. Albania figures in these works as a backdrop to questions of socialist modernization, but by 1964 a change is perceptible in the representation of Albania. Ethnic identity had become a powerful sustaining force for the writer. At the same time, in the context of the regime's move towards an openly nationalistic socialism, Kadare began to experience the conflict between the regime's politicized nationalism and his own now deeply felt patriotism. Over the years this conflict would become a more or less open battle for the voice of Albania. In the mid 1960s, however, as the writer was still finding his way, we can sense confusion, notes of accord if not concord, and the difficulties of the young writer in establishing an Albanian voice which was not that of the regime.

Unmastered Past: *The General of the Dead Army*, 1962–1963

Kadare's second novel, *The General of the Dead Army*, would be his first great success — outside, if not within, Albania. *The General* was written in its first version in 1962 and published the following year; it was not finalized until 1967 in the version which was translated into French in 1970 and included in the Fayard works edition in 1998. The idea for the novel was born in the café of the Hotel Dajti where the writer met an Italian diplomat charged with the mission of locating, exhuming, and repatriating the bodies of fallen Italian soldiers from the occupation and the war.[89] It seems that the project did not take place, although it is entirely possible that the Italian request to repatriate fallen soldiers was not immediately rejected at this time. After the break with the Soviet Union, the regime appeared to be open to the possibility of rapprochement with Western governments.

The time is late 1961. Contact with the Soviet Union has been broken and the blockade is underway. An Italian military mission has been given permission to locate and repatriate the bodies of the soldiers who fell during the military campaign of 1939–43. A middle-aged Italian general and a high-ranking military chaplain are to spend two years supervising the work. They also have a special charge from a still youthful and beautiful aristocratic widow to bring back the remains of her husband, Colonel Z., giving closure to years of uncertainty. Scion of a distinguished and aristocratic family and decorated war hero, Colonel Z. was in charge of the Blue Battalion which executed Italian deserters during the Albanian and Greek campaigns. He disappeared without trace towards the end of the Italian campaign in Albania in 1943. Kadare's plot is constructed around the fate of Colonel Z. and the mission to repatriate his remains.

Given the history of Italian occupation of Albania, the general is not portrayed as negatively as one might expect. He verges on caricature, to be sure, but is represented with a warmth of characterization which contrasts with the chaplain and with the Albanian figures.[90] Preening, self-indulgent, and egotistical, incapable of understanding his hosts' culture, he is anything other than threatening. But his ignorance and self-indulgence are offset by a certain harmlessness and even ingenuousness. Full of his own importance vis-à-vis the generals who had led their men to disaster twenty years earlier, he sees himself as a national saviour and representative of a 'great and civilized country', returning the tens of thousands of Italian soldiers, betrayed by their leaders' incompetence, to their national soil. He views his mission in terms of a history of noble warfare stretching back to the Greeks and the Trojans, to the solemnity of Homeric funeral rites. His pretensions to soldierly values are laughable. As a peacetime general, who did not experience active service during the war, he is a comic and slightly ridiculous figure.

The General entertains erotic fantasies about Colonel Z'.s beautiful widow, Betty, imagining that he might woo her on his triumphant return, having laid to rest the remains of her dead husband. (The name, 'Betty', surprisingly perhaps, suggests Anglophone elegance to Italian and Albanian ears.) His jealousy of the dead Colonel and competition with the chaplain for the — imagined — favours of Betty provide a note of lightness in the otherwise unrelievedly grim story. The Italian general, the chaplain, and the post-war Italy evoked through the figures of Colonel Z'.s family and widow act as a foil to the representation of post-war Albania. This Italy is a post-war European country oriented towards the future and the West. The image of a Western country intent on a superficial and cosmetic confrontation with its past, which will enable it to move on into a promising future as part of Western Europe, is counterposed strikingly against that of an Eastern country whose communism has concreted over past damages and which remains in thrall to its unlaid ghosts. At one level the novel is a critique of post-war Italian politics and society, of a defeated imperialistic and militaristic regime which wreaked havoc in Albania and which now, thanks to its Western European identity and with American support, can turn its back on the history of failed imperialism. However, Kadare is not primarily interested in Italian guilt or responsibility in *The General of the Dead Army*. In post-war European countries literature played an important role in the process of coming to terms with the past. In the Federal Republic of Germany in particular, where the burden of Nazism was felt so keenly by the younger generations from the 1960s onward, *Vergangenheitsbewältigung* ('coming to terms with the past') became the dominant theme of post-war literature. In Italy, or France, this was scarcely the case, and while Italy contributed to the post-war construction of Western European democracy, little national retrospection took place regarding the depredations of Mussolini's regime in the erstwhile colonies and occupation zones.[91] The theme of 'mastering the past' lies at the core of *The General of the Dead Army*. However, it is the Albanian, not the Italian past, which is the focus of Kadare's novel. Kadare acknowledges that he wrote this novel when he was young, and without first-hand knowledge of post-war Western Europe.[92]

Life and Death in Albania

The Albania of communist modernity lies superimposed over the unmastered past like an unhealed scar. The bitterness and resentment of still-grieving mothers, fathers, sisters, and wives emerges throughout the novel, coming to a climax in the disruption of the wedding ceremony at the end. The point made over and over is that Albania has not been able to overcome its past. Kadare would later develop at length the metaphor of congealment or frozenness to describe this state of national paralysis. Despite the regime's propagation of national communism, the creation of the Albanian 'new man', and the socio-economic modernization, a sense of the dislocation of past and present predominates. While Kadare is not an enemy of modernization, the sense of loss of authenticity is palpable, rendering the novelistic present dismal and colourless. This is not naive anti-modern romanticism or reactionary nostalgia for the kingdom of Zog or the stability of Ottoman colonialism, although romantic elements are present in Kadare's evocations of the national past. In this representation of Albanian history, Hoxha's socialist modernity begins to be seen as a symptom of the depredations of the past, rather than as a cause of socio-political distress in the present.

The novel opens amid the rain and sleet of November, Kadare's familiar trope of the 'winter of discontent' under communism. It is a cold, wet, and grey day. The signs of Albanian modernity, the airport, the roads and the buildings are black and grim. While the Italians have moved on, seeking the repatriation of the bodies of their fallen countrymen in order to find national closure, the past has not yet ended for the Albanians. They remain under the spell of the dead army, nursing the unhealed wounds of an unfinished war, constrained to remember but not come to terms with their tragic history. The landscape itself seems to warn of the dangers of the past, as the general looks out over the land that he is about to begin excavating:

> L'armée était là, en bas, hors du temps, figée, calcifiée, recouverte de terre. Il avait pour mission de la faire se relever de terre. Et cette tâche lui faisait peur.

C'était une mission contre nature, qui devait recéler quelque chose d'aveugle, de sourd, d'absurde. Qui devait porter en soi des conséquences imprévisibles. (*Le Général* 16)[93]

The army was there, below him, outside time, frozen, petrified, covered with earth. It was his mission to draw it up from the mud, and the mission made him afraid. It was a mission that exceeded the bounds of nature, a mission in which there must be something blind, something deaf, something deeply absurd. A mission that bore unforeseeable consequences in its womb. (*The General* 4)[94]

History holds secrets that the general will not come to terms with over the duration of his mission. The Albanian past is covered by a thin layer of earth and it still harbours virulent forces of destruction. The country is occupied by *thanatos* in the form of the dead army, harbouring dormant microbes of war waiting for light and air to revive them twenty years on.

'Le microbe reste vingt ans enfoui sous terre et recouvre soudain toute sa virulence. C'est effrayant . . ., commenta le général. 'Il en va pourtant ainsi, fit le prêtre. Au premier contact avec l'air et le soleil, il reprend vie'. 'Comme un fauve qui se réveille de sa léthargie hivernale'. (*Le Général* 209)

'The germ can stay buried there for twenty years, then suddenly jump out as virulent as ever. It's terrifying, remarked the general. 'But true', the priest added. 'At the first contact with air and sunlight it returns to life'. 'Like a wild animal coming out of hibernation'. (*The General* 172–73; translation altered for accuracy, PM)

Death comes out of the blue as one of the workmen is infected from contact with human remains and dies, a late victim of the Italians whom he had fought against twenty years earlier. For his wife the job of digging up the graves represents the return of the past:

'Elle se faisait beaucoup de mauvais sang. Elle l'avait attendu tant d'années, durant la guerre, et voilà qu'à présent il lui semblait y être reparti'.
  'C'est ce que lui-même nous disait tout le temps: J'ai eu affaire avec les fascistes leur vie durant et maintenant qu'ils sont morts, il faut encore que je m'occupe d'eux!'
  'Hé oui! Il s'est battu tant d'années contre eux, il les a vaincus, mais ce sont eux qui ont tout de même fini par l'avoir. Quelle poisse!'
  'On dirait une vengeance postume'.
  'Ils ont attendu vingt ans pour se venger'. (*Le Général* 213)

'She worried about him constantly. She had waited for him so many years during the war, and now she felt somehow that he was away fighting again'.
  'He was always saying much the same thing himself: '"The Fascists kept me busy while they were alive, and now that they're dead I'm still having to hunt for them, they're still keeping me busy!"'
  'Yes! He fought against them so many years, and he beat them. But it was them that got him in the end. What pig luck!'
  'Like a revenge after death'.
  'They waited twenty years for it too. But all the same, when he fought them he fought them fairly, in open war, whereas they killed him with a rusty button like filthy cowards'. (*The General* 176)

The mission of unearthing the past is deeply abhorrent to the general. In this novel about death, he is, paradoxically, the representative of life, and his mission seems absurd and unnatural. Like the West German general he later meets on a similar mission, he is a figure of *eros* despite his age and his profession.

> Le général buvait son cognac á petits traits en promenant son regard autour de lui, un regard qui lui donnait á mesurer combien l'atmosphère ambiante lui était étrangère. Il se sentit soudain tout à fait seul. Seul au milieu des tombes de ses compatriotes morts. Au diable! Il aurait voulu chasser de son esprit la vision de ces tombes, les sépultures de ses 'frères', ne plus y penser, à aucun prix. [. . .] Il était vivant, lui. C'était un droit qu'il tenait de la nature. (*Le Général* 35)

> The general sipped at his cognac and let his eyes wander about him, realizing as he did so how foreign the whole atmosphere of this place was to him. He suddenly felt quite alone. Alone among the graves of his dead countrymen. Dammit! he wanted to rid his mind of the sight of those graves — those places where his 'brothers' lay buried — and not think about them again at any price. [. . .] After all he was still alive. It was a right conferred by nature itself. (*The General* 20)

The general is thus a foil to the real subject, which is the suffering that the Italian campaign caused to Italians and Albanians alike. Through the story of the exhumations in an endlessly grey and rainy countryside, the stories of Italian deserters are told and the disastrous effects of the occupation on the lives of the Albanians emerge. Only in the idyllic Albania of the past does the sun shine and the birds sing.

In his ignorance the general assumes that the Albanians have turned their back on the past just as the Italians have. 'Il y a beau temps que la guerre a pris fin. Le passé est oublié' (*Le Général* 244, 'It is a long time since the war was over. The past is forgotten', *The General* 199), he tells the priest later in the novel. It is the dead Colonel Z., not the living general, who represents death and killing, and who embodies the inhumanity, brutality, and perversion implicit in war. Colonel Z. was not a warrior, fighting the Albanians. His role was to execute those of his own nation who chose life as deserters rather than death as soldiers in the service of fascist imperialism.

Unlike the general, the chaplain experienced the Italian campaign. He speaks some of the language and thinks he understands the culture of the Albanians. He straddles past and present, representing the continuation of Italian imperial and fascist attitudes. His knowledge of the Albanians is a set of clichés from Italian fascist imperialism about their warlike nature and their death-oriented culture of Kanun and vendetta.

> 'Les Albanais — par nature, justement — sont portés à la guerre' exposa le prêtre. [. . .] sans guerre et sans armes, ce peuple s'étiolerait, ses racines se dessécheraient et il finirait par disparaître'.
>   'Alors qu'avec des armes et par la guerre, il se régénéra?'
>   'C'est qu'ils croient, même si c'est justement par les armes qu'il disparaîtra plus rapidement encore'.
>   'D'après vous, la guerre serait pour lui une espèce de culture physique qu'il ferait pour se dégourdir les membres et entretenir son souffle?' [. . .]

> 'En d'autres terms, avec ou sans armes, ce peuple est voué à disparaître?' (*Le Général* 163–64)

> 'The Albanians are given to war by their very nature', the priest said. [. . .] deprived of war and weapons this people would wither away, its roots would dry up and it would eventually just disappear'.
> 'Whereas with war and weapons it will always regenerate itself?'
> 'So they believe. Though in fact weapons will reduce them to non-existence even more rapidly'.
> 'According to you then, war is a sort of sport for them, an exercise they need in order to keep their circulation going and stay fit?' [. . .]
> 'In other words, with weapons or without, they are a people doomed to annihilation'. (*The General* 132–33)

Later he similarly expatiates on the morbid Albanian culture of Kanun and vendetta.

> 'Il faut reconnaître en toute objéctivité que chez les Albanais, il n'y a pas beaucoup de criminels de droit commun. Les meurtres qu'ils commettent sont toujours conformes à des normes dictées par d'anciens usages. Leur vendetta ressemble à une pièce de thèâtre composée dans toutes les règles de l'art, avec un prologue, une tension dramatique qui va croissant, et un épilogue comportant inévitablement la mort. Cette vendetta pourrait être figurée par un taureau furieux lancé à travers monts et ravageant tout sur son passage. Ils lui ont pourtant accroché au cou quantité d'ornaments et de parurues qui répondent à leur conception du Beau, de sorte que, lorsque la bête est lâchée et qu'elle sème pourtout la mort, ils puissent en même temps goûter diverses satisfactions esthétiques'. (*Le Général* 164–65)

> 'The Albanians are not criminals in the common law sense. The murders they commit are always done in conformity with rules laid down by age-old customs. Their vendetta is like a play composed in accordance with all the laws of tragedy, with a prologue, continually growing dramatic tension, and an epilogue that inevitably entails a death. The vendetta could be likened to a raging bull let loose in the hills and laying waste everything in its path. And yet they have hung around the beast's neck a quantity of ornaments and decorations that correspond to their conception of beauty, so that when the beast is loosed and even while it is spreading death on every side, they can derive aesthetic satisfactions from those events at the same time. [. . .] for centuries now the Albanians have been acting out a blood-thirsty and tragic play'. (*The General* 134–35)

The young Albanian historian and specialist adviser to the mission, who comes in as the priest is speaking, dismisses this type of language as a form of genocide, 'to spread the notion that the Albanian people is doomed to annihilation, to make people familiar with it and accept it' (*The General* 136, 'de préparer l'opinion internationale à l'anéantissement du people albanais et d'en propager l'idée', *Le Général* 167). And indeed, once he has left, the general and the priest continue to discuss the Albanians in exactly these terms: 'All we ask is that they should exterminate themselves. And the quicker the better' (*The General* 137; 'Libre à eux de s'entretuer, et aussi vite qu'il leur plaira!', *Le Général* 167). Their attitudes represent the views of centuries of foreign invaders, for whom Albania is simply territory to annex or colonize. Neither the general nor the chaplain understands the wider context of Albanian culture and history or recognizes the broader implications of the war, or of questions of Italian culpability in occupying Albania.

In the course of their searches the general's team locates the bodies of Italian deserters, Germans, Greeks, a British pilot, and even the remains of Turkish fighters from an earlier era in the ancient fort at Gjirokastra. The dead bodies are all the same; only the insignia of identification differ. Albania is a land occupied not just by the Italians, but by a range of foreign aggressors over its history. It is this history of foreign occupation and its effect on his nation, rather than the particularities of the Italian campaign, which is the focus of Kadare's novel. Responsibility for the Albanian present is directed towards those foreign states and empires that contributed to the disappearance of Albania from history after the fall of Rome. It lies with the Byzantines, the Normans and the Venetians, the Ottomans; after 1913, with the European powers who carved up the Balkans; and in the 1930s and 1940s, with the Italians, the Greeks, and the Germans who invaded their country.

In the vicinity of Gjirokastra the general's car is stopped by an old peasant and his grandson, carrying with them the remains of an Italian deserter who had worked for the peasant before being killed by the Blue Battalion in 'that unforgettable autumn' of October 1943. As the soldier's body is measured up against the records and found to be exactly six feet one inch in height, the general and the chaplain both note to themselves that his dimensions match those of Colonel Z. There is no medallion to identify him, but he left behind a diary covering the period 25 February until 7 September 1943. In this bleak work the only glimpses of summer happiness occur in the pages of the deserter's diary. As a miller's labourer devoid of a name and an identity, he comes to appreciate the rhythms of Albanian peasant life and to experience moments of contentment and existential tranquillity in this limbo between identity and forgottenness. This unknown soldier, who began the war as a loyal Italian in the 'Iron Regiment', and who lost his name and his identity when he gave his medallion away to the daughter of the miller as a wedding present, has also partaken of the timelessness of traditional life. Against the chaplain's evocation of a bloody culture of vendetta, the deserter's diary reveals an idyllic rural life untouched by violence or bloodshed. The sudden end to the deserter's diary, as he is located and executed by the Blue Battalion, introduces a note of personal tragedy into the weary and cynical account of death and exhumation.

We see the past through the eyes of the general, for whom it is a distasteful arena of death; the chaplain, for whom it remains a series of fascist clichés about national cultures; the nameless prisoner, for whom it is a springtime respite from war; and the government adviser to the mission, a young Albanian historian, for whom it is a record of foreign interventions, against which the Albanians had to generate some sort of protective structure. The young post-war Albanian specialist thus provides a key to Albanian history and the present. He does not deny the reality of the Albanian culture of vendetta, but he sees it in an entirely different light from the chaplain, for whom it is an unchanging national identity based on fascist attitudes towards race. For the historian, vendetta is an ancient code which became fossilized in the course of Albanian history as a result of the imposition of foreign legal and administrative structures onto the Albanians, and of the disruption of the processes of historical development that occurred with the Ottoman occupation. For him, the historian, the Albanian present has always been the product of its past. Kadare does not explicitly link the historian's views to the present, but the current regime, with its policy of faceless modernization, is implicitly also a product of these same historical forces. In its need to remake Albania as a modern and independent nation, the regime has cut its ties with the past, displacing ethno-national identity in the interest of a gloomy and characterless prosperity based on an internationalist doctrine of modernization. Enver Hoxha is not mentioned by name, but the implication of the ending in particular is that the country has come under the sway of a powerful and deadly regime. Fatos Lubonja, in a rather stronger critique of Albanian history, writes of a historical syndrome of alternation between foreign powers and home-grown tyrants born of Albania's history of occupation. His country's attempts at self-liberation have, for Lubonja, been characterized by dependency on local strongmen.[95] In Kadare's later fictional historiography, the figure of Ali Pasha in *The Niche of Shame*, typifies the local *bajraktar* or chieftain as national leader. (The only national leader who does not appear directly in Kadare's work is Scanderbeg, partly because he had been so completely subsumed into the cult of Enver Hoxha, but also because he represented an exception in Albanian history.) The point of the long discussions of Albanian history and culture in *The General* is to emphasize the relationships between past and present, rather than to criticize the regime. *The General* does not mount a critique of socialism so much as a critique of the regime's response to the nation's history. The socialist present in *The General of the Dead Army* is so over-determined by the traumas of history that it cannot live with the past, but must bury it, refusing to accept or come to terms with its history. The Italian 'coming to terms with the past' may be false and chauvinistic, but at least it represents historical movement and orientation toward life, compared to the stagnation and morbidity of the Albanian situation.

Return to Life

Two arduous years are spent searching for and exhuming bodies, measuring, marking, identifying, and bagging them to be sent home. Like so many of Kadare's foreign protagonists, the general begins to be drawn into the Albanian world of the dead. His everyday life becomes dominated by nightmares, sleeping pills, drunkenness, and hangovers as the environment of death and decomposition seeps into his spirit.

> Depuis qu'il avait remarqué que, non seulement dans ses conversations, mais dans tous les épisodes de sa vie s'introduisaient peu à peu des éléments étrangers, des phrases de visiteurs qu'il avait reçus chez lui, des fragments de lettres ou de journaux de soldats morts, il avait fait effort pour endiguer ce flux. Mais celui-ci s'était révélé si puissant que des mots, des phrases, parfois des récits entiers de disparus envahissaient son cerveau. [. . .] Et sa crainte qu'à employer des phrases ou des mots de personnages du royaume des ombres, lui-même ne finît par s'y intégrer, s'était désormais dissipée. Il était devenu un des leurs; jour après jour, saison après saison, il était entr dans cet univers et, quoi qu'il fît désormais, il ne pourrait plus en sortir. (*Le Général* 198–99)

> Since he had noticed that, not only in his conversation but in every episode of his life, alien elements were creeping in little by little, the words of visitors he had received, fragments of letters or diaries of dead soldiers, he had tried to dam up this flow. But this had proved so powerful that the words and phrases, sometimes entire narratives by the dead men, kept invading his mind. [. . .] And his fear that if he kept making use of sentences or words deriving from people in the kingdom of the dead, he would fetch up there himself, this fear did finally pass. He had in effect joined up with them; day after day, season upon season, he had entered this universe and, never mind what he did now, there was no escaping it any more. (*The General* 163)

Finally the general and the chaplain come to the end of their mission. The earth has kept back its portion, handing back most, but not all of the Italian soldiers (185). The general imagines the burial ceremonies for his dead army. Charon, the mythological carrier of souls across the Styx, enters their names into his ledger as the workmen place the blue bags of remains into the coffins. The general's dead companies, battalions, regiments, and divisions will dissolve into 'no more than a few tons of phosphorus and calcium' (*The General* 186; *Le Général* 230). However, the remains of Colonel Z. have not turned up and his fate remains a mystery.

As the general leaves the mountains and high plains for the lowland, the capital and the journey home, he feels the relief of a survivor. The distinction between life and death begins to return as he feels the signs of life again. In his final nightmare he sees himself retained at the last moment. 'L'ultime tourment de ce pélerinage: après avoir fait mine de le laisser partir, au tout dernier moment, les montagnes, à la lisière de leur royaume, avaient tenté de le faire rebrousser chemin' (*Le Général* 232, 'The final torment of this pilgrimage [. . .] happened in a flash, the way nightmares come: after pretending to let him go, the mountains at the last moment, right on the border of their territory, had sought to force him back', *The General* 188). At this point Kadare emphasizes again the characterization of the general as a 'peacetime general', who was a junior recruiting officer during the period of the Albanian occupation, and who did not see active service.

Arriving at a country village on the eve of a marriage festival, sick to death of his morbid occupation, the general has already begun to turn away from the realm of death. Colonel Z. disappeared in this area, but the general no longer even wants to find his remains.

> 'A parler franc, je ne tiens pas tellement à le retrouver, articula-t-il lentement. Ce soir, je ne tiens d'ailleurs à retrouver aucun mort. Pour ma part, je me réjouis de voir ce calvaire prendre fin, alors que vous tenez absolument à m'embarquer dans une nouvelle histoire'. 'Mais c'est notre devoir . . .', protesta le prêtre. [. . .] Le général était d'excellente humeur. Ce long et pénible périple, qu'il évoquait comme une vision d'épouvante était enfin terminé. Mais il ne s'agissait en rien d'un pèlerinage. C'était une marche à travers les ténèbres de la Mort. (*Le Général* 234)

> 'To be honest, I'm not particularly anxious to find him. This evening I have no urge to find any dead men at all. For my part I just feel utterly delighted to have reached the end of our ordeal. And here you are wanting me to set off on some new quest'. 'But it's our duty...', the priest said. [. . .] The general was in good humour, very good humour. The long and arduous pilgrimage

that he saw in his mind as a vision of terror was at last at an end. But it wasn't a pilgrimage. It had been a march through the valley of the shadow of death. (*The General* 190)

In this reawakening to the world of the living, the general listens to the sounds of the Albanian countryside which we had last heard in the notebook entries of the Italian deserter, the sounds of idyllic nature, a traditional and peaceful image quite different from that of the mud, icy rain, and bleak rocky mountainscapes of the dead army:

C'était une maison à étage entourée d'un jardinet, et, du balcon, on découvrait une partie du village. Le général entendit le cliquetis d'un seau et des voix de femmes en provenance d'un puits voisin, les beuglements solitaires des vaches, les sons d'un poste de radio qu'on venait de mettre en marche, et toujours les cris des gamins qui jouaient et couraient en tous sens sur la place. (*Le Général* 235)

There was a little garden all around the bungalow, and a view of a section of the village from the veranda. The general could hear the clinking of a bucket and women's voices from a nearby well, the lonely lowing of distant cattle, the sound of a radio that had just been switched on, and the cries of the children still at play, running to and fro across the square. (*The General* 191)

Settling into his quarters, the general hears the drumbeats announcing a village wedding. At this point he stands in the balance between past and future, death and life, Albania and Italy. The call of life is strong after two years in the realms of death and he wants to attend the village wedding to rid himself of the associations of death. The chaplain, still associated with the past, the dead soldiers, and mourning warns him not to go, but the general insists. They appear as figures of death in their black capes which contrast so strongly with the colours of the wedding guests. At first the general cannot adjust to this vision of life after his eighteen-month mission as an envoy of the dead:

La fête, à présent, lui faisait l'effet d'un grand organisme invertébré mais puissant qui respirait, remuait, murmurait, dansait tout en remplissant l'atmosphère de son haleine chaude, grisante et trouble. [. . .] Le général sentit un souffle chaud et une douce émotion lui inonder la poitrine. Il avait la sensation de se délasser dans un bain de sons et de lumière. Et ces sons, ces flots de lumière qui se déversaient sur lui comme d'une tiède fontaine le réchauffaient, débarrassaient son corps de toute la boue des cimetières, de cette boue qui dégageait une odeur de moisi et de mort. (*Le Général* 240–41, 243)

Now the feast seemed to him like a great organism, powerful and amorphous, breathing, moving, murmuring, dancing, and filling the whole atmosphere around him with its warm, disturbing, intoxicating breath. [. . .] The general felt a warm breath of tender emotion flooding through his breast. He had the sensation of being laved in a delightful bath of sounds and light. And the waves of sound and light pouring over him like the waters of a healing spring were warming him, purifying his body of all that graveyard mud, that foul mud with its unmistakable odour of putrefaction and of death. (*The General* 196, 198)

The chaplain reminds him that they are the symbols and even harbingers of death for these people at this wedding, but he refuses to believe him.

'La mort . . . Je ne crois pas que nous l'ayons inscrite sur notre figure . . .', riposta le général. [. . .] 'Il y a beau temps que la guerre a pris fin. Le passé est oublié. Je suis certain que personne à cette noce ne songe aux vieilles inimitiés'. (*Le Général* 243–44)

'Death . . .? I don't think it's written on our faces, [. . .] It is a long time since the war was over. The past is forgotten. I am certain that no one at this wedding has a thought for past enmities'. (*The General* 199)

Inebriated and overwhelmed by the beat, the general joins the wedding dance, drunkenly mistaking ritual for merriment.

Le tambour retentit de nouveau comme un grondement de canon. La clarinette reprit sa lamentation, les violons l'accompagnèrent de leurs voix minces, semblables à des voix de femmes. [. . .] Le tambour tonnait avec toujours plus d'emportement, les cris de la clarinette se déversaient à flots redoublés, semblables aux sanglots sortis de la gorge d'un titan, et les cordes des violons vibraient, éperdues. Le tambour battait de plus en plus vite, et maintenant, à travers la complainte, on eût dit que de gros rochers déboulaient du haut des montagnes. Toujours debout, le général [. . .] vit comme à travers un voile les visages en sueur des musiciens, le pavillon de la clarinette osciller de bas en haut, tel un canon de DCA braqué sur une cible mobile, les yeux clos des danseurs en extase. Puis le tambour se tut, les cordes se relâchèrent comme par enchantement. (*Le Général* 249–51)

The drum beat out its summons yet again, like cannon firing. The clarinet resumed its lamentations, while the violins accompanied it with their slender, almost feminine voices. [. . .] The drum was beating with redoubled fury, the cries of the clarinet were pouring out in wilder and stronger waves, like sobs emerging from the throat of some Titan, and the violins' strings were vibrating like lost souls. The drum beat quicker and quicker, so that now, through the lament, it was as though great rocks could be heard thundering down from the mountains. The general [. . .] stood there seeing the sweating faces of the musicians, the mouth of the clarinet swaying up and down like the barrel of an anti-aircraft gun following a moving target, the closed ecstatic eyes of the dancers. Then the drum fell silent, the violins relaxed, and there followed an enchanted calm. (*The General* 205–06)

The wedding dance is one of Kadare's most powerful images of Albanian ethno-cultural identity. Here the dance recapitulates Albania's recent history of war and occupation. The general is both drawn to and burned by it. Like the epic poem sung to the *lahuta* accompaniment in *The Palace of Dreams*, the dance is an image of culture as life or as the life-giving bond of the community. In the historical environment of the Albanians continuity has only been possible through this medium operating through music and the pared down, ritualized language of the epic.

An old woman, Nice, sits in the background, silently cursing the foreigner who occupied the land and killed her family. Old Nice is outraged as the general glibly turns from past to present, death to life. For her, death and the past are not so easily forgotten. She breaks the silence with howling sobs, abusing the general. The only word he understands is '*vdekje*' (death). She disappears into the night and returns shortly to throw a muddied sack of bones before his feet, the remains of Colonel Z. She is his killer. Her fourteen-year-old daughter committed suicide twenty years earlier after being raped by Colonel Z. In retaliation the old woman killed the colonel, burying him under her doorstep the night her daughter died. The irruption of the bitterness and the tragedy of the war breaks the general's alcohol-induced dream of turning his back on death and the past, and forces him back to his role as the general of death:

> Il enfila alors son imperméable et, reprenant le sac, le hissa cette fois sur son épaule et sortit, courbé, mortifié sous ce fardeau, comme s'il portait sur son échine toute la honte et le poids de la terre. (*Le Général* 261)

> He put on his coat, took up the sack once more, hoisted it slowly up onto his shoulder, and left that place, bent beneath his burden, mortified, as though he were carrying all the shame and the weight of the earth on his back. (*The General* 215)

Nearing the completion of his mission, he had begun to turn back towards life, Italy, and the future, and the dance seemed attractive to him in its passion and intensity. But he does not understand this intensity as a product of a national history of destruction, of a history that generated vendetta and Kanun. Old Nice represents the truth of history and death, against the general's falsification of history and life. She is the image of her country, mortally wounded and bitterly resentful of the world that has abused her and passed on. These are the forces which moulded Albania over its history.

On the road again that night, haunted by the presence of death and the memory of the old woman, the general finds himself headed back down towards the underworld:

> Soudain réveillée par les phares, la route ensommeillée et pâle sortait un instant du chaos de la nuit pour y replonger aussitôt. De chaque côté surgissaient de loin en loin les bornes kilométriques, toutes blanches. D'une blancheur mauvaise, à donner le frisson. Elles faisaient au général l'effet de pierres tombales. (*Le Général* 268–69)

> The road, wakened by the sudden onslaught of their lights, was perpetually emerging for an instant from the chaos of night, pale and still half asleep, only to sink back into it as soon as they had passed. Every so often pairs of very white milestones flashed past on either side. Their whiteness was unpleasant. It sent a shiver up the spine. They made the general think of tombstones. (*The General* 222)

In an attempt to free himself from the realm of death the general throws the sack into the river, impetuously consigning Colonel Z.'s remains to oblivion in the turbid depths. He turns away from death and back to life, rejecting Albania and the past for Italy and the future. As the sack sinks, the general feels relief, in spite of his dawning realization that he has just ruined his chances of preferment at the hands of Colonel Z.'s thankful family, or of gratitude and recompense from the adorable widow, Betty. Even the chaplain experiences a momentary sense of reprieve. The general's return to life has not brought insight or understanding — few Kadarean protagonists achieve this — but at least he is back in the land of the living. Albania, the realm of death, is left behind. But his experience has not left him untouched. Back in Tirana as he fumbles with a large denomination note in a bus he is mistaken for an Albanian by an old man. Like Bill in *The File on H.*, the general has been changed by Albania and is no longer completely foreign. Albeit fleetingly, he too has inhabited the realms of death.

> 'C'est un étranger, camarade,' dit un grand garçon d'une voix posée en s'adressant à la receveuse. 'Pas la peine de me faire un dessein', répondit-elle, et elle se mit à compter pour lui rendre la monnaie. 'Ce doit être un des nôtres revenu d'Amérique', intervint un vieillard assis près de la receveuse. Il y en a qui ont complètement oublié l'albanais'. 'Non, grand-père, c'est un étranger, j'en suis sûr et certain', insista le garçon, qui parlait posément. 'Écoute plutôt ce que je dis', entêta le vieillard; moi, je les reconnais à vue d'œil, c'est l'un d'eux'. [. . .] 'Mon Dieu, se dit [le général], même si j'étais une ombre, ils devraient me montrer plus d'égards!' (*Le Général* 278–79)

> 'He is a foreigner, comrade', a tall youth with an oddly sedate way of speaking said to the conductress. 'So it seems', she answered, and began counting out change. 'He must be an Albanian just back from America', an old man sitting behind the conductress broke in. 'There are some that forget our language completely over there'. 'No, grandad, he's a foreigner, I'm sure of that', the sedate-voiced youth repeated. 'Oh no', the old man insisted, 'you mark my words, he's an Albanian just come home again. I can recognize them at a glance, I tell you. [. . .] My goodness, [the general] thought, even if I were a shade they ought to show me a little more respect! (*The General* 230–31)

While criss-crossing the country the general encounters a West German lieutenant-general on a similar mission. They meet again in Tirana. Both have made the transition back to life. To the Italian's story of his irrational desire to dance at the wedding, the German adds his own story of the conflict between life and death. While excavating bodies at a provincial stadium, he notices a girl who watches and waits for her boyfriend at soccer-practice every day. As they leave arm in arm he feels 'un tel vide autour de moi, j'avais le cœur si gros que le monde me semblait désert et dépourvu de sens, à l'instar de ce stade obscur et vide' (*Le Général* 295, 'such an emptiness all around me, I felt my heart so heavy that the whole world seemed to me as abandoned and as meaningless as that dark, empty stadium', *The General* 245). The Italian general understands his German colleague's malaise.

> 'Ce qui vous a troublé en elle, il me semble, c'est la jeunesse, la manifestation même de la vie. Il y a si longtemps que nous courons par monts et par vaux à renifler comme des hyènes la mort là où elle est tapie, en cherchant de mille manières à la faire sortir de sa tanière. . . Nous en arrivons presque à oublier tout ce qu'il y a de beau sur terre . . .' (*Le Général* 296)

> 'What disturbed you in her, it seems to me, was her youth, the fact that she seemed such an absolute manifestation of life. It's such a long time now that we've been running up hill and down dale sniffing for death like hyenas, trying to find ways of coaxing it or smoking it out of its lair, that we have almost forgotten that beauty still exists on this earth'. (*The General* 246)

It seems that he has indeed learned something in his encounter with Albania. The ageing German's sense of falling in love with an unknown girl, like the Italian general's desire to dance at the wedding, is an expression of *eros* against *thanatos*. It is this that renders each of them, the Italian in particular, surprisingly positive figures in this novel of wartime memories. Unlike the Albanians they can return home to life and the future.

After throwing the Colonel's bones into the river, it appears likely that the general, with the tacit approval of the chaplain, will substitute the remains of the unidentified soldier for those of Colonel Z. in order to fulfil his obligations to the Italian government and to the Colonel's influential family. The past will continue to be falsified by the Italians as they celebrate the return of their hero and move into the future. The government of Italy has moved beyond the tragic past, even if the general entertains fantasies of leading Italy's post-war armies successfully to a new imperial future thereby undoing the failures of history. The Italian soldiers are repatriated, laid to rest, the remains of the Colonel will be interred in his marble tomb and life will go forward. The Colonel's widow will be free to remarry and his family to grieve for a legend and a national hero. Italy will enter the new decade as a modern European post-war polity. Albania, by contrast remains frozen in the past. Any potential bitterness at the fortune of the Western Europeans is undercut by the comedy of the characterizations: the self-satisfied and rather pathetic Italian and the comically grotesque one-armed German with his curious turns of phrase. Of course the writer could not allow himself to express such bitterness, even if he wanted to. Even in the political limbo of the period directly after the break with the Soviet Union, such open expression of desire for rapprochement with the West was unthinkable. It would have breached the conditions of Aesopian language by expressing too strongly Kadare's rejection of the regime and socialism. Moreover, Kadare's representation of the Italian failure to confront the past renders his critique of post-war Western Europe clear. The irony of the situation is unmistakeable. The Italian and the German Generals represent the two fascist aggressors, defeated in the Second World War, moving into a post-war European West symbolized by life and *eros*, not death. Albania, the victim, is left behind, a land of death, mired in the past.

National Day

The general's last day in Albania is 28 November, the day of national liberation from the German occupation. On the evening before, he and the German general watch the preparations for the following day's procession on the main boulevard from the University to Scanderbeg Square.

> A l'autre bout du Boulevard, du côté de l'Université, se profilaient de gros carrés sombres qui se mouvaient vers eux. Le bruit sourd des pas s'entendait à présent plus distinctement, et les ordres brefs, tranchants, résonnaient, glacials, dans le noir de la nuit. Les deux généraux étaient accoudés à la balustrade, les yeux braqués dans cette direction. Comme les carrés s'approchaient du pont, ils distinguèrent les froids reflects des caques et des baïonnettes mouillés, les longues colonnes de soldats, les officiers sabre au clair, les espaces vides entre les compagnies et les bataillons. Le sol tremblait sous les lourdes bottes et les ordres secs retentissaient comme un cliquetis de baïonnettes. Les formations ne cessaient d'approcher; tout le Boulevard fourmillait à présent de soldats et les reflets des lampadaires sur les casques paraissaient aussi mystérieux et froids que ceux d'un monde en décomposition. [. . .] Le Boulevard n'était plus

FIG. 6 (above): The famous
Hotel Dajti, once the meeting
place for VIPs and functionaries
in Tirana, now in disrepair.
(Photo: Peter Morgan.)

FIG. 7 (right): The entry of the
National Liberation Army into
Tirana, November 29, 1944,
commemorated in the National
Day celebrations at the end of
The General of the Dead Army.
(Source: *40 Years of Socialist
Albania*, Tirana: 8 Nëntori
Publishing House, 1984.)

maintenant que troupes, métal, pas cadencés, vrombissements de moteurs et commandements secs, et tout cela, tel un seul et même corps, se dirigeait vers la place Skanderbeg. (*Le Général* 310–11)

At the far end of the boulevard, near the University, big, dark squares were advancing towards them. The heavy ('muffled', PM) tramp of feet could now be more clearly distinguished, and the orders, sudden and brief, carried icily through the darkness of the night. The two generals remained there, leaning on the balustrade of the balcony, eyes fixed on the advancing shapes. As the dark squares neared the bridge they could make out the cold reflections on the wet helmets and bayonets, the long columns of soldiers, the officers with drawn swords, and the gaps between companies and battalions. The earth shook under the heavy boots, and the curt cries of command rang out like bayonets clashing. The formations kept coming; the whole boulevard was now teeming with soldiers, and the street lamps lining the roadway were reflected to infinity on the wet, shiny helmets, looking as cold and mysterious as a world going putrid. [. . .] The boulevard was now all troops, metal, marching feet, thundering engines, abrupt commands, and all of it, as in a single body, streaming relentlessly on towards Scanderbeg Square. (*The General* 258–59)

This vision of the National Day army brings to mind the general's dead army, marching past 'dans leurs sacs bleus à lisérés noirs' (*Le Général* 312, 'in their blue bags with their black edgings', *The General* 259), and plunges the general into drunken despair once again as he contemplates 'cette vaste étendue de mort' (*Le Général* 312, 'that vast stretch of death', *The General* 260) which is beyond his understanding. The imagery of 'a world going putrid' is strikingly unexpected. So far contemporary Albania has appeared in muted terms as a place of modernization, a colourless but relatively benign communist polity, with no explicit reference to the dictator or the regime. The peasants in the countryside where the general spends most of his time seem unaware of modern politics, and the general's contact with the archaeological specialist, the translators, the diplomats and other members of the intelligentsia and the nomenklatura, remains minimal. However, in the final pages this blandness of representation of the Albanian present is dramatically broken. The National Day procession is an irruption of *thanatos* into the present, a ghastly reminder of the laws of history, of the power of the past. The image is one of both life and death: of the ant-like teeming activity of the soldiers ('fourmillait') and the putrescent colourlessness of dead matter. The body of soldiers is a strikingly militarist image, comparable to Golding's images of the fascist body corporate at the beginning of *The Lord of the Flies*. Contemporary communist Albania is a military machine focused on the threat from outside, when in fact the germs of death lie buried deep within. *The General*, like *The Great Winter* ends with an image of cold war, of the freezing of relations between Albania and the rest of the world. Albania is isolated from its communist ally and protector, the Soviet Union, and the Chinese are not yet on the literary horizon, despite the high-level diplomatic activity occurring between China and Albania at this time. The West is seen as moving off into post-war prosperity and freedom while Albania is stuck between a frozen past and an over-determined, traumatized present.

   Modernization and the past are the central themes of *The General*. The one follows from the other. Is communist modernization the key to moving on and overcoming Albania's tragic past? Can history be buried beneath a layer of modernity? Or will it keep resurfacing, as a virulent and deadly bacterium, or bitter and vengeful as old Nice, until everything has returned to earth. How can the nation move on? By means of the archaeological metaphor of the dead army Kadare juxtaposes the relationships of death and life, past and present, Albania and Italy. The opening of the graves releases stories of suffering, torment, and cruelty on both sides. Several views of the relationship between past and present are presented. In one of the unnumbered chapters interspersed throughout the novel, the voice of a dead peasant expresses the tragic pre-Christian and pre-Islamic worldview of traditional Albania:

> La terre, elle ne ment jamais. Sur elle l'herbe croît chaque année, et elle nous accueillera tous, comme elle nous l'a promis . . . Cette fosse au lieu-dit le Crêt du vent, vous n'y trouverez pas une once de vérité. Rien que le silence et les ténèbres. Ou plutôt quelque chose que vous autres, vivants, ne pouvez pas comprendre. Mieux vaut donc ne pas m'interroger. Le voudrais-je que ma langue se refuserait à vous répondre. . . . Ça vaut d'ailleurs mieux pour vous!. . . (Le Général 222)

> The earth — the earth never lies. The grass grows up on it each year and it will be our lodging, for all of us, that is its promise . . . As for the grave at the place they call Wind Ridge, you'll not find an ounce of truth if you look for it there. Only silence, shadows. Or rather something that you living folk, you'll never be able to grasp. Better to ask me no questions. My tongue would refuse to answer you even if I wanted it to . . . Which is just as well for you! . . . (The General 181)

Everything sooner or later will return to the earth which bore it. The past is simply past and the present and future will occur as a result of actions and events in the past which are unchangeable. Hence the present must be simply accepted. The regime's Stalinism represents a radical denial of this traditional nihilism. Communism is a modernizing ideology based on a post-Enlightenment doctrine of the dialectical relationship between past and present. As Stalin had done in the Soviet Union, Hoxha in Albania used the communist strategy of unitarian government to accelerate historical progress, utilizing what S. N. Eisenstadt refers to as a selection and totalization of the 'Jacobin ideological elements of society'.[96] However, the young writer, like so many intellectuals of the founding years of the different socialist states, recognized the conflict between freedom and control in the socialist project. He felt it personally in the constraints on his own activities and he observed it throughout Albanian society. A possible way forward is suggested through the sympathetic figure of the young Albanian archaeologist, who mediates between past and present, Albanian and Italian, regime and populace. An intellectual sharing the generation and class of the author, he understands the need to both dig down into the past and to move forward into the future.

A further, at this stage still not fully developed, conceptualization of history, change, and the relationship to the past is presented in the dance and the epic songs of Albanian traditional culture. The general dances to music which has incorporated into itself the experiences of the war. It is an ambiguous image: the dance is both a captive to the past and an attempt to master the past by bringing it into the present.

This theme of traditional culture as the Albanians' means of mastering the past by incorporating it into the epic history of change and development will become a central part of Kadare's romantic nationalism. The epics which are the subject of the later novel, *The File on H.*, change and develop, gradually taking into themselves the events of the present, shaping and simplifying them into the stuff of collective memory. At the end of the revised version of *The Great Winter*, Enver Hoxha's combat with Khrushchev in 1960 emerges from the consciousness of the people in the form of the *issa* or heroic song. History moves forward, both changing and remembering the cultural archetypes of eternal Albania.

Kadare's critique of the regime in *The General* remains relatively muted until the final image of the National Day procession. Until that point, the Italian mission to recover the past and give it the patina of glory that will release their nation into the Western European future is the focal point. The Italian model of mastering the past may be suspect, but it enables movement forward. The Italian adventure in Albania remained conveniently inconspicuous in a communist corner of South-Eastern Europe.[97] Encased in marble and the rhetoric of national glory, the exploits of the fascist government can be considered closed, leaving Italy free to join Western Europe. The Italians are pompous, hypocritical, and false. But Albania, too, appears unable to come to terms with its past, refusing any version that is not part of the exaggerated cult of partisan heroism and national-communist victory. The question of how Albania is to move on is raised, but not answered, merely adumbrated in the final ambiguous image of the Albanian national day of death.

In *The City without Signs* Kadare had taken aim at bureaucracy and corruption — critical but still relatively safe themes for the young writer at this point of cultural thaw in Albania. In *The City* there is a sense of the mistreatment of history, a sense that the mute past has been violated by the protagonists and by government officials willing to collude with a reading of history which supports their careerist motives. *The General* deepens the critique of history in the dictatorship by implicitly accusing the regime of having buried the past beneath a militaristic and despotic socialism after the disastrous war with Italy and Germany. In his next novel, *The Monster*, which was written in 1965 and lies between the two versions of *The General*, this critique is strengthened in relation to a regime which misuses history in order to perpetuate its hold on power.

The General was not well received. While many recognized the power and the quality of the writing, the message of the novel was hardly likely to curry favour. After the break with the Soviet Union a certain openness to the West was detected, primarily in the sympathetic portrayal of the general himself, as was the absence of positivity about the socialist present. The dangerous rumour began to circulate that Kadare was an agent of Western governments.[98] Moreover, the novel was soon translated and was well received in Bulgaria and Yugoslavia, both revisionist enemies of Albania. With its negative portrayal of the present and no mention of the Party or its leader, it was read by revisionist Yugoslavs as a critique of Albanian communism. Some around the dictator began to sharpen their knives, sure, now, that the young author was hostile to the regime, and that he could be discredited in the eyes of the supreme leader. The talented writer, who had come to the notice of the regime and was viewed by the dictator as a potential laureate of Albanian communism, was not untouchable. His honeymoon with power was over.

Threat, Infiltration, and Terror in *The Monster*, 1965

Perhaps the official coolness towards *The General* provoked Kadare. Looking back from the 1990s he writes that he felt that he had compromised with *The General* and that he wanted to give his imagination free rein in his new novel, *The Monster*.

> *Le Monstre* fut quelque chose d'absolument nouveau. Il est paru en 1965, soit après *Le général*, dans une revue littéraire. A l'époque, j'avais décidé que tout ce que j'écrirais devrait chaque fois avoir une nouvelle forme.[99]

> *The Monster* was something entirely new. It appeared in 1965, after *The General*, in a literary journal. At that time I had decided that everything I wrote should take a different form.

The comment suggests a certain personal dissatisfaction, as well as an intention to stretch the boundaries, of his own imagination as well as of literature and socialist society. Perhaps at this stage he was giving free rein to the different, even opposed feelings, hopes, and dreams of life back home in his native land. He had been willing to make his obeisances to the dictator in order to give expression to the early romantic nationalism of 'What are these mountains thinking about?', and in *The General* he had sought the deeper causes of the contemporary malaise, those forces of history which had determined the nature of post-war socialist change and development. At this turning point between 1962 and 1964, as the dictatorship began to radically narrow and harden its social and cultural policies, setting them into place for the next two decades, the young writer recognized what was coming. Everything, from the choice of hairstyle through to literature and thought, was subjected to increasing control. The restrictions that he had accepted unwillingly as the conditions of return to his native language and culture, and which the promise of fame and success initially rendered less onerous for the ambitious young man, were beginning to bite. And in donning the mantle of the national writer, he would be accepting not only the curbs and restrictions but would be entering a pact with the regime and taking on a responsibility for what was to come. In the image of the national day procession at the end of *The General* and in the following audacious work, *The Monster*, he profited from the short period of transition to give full rein to his fears. With these two works Kadare bids farewell to the callowness of *The City* with its derivative theme of Westernized youth, and achieves his recognizable adult novelistic voice. He has entered the Aesopian world of the conflict between writer and regime.

Looking back from the 1990s, Kadare wrote that he tried to write normal literature in an abnormal environment.[100] The power of *The Monster* derives from the striking opposition of the ordinary and the extraordinary in two main narrative strands, the one an idyllic and completely ordinary love story, the other a bizarre and surreal evocation of Tirana in a state of emergency, under siege from shifting and indefinable forces symbolized in a mysterious Trojan Horse standing outside the city. Around the archetypal motif of the love story, mirroring the writer's own life (he married Helena shortly after returning from Moscow), Kadare weaves a brilliantly imaginative plot around the theme of siege and terror. Where Gogol's dead souls hover in the background of *The General*, the Horse of Troy, the archetypal European symbol of war and the threat of foreign infiltration, provides the inspiration for *The Monster*. Kadare introduces a new element into the ancient story of Troy. His Wooden Horse stands eternally outside the gates of the city, harbouring dangerous agents and transforming itself over the centuries in a surreal image of political terror. The theme of the fear from outside masking the danger from within, which emerges at the end of *The General*, moves to the centre of focus in *The Monster*.

> Troie ne chute pas; le cheval reste éternellement à sa place. Les citadins vivent dans une anxiété permanente. Ils se disent: 'Voilà trois mille ans que cela dure, le cheval est toujours là, comment vivre dans ces conditions?'[101]

> Troy doesn't fall; the horse stays forever where it is. The townspeople live in a state of permanent anxiety. They tell themselves: 'It has lasted for three thousand years, the horse is still there, how can we live under these conditions?'

A young man returns from study in Moscow, falls in love with a girl, and lives happily ever after. Gent Ruvina is an academic and writer, working on a study of the siege of Troy. Lena is called Helen of Troy because of her platinum hair. She is engaged to the art-historian and museum curator, Max. Both Lena and Max come from powerful clans and the marriage has been organized by their families for reasons of status and power. Max is a bureaucrat, member of the nomenklatura, and scion of an influential family. Gent and Lena elope on the eve of the wedding, leaving the jilted bridegroom thirsting for revenge. The story takes place over a year from Gent's return in October (probably 1961) through to autumn the following year, by which time Lena is pregnant. In the Tirana of this time Kadare's Trojan Horse takes the form of an abandoned van lying on the outskirts of the city, dilapidated but still intact, raised above the damp ground on four short piles. In the light of day it stands out clearly, but when night falls it seems to move, disappearing into the night and fog:

> Quand la nuit ou la brume tombaient sur la plaine, ses contours s'estompaient et il s'effaçait à la vue comme s'il n'eût pas existé. C'était surtout le cas vers la fin d'octobre. [. . .] cela ne faisait pas longtemps qu'on le voyait là et nul, au début, n'aurait su dire d'où il était sorti, ni qui l'y avait mis. (*Le Monstre* 7)[102]

> When night or fog fell onto the plain, its contours became blurred and it disappeared from view as if it had never existed. This was particularly the case towards the end of October [. . .] it wasn't long ago that it was visible and no-one, to begin with, could say where it had arisen from or who had put it there.

Lena's jilted fiancé, Max, bridges both worlds, contemporary Tirana and the inside of the Wooden Horse, linking the two stories, the ordinary and the extraordinary. He collects weapons capable of causing appalling wounds. At the time of their engagement he told Lena that he would kill her if she were ever unfaithful to him, and now he plans to murder her and Gent one warm summer night. The historical-mythological parallel for the revenge of Max/Menelaus is set up early in the novel: 'Il m'a simplement déclaré que si je le trompais, il me tuerait avec l'une de ces terribles armes anciennes qui se trouvaient là' (*Le Monstre* 17, 'He told me clearly that if I'm unfaithful to him, he will kill me with one of those terrible ancient weapons which he has there'), Lena tells Gent shortly after they meet.

The Trojan Horse and its Agents

On the anniversary of Lenin's birthday on 23 April 1960 Politburo candidate member Ramiz Alia delivered a speech critical of Yugoslav revisionism. The Trojan Horse features in Alia's speech as the stock image of ideological revisionism and inner decay. The revisionists seek to infiltrate the countries of socialism, he wrote,

> like the Trojan Horse [. . .] in order to undermine them from within and . . . to overthrow the Marxist-Leninist parties and the peoples' democratic regimes. Above all, at present, when one can perceive symptoms of a détente in international relations, the danger of revisionism, of dissemination of illusions on the question of building socialism, on the class struggle, and on the problems of peace, becomes greater [. . .][103]

The Albanian state, he declared, must continue to unmask 'the aggressive policy of imperialism and its dangerous attempts to prepare for war . . . [and] impose the policy of peaceful coexistence upon the enemies of peace'.[104] Political fear became part of the fabric of everyday life in Kadare's Tirana. Fatos Lubonja, who grew up in Tirana in the 1950s and 1960s, writes of the ubiquitous warnings to 'be vigilant of 'wooden horse revisionism'.[105] The Yugoslav journalist Miodrag Djukic comments that the siege-mentality and fear of foreign enemies were an 'obsession' of Hoxha and the regime: 'The whole world conspires against little Albania [. . .] For 35 years, the public media have bombarded the population with messages, emphasizing the need for "vigilance and caution" calling on the people to prepare to defend their country'.[106] The image of the Trojan Horse, offered to an idyllic Albania by a duplicitous ally and false friend, was relentlessly cultivated by the regime.

In *The Monster* Gent returns at the time of the break with Moscow to a country bombarded with warnings against revisionism, the internal enemy and the danger of infiltration.

> Peu après, on annonça officiellement que les étudiants ne repartiraient plus. Avec le froid et les pluies d'automne, les relations entre les pays du camp socialiste devenaient de plus en plus fraîches et, quoique la radio et la presse n'en fissent point état, la tension était désormais notoire. Les rumeurs allaient bon train: trahison, prise de la citadelle socialiste de l'intérieur, vigilance à l'endroit du nouveau cheval de bois qui se profilait à l'horizon. (*Le Monstre* 16)

> A short time later, it was announced officially that the students would not be returning. Along with the cold and rain of autumn, relations among the countries of the socialist bloc became colder and colder. And while the tense relations were not mentioned at all in the radio or the press, it was well-known by now what the situation was. The rumour-mills were gathering steam: capture from within of the socialist citadel, vigilance towards the new Trojan Horse standing out on the horizon.

Khrushchev's post-Stalinist revisionism is the Trojan Horse of an imperialist power at once cajoling and threatening Albania should the country not acquiesce to the new Soviet version of communist doctrine. A film of the sacking of Troy has been playing and the image of the horse outside the gates occupies the popular imagination. At a picnic the change in social relations becomes palpable as the image of the van enters people's consciousness:

> On était resté un bon moment sans relever sa présence, mais, un jour de printemps, au cours d'un pique-nique [. . .], certains émirent le soupçon que ce fourgon abandonné abritât des gens animés de mobiles subversifs. (*Le Monstre* 7–8)

> For a good while its presence went unnoticed, but one spring day, in the course of a picnic, some people voiced the suspicion that the abandoned van was harbouring characters with subversive motivations.

Apparatuses have appeared overnight, jamming foreign broadcasts. Even those who earlier dismissed the rumours and fears now are incredulous to hear them questioned. Gent notices things which he never noticed before (18) and revising his letter to Lena at the end of chapter two, he crosses out the words, 'big abandoned van' in favour of 'large Wooden Horse'.

> 'Tu vois', lui disait-il quand ils écoutaient la radio ou lisaient dans quelque revue littéraire des vers brodant sur ces thèmes. 'Nous ne sommes pas les seuls à evoquer l'histoire de Troie . . .' (*Le Monstre* 16)

> 'You see', he said to her as they were listening to the radio or reading verses touching on these themes in some literary journal or other. We are not the only ones to mention the history of Troy. . .

In a café a loud-speaker carries reports of political tensions, recriminations, and threats of war. An advertisement for a chess championship, strongly associated with the Soviet Union merges, via the image of the horse-headed playing piece, the Knight, on the advertising poster, with the wooden horse of Troy:

> Dans un bâtiment proche de la Poste se déroulait un championnat d'échecs. Sur la façade, on avait disposé une grande affiche avec, en arrière-plan, la silhouette d'une sorte de cheval. (*Le Monstre* 30)

> In a building near the post-office, a chess championship was taking place. In front a huge poster had been put on display, with the silhouette of a sort of horse in the background.

Walking home, Lena looks for the imaginary Trojan Horse and in the dialogue gives expression to the extent to which the story of the Trojan Horse, Gent's doctoral thesis on Troy, the contemporary environment of *entente* between Albania and the Soviet Union, and her own fear of Max's revenge flow together in her consciousness:

> 'Sais tu ce que je cherche des yeux?' fit-elle au bout d'un moment. 'Ton cheval de bois'. [. . .] 'Tiens, là, sur la droite, se découpe une tache noire isolée. C'est peut-être lui?' 'Peut-être', fit Gent. 'A la fac, hier, on parlait ouvertement du schisme au sein du camp socialiste. Comment marche cette . . . thèse de doctorat?' [. . .] 'Parfois, j'y pense pour de bon: si le Cheval de Troie apparaissait

un jour aux abords de la ville . . .' 'Mais il y est apparu! — Pas dans un sense imagé, mais en réalité, en . . . J'ai failli dire en chair et en os!' s'exclama-t-elle en riant. 'Fait de planches et de clous, comme autrefois'. 'Cela revient au même'. 'Depuis que tu m'as parlé de tes notes, je me suis souvent dit: et si le Cheval surgissait et que dans son ventre se trouvât mon ex-fiancé revêtu de cette cotte de mailles?' (*Le Monstre* 84)

'Do you know what I was looking for', she said after a moment's pause. 'Your wooden horse'. [. . .] 'Look, over there on the right. You can make out an isolated black spot. Maybe that's it?' 'Perhaps,' said Gent. 'Yesterday at university they were talking openly about the split in the communist camp. By the way, how is your doctoral thesis coming along?' [. . .] 'Sometimes I seriously think: if the Horse of Troy were to appear one day on the outskirts of the city, in . . . I wanted to say in the flesh', she exclaimed, laughing. 'Made of planks and nails, just like it used to be'. 'It amounts to the same thing'. 'Ever since you spoke to me about your notes, I have often asked myself: what if the Horse were to appear one day and my ex-fiancé were to be found there dressed in his coat of mail?

With each repetition, the motif of the Trojan Horse becomes more deeply fixed in the consciousness of the protagonists. Lena in particular projects the fear of Max into images of threat from outside. And Gent, working on his doctoral thesis on the fall of Troy, muses on the political context of the Horse, the gift of the Soviet Union, which is poised to strike at the heart of the Albanian state. The message of the novel could, perhaps, be taken as a confirmation of the regime's fears. Albania is a small isolated and besieged Troy against which the imperialist Greeks (Soviet Union) are waging war as a coalition of states bound by a single, pan-Hellenic (pan-Slav) ideology. However, where the enemies of the regime are clearly identified as the agents of the Soviet Union, the novel explores the social consequences of the creation of an environment of fear and suspicion: 'Tout le monde se sentait d'une manière ou d'une autre menacé, parfois sans savoir au juste par quoi' (*Le Monstre* 67, 'everyone feels threatened in one way or another, sometimes without knowing quite by what').

Lena becomes the mouthpiece for the thought which lies at the heart of the novel and which puts the whole edifice of the political analogy into doubt, namely the possibility that the Horse is not the product of Soviet interference, but is an internal tactic of intimidation and control exercised by the Albanian regime:

Soudain, elle lui fit face. [. . .] 'Et s'il n'y avait rien de vrai dans tout cela?' dit-elle d'une voix glacée. 'Quoi? Qu'est-ce qui ne serait pas vrai?' 'Tout ce qui nous entoure: le Cheval de bois, cette tension, la montée des périls. Si tout cela n'était que pure invention?' 'Une invention de qui?' 'Je l'ignore. Je ne sais trop moi-même. Il se peut que je déraisonne'. (*Le Monstre* 94)

Suddenly she looked at him [. . .] 'And what if there was nothing true in all of that?' she said in an icy voice. 'What? Nothing true in what?' 'Everything around us: the Wooden Horse, the tension, the growing dangers. If all that were nothing but fabrication?' 'Fabrication by whom?' 'I don't know. I don't really know anything. Maybe I'm just talking nonsense'.

Lena's fear that the monster is not a threat from outside, but is the product of internal political machinations, suggests a sinister state of affairs. In this closed political environment it is difficult for the individual to know what is true and what is false. Everything seems nebulous, cloudy, and capable of sudden change. Are the threats from outside and the fears of subversion within genuine or have they been created as a means of internal control?

The environment of the six men in the Horse is shot through with ambiguity. It is at once the draughty abandoned van, a run-down Tirana ministry building and the ancient Horse of Troy. The agents inside represent a broad spectrum of the people — Lena's fiancé (Max), an ordinary white-collar worker (Robert), an Illyrian (Acamante), a foreigner from a socialist country (Milosz), and a figure of European literature from Homer to Kafka (Ulysse K.). Their commander is the sinister Builder, responsible for the construction of the Horse.

> Le constructeur se mit à évoquer les heures sombres et humides au cours desquelles avait été construit le cheval, les hommes qui transportaient et clouaient les planches et les poutres de sapin, tandis que lui-même dirigeait les opérations dans le chaos de cette nuit. Il décrivit le lever du jour et comment, dans la pénombre glacée, le Cheval se dressa, majestueux et redoutable, devant des centaines d'yeux exorbités de peur. (*Le Monstre* 103)

> The builder began to evoke the dank, dark hours over the course of which the horse was built, the men who transported and nailed the planks and the beams of fir, while he directed the works in the chaos of that night. He described the beginning of the day and how, in the icy half-light, the Horse rose up, majestic and formidable, before hundreds of eyes bulging with fear.

His men are at once Greek infiltrators, Albanian bureaucrats, and revisionist spies. This ambiguity persists throughout. They are both subversives hiding in the wooden horse dreaming of rape and pillage, and frustrated office workers and functionaries chafing with the boredom of their everyday life:

> 'Tu veux te mettre quelque chose sous la dent?' demanda Milosh. 'Non, merci. J'ai cassé la croûte dans une rôtisserie'. [. . .] 'Dis-moi quelque chose des femmes', dit-il d'une voix suave. 'Y en a-t-il de bien roulées dans les rues?' (*Le Monstre* 30)

> 'Do you want a bite to eat?' asked Milosh. 'No, thanks. I had a snack in a grill'. [. . .] 'Talk to me about women', said a mellow voice. 'Are there any good sorts knocking around on the streets?'

Inside the Horse agents await the day when the gates of the city will be opened, the van brought inside and they will finally emerge to wreak havoc and destruction. They are cold, sick, bored, and morose with their millennial wait for the gates to be opened, and the longer they wait, the more lurid become the fantasies of murder, rape, and destruction with which they entertain themselves. The anticipated entry and destruction of the city and the atrocities that follow are related with sadistic relish. The Trojan weakening of defences in ancient legend is reiterated in modern form as the Albanians cut their power-lines in order to allow the entry of the horse, and the sacking and plundering of the city echoes that of Troy, as a latter-day Hector is abused and butchered and Helen is hunted down:

> Les mains et le visage couverts de sang, ils arrivaient d'un pas rapide du côté

du stade, traînant un homme par les bras et les cheveux. L'homme se débattait, cherchait à leur échapper, mais à chacune de ses tentatives, ils le frappaient à coups de tessons de bouteille de bière. Ils avaient dû briser cette bouteille à dessein, chacun s'armant d'une de ses moitiés. [. . .] Sur le perron du grand bâtiment de l'Université, le Constructeur aperçut Max traînant quelqu'un par les cheveux. D'une main, il tenait haut levée sa vieille lance, tandis que l'autre empoignait une touffe étincelante de cheveux blonds cuivrés. 'Il a trouvé Hélène', se dit le Constructeur. 'Dommage qu'il doive souiller de sang de si beaux cheveux'. (*Le Monstre* 132–34)

Their hands and faces covered in blood, they ran down alongside the stadium, dragging a man by the arms and the hair. The man was struggling to escape, but with each of his attempts, they struck him with pieces of broken beer-bottle. They must have broken the bottle for that purpose, each of them arming himself with a piece. [. . .] On the steps of the main university building the Builder saw Max dragging someone by the hair. With one hand, he held aloft his ancient lance, while with the other hand he grasped a gleaming tuft of coppery-blond hair. 'He's found Helene', the Builder said to himself. 'Pity that he will have to dirty such beautiful hair with blood'.

The description of the sexual cruelty, generated by Max's desire for revenge, is terrifying.

'Je pourrai le faire en avril, par une tiède nuit de clair de lune', reprit Max d'un air sombre. 'J'attendrai, je sais que cette nuit viendra, quand tous deux, oubliant toute précaution, sortiront de la ville et viendront se promener dans la plaine désolée qui apparient à tous. Alors j'empoignerai cette lance antique et descendrai lentement, lentement à terre. Je les trouverai peut-être blottis dans les bras l'un de l'autre, couchés sur l'herbe printanière, grisés par l'amour et les senteurs de la plaine. [. . .] Tu n'ignores pas, Acamante, quelle plie horrible peut laisser une telle lance de style antique. [. . .] Une énorme plaie rouge, avec, sur les bords, les déchirures causés par l'extraction du fer. [. . .] — Une plaie qui laissera terrifiés tous les contemporains. (*Le Monstre* 34–35)

'I could do it in April, on a balmy clear moonlit night', Max replied darkly. 'I would wait, I know that a night like this will come, when the two of them, forgetting all precautions, leave the city and go for a walk on the empty plain which belongs to everyone. Then I'll grasp my ancient lance and I'll go softly, softly along the ground. I'll find them, maybe nestling in each others' arms, lying on the grass in springtime, drunk on love and the scents of the plain. [. . .] You don't know, Acamante, what horrible wounds an ancient lance of this type can cause. [. . .] An enormous red wound with lacerations around its edges caused when the metal blade is withdrawn. [. . .] A wound which leaves our contemporaries terrified.

It is the figure of the Builder, however, who represents the most dangerous political aspect of this novel. He is the archetypal creator of political weaponry and the architect of power and control. Friendship, subversion, infiltration, penetration, and violent aggression are his strategies, not his ends. He does not revel in the violence for its own sake and he is oblivious to the opportunities for plunder. Satisfied with the outcome of his work, the intellectual returns to the Horse, leaving his lieutenants to finish the job. Already the refugees are fleeing the city, their appearance unchanged since millennia:

Parvenu près de l'amphithéâtre, il aperçut le premier groupe de réfugiés qui se déversait comme un torrent tumultueux par une rue étroite. Pour la plupart, il s'agissait de femmes pressant des enfants contre leur sein, de vieillards qui marchaient avec peine; çà et là, parmi eux, quelques hommes d'âge moyen. L'un d'eux, blessé au visage, portait dans se bras son père très âgé. Leurs visages étaient ravagés par le feu. Visiblement, ils avaient tout juste échappé aux flammes et aux balles et maintenant, ils cherchaient à quitter la ville en toute hâte. [. . .] Certains tenaient entre leurs mains des statuettes qui lui parurent ressembler tantôt à des pénates domestiques, tantôt à de petits bustes de Marx. (*Le Monstre* 136–37)

Having almost reached the amphitheatre, he saw the first group of refugees pouring down a narrow street like a wild torrent. They were, for the most part, women holding infants close to their bosom and old people walking with difficulty; here and there among them some middle-aged men. One of them, wounded in the face, carried his old father in his arms. There faces were ravaged by fire. Clearly they had just escaped the flames and the bullets and now they were trying to flee the city in all haste. [. . .] Some held in their hands tiny statuettes which at one moment looked like the gods of the hearth and at the next like little busts of Marx.

The Builder quickly tires of the torture, rape, and theft. He leaves that to his underlings whose horizons extend only to ruthless brutality. He returns to the quiet of the Horse to savour victory in the abstract. He uncannily mimics the gestures of a dictator and Kadare suggests the ways in which dictatorial control feeds on personal motives, utilizing and manipulating individual energies, creating victims and perpetrators, rewarding and punishing in the cause of an overriding political aim. The single-mindedness of the Builder is the most threatening aspect of the story, for it harnesses the fears, desires, and capabilities of disparate individuals, making one of many. The Builder is the first of Kadare's Hoxha figures, and 'engineers of human souls', whose demagogic paternalism masques his megalomania. His long monologue in the middle of the novel is a study of the deformations of the dictatorial mind.

Chaque fois que le besoin s'en ferait sentir, mon Cheval apparaîtrait soudain à l'horizon des peuples et des cités rebelles, il pèserait et répandrait son ombre sur leur conscience, suscitant perpétuellement le doute, l'appréhension, l'effroi. Aucune horde barbare, aucune épidémie de peste, aucune dictature ne pourrait se révéler aussi efficace. [. . .] Il pouvait se manifester sous n'importe quelle forme, et tout aussi bien disparaître sans laisser de traces. [. . .] Dans ce monde où il semblait que tous les malheurs eussent déjà été inventés, j'ai créé une nouvelle terreur, plus totale que n'importe quelle autre: la terreur politique. (*Le Monstre* 104–05)

Whenever the need made itself felt, my Horse would appear suddenly on the horizon of rebellious peoples or cities. It weighed on and spread its shadow over their consciousness, perpetually evoking doubt, arousing fear and terror. No barbarous horde, epidemic of plague or dictatorship could turn out to be as effective as this. [. . .] It could reveal itself in any form whatsoever, and just as easily disappear without leaving any trace. [. . .] In this world in which it seemed that all the possibilities of misfortune had already been invented, I had created a new terror, more comprehensive than any other: political terror.

Gent's Dissertation on the Fall of Troy

A form of gloss on the political story is woven into the novel through excerpts from Gent's speculative notes in preparation for his doctoral thesis on the fall of Troy, and in fragments of a novel about Lena and himself which appear in italics alongside the events on which they are based. Chapters 10, 11, and 12, each of which bears a subtitle, form a sequence in which the fall of Troy is retold from the Trojan perspective. One strand of narrative follows Helena back to Sparta and everyday married life with Menelaus, suggesting the life that Lena would have led with Max, contented and superior in his knowledge of having conquered and survived. Another strand explores the fate of the Trojan high priest, Laocoon, after the sack of the city. Sensing danger, Laocoon warned the Trojan ruler, Priam, against opening the gates for the Greek gift. However, in a scenario reminiscent of Hoxha's court politics, he falls into disfavour and is purged. In Gent's dissertation, he is the image of the intellectual in a dictatorship, warned against telling 'the truth to power' and executed for doing so.

> L'après-midi, à la réunion du Conseil, j'eus l'impression que tout un chacun était au courant de mon entretien avec le roi. Les regards de mes adversaires s'étaient faits plus perçants que jamais. [. . .] J'y suis accusé d'être un ennemi de la paix, partant, la cause des souffrances endurées par les Troyens, etc. On demande que je me démette. Mais c'est le moins de ce qui est exigé. J'ai comme l'impression qu'on y réclame davantage. Peut-être ma comparution devant quelque tribunal. La prison, donc; après cela, pourquoi pas, la mort. (*Le Monstre* 158–59)

> That afternoon at the meeting of the Council, I had the impression that everyone was aware of my meeting with the king. The looks of my enemies were more piercing than ever. [. . .] I was accused of being an enemy of peace and therefore a cause of the sufferings endured by the Trojans, etc. They called for my resignation. But that's the least that they have demanded. I have the impression that they will insist on more yet. Maybe my appearance before some tribunal or other. Prison, then; after that my death — why not?

The forgotten Trojan bard, Thremoh, Gent's anagram for the Trojan Homer, escapes the destruction, seeks exile in Hittite lands, and writes the Trojan version of the siege and fall of Troy.[107] However, his version, even in its written form on the new cuneiform tablets of his superior host civilization, is treated with incomprehension and suspicion in his new homeland. Laocoon comforts himself with the thought that at least Thremoh will have preserved the truth about the siege of Troy, that artistic truth will have been preserved even when the city and the minutes of the meetings of the ruling house and the records of its political decisions will have been destroyed by fire and the rampages of the invading Greeks. However Thremoh among the Hittites is the archetypal writer in exile, treated with distrust by a people who do not understand his language or his motives. The Thremoh episode tells the story of the lost literature of history. The narratives of the conquered are not heard: their poets in exile lose the living language and are no longer able to put experience into poetry, and the fate of those few fragments that are preserved is to disappear among the detritus of history. The living word of the bard is consigned to the unfreedom of the cuneiform tablet, and the organic link between literature and life is broken. Political conflict, symbolized in the siege of Troy, ends the organic, chthonic, and communal act of literary remembering. The oral, bardic aspect dies. The act of writing and of the creation of the literary and historical record takes its place. However, its existence is not ensured. In exile Thremroh is unable to complete his mission to save Troy in words. The clay tablets are lost in the decline of the Hittite empire and end up as the paving of a courtyard. Shattered by the hooves of Tamerlane's army, they finally disappear beneath the desert sands. Archaeologists have found one fragment, on which the last half of the fourth line alone is preserved: 'Peut-être pleurerez-vous Troie, mais il sera trop tard, à jamais trop tard' (*Le Monstre* 173, 'Perhaps you will weep, Troy, but it will be too late, forever too late'). The disillusioned and embittered poet dies in exile and his work is lost in the steppes of Central Asia, Kadare's symbol from early on of the Soviet Empire.

This theme, of the writer's exile and the loss which comes of it, preoccupied Kadare and goes some way to confirming his claim in *The Weight of the Cross* that he considered seeking exile in Czechoslovakia (at that stage the most progressive of the socialist states in terms of its oppositional subculture) as early as 1962. Thremoh's flight to the Hittites reflects Kadare's fear that he would be submerged and disappear in the Soviet environment and that his language and its literature would be lost. This fear underwrote his return to Albania. Albanian culture had survived against so many odds. He must continue to contribute to the vitality of his country which had survived partly in its poetry and song. It would be his role to commit that identity to writing, just as Thremoh had done. But the task must be carried out in Albania, drawing on the creative nourishment of his language and culture in spite of political repression. Kadare's romantic nationalism has accompanied him throughout his writing life, and this early theme of writing and cultural loss would be elaborated in detail in the literary essay *Aeschylus or the Great Loser* after Hoxha's death and in the final years of the regime.

At the end of the novel the Horse turns back into an abandoned van and appears nothing more than a harmless wreck. Some picnickers throw empty bottles at it. But the threat has not completely dissipated. Shortly afterwards a pair of lovers are found dead, grotesquely mutilated in a spot favoured by Gent and Lena. The girl is platinum blond, like Lena. But she is someone else, and Gent continues his academic career unharmed. The romantic idyll ends with the promise of Lena's pregnancy, foreshadowing an uneventful life of love, marriage, children, and contentment in a featureless, ahistorical present. The political novel ends with terror in the image of Gent as Laocoon. In a surreal final configuration he finds himself alone on the immense expanse of the plain, awaiting the emergence from the mud of the massive snakes which will punish him for his provocation of the gods.

> Se traînant dans la boue, ils s'avancent vers lui. Il a la sensation d'être pétrifié sur place, transformé en une statue de marbre, à l'image de Laocoon . . . (*Le Monstre* 218)

> Dragging themselves through the mud, they advance towards him. He has the feeling of being turned to stone on the spot, transformed into a marble statue, in the image of Laocoon . . .

As Laocoon, his face gashed by monstrous fangs, he stands there, mouth open wide to tell of the terrible events, but he cannot speak. Laocoon would become a European icon of the representation of suffering in art as he is strangled by sea serpents sent by the gods. The ancient sculpture, subject of debate in Western aesthetics since Winckelmann and Lessing regarding the relationship of art to truth and of aesthetic expression to human suffering, continues to say the unsayable to masses of Western tourists incapable of understanding the obvious.

> Il se trouve au musée du Louvre, à Londres, à Madrid, entouré d'une innombrable foule de flâneurs et de touristes. [. . .] Les gens se montrent les uns aux autres les estafilades laissées par les monstres sur son visage. Il veut ouvrir la bouche pour raconter les faits tels qu'ils se sont produits, mais le marbre dont il est fait l'en empêche. (*Le Monstre* 218)

> He is to be found in the museum, in the Louvre in London and in Madrid, surrounded by innumerable tourists and passers-by. [. . .] The people point out to each other the gashes to his face left by the monsters. He wants to open his mouth to tell the facts of how they happened, but the marble of which he is made prevents him.

Victim of a vicious regime, flailing and uttering cries of terror and pain, the writer is rendered at once visible and inaudible. He becomes the aesthetic image of the problem, as the mouth which cannot speak and the body which cannot move as it is punished by the serpents of the gods. Unable to enunciate what has happened to him, he must rely on himself as the image of the regime, the material which exposes itself in order to expose the evils of its political environment. Laocoon is the intellectual in an oppressive and physically threatening regime, whose body is hostage to his art. He is at once cut off from the world and the object of the world's attention. Laocoon is the image of the writer in Stalinist Eastern Europe. Object of the world's gaze, yet unable to articulate his situation, he can do no more than show himself, in the hope that the aesthetic sphere can generate understanding where the political sphere has failed.

Only the writer and intellectual, Gent, is able to make something constructive of the abandoned van. Kadare thus begins to tell the story of the education of the writer. In the changing image of the Horse he finds the material of his political self-education, seeing its effect on himself and his loved one, observing the ways in which it skews public and private communication. Gent's notes represent an extended, quasi-fictional musing on the workings of fear in the dictatorship. The strange, surreal texture mirrors the workings of the creative writer's mind, enabling Kadare to articulate the process of becoming for a writer in an environment in which political terror infiltrates the consciousness of individuals and the public sphere alike.

> L'événement (la chute de Troie) se situait tout à la fois dans le futur et le passé des personnages. Par endroits, ceux-ci restaient immuables alors que Troie se transformait sous leurs yeux, changeant de forme jusqu'à devenir une cité moderne, avec cafés, aéroport, etc. Ailleurs, c'était elle qui se figeait cependant qu'eux-mêmes se transformaient, traversaient différentes époques, jusqu'à se métamorphoser en personnages de notre temps. (*Invitation* 83, 85)

> The event (the fall of Troy) is situated both in the future and the past of the characters. Sometimes they remain immutable while Troy transforms itself beneath their eyes, changing form to become a modern city with cafes and an airport, etc. At other times it is the city which freezes, however, while the characters change, passing through different eras until they turn into characters from our time.

The transformation of the Horse of Troy into an allegory of political terror over history allows Kadare to explore aspects of consciousness and culture in the dictatorial state. The Horse moves ominously through time and space, materializing and disappearing in response to the fears, dreams, and nightmares of the protagonists, past and present. It comes to represent not the threat from outside but the fears from within, its transformations following the contours of the characters. The threat from outside generates a new dynamic of power and intimidation inside the polity. Factions become increasingly powerful in the new situation. Dissent and dissension are ruthlessly persecuted until the threat on the horizon appears mysteriously within the walls. Spies and infiltrators are blamed for opening the gates, but in fact the monster was always on the inside. *The Monster* marks a new awareness in the writer of the dynamics of the monopoly of power. If Kadare uses the Trojan Horse as a metaphor of (Soviet) revisionism, he does so in such a way as to explore the workings of political threat and terror rather than to advocate the anti-Soviet policies of the regime. It is not the external, but rather the internal enemy which is identified in the ubiquitous image of the Trojan Horse. In the environment of Albanian ideological purism and isolationism Kadare focuses on the metaphor of the Horse itself, the primal image of political power and moral guilt. Kadare reveals not the danger from outside, but the workings of the siege mentality and the ways in which fear can be manipulated.

> J'avais plus ou moins accompli cette descente en 1965 lorsque, avec l'image du cheval de Troie, j'avais mis l'accent, plus que sur l'idée de trahison intérieure, principale hantise des communistes, sur une autre idée: l'angoisse et la terreur d'État. J'avais imaginé le Cheval comme une pression s'exerçant sans relâche, des années durant . . .[108]

> I had more or less accomplished that slope in 1965 when, with the image of the Trojan Horse, I placed the accent on state terror and the distress it causes rather than on the idea of betrayal from within, the main obsession of the communists. I imagined the Horse on the horizon of our lives as a form of pressure applied relentlessly over years . . .

Brilliant imaginative riffs give the novel its power: the surreal transformations of the Horse, the doubling of identities of those within the Horse with those on the outside, and the historical digressions — the story of Menelaus and Helena back at home in Sparta after the war, and the fate of Thremoh, the Trojan Homer, in exile, and the depiction of life inside the Horse as everyday life in the dictatorship, a dreary succession of ordinary days of waiting fuelled by lurid fantasies of rape, pillage, and destruction. The idyllic love story, too, has a personal element, reflecting the role of Kadare's wife Helena in his creative life. Helena had written to the writer in Moscow, introducing herself as a school-student and admirer of his work, and subtly reproaching him for his absence. 'Discrètement, avec douceur, cette voix me rappelait que la littérature [. . .] n'était pas du tout dépassé' (Discreetly, sweetly, that voice reminded me that literature [. . .] was in no way outdated').[109] As a novel, however, *The Monster* is, perhaps, less than the sum of its parts.

Idyllic, unchanging communist Albania turns out to be built on political terror. Kadare writes that he was disappointed with the reception of the novel, which was prohibited from book publication. However even in the still relatively free context of the early 1960s, before the crackdown of the cultural revolution, it is remarkable that it was published at all in 1965, even shortened in a literary journal such as *Nëntori* with limited exposure. The text of *The Monster* published in French in 1991 is a translation of the edition published in Albanian in Tirana in 1990 shortly before the fall of the regime. Powerful protective forces were clearly still at work. The dictator knew that he had a writer of outstanding promise within his grasp and Kadare's period of grace was not yet exhausted.

The cool reception of *The General of the Dead Army* and the prohibition of *The Monster* came as a shock to the successful young writer whose ambitions had been fired by the dictator's intervention on his behalf in 1961. The poem 'Laocoon' (1967) gives expression to Kadare's sense of having fallen from favour.[110] The high priest of Apollo is shunned by Priam and the dominant court faction after advising the king not to allow the Wooden Horse inside the gates of Troy. The dissenting priest tells the truth about his city and its factions, and the king's decision to ignore him will have fatal consequences for the greater community. This conflict represents the beginning of the struggle over the voice of Albania that began in the early 1960s, would occupy the dictator and the writer for the following decades, and which took on personal qualities unique in the history of the European socialist dictatorships.

China and the Albanian Cultural Revolution, 1965–1968

In January 1961 both Enver Hoxha and Mehmet Shehu were still speaking of the Soviet Union in glowing terms after signing a new improved trade agreement. Behind the scenes, however, the Soviet government had affirmed that only top-level discussions between the leaders could mend the break and lead to ongoing relations — and Hoxha was not willing to return to Moscow. He had found a new ally whose political ideology was more acceptable, and whose geographical distance rendered it militarily unthreatening. In 1957 Mao's then vice-chairman and leading diplomat, Chou En-lai, had visited Poland and Yugoslavia with the mission of encouraging disaffected Eastern European countries to switch allegiance from the Soviet Union to China. Chou was unsuccessful; however, the Chinese overtures to Eastern Europe were not lost on Enver Hoxha, who first visited the country in 1956, and invited defence minister Peng De-huai to Tirana in 1959.[111] The Chinese connection was followed up during the early 1960s by increasingly close diplomatic, cultural and ideological, and economic ties. Albanian Deputy Prime Minister Abdyl Këllëzi visited China in February 1961 to conclude a technical assistance agreement which would see Chinese influence in the country grow dramatically as Soviet influence waned. Within one week of ordering all Soviet specialists out of the country, leading to cessation of work on the new Palace of Culture in Tirana, the Albanians were concluding an agreement with China underwriting the Third Five-Year plan.[112] At the meeting of the Chinese-Albanian Friendship society Këllëzi spoke of the 'great and unbreakable' friendship between the Albanian and Chinese peoples, based on 'the immortal principles of Marxism-Leninism' and on the 'joint struggle for national liberation and for the sacred cause of building socialism and communism in our two countries [. . .] against USA-led imperialism and its lackey, the Belgrade Tito clique which represents modern revisionism and in our unswerving struggle for the defence of the purity of Marxism-Leninism'.[113] His counterpart, Chiang Nan-hsiang, replied in kind, paying tribute to the 'heroic Albanian people' and 'their glorious revolutionary tradition under the correct leadership of the Albanian Party of Labour headed by Comrade Enver Hoxha, the long-tested Albanian leader'.[114] In 1964 Chinese Premier Chou En-lai paid a ten-day state visit.

World attention at this time was focused on Mao Tse-tung's ambition to undermine Khrushchev and Brezhnev by presenting the Chinese model as an alternative to Soviet 'great-power chauvinism'. The alliance with Albania suited Mao Tse-tung's ambition to extend China's global influence[115] and he was willing to sacrifice a great deal to drive a wedge into the Soviet domination of Eastern Europe.[116] In the context of the major issue in world communism at this time, namely the ideological differences between China and the Soviet Union and of the Cold War, Albania's role as the Chinese regime's only ideological ally in Europe was relatively minor. On the tenth anniversary of Stalin's death in 1963, Albania alone of the Eastern European states paid homage to the discredited Soviet leader. And in 1965 Hoxha strengthened his critique of Soviet Marxism, now led by new General Secretary Leonid Brezhnev, for aiming to share domination of the world with the imperialist West led by the United States, and thereby implicitly continuing his support of Chinese policy. Albania was small fry in the stakes for global communism; however, the Chinese interest could be turned to Albanian advantage by someone as clever as Ever Hoxha. The Chinese–Soviet hostility over ideology was played down and prominence given to Hoxha's doctrinal battles with the former ally. Hoxha manipulated the affair to his own benefit, pursuing a pro-China policy in order to cement his power and find a new source of industrial and technological support and financial aid. Chinese subventions in the form of cash, kind, and personnel flowed into the country and political, trade, and cultural delegations flew back and forth. By this time the Cultural Revolution was underway as Mao Tse-tung purged the Party of enemies and remaining members of the old guard.

In spite of the political frost that began in 1964, and strange as it may seem in retrospect, many intellectuals continued to hope into the late 1960s that Hoxha would move westwards in orientation, despite his courting of communist China since early in the decade. As late as 1970, writes Kadare, he was not the only Tirana intellectual to 'have the conviction that independently of its grotesque friendship with the Chinese', Albania was about to leave the communist world once and for all and 'return to its continental family, Europe'.[117] Hoxha would bring about the secession from communism by making the break first with European socialist states and using the Chinese alliance as a 'mask' while waiting for gestures of friendship (and support) from the West.[118] Despite the influx of Chinese funds, aid, and technological and specialist support from 1961 onward, the ideology of Maoism did not penetrate deeply into Albanian socialism. Neither Hoxha nor the regime espoused Maoism, preferring to view Mao publicly for a while as an ally and co-supporter of the true — Stalinist — line of Marxism against Soviet revisionism. And Hoxha made some surprising gestures, including the invitation to speak French and English at Politburo meetings, which led people to hope that he was preparing to make overtures to Europe. However, the hardened Stalinists, including Kadri Hazbiu and Hysni Kapo, created a fear campaign, suggesting that if Enver Hoxha were to make the fatal mistake of opening the country to the West, it would bring about his downfall.[119] The pro-Western intellectuals' hopes did not materialize. As Kadare noted in relation to the prohibition of *The Monster*, the turn towards frost occurred around 1965 when Hoxha reneged on his strategy of rapprochement with the West and initiated his country's own cultural revolution.[120] A new era of harshness began.[121]

As early as 1963, Hoxha had begun his campaign against aspects of Albanian traditional value systems, condemning arranged marriages, feuding and vendetta, and the rising birthrate as obstacles to progress.[122] At the 15th Plenum of the Central Committee on 26 October 1965, and again at the 5th Party Congress in early November the following year, Hoxha spoke on the role of creativity in building a socialist society and established a particularly Albanian aesthetic with his call for a socialist literature 'national in form and socialist in content'.[123] Writers and artists are charged with the 'sacred duty and the heavy burden of responsibility' for educating the masses. However, the party takes ultimate responsibility. The Party, he writes,

> will always give powerful support to the good works, the correctly inspired works, those that educate, mobilize and open perspectives. Mistakes are made and will be made [. . .] They should be corrected; criticism should be constructive and not denigrating, and he who is criticized should respond, not with petty-bourgeois pride [. . .] but with an open heart. With those who are confused in their works from the ideological, political and artistic point of view in content or in form it is the duty of the Party to correct them with patience.[124]

This speech initiated a much stronger involvement of the state in literary affairs.

In 1964 the influences of Western music were condemned at the Second National Song Festival. An attack was launched in *Drita*, the weekly journal of the Albanian League of Writers and Artists, on recent trends in Soviet writing, naming Yevtushenko and Solzhenitsyn as deleterious influences. Three young Albanian writers were accused of neglecting the requirements of socialist realism in recent works. Artists and intellectuals were the targets of the new program, and in January 1966 forty members at a meeting of the League of Writers and Artists resolved to go into the country to live and work among the people. In the following month the first major policy action of the Albanian cultural revolution took place with the dispatch of twelve high-ranking party officials to do grass-roots work in different parts of the country. According to Prifti this was not so much a purge as a statement of new revolutionary ideology in action as party officials were brought 'back to the masses'. The Chinese influence was unmistakeable. During March the changes continued with the announcement of measures in an 'Open Letter to the APL Central Committee' to reduce bureaucracy, reorganize the Party and state apparatus, and 'modernize' the armed forces through measures such as the elimination of ranks and insignia and the reintroduction of political commissars.[125] In early 1966 the Central Committee introduced a set of far-reaching economic and governmental policy changes, influenced by the Chinese Cultural Revolution. An open letter to the people criticized the survival of 'liberal and petty bourgeois' remnants of pre-communist culture. Further cohorts of party officials were sent into the countryside, the administration was cut back dramatically and in the army all military insignia of rank were annulled.[126] Religion was not targeted until later, when, at the 5th Party Congress in November 1966, Hoxha attacked 'regressive' religious practices, among which he included the traditional custom of marrying off girls of the ages of thirteen to fourteen, and in particular the local Muslim custom in Lezhë of selling girls into marriage. Attacks on religion would increase over the following year as Albania became the world's first officially atheist nation in 1967.[127]

Enver Hoxha was, no doubt, impressed with Chairman Mao's methods — or at least results — but he had no need of the type of 'great purge' that took place in China from 1965.[128] He had been carrying out regular purges since the break with Yugoslavia in the late 1940s, ostensibly on ideological grounds, but practically to ensure his total control of the country. In 1961 he had even pre-empted Mao's strategy of empowering young people in order to disabuse the old guard of any notions of credit or authority on the basis of age and their partisan experiences.[129] Eric Faye writes that although intellectuals and writers were sent to the country in order to learn from the life of the proletariat and workers, this did not constitute a Chinese-style cultural revolution of harassment and imprisonment.[130] Prifti, too, writes that 'at no time did the Albanian cultural revolution go much deeper than the traditional self-criticism among party cadres. The practice of public humiliation of functionaries conducted by the Red Guards in China did not occur in Albania'.[131] Compared to the Chinese Cultural Revolution, 'the Albanian variety was moderate, orderly for the most part, and at all times under the direction and control of the party'. Unlike its Chinese counterpart, 'which was basically political in nature and involved a fierce intra-party struggle', Albania's revolution was 'a technique of economic and social mobilization', adopted by the leadership in order to implant socialism more deeply.[132]

Hoxha was using the model of the cultural revolution to change the direction of national development, moving from the Stalinism of the previous decades to a new cult of personality around himself and his inner circle.[133] At the same time measures such as reduction of the bureaucracy, abolition of religion, and annulment of all military insignia of rank in the armed forces indicated a new direction in policy dictated by the economic decline which attended the loss of Soviet aid and the failure to find equivalent replacement.[134] In 1967 at the 5th Congress of the Party of Labour of Albania Hoxha announced that the period since the 4th Congress

(1961) had been the most difficult in the party's history, but claimed significant increases in investment and output during the 3rd Five-Year plan (1961–65). In September Albania withdrew from the Warsaw Treaty Organization which it had been an original member of since 1955, although it had been excluded since 1961. The following year Hoxha would opportunistically condemn the Soviet invasion of Czechoslovakia and 1969 would see a build-up of armaments from China (although Soviet-made) in response to the presence of the Soviet fleet in the Mediterranean and the occupation of Czechoslovakia.

Chinese communism was a shock for Kadare. He visited China in 1967 early in the Cultural Revolution as part of a delegation of writers, and became aware of the use of terror against writers and intellectuals.[135] He attended a banquet given by Chou En-lai, with Mao, Jiang Qing, and Lin Biao present. At this time the Chinese Union of Writers was disbanded and literature was denounced as anti-revolutionary and unnecessary by Mao Tse-tung. Western classics such as Cervantes and Shakespeare were condemned and Chinese literature disappeared from view for over a decade. In Kadare's imaginative geography, the steppes of the East had already come to symbolize the oppressive uniformity of Soviet ideology and power, in, for example, 'On a Lost Train in the Winter Night'. The symbolism of the Soviet steppes would be extended into the arid deserts of western China as Kadare enlarged his literary geography to include the Eastern despotisms. From the symbolic plains of Asia the worst excesses of political oppression emerge, from the Ottomans, the Mongol hordes and, beyond them, the communist Chinese. He would later use his experiences in his novel of the Albanian–Chinese friendship, *The Concert* (1978), in which the brooding and mysterious figure of Mao Tse-tung exercises absolute power from a mountain fastness. The experience of Chinese communism provided a foil to the Albanian and Soviet situation and would even temper his attitudes to the long night of the Ottoman occupation. 'Le Concert a été mon incursion la plus profonde à l'Est' ('*The Concert* was my most profound foray into the East'), he later wrote.[136]

Kadare has been criticized for utilizing clichés of Eastern despotism. However, there is a logic to his literary symbolism given the time and place of writing. All political systems, as structures of power, represent the possibility of constraint and unfreedom in Kadare's symbolic history of humanity. 'The Pyramid of Kheops' (1967) is an image of both civilization and oppression. Later, observing the construction of the glass pyramid in the Louvre in Paris and thinking of the museum and monument to Enver Hoxha in central Tirana which was begun in 1988 after years of planning, he began work on a novel that would explore the ambiguities of the Egyptian monument.[137] 'L'enfer', he writes, 'est le commencement des lois, de la légitimité. [. . .] L'enfer est le premier code pénal de l'humanité' ('Hell is the beginning of law, of legitimacy. [. . .] Hell is the first penal code of humanity, the concept of law begins with Hell').[138] Culture is a part of human order and encompasses constraint and loss as well as structure and memory. Even writing, 'cette grand aventure de l'humanité' ('that grand adventure of humanity'), contains the antinomies of human culture: 'Elle est faite de nuances aussi sublimes que tragiques. D'éléments imposants et monstrueux, tout à la fois triomphants, redoutables, mordants, lumineux et terribles' ('it comprises shadings as sublime as they are tragic. Of elements both imposing and monstrous, at once triumphant, formidable, biting, luminous and terrifying').[139] In his late novel, *The Pyramid*, Kadare counterposes against the beautiful if oppressive monument of Kheops, the ephemeral and ghastly pyramid of skulls erected by Tamerlane. The polished marble of the Pyramid of Kheops glows and attracts cries of wonder in the poem and the later novel (1988–1992). Its massive, tranquil, and beautiful solidity aestheticizes power, and it proves to be greater than the pharaoh who commissions it. Later, in 1993, Kadare would use *The Great Wall of China* to consider themes of separation, confrontation, and re-engagement of civilizations after the fall of the socialist 'wall'. Whereas Kheops initiates history with his pyramid, the further eastern, nomadic despotism of Tamerlane represents extreme brutality and political oppression, cultural annihilation, and the end of history. Ottoman, Soviet, and even Albanian oppression pale into comparison against Tamerlane's and Genghis Khan's empires of destruction.

The New Sobriety: Internal Exile to Berat

The General and *The Monster* were products of the prosperity of the 1950s and the thaw of the early 1960s. The situation changed dramatically in the mid 1960s. In the new environment of frost, artists, writers, and intellectuals were in danger if they stepped out of line. As Kadare testifies and Maks Velo has documented, the situation of intellectuals in Albania at this time was comparable to the Soviet Union of the late 1930s, with many persecuted, imprisoned, sent to labour camps, tortured, shot, or otherwise killed during interrogation.[140] Until 1968, writes Kadare, he treated the machinery of political control and intimidation with contempt. Indeed, part of his success lay in not taking the regime seriously.

> A l'époque, non, je ne craignais rien. Envoûté par la littérature et mon officine d'écrivain, je trouvais falot tout l'univers environnant. La dictature, le Parti, son chef, leurs discours, les flagorneries, les menaces, les vociférations: autant de choses que non seulement je ne prenais guère au sérieux, mais que je considérais comme de la vulgaire pacotille.[141]

> At that time I didn't fear anything. Enchanted by literature and my writer's office, I found the world around me dull. The dictatorship, the Party, its leader, their speeches, the toadying, the threats, the outcries: I didn't take any of them seriously, nor did I consider them anything other than vulgar rubbish.

Stalin had been dead for fifteen years and the likes of the Soviet terror would not occur in Albania — or would it? His first experiences of the cold wind of political frost were about to take place. Kadare realized that he too could fall further when he was sent along with other writers to the country to learn about life alongside the peasants and workers.

> Dans les pays de l'Est, il existait deux sortes to peur: l'une, terrible, incurable; l'autre, banale, passagère. Celle-ci, tout comme elle s'emparait de vous dans des circonstances et pour des raisons définies, pouvait tout aussi bien vous quitter. En revanche, la première, l'incurable, était on ne peut plus spécifique. Elle s'insinuait par des voies mystérieuses, dont l'une était le culte du dictateur. Dans

Fig. 8: Ismail Kadare in China at the Great Wall in 1967.
(Photo: Private collection of Ismail Kadare.)

les souterrains de la conscience, il arrivait que cette adoration se mît à fermenter peu à peu jusqu'à se transformer insensiblement en peur. Puis se produisait le processus inverse: cette peur se muait en adoration, et ainsi, tour à tour, chacune engendrait l'autre. (*Le Poids* 315)

In the countries of the East, there are two sorts of fear: the one, terrible, incurable; the other banal, temporary. The latter form takes hold of you under clear circumstances and for definite reasons and it can let go of you in just the same way. The former, on the other hand, the incurable form, could not be more specific. It crept its way in through mysterious pathways, one of which was the cult of the dictator. In the subterranean passages of conscience, that adoration began to ferment, gradually turning into fear. Then the opposite process occurred: the fear transformed itself into adoration and thus by turns each engendered the other.

Kadare was sent away from Tirana to the country to 'dip his hands in the mud'. In fact, he writes, he continued to work as cultural correspondent for the review *Drita* during this period in the southern town of Berat from 1966 to 1968.[142] He alludes to the model of the Chinese Cultural Revolution, but the experience seems to have been more comparable to the East German programme of the 'Bitterfeld Way' of learning from and working side-by-side with the proletariat, than to Chinese re-education through ruthless physical humiliation and degradation.[143] Kadare was not subjected to the abuse that characterized the treatment of the Chinese intellectuals and party officials. The punishment was minor, but the point was clear. Along with the official prohibition of *The Monster*, it was an unaccustomed snub for the young author. The banishment from his beloved Tirana constituted a warning not to overstep the boundaries.[144] The experience of Berat and the 'frost' of the late 1960s opened Kadare's eyes to the personal effects of the terror he had imagined in *The Monster*. In 1968 he experienced for the first time a self-criticism, and witnessed the humiliation of his friend, the naturalist writer Dhimitër Xhuvani.[145] In 1969 two dramatists were imprisoned for eight years each for incurring Hoxha's displeasure with a piece which won a national prize.[146] Kadare realized in the 'cruel year' of 1967 that he would have to toe the line, and he became a member of the Union of Writers, and a hence a professional full-time writer drawing a state salary, in 1969.[147] In 1970 he was nominated as a Deputy of the People's Assembly and in 1972 became a member of the Albanian Party of Labour. These were ceremonial roles, which he was not at liberty to refuse without serious consequences, and they were necessary for his continued existence in Tirana.[148] By the second half of the decade the contradictions of Kadare's existence had come out into the open. The works of these years hold the key to Kadare's development as the conflict between modernization, tradition, ethno-national identity, and socialism become more pronounced under the force of the dictator's gaze. Success and compromise had become irreconcilable with literary imagination and existential authenticity.

In the 1967 story, 'The Song', a young Albanian's wish that his life might be celebrated in epic song comes true.[149] Waylaid and shot in a blood feud, he ends up remembered as a nameless corpse on the side of the road in the song of marriage of an unrelated family. In this work the romanticism of the peasant imagination contrasts powerfully with the critical realism of the narrative voice, leaving the conflict between traditional and modern consciousness unresolved in the irony of the ending. The romanticism of 'What are these mountains thinking about?' is matched by a sceptical modern narrative consciousness, aware of the brutal reality of the traditional customs of feud and vendetta as prescribed by the Kanun. The facile resolution of the conflict between tradition and modernity in 'The Nude', for example, becomes strained in the later stories as the constraints on writing and freedom of expression were increased and the writer was forced to meet the demands of the new sobriety.

Questions of political orthodoxy, traditional attitudes, aesthetic individualism, and socialist realism emerge in the 1968 story, 'Winter Season at the Cafe Riviera'.[150] A university student takes a job in a city cafe in a gesture of socialist worker solidarity. He is shocked to discover that office workers, functionaries of the nomenklatura, and even Party members use the premises to arrange marriages, either to offload unwanted girls or for financial gain, in contravention of socialist principles. The young worker's colleagues react with hostility and suspicion to his demand that private morals be brought into line with official doctrine and public expectations. For Kadare's young socialist intellectual the issue revolves around the principle of arranged marriages, sometimes involving girls under the legal age limit. It is not a matter of religious belief, but rather of women's rights. The issue of the liberation of women from the repressive customs of the past was one of the aspects of socialist modernization most enthusiastically received by young people influenced by post-war Western and Eastern European models of equality.

The young Kadare was a modern intellectual in every respect: as an atheist as well as a believer in women's rights and social liberalization. Religion, particularly Islam, is for the most part represented negatively in these early works. In 'Winter Season at the Cafe Riviera' the issue of modern socialist civic morality seems clear-cut. Obsolete socio-religious practices have no positive aspect. However, the focus turns towards two adjacent matters: art and the role of the Party. The waiter encourages a young painter to depict the engagement preparations which are carried out in the cafe from a socialist point of view, revealing the ugliness of the custom and of those perpetuating it. The painter cannot, however, since there is no positive aspect to be gained from it. The subject will not yield to the requirements of socialist realism and hence must be passed over in silence by the socialist artist. The critique of the rigidity of socialist aesthetic dogma remains implicit. Finally the politically correct young waiter falls foul of a group patronized by a powerful minister and is denounced for holding class attitudes. Collusion between the manager and a colleague, and the suggestion that bribes are being taken, imply nepotism and corruption in or around the Tirana Party. The waiter is fired and the story ends with him in a state of indecision as to what he should do. He considers approaching the relevant Party committee to discuss the problem but is now unsure whether this is a wise move. The final image of the story, the entrance to the Committee building, is ambiguous in its implications.

> Le bâtiment du Comité se dressait là, en face, avec des lustres allumés derrière toutes ses larges baies vitrées, et c'est seulement à cet instant que je me rendis compte que je m'étais dirigé vers lui sans trop savoir comment. ('Saison d'hiver', Œuvres 9:582)

The Committee building stood out there, opposite me, its lights shining through all of its large bay windows, and in that moment I realized that I had headed for it without really knowing how.

The entrance is bathed in clarity and light, but, after all that has happened, it is by no means clear whether the lavishly lit windows represent Party excess and corruption or whether they are an icon of socialist enlightenment. The process of modernization from above and the instilling of socialist principles into the populace are fraught with problems in the environment of Party corruption where socialist dogma has replaced sophisticated and flexible principles of literary and artistic representation.

Tradition and Modernity in *The Wedding*, 1968

On 7 February 1967 Enver Hoxha urged his people to 'hurl the remnants of the past into the flames of the revolution'.[151] Complaints had often been made that Kadare ignored the workers and the factories, preferring to confine his focus to the Tirana intelligentsia and to subjectivist, formalistic experimentation.[152] In his new novel, *The Wedding*, he sends his writers out to the country, a crew from the New Albania Film Studio shoots a documentary on backward customs and religious superstitions, and the newly constructed textile mill is named after Mao Tse-tung.

The experience of political 'frost' in Berat was the main motive for the reworking of the 1961 story, 'Strange Wedding', into the novel, *The Drum-Skin*, which was serialized in *Nëntori* in 1967 and appeared in book-form in the following year, renamed *The Wedding*. This work was partly written in Berat where Kadare was sent to work with the people and engage with everyday socio-political reality as cultural correspondent for the review *Drita*. It was substantially rewritten and shortened for republication in 1981 and was included in the Fayard *Œuvres* edition under its original title in 2000. A translation into English appeared in Tirana in 1968.

It is sadly ironic that the fear which Kadare had portrayed so audaciously in *The Monster* manifests itself as a motive force in the writer's reworking of *The Strange Wedding*, marking the end of Kadare's honeymoon period under the dictatorship. In *The Wedding* we can see the effect of political constraint on a writer who was well-disposed to modernization, but for whom the duress of the socialist regime generates tension and resentment. The Albanian cultural revolution appears to have achieved its aim. Despite Kadare's acquiescence in the demand that he produce an Albanian form of socialist realism, however, a powerful tension nevertheless survives in this story between the old and the new. The rediscovery of the old is surcharged with resentment at the failure of the new. The work does not represent a complete capitulation to the demands of the regime.

With reference to both the legend of Rozafat and to Andrić's *Bridge over the Drina* Kadare takes the classic Balkan theme of the disruption of traditional identities through modernization, in this case transport and communication. A socialist construction crew turns up to a 'station without a name' where there was once a religious shrine, destroyed, presumably, as a result of official atheism and the new cultural revolutionary policies, in order to extend the railway line.[153] But one morning they discover that their work has been sabotaged. An official report traces the damage back to the drunken antics of guests at a wedding celebration which has just taken place (hence the early title, 'The Drum-Skin', referring to the traditional goatskin drum beaten at the wedding ceremony). Katrina, a liberated village girl, is marrying her sweetheart, the socialist hero, Xhavid, against her father's wishes. She has been betrothed to another since the age of ten but has been liberated by socialist education and work. It turns out to be the father together with the jilted betrothed villager and the go-between who damage the railway tracks as an act of revenge. The case arouses national interest in the newspapers and a writer and a newspaper reporter arrive to cover the story. The reporter, sent from Tirana to cover the facts, completes his piece as demanded by his editor.

> 'I must write something about the builders, about the work which is going here. That is what we planned at the Editorial Board'. 'Isn't it the same thing', interrupted the writer, 'Aren't these the builders, the heroes of labour, fitters, plumbers, carpenters? Here you have them all, sitting at tables, dancing, drinking'.[154]

The pair disagree over the nature of change. For the cynical reporter the essence remains the same while the form changes, whereas for the writer 'it is precisely the essence that changes while the form remains more or less the same' (*Wedding* 12). This discussion appears to give support to the writer's belief in the possibility of the 'new man' of socialism. However, all is not quite what it seems, for the writer's deeper probing of the essence of Albanian life reveals a human texture which the reporter ignores. '"We wait for things to 'crystallize,'"' continued the writer, "We keep a certain distance from events. That is why there is more mould than living things in our books"' (*Wedding* 14). As in 'Winter Season at the Cafe Riviera', their interchange raises the issue of the role of literature in socialism as the writer justifies the new line of the cultural revolution:

> 'The writer's face must be scorched by the breath of time just like that of a stoker feeding coal to the furnace at the metallurgic plant'. 'That's right! But you have accustomed your readers to bad habits, too' the newspaperman remarked. 'For instance, if you were to include these remarks we are making at this wedding party in your novels, I can imagine some reader biting his lips. I am sure these things would look to him like 'reportage' rather than 'a novel' because by reading bad books he is used to separating real life from books'. (*Wedding* 15–16)

Kadare uses stock motifs calculated to please the powers that be: the village girl liberated by socialist education and work from an arranged marriage and life of servitude; the heroic factory workers, one of whom becomes a martyr in an industrial accident; the drunken, Westernized, layabout son of a powerful minister who discovers socialism and becomes a hero of labour on the provincial factory floor; the degraded and corrupted dervishes, the foolish and intellectually sloppy Tirana intellectual from the Folklore Institute; the hard-nosed but well-meaning newspaper reporter who sees everything in black-and-white ideological terms. However even in this most conciliatory novel of socialist realism, Kadare's evocation of the depth, complexity and tragedy of Albanian traditional life contrasts with the superficiality of his positive heroes and heroines.

The reporter returns to Tirana, satisfied that he has covered the facts and hence the truth. Noting to himself that the bride's family is not present and that only her father turns up alone, the writer remains to find out what the truth of the matter is. In Katrina's father, the simple mountaineer, the writer recognizes a depth of character absent in the ideal figures of modernity. 'His long and weather-beaten face looked like a wood carving which had stood out in the sun for a long time and had been worked on by the wind and rain' (*Wedding* 21). The old man, father of the bride, cannot forget the events of his own ill-starred wedding. 'All this wedding party seemed more like a funeral to him and his thoughts turned to his own distant wedding nearly half a century ago [. . .] it was rumoured that a sorcerer had cast a spell on their way' (*Wedding* 25–26). At his wedding an argument broke out between his older brother and a drunken guest, leaving the brother dead and the new bridegroom obliged to kill in turn in accordance with the law of the Kanun. After three days of inaction, coffee is served under the knee to him, signifying social condemnation, a scene familiar from Kadare's later novel, *Broken April*. He kills to release himself from the shame. In a section which was excised from the 1968 version the writer sympathizes with the old man:

> 'Il a son drame à lui', observa l'écrivain. 'Tu me connais, je ne suis pas un sentimental; tout de même, sa condition me touche. Il est dur, pour un homme des montagnes, de rompre avec le *Kanun*. Parfois, à dire vrai, on ne sait trop où se termine la montagne et où commence le *Kanun*'.[155]

> 'He has had his dramas too', observed the writer. 'You know me, I'm not a sentimentalist; but all the same his situation touches a cord in me. It is hard for a man of the mountains to break with the Kanun. Sometimes, to tell the truth, it's difficult to tell where the mountains finish and the Kanun begins'.

Nor, however, is the situation of the young woman oversimplified. At the intervention of her Party comrades, her father allowed her to work on the railway, but only on the condition that she return to be married to her betrothed. Katrina's inner monologue reveals the problems of women in traditional rural Albania. Her anger at the go-between, rather than at her father or her betrothed, is intensified in the image of the snake:

> He wants to deprive me of the beautiful highways, cities, the sea, the trains and my companion. In compensation for all these he wants to give me a half-lit nook and the solitude of subjugation to a forty-year-old man I have never seen. He wants to deprive me of my bobbed hair, clean underwear, wall bulletins, books and songs, and in their place to give me a black kettle, a lash rope to haul firewood, filth, and beatings. He wants to snatch away socialism from me. [. . .] I hear the hiss of the serpent. It looks for a crack through which it can strike. He approaches then sneaks away again. I used to be frightened by his shadow, by the lump on his neck, by his carbine. (*Wedding* 178–79)

The other privileged themes of socialist realism — of labour, the positive hero and the creation of the classless society — are treated perfunctorily. The representation of the degraded dervishes drinking alcohol and enticing young girls for sex at the holy shrine does the writer little credit, regardless of whether it arose from his dislike of religion or from the need to appease the regime's new strictures against religion.

> The writer puffed on his cigarette. 'There is no end to outrages like these committed in churches and monasteries!' he ruminated to himself. 'At times I feel like getting up here and telling my whole story to arouse the indignation of all these workers who would certainly set fire to the monastery'. (*Wedding* 64)

Using imagery reminiscent of 'What are these mountains thinking about?', suggesting the symbolic identification of Enver Hoxha with the mountainous backbone of the country, the writer speaks of the changes taking place throughout the land:

> 'Albania is being shaken up' said the writer. 'The mountains are squaring their shoulders. You know what that means? The mountains want to shake off the Canon, old prejudices and superstitions from their backs. This requires a gigantic effort. The Canon is tough and nearly as old as the mountains. At times one can't tell where the mountain ends and the Canon begins. . . . Nevertheless the impossible is happening. Imagine what colossal force the revolution has wakened'. (*Wedding* 57)

In the important speech which laid down the lines of the new cultural policy, 'Literature and the Arts Should Serve to Temper People with Class Consciousness for the Construction of Socialism', Enver Hoxha made reference to the ancient Albanian legend of Rozafat.[156] The modern workers of Albania, he announced, 'have laid down their lives while working to build the dams just as in our beautiful legends about the building of bridges and castles'.[157] Kadare uses his alter ego, the writer, to build the leader's reference to the Rozafat legend into his story:

> 'A little while ago one of the old men sitting at the small table said that this new town demands a sacrifice'. [. . .] 'It demands that life in this new town should begin with death'. 'Why?' 'Because it is a legend. It respects no projects and plan and technical laws. It respects only obscurity which has given birth to it'. As he spoke he realised that he was steadily plunging into the past. [. . .] he saw thousands of young wives taking the road uphill or along river banks where walls to surround castles and bridges to span rivers were being built; and all those young wives were carrying in their hands the dinners for their husbands who were building these walls and these bridges. Which one of them is Rozafat who will be buried alive in the foundations of the Shkodra castle? (*Wedding* 170)

Rozafat becomes for Kadare a trope of the sacrifice and suffering of individuals for the progress of the collectivity. It is an early version of the tragedy of modernization. He would use it as the centrepiece for his later historical novel, *The Three-Arched Bridge*. The old man represents the continuities of tragic consciousness between past and present which the leader alluded to in his speech, but which socialism must break if it is to succeed. The point of socialist realism, in the 'positive' figures of the novel, such as Katrina and Xhavid, is precisely to break this link between past and present. The old man pays no heed to the ubiquitous Party slogans. The comedy of socialism does not register in his tragic consciousness.

> The foundations of castles and bridges stretch far and wide through the edifices of centuries. Today, in our time, they extend far and wide in the buildings of the worksites. They lie sheathed in scaffolding, blocks of concrete, under cranes, motor pumps, and deep down there the legend is breathing its last. It demands nourishment. It is famished. After hundreds of years, its call is almost inaudible, yet every one of us occasionally hears its echo as we hear the rain while we sleep. Why does one lose one's balance when walking over the narrow board across an open foundation? Because of the call of the legend. 'Come down!' it cries. Its voice is faint, even inaudible. Nevertheless, you feel its pull, and at the danger you hurry to regain your balance and not tumble into the pit below. (*Wedding* 170–71)

In the construction projects of socialism he sees the reiteration of the sacrifice of Rozafat — but in a way very different from that envisaged by the leader whose passing reference was to a heroic positivity. The powerful chthonic pull of legend belongs to Enver Hoxha's past, not to the present. He had established the Institute of Folklore in 1960 and placed 'folklore specialists' throughout the towns precisely in order to consign this material to the past, rendering it a dead, fossilized museum culture, not a part of the fabric of modern life. Kadare sees things differently even in this most socialist realist of his works. In the representation of the wedding dances the author replays the tragic history of Albania and reinforces the theme of Albanian traditional life:

> It occurred to him [the writer] that these movements of feet and hands are the most ancient alphabet the people have created and interpreted. This living circle has gathered into a white skein all the long threads of boredom and their sudden breaks, all the fathomless griefs and gleams of unrestrained gaiety. From what depths of a nation's soul does all this turmoil spring and to what depths does it return? . . . 'What is the use of the books I have read if I am not able to read these dances properly?' S.K. thought to himself. (*Wedding* 165)

In the Rozafat legend and in the wedding ceremony the positive and the negative aspects of social progress are rendered irrelevant by the force of ethnic identity. This episode is comparable to the ending of *The General* and to Marc-Alem's discovery of his ethnicity in *The Palace of Dreams*. Albanian ethnicity is represented as a chthonic force of the collective imaginary against the ethos of socialism evoked in Katrina and Xhavid. The earlier discussion of the nature of historical change is brought to mind as the old man sinks back into the past, and as the wedding guests participate in the ancient language of dance. No further conclusions are drawn. The question remains open, however, whether a political system that does not come to terms with this deep-lying force in its attempts to move forward beyond primitive social practices is likely to succeed.

At daybreak the wedding guests repair the damaged rails and the novel ends with an image of victorious socialist modernity as the train arrives and leaves again with only six minutes' delay. Nevertheless, the references to the Rozafat legend and the powerful sense of ethnicity in the wedding celebrations cannot be denied, even in this most questionable of Kadare's works. *The Wedding* is the only work which Kadare subsequently rejected as compromised by its deference to socialist-realist criteria.[158]

In the process of revision for book publication, the title of this work was changed from *The Drum-Skin* to *The Wedding*, in order to reduce the prominence of folkloric motifs, many deletions of folkloric material were made, and the evocations of a positive socialism were strengthened. Citing Enver Hoxha's speech, 'The Further Revolutionization of the Party and the State', the author of the afterword to the English translation of *The Wedding*, published in Tirana in 1968, notes that Albanian socialist life 'is proceeding ahead at an unprecedented speed, sweeping away all outdated concepts, trampling underfoot all backward and reactionary survivals'.[159] This speech and the 5th Congress of the Party in the same year are evoked in the 1967 version of novel.[160] The author's socialism is praised and any suggestion of romantic sympathy for the past is denied:

> This literary work treats many problems preoccupying our present society: the creative work of our working class, the struggle against the old world-outlook, the campaign against bureaucracy, the education and re-education of the new man, the link established between the intellectuals and the masses, the devotion and many other aspects of the life of our own days. [. . .] In *The Wedding* we have no principal hero around whom the others may hover, we have no hero we could align with the outstanding heroes of our literature. This is written for the masses and the masses themselves are the heroes. [. . .] The protagonist in this work is the revolution. (*Wedding* 195–96)

The official critique of the original title was astute. *The Wedding* did indeed foreground the call of traditional ethnicity against socialist modernization. In this work the opposition between past and present, tradition and modernization, *ethnos* and *ethos* emerges. The earlier preoccupation with nepotism and corruption in the Party are rendered secondary as the writer begins to engage at a deeper level with the failings of socialism, namely the destructive potential of political unfreedom. Conflict continues to be expressed between the recognition of the possibilities of communist modernization, of education and the enfranchisement of women on the one hand and the romantic attachment to tradition and traditional cultural values. In *The Wedding* it is the dogmatism, the enforced comradeship and the denial of human nature which come across as so unpalatable, not modernization itself, which is positively represented in the form of emancipation of women and the liberation from the brutalities of traditional life and the Kanun. The focus is not on the corruption and ideological manipulation of the system as in *The City without Signs*; there is little of the sense of terror of *The Monster* or the grey oppressiveness of *The General of the Dead Army*. However, these early works were written during the thaw; *The Wedding* was a product of the frost of the late 1960s.

Conclusion

In the works discussed in this chapter the foundations of Kadare's writing life were laid. In *The City without Signs* we read of post-war youth, liberation from traditional roles, and the blights of careerism, corruption, and the weakness of the Party to ideological manipulation. In *The General of the Dead Army* Kadare recognized the co-existence of two Albanias, the modernizing communist present and the traumatized, silenced past, and suggests the necessity of coming to terms with the past in order for the nation to move beyond the culture of death. *The Monster* used the language of European surrealism to explore the effects of the isolation of Albania, coming to the classic Central European recognition of the inseparability of politics and the private sphere, as the vocabularies of fear and the foreign merge in the imaginations of contemporary Albanians. In *The City* Kadare attacked careerism, bureaucracy, and the dangers of ideology. In *The General* he found a vehicle for his sense of the betrayal of the past in post-war Albania; and in *The Monster* he deepened his perception of the insidious nature of propaganda and the political rhetoric of terror and xenophobia. These novels are all critical, but do not mark the complete rejection of the program of modernization, although they are powerfully alert to the sinister potentialities of the regime. In *The Wedding*, product of the new frost and his weakest work, Kadare offers his most propitiatory contribution to the debate about modernity versus tradition. He refers to it as 'the most schematic of his works and the least deserving of praise'.[161] However, even this work, which represents so strongly the achievements of modernization, improvements in the role of women and in education, the development of civic consciousness, and the progress of the nation, are suffused with a sense of ambivalence. Ancient Balkan themes hover in the background as the offended spirits of the past make their presence felt in an act of sabotage. Who will be the victim of sacrifice in the new legend of Rozafat? As in *The General*, the marriage celebration in *The Wedding* becomes an image of traditional Albanian life and of an eternal Albania against which the Albania of communist modernization seems such an empty and soulless affair.

In these works Kadare revealed himself to be a young writer of imagination and audacity, fresh from Moscow, well disposed towards the modernization of his country but increasingly aware of the negative aspects of communist progress. In all three works there emerges the image of an 'other' Albania different from that of the regime. The young writer becomes aware of aspects that he cannot integrate into a positive, let alone a socialist, realism. The relationships between ideology and power, the rejection of the Albanian past as the 'new Albania' and the 'new man' are created, and the potential of the regime itself to become the inner 'monster' — these themes will cohere during the 1970s into a set of literary ideas which not only express opposition to the regime and its vision of the new Albania, but also penetrate to the heart of the dictatorial system, finding in the writer himself the nemesis of and counter-ego to the dictator.

Notes to Chapter 2

1. On Gjirokastra, cf. Ismaïl Kadaré, and Gilles de Rapper, *L'Albanie entre la légende et l'histoire* (Arles: Actes Sud, 2004), pp. 92–96.
2. 'Facteur' and 'modeste fonctionnaire', Sinani, p. 147.
3. Ismail Kadare, 'The Art of Fiction', interview with Shusha Guppy, *Paris Review*, 147 (1998), 194–217 (p. 203).
4. Kadaré/Bosquet, pp. 8–10; Kadaré, *Le Poids*, pp. 323–33.
5. Kadaré/Bosquet, p. 12.
6. Cf. Kadare's observations on Haxho Hoxha's comment, 'nous avons eu a voir avec les Kadares' ('we have things in common with the Kadares'), *Le Poids*, p. 323.

7. On Kadare's early attitudes to communism, see Ismaïl Kadaré, *Entretiens avec Eric Faye* (Paris: Jose Corti. 1991), p. 97; Champseix and Champseix, *L'Albanie ou la logique du désespoir*, p. 218.

8. Robert Elsie, 'The National Role of the Albanian Literary Journals', in *History of the Literary Cultures of East-Central Europe: Junctures and Disjunctures in the 19th and 20th centuries*, III: *The Making and Remaking of Literary Institutions*, ed. by Marcel Cornis-Pope and John Neubauer (Amsterdam and Philadelphia: John Benjamins Publishing Co., 2004), p. 93.

9. There is some dispute over the exact date. Faye cites 1953 as the date of publication of *Youthful Inspiration*, Kadaré, *Œuvres*, I, 20; Kadare cites 1953, *Le Poids*, p. 297; Samoïlov cites 1954, Sinani, p. 41; and Robert Elsie cites 1954, *Dictionary of Albanian Literature* (Westport, Conn.: Greenwood Press, 1986), p. 72.

10. Kadare, *Le Poids*, p. 297.

11. Sinani, pp. 35–37.

12. Sinani, p. 136. Nexhmije Hoxha was a partisan alongside Enver in the famous 'Seventh Brigade' during the war. In the regime she headed the Central Committee's Directorate of Education and Culture, which included the prestigious Institute of Marxist-Leninist Studies, and was editor of the *Albanian Woman* from 1943. She served on the Central Committee from 1948. As director of the Institute of Marxist-Leninist Studies since 1966, she focused on the fields of propaganda, the press, education, and culture. She was a doctrinaire and hard-line Stalinist, for whom Khrushchev presaged Gorbachev as the beginning of the end of the Soviet Union. Jacques, p. 639.

13. 'Cette usine à fabriquer des écrivains conformistes destinés à tout l'empire communiste.' 'That factory to produce conformist writers destined for the whole of the communist empire', Sinani, p. 203; cf. Kadare, *Le Poids*, p. 297. Kadare writes that he had become well-known as a poet in Albania by the time he left for Moscow. Kadaré, *Invitation*, p. 78; Ismaïl Kadaré, and Denis Fernandez-Récatala, *Temps barbares: De l'Albanie au Kosovo, Entretiens* (Paris: L'Archipel, 1999), p. 44.

14. Vrioni, p. 222.

15. Kadaré/Bosquet, p. 21.

16. Kadaré/Bosquet, p. 19.

17. Kadaré/Faye, p. 68; Kadaré/Bosquet, pp. 16ff.

18. Pearson, III, 557.

19. Jung Chang, and John Halliday, *Mao: The Unknown Story* (London: Vintage, 2006), pp. 519–35; Griffith, p. 47.

20. Pearson, III, 570–71.

21. The Australian communist and writer, Dymphna Cusack, visited Albania in 1959 and produced a glowing reportage of the modernization programmes of the country in *Illyria Reborn* (London: Heinemann, 1966). The high-ranking communist Liri Belishova, whom Cusack interviewed as living proof of the sexual egalitarianism of communism, was toppled in 1960 and consigned to thirty years in labour camps. Nevertheless, this image of Albania is one which committed communists and sympathizers aspired to, and which appealed to intellectuals inside and outside the country. In the early years in particular this vision blinded many such as Cusack to the realities of the dictatorship and provided others with a utilitarian alibi for the curtailment of rights and freedoms.

22. Peter R. Prifti, *Remote Albania: The Politics of Isolation* (Tirana: Onufri, 1999), p. 18; Griffith, Document 14, p. 263.

23. Pearson, III, 602.

24. Kadaré, *Printemps albanais*, p. 160; *Albanian Spring*, p. 154.

25. Agnes Heller, 'Existentialism, Alienation, Postmodernism: Cultural Movements as Vehicles of Change in the Patterns of Everyday Life', in *Postmodern Conditions*, ed. by Andrew Milner, Philip Thomson, and Chris Worth (Clayton, Victoria: Centre for General and Comparative Literature, 1988), pp. 5–6.

26. Deming Brown, *Soviet Russian Literature since Stalin* (Cambridge: Cambridge University Press, 1978), pp. 216–17.

27. Tönnes, p. 246.

28. Hosking, p. 532.

29. Ismail Kadaré, 'Le Nu', Œuvres, I, 519–31.

30. Kadaré/Bosquet, facing page 96.

31. Kadare, Le Poids, pp. 299–300.

32. Cf. Kadare's objection to this, Le Poids, p. 299.

33. 'Le ciel est sans forme comme une cervelle d'idiot'. 'The sky is without shape, like the brain of an idiot'. Ismail Kadaré, Le Crépuscule des dieux de la steppe (Paris: Gallimard, 1996), pp. 107–08; Kadaré/Bosquet, p. 21.

34. Kadaré/Bosquet, p. 23.

35. Ismail Kadaré, La Ville sans enseignes, trans. by Jusuf Vrioni (Paris: Stock, 1996), p. 57. All further French references are indicated in brackets after the text. Following translations are my own.

36. On the situation of young people under the regime, see Tönnes, p. 210.

37. The Poetry of Yevgeny Yevtushenko 1953 to 1965, ed. and trans. George Reavey (London: Calder and Boyars, 1966), pp. 63–64.

38. Hosking, p. 23.

39. Hosking, p. 23.

40. Hosking, p. 23.

41. Ismail Kadaré, Un climat de folie, suivi de La Morgue et Jours de beuverie, trans. by Tedi Papavrami (Paris: Fayard, 2005), pp. 157–205.

42. Kadare quoted in Champseix and Champseix, L'Albanie ou la logique du désespoir, pp. 217–18.

43. According to Griffith, the Soviets withdrew all scholarships from Albanian students in late August 1961 and expelled all remaining students shortly after. The article in Zëri i Popullit of 25 March 1962 identifies the period from the Bucharest meeting in June 1960 until the Moscow conference at the end of the year as the breaking-point in Albanian–Soviet relations. This would explain the repatriation of Kadare in late 1960 not long after the Bucharest meeting, when relations had deteriorated, but before the official Soviet expulsion of students. Griffith, p. 85, and Document 26, p. 337.

44. Vrioni, pp. 153, 223.

45. Vrioni, pp. 215–20.

46. Vrioni, p. 211.

47. Nicholas C. Pano, 'Albania: The Last Bastion of Stalinism', in East Central Europe: Yesterday, Today, Tomorrow, ed. by Milorad M. Drachkovitch (Stanford, Calif.: Hoover Institution Press, Stanford University, 1982), pp. 187–218 (200).

48. Griffith, pp. 46–47, 168.

49. 'Let the Plotters and Revisionists of Belgrade Be Unmasked Through and Through', Zëri i Popullit, 17 July 1960, translation in Griffith, Document 2, p. 185; 'Report of Enver Hoxha to the Fourth Congress of the PPSh', Zëri i Popullit, 14 February 1961, document 6 in Griffith, pp. 197–222. 'Our relations with Italy have been developing more or less normally, especially in the field of trade. The conclusion of an agreement on reparations is a step forward. But the installation of rockets on Italian soil must be mentioned as a negative factor. We cannot help but feel uneasy about the transformation of Italian territory into an imperialist base for aggression against our country and the other countries of the socialist camp. We are anxiously following the actions of the Italian government in this respect, and as we have stated, we cannot stand by with our hands folded.' Griffith, p. 211.

50. Griffith, p. 83.

51. Translated in Griffith, Document 6, pp. 211–12.

52. Kadaré/Bosquet, pp. 40f.

53. Vrioni, p. 232. Jon Halliday writes that Hoxha 'was very cultured [. . .] by far the best-read head of any Communist party in the bloc. On visits to other countries in Eastern Europe, he often comments on the philistinism of his bloc colleagues. Hoxha knew fluent French, and had a working knowledge (either verbal or written) of Italian, Serbo-Croatian, Russian and English. The range of references in his memoirs is not what one would expect from a Balkan ex-Muslim Stalinist.' Enver Hoxha, The Artful Albanian: Memoirs of Enver Hoxha, ed. Jon Halliday (London: Chatto & Windus, 1986), p. 6.

54. Kadaré/Bosquet, p. 103.

55. Cited in Schreiber, p. 107.

56. Bernd Jürgen Fischer, *Albania at War 1939–1945* (West Lafayette: Purdue University Press, 1999), p. 272.

57. Tönnes, p. 134; Sinani, pp. 188–93. 'The persecution of intellectuals [. . .] and the break with virtually all cultural traditions created a literary and cultural vacuum in Albania that lasted until the sixties, the results of which can still be felt today'. Robert Elsie, 'Evolution and Revolution in Modern Albanian Literature', *World Literature Today* 65.2 (1991), 256–63 (p. 258).

58. Griffith, pp. 26–27.

59. Vrioni, pp. 227–28.

60. Kadaré/Bosquet, pp. 29–30.

61. Kadare, *Le Poids*, p. 313; see also *Le Poids*, pp. 552–53.

62. Kadare, *Invitation*, p. 256.

63. Kadaré/Bosquet, p. 29; Kadaré/Faye, *Entretiens*, pp. 70, 78; Vrioni, p. 278.

64. Vrioni, p. 277.

65. Vrioni, p. 213.

66. Ismail Kadare, 'Le vieux cinéma', ed. and trans. by Michel Métais, *Ismaïl Kadaré et la nouvelle poésie albanaise* (Paris: Pierre Jean Oswald, 1973), p. 22; 'The Old Cinema', trans. and ed. by Robert Elsie, *An Elusive Eagle Soars: Anthology of Modern Albanian Poetry* (London: Forest Books, 1993), p. 82.

67. Ismaïl Kadaré, 'La Vérité des souterrains', interview with Stéphane Courtois, in *Le Dossier Kadaré*, ed. by Shaban Sinani, trans. by Tedi Papavrami (Paris: Odile Jacob, 2006), pp. 141–205 (p. 203).

68. Kadaré, *Invitation*, pp. 15, 75; Kadaré/Bosquet, p. 125; Kadaré/Faye, *Entretiens*, p. 53.

69. Ismail Kadaré, 'A bord d'un train perdu dans la nuit hivernale', *Œuvres*, IX, 539–44.

70. According to Milovan Djilas, Stalin allegedly made a crude gesture of swallowing in relation to Yugoslavia's relationship to Albania, Pearson, III, 257.

71. Pearson, III, 343; cf. also III, 494–95, 514.

72. Kadaré/Bosquet, p. 38.

73. Kadaré, *Le Poids,* pp. 298–99.

74. Kadaré, *Printemps albanais*, pp. 57–58; *Albanian Spring*, pp. 60–61.

75. Kadaré, *Le Poids*, pp. 299–301.

76. Dalan Shpallo, 'Karakteri kombëtar — problem thelbësor për letërsinë dhe artet', *Nëntori* 5 (1976), p. 14, quoted in Tönnes, p. 219. My translation of Tönnes.

77. Tönnes, p. 6. My translation.

78. Kornai, pp. 4–9.

79. Ismail Kadare, 'Nostalgie de l'Albanie', in Métais, *Ismaïl Kadaré et la nouvelle poésie albanaise*, p. 17.

80. Ismail Kadare, 'Longing for Albania', trans. by Robert Elsie in Elsie, *An Elusive Eagle Soars*, p. 79.

81. Cf. Ismail Kadaré, 'L'Irruption de Migjeni dans la littérature albanaise', in Migjeni, *Chroniques d'une ville du Nord et autres proses*, trans. by Jusuf Vrioni (Paris: Fayard, 1990), pp. 9–121, and the chapter on Poradeci in Kadaré, *Invitation*, pp. 113–36.

82. Tönnes, pp. 130–98.

83. Ismail Kadaré, 'A quoi pensent ces hautes montagnes?', in Métais, *Ismaïl Kadaré et la nouvelle poésie albanaise*, pp. 69–79 (p. 69). All further French references are indicated in brackets after the text.

84. Ismail Kadaré, 'What are these mountains thinking about', in Elsie, *An Elusive Eagle Soars*, pp. 86–96 (p. 86). All further English references are indicated in brackets after the text.

85. Mehmet Shehu, 'Qu'il vive autant que les montagnes', cited in Schreiber, p. 151.

86. Koço Bihiku, *Histoire de la littérature albanaise* (Tirana: Editions '8 Nëntori', 1980), p. 206.

87. Kadaré, *Le Poids*, p. 308.

88. He would later have his manuscripts sent via intermediaries to Kadare's French publishers. In retrospect Kadare suspects Hoxha of jealousy of successful writers such as himself, Kadaré/Bosquet, p. 103.

89. Kadaré/Faye, *Entretiens*, p. 52; Eric Faye, 'Souvenirs d'une autre Europe: Rencontres avec Ismail Kadaré à Tirana, avril 1990', *L'Oeuil de Bœuf*, 20 (May 2000), 19–28 (p. 20). Eric Faye,

'Introduction,' Kadaré, *Œuvres*, VI, 166: '*The General* finds its origins in the visit to Albania made by an Italian army chaplain, who came fifteen years after the end of the Second World War, to search for the remains of soldiers buried around the country. Kadare met this man briefly at the Hotel Dajti in Tirana, where some passages of the novel take place. He splits the figure into two characters, in order to separate the military and the religious aspects.' Kadaré/Faye, *Entretiens*, p. 52; my translation.

90. Kadaré/Bosquet, pp. 13, 25.

91. Cf. Alessandro Roselli, *Italia e Albania: relazioni finanziarie nel ventennio fascista* (Bologna: Il Mulino, 1986). This study excludes the type of national historical and moral analysis that characterizes the German *Vergangenheitsbewältigung* ('coming to terms with the past') in which questions of national responsibility are confronted. Italian scholars have paid relatively little attention to the national and moral aspects of the interventions in Albania under the Italian fascist government. Cf. Ray Moseley, *Mussolini's Shadow: The Double Life of Count Galeazzo Ciano* (New Haven: Yale University Press, 1999), pp. 50–57.

92. 'Sans être moi-même au courant de la propagande anti-albanaise (j'étais très jeune et j n'avais aucun moyen de savoir ce que l'on pensait vraiment de l'Albanie, en Occident), j'ai décrit dans *Le Général de l'armée morte* des personnages occidentaux alors que je n'en avais jamais rencontrés en chair et en os.' 'With no knowledge of anti-Albanian propaganda (I was very young and did not have any means of knowing how the West thought of Albania) I described Western characters in *The General of the Dead Army* without ever having met any in the flesh.' Paul de Sinety et Jean-Luc Tingaud, 'Entretien avec Ismail Kadare', *L'Oeil de Boeuf*, 20 (May 2000), p. 7.

93. Ismail Kadaré, *Le Général de l'armée morte*, trans. by Jusuf Vrioni (Paris: Albin Michel, 1970). All further French references are indicated in brackets after the text.

94. Ismail Kadare, *The General of the Dead Army*, trans. from the French by Derek Coltman (London: Harvill Press, 2000). All further English references are indicated in brackets after the text.

95. Fatos T. Lubonja, 'Pyramids of Slime, editorial' (1997), in *Përpjekja/Endeavour: Writing from Albania's Critical Quarterly*, ed. by Fatos T. Lubonja and John Hodgson, trans. by John Hodgson (Tirana: Botime Përpjekja, 1997), 83–92 (p. 84).

96. Samuel N. Eisenstadt, 'The Breakdown of Communist Regimes and the Vicissitudes of Modernity', *Daedalus*, 121 (1992), 21–41 (p. 33).

97. Ilaria Poggiolini, 'Translating Memories of War and Co-Belligerancy into Politics: The Italian Post-War Experience', in *Memory and Power in Post-War Europe: Studies in the Presence of the Past*, ed. by Jan-Werner Müller (Cambridge: Cambridge University Press, 2002), pp. 232–33.

98. Kadaré, *Le Poids*, p. 304.

99. Kadaré/Faye, *Entretiens*, p. 32.

100. Kadaré/Courtois, 'La Vérité', p. 196.

101. Ismail Kadaré, 'Sur quelques-uns de mes livres', entretien avec Ismail Kadaré par Shusha Guppy, *L'Oeil de Boeuf*, 20 (May 2000), 69–71 (p. 69).

102. Ismail Kadaré, *Le Monstre*, trans. by Jusuf Vrioni (Paris: Fayard, 1991).

103. Griffith, p. 36.

104. Griffith, p. 36.

105. Fatos Lubonja, 'Between the Glory of a Virtual World and the Misery of a Real World', in *Albanian Identities: Myth and History*, ed. by Stephanie Schwandner-Sievers and Bernd J. Fischer (Bloomington: Indiana University Press, 2002), pp. 91–103 (p. 98).

106. Miodrag Djukic, *Anti-Yugoslav Pretensions of Enver Hoxha* (Belgrade: Tanjug News Agency, 1984), p. 58, quoted in James S. O'Donnell, *A Coming of Age: Albania under Enver Hoxha* (Boulder: East European Monographs, distr. by Columbia University Press, New York, 1999), pp. 201–02.

107. '*Thremoh*', an inversion of the name *Homer*, translates as 'Little Homer', the *–th* suffix in Albanian having a diminutive function.

108. Kadaré/Bosquet, p. 182.

109. Kadaré, *Invitation*, p. 79.

110. 'En 1967, je composai le poème "Laocoon", qui n'était en quelque sorte qu'une bougie allumée sur la tombe de mon roman'. 'In 1967 I composed the poem, "Laocoon" which was nothing other than a candle lit on the grave of my novel'. Kadaré/Bosquet, p. 185; cf. Kadaré/Faye, *Entretiens*, p. 44.

111. In fact, Peng's intentions were quite different to Chou's. While on this official visit to Eastern Europe he was secretly seeking help to undermine Mao Tse-tung at the time of the devastating famines and the 'Great Leap Forward'. Chang and Halliday, pp. 494–96, 541–42.

112. Pearson, III, 584–86.

113. Quoted in Pearson, III, 586.

114. Pearson, III, 586.

115. The first Chinese satellite was launched in 1970, heralding the spread of world Maoism with the anthem 'The East is Red', Chang and Halliday, p. 700.

116. Chang and Halliday, pp. 495, 558–71.

117. Kadaré, *Le Poids*, p. 330; cf. also Kadaré, *Le Poids*, p. 317; and Kadaré/Bosquet, p. 49: 'Enver Hoxha avait perdu tout espoir de se voir absourdre par l'Occident et admettre en son sein, comme Tito. C'est alors qu'il décida de s'allier à la Chine'. 'Enver Hoxha had lost all hope of seeing himself absolved by the West and admitted to its breast, as Tito had been. It was then that he decided to ally himself with China.' According to Prifti, Albania had established diplomatic relations with ten Western European nations. 'Tirana's intense activity vis-à-vis the West at this time signalled the start of what may be called Albania's "opening to the West".' *Remote Albania*, p. 34.

118. Kadaré, *Le Poids*, p. 330.

119. Kadaré, *Printemps albanais*, 206 (n. 15); *Albanian Spring*, p. 197 (n. 15).

120. Kadaré/Bosquet, pp. 30–31; Kadaré, *Le Poids*, pp. 305, 551 (fn. 3).

121. Kadaré/Bosquet, pp. 49, 65.

122. Jean-Paul Champseix writes that Hoxha detested the backward and oriental aspects of his country, 'Itinéraire d'une œuvre inespérée', *L'Oeil de Boeuf*, 20 (May 2000), 39–48 (p. 39); on the regime's attitude toward Albanian tradition, cf. Kadaré/Courtois, 'La Vérité', p. 181.

123. Enver Hoxha, 'Literature and the Arts Should Serve to Temper People with Class Consciousness for the Construction of Socialism', closing speech delivered at the 15th Plenum of the CC of the PLA, 26 October 1965, in *Selected Works*, III: *1960–1965* (Tirana: Nëntori Publishing House, 1980), pp. 832–59 (p. 843).

124. Hoxha, 'Literature and the Arts', p. 846.

125. Prifti, *Remote Albania*, pp. 21–22.

126. Pano, p. 201.

127. Tönnes, pp. 60–64.

128. Chang and Halliday, pp. 624–40.

129. Kadare refers to the events of 1961 in Kadaré/Bosquet, p. 30 and *Le Poids*, pp. 311 and 361.

130. Eric Faye, 'Introduction', Ismail Kadaré, *Œuvres*, IX, 12.

131. Prifti, *Remote Albania*, p. 23.

132. Prifti, *Remote Albania*, p. 27.

133. Hoxha was not alone in using the move against Stalin as a pretext for focusing the cult of personality on himself. On posters of the Chinese Communist Party Mao had become the fifth classic figure of Marxism (after Marx, Engels, Lenin, and Stalin) but after Khrushchev's denunciation of Stalin Mao's portrait was drawn larger than the others, 'a pleasure which he had not permitted himself during Stalin's lifetime or prior to the Twentieth Party Congress'. Medvedev and Medvedev, p. 72.

134. Pano, p. 201.

135. Kadaré/Bosquet, pp. 50–51. This was the last delegation of Albanian writers to visit China, since the Chinese Union of Writers was dissolved shortly afterwards. Kadaré/Faye, *Entretiens*, pp. 71, 73–75.

136. Kadaré, *Invitation*, p. 241.

137. 'La Pyramide de Cheops', Ismail Kadaré, *Poèmes 1957–1997* (Paris: Fayard, 1997), pp. 64–65; cf. Kadaré/Bosquet, pp. 178–80, Kadaré, *Invitation*, p. 242.

138. Kadaré/Faye, *Entretiens*, p. 25.

139. Kadaré, *Invitation*, p. 13.

140. Kadare repeatedly refers to similarities between the Albanian situation at various points in the 1970s and the Soviet Union at the height of Stalin's purges in 1938 and 1939. Kadaré, *Le Poids*, pp. 314, 544; Velo, pp. 7–9.

141. Kadaré, *Le Poids*, p. 314. Cf. Kadaré/Courtois, 'La Vérité', pp. 176, 203.
142. The dates of Kadare's banishment to Berat are not entirely clear. Kadare gives 1966–68, but was in Tirana for periods during this time; Eric Faye gives the dates 1967–69, apparently on the basis of information from Kadare in his general introduction to the Works edition, *Œuvres*, I, 23. Cf. Kadaré, *Invitation*, pp. 86–87. The most reliable source of information on this aspect of the cultural policies of the regime is Luan Rama, who gives the dates 1966–68 as the period of Kadare's discharge to Berat. Rama, p. 45.
143. Kadaré, *Invitation*, p. 86.
144. Kadaré, *Invitation*, p. 87, 168–69; *Les Poids*, p. 304.
145. Kadaré/Courtois, 'La Vérité', p. 155. 'L'autocritique est un outil destin à mutiler l'être et à obtenir sa soumission'. 'Autocriticism is a tool desigend to mutilate a person's being and to obtain his submission'. Kadaré/Courtois, 'La Vérité', p. 162.
146. Rama, p. 58.
147. Kadaré, *Le Poids*, p. 305.
148. Kadaré/Faye, *Entretiens*, p. 47; Kadaré/Bosquet, pp. 66–68.
149. Ismail Kadaré, 'Le Chant', *Œuvres*, IV, 537–40.
150. Ismail Kadaré, 'Saison d'hiver au café Riviera', *Œuvres*, IX, 545–82.
151. Hoxha, *Selected Works*, IV, 209–20.
152. Kadaré/Faye, *Entretiens*, p. 33.
153. The 'monastery' in the English translation published in Tirana in 1968 is a *tekke* or Bektashi or Sufi shrine in the Albanian.
154. Ismail Kadaré, *The Wedding*, trans. by Ali Cungu (Tirana: 'Naim Frashëri Publishing House, 1968), p. 14. The English translation, published in Tirana is used unless otherwise stated. An early, shorter version of the novel, dated 1967, has been included in *Œuvres*, IX, 23–146.
155. Ismail Kadaré, *La Peau de tambour*, *Œuvres*, IX, 69.
156. Elsie notes that this story of 'a woman being walled in during the construction of a bridge or castle in order to stabilise the foundations' is widespread in Albanian oral literature. Three brothers, masons, are building the foundations of a castle. The foundations collapse mysteriously at night, until an old man tells the brothers that if the first of their wives who appears the next day bringing food is buried alive in the walls, the foundations will hold and the castle will be finished. The older brothers warn their wives not to come; the youngest remains true to his word (*besa*) and his wife appears, only to be immured. 'Even today, at the foot of the castle, the stones are still damp and mildewed from the tears of the mother weeping for her son'. Elsie, *A Dictionary of Albanian Religion, Mythology and Folk Culture*, pp. 218–21.
157. Hoxha, 'Literature and the Arts', p. 837.
158. Cf. Kadaré, *Invitation*, pp. 86, 88, 'Il apportait la preuve de ma totale soumission au dogmatisme.' 'It provided proof of my total submission to dogmatism.' Cf. also Kadaré/Bosquet, p. 150. Kadare repeated this criticism to me in an interview held on 6 November 2004.
159. Enver Hoxha, 'The Further Revolutionization of the Party and the State', speech delivered at the joint meeting of the basic party organizations of the Kërraba coal mine, the 'Enver' plant, the 'Wilhelm Pieck' agricultural cooperative, the army detachment No. 5009 and the University of Tirana, in *Selected Works*, IV, 209–21. A[li] K[ungu], 'An Assessment of I. Kadare's *The Wedding*', Afterword to *The Wedding*, pp. 195–97 (p. 195).
160. Kadaré, *La Peau de tambour*, *Œuvres*, IX, 41.
161. Kadaré, *Invitation*, p. 86.

CHAPTER 3

Maturity and Political Responsibility

The Writer and the Dictator

The Hoxhas and the Kadares

Kadare felt a closeness as well as an intellectual and emotional ambivalence towards Enver Hoxha. The two families were neighbours in Gjirokastra, and Kadare remembers the mixed signals he received from his family regarding the Hoxhas. His maternal grandmother tells him secretively that they 'have things in common with the Hoxhas', while his father disapproves of the family he refers to as '*psefto*', a pejorative word of Greek origin meaning, a liar or a fake.[1] Kadare's father worked as a court bailiff, a position that revealed to him many of the townpeople's secrets. Class relationships are finely calibrated in the town. The Hoxhas are less sophisticated and Westernized than the Kadare family, at least on the mother's side. The 'Hoxha boy's' dandyism, too, is disapproved of by the father, although by the time of Kadare's birth, Enver was in his late twenties and was about to return from France and Belgium to work as a schoolteacher in Korça, before moving to Tirana where he ran a café and kiosk that was a centre of communist activity from 1939. Both grandmother and father appear to know things about Enver which remain a secret. Later the rumour of his homosexuality circulates, bringing all who hear it into danger. Kadare himself would be endangered by a foreign critic's imputation that a homosexual figure in Kadare's novel, *Chronicle in Stone*, was reminiscent of Hoxha.

In the complex and, in his early years, by no means unattractive figure of Enver Hoxha, Kadare thought that he had found a way of changing the political face of Albania. 'For the first time', he writes, 'I realized that a dictatorship may be made of harder material than the dictator himself'.[2] With his fondness for France, his experiences as a student and young man, and the dandyism which rendered him such a different phenomenon from the other Eastern European leaders, Hoxha appeared to Kadare to have a chink in his armour. However, the project of gaining access to the dictator via his weaknesses proved to be disastrous. Those points of weakness were also the highly sensitive receptors of danger. According to Kadare, the Yugoslav government threatened to release secret wartime material on Hoxha in order to keep him under control on the Kosovo question in 1981 when trouble broke out in the province.[3] Kadare wrote in 1993 in the introduction to Bashkim Shehu's post-communist memoir, *Autumn of Fear*, that 'the homosexuality of the dictator was responsible for the deaths of hundreds of people, amongst whom were those most close to him'.[4] One of the regime's faithful retainers, L. Peçini, was charged with keeping watch for any suggestion of emergence of the 'supreme rumour' of Hoxha's homosexuality, a task which earned him summary execution without trial after many years of service.[5]

'Prometheus', 1967

The suggestion that the writer might be anything other than the amanuensis of history's progress is a heresy against the doctrine of socialist realism. In *Chronicle in Stone* the child uses a mirror to reflect light down to the nether world of the water cistern deep in the cellar, reminding the imprisoned raindrops of their provenance among the upper realms of light and air. This image indicates why the writer could wield such influence in the socialist state so dependent on words to shape reality. At one level the communist dictatorships were collective writing enterprises dedicated to the propagation of the idea over reality, of dogma over truth. Inasmuch as a writer constructs an alternative world, he reverses this relationship. But he nevertheless works with the same tools. No writer in a dictatorship has been more aware of this relationship than Kadare. As he matured, Kadare came to realize that the writer and the dictator share something in their control over the worlds of imagination and reality.

The symbolic oppositions of above and below, of civilization and nature, knowledge and ignorance, power and captivity, order and freedom, modernity and tradition, ideal and ethnicity, communism and Albania, suffuse Kadare's work. The writer, as bringer of light, operates between these levels of existence, between Olympians and mortals. Zeus' punishment of Prometheus, confinement in the depths of the abyss, becomes the dominant metaphor in the late works of the fate of the writer. However, in the late essay *Aeschylus or the Great Loser* and the post-communist comedy *Bad Season on Olympus* Kadare reinstates Prometheus to his position among the gods. Kadare's representation of the battle between the writer and the dictator as that of Prometheus and Zeus, the son and the father, ego and alter ego, represents one of the most profound and complex explorations of the links between imagination and power in the European tradition.

Prometheus loved the human race that had ceased to obey Zeus. The father of the gods decided that this corrupted race of beings must be annihilated and a new humanity created, untouched by the past. Prometheus' name, 'Forethinker', links him to the writer and poet. He knows the secret of Zeus' future and hence is indispensable to the god. Prometheus is thus the nemesis of the dictator. In bringing fire to mankind, Prometheus both transgressed against the absolute decree of the supreme god and sowed the seeds of an immortal ambition which would be the cause of endless conflict between those with and those without power, between fathers and sons, rulers and ruled. He took on the role of a god to mankind, supplanting Zeus, and showing the way to self-determination. Aeschylus' *Prometheus Bound* is believed to be part of a trilogy on the hero, the existence and subject of which are conjectural. It is believed that the three plays dealt with Prometheus' original transgression, his punishment and his release. For Voltaire Prometheus was a great myth of the Enlightenment, of the emergence of mankind from the

FIG. 9 (right): The Kadare house in
Gjirokastra, under reconstruction as a
museum, 2008.
(Photo: Peter Morgan.)

FIG. 10 (below): The Hoxha house in
Gjirokastra, now an ethnological museum.
(Photo: Peter Morgan.)

inarticulate depths to the heights of clarity and control, although that era's greatest representative, Johann Wolfgang Goethe, sensed a new oppressive patriarchy in the secular order of the rebel, remaking the image of mankind in his own likeness.[6] In Shelley's romantic sequel to Aeschylus and rejection of Goethe, 'Prometheus Unbound', the hero's knowledge enables him to bring about an era of utopian happiness, banishing for ever the conflict symbolized in the figure of the patriarch Zeus. Kadare uses the figure of Prometheus throughout his writing, like Goethe, cutting the cloth of the myth according to his wants, to explore the contradictions and the similarities in the figures of the writer and the dictator.[7]

In 1965 Enver Hoxha quoted Marx's tribute to Prometheus as the 'noblest saint and martyr' in European culture.

> Aeschylus made Prometheus, the hero of mythology, a symbol of the fighter for the happiness of mankind. Whoever has read 'Prometheus' will remember the words of the hero to Hermes, the servant of the gods: 'Be sure, I would never want to exchange my miserable fate for your servitude, because I would rather be bound with chains to this rock than be the obedient lackey of Zeus. . . . In a word, I hate all the gods'.[8]

Yet, speaking of a planned opera by Kristo Kono on this hero of mythology, he observed that rather than turning back to the ancient Greeks, Kono should focus his energies on something 'purely Albanian, beautiful and inspiring not only to our own people, but also to people outside the borders of Albania'.[9] The figure of the fifteenth-century national hero, Scanderbeg, seems the obvious subject. Kadare is likely to have been aware of Hoxha's speech and its programmatic statement; however, he avoided representing Scanderbeg other than as the absent saviour in the novel, *The Castle*, choosing Prometheus instead as his hero. Kadare's three-part short-story 'Prometheus' dates back to 1967 in its first version. The choice of this all but proscribed subject for his ongoing reflections on the relationship between himself and the regime represents a quiet declaration of war on Hoxha's national aspirations. Building on Aeschylus' tragedy, Kadare introduces the allegory of the relationship between the writer and the dictator as an existential conflict on a personal as well as socio-political level. The mythical figures of Prometheus and Zeus became the central metaphor for the relationship between politics and literature, power and imagination for the writer.

In this early version of the story we can already sense the writer's closeness to the dictator, his intimate knowledge of, and fascination with, the way power works. The story is a reflection of Kadare's realization, after having considered the possibility of exile in 1962, that Albania and its dictatorship will determine not only his life, but also his creativity. He will share the fate of Prometheus.

> Ce qui la veille paraissait horrible devenait normal le lendemain, et ainsi jour après jour, de plus en plus sombrement, just quà'ce matin impossible à oublier où advint ce qui laissa la plupart incrédules: le départ en exil. [. . .] De fait, plus que par ses chaînes, Prométhée était déprimé par un sentiment d'abandon.[10]

> That which seemed horrible the day before became normal the day after. And so it went on, with the days becoming darker and darker until, finally, that unforgettable morning arrived, when my departure into exile left everyone in

> a state of disbelief [. . .] Indeed, Prometheus was depressed more by a sentiment
> of abandonment than by his chains.

Prometheus, the rebel and saviour of mankind, remains determined by his
relationship to Zeus, king of gods and holder of supreme political power. This
Prometheus is the alter ego of the writer who, in the late 1960s is beginning to
engage with the complex personality of the dictator, trying to fathom the ways
in which power works through this figure and to judge whether any constructive
relationship can be established with the holder of absolute power. Zeus' punishment
determines Prometheus' universe and his sense of self. He is defined by his
relationship to the eagle and its master.

The story begins in the depths of the earth to which Prometheus has been
hurled by the furious god after refusing to recant his support for mortals and
realign himself with the interests of Olympus. He lies in darkness, pinned down
by the rocks and stones which have been dropping onto him for millennia. This
Prometheus is the writer of 1967, whose first experience of being 'burnt by the
sun' generates this allegory of the relationship between dictator and writer, power
and imagination.[11] Echoes of self-criticism and the fate of lesser figures underwrite
Prometheus/Kadare's evocation of his fall from grace: 'Après les clameurs, les
polémiques, les accusations, les cris "Avoue ta faute!", suivis du fracas de sa chute,
la surdité du sous-sol paraissait cent fois plus profonde' ('Prométhée' 62, 'After the
outcries, the polemics, the accusations, the cries of "admit your error!", followed
by the crash of his fall, the deafness of the underground seemed one hundredfold
more profound'). However, Prometheus' fall to the depths of suffering is also an
existential plunge into the murky realms where comprehension of the effects of
power can best be achieved: 'Les profondeurs du sol étaient sans doute l'endroite
qui se prêtait le mieux à l'évocation des événements de la surface' ('Prométhée'
62, 'The depths of the earth were without doubt the place which lends itself best
to the evocation of the events on the surface'). He recollects events such as his
hastily arranged appearance before the supreme leader, the time when he began
to recognize the gestures and the feints of power. 'Lui, Prométhéé, avait appris
à discerner l'authentique courroux du maître des ses colères feintes' ('Prométhée'
62–63, 'He, Prometheus, had learned to distinguish the master's genuine rages from
the pretend ones'). The battle between the tyrant and the rebel is about power and
knowledge. Zeus has power over life and death, but Prometheus has knowledge
that renders him both dangerous to the god and a potential ally. He alone has the
ability to see into the god's future and to know what form Zeus's end would take.
The rebel knows that the god values this power, and that he, Prometheus, is more
valuable to the god as a figure who has compromised in order to save himself than
as a corpse. This is his only source of strength:

> De temps à autre débarquaient des messagers clandestins de Zeus pour lui
> soumettre les conditions d'une possible réconciliation. [. . .] Zeus lui promettait
> sa grâce; en échange, lui, Prométhée, s'engagerait à ne pas ébruiter un secret
> qu'il était seul à détenir. Il avait ri à part soi. Voilà donc comment s'expliquait
> la longue patience du tyran . . . ('Prométhée' 64)

> From time to time the secret messengers of Zeus turned up to present to him

the conditions of a possible reconciliation. [. . .] Zeus promised him a pardon; in exchange he, Prometheus, would agree not to divulge a secret which he was the only one to possess. He had laughed to himself. So that's what explained the tyrant's patience for so long.

Kadare is possibly alluding to the secrets of Hoxha's life in France and Belgium before the war and/or the rumour of his homosexuality; however, the secret is also about his regime, that its claims to socialism and modernization are merely a pretext to retain absolute power. Like all dictatorial regimes which keep impeccable records of their crimes, the Hoxha regime sought to justify and validate itself by documenting the workings of its justice. The vast archives of the Eastern European state security systems disguised the original sin of the dictatorships, namely that absolute power was their first and only law. (Kadare often referred to the upper echelons of the regime in Tirana as 'Olympus'.)

The first level of punishment of the writer who has come to the negative attention of the dictator is exclusion from the realms of comfort and privilege. Zeus offers repatriation into the immortals' home, but Prometheus refuses, knowing that he is not powerless.

> Prométhée avait ricané au visage du messager et, de toute la force de ses poumons, avait crié: Non! C'avait été son dernier après-midi sur terre. [. . .] quelques instants plus tard, il avait été précipité sous terre. ('Prométhée' 64)

> Prometheus had laughed in the face of the messenger and, cried out with all the force of his lungs: No! That was his last afternoon on earth. [. . .] some moments later, he was cast down.

Hauled back up to his rock for a second time, Prometheus will be prey to the eagle of Zeus, symbol at once of the dictator and of Albania, until one day, after millennia, the eagle fails to appear and the hideous wound begins to heal. Release dismays the rebel:

> Au cinquième jour, il demanda soudain: Que se passe-t-il? Il lâcha ce cri sans joie, presque avec épouvante, comme s'il se fût réveillé d'un cauchemar. Où était l'aigle, pourquoi ne venait-il pas? ('Prométhée' 66)

> On the fifth day, he suddenly asked: What's happening? He cried out without joy, almost with terror, as if he had been visited by a nightmare. Where was the eagle, why didn't it come?

He has become determined by his suffering, unable to imagine life and circumscribed by his pain, focused entirely on the next attack.

> Alors, que s'est-il produit? faillit-il hurler. L'avait-on oublié? Ne constituait-il plus un problème? De nouvelles affaires plus pressantes avaient-elles surgi au premier plan? Ou bien, dans ses journées de délire, lui-même avait-il révélé inconsciemment ce qui intéressait le tyran de sorte qu'à présent plus personne ne se préoccupait de lui? Si l'aigle ne revient pas, c'est ma fin assurée, se dit-il avec rage. ('Prométhée' 66–67)

> So, what has happened? he almost called out. Had they forgotten? Wasn't he a problem any more? Had new, more urgent affairs come up? Or maybe, during his days of delirium, he had unconsciously revealed something of interest to the

tyrant? So that now no one bothered with him any more? If the eagle did not return, that's the end of me, for sure, he said to himself in a rage.

Suspecting the well-meaning intervention of a third party he succumbs to self-pity, forgotten on a lonely rock in the Mediterranean, except for the occasional visit from a delegate of Amnesty International. But then he descries a huge bird winging its way towards him:

> Quand celui-ci fut planté, rouvrant la plaie tout juste refermée, Prométhée en même temps qu'un hurlement de douleur, lança les mots: Je suis sauvé! qui, comme la clameur d'un fou, se confondirent avec sa plainte. ('Prométhée' 67)

> When it [the eagle] was standing by him, tearing open the freshly healed wound, Prometheus, wailing in pain, screamed out: I'm saved! Words which, like the clamour of a madman, were mixed up with his groans.

His suffering has also become his *raison d'être*, his existential proof of his identity and his power.

The final section, written after the events of 1989 in Eastern Europe, switches from Prometheus' third person to the writer's first person, taking on the exculpatory tone of Kadare's autobiographical works of the 1990s in reviewing the writer's role under the dictatorship. The Prometheus complex, the themes of the dialectic of power, and of the possibility of transformation of the rebel into the patriarch are implicit in Kadare's figure. The 1967 story reveals the writer's engagement with the dictator to have been personal and individual from the beginning. His battle with the dictatorship would become at the same time a personal battle with the dictator for the voice of Albania.[12] Over the following decades Kadare would explore this relationship in terms of its existential, psychological, and intellectual ramifications. This theme would recur in forms as different as the essay, *Aeschylus or the Great Loser* (1985), and the post-communist comedy, *Bad Season on Olympus* (1996), Kadare's only dramatic work. In the post-communist context Kadare toys with the image of a Prometheus 'unbound' and sharing power as the deputy and successor of Zeus, a role which the author played briefly in the hope of achieving a smooth transition from dictatorship to democracy in the newly formed Democratic Front in which he appeared alongside figures from the regime, such as Nexhmije Hoxha. In this work, the writer reveals a black humour which is one of the keys to his transition into the new writing context.

'Heavy ore of memory': *Chronicle in Stone*, 1970[13]

During a period of relative reclusion and quiet beginning in 1969 Kadare was beginning research on *Winter of Great Solitude*, the novel based on archival records of Hoxha's break with Khrushchev in 1961. At this time, he writes, he completed various works, including the autobiographical memoir *Chronicle in Stone* and the historical novel *The Castle*.[14] In *Invitation to the Writer's Studio* Kadare describes *Chronicle* as belonging among his earliest works in conception. The idea for the novel was born during a skiing trip outside Moscow:

> Je ne me souviens pas bien comment l'engagea la conversation, mais on sait bien que dans un groupe de gens de nationalités diverses, rien n'est plus courant

> qu'un échange de vues sur la localité d'origine de chacun. On parlait de villes extraordinaires, magnifiées dans les esprits par la nostalgie et l'éloignement, de villes étrangement ensoleillées ou éclairées par la lune, avec des espaces verts, des lacs, des ponts qui se dressaient la nuit comme des fantômes. [. . .] Subitement, je me sentis envahi d'une nostalgie immense, associée, comme il est fréquent en pareil cas, à un sentiment de culpabilité. (*Invitation* 15–16)

> I don't remember how the conversation started, but it's well known that in a group of people of different nationalities, nothing is more usual than an exchange of views on everyone's places of origin. We spoke of extraordinary cities, magnified in people's spirits by homesickness and distance, of cities drenched in sun or glowing in the moonlight, with green spaces and lakes and bridges which loomed out of the night like ghosts. [. . .] Suddenly, I felt an immense nostalgia overcome me, associated, as is often the case, by a feeling of guilt.

Amidst the excitement of cosmopolitan Moscow, the writer is struck by the uniqueness of his place of birth and experiences a wave of nostalgia for his home town. Later in *Invitation* he further links the origins of this novel to the experience of expatriation:

> Entre ces deux romans dont l'idée m'est venue à l'étranger, il existe un lien particulier [. . .] La *Chronique* a été conçue *là-bas* et porte sur des événements et des personnages d'*ici*, alors que le *Crépuscule* est né *ici* et concerne le monde de *là-bas*. (*Invitation* 20).

> A particular link exists between these two novels, both of which occurred to me when I was in a foreign country. [. . .] *Chronicle* was conceived *there* and is about events and characters *here*, while *Twilight* was born here and is about that world *there*.

The contextualization of the original idea for the *Chronicle* in the conversations at the Gorki Institute reinforces the sense of distance and perspective which is powerfully evoked in the epilogue to the novel as the adult writer experiences flashes of memory in the bright modern boulevards of foreign cities. In 1964 Kadare published approximately thirty pages of descriptive episodes from his childhood under the title 'The Southern City', in the journal *Nëntori*. These were extended and republished in 1967 in a collection of short stories, *The Southern City: Short Stories and Reportages*. The completed full-length novel appeared in 1971. According to Arshi Pipa, the epilogue was added in 1978.[15]

Perhaps one of the lessons of *The General of the Dead Army* was that the private past precedes the public past and that the way to the nation is through individual and personal memory. The archaeological metaphor of national past and socialist present raised the problematic relationship of history and individual identity. At the end of this novel the tragic old woman, Nice, represents on a personal level the unanswered questions of the past. *Chronicle in Stone* is about the meeting of two worlds, as seen through the eyes of the child and retold from his adult perspective. The child does not yet understand the nature of this meeting; the adult writer, looking back, recasts his fragmented childhood memories, together with documents and imported reminiscences and recollections, as a chronicle, a narrative structured by the passage of time. Memory is allowed open and free access to the origins and development of consciousness. The contrast with the dislocation of past and present in *The General* could not be greater. The obligations of socialist realism and doctrine have no place in this memoir of the writer's childhood from around 1939 until early 1944, the period immediately preceding the establishment of the regime.

A powerful sense of past and present is created through the loose association of events, places, and personages. To the contrast between objective and subjective time frames is added the sense of historically determined subjectivity as the relationship between the child's perception and the adult voice deepens. The overwhelming, often elegiac, sense of time passing gains a further aspect in the chronicle of decline and destruction, as the traditional life of the Albanian Ottoman town fragments and ends in civil violence. The march of history continues as the child plays, interacts with family and friends, encounters the new and the strange, learns to read, begins to think for himself. In the act of remembering the adult voice revisits its origins. By the end of the story the voice of the narrator exists in a history, and an adult identity has formed in organic relationship to its environment. Everything is in flux and the child's consciousness is formed in the process of observation of events and characters. It is this process of formation of the child's consciousness which lies at the core of the work, explaining the adult writer's view of the present as the outcome of a history characterized by breakdown and violence. Memory re-establishes continuity for the adult who has travelled so far from his origins in the final epigraph.

Nature and Nurture in Gjirokastra

In *The City without Signs* Gjirokastra was the depressing provincial destination of the young Tirana intellectual. In *Chronicle* it is a living entity, the symbol of an ancient culture. The physicality of the country — of mountains, valleys, rivers and of the town itself, which begins to emerge in *The General*, re-emerges as the *writer's* native land in *Chronicle in Stone*. The work opens with images of the precariousness of human order on the Albanian landscape. History is natural history, not human history, and the man-made is insignificant in the timescale of the rocks and water which make the town. It is imagined as a prehistoric creature with a carapace of stone, cast up onto the mountainside after a storm.

> C'était une ville étrange qui, tel un être préhistorique, paraissait avoir surgi brusquement dans la vallée par une nuit d'hiver pour escalader péniblement le flanc de la montagne. Tout dans cette ville était ancien et de pierre, depuis les rues et les fontaines jusqu'aux toits des grandes maisons séculaires, couverts de plaques de pierre grise, semblables à de gigantesques écailles.[16]

> It was a strange city, and seemed to have been cast up in the valley one winter's night like some prehistoric creature that was now clawing its way up the mountainside. Everything in the city was old and made of stone, from the streets and fountains to the roofs of the sprawling age-old houses covered with grey slates like gigantic scales.[17]

But the image is not threatening. While life is hard in the city, leaving the child scraped and bruised, it is a nurturing environment:

> On avait de la peine à croire que sous cette puissante carapace subsistait et se reproduisait la chair tendre de la vie. (*Chronique* 7)

> It was hard to believe that under this powerful carapace the tender flesh of life survived and reproduced. (*Chronicle* 11)

During a storm the child's parents realize that the water cistern below the house is in danger of overflowing and undermining the foundations. The hinged guttering must be disconnected and the over-filled cistern emptied. The child imagines the fall of the raindrops into the cistern below the house as a descent from freedom to unfreedom, from the realm of the gods to the gloomy, sunless netherworld which in Kadare's writing is associated with the Albania of the present.

> Là prenait fin leur vie libre et joyeuse. Dans le réservoir sombre et sourd, elles devaient évoquer avec une morne tristesse les espaces célestes qu'elles ne reverraient jamais plus, les villes extraordinaires au-dessous d'elles et les horizons déchirés d'éclairs. [. . .] Pour le moment, elles ne se doutaient de rien. Elles couraient, joyeuses et bruyantes, sur les pierres plates, et en écoutant leur bruit j'éprouvais pour elles comme de la compassion. [. . .] je méditais, me demandant qui, de l'homme ou de l'eau, supporte le plus difficilement la captivité. (*Chronique* 9–10)

> Here the raindrops' life of joy and freedom ended. In the dark and soundless cistern they would recall with dreary sorrow the great spaces of sky they would never see again, the strange cities below them, and the lightning-ripped horizons. [. . .] But for the moment they knew nothing of their fate. They ran, happy and noisy, across the flat slate, and I felt sorry for them as I listened. [. . .] I lay wondering whether man or water suffered more in captivity. (*Chronicle* 13–14)

If the stone town nurtures life, the cistern confines the forces of nature. Lying under the house, it is an obstacle to the natural cycle of rain and evaporation:

> J'imaginais les gouttes innombrables roulant sur les surfaces inclinées, se hâtant de rejoindre le sol, pour demain s'évaporer et remonter là-haut dans le ciel blanc. Elles ne se doutaient pas que sous les avant-toits les attendait un méchant traquenard, la gouttière. Et, au moment où elles s'apprêtaient à sauter à terre, elles se trouvaient subitement prises dans l'étroit tuyau avec des milliers de leurs compagnes, et se demandaient apeurées: 'Où allons-nous, où nous mène-t-on?' Puis, sans s'être bien ressaisies de cette course folle, elles étaient jetées brusquement dans une prison profonde, la grande citerne de notre maison. (*Chronique* 9)

> I pictured the countless drops rolling down the sloping roof, hurtling to earth to turn to mist that would rise again in the high, white sky. Little did they know that a clever trap, a tin gutter, awaited them on the eaves. Just as they were about to make the leap from roof to ground, they suddenly found themselves caught in the narrow pipe with thousands of companions, asking 'Where are we going, where are they taking us?' Then, before they could recover from that mad race, they plummeted into a deep dark underground prison, the great cistern of our house (*Chronicle* 13)

The imagery of freedom and imprisonment, however, contrasts with that of order and chaos. Nature is a potentially disruptive force and the incarcerated raindrops represent a threat.

> Je m'approchai de l'orifice et regardai vers le bas. Des ténèbres. Rien que des ténèbres et un sentiment de peur. 'Oooh', fis-je doucement. Mais la citerne

FIGS. 11(a) & 11(b) (above and centre): Gjirokastra, city of stone. (Photos: Peter Morgan.)

FIG. 12 (below): The citadel in Gjirokastra, place of refuge during the bombing raids of World War II, as described in *Chronicle in Stone*. (Photo: Peter Morgan.)

ne me répondit pas. C'était la première fois qu'elle restait sourde à mon appel. Je l'aimais beaucoup et me penchais souvent sur sa grande bouche pour parler longuement avec elle. Elle s'était toujours empressée de me répondre de sa voix caverneuse.

'Oooh!' fis-je une nouvelle fois, mais elle se taisait encore. J'en conclus qu'elle devait être très fâchée.

J'imaginais comment les innombrables gouttes de pluie rassemblaient leur colére, là au fond. Les anciennes qui y languissaient depuis longtemps s'unissaient aux nouvelles venues, aux gouttes déchaînées de l'orage de cette nuit-là, pour commettre avec elles quelque vilaine action. [. . .] A aucun prix il n'aurait fallu laisser les eaux de la tempête pénétrer dans notre sage citerne et la pousser à la révolte. (*Chronique* 12)

I went to the opening and looked down. Gloom. Gloom and a sense of fear. 'A-oo', I said softly. But the cistern didn't answer. It was the first time it had refused to answer me. I liked the cistern a lot and often leaned over its rim and had long talks with it. It had always been ready to answer me in its deep cavernous voice.

'A-oo', I said again, but still it was silent. I thought it must have been very angry.

I thought about how the countless raindrops were gathering their rage down below, the old ones that had been languishing there so long getting together with the newcomers, the drops unleashed by tonight's storm, plotting something evil. [. . .] the waters of the storm never should have been let into our well-behaved cistern to stir up rebellion. (*Chronicle* 15)

The presence of unruly forces plotting against domestic and civil order alarms the boy, who remains an onlooker as the adults frantically empty the tank in order to safeguard the house. The captive, displaced entities threaten the balance which has been established between the house and its environment and which depends on the timely intervention of the father to release them back into their natural course.

Après chaque seau versé, je disais silencieusement à l'eau: 'Va-t'en, va-t'en au diable, puisque tu n'as pas voulu rester dans notre citerne!' Chaque seau était plein de gouttes captives et je pensais que l'on aurait avantage à pouvoir en faire sortir d'abord les plus méchantes et les plus querelleuses pour diminuer le danger. (*Chronique* 13)

As each bucket was emptied out, I said silently to the water, 'Go on, get the hell out, if you don't want to stay in our cistern'. Each bucket was filled with captive raindrops, and I thought it would be good if we could weed out the nastiest ones first, the ringleaders; that way we could lessen the danger. (*Chronicle* 16)

The image cluster of freedom, imprisonment, and rebellion is indicative of a recurring theme of confinement and control, foreshadowing questions of change with which Kadare will concern himself throughout his creative life. The sense of the hierarchy of forces in the vertical metaphor of above and below, colours the child's early experiences, creating the cognitive structures for his understanding of power. Later in bed that night the boy imagines himself and the house flooded down the hillside along with the cistern and its overflowing water. The dualistic universe of above and below and of the displaced entities — water, river, mankind — which expend their lives in rage and conflict, frightens the child. In the dialectic of anarchy and order which is the subject of this novel, the writer-as-child seeks stability and safety. Danger comes from chaos, anarchic energy, destructive nature. Threatened by powerful forces from every side, the boy seeks security in the *status quo*, before the waters of the cistern were stirred up. He seeks to mitigate the conflict, to keep the powers of disorder at bay, and to liberate the rebellious elements in order to protect the house and to safeguard his existence. Once the dangerous water-level has been reduced and the forces of anarchy expelled, the boy resumes his dialogue with the water. However, the cistern answers, 'd'une voix rauque, qui m'était étrangère' (*Chronique* 17, 'in a hoarse, strange voice', *Chronicle* 19) and the child realizes 'que sa colère s'était calmée, mais pas tout à fait cependant, car sa voix était plus sourde que d'habitude' (*Chronique* 17, 'that its anger had eased, but not completely, for its voice was duller than usual', *Chronicle* 19).

Unnoticed by the adults, the child begins to explore his own imaginative powers as the nascent creative writer and artist. Mirrors, spectacles, and windows play an important role. They are associated with light, sight, blindness, and visual unclarity. In *Chronicle* and elsewhere windows are misted or distorted by rain, the ageing dictator has become increasingly blind, the youthful rebels wear dark glasses, and the child with bad eyesight finds a lens which clarifies the outlines of his world. Kadare remembers himself playing with a piece of mirror in order to reflect the sky down to the imprisoned souls below.

> Il n'y avait que moi, agitant un petit miroir, leur envoyais parfois un petit pan de ciel, pas plus grand que la paume de la main, que jouerait un moment sur la surface de l'eau, fugace souvenir du ciel sans fin. (*Chronique* 10)

> The only slice of the heavens they would see henceforth would be no bigger than the palm of my hand, on the occasions when I used a pocket mirror to send a fleeting memory of the endless sky to flicker on the surface of our reservoir. (*Chronicle* 13*)

This is the archetypal artist's role, distanced, disengaged, and mediating between the upper and the lower worlds. Thanks to his creative gift he too has power to cast light down. His position is a privileged and slightly dissociated one, and hence has something of the realm of freedom about it. He is at liberty to stand on the sidelines, observe, write, and think. He reflects down to the waters of the cistern the light which reminds them of the possibilities of freedom, a potentially unsettling act of subversion of the regained order. Kadare manipulates reality in such a way as to reflect light back on life itself. But the activity is ambiguous: does the memory of freedom help or hinder the raindrops in their imprisonment? 'Je méditais, me demandant qui, de l'homme ou de l'eau, supporte le plus difficilement la captivité' (*Chronique* 10, 'I lay wondering whether man or water suffered more in captivity', *Chronicle* 14). There is no question of identification, of the artist becoming the mouthpiece for these raging souls. The child will experience late childhood and early adolescence as times of war, civil upheaval, and revolution. Change is a menace and a danger. The writer's early response to this environment of change is to situate himself between the two sides, to take the classic position of the artist vis-à-vis the real world, standing apart and reflecting on reality in order to comprehend. Later, in the dictatorial environment he would be criticized from both sides for not clearly showing his colours or identifying himself as either a dissident or a supporter of the regime.

Next morning the child views the aftermath of the storm. The river has over-flowed its banks, threatening the bridge, archetypal Balkan image of stability.

> Toute la nuit, il avait dû, à son habitude, s'efforcer de franchir l'arche du pont, la secouant comme un cheval emballé qui cherche à se débarrasser du bât qui le blesse. [. . .] Comme, finalement, il n'avait pu passer le pont il s'était rué sur la route et l'avait engloutie. A présent, démesurément grossi, il tâchait de la dissoudre en lui. Mais elle était coriace, accoutumée à ces violentes attaques, et maintenant, à coup sûr, elle se tenait, tranquille, sous les eaux troubles et rougeâtres, attendant qu'elles se retirent. [. . .] Je contemplais le paysage transfomé durant la nuit, songeant que, si le fleuve haïssait le pont, la route éprouvait la même haine pour le fleuve, les torrents pour les murs et le vent pour la montagne, qui l'arrêtait dans sa fureur [. . .] (*Chronique* 15–16)

> It must have tried all night, as usual, to knock down the bridge, shaking it like a pack-horse trying to throw off a painful load. [. . .] Having failed to sweep away the bridge, the river had turned on the road and swallowed it whole. Immensely swollen from this gulp, the river was now busy digesting the road. But the road was tough, accustomed to these unexpected attacks, and now lay patient under the swirling reddish waters, waiting for them to withdraw. [. . .] I looked out at the countryside, transformed during the night, and thought that if the river hated the bridge, the road surely felt the same hatred for the river, and the torrents for the walls and the wind for the mountain that checked its fury. (*Chronicle* 18–19)

In *Albanian Spring* the battle between the dictator and the writer would be represented in similar terms as a fight to the death between two different, but equally matched adversaries. The town, though, is something different to the bridge, symbol of human intervention in the natural environment. It is prehistoric and eternal, a natural formation of rocks and stone, pre-dating memory or history and calmly withstanding the elemental battles, its 'cuirasse de pierre' ('stone carapace') protecting 'la chair tendre' (*Chronique* 7–8; 'the tender flesh', *Chronicle* 11–12) of life.

> Tous ensemble, ils haïssaient la ville qui s'étendait, humide, grise, et dédaigneuse, au milieu de cette haine dévastatrice. Je l'aimais, car, dans cette guerre, elle était seule contre tous. (*Chronique* 16)

> They all must have loathed the city which spread wet, grey, and disdainful in the midst of all this destructive hatred. But I loved the city, because it stood all alone against the others in this war. (*Chronicle* 18)

Its heart is the ancient fort built in defiance of the Turkish invaders, in which the townspeople find shelter from British and German bombers as the war proceeds.

Meanwhile the storm has entered into a truce with the earth, but it will only be temporary, the most that can be hoped for in this place of endemic conflict.

> Je [vis] avec joie que loin, à une distance que je ne pouvais mesurer, était apparu en arc-en-ciel, comme un pacte de paix à peine conclu entre la montagne, le fleuve, le pont, les torrents, la route, le vent et la ville. Mais l'on devinait bien que ce n'était là qu'une courte trêve. (*Chronique* 17)

I [. . .] looked out and saw with joy that far off, at a distance too great to measure, a rainbow had appeared, like a peace treaty [just concluded — PM] between mountain, river, bridge, torrents, road, wind, and city. But it was easy to see that it would be no more than a short truce. (*Chronicle* 19)

Modernity

Change is coming to the town in the form of modernity, seeping in at the edges and gradually suffusing the fabric of social interaction, loosening and dissolving ancient ties. Not even the plagues of the previous millennium, nor the Turkish occupation four hundred years ago, have prepared the townspeople for this revolt from within.

> Les paroles se défaisait brusquement du sens qu'on leur accordait d'habitude. Les expressions de deux ou trois mots se fragmentaient douloureusement. [. . .] Les mots avaient une force déterminée à leur état figé, normal. Mais maintenant qu'ils se diluaient, se désassemblaient, ils émettaient une énergie formidable. Je redoutais leur décomposition. Je m'efforçais par tous les moyens de la prévenir, mais en vain. Dans ma tête se créait un véritable chaos, où les mots se livraient à une danse macabre, hors des confins de la logique et de la réalité. [. . .] Tout se bouleversait, se brisait, s'effritait. [. . .] Le monde se désagrégait sous mes yeux. C'est sûrement à cela que faisait allusion la mère Pino lorsqu'elle parlait constamment de 'la fin de tout'. (*Chronique* 98–100)

> The words were casting off their usual idiomatic sense. Expressions made up of two or three words would agonizingly decompose [. . .] Words had a certain force in their normal frozen state. But now, as they began to melt and break apart, they released a stunning energy. Their decomposition scared me. I did all I could to stop it, but in vain. Chaos reigned in my head as words, devoid of logic and reality, abandoned themselves to their *danse macabre*. [. . .] Everything was upside down, falling apart, breaking up. [. . .] The world was falling apart before my very eyes. Surely that was what Kako Pino meant when she constantly repeated, 'It's the end of the world'. (*Chronicle* 89–90)

In an episode which foreshadows the ending of the Albanian–Ottoman class structures, the child watches as fire, set by communist agitators, consumes the city hall and the deeds and titles office.

> Moi, j'avais presque collé mon visage à la vitre, les yeux fixés sur la rue qui bouillonnait de monde. De temps en temps, le carreau s'embuait. Les terrains et les maisons, affranchis du pouvoir des titres, avaient commencé à s'écarter, à se mouvoir. Les distances s'effaçaient, les murs tendaient à sortir de leurs fondations, quelque chose sous eux, l'ancre séculaire qui les maintenait, s'était rompu. Les maisons de pierre, se déplaçant, s'approchaient de façon menaçante les unes des autres, risquaient de se heurter, de se détruire.
>   'Ils brûlent! Ils brûlent!'
>   Seules les rues, qui appartenaient à tout le monde, tentaient de maintenir un ordre relatif dans ce chaos. [. . .] 'Le Reichstag aussi a brûlé', dit Javer, en poussant le globe du doigt. (*Chronique* 223–24)

> I plastered my face to the window pane and looked out at the teeming street. Now and again the pane misted over. The land and houses, freed from the power of the deeds, strained to break from their foundations. Something deep

FIG. 13 (above): A *kulla* or traditional family dwelling in Gjirokastra. (Photo: Peter Morgan.)

FIG. 14 (below): Traditional interior, the Hotel Kalemi in Gjirokastra. (Photo: Peter Morgan.)

below them, which had anchored them for centuries had gone. The stone
houses in motion roamed dangerously near one another, risking collision and
destruction.

'They're burning, they're burning!'

Only the streets, which belonged to everyone, tried to maintain some
degree of order in the chaos. [. . .] 'The Reichstag also burned like this', said
Javer, pointing to a place on the globe. (*Chronicle* 194)

The prime suspect for the fire in the municipal offices is the deranged boy who
searches the town at night for the body of his lover, thrown into a city well by her
outraged parents.

A la nouvelle que la police avait arrêté au milieu de la nuit le jeune homme au
pétrole et à la corde, tout le monde pensa qu'on avait enfin capturé le Néron de
la ville. Mais il apparut que ce n'était pas Néron, mais Orphée, qui cherchait
son Eurydice dans les puits de nos cours. Procès. Mesures exécutoires. Tous
les procès sur les biens-fonds sont temporairement suspendus en raison de
l'incendie du cadastre. Demain: *Grand-Hôtel* avec la célèbre artiste Greta Garbo.
(*Chronique* 227)

When the police arrested the young man with the kerosene and the rope in
the middle of the night, everyone thought that the Nero of the city had been
caught at last. But it turned out he was not Nero but Orpheus, seeking his
Eurydice in the wells of our courtyards. Trial. Executive measures. Property.
All suits having to do with real estate are temporarily suspended because of the
burning of the registry of deeds. Cinema tomorrow: *Grand Hotel*, starring the
famous actress Greta Garbo. (*Chronicle* 197)

The practice of drowning or asphyxiating disobedient daughters occurs several
times in the novel. In the light of the inhumanity of such aspects of traditional life,
the communist rebels appear to offer progress. The young man who spends his
nights searching the town's wells and cisterns powerfully represents the perversion
of human feelings in this environment. That he is mistaken for a terrorist is ironic,
since he is a symptom not a cause of the problems.

The Reichstag fire of 27 February 1933, symbol of the Nazi dictatorship and of
the reigniting of the European conflagration, appears as the harbinger of things
to come in the Albanian town on the fault line between Ottoman past and Soviet
future. At the same time American cinema has arrived. *Grand Hotel* tells the stories
of a group of characters whose paths cross in a classy Berlin hotel one weekend
in 1932. Neither Nazism nor the crisis of the Weimar Republic appears in the
depoliticized stories of innocence, fraud, and death, although Hollywood has
not been entirely successful in expunging the pervasive sense of criminality, loss
and alienation from Vicki Baum's original novel, *Menschen im Hotel* (1929). The
apparently random linkages of the chronicle manifest the workings of history, the
convergence of the 'non-contemporaneous' (Bloch) events of the Balkan town
into a broader European narrative of conflict and upheaval. Modernity will come
suddenly as the partisans set up a Soviet communist state and put an end to the
traditions and ways of life which both sustain the community and civic order, and
perpetuate pre-modern barbarity. Under the pressure of occupation, collaboration,
reprisal and retribution, civil society, based on Ottoman foundations, breaks

down. The traditional enmities between the wealthy urban Ottoman *agas* and the
Christian Orthodox peasants are exacerbated by military occupation. Class, marked
by religion in this typically southern Albanian environment, is the first point of
fragmentation. Finally even clans and families are split by something new, modern,
and hitherto unknown. The old Muslim women in the salon upstairs, observing
the world below through their lorgnettes, represent the combined voice of ancient
and eternal Albania. These figures, in whom the young writer finds the ancient
choric voice of Albania, are hardly the stuff of communist doctrine. They provide a
background lament as things go from bad to worse under the successive occupations
of Greeks, Italians, and Germans during the late 1930s and early 1940s when the
writer is still a child. They give expression to something which the child also, in
his unreflective way, recognizes, namely that in this changing world, it will be the
younger generation of intellectuals who will take responsibility for the new order.

In the wake of the Italian occupation and the increasing misery, the people turn
to traditional magic as a means of warding of further evil. The budding intellectuals
and political radicals, Isa and Javer, interpret the return of pre-Muslim practices in
terms of the interests of the occupation forces:

> Dans la cour de Mane Votso, Illyr et moi écoutins Javer et Isa parler de
> sorcellerie. [. . .] Nous les entendîmes prononcer plusieurs fois les mots de
> 'mysticisme' et de 'psychose collective', puis Isa demanda à Javer: 'As-tu lu
> Jung?'
> 'Non', dit Javer [. . .] 'Tout cela es fort clair. La réaction a intérêt à cette
> psychose, car elle détourne l'attention des gens des problèmes du temps. Tiens,
> voilà ce qu'on écrit dans le journal: "Les pratiques de magie appartiennent en
> quelque sorte au patrimoine folklorique d'un people".'
> 'Théorie fasciste!' dit Isa. [. . .] Ces barbares, avec leurs plumes sur la tête,
> sont prêts à ressusciter les coutumes médiévales pourvu que'elles soient de
> quelque avantage à Mussolini'. (*Chronique* 50–51)

> In Mane Voco's yard, Ilir and I listened to Javer and Isa talking about witchcraft.
> [. . .] Several times we heard them use the words 'mysticism' and 'collective
> psychosis'. Then Isa asked Javer, 'Have you read Jung?'
> 'No', said Javer. [. . .] 'All this is clear enough. This psychosis serves the
> interests of the reactionaries by diverting public attention from the real
> problems. Here, look at the newspaper: "Magic is in some sense part of the
> folkloric heritage of the people".'
> 'A fascist theory', said Isa. [. . .] 'Those barbarians with feathers in their
> hats are happy to resurrect any medieval custom, as long as Mussolini can get
> something out of it'. (*Chronicle* 46–47)

These practices were in fact part of the fabric of folk, Muslim, and Christian
beliefs and rituals of the mental life of the people. The new ideas of the young
radical intellectuals, Isa and Javer, represent another layer of belief, which will
be superimposed over the existing layers as has been the way in Albania for
centuries.

Unlike the old women, these young intellectuals have a life before them. In
the environment of occupation, social disintegration and civil war, and with the
communism of foreign-trained intellectuals such as Enver Hoxha filtering back

into the country from the mid-1930s onward, young people find themselves in the situation of either taking or losing control of their lives. The apocalyptic situation of the end of the world is for them one where all is to be lost or won. Kako Pino's refrain is comical in this episode, but it turns out to be true, as she is found hanged in the final pages with the word 'saboteur' scratched across her body. The culprit is not named — it could be the Germans, or Javer revenging the execution of Isa.

> 'Des garçons et des filles se réunissent dans les caves pour chanter des chants interdits. Ils veulent renverser le vieux monde, disent-ils, et en construire un nouveau. [. . .] On dit que ce monde nouveau, il va falloir verser du sang pour le bâtir'. 'Je le crois. Si, pour un pont qu'on construit, on immole une bête en offrande, qui sait ce qu'il faudra pour bâtir un monde nouveau'. 'Un hécatombe'. (*Chronique* 255)

> 'Young boys and girls are getting together in the cellars to sing forbidden songs. They want to overthrow the old world and build a new one. [. . .] They say that blood will have to be spilled for this new world to be built'. 'That I can believe. If an animal has to be sacrificed when a new bridge is built, what will it take to build a whole new world?' 'A hecatomb'. (*Chronicle* 221★)

Javer and Ilir are prototypes of the communist partisans and intellectuals who would make up the post-war ruling party. Isa is executed after assassinating the Italian commander, and Javer goes underground after killing his uncle in reprisal for Isa's death, and carrying out further retaliatory murders of fascists and saboteurs. He will re-emerge in the battle for Tirana at the end of the war in the 1974 novel, *November of a Capital*.

Glasses become the motif of the intellectual, symbolizing the new way of seeing that would turn Albania into a modernizing communist state. Early in the novel Mane Voco's son Isa begins wearing glasses.

> Ils parlaient d'Isa, le fils aîné de Mane Votso, qui venait de faire la semaine dernière quelque chose d'inouï, il avait mis des lunettes. 'Quand j'ai appris ça,' disait Djedjo, 'je n'ai d'abord pas voulu en croire mes oreilles, puis je me suis levée, j'ai jeté mon fichu sur ma tête, et j'ai couru chez Mane. Le malheureux se dominait, mais les femmes de la maison, elles, avaient le visage défait. Elles paraissaient pétrifiées'. (*Chronique* 21)

> They were talking about Isa, Mane Voco's older son, who had done something unheard of: he had started wearing glasses. 'When they first told me', Xhexho said, 'I couldn't believe my ears. I got up, threw a scarf on my head, and went to see Mane Voco. The poor man was taking it bravely, but the women looked stunned, as if they'd been turned to stone'. (*Chronicle* 23★)

Isa's glasses are 'the only thing that seemed alive on his battered face' (*Chronicle* 229, 'sur son visage massacré, seuls ses lunettes paraissaient vivantes', *Chronique* 264), when he is mutilated and hanged. The young revolutionary, Enver Hoxha, too wears glasses:

> 'On dit que c'est lui qui dirige maintenant le combat. Et c'est lui aussi qui a, paraît-il, inventé cette nouvelle guerre dont je te parlais tout à l'heure'.
>   'J'ai de la peine à y croire, dit grand-mère. C'était un garçon si bien élevé'.
>   'Oui, bien élevé, Selfidjé, mais on dit que maintenant il s'est mis une paire

> de lunettes noires pour ne pas être reconnu et qu'il s'occupe de la guerre. (*Chronique* 261)

> 'They say he's the one leading the war now. He's also the one who invented this new war I was telling you about'.
> 'That's hard to believe', said Grandmother. 'He was such a well-behaved boy'.
> 'Yes Selfixhe, very well behaved. But they say he wears dark glasses now so he won't be recognized and that he's the one running the war'. (*Chronicle* 227)

Enver Hoxha is mentioned several times, as the local boy who went to study 'dans le pays des Francs' (*Chronique* 261, 'in the land of the Franks', *Chronicle* 226), and as 'un commissaire nommé Enver Hodja' (*Chronique* 307; 'a commisaire called Enver Hoxha', *Chronicle* 267) who says that there will be communism in the new Albania.

> Sur un reste de mur de la maison écroulée était affiché un avis. [. . .] 'On recherche le dangereux communiste Enver Hodja; âge: la trentaine; taille: haute. Porte des lunettes de soleil. (*Chronique* 259)

> A notice was posted on what remained of a wall of the ruined house. [. . .] 'Wanted: the dangerous Communist Enver Hoxha. Aged about 30. Tall. Wears sunglasses. (*Chronicle* 225)

The sunglasses are an ambiguous image signalling both sightlessness and a sinister version of the glasses of the intellectuals. If the glasses of the intellectuals give access to the worlds of modernity, of Marxist-Leninist dogma as well as Hollywood film, the black eye sockets of Kadare's blind seers are the means of access to the underworld of Albanian reality. The darkness of the cistern is associated with the blind poet, Homer (*Chronique* 56, *Chronicle* 52). The boy recognizes the 'majesty of blindness in the crones' (*Chronique* 98, *Chronicle* 89) who function as the voices of human experience. They reappear in the *Great Winter*, petitioning the leader, Enver Hoxha. As the partisans enter the town, the Muslim cleric, Sheikh Ibrahim, blinds himself in desperation, claiming, 'Je ne veux pas voir le communisme!' (*Chronique* 278; 'better no eyes at all than to see communism', *Chronicle* 241). While Islam, the religion of the Ottoman upper class, barely figures in the socio-cultural environment of the child, the Muslim cleric's self-blinding suggests a turning away from the light of communism and modernity for the dark past of the Ottoman 'night'.

The spectacles of the intellectual, the harbingers of change, also affect the author-as-child, bringing clarity and the hard lines of modernity to him, the following generation, as well. He finds a spectacle lens in his grandmother's chest.

> Subitement tout ce qui m'entourait me parut se secouer. Les contours des choses se contractèrent, se clarifièrent impitoyablement. [. . .] Et pourtant il ne me plaisait pas ainsi. J'étais habitué à le voir derrière une couche de vapeur, où les contours des objets se joignaient ou s'écartaient sans contrainte, sans obéir à des règles rigoureuses. [. . .] derrière ce verre rond, le monde me paraissait rigide, assujetti à des règles, avare, ne donnant aux objets existant rien de plus que ce qu'ils avaient. (*Chronique* 23–24)

> Suddenly the world around me trembled. The edges of things seemed to tighten, to get ruthlessly sharp. [. . .] But I didn't like it. I was used to looking

at the world through a puff of steam, so that the edges of things ran together
and separated freely, not according to any fixed rules. [. . .] through that round
glass the world looked rigid and mean, full of rules, showing no more than
what there was. (*Chronicle* 25★)

The glasses establish a link between the child and the young revolutionary
intellectuals, only a decade older than he, who will become the cadres of the new
regime in the late 1940s and 1950s. The 'ruthlessly sharp' outlines created by the
glasses both appal him and enable him to see more clearly the films which nurture his
imagination and to read the books introduced to him by Isa and Javer: Shakespeare's
Macbeth and the psychology of Carl Gustav Jung. The Italian brothel, the glasses,
later the aeroplanes of the British and the Germans, are signs of a modernity which
will change the world from the traditional one of usage and familiarity to one
determined by the rules of economics and efficiency. The 'new and bright' world
of communist enlightenment contrasts throughout Kadare's work with the misty
world of eternal Albania. The image of the present with its sharp lines and piercing
light has little of the positive spin of Western modernity; rather it is the harbinger
of the type of economic efficiency, rule-bound bureaucracy, and uncompromising
scrutiny which would characterize communist social planning and everyday reality.
In the symbolic scheme of the work, the writer-as-child is located between the two
worlds. He takes the lens he has found in his grandmother's attic to the cinema in
order to see clearly. It enables him to escape the nether world of fog and haze. But
it also turns his world into a set of precise details, a society of contracts against the
old, hazy community of nature, accommodation, and mutual compliance. The lens
is the counterpart of the mirror that the boy uses to reflect a piece of the sky, of
'freedom', to the imprisoned waters of the cistern below. Light, in its reflected and
refracted states, is the medium of the writer. It is an attribute of the upper world but
like the fire of Prometheus, it is dangerous, shining fiercely into the dark corners
where life exists.

  As the British bombing raids increase in frequency the citizens abandon their
homes for the cellars of the citadel, the heart of the ancient city.

> Dans les propos de certains gens, la citadelle était de plus en plus associée au
> Moyen Age. La forteresse était ancienne. Elle avait engendré la ville. Et nos
> maisons ressemblaient à la citadelle un peu comme les enfants ressemblent à
> leur mère. (*Chronique* 205)

> Certain people were associating the citadel with the Middle Ages more and
> more. The fortress was very old. It had given birth to the city, and our houses
> looked a little like the citadel the way children look like their mother. (*Chronicle*
> 179)

Here the boys experience history in the journey downwards and inwards to the
medieval origins of their town. Like Dante in the *Inferno* they hear the stories of
the past, of the Ottoman times which shaped and distorted the nation's identity.
The severed head of a disobedient pasha rolls past them and the chained and rotting
bodies of officials who had fallen foul of the Porte haunt this place. This Ottoman
motif of beheading will provide Kadare with one of his most important symbols
for the failure of Albania to have found a modern leader after the early uprising of

Scanderbeg. (It provides the central motif of the later historical novel, *The Niche of Shame*.) The Ottoman practice of capturing and beheading any figure of opposition represents for Albanians a syndrome of the loss of potential leadership and the focus or centre of the nation's spiritual as well as material forces.

Chronicle in Stone ends with the occupation of the town by the Germans.

> Au crépuscule, la ville qui, au fil des siècles, avait figuré sur les cartes comme une possession des Romains, des Normands, de Byzance, des Turcs, des Grecs, des Italiens, se retrouvait, en regardant venir le soir, dans l'empire allemand. Lasse, étoudie par le choc, elle ne donnait aucun signe de vie. (*Chronique* 311)

> At dusk the city, which through the centuries had appeared on maps as a possession of the Romans, the Normans, the Byzantines, the Turks, the Greeks, and the Italians, now watched darkness fall as a part of the German empire. Utterly exhausted, dazed by the battle, it showed no sign of life. (*Chronicle* 271)

In the winter of 1943/44 between the departure of the Italians and the arrival of the Germans, the Ballists and the communists battled for power while engaging fire with the exhausted Italian battalions and secretly negotiating with representatives of the Allied powers. The southern countryside and the towns, Korça, Gjirokastra, Elbasan, and Berat were occupied by the partisans.[18] The hatred between the communists and the Ballists, the followers of the Balli Kombëtar or National Front, is palpable in Kadare's novel. After the execution of Isa, Javer assassinates his uncle, Azem Kurti, a Balli Kombëtar commander responsible for Isa's arrest. The killing of Azem Kurti is described in graphic detail as Javer takes a pistol from his pocket and kills his uncle at the family dinner table. The deed sets off a spate of retributions. Once the town is in the hands of the partisans, summary justice is meted out to those considered to have collaborated with the Ballists, the internal 'fascist' enemy of the communists. The tanner Mak Karllashi and his son are executed in front of their doorway and the daughter who refuses to leave her father's side is also gunned down. When the partisan responsible for the girl's death is executed shortly after, the imposition of summary justice suggests that the uncompromising liquidation of 'fascists' and the re-establishment of order will be the overriding priority of a partisan government. The chronicle ends with the arrival of the German tanks. The partisans return to the hills and the citizens seek refuge in the outlying villages until the surrender brings about the cessation of German bombing.

Kadare does not end with the victorious re-emergence of the partisans after the German retreat. The appearance of the partisans is carefully placed in the interval between the Italian withdrawal and the German occupation, in order to avoid the political problems associated with the representation of the beginning of the new era. The execution of Mak Karllashi by the partisans remains an episode and the chronicle ends with the town, not the politics as its focal point. The stone town, which supports life in its cracks and crevices, has again proved itself to be more lasting than any of the occupying forces. That it is an ecosystem for its people, Gjirokastrans and Albanians, and not for political regimes, has been demonstrated yet again with the departure of the Italians and the Germans. Presumably it will survive the communists. However, the ending is not confrontational. Kadare's aim is to establish a continuity. The sense of break between past and present identified at the end of *The General* has been overcome with the image of continuity in the town as a life-world. Despite the violence, upheaval, destruction, civil unrest, and mutual hatred which occur as the traditional order breaks down, the town survives, and while individuals die and are killed, their stories survive in the history of the town. The final death is that of Kako Pino, the harmless old woman who makes up brides for their weddings and whose cosmetic instruments are mistaken for a saboteur's equipment. Life will go on, the child becomes the man and the adult writer remembers the people whose footsteps, faces, and voices are imprinted in the rough cold stone of the city, giving him the language and the memories which will survive even during the darkest years of the dictatorship. The author's postscript represents the town as the stone remnants of the accrued wisdom and experience of the old women, the bearers of ancient and eternal Albanian identity in spite of their individual fates. Kako Pino, Grandmother Selfixhe, and others are etched into the author's memory:

> Aux coins des rues j'ai cru discerner quelques traits familiers, comme des traits humains, des ombres de pommettes et d'yeux. Elles sont là, éternelles, pétrifiées, avec les empreintes qu'ont laissées sur elles les tremblements de terre, les hivers ou les fléaux humains. (*Chronique* 317)

> At the street corners, where walls join, I thought I could see some familiar lines, like human features, shadows of cheekbones and eyes. They are still there, frozen for ever in stone, along with the traces left by earthquakes, winters, and scourges wrought by men. (*Chronicle* 277)

History lies at the heart of *Chronicle in Stone*: as natural history, as social and personal history, memory, remembrance and memoir, chronicle and documentation. The fragmented texture, including childhood memories along with adult reflection, interleaved sections of anonymous chronicle along with episodes of town life, renders the work tentative and exploratory. Nevertheless, the sequential nature of the chronology foregrounds the relationship of past to present, although in ways very different from those ordained by historical materialism. *Chronicle in Stone* is also Kadare's most intimate and personal work whose opening suggestions of whimsical humour are undercut by episodes of cruelty and tragedy.

The stone town bears the traces of its human and natural history; however, it is the writer who recognizes the lines of human experience alongside those of climate and change. *Chronicle* marks an important step forward in Kadare's development by linking the writer directly to the land through individual experience and identity and radically contradicting the requirements of socialist realism. Kadare places subjective authenticity at the centre of his creativity in this important novel. While earlier works such as *The Monster* and *The General* were written in a spirit opposed to socialist realism, *Chronicle* takes the rejection further by placing the creative consciousness at the centre of personal memory and national identity. The author here, for the first time, is explicitly the carrier of group memory and identity. Individual creative consciousness, not objective history, embodies and gives voice to the nation. At this stage the challenge to the dictator and the regime remains implicit: it is the writer, not the dictator who is the voice of the nation. Not the 'new man' of Albanian communism, but the eternal Albania of the writer's memory and creative consciousness will be the subject of its history. This is the beginning of a battle to the end for the voice of Albania between the writer and the dictator. It is Kadare's great theme, linked with his portrayal of his country as an *ethnos* wider and deeper than communism or modernity. In *The Twilight of the Steppe-Gods* written half a decade later, Kadare will retrospectively formulate his return to Albania as a *descente* in order to rescue his native land. As Constantine, the Albanian Orpheus, who passes between life and death to rescue his beloved sister Doruntine, Kadare will cross between literature and reality in order to redeem Albania from its confinement under the dictatorship.

The appeal to memory in *Chronicle* constitutes the beginning of an answer to the final question of *The General of the Dead Army*: where to go from here? How can past and present be re-connected? Can this connection be made positive? How can we come to terms with history, rather than burying it in the frozen soil where it harbours its destructivity or rewriting it in accordance with dogma and political convenience? The writer's answer is personal. He seeks the origins of his subjectivity and his adult identity. In doing so he suggests answers to further questions about his country. For in his memories lie clues to the denial of the past. Where the past remains closed in different ways for Italians and Albanians alike in *The General*, *Chronicle in Stone* revisits the childhood of the writer, taking the first step towards a reconnection of past and present. In the stories of the inhabitants, whose lives are fleeting moments in the history of the town, the continuities of the centuries are preserved, from the magical practices dating from earliest times through Christian and Muslim, Byzantine, and Ottoman civilizations to the dawning of the new era of communism amid flames and summary executions at the end of the work.

Chronicle in Stone was denounced in June 1971 in a letter to Ramiz Alia, published in part in the daily newspaper *The Courier*. The sender, a teacher and young writer in Berat, criticizes the work for its lack of socialist principles, its ugliness, and its surrealism, and suggests that it be withdrawn from circulation. The novel defies the regime in form as well as content. At this still relatively early stage in Kadare's career, modernization and ethnicity, communism and Albania have taken shape as contradictory forces. The figure of Enver Hoxha appears, but the work remains primarily a study of the past as the 'concrete pre-history of the present'.[19] *Chronicle in Stone* documents the formation of the writer's consciousness in the era preceding the communist *Gleichschaltung*. In counterpoint to the encomiums to Hoxha's Stalinist purism and Albanian patriotism at the high point of the regime, Kadare reminds his fellow countrymen of the origins of Albanian communism in civil war, terror, revenge, and summary justice.

Moreover, it is the 'subjective authenticity' of the narrative voice, not the objective authenticity of socialist realism, which gives meaning. In the city of his birth the child finds the images that will accompany him through life, and with which he begins to construct an alternative Albania in words and memories to that of the dictatorship. Over the following decade Kadare will reformulate his relationship to the dictator and the regime, experimenting with the idea of the 'corrective mask', the Enlightenment model of political education by precept and literary example; later he will become more and more preoccupied with the innate conflict between the writer and the dictator, building in the figure of Prometheus an alter and counter-ego of dictatorial Zeus. In *The Twilight of the Steppe-Gods* he describes his recognition that the creative imagination, the mirror which sends a 'slice of sky' to the imprisoned ones below, has become his existential justification for returning to his captive nation.

'Opening the Doors of the Prison': *Winter of Great Solitude, 1969–1973*

By 1969 Kadare had begun to gain a profile beyond Albania. In 1970 Jusuf Vrioni's translation of *The General* was authorized for publication in France by Albin Michel. A French magazine referred to Kadare and Hoxha as the two best-known Albanians for the rest of the world. Other members of the Union of Writers, such as Dritëro Agolli, were consumed with envy.[20] In addition Kadare's prominence was beginning to encroach on Enver Hoxha's aspirations. He too wanted to be admired in the West for the education and literary gifts which he traced back to France.[21] By 1970 Hoxha was rumoured to be thinking of dedicating a greater part of his time to reflection and writing, with a book about his childhood already finished (*Years of Childhood*) and one about the break with the Soviet Union (*The Khrushchevites*) under way. He was sixty-two years old. Since the 1950s he had achieved levels of control only dreamed of by his Eastern European colleagues. Hoxha's literary ambitions constituted an extra threat to Kadare, who writes of the situation:

> Pour la première fois, je me rendis compte de ce qu'il y avait de terrible à être connu dans un pays stalinien dirigé par un tyran aussi féroce que rusé et qui, par malheur, se targuait d'être lui aussi écrivain.[22]

> For the first time I realized that it was terrible to be known in a Stalinist country under the control of a tyrant as ferocious as he was cunning and who, unfortunately, also claimed to be a writer.

Kadare's enemies in the Sigurimi, or Directorate of State Security (the secret police service under Mehmet Shehu), and the old guard of the Politburo repeatedly referred to him as an agent of the West. This was one of the most dangerous accusations that could be made in this state obsessed by external threats. As his international profile emerged, so too did his need of a writing strategy to protect himself at home from both the paranoia of the dictator, and from his old enemies on the left and in the Sigurimi.[23] Until this point Kadare was considered to be both a writer of talent and a writer whose talent was dangerously inclined towards decadence and subjectivism.

   The aspect of Enver Hoxha as patriot and wartime partisan leader had appealed to the young Kadare. When he discovered as a child that Hoxha, 'the man who led the Resistance', was from his own quarter in Gjirokastra, he was amazed and impressed. As communist partisan leader Hoxha had liberated Albania from Italian and German occupation and in 1961 he achieved that which no other European communist leader had managed: the liberation of Albania from the Soviet bloc. Kadare remained impressed by this one world-historical achievement of the Albanian leader:

> Dès le début, j'avais douté de la bonne foi d'Enver Hoxha dans cette prise
> de décision. Je savais que le mobile essentiel qui l'y avait poussé était son
> destin personnel, non celui de l'Albanie. Quoi qu'il en fût, cela était de peu
> d'importance en regard de l'acte lui-même. Et cet acte était considérable: la
> sécession de l'Albanie n'était ni tactique ni de pure forme. Elle était totale,
> solennelle, irrémédiable. Sincère ou non, Enver Hoxha méritait, pour cet acte,
> de prendre place dans l'Histoire plus qu'au titre de chef de la Résistance au
> cours de la guerre. (*Le Poids*, 331–32)

> From the beginning I doubted Enver Hoxha's good faith in making this
> decision. I knew that the main motive driving him was his own destiny and
> not that of Albania. Be that as it may, this was of little importance in relation
> to the act itself. And that act was considerable: the secession of Albania was
> neither tactical nor formal. It was total, serious, irremediable. Sincere or not,
> Enver Hoxha deserved for this act, to take his place in History, more than he
> did as leader of the resistance during the war.

With these mixed views, around 1969, Kadare began to contemplate a strategy
which would both flatter and educate the dictator and create a protective alibi
for himself for his future work. He traces the origins of the idea back to a poem
written in the 1960s, 'The Sixties', in which Enver Hoxha appears as an epic figure
redeeming his tiny nation from the clutches of the Soviet monster.[24] Planned as an
accolade to Hoxha in the style of the hymns to Stalin, it also evoked the lasting
impression of the national hero, although Kadare passes it off in *The Weight of the
Cross* as nothing more than a piece of political expediency designed to stay on
the good side of the regime.[25] The poem received lukewarm praise from official
quarters. It was clearly not tribute enough from the national laureate-to-be. 'Que
voulez-vous de moi? étais-je tenté de dire à la cantonade' (*Le Poids* 318; 'what do
you want from me? I was tempted to say to them all'). But he now was planning a
novel that would stave off the attacks for some time.

At this time Kadare writes that he was still convinced that the break with the
Soviet Union would lead to rapprochement with the West. Kadare's model at this
stage is Marshal Tito, hailed in the early 1970s as offering a potential third way
between Soviet communism and the West. Kadare was bitter at the Europeans' lack
of initiative in offering the hand of friendship to Albania at this point when the
country appeared to be teetering between East and West.[26] The failure of the West
to respond to Hoxha's manoeuvre, leaving him stranded and the Albanian people
abandoned, was for Kadare a 'second Yalta'.

> L'Occident a pardonné a bon nombre de dictateurs et il pardonnera encore
> à d'autres, y compris à Bokassa et à Pinochet, mais à lui [Hoxha], non. Aussi
> bien l'occident ne fait-il aucune distinction entre Enver Hoxha et l'Albanie. En
> même temps qu'au dictateur, il tourne le dos au peuple albanais et l'abandonne
> à son sort. (*Le Poids* 335)

> The West has pardoned a good number of dictators and will pardon more again,
> including Bokassa and Pinochet, but not him [Hoxha]. The West makes as good
> as no distinction between Enver Hoxha and Albania. At the same time as it
> turns its back on the dictator, it abandons the Albanian people to their fate.

The new work would be based on Hoxha's world-historical role in the epic break with the Soviet Union. Kadare read psychoanalytic literature in order to try to understand Hoxha's behaviour, attempting to catch the dictator in his 'trap', and finally comprehend the man (*Le Poids* 346). *The Winter of Great Solitude* was to be Kadare's alibi and his protection over the following decade. Hoxha would appear at a moment of hope.[27] The fictional representation of the leader would be designed as a 'mirror' for the dictator, showing him at his best, cleansed of dictatorial traits and offered as a 'corrective mask'. Having presented the idealized image of the dictator and become a household name, Kadare could no longer be simply dispensed with. This novel would 'open the doors of the Prison'.[28]

Kadare gained access to the documentation of the meetings of Hoxha, Shehu, and the other members of the Albanian delegation with Khrushchev and the Soviet leadership at the meeting of eighty-one world communist leaders in Moscow in 1960. The omnipresent Nexhmije supported and facilitated his request, opening the secret archive to him. Her reasons for doing so are conjectural but interesting. Nexhmije was a hard-line Stalinist devoted to maintaining the stability of the regime, her own and Enver's position. She was wily enough to recognize in Kadare potentially a valuable ally as well as a dangerous enemy by 1970 when his reputation had reached France (and probably before). Perhaps Nexhmije saw in this novel the means of making or breaking Albania's only alternative voice to the regime. If Kadare were given the freedom to make irreparable mistakes in this novel about Hoxha and the break with the Soviet Union, he would be discredited for life, particularly with Enver, who had protected him in the past. If he succeeded in writing a novel acceptable to the regime, he would become unattractive to his supporters in the West. For Nexhmije, who saw the world in black-and-white, the possibility of Kadare's stepping the fine line between these two extremes was unlikely.

In 1971 Nexhmije invited Kadare to discuss the novel with her. It was at this time that the writer's only private meeting with the dictator took place. During the meeting with Nexhmije, Enver walked into the room 'by chance' and chatted with Kadare for several hours about literature. The famous photograph of Kadare, Hoxha, and Kadare's infant daughter was taken at this meeting. Hoxha charmed the writer with his famed European urbanity, speaking for hours about the Moscow conference, his youth, his love of France and his origins, mentioning in passing Kadare's recent memoir, *Chronicle in Stone*, and their common origins in Gjirokastra. The intensity with which Hoxha spoke of France and his youth brought to the author's mind the 'supreme rumour' of Hoxha's homosexuality, which was such a dangerous topic, but which in this context seemed to promise some hope in a character so different from his Eastern European colleagues, 'those withered flowers of the dry Marxist-Leninist steppes' (*Le Poids* 344).

> On était tenté de lui dire: Ne te soucie pas de cette rumeur. Dans le monde d'aujourd'hui, elle ne jette sur toi aucune ombre. Tant d'hommes éminents, délicats et raffinés, n'en ont pas été atteints dans leur image. Au contraire elle te singularise, te distingue de l'impuissance de ce nabot stérile de Lénine ou de la longue masturbation monacale d'un Staline. (*Le Poids* 344)

> One was tempted to say to him: Don't worry yourself about that rumour. In today's world it doesn't reflect badly on you. So many eminent men, refined

and sensitive, have not suffered in their image because of it. On the contrary, it
singles you out, distinguishes you from that impotent and sterile runt, Lenin, or
from the extended monastic masturbation practices of someone like Stalin.

Kadare wrote quickly, substantially finishing the manuscript of *The Winter of Great
Solitude* by the end of 1971. An acquaintance told him that the novel would be like
a ring through the nose of a bear, making Hoxha dance to his music (*Le Poids* 347).
He would disarm the dictator with its beauty, appealing to his subtle and refined
taste in literature. Everything in the novel was true, writes Kadare, except the
portrait of the dictator.

> D'un certain point de vue, il était exact: les mots, les gestes, les dialogues
> appartenaient tous au personnage. Mais il était incomplet. Il y manquait les
> taches et les ombres, sans compter ce qui constituait le clé de tout: la véritable
> raison qui avait poussé le personnage à cette folle audace. (*Le Poids* 348)

> From a certain point of view it was exact: the words, the gestures, the
> conversations all belonged to the character. But it was incomplete. It lacked
> the blemishes and the shadows, not to mention the key to everything in his
> character, the true force behind that brazen insanity.

A section was shown to Kadare's friend, Todi Lubonja, director of state broadcasting
and television, who passed it on to Ramiz Alia at the latter's request. It seems likely
that Hoxha read the manuscript, which Kadare had given to Ramiz Alia; indeed,
he may well have instigated Alia's request.

The Winter of Great Solitude

The story is set in the winter months between September 1960 and March 1961, the
time of the break between Moscow and Tirana. Journalist and translator, Besnik
Struga, is chosen to accompany the Albanian delegation to Moscow for the summit
meeting of the eighty-one heads of international communist organizations in
November 1960. The plot moves quickly to the Moscow meeting, which takes up
Book Two and is based on Kadare's access to the then secret files. Discussions at the
meeting touch on the importance of the Vlora naval base, Khrushchev's flippant
comments regarding Soviet reserves in the aftermath of the previous summer's
wheat shortages, the cooling of relations, and the need for socialist solidarity.
The well-known members of international communism are present: Andropov,
Kosygin, Mikoyan, Ulbricht, Ho Chi Minh, Gomulka, Dej, Thorez, even 'La
Pasionaria', the Spanish partisan, Dolores Ibarurri. Kadare emphasizes the heroic
opposition of Hoxha and Khrushchev in which the suffering, fighting Hoxha is the
underdog, isolated and bullied by the Soviet Union and its sycophantic member
states and global allies. 'Confusément [Khrouchtchev] devine que c'est l'autre qui
a raison. [. . .] Pour sa part, Enver Hoxha est complètement transfiguré' (*Le Poids*
333, '[Khrushchev] vaguely senses that the other is right. [. . .] For his part, Hoxha
is completely transfigured'). There is little discussion of ideological issues other than
the broad need for solidarity and the role of the Soviet Union as the world leader
of socialism. Kadare consolidates the historical break, implying that it occurred at
the 'heroic' confrontation of the two leaders, whereas in fact it had been brewing

FIG. 15 (above): V. Kilica's idealized portrait of Enver Hoxha as communist resistance leader, 'The Dawn of November 8, 1941'. (Source: *40 Years of Socialist Albania*, Tirana: 8 Nëntori Publishing House, 1984.)

FIG. 16 (below): The meeting of Ismail Kadare and Enver Hoxha (with Kadare's daughter) at the time of writing of *The Winter of Great Solitude* in 1971.

for well over a year and had its roots in broader political issues. Although primarily engaged as a journalist and translator, Besnik Struga interprets for Hoxha at the Moscow summit meeting. At a difficult point in the proceedings, during a stressful and exhausting day, he makes a mistake in the translation of a Russian proverb. This contributes to the heightening of tension, to bitterness and disagreement between the two leaders and to the criticism and ostracism of the Albanians by other members of world communism. While Enver Hoxha dominates the Moscow meeting in Book Two, the rest of the plot revolves around the translator, Besnik, his family and friends, and in particular around his relationship with his fiancée, Zana. This is the point of contact between the great world of politics and the small world of personal relationships. For as an indirect result of Besnik's involvement in the Moscow meeting, his relationship with Zana suffers and finally breaks up.

Besnik returns to Albania distraught at the role he has played at the conference, but is constrained to remain silent on the topic of what transpired until the regime formulates its response and clears the embargo imposed on members of the delegation. Preoccupied with his failure and the fate of the nation, he is evasive with Zana about the date of their wedding. She, fearing that he has found another woman in Moscow, turns to alcohol and in a drunken moment seduces her French tutor and neighbour, Marc, the son of a disgraced bourgeois family in the flat below. Zana's mother, Liria, decides to end her daughter's relationship with Besnik once and for all by denouncing him to his boss and local Party member. Besnik is required to make an official explanation of his behaviour, but refuses on the grounds that this is none of the Party's business. His application for Party membership, the passport to professional success, is postponed, further exacerbating his emotional and psychological crisis.

Kadare paints a broad canvas of secondary figures. Besnik's father Kristaq is an ex-partisan and hero of the Albanian communist movement, famous for having blown up the tomb of the Queen Mother during the resistance. His younger brother, Beni, is typical of Kadare's disaffected young people of *The City without Signs*. Beni drinks too much, spends his time hanging around with his friends listening to popular music, and grows his hair long. Constantly reminded of the achievements of his father's generation, he lacks self-esteem and a sense of direction but is rehabilitated in the novel after discovering self-fulfilment through work and self-sacrifice in the communist cause. Zana's family, too, is represented in detail. She is the daughter of a prominent family of intellectuals. Her sister, Diana, is married to a leading writer, Skender Bermema (who reappears in *The Concert*). The Bermemas become embroiled in scandal when a young relative is engaged to the son of an ex-Party member, excommunicated after the events of 1956 in Hungary. Below the Bermemas live old Nurihan and her son Marc on the ground floor of their dispossessed house. Nurihan listens to foreign radio broadcasts and gossips with her friends and cronies, embittered remnants of the bourgeoisie and land-owning gentry, who include Rrok Simonjaku, proprietor of a second-hand goods store in the city.

The figures representing the past, particularly old Nurihan and her friends, cower over their radios, hoping to hear signs of political change from long-wave broadcasts. Kadare harbours little sympathy for these figures of the past, even though he also makes some minor narrative gestures to render them less unsympathetic. When Beni, the scion of a partisan communist family and younger brother of the protagonist, Besnik, is involved in a drunken scuffle, the old bourgeois, Rrok Simonjaku does not identify him to the police. Nevertheless, Nurihan and her friends are conniving, snide, and nasty. In the second version (*The Great Winter*) a doctor is released from prison after fifteen years for having sewn jewels and gold into cadavers while completing death certificates and autopsies, so that their families might reclaim the treasures later on. It is hard to believe that a figure such as Jusuf Vrioni, Kadare's colleague and translator who suffered miserably on account of his privileged pre-war class background, could not have been affronted by these portrayals. And yet, one of the most sympathetic portrayals in the novel is of Nurihan's son, Marc, a cellist with the symphony orchestra, whose fate has been determined by the class status and wartime actions of his family.

The break with Zana and the ensuing disappointment in Besnik's personal life has its origins in the meeting in Moscow. However, it comes to a crisis as a result of the unethical behaviour of Zana's mother and the complicity of Party members. It is in the nature of the Party that personal issues became politically charged. The regime is implicitly criticized for creating a perverted and artificial life-world among the nomenklatura and the professional and educated classes in the capital.

Alone and adrift after Zana has called off their relationship, Besnik seeks a sense of inclusion in the wider community. In an epiphanic moment he recognizes his place in the communist scheme of things as he comes to the realization that even he in his role as translator contributed to Albania's independence. Nevertheless, by the end of the novel, the outlook is distinctly bleak. Besnik's emotional life is in tatters, the country is still suffering from a bitterly cold winter, despite the late stage of the year and the final image is of people struggling against snowstorms to repair television and radio antennas which will no longer receive news or information from the outside world. The West is out of bounds, and even the Warsaw Pact countries are now blockaded. Only relations with China are strengthening. The novel ends with the death of Nurihan and the birth of Diana Bermema's child on a cold day at the end of winter 1961.

Besnik Struga is peripheral to the epic events of the Moscow meeting, and his fictional mistake in interpreting, which drives the plot line, is trivial in the scheme of things. The extent to which it contributes to the break between Hoxha and Khrushchev, or whether it is simply the factor which undermines Besnik's peace of mind, is unclear. However, this indirect relationship between the private and the public, the personal and the political lies at the heart of the novel's message. At the end Besnik is shown to have achieved a sense of personal resolution through his conviction that he has in his own way contributed to Albania's maintenance of her national integrity, despite the translation mistake and the loss of Zana. The narrative reflects Besnik's thoughts in the final paragraphs, his hopes that Zana would return to him, his sense of loss as he realizes that she is gone forever, and his consolation that the nation, at least, had been saved, even if he has been sacrificed.

> Le peuple avait supporté le coup. Il avait grimacé de douleur, et, sous l'épreuve,

s'était peut-être recroquevillé sur lui-même, crachant parfois son amertume, mais il avait conservé la vie. Les pertes creusaient bien çà et là des trous profonds sur sa large poitrine, mais les pertes ajoutent parfois à la grandeur d'un people. À moi aussi, la perte a apporté quelque chose, songea-t-il. Il sentait au fond de lui un calme étonnant, fait de pureté et de chaleur. En fin de compte, toute cela avait été on ne peut plus simple: parmi les armées innombrables du communisme, il était un simple soldat, quasi anonyme, au milieu du XXe siècle, sur qui l'époque s'était déchargée d'une partie de son poids. Le hurlement de la sirene semblait s'être fiché dans le ciel. Je t'ai attendue tout l'après-midi, pensa-t-il. Je t'ai attendue dans les siècles des siècles . . .[29]

The people had withstood the blow. During the ordeal they grimaced with pain and may have flinched, spitting with the bitterness of it all, but they stayed alive. The losses were large, leaving gaping wounds here and there, but losses can add to the grandeur of a people. For me, too, loss brought something, he said to himself. Deep within himself he felt an inner calm, a strange mixture of purity and warmth. After all was said and done, it was now completely clear: in the armies of communism he was one of so many, just a simple, almost anonymous, foot soldier in the mid-twentieth century, on whom history had laid part of its heavy burden. The howl of the siren seemed to have become a part of the sky. I've been waiting for you all afternoon, he thought. I've been waiting for you for centuries.

This novel of the simple soldier of communism nevertheless ends not with his country but with his loss. The theme of the sacrifice of the personal for the public could not be clearer — nor any more questionable in Besnik's thoughts despite the epic-heroic tenor of the writing.

While Kadare can be seen to have fashioned Enver Hoxha into a positive hero of socialism and to have painted a broad epic canvas of the events of 1961, the novel ends on an ambivalent note as the economic, cultural, and social consequences of the break in relations begin to affect everyday life. The Soviet and Warsaw Pact ambassadors and technocrats depart, leaving Albanian projects unfinished and dangerously undermanned. Hoxha's 'heroic' actions affect the whole of his country in disastrous ways. Not only is the freeze political; it hardens relationships all the way down from the summit in Moscow to the most intimate levels of interpersonal relations. The stubborn intransigence of the leaders is replicated at all levels as characters either conform or are excluded from society. Interpersonal relationships seem afflicted by obstacles to communication that are born of personal insecurity, social distrust, and entrenched political taboos. Above all, the embargo on the events in Moscow, which was not officially lifted until late in 1961, affects the relationship of Besnik and Zana, who appear incapable of speaking openly and freely, even in private, or of trusting one another. This is hardly surprising, given the ideologically hardened attitudes of those around them, the distress which the Bermema family suffers as a result of a distant cousin's engagement to the relation of a 'class enemy', Zana's circumspection and narrowness, and Besnik's ambitions and insecurities. The next step up from the family in social affairs, the workplace, is dominated by the Party and by the nepotism and malice of figures such as Besnik's boss, who is delighted to have a pretext to exclude his junior colleague from Party membership. It is the Party which colludes with Liria in denouncing her future son-in-law for purely personal reasons, and the upper levels of the Party and the nomenklatura are characterized by political correctness, intimidation, and manipulation.

The literary trope of a harsh winter survived is undercut from the beginning by Kadare's implication that winter has become the permanent state of Albanian social life. He begins the novel with an image of the inhabitants of Tirana struggling to re-erect their radio and television antennas in the September storms, and finishes with the same image on the snowbound roofs of the capital. Throughout the novel, and in its sequel, *The Concert*, radio contact with the rest of the world becomes a metaphor for the state of Albanian isolation. With its echoes of Shakespeare's *Richard III*, the ambiguous original title of the work, which the writer was obliged to change for the revised version, directs the reader's attention to the dubious nature of Albanian 'solitude'. Access to the world via radio and television would diminish, not increase, as the previously accessible Italian and Yugoslav broadcasts were scrambled and punishments raised for illegal listening. Enver Hoxha's ideological purity achieves a 'great solitude' which appears to do little for the inhabitants of Albania in the novel. Dashnor Mamaqi, the secretary of the Tirana Committee of the Party, identified the tone of disappointment and unhappiness in his 1973 critique of the novel: 'L'atmosphère y est lugubre et le roman est traversé d'une sorte d'angoisse existentialiste' ('the atmosphere is gloomy and the novel is permeated with a sort of existentialist anguish').[30]

Winter of Great Solitude is a flawed work, but it is pivotal in Kadare's development as a writer. For here he engages with the figure of Enver Hoxha, the holder of power since the communist takeover in 1945 and a figure whose name had become synonymous with the nation. The novel has been widely criticized for pandering to the image of the dictator as a man of ideological conviction, inner strength, and international importance when in fact his involvement was self-seeking, ideologically devious, and determined by the conflict between the two communist superpowers, China and the Soviet Union. However, this novel also represents an important stage in the writer's engagement with the dictator. Here for the first time Hoxha is represented in detail as a realistically conceived figure, not as an intangible presence, or as an allegory of power in historical costume. The structure of the dictatorship — the committee system, the Party, the nomenklatura, and the politicized society of the capital — is also represented, where in earlier works the relationships of power between the bureaucrats and the dictator were nebulous and indefinable. In the context of the regime, the possibility of realistic representation of these aspects of contemporary life (in particular Liria's denunciation of Besnik) was predicated on the idealization of the dictator.

And yet this idealization is more than just a strategy of representation. Kadare's admiration for the fighter and patriot and for the land that he represents is palpable. In the revisions for the second (1976) edition he shifts the focus slightly, underscoring Hoxha's role as an instrument of history, of the birth of the modern nation. Hoxha's personality is still predominant, but it is increasingly viewed as a product of historical circumstance, without which the nation would not have survived the post-war reorganization of the Balkans. Albania is more than Enver Hoxha. In this version Hoxha represents history, the problematic coming to self-determination of a country that was accustomed to tutelage. Kadare was not the only Eastern European intellectual to accept Stalinism as a modernizing force, but he was clearly moving beyond this position by the mid-1960s. In *The Great Winter* he brings together his admiration of Enver Hoxha the partisan and patriot with a profound questioning of Hoxha's nationalistic communism at that point in 1960 when the post-war order of Europe was being sealed in the east as well as the west.

Reception of 'Winter of Great Solitude'

By the end of the 1960s things seemed to be looking up again after the first years of the cultural revolution. Social and cultural life improved, the alliance with China was no longer taken seriously, and rumours circulated that Hoxha was about to make a pronouncement against the cultural revolution. Hoxha's cultural predilections for French and European music and literature were widely known and it was announced that the dictator had encouraged his colleagues in the Central Committee to express themselves freely in French and English as well as Albanian.[31] Hoxha had put the liberal Ramiz Alia above the old guard warriors, Mehmet Shehu and Hysni Kapo, as the 'human face' of Stalinism. Significant numbers of the intelligentsia hoped, naively perhaps, that Hoxha was waiting for signs of an approach from the West, and that the Chinese alliance was simply a holding action, designed to keep the Soviets at bay until Western contacts could be established.

In retrospect Kadare represents the writing of the novel in terms of a thaw in Albanian relations, both internally and with the Western world. Todi Lubonja, the director of radio and television, encouraged Kadare to persevere with this work, which would help the dictator to liberate himself from his demons. Kadare refers to Lubonja, along with another highly placed liberal official and friend, Agim Mero, both of whom supported him in his work, as 'Gorbachevs before their time' (*Le Poids* 353). Lubonja was aware of the dangers inherent in Kadare's project, but the writer was excited by the prospect of the dictator taking on the challenge offered to him.

> J'avais parfois l'impression qu'à l'instar d'un combattant qui, dans un duel, attire son adversaire sur un terrain qui lui est favorable, j'avais entraîné le tyran dans le repaire de la littérature où je me sentais maître [. . .]. Là, dans cet espace découvert, loin des gardes, des courtisans, de la doctrine et de la dictature, je croyais pouvoir l'emporter. Le temps de lui mettre le masque. Puis ce masque lui-même lui imposerait sa contrainte. (*Le Poids* 352).

> I sometimes had the impression that, like a combatant who draws his duelling partner onto more favourable ground, I had led the tyrant to the field of literature, where I felt myself to be the master [. . .]. There, I thought, exposed and separated from the guards, the courtesans, the doctrines, and the dictatorship, he could be prevailed over. That would be the chance to attach the mask. Then the mask itself would curb and constrain him.

The novel was intended to suggest a possible option for Hoxha in this environment, namely withdrawal from the day-to-day running of the country. The 'frail' Alia was in every way a man designed to do the leader's bidding.[32] The old Stalinist war-horses, Mehmet Shehu and Hysni Kapo, could be further demoted, and the dictator could work towards attenuating his Stalinist image with a less criminal Leninism.[33] However, all was not what it seemed in this most opaque of political environments and Hoxha, like the sultan in *The Palace of Dreams*, was about to strike.

Ramiz Alia read the complete manuscript of *Winter of Great Solitude* in the autumn of 1972. Several months passed in which the writer heard nothing. The atmosphere of detente and optimism in the capital since the end of the 1960s continued into the winter of 1972. Hoxha returned from winter holidays in Vlora at the end of the year. In a passage evocative of *The Palace of Dreams*, Kadare describes the sudden chill which hit the city:

> Dès le lendemain se répandit une rumeur de mauvaise aloi: il se passait quelque chose. Telle une larve effrayante, la rumeur se métamorphosa jour après jour (il s'est produit quelque chose de fâcheux . . . le camarade Enver est très en colère . . . vraiment, c'est quelque chose de grave . . .), jusqu'au moment où se répandit cette formulation inquiétante qui ne laissait nul espoir: 'un groupe . . . autrement dit . . . un complot . . . dans le secteur de la Culture'. (*Le Poids* 356)

> From the day after [i.e. Hoxha's return] a rumour began to spread which did not bode well. Something was up. The rumour mutated day by day into something else, like some sort of monstrous larva (something bad has happened . . . Comrade Enver is furious . . . it's something really serious . . .), until that alarming formulation which annihilated all hope: 'there is a group . . . in other words . . . a conspiracy . . . in the cultural sector.

In his reading of the situation Kadare suggests that Hoxha himself was at an impasse at this time, still hoping for an approach from the West, but isolated from the Soviet Union and feeling exposed and humiliated by the Chinese after Mao Tse-tung's 'revisionist' moves, in particular the interest in rapprochement with the United States, first expressed via intermediaries in 1970, which resulted in Nixon's visit to China in February 1972.[34]

The strategy of creating an alibi for his writing by offering the dictator an idealized image, which would function as the model of the 'good dictator', was a risky move. Politically astute, even cunning as he was, Kadare was no match for Hoxha. Over-confident, even optimistic about the changes in policy towards China, he had not seriously accepted the possibility of complete seclusion, and failed to foresee the frost of the early 1970s. Encouraged by the restlessness of young people and the sense of social and cultural change as well as by the engagement of progressive intellectuals such as Lubonja and Paçrami, he had played his card. He and his novel were caught up in the ensuing political machinations.

The rumour of the book's existence polarized the two main factions around Hoxha: the old-guard Stalinists whose power base lay in the Sigurimi, and the liberals, headed by Ramiz Alia, but held in contempt by figures such as Nexhmije Hoxha, Mehmet Shehu, and Hysni Kapo. In addition Nexhmije, wife of the leader, hard-line Stalinist, and a partisan combatant in her own right during the war, had a great deal of influence as a member of the Central Committee and as a power behind the throne along with Kapo in particular.[35] The manuscript was passed back and forth among the factions, each sizing it up for their political purposes for or against the author, given the extremely touchy subject of the supreme leader himself.

Enver Hoxha withdrew into ominous silence. The novel was neither hailed nor prohibited, but lay in check between the dictator and the factions around him.

Time was passing, the West showed no interest in rapprochement, and the dictator had to make a move. At a meeting of the Central Committee he drew attention to ideological deviations and announced the existence of a conspiracy close to the heart of government. As ever, he would divide and rule, and internal political intrigue would be used to justify increased vigilance and control. Meanwhile Kadare's manuscript was authorized for publication and sent to the printer. It appeared in January 1973 in a print run of 25,000 copies which was soon sold out.[36] On its appearance, Kadri Hazbiu, Minister for the Interior declared, 'I read forty pages of it and I spat forty times'.[37] Each side thought that it had won, and hoped to see Kadare's scalp held aloft as a tribute to liberalism or to orthodoxy.

The crackdown occurred in early 1973. As part of the terror, a press campaign was launched against the novel, accusing its author of anti-socialist activity and hostility towards the dictatorship of the proletariat and the class struggle. Not surprisingly, the use of the word 'solitude' in the original title, with its suggestion of criticism of the Supreme Leader, was controversial. The newspapers were flooded with critical letters (an important mode of 'popular' denunciation[38]) and meetings were convened to discuss the work. Kadare suspected at the time that Nexhmije was behind the campaign to use the novel against him, and gives substance to his accusations in the light of revelations which came about after 1991.[39] Hoxha himself remained quiet, proof for Kadare that he was tempted by the possibilities of self-representation and change implicit in the representation of him in the novel. However, he is put into a difficult situation, with his wife, Nexhmije, the Sigurimi, and the old-guard 'left-wing' pressing for retaliation against the writer and his supporters, the Soviets watching with interest (he assumes) and waiting for his response, and the liberals hoping for change. Hoxha knew that he would not find a writer to match Kadare. If the novel were banned, his flattering image as the hero of Albanian independence and nemesis of the Soviet revisionists would have to disappear from view. The Soviets would rejoice and the left wing of the Party would appear victorious. If the novel were allowed to remain in circulation, he would remain in debt to this writer who was nevertheless challenging him both through his representation of an Albania alone and impoverished in the post-war world, and as the spokesman for Albania in France and the world.

A request for the withdrawal from circulation of *The Winter of Great Solitude* was submitted in May 1973 to the Central Committee by the Secretary to the Committee of the Party of Tirana. The reasons cited were Kadare's misrepresentation of the history of the break between the Soviet Union and Albania, the inclusion of themes of existentialist anguish, 'contemporary bourgeois theory of the sexual revolution', surrealism, generational conflict, alcoholism, prostitution and other social ills, and an attitude of 'ancestral' rather than 'socialist patriotism'. Initiated by this critique, a controversy raged for several months over the novel.[40] In a further denunciation of May 1973 from the Elbasan Regional Committee the theme of 'the moral degeneration of youth' and 'feminist tendencies' are highlighted as inappropriate for Albanian literature.[41] The novel remained in circulation, but the crackdown took place, strengthening the dictatorship and giving the liberals to understand that they should not take heart at their apparent victory.

Kadare revised the manuscript, as required, and submitted it for discussion by the Party and committees. In the official response by Dalan Shpallo in November 1973, the revisions are taken into account but considered insufficient. A further list of requirements was drawn up, and Kadare's ongoing 'revisionism' was noted, along with the absence of positive figures among the intellectuals and their nostalgia for Russia, the ironic treatment of socialist principles, and implicit endorsement of 'liberalism'. The depth and detail of the official responses and analyses to the novel are an indication of how seriously literature and the written word were taken in Albania and in the socialist countries in general. Dashnor Mamaqi identifies problems of emphasis in the meeting with Khrushchev, in which prominence is given to Khrushchev's revisionism rather than to the concrete political questions of the wheat, Albano-Soviet diplomatic relations, and the importance of the naval base at Vlora. Not only the sense of 'existential distress' but also the social relationships are perverted. Even Beni, who, from an outsider's perspective, seems to fulfil the role of the socialist hero in the end, is criticized for his egoism and lack of disinterested patriotism. His and other people's love of their nation is identified as 'ancestral' rather than 'socialist patriotism, and the young people in particular lack altruism and show too much egoism.[42] The 'enemy within' (Nurihan, Rrok, Hava) is drawn too positively, and the writer places too much narrative interest in the battle between 'the capable and the incapable in socialism' (i.e. in the bureaucracy), showing the latter to be successful in using the structures to their own benefit. The partisan generation are generally 'depicted in states of spiritual, physical, and psychical decay', while those seeking entry to the Party are 'hesitant or immoral'. The inclusion of prostitution and alcoholism in socialist society is untruthful, the social influences of current bourgeois theory, existentialism, and the 'sexual revolution' are palpable, and the literary influences of 'the surrealists and other decadents' are identified. Mamaqi's thorough and acute critique ends with the submission that the novel be withdrawn.[43] These criticisms are echoed by Dalan Shpallo in his review of Kadare's first rewritten version in November 1973.[44] Considerable attention is paid to the representation of ideological and other differences in the Moscow meeting in Part Two, and questions of perspective, such as Besnik's implied distinction between himself and the Party in terms of 'them' and 'us', and of Kadare's ironic treatment of the conventions of socialist realism are raised. While little attention is paid to the novel as fiction, Shpallo draws attention to the weakness in the relationship between Besnik and Zana which drives the story and objects to the author's failure to have created a happy ending without having Besnik disobey Hoxha's command not to break his embargo on all mention of the Moscow meeting.[45]

As can be seen from these criticisms, the agents of review and censorship of literature were neither obtuse nor naive. Even given the formulaic nature of the identification of faults in the novel, some repetition of vocabulary implies that these reports were circulated informally. Kadare responded as he had to, by revising the work. Most of the inserted material concerns the representation of the older generation, which was a major item in the list of faults. It is clear that the sensitivity of the old guard to their representation in the work of this younger writer is a touchy topic. The representation of dissolute youth, also a major point, is not significantly changed in the novel. In fact Beni's redemption as a communist worker occurs in the first version. In her comments on the 1977 revised edition of the novel, Nexhmije Hoxha drew attention to the representation of Enver as 'disassociated from the government and the Party'. The amount of attention given to the pro-Soviet figures from the past, Liri Belishova, Koçi Xoxe, and Maqo Çomo, is criticized along with the representation of the Party bureaucracy.[46] In response to these criticisms Hoxha reappears in chapter 18 of the revision applauded by the students who will be repatriated as a result of the break, and again in a flashback as partisan leader. The flashbacks and reminiscences of the partisan generation vividly bring to life the experiences of hardship, deprivation, and courage of this generation. The episode in which Besnik's mother, Rabo, and the children are threatened at night in the wild by a she-wolf is striking and unforgettable as are the memories of his father, Kristaq, of the last months of the war. The representation of the counter-revolutionaries and of the bureaucracy and the 'existential anguish' of the post-war-generation protagonists are retained under the new, but also ambiguous title of *The Great Winter*. A major change of perspective is brought about in the revision through the inclusion of a supernumerary, penultimate chapter. This added chapter emphasizes Besnik's redemption by idealizing his heroic mediocrity (i.e. in a brilliantly oblique response to the critique of the unhappy ending), and strengthens the historical perspective. Besnik sits in his office reviewing letters that have been sent to his newspaper from throughout Albania in the wake of the events of the previous winter. Unlike other letters about current events, these letters about the winter of 1960 already begin to take on the contours of epic. 'Les dimensions des choses y étaient transformées et elles renfermaient d'anciens éléments épiques' ('the dimensions of things were transformed, incorporating elements of ancient epic').[47] As in the later *File on H.*, recent events are gradually pared down to their essentials in the sparse language of epic song. The events of Moscow are reduced to the symbolic details of the season, the hero, the journey and the quest.

> Où vas-tu en cet automne,
> Cette froide saison, Enver?
> La route de Moscou n'est pas bonne
> Et le gel fend la terre.
> [. . .]
> Mais tu as bravé rois et tsars,
> Tu as bravé les canons,
> Tu as poussé la porte du Moyen Age
> Et tu es entré dans le chateau. (*Le Grand hiver* 553)

> Where are you going this autumn time,
> In this cold season, Enver?
> The way to Moscow is not fair
> And the ground is split with rime.
> [. . .]
> But you have challenged kings and tsars,

> You have defied their cannon,
> You have pushed open the doors of the Middle Ages
> And have entered into the castle.

In this section, too, the 'ancestral' patriotism that was criticized in the first version is emphasized, reflecting Kadare's growing sense of national identity in opposition to that of the regime. Nevertheless, the ending of the novel is strongly pro-Albanian and anti-Soviet. Little mention is made of the West, other than as the source of counter-revolutionary bourgeois gossip of old Nurihan and her friends. Besnik discovers his role in the events transformed into epic stanzas:

> Le tourdjouman ne traduit pas bien,[48]
> Ou ne connaît-il pas le russe? (*Le Grand hiver* 556)

> The interpreter doesn't translate well,
> Perhaps he doesn't know Russian?

Besnik is astounded. This minor detail may also gradually disappear in the epic process of reduction, but the motif emphasizes the merging of Besnik's fate into that of the nation. These words come to the aid of the drowning man like floating branches in a flood.

> Au sentiment d'émerveillement de se découvrir là où il est rarement donné à quelqu'un de se voir, se substitua une émotion particulière, de celles qui semblent avoir le pouvoir de désincarner l'homme. Il n'eut pas conscience du temps que dura cet état d'envoûtement. Les vers étaient encore là, sur la table, deux rameaux brisés, que les flots de l'épopée poussaient vers lui. (*Le Grand hiver* 556)

> He was amazed at finding himself in a place where it is only rarely granted to anyone to see himself. His amazement gave way to another feeling, of appearing to see himself disembodied. He lost sense of time, unaware of how long the state of enchantment lasted. The verses were still there, on the table, two broken branches, surging toward him in the epic flood.

They and he will disappear into the depths, leaving only the oceanic totality in the process of epic inclusion and transformation. In explicitly placing Besnik's role into a romantic flow of ethno-national history, Kadare strengthens the theme of his protagonist's submission to the greater good of socialism, emphasizing the communal element where in the earlier version the sense of personal loss predominated. At the same time, Kadare's 'ancestral patriotism' also suggests a flow of history deeper and broader than the present or the post-war — communist — era. In the heroic song even the activities of Enver Hoxha are merely the most recent phenomenon in the chronicle of eternal Albania, taking up a few lines at most. The author thus, in the second version, signals a more distanced view of the epic-heroic figure of the dictator. He, too, is merely a figure in Albanian history, alongside Constantine, Scanderbeg, and Ali Pasha, on the path toward nationhood and national identity.

Nexhmije's detailed corrections and emendations of the reworked manuscript shed light on her character and on an aspect of the regime.[49] She provides a list of phrases and expressions which need to be changed and suggests alternatives. Nexhmije's interventions are multiple, minor, even pettifogging. Nexhmije lacked Enver's brilliance and cunning. She contributed the force of a dogmatic fundamentalism.[50] Underlying her comments, however, is a recognition of the importance of the text and of the necessity of providing the correct formulations for the guidance of the people. She, like other powerful figures, intended that Kadare would either change or be destroyed.[51] The dramatist and faithful party-liner, Uruçi, wrote to Nexhmije supporting the novel and its author and was deported for his pains.[52]

Ultimately this novel would be remembered in terms of the representation of Hoxha and of his heroic stand against Khrushchev. All mention of the irony and political satire is avoided in the official history of Albanian literature of 1980:

> Le côté le plus fort du roman réside dans le tableau de la lutte que mena le fondateur et le dirigeant du Parti, le camarade Enver Hoxha, dans la réunion des 81 partis communists et ouvriers, tenue à Moscou en novembre 1960. [. . .] Kadare a su brosser avec chaleur et véridicité les qualités de marxiste-léniniste éminent et de révolutionnaire sans défaillance du camarade Enver Hoxha, son hardiesse, son esprit de principe élevé, son sang-froid devant les situations extrêmement difficiles, sa confiance inébranlable dans la justesse du marxisme-léninisme, dans les forces du peuple albanais, dans la fermeté du Parti qui a engagé sa lutte contre les nouveaux ennemis du mouvement communiste mondial.[53]

> The strongest aspect of the novel lies in the scene of conflict in which the founder and leader of the Party, Comrade Enver Hoxha takes on the 81 communist and workers' parties at the reunion in Moscow in November 1960. [. . .] Kadare knows how to depict with warmth and truthfulness the pre-eminent, revolutionary Marxist-Leninist virtues of Comrade Enver Hoxha, his bravery, his heightened sense of principle, his sang-froid in situations of extreme difficulty, his unwavering confidence in the rightness of Marxism-Leninism, in the power of the Albanian people, and in the steadfastness of the Party, which has sallied forth into battle against the new enemies of world communism.

The fully emended version of *Winter of Great Solitude* was republished in 1978 under the title *The Great Winter*.[54] (It had been referred to by this title earlier on, for example in the request for censorship dated 8 May 1973 from the Central Committee.) This revision was the version first translated into French and published in Paris in 1978. The original version has since been published independently in French and has been included in volume 7 of the Fayard *Œuvres* as the first part of a diptych along with *The Concert*, Kadare's semi-sequential satirical novel about the Albanian–Chinese alliance.

Corrective Mask

The belief in pedagogy and the possibility of correction was ubiquitous in the Marxist-Leninist regimes. It underwrote the rituals of self-criticism and the show trials; it enabled political change and invited manipulation. There was an entrenched belief in the upper echelons of the regime, often cynically applied and misused, that everyone could be brought to recognize the right path through assiduous study of the appropriate dogmas and teachings. A Stalin or an Enver Hoxha could use the processes of self-criticism and correction to identify, break down, and, if necessary, liquidate opposition. Hoxha learned this lesson in 1948 when himself was cornered by the pro-Yugoslav Koçi Xoxe over his infraction of the Party line regarding relations with Yugoslavia.[55] In *The Great Winter* Kadare tried to manipulate this homage to the belief in change and improvement, turning the regime's strategies back on itself. Just as socialist realism aimed to provide an iconic image of life in the communist future by showing the positive and progressive workings of history in individuals and communities, so Kadare hoped to encourage the dictator to view himself in terms of a positive dialectic. He tried to turn this thinking back onto the regime itself, believing that literature could act as a 'corrective mask', which, accepted by the dictator as his 'good' face, would exert an ameliorating effect:

> C'est ainsi, petit à petit, devant ce dossier hivernal, que naquit en moi l'idée du *masque* correcteur. Un masque qu'il accepterait de porter en viendrait-il à corriger les traits du tyran? (*Le Poids* 337)

> And so, little by little as I was working on the wintry file, the idea of the corrective mask was born in me. Would it correct the traits of the tyrant, a mask like this, that he himself would wear?

The idea of using literature and the imagination to educate the powerful more or less subtly in the right use of power can be traced back to antiquity (Seneca's *De clementia*) and throughout the Middle Ages. As the *Fürstenspiegel* or 'mirror for princes' it became an important form of political literature in the absolutist period, exemplified in works such as Eramus's *Education of a Christian Prince* (1516), and François Fénelon's *Télémaque* (1699), written in order to educate and instil a sense of duty into the future kings of France and Burgundy. Literature in the dictatorship, too, Kadare hoped, would provide gentle but firm pressure, a brace, to allow the healthy development of the socialist regime. 'Like Erasmus in the *Praise of Folly*', write Elisabeth and Jean-Paul Champseix, Kadare hoped to be able 'to transform the tyrant, by offering him a "corrective mask." He would agree to wear it and would become its captive'.[56] But it was in vain. Unlike his wife, Enver Hoxha knew that he, the dictator, was above correction, even from his nemesis the writer.

At this stage, Kadare still thought that the 'corrective mask' might serve the ruler's covert intention to seek rapprochement with the West. He knew that Hoxha's motivating interest was his personal vanity, not the fate of Albania. Like Tito he might be flattered by the attentions of the West if he received the right encouragement and pretext.

> Les agissements malfaisants qu'il avait commis jusqu'alors pouvaient lui être pardonnés, comme ils l'avaient été à Tito. (Il convient toutefois de préciser qu'à l'époque il n'avait pas encore perpétré la plus grande part de ses crimes.) [. . .] Désormais, il lui était possible de s'acheminer dans une autre voie, avec un autre visage ou un autre masque, comme l'acteur qui réapparaît sur scène dans un rôle différent. En faisant sien ce masque, il pouvait s'y adapter, tout comme le bandit italien capturé par erreur par suite de sa ressemblance avec le général Rovere et qui fut si ravi de cette confusion qu'il accepta d'être fusillé à sa place comme héros, pourvu qu'on ne le privât pas de ce masque prestigieux. (*Le Poids* 332–33)

> The harm which he had committed up until then could have been pardoned for him as it had been for Tito. (We must keep in mind that by that stage he had not yet perpetrated the most heinous of his crimes.) [. . .] From then on it would have been possible for him to move towards a different path, to adopt a different countenance or to change his mask, like an actor who reappears on the scene in a different role. In making this new visage his own, he could adapt himself to it, just like the Italian crook captured by mistake and believed to be General Rovere. He was so flattered by the mis-identification that he agreed to be shot in the general's place, provided that he not be deprived of his prestigious mask.

The reference to Roberto Rossellini's 1959 film, *Generale delle Rovere*, perhaps reveals Kadare's underestimation of Hoxha at this time as a partisan leader gone astray rather than as a narcissistic and pathological megalomaniac. Rossellini's film contains an element of fairy-tale or operetta in the transformation of conman to hero. Bertone, the petty criminal with a good heart at the time of the Allied armistice in Italy, chooses patriotism over capitulation after being caught by the Nazis. Like Brecht in *Arturo Ui*, Kadare fails to recognize the true nature of the beast. *Winter of Great Solitude* was the only work in which Kadare deliberately tried to intervene in the political processes, occupying a space between his 'second world' of literature and the 'first world' of reality. Other works took political themes, such as *November of a Capital*, the short novel about the liberation of Tirana by the partisans in 1944, written in 1974 in the wake of *The Great Winter*. And he continued to write more or less obliquely about political themes. But he never again engaged the dictator directly in the political field.

In retrospect Kadare is defensive of his decision to write *The Great Winter*:

> Je ne me suis jamais repenti de la voie que l'ai choisie. Sans le roman *Le Grand hiver*, quatre-vingts pour cent de mon œuvre n'auraient jamais pu être écrits. (*Le Poids* 329)[57]

> I never regretted having chosen this path. Without the novel, *The Great Winter*, eighty per cent of my work would never have been written.

The novel created an alibi for the completion of other works. From 1969 when he applied for access to the files until 1972 when the novel was finished, Kadare was left alone. During this period he wrote the historical novel *The Castle*, and the autobiographical *Chronicle in Stone*. With the storm that broke over *The Great Winter* in 1973 and with the hardening and isolation of the dictatorship, his period of protection was over.

The Purge of the Liberals and the End of the Chinese Alliance, 1973–1978

In *The Weight of the Cross* Kadare reads the events of 1973 and the new frost in terms of the reception of his novel. However, the regime was confronted with a range of internal and external problems with which it had to deal. The novel *Winter of the Great Solitude* and the affair surrounding it were symptomatic of broader contextual issues. According to Bernard Tönnes, Hoxha 'clearly recognized, that a spiritual climate had come about whose pluralistic tendencies threatened to fragment the monolithic "unity of the nation" that he had propagated'.[58] During this crucial period decisions would be made which would determine the final phase of the regime.

On 17 January 1968, a monument was unveiled in Scanderbeg Square to celebrate the 500th anniversary of the death of the Albanian national hero.[59] The statue of Scanderbeg displaced that of Stalin and was strongly associated with the leader, Enver Hoxha. 'Just as the Albanians then dared to stand alone under Scanderbeg, so they would now under Hoxha', proclaimed Mehmet Shehu at the opening.[60] The statue heralded a new direction in the nation's development, away from the alliance with the Chinese Stalinist 'big brother' Mao Tse-tung and towards a new isolationism, embellished as Albanian nationalism. In the following year, Ramiz Alia, the Party's 'cultural commissar', noted that the main task of the Party now was 'to cleanse the superstructure of [Albanian] society of everything alien to it', linking the nationalism of the Party to the coming cultural revolution.[61] Hoxha-as-Scanderbeg officially replaced Stalin as the heir and continuation of Marxism-Leninism and the fourth member of the leadership of world communism, Mao Tse-tung, disappeared altogether.

In fact, the alliance with China had begun to weaken quite early as a result of the failure of the new ally to provide the level of goods and services expected by the regime. While China still provided a huge subsidy to Albania in 1970, by the time of the 6th Albanian Party of Labour conference in November 1971, relations had cooled dramatically and no Chinese delegation attended. Mao's 1972 meeting with Richard Nixon marked the beginning of the end, after which Chinese socialism, like that of Yugoslavia and the Soviet Union, was irremediably corrupted by the ideological 'revisionism' of Chairman Mao's 'three-worlds' theory of global power relations. For the next five years, until the break in 1977, the relationship with China would remain troubled. In September 1976 Mao Tse-tung died and leadership of the Party passed to relative moderates, leaving Hoxha further isolated in both political and doctrinal terms. At the 7th Party Congress Hoxha announced less reliance on China. The discovery of a conspiracy led to purges of Soviet-trained senior officials. In 1977 after sixteen years of 'unbreakable friendship', attacks on China began to appear in the press, and an article, probably by Hoxha himself, was published in *Zëri i Popullit* criticizing the 'three-worlds' theory with which the Chinese leadership justified its new openness to the United States and the West. Chinese aid had been dramatically reduced and the invitation to Marshal Tito to visit China was viewed as an insult to Albanian–Chinese relations (although Albanian-Yugoslav relations improved and trade increased over the same period). In a scenario familiar from 1961, Chinese workers were withdrawn from Albania, although diplomatic ties were retained. Far from masking a turn towards the West, as had been hoped by many, the Chinese alliance masked the regime's turn inward towards a grim politics of isolation. For the rest of the post-war period Albania became even more of an enigma on the edge of Europe.

The second problem faced by the regime at this time was generational. In the early 1970s people under thirty made up over 60 per cent of the Albanian population.[62] As with the rest of Europe, the post-war generation was coming of age and was beginning to move from passive resistance to more active opposition to the oppressive regime of their fathers' generation and the centralized control of the Party. They did not remember the war years, which were so formative for the attitudes of the older generations. Generational differences had been foregrounded by Kadare in his earliest work, *The City without Signs*, but youth and 'youth culture' became a major issue in 1972 when hooliganism, youth crime, and failures and expulsions of students from the University of Tirana increased, leading Enver Hoxha to ask: 'how can Communists, whose children turn into hooligans, vagabonds, and purveyors of extravagant bourgeois fashions and tastes, be in the vanguard and set and example for others?'.[63] In addition to the existentialist intellectual influences of Kierkegaard, Sartre, Camus, and Marcuse, various 'alternative' scenes developed, influenced by Italian (and Yugoslav) television[64], and characterized by the long hair, jeans, and miniskirts of the European and American youth movements.[65] Tönnes notes concern at rising levels of alcoholism among students.[66] Where youth vagrancy or dropping out in the West was a form of protest against consumer society, in Albania, according to Tönnes, it was directed against the 'Spartan discipline and spiritual sterility of the Party'. Young people were sick of having their lives planned out for them. They were not able to choose their fashions, vocation, place of work, or where they could live. They were consigned anonymously to employment positions 'as if they were soldiers in a nation at war'.[67] Of course, behaviours which in the West would scarcely have raised an eyebrow even then were quickly identified as youth rebelliousness by the puritanical ideologues in the Albanian environment.[68] Influenced by the earlier Soviet wave, Kadare himself had been a forerunner and representative of this generation. His early works are full of young people influenced via the media by Western fashions.

The young artistic intelligentsia had become more confident in arguing that Albanian socialist realism had nothing to fear from comparison with Western works, a line which was urged strongly in the context of world youth solidarity at the Sixth Congress of the Youth League in October 1972. At a song-festival held in late December 1972, which turned into something of an Albanian *Woodstock*, calls were made for global youth solidarity. In the report of the LYUA (Labour Youth Union of Albania) to the Party of 1974 the separation from Europe and the world was a major issue.

Signs of political opposition to the policy of isolation were also emerging in the political sphere. With the tacit support of the Chinese, Politburo member, Deputy Chairman of the Council of Ministers, and Minister for Defence, Beqir Balluku, supported the creation of a wider defence network along the axis Bucharest–Belgrade–Tirana. Balluku also criticized Hoxha's policy of isolationism and defence strategies (the concrete bunkers built at great cost throughout the impoverished country against attack from the West). The implicit critique of the new nationalist isolationism was a provocation to Hoxha, who used it as a pretext for a major series of purges of liberals. Hoxha's strategy was, as ever, partial and oblique to begin with. He set about cleaning up the 'pollution' in the areas of culture, literature, and entertainment. In the wake of the broadcast of the song festival, complaints came pouring in to the newspapers and local party offices throughout the country about the bourgeois and revisionist poison that this festival represented for the nation's youth. In 1973 Hoxha called a meeting to discuss the report of the Labour Youth Union of Albania (LYUA) in which complaints were aired about the failure of the leadership to understand 'the concerns, requirements, interests, and problems' of young people, the focus on the partisan generation in education, films, theatre and literature, and the repressive isolationism that separated young people from their peers in the communist East, not to mention capitalist West.[69] The leaders of the youth movement, Agim Mero, Rudi Monari, and Asim Bedalli, were arrested. In mid-1973 Todi Lubonja the director of media and television, was arrested and imprisoned, an 'Albanian Bukharin' in Kadare's words, and scapegoat for the liberal intelligentsia.[70] Lubonja was associated with more liberal thinking in the upper echelons of the regime. He was a friend of Kadare and advocate of the novel *Winter of Great Solitude*. The purge of liberal party officials included the writer, cultural functionary, Central Committee member, President of the Albanian Popular Assembly and General Secretary of the Council of the National Front, and editor of *Zëri i Popullit*, Fadil Paçrami and most of the leading figures of the Albanian Union of Writers (with the exception of Dritëro Agolli).[71] Lubonja and Paçrami were accused of 'bourgeois liberalism' and were sentenced to long periods of incarceration. Hard-liners called for Lubonja's execution.

In the following year Hoxha carried out a direct attack on leading political figures such as General Beqir Balluku. Balluku had been a loyal supporter of Hoxha and the Albanian Party line, especially in 1956 (when Hoxha was criticized for ignoring the conclusions of the 20th Congress of the Soviet Communist Party), and in the battles with Khrushchev in 1960–61.[72] He was denounced at the Fourth Plenum in June 1974, removed from office, and is believed to have been executed as an 'arch-traitor' working for Chou En-lai in the interests of China.[73] In 1975 the director of the State Planning commission, Abdyl Këllëzi, the minister of industry and mines, Koço Theodhosi, and the minister of trade, Kiço Ngela, were identified as conspirators 'inspired by foreign revisionist enemies' in the wake of moves to loosen up the tightly centralized economic system and were purged.[74] Even Ramiz Alia, Hoxha's new second-in-command, was under threat. But then something happened which was typical of Hoxha's dictatorship. Ramiz Alia was not only spared: he was promoted.

> Mais puisque, dans l'esprit du tyran, son dauphin potentiel était toujours porteur, en même temps que de la promesse de la couronne, du signe de la mort, précisément à cet instant, alors qu'il était sur le point de l'expédier sous terre, voilà qu'il décide le contraire: non seulement de lui accorder la vie sauve, mais d'en faire officiellement son successeur. Ainsi, comme il advient souvent sous les dictatures quand les relations entre les événements sont de caractère onirique, cet oisillon effrayé et transi de Ramiz Alia tire son épingle du jeu tandis que les deux vieux loups du régime, M. Shehu et H. Kapo, qui se sentaient plus près que jamais des cimes du pouvoir, sont voués au trépas. (*Le Poids* 373)

> In the mind of the tyrant, the heir apparent was always the bearer of the promised crown and of the sign of death. Just at the moment when the tyrant is on the point of expediting his potential heir to the nether regions, the next

thing you know, he has decided to do the opposite: not just grant him his life, but to make him officially his successor. Because of this, as happened often in the dictatorships where the relationships between events are of a dream-like nature, the scared and fearful fledgling, Ramiz Alia, pulled out of the game while he still could. The two old wolves of the regime, M. Shehu and H. Kapo, were thus left high and dry. Just at the point where they thought they were closer than ever to the summit of power, they were doomed.

Kadare would represent the contradictory and dreamlike workings of the dictatorship in his greatest novel, *The Palace of Dreams*, in which the promotion of the weak and biddable Mark-Alem follows in the wake of the sedition of the Quprili family and the execution of his cousin Kurt in scenes of wild political intrigue.

Hoxha showed extraordinary cunning in turning this groundswell of opposition to his isolationist policy into an alibi for making the complete break with the socialist as well as the capitalist world. The denunciation of Balluku as an agent of China led to the ending of relationships with the Asian communist power and to complete political and social isolation. The extent of the terror waxed and waned in response to specific incidents, but the 1970s and early 1980s were characterized by extreme and unpredictable acts of repression at the hands of the dictator and his inner circle. Whereas in the Soviet Union the Brezhnev era was characterized by the stability which was a long-term outcome of Khrushchev's realignment of government with the Party, in Albania the era after the break with the Soviet Union was typified in Hoxha's reduction of the real powers of the Party and its committees and, as the 1980s began, increasingly aberrant, paranoid behaviour.

The policy changes effected during the period of the frost from around 1972 until 1976 were cemented into place through the adoption of the new constitution, which replaced the Soviet-inspired Constitution of 1946. While the decision to draft a new constitution was made at the 6th Congress of the Party in November 1971, the 1976 document, according to Prifti, was based on the need to justify the 'great socio-economic transformations' that had taken place by 1975, rendering the old constitution obsolete after the end of the transition into complete socialism with the full nationalization of agriculture, industry, and property. The new document also placed the Communist Party at the centre of power, where the old constitution barely mentioned it.[75] The 1976 constitution emerged 'as a militant and consistently oligarchic and state-oriented document', confirming the Party under Enver Hoxha as the driving force of the Albanian nation.[76] The official name of the country became The People's Socialist Republic of Albania, the Party of Labour of Albania was the sole directing political power, and the First Secretary of the Central Committee was Commander-in-Chief of the Armed Forces (i.e. taking Balluku's old role) as well as Chairman of the Defence Council. Private property and taxation were abolished, equal rights were formally attained for both sexes, religious foundations were declared void, and the practice of religion declared illegal (recognizing the state of affairs that had existed *de facto* since 1967). Measures such as the abolition of military rank and the so-called democratization of the armed forces had been adopted from the Chinese at the time of the Cultural Revolution in 1967–68, but also appealed to Hoxha and Shehu as a corrective to modernizing voices in the regime who favoured an 'elitist army not under direct control of the Party'.[77]

'The Red Pashas', 1974

The two works that Kadare wrote in 1974 illustrate the ambiguity of the writer
and his situation. *November of a Capital*, the short novel of the liberation of Tirana
in 1944, continued the story of the young communist partisan Javer in *Chronicle in
Stone*. It is a politically safe tale, in which any suggestion of impropriety in the figure
of Enver Hoxha is avoided and the partisans are lauded as saviours of the nation.
In January 1974 Kadare wrote the poem, 'At Midnight the Politburo met . . .',
commonly known as 'The Red Pashas'. In this work Kadare accuses those around
the dictator of the major responsibility for the corruption, nepotism, and disarray
of the country. The poem belongs to a tradition of Central European political
literature in which it is not the king or leader, but his corrupt advisers who are to
blame for the ills of the country. This literary product of enlightened absolutism
sought to improve politics by appealing to the sovereign to cleanse his government
of its corrupted servants. It was most successful in those cases where the critique
exposed the contradictions of enlightened absolutism: of the systemic weakness
which gives power to a weak mortal, in works such as Voltaire's *Le taureau blanc*,
Schiller's *Kabale und Liebe* or Lessing's *Emilia Galotti*. In post-revolutionary Soviet
literature, for example, Lenin is surrounded by fallen or corrupted communists, or
the ideal of communism is surrounded by a corrupted praxis. It is also a form of
'corrective mask'. Kadare's poem was thus not a direct attack on Hoxha, but rather
on the Party, including the Politburo and the nomenklatura.

> Les Etats ne se détruisent jamais à partir du toit
> Même si la pluie s'infiltre par ça et là.
> Ils se détruisent par les fondations. A cette loi
> L'état socialiste obéit aussi.[78]

> States are not destroyed from the rooftops
> though the water seeps in somewhere,
> They're destroyed from their foundations.
> Socialist states are subject
> To this principle too.[79]

The 'red pashas' undermine the Revolution and pillage the bloodied insignia of
wealth and power from the tombs of the pre-revolutionary aristocracy, the beys
and the landowners:

> Sont enterrées les classes renversées:
> Pachas, beys, grandes familles
> Ils se précipitent, retournent les corps ensevelis
> Qu'ils dévêtent dans un élan sinistre.
> Les habits des puissants ensanglantés
> Avec médailles et galons, ils les endossent vite

> Here is where the overthrown caste was buried,
> The pashas, beys, and noble families,
> they attack, turn the bodies over and begin
> Without delay to strip them bare.
> The bloodstained robes of the former rulers
> They don quickly, with orders and medals.

The ink of the bureaucrat becomes the blood of the victims, scrubbed away in the night:

> Non pas baveux et souillés d'encre
> Comme des imbéciles heureux ho, ho, ho,
> Mais perfidement
> Avec les mains ensanglantées
> Jusqu'aux coudes.
> [. . .]
> Regarde,
> Ils semblent laver les corps.

> Not with Pelikan ink they're covered,
> That fine, eccentric bunch, ha, ha,
> No, they are evil,
> I see them with their hands
> Bathed in blood up to the elbows.
> [. . .]
> But take a look,
> It appears they are washing the bodies

Hoxha is imagined as identifying the rot and cleansing the country by revisiting it with the torch of communism and putting to flight the phantoms taking over the new roles of power in the guise of the 'red pashas'.

> Enver Hoxha à l'œil vigilant
> Etait le premier qui eut un doute
> Et alors, dans les fondations de l'Etat
> Il descendit comme dans la grande ballade
> Un flambeau rouge à la main
> La terre trembla
> La flamme sur eux tomba.
> Et il les vit corrompre le sang des martyrs
> Et se partager les manteaux il les vit.
> [. . .]
> Il n'était pas le Christ pour les chasser
> De l'Etat avec un fouet et un bâton.
> Il fit se lever la classe ouvrière
> Pour river les bureaucrates.

> Enver Hoxha with his eagle eye
> Was the first to have doubts about them.
> He then descended to the foundations
> Of the state, as in the great ballads of old.
> He bore a red torch in his hand,
> The very earth quivered,
> The light of the fire fell upon them,
> And he saw them effacing the blood of our martyrs
> As they were dividing up the cloaks.
> [. . .]
> He was not Christ, to drive them from power
> With a whip and a club.
> He raised the working class
> To make Communism thrive.

FIG. 17 (above): Ismail Kadare at the time of 'The Red Pashas'.
(Photo: Private collection of Ismail Kadare.)

FIG. 18 (below): Ismail and Helena Kadare in 1978.
(Photo: Private collection of Ismail Kadare. Copyright M. Maillot.)

While there is perhaps some ambivalence in the negative comparison with Christ, the poem is aimed squarely at the socialist bureaucracy and belongs to a genre which was common in socialist environments, namely the critique of the apparatchiks and careerists. It is comparable in some ways to traditional Catholic anti-clericalism. Hoxha appears as a saviour, the classic 'good ruler', who acts in the interest of the people against his corrupted functionaries as soon as he becomes aware of their nefarious activities. However, the key to this type of critique in the absolutist tradition was the implicit understanding that the corruption is systemic, that even if the particular ruler is good, the system itself is fatally flawed. Most striking, perhaps, was the bloodthirsty imagery, which was shocking in the context of the traditional communist paeans to the country's leaders.

Dritëro Agolli the President of the Union of Writers, alerted Pirro Kondi, member of the Central Committee, to the themes of crisis and counter-revolution in the work, writing that Kadare shows the Party as 'no longer able to govern'.[80] As a result, the poem was withdrawn from publication and submitted for Party discussion. A meeting was called and Agolli presented a detailed critique, noting the ideological and historical errors and relating them to Kadare's earlier work. The poem was judged to be more than just a critique of corrupt bureaucracy: it was anti-socialist, and revisionist, showing influences of Western ideologies and the critiques by figures such as Djilas (theorist of the 'new class' of socialist bureaucrats) and Togliatti.[81] The unknown factor in Hoxha's attitude towards Kadare underpins the carefulness with which the poem's positive representation of the leader is questioned. The memory of the leader's intervention on behalf of the young renegade writers in 1961 was not quickly forgotten. If Kadare sought to drive a wedge between Hoxha and the Party, the latter in its response emphasized the revolutionary unity of the people, the Party and the leader, and the schismatic role of the writer.

On 25 October 1975 Kadare was obliged to submit a self-criticism before a committee of the Party held in the offices of the Union of Writers. The author admitted to having written and submitted for publication a work 'hostile, anti-revolutionary, directed against the Party line, against the regime, the dictatorship of the proletariat and the people'.[82] Kadare's speech seems provocative as the writer reminds his listeners that his long history of ideologically unsound writing has been extraordinarily successful both in Albania and overseas. However, there is more to the story than meets the eye. Kadare knew that his enemies in the party were mainly on the so-called 'left', of the old guard, or Nexhmije Hoxha and the Sigurimi. He also knew that the accusation of ideological confusion was a relatively harmless one in his situation. He could afford to admit to errors in tact and judgement, blaming them on his insufficient education in Marxism-Leninism.[83] In the criticism of this work was embedded a more threatening accusation. Kadare was warned that writing for a foreign audience would alienate him from his duty as a communist writer. The implicit accusation of subversion, of being an agent for the West, was extremely dangerous and Kadare knew that his enemies on the left were pushing their accusations in this direction as far as they dared. He must avoid any association with this cardinal sin in Enver Hoxha's universe, while accepting responsibility for other less threatening misdemeanours. Hence he accepted many of the lesser charges of arrogance, ideological confusion, even revisionism, but obdurately rejected imputations of treasonous activity. The members of the Union of Writers were not necessarily well-disposed towards Kadare, but they were not his worst enemies; the other members of the committee drawn from the Politburo were potentially more dangerous. Those judging Kadare, however, also needed to keep their wits about them. Hoxha might turn on them in a move calculated to divide and rule as he had done in 1961. At the second sitting in which members were required to respond to the self-criticism, the atmosphere was less aggressive.

In *Autumn of Fear*, the documentation of his family's fall, Bashkim Shehu writes that he had warned Kadare in the early 1970s of the attempts by powerful members of the regime to bring him down.[84] Kadare was considered an agent of foreign secret services by some of the most powerful figures in the regime, including Shehu's father, Mehmet, at that time still the second-in-command to Hoxha.[85] Rumours and allegations of espionage were raised again and again by Kadare's enemies in the regime. In a letter to Kadare, written in 1991 after Shehu's release from prison, Shehu informs the writer that in 1981 as a result of his father's fall from grace, he had been interrogated by the Sigurimi over the course of a week. Even the Vice-Minister of the Interior, Rexhep Kolli, was involved in combing for evidence to support the accusation that Kadare was a long-standing enemy of the people, engaged in espionage against the Albanian state. Hence Kadare's self-criticisms for anti-revolutionary thinking, ideological confusion, and bourgeois false consciousness remained anodyne despite the fullness of the documentation; the real danger lay in the background and remained unspoken at the second sitting.

As part of the ritual of self-criticism the culprit was required to suggest a punishment appropriate for his misdemeanours. Kadare proposed banishment from Tirana in order to 'reflect on the ways in which he might make good his errors' in rural central Albania.[86] The Party Secretary informed him that 'on orders from above' he should 'leave the city immediately and abstain from literary work'. The message was clear: to stop writing would mean to change his identity completely, to cease being Ismail Kadare. The plan to change the dictator had backfired badly:

> 'Ecoute', me dit-il. Ce que veut le Parti, c'est que tu changes radicalement'. [.
> . .] Avec ses signes annonciateurs, ses symboles interprétés par la psychanalyse:
> les papillons, les vers à soie, le travestissement . . . Tout cela, je l'avais cherché
> en songeant au dictateur, sans me douter un seul instant que le sort me l'avait
> réservé à moi-même! Je devais donc me tranformer. [. . .] Peu à peu, je pris
> conscience de la vérité nue. Mon interlocuteur me signifiait clairement que je
> ne devais plus écrire, hormis quelque reportage ou croquis. Plus tard, peut-être,
> un petit récit, au mieux une nouvelle, mais un roman, jamais plus. Un roman,
> non, répéta-t-il. (*Le Poids* 383–84)

> 'Listen', he said to me. 'What the Party wants is for you to change radically'.
> [. . .] Using psychoanalysis I had researched the warning signs in the dictator.
> The symbols, the butterflies, the silk-worms, the dressing up . . . I went on
> dreaming, without doubting for a moment what fate had in store for me. It was
> I who had to change. [. . .] Little by little I became aware of the hard reality. My
> interlocutor indicated clearly to me that I was not allowed to write any longer,
> apart from the odd reportage or sketch. Later, maybe, a short story, or perhaps
> a novella, but a novel? Never again. 'A novel, no', he repeated.

Yet the controversy brought literature to the attention of the whole country, not just the Party, the intellectuals, and the nomenklatura. The country's leading writer had dared to criticize the regime.[87]

'The Red Pashas' became a focal point in the controversy over Kadare's status under the dictatorship. It was written in early 1974 at the time of frost associated with the break with China and the turn inward under the guise of Albanian nationalism. Kadare sent the manuscript to the magazine *Drita* in the second half of October 1975.[88] From that point on its fate was unclear. It was not published and the manuscript disappeared. Kadare's critics subsequently questioned whether it had existed at all, suggesting that Kadare had fabricated the story of the critical poem after the fall of the regime in 1990 in order to distance himself from the government and profile himself retrospectively as a dissident intellectual. Looking back from an environment of photocopiers, digital copies, and freedom from censorship, it may seem strange to us that a document such as this could disappear so entirely from view. However, in the environment where access to copying was restricted, where loose or unfinalized formulations in manuscripts and drafts could be dangerous if seized by the authorities, and where the finalized version disappeared into the type of secretive bureaucracy that Kadare would depict in *The Palace of Dreams*, all traces of a work could indeed vanish. The artist and writer Maks Velo published a documentation of the controversy in Albania in 2002, and the then general director of the Albanian national archives, Shaban Sinani, set about searching for the manuscript in the regime's archives. He discovered it, and, with the author's permission, published it, proving that it existed.[89]

The deep ambivalence in Kadare's early writing about the dictator lent depth to the images of the tyrant in Kadare's work, and fuelled the suspicions of his detractors that he was sympathetic to, and a participant in Albanian communism. But Kadare was not sympathetic to Hoxha or to communism as an ideal or an ideology, although he certainly welcomed aspects of the modernization of his country. During the 1960s he saw in Hoxha a figure of national significance, as a particularly Albanian type of leader and patriot. Later he would recognize the narcissistic psychopath, regarding Hoxha with the abhorrence that comes of intimacy, of the closeness of their family backgrounds, and with an Oedipal intensity as he competed with him for the voice of Albania. Kadare would increasingly view his battle with Enver Hoxha as a personal mission to save the soul of his native land. The details of politics, even of the nature of communism, became less and less important to him. He saw himself increasingly as Prometheus to Hoxha's Zeus. The era of Kadare's ambivalence ended with *Winter of Great Solitude*.

After the crisis of the mid-1970s over *The Great Winter* and 'The Red Pashas', traces of the early defiance remained but the older writer became more self-conscious, cautious, and premeditated.[90] The outcome was a tacit stand-off between the writer and the dictator which would obtain until the publication of *The Palace of Dreams* a decade later.

> Je finissais par rester seul face au tyran, avec ce masque dont je m'évertuais encore à recouvrir ses traits, tandis que lui, gesticulant, tenant de le repousser, cherchait à m'éborgner. Dès lors, tout devenait limpide: ce masque le blessait.
> (*Le Poids* 374)

I finished up face to face with the tyrant, with that mask in which I had tried my best to conceal his characteristics, while he, gesticulating wildly and pushing it away, tried to poke my eyes out. From then on everything became clear: the mask was wounding him.

Kadare's 'Second Chronology'

As a young man Kadare showed a certain arrogance towards the regime and the powers that be. There was also a component of bluff in his first showdown with the old guard in 1961 over the writing of the post-war generation. As a member of the intelligentsia since returning from Moscow, he had entered directly into an echelon of the regime that put him on first-name terms with the holders of power. Figures such as Ramiz Alia, Nexhmije Hoxha and even, after the late 1960s, Enver Hoxha, were closely aware of his activities. The interpersonal dynamics of this regime, as of others in the Eastern bloc countries, were complex, and clan or family allegiances, personality, and usefulness or instrumentality all played a part. Those who crossed Hoxha on political issues were quickly dispatched into labour camps or to execution squads. Figures such as Liri Belishova and Todi Lubonja received long prison sentences, and those threatening his personal power, such as Koçi Xoxe, Hysni Kapo, or, later, Mehmet Shehu, were liquidated in one way or another. Writers, particularly Catholic writers, had been executed in the late 1940s, often as a part of the general policy of terror.

> En Albanie, après l'exécution, en 1945, de plusieurs écrivains catholiques comme Anton Harapi, il n'y eut plus d'emprisonnement d'autres personnalités éminentes de la literature en dehors de deux écrivains réputés, Dhimitër Pasko et Petro Marko, emprisonnés en 1947 puis amnesties un an plus tard.[91]

> In Albania, after the execution in 1945 of several Catholic writers, such as Anton Harapi, imprisonment of eminent literary figures did not occur, with the exception of the two well-known writers Dhimitër Pasko and Petro Marko, who were imprisoned in 1947 and then pardoned a year later.

Others, such as the great national poet Lasgush Poradeci (born in 1900), who belonged to earlier generations and refused to be drawn into any relationship with the regime, were ultimately consigned to oblivion and 'a slow death' in rural backwaters.[92] While at a certain level of eminence, there was some safety for writers, a wrong sentence or public utterance by a little-known figure and/or political dissident could result in draconian punishments or even death. Maks Velo has documented the numbers of little-known writers and artists, whose fate would not be reported overseas to the detriment of the dictator's reputation, who suffered extraordinary judgments, ranging from long periods of imprisonment, often in solitary confinement, to labour camps and execution.[93] The unknown young poets Trifon Xhaghika, Vilson Blloshmi, and Genc Leka were shot merely for having written poems that were too lyrical. Reading their poems describing the advent of autumn, the falling leaves, the mist on the fields, and the departure of the migrating birds, Kadare reflects on their lost lives and his own survival. 'Tout était flou, comme dans *Le Procès* de Kafka. Je sentis que tous estimaient que c'était bien peu. Pour de telles accusations, d'autres étaient allés directement en prison, voire devant le peloton d'exécution' ('Everything was hazy, just as in Kakfa's *Trial*. [. . .] I felt that everyone considered this light [i.e. the punishment]. Others had been sent directly to prison, not to say in front of the firing squad for the same accusations').[94] His own crimes, he writes, were serious, but others were punished, not he. 'J'étais conscient que certains payaient pour les autres afin d'alimenter la terreur' ('I was aware that some of them were paying for others, to feed the terror').[95] Unknown individuals such as minor poets or expendable bureaucrats would be sacrificed in order to keep the powerful in line.[96] Kadare was both exposed to and protected from physical threat, but this itself constituted a form of everyday terror which relied on opacity and unpredictability for its effect. Kadare's description to Alain Bosquet of Hoxha's strategies reveals the leader's cynicism in dealing with writers:

> Sa tactique à l'égard des écrivains les plus en vue consistait à ne pas les attaquer. Se croyant non seulement le plus grand homme d'état, mais aussi l'intellectuel albanais le plus éminent de tous les temps, il repoussait l'idée que l'on pût reprocher d'avoir attaqué un écrivain.[97]

> His tactic towards the better-known writers consisted of not attacking them. Believing himself to be not only the State's leading person but also the most eminent Albanian intellectual of all time, he rejected the idea that he should ever be reproached for having attacked a writer.

Hoxha and the regime believed that figures such as Kadare, who did not hold power directly, were of more use alive than dead or incarcerated. Such figures could bargain for freedoms that both greater and lesser figures could not. Kadare was aware of this aspect of his relationship to the holders of power. The regime's strategy worked to a certain extent. Both sides understood the rules of the game:

> Étrangement, le seul élément à me donner courage était ma propre arrogance. [. . .] sous les dictatures, le comportement qu'on affiche joue un rôle determinant. L'arrogance non seulement redonne du cran, mais elle 'suggestionne' autrui, voire la dictature elle-même. Le problème est que cette attitude, on n'en est pas maître. Un beau jour, elle peut vous quitter et vous vous sentez tout à fait incapable de la recouvrer. Elle est la première à abandonner l'individu au seuil de la soumission. (*Le Poids* 407)

> Strangely, the only element which gave me courage was my arrogance. [. . .] under dictatorships, the behaviour which one displays plays a determining role. Arrogance not only restores your courage, but also 'suggests' it to others, or even to the dictatorship itself. The problem is that you are not the master of this attitude. One fine day, it can leave you and you feel yourself completely unable to recover it again. It is the first thing to abandon an individual on the threshold of giving in.

However, the rules were rendered opaque and unpredictable by Hoxha, whose complex personality was in conflict with itself, one part of his mind plotting against the other.[98] In the early days, Kadare's youth, precociousness, and success were exploited by Hoxha in his strategy of weakening the old guard. After the publication of *The General* in France Kadare relied on the perception of his success in the West in order to maintain his position. He realized that he could not afford to lose his confidence in this contest. In the 1970s, however, Kadare's sources of external support weakened. After the success of *The General* in France and despite the beginnings of an international reputation, he felt abandoned by Europe.

> D'Europe ne me parvenait aucune voix. Depuis trois ans, aucune traduction de mes œuvres n'y avait été publiée. Cela faisait deux ans que je ne répondais plus à aucune invitation. Je me sentais abandonné. (*Le Poids* 406–07)

> No-one called me from Europe. I heard nothing. For three years no translation of my works was published there. For two years I was unable to respond to any invitations. I felt abandoned.

Kadare's first test had come with the scandal of *Winter of Great Solitude*. For a while the writer checked the dictator and a sinister silence emanated from the centre as Hoxha considered his next move. That move, when it came, was typical of Hoxha's manipulative brilliance. The humiliation of Kadare, the punishment of being sent to the country to work alongside the people, and the nominal prohibition of any further novels were mild in comparison to the penalties meted out to others for less provocation. However, Hoxha made his point. The obligation to carry out a formal self-criticism in 1975, repeated in a more threatening public environment in 1982 as a result of the publication of *The Palace of Dreams*, represented significant heightening of the stakes in the cat-and-mouse game which lasted from 1975 until the death of Enver Hoxha in 1985. Nothing would happen without the dictator's imprimatur. This saved Kadare from secret reprisals of enemies among the old guard Stalinists, the Sigurimi, and the Union of Writers. While threats, set-ups, and denunciations were common, no-one dared move without Hoxha's instigation. But the writer could never feel secure. And as the dictator aged and became sick and even more unpredictable by the late 1970s, Kadare's sense of danger increased. His main fear at this time was not of the tortures, detentions, and other chastisements routinely meted out to less well-known figures. His concern was for his life as a writer. Looking back from the 1990s he refers to some of the more subtle ways in which writers could be silenced, namely by reduction of their possibilities, forcing them into a slow decline into desuetude.

> Plus tard, quand on ferait l'historique de cette période de notre littérature, on dirait peut-être: A l'époque, vers la fin des années cinquante ou au début des années soixante, apparut un écrivain aux débuts prometteurs, mais tombé ensuite dans l'oubli, Ismail Kadaré. Après quelques success initiaux en poésie et en prose, il versa dans des œuvres conformists . . . Ou encore: Après les quelques espoirs qu'il avait donnés au début, il fut, dans des conditions demeurées obscures, impliqué dans un group 'hostile' et condamné à une peine d'emprisonnement; reconnu plus tard innocent, il renonça jusqu'à la fin de ses jours à la littérature, se consacrant par intervalles à des traductions de poètes de second ordre comme Smirnenski ou Nekrassov. (*Le Poids* 329–30)

> Later, when the history of that period in our literature was being written, they might, perhaps, have said: At that time, towards the end of the fifties or at the beginning of the sixties, Ismail Kadare made his debut as a promising writer, but subsequently was completely forgotten. After some initial success in poetry and prose he produced more conformist works . . . Or maybe: After the initial hopes of his beginnings, he was implicated under circumstances which

have remained unclear with a group 'hostile' to the regime and condemned to serve a prison sentence; acknowledged afterward to have been innocent, he renounced literature for the rest of his life, devoting himself for short periods to the translation of second-rate poets such as Smirnenski or Nekrassov.

From the late 1960s onwards Kadare would develop various inner strategies to deal with the threats and intimidation of life under the regime. Self-protection came in the form of a belief in the literary life, borrowed from the modernist conception of the artist as occupying two worlds. Against the reality of the present and the dictatorship, he posited the 'second chronology' of the writer, in which the word meant more than the fact. The 'ivory tower' of the writer is not a world of unreality and escape but is a 'second chronology' of respite and strength in the dictatorship.

> Cette maison immémoriale est connue sous diverses appellations: demeure céleste, tour d'ivoire, Parnasse, réclusion volontaire, etc. En ce qui me concerne, je la qualifierais sobrement de 'temps second' de l'écrivain [. . .][99]

> That immemorial dwelling is known by various names: celestial abode, ivory tower, Parnassus, place of voluntary imprisonment, etc. In my case, I would describe it more plainly as the 'second time-frame' of the writer [. . .]

In *Invitation to the Writer's Studio* Kadare gives an inventory of names, places, themes, and characters which allow us to judge the depth and breadth of his other, internal and literary universe.[100] The coherence of this world is striking, as is its thematic continuity throughout Kadare's writing life. With its characters and cities, lands, seas, underworlds and legends, the Kadarean universe shows how superficial and circumscribed Albanian reality had become for him under communism. Here too we find the answers to questions regarding the distortions, the surrealism, and the refractions of reality which have perplexed commentators:

> Ainsi travestie, tranfigurée, brouillée, l'Albanie me paraissait plus proche, et, par-dessus tout, mieux immunisée contre le régime communiste.[101]

> Thus disguised, transfigured, clouded over, Albania appeared closer and above all else, better immunized against the communist regime.

To this trope of the separation of life and art he brings a new element, which would lead inexorably to his confrontation with the leader. For in this second, literary life, he is a keeper of the nation, a Herderian guardian of the temple,[102] whose role must at some stage come into conflict with that of the dictator. Kadare's first strategy to deal with this competition for Albania is to try to change Zeus. He would educate the tyrant, tempting him with a 'corrective mask' in which he would be both flattered and chastised. In retrospect from the late 1970s, he recognized the naivety of his early hope to be able to induce the dictator to change his ways. However, in the context of the late 1960s the project seemed feasible and it led to the creation of Kadare's most controversial work, *The Winter of Great Solitude*.

The fiction of the 'second chronology' provided inner strength for the writer, but he had to come to some compromise with the world of political reality as well. In 1971 Kadare considered his situation and at the beginning of 1972 joined the Albanian Party of Labour. In a later interview with Stephane Courtois, Kadare gave his reasons for taking this decision. His response is indicative of the complexity of issues of collaboration in an environment such as communist Albania, but also clarifies issues of personal and social morality which have been raised in regard to the writer. Kadare admits that neither then nor at any time did he have a need to join the Party; on the contrary, he had many reasons for not joining. He was not a communist by conviction and he found the long meetings tiresome and boring and the Party discipline demeaning. However, he did have two quite different motivations. The first was that the publication in France in 1970 of *The General of the Dead Army* enabled him to become the only Albanian member of the 'club' of free European writers, and the only Albanian writer well-received in Western Europe. For the writer in anti-Western, anti-European Albania, he needed to join the Party in order to counterbalance his membership of that 'other' party.

> Dans l'Albanie stalinienne, traversée par la haine de l'Occident et persuadée d'être également haïe, l'estime de l'Occident pour un écrivain était perçue comme un paradoxe dangereux qui faisait perdre les repères de l'ordre communiste. C'est pour cela qu'il fallait briser rapidement cette menace.[103]

> Stalinist Albania was permeated with hatred of the West and was convinced that the hatred was mutual. For a writer to be well-regarded in the West was a dangerous and paradoxical situation. A writer in this situation lost his points of reference in the communist order. For this reason I needed to move quickly to destroy that threat.

Hence, he replies, he joined the Party. The second reason is that membership of the Party was by no means to be taken for granted. Many applied but were rejected, and while it would have been possible perhaps to formulate a polite refusal, Enver Hoxha had personally supported the Party's invitation to Kadare. A refusal in this case would have been tantamount to defiance of Hoxha. In one sense Kadare's entry into the Party represented the beginning of the complex game of cat and mouse which would characterize the famous writer's relationship with the dictator. Membership of the Party represented his commitment to his country and its culture rather than to a club of free Western European writers, and hence signalled his engagement as an adversary from within.[104] While figures around the dictator, such as his wife, Nexhmije, were incapable of understanding this, Enver Hoxha surely did understand the unwritten rules of the battle with his leading writer. In this sense, Kadare's membership of the Party simply continued the line of commitment and engagement which he had commenced on returning from Moscow and which he corroborated in refusing to seek exile in Finland in 1962 or during any of his subsequent visits to the West. As he writes in the early 1990s, the role of the dissident exile was not for him;[105] however, by staying within the borders of his country he knew that he had to play by a set of moral and aesthetic rules which he himself formulated. The central one for him throughout the period of the regime was that while he collaborated on issues of self-criticism and on the required formalities of self-abasement and party discipline he did not denounce any of his compatriots,[106] and he did not compromise the truth of his writing.

> Je compris que j'étais mis à l'épreuve. Est-ce que je préférais être le 'chouchou de la bourgeoisie', ou est-ce que j'accepterais de montrer que mon pays (qui, dans leur esprit, était confondu avec le Parti) était plus important que

la bourgeoisie? On comprend que la mauvaise décision aurait été fatale. J'ai donc 'choisi mon pays', et je ne le regrette pas. [. . .] À mon sens, perdre la vie pour une simple carte du Parti aurait voulu dire que vous preniez toute cette bouffonnerie trop au sérieux.[107]

I understood that I was being put to the test. Would I prefer to be the 'darling of the bourgeoisie', or would I agree to show that my country (which, in their minds was confused with the Party) was more important than the bourgeoisie? You must understand that the wrong decision would be fatal. So I 'chose my country' and I don't regret having done so. [. . .] I was not about to lose my life just for a Party card. That would involve taking their buffoonery far too seriously.

A Note on Publication, Editors, and Censorship

Publication in Albania was strictly controlled by the regime, but there was no official pre-publication censorship. 'Le censure n'a jamais été instituée chez nous, toutes ces œuvres furent sévèrement critiquées, ou interdites pour un plus ou moins long temps, mais seulement après publication' (*Invitation* 254, 'Censorship was never instituted, all of these works were severely criticized or prohibited for a longer or a shorter time, but only after publication'). All publications were state-controlled and works were published on the basis of the authorization of the editor-in-chief of the press or the journal to which a manuscript was submitted. (The possibilities were limited, given that all material was published by the state.) As can be seen from the following description by the writer, Fatos Arapi, the absence of formal pre-publication censorship was made up for in the long process of negotiation between the publishing editor, the writer, and the various levels of political power and responsibility:

> The manuscript of a book was deposited at the publishing house and it was the chief editor who designated an editor responsible for its political content. He was the first censor. Afterwards, two others were responsible for providing political and ideological feed-back and criticism. Later, it was the turn of the vice-director and after that of the director of the publishing house. If a well-known writer was involved, the book was consigned to the Central Committee's office of book publication. After that, the director of book publication in the Ministry of Culture took charge, etc.[108]

The editors of the state publishing organizations in the European socialist states operated as mediators between the writers, the regime and the reading public. Their role was a finely calibrated one. Many of these figures were writers themselves or harboured writing ambitions; many were motivated by genuine literary interest and even a spirit of improvement, amelioration, or bettering of the situation, if not dissident or even outspoken in any way. Kadare's editor in Moscow, David Samoïlov, is typical of this type of communist intellectual. Samoïlov advised Kadare not to include certain poems, or at least to delete certain provocative lines, and warned the young writer that should he publish the material, he, Samoïlov, as editor would have to distance himself in the introduction, according to commonly understood formulae regarding the writer's promise and youthful impetuosity. Still inexperienced in the ways of dictatorial censorship and control, Kadare insisted. Fortunately for him, the book was published after he had left the Soviet Union. However, he retains to this day a powerful gratitude towards, and understanding of, Samoïlov's position at this time.[109]

The responsibility of the editor was great. References were sought from appropriate readers of the manuscripts and corrections, modifications, and changes sought from the author. In the case of *Winter of Great Solitude*, for example, one of the readers, the literary historian and professor Dalan Shpallo, writing in late 1973, compares the author's revisions to the 1972 published version, undertaken in response to official and unofficial criticisms, and concludes that the author 'has taken a good number of the reprimands into account and has in some cases made perceptible changes to the work at certain sensitive points. Certain weaknesses, deficiencies, dubious phrasings have been avoided'.[110] The complex dynamics of creative writing, editorial critique and feedback, revision and publication in Albania, as elsewhere in socialist Eastern Europe, should not be underestimated. There was not a black-and-white opposition of writer and censor, but rather a collaboration in which the censor and the creative writer were in closest contact with each other, sometimes even in the same person.[111] Not only were the processes of inner censorship well developed,[112] but reviews and critiques were written by close associates (such as Dritëro Agolli) and changes were made or rejected on the basis of editorial suggestion or the warnings of friends.[113] The Sigurimi too were involved in the surveillance of writers, and collected evidence of dissent from colleagues, associates, and friends, from draft manuscripts and published works.[114] When the 'liberal' Todi Lubonja was toppled in the wake of the crisis surrounding publication of *The Great Winter* the diary of his son, Fatos, was discovered during a search of the family's home in the early 1970s. The young man was sentenced to fifteen years' prison on the basis of his privately critical comments, although this episode cannot, of course, be separated from the political coup against the Minister.[115] Kadare writes that the Sigurimi sought access to the tape-recorded first draft of *The City without Signs*, and that he was warned about its content by his friend Drago Siliqi.

After publication of a work, letters from readers or complaints from members of the nomenklatura could lead to prohibitions on republication, and to campaigns of persecution:

> Un article dénigrant *Le Monstre* suffit à exclure ce récit de la littérature albanaise. Une critique de quelques lignes lue au cours d'un certain plénum parvint à elle seule à étouffer *Le Palais des rêves* [. . .] Dans le cas de *Clair de lune*, c'est une brève note d'une lycéenne, dans le journal de la jeunesse, qui atteignit le même but. (*Invitation* 255)

> One article denigrating *The Monster* was sufficient to exclude that story from Albanian literature. A critique of a couple of lines read during the course of a certain plenum was enough to smother *The Palace of Dreams* [. . .] In the case of *Clair de lune* a school-girl's brief note in the youth journal achieved the same goal.

Exile in the Myzeqe, 1975

In 1975, in the wake of the affairs of *The Great Winter* and 'The Red Pashas', Kadare was sent 'amongst the mud and the people' ('au milieu de la boue et du peuple') first to Fier and then out beyond Semani into the 'mire of the Myzeqe'. He was to desist from writing and learn to contribute productively to his nation's welfare. It was only a 'semi-relegation', and Kadare was able to return periodically to Tirana.[116] Intellectuals had been sent out all over the country, so Kadare was not alone. The situation in the Myzeqe bordered on the surreal. Kadare appears to have refused to carry out the work allotted to him — laying concrete — with impunity, as insupportable for a writer and intellectual. After this a form of stand-off occurred:

> On ne parvint pas à savoir ce qui s'était passé en coulisses. [. . .] Ce fut un sorte de cessez-le-feu à l'issue duquel personne — pas même nous — ne savait comment les choses allaient tourner, pourquoi nous étions là, combien de temps nous y resterions encore. (*Le Poids* 396)

> We didn't get to know what had happened behind the scenes. [. . .] It was a sort of cease-fire, at the end of which no-one — not even we — knew how things would turn out, why we were there, or how long we would stay there.

Kadare's colleague, the ex-partisan and communist writer Leon Qafzezi, along with Llazër Siliqi, had spoken in the writer's favour, albeit ineffectually, at the Party meeting at which Kadare was officially censured. Qafzezi was a robust and outspoken character, a committed communist whose open views on sexual morality brought him into conflict with the prudish Party. To Kadare's surprise, Qafzezi was sent with him to the Myzeqe. It is indicative of the regime's perversion of relationships that Qafzezi, with whom Kadare shared a sense of friendship and collegiality, should have been charged with keeping the writer under surveillance. He had finally been degraded to the point where he had to spy on his friend.

Kadare's punishment, as he realized, was far from draconian by the standards of the time and place,[117] but the regime had made its point. He had overstepped the limits and was put on notice. Kadare remained in the Myzeqe for only a period of months, but even this nominal exile ended once and for all his illusion that he could influence the dictator for the benefit of the country. He recognized with chagrin the naivety of his intention of applying a 'corrective mask' to the dictatorship through literature. The corruption and nepotism of the communist system ceases to be a point of focus from this time onwards and the image of a rotted and decaying present-day Albania takes its place.

> L'Albanie se défaisait sous nos yeux. Telle une icône vermoulue, elle vieillissait jour après jour, se défigurait, s'étiolait. S'il me restait encore quelque bonne raison d'être écrivain [. . .] la seule, la première et la dernière raison était celle-là: essayer de restaurer l'icône. Pour que les générations à venir, quand elles gratteraient le vernis de cette époque sans merci, redécouvrent l'image intacte. (*Le Poids* 401)

> Albania was coming undone before our eyes. Like a worm-eaten icon, she aged day by day, becoming disfigured and sickly. If there was any good reason for

me to remain a writer [. . .] this was the only one, the first and the last reason: to try to restore the icon. So that the generations coming, when they scratched hard at the varnish of that epoch, would rediscover the intact image.

In the aftermath Kadare completed the 'family novel' *The Secular Chronicle of the Hankonis* (later renamed *The Chain of the Hankonis*), a unique work in his oeuvre covering the history of the Hankoni family from 1703 when Basri Hankoni perjures himself in order to gain possession of a disputed field in Gjirokastra. The family reaches the pinnacle of wealth and prestige in the Ottoman province but by the first year of the new century has fallen back into provincial insignificance. The history of Ottoman Albania is explored in relation to Kadare's own family and clan in Gjirokastra, deepening the image of 'eternal Albania' in his work. In his autobiography Kadare describes the origins of this work with reference to the house of the Hoxha family, only two hundred steps from his own and, of course, lovingly preserved by the regime.

> Ce n'est sans doute pas un hasard si j'entamai cette nouvelle phase de mon travail par la *Chronique des Hakoni* [sic], une nouvelle où réapparaissait çà et là le fantôme de ma maison, désormais à demi en ruine. (*Le Poids* 405)

> It is without doubt not by chance that I initiated that new phase of my work with the *Chronicle of the Hakoni* [sic], a novella in which here and there the spirit of my home appears, from that time onward, a semi-ruin.

The regime, he writes, took a perverse joy in allowing the Kadare family home to fall into decay while turning the Hoxha home into a museum and place of adoration.[118] The level of counter-identification against the dictator as the voice of Albania implicit in the claim for the familial home as a valid site of national memory provides a window into Kadare's self-perception at this critical time. Kadare's metaphor for his relationship with the dictator has changed from mentoring to competition for the voice and memory of Albania. He speaks of 'restoring the icon' of national memory, and autobiographical reference to the change in his relationship to the dictator is borne out in the change in direction of his work during the second half of the decade. 'Il fallait redonner vie à des images perdues, à des routes, des ponts, des villes, des auberges, des églises, des monastères et des cathédrales' (*Le Poids* 405, 'It was necessary to give life back to the lost images, to the roads, the bridges, the cities, the inns, the churches, the monasteries and the cathedrals').

The Education of the Writer: *Twilight of the Steppe-Gods*, 1976

If Kadare's first autobiographical novel, *Chronicle in Stone*, documents the writer's discovery of subjective authenticity as the conduit of individual, national, and ethnic identity, *The Twilight of the Steppe-Gods*, written approximately five years later, charts the writer's awareness of the sacrifices involved in committing himself to literature in the communist environment. Both works portray aspects of the writer's coming to terms with himself, his vocation, and his nation. *The Twilight of the Steppe-Gods* revisits the break with the Soviet Union from the subjective viewpoint of the young writer, at the critical point where national and individual history intersect, namely at the time of his enforced return to Albania in 1961. The autobiographical fiction confirms the authenticity of the subjective voice against socialist realist doctrine. The young writer comes to recognize the extent to which his Albanian identity is rooted in language and culture, and hence the necessity of returning to his native land in spite of the oppressive nature of the regime there. The situation is not unlike that of twentieth-century Indian and other post-colonial writers who returned to their native lands after a privileged education at the centre of the empire. They discover themselves between both worlds. Home seems no longer the same and the empire has revealed its oppressiveness. A decade and a half after his return, having witnessed the dictator's consolidation of power over the regime and the people, Kadare looked back with very different eyes.

The Gorki Institute and the 'De-Nationalised' Writers of the Soviet Union

Twilight of the Steppe-Gods begins in the summer of 1959 in a Soviet writers' retreat at a seaside resort near Riga. The young Kadare is bored with the company of mediocre middle-aged writers from throughout the Soviet Union. The theme of youth, disaffection, and generational perspective arises as he meets a Ukrainian girl with whom he can discuss taboo topics such as the suicides of Fadeyev and Mayakowsky, the superficiality of socialist realism, and the failure of Soviet culture to have produced an interesting or profound literature. For the youngsters the reality of the ageing, tired, and submissive writers contrasts with the socialist-realist idealism of their works. They are surprised and disillusioned by the gap between literary imagination and daily life for these symbols of the revolution. Kadare feels as though he is living in a museum of preserved specimens:

> En outré, cette dichotomie du monde avait quelque chose d'anormal, je dirais même d'effrayant, qui me rappelait souvent les êtres monstrueux que j'avais vus macerant dans des bocaux au musée des sciences naturelles. (*Le Crépuscule* 15)[119]

> In addition, the dualism of that world had something abnormal, I would even say something frightening, about it. It reminded me often of the monstrosities which I had seen in jars of formalin at the museum of natural sciences.

The Soviet writers in Riga represent the older generation, for whom the formulae of socialist realism and the history of the revolution have become second nature, and whose reality does not intrude into the idealized realms of the Soviet hero. They have experienced Stalinism and the war and are exhausted and happy to have found some sort of niche where they can live out the rest of their lives in peace and comfort. Opposite Kadare's room is that of Paustovsky who taught at the Institute from 1948 until 1955 and was now writing his memoirs, The *Story of a Life*. Later in the novel he will reappear in the context of the Pasternak denunciations, obliged to be present, but speaking neither for nor against his colleague.[120]

The Moscow Gorki Institute for World Literature was the premier training facility for the writers, critics, and literary nomenklatura of the Soviet Union. However, Kadare's fellow students there include a wider selection of Soviet types than the retired, successful, and exhausted writers of post-war socialist realism whom he meets at the seaside retreat in Riga. At the Institute are people at all stages of their lives, accommodated in the vast building in the centre of Moscow for a variety of reasons. He encounters writers from the length and breadth of the Soviet Union, who have 'played the game' and survived the Stalinist era only to find themselves in a form of limbo. Many have suffered the dramatic reversals of fortune which were so common in the Soviet system, as a result of bad judgement, political change, or intrigue. Some, like his friend, the exiled Greek communist Petros Antéos, are outsiders who refuse to compromise in the post-war environment of 'real-existing socialism'.[121] Some have failed to make the transition from partisan to apparatchik and have fallen by the wayside. Others, such as the melancholy Lithuanian Jeronim Stulpanz, are still young but seem destined to suffer the fate of the Soviet writer, to live in a state of perpetual inauthenticity, the result of the dishonesty of their writing. The images of life in the Institute become more and more bizarre as the young writer witnesses the scenes of degradation and humiliation of the writers around him. He explains to his new Russian girlfriend Lida how in cathartic group 'vomiting' sessions the drunken writers metaphorically and physically regurgitate those subjects that they will never dare commit to writing.

> 'Le vomissement des sujets. C'est comme ça qu'ils l'appellent. Des nuits comme celle-ci, ils se racontent des sujets d'œuvres qu'ils n'écriront jamais. Certains se mettent alors à vomir et c'est à cela que ces séances doivent leur nom. [. . .] Ils écrivent d'autres choses, qui sont souvent tout le contraire'. (*Le Crépuscule* 118–19)

> 'The regurgitation of subjects. That's what they call it. On nights like this, they recount the subjects of works that they will never write. Some then set about vomiting and it is from them that the sessions derive their name. [. . .] They will write other things, which are often completely the opposite'.

In these outbursts the real content of Soviet literature is to be found:

> Des fragments de sujets énoncés a voix plus ou moins basse pénétraient dans mes oreilles, tantôt à ma gauche, tantôt à ma droite. Il y avait là des secrétaires de partis boiteux qui volaient les porcs des kolkhozes, des ministres imposteurs, des généraux balourds et décrépits, des membres du praesidium, du Bureau politique, des individus qui croyaient en Dieu, s'espionnaient les uns les autres, et enterraient une partie de leur traitement sous les isbas en prévision des mauvais jours. Certaines nouvelles décrivaient les luxueuses datchas des hauts fonctionnaires, leurs beuveries, les pots-de-vin qu'ils recevaient et les danses nues de leurs enfants. D'autres évoquaient des espèces de révoltes, sinon de véritables insurrections, dans diverses régions du pays, parlaient de massacres assourdis, de prolifération religieuse, de déportations, de prisons et de crimes, de monstrueuses différences de salaires entres les ouvriers, 'maîtres du pays', et les cadres supérieurs du Parti et de l'État, 'serviteurs du peuple'. (*Le Crépuscule* 124–25)

> Bits of subjects expressed in low voices penetrated my ears, sometimes from the left, sometimes from the right. There were limping party secretaries who stole pork from the kolkhozes, fake ministers, oafish and decrepit generals, members of the presidium, of the Politburo, individuals who believed in God, who spied on others and who buried a part of their salary underneath their *isbas* 'for a rainy day'. Some stories described the luxurious dachas of high party officials, their drinking, the bribes that they received, and their children's dancing in the nude. Others evoked different sorts of things, revolts, if not true insurrections, in various areas of the country, they spoke of covered-up massacres, of the increase

of religious belief, of deportations, of prisons and crimes, of the monstrous differences in salary between the workers, the 'masters of the country', and the upper-level cadres of the Party and the State, the 'servants of the people'.

The dormitories of the Institute are a Dantean *Inferno* in which each floor-cum-circle houses a different type of Soviet writer:

> Premier étage: c'est là que logeaient les étudiants des premières années, ceux qui n'avaient encore commis que peu de péchés littéraires. Deuxième étage: les critiques littéraires, les dramaturges conformistes, les vernisseurs de la vie. Troisième . . . cercle: les schématiques, les flagorneurs, les slavophiles. Quatrième cercle: les femmes, les libéraux, les désenchantés du socialisme. Cinquième cercle: les calomniateurs, les délateurs. Sixième cercle: les dénationalisés, ceux qui avaient abandonné leurs languages et qui ecrivaient en russe . . . (*Le Crépuscule* 117)

> First storey: students in their first year, who have not yet committed much in the way of literary sins, are accommodated here. Second storey: literary critics, conformist playwrights and people who embellish life. Third . . . circle: the simplifiers, sycophants, Slavophiles. Fourth circle: women, liberals, those disillusioned with socialism. Fifth circle: slanderers and informers. Sixth circle: the de-nationalized, the ones who have abandoned their native languages and who write in Russian.

This last group have abandoned their native languages in order to write in the language of supranational world communism. Kadare earlier refers to the 'aridity' of socialist literature since Lenin (*Le Crépuscule* 45) and in his contact with his fellow-students he experiences a vision of the wretched, dying, and abandoned languages of Eastern Europe:

> Je [. . .] me retrouvai à nouveau dans le couloir du sixième, où les dénationalisés s'étaient maintenant mêlés les uns aux autres et parlaient toutes leurs langues mortes ou agonisantes à la fois. C'était un cauchemar effroyable. Défigurés par l'ivresse, transpirants, poisseux, avec des filets de larmes sèches sous leurs yeux rougis, ils parlaient d'une voix rauque les langues qu'ils avaient désertées, se frappaient la poitrine du poing, sanglotaient, juraient de ne jamais les oublier, de les parler en rêve, s'accusaient de lâcheté pour les avoir abandonnées là-bas, à la merci de la montagne ou du désert, elles, leurs mères, pour cette marâtre qu'était la langue russe. [. . .] Parmi ce chaos de mots de langues mortes ou malades flottaient des phrases ou des expressions russes. Elles se manifestaient çà et là comme de petites îles, perdues sur cette mer obscure de leur subconscient collectif. 'Ma langue m'apparait comme un fantôme!' criait par moments l'un d'entre eux, comme s'il se réveillait, épouvanté. Je frémis. A quoi pouvait bien ressembler le fântome d'une langue? (*Le Crépuscule* 130)

> I found myself in the corridor of the sixth again, where the de-nationalized writers were mixed up with each other and spoke all of their dead and dying languages at once. It was a terrible nightmare. Disfigured through drink, sweating and clammy, with trails of dried tears running down from their reddened eyes, they spoke in rough voices the languages that they had abandoned, striking themselves on the bosom with their fists, sobbing, swearing never to forget their languages, speaking them in their dreams, accusing themselves of cowardice for having left them behind, to the mercy of

the mountains and the deserts, them, their mother tongues, abandoned to the
cruel Russian step-mother. [. . .] Russian phrases turned up amidst the chaos of
dead and sick languages appearing here and there like little islands, lost in the
dark sea of their collective unconscious. 'My language has appeared to me like
a ghost!' they cried out to each other, as they woke up, terrified. I shuddered.
What would the ghost of a language look like?

The vision of a group of poets, estranged from their national languages and lost
in a desert of Russian, is a terrifying vision of his own future. These writers, who
have turned their backs on their languages in order to write in the language of
Soviet Marxist-Leninist doctrine and Russian cultural hegemony, arouse Kadare's
revulsion. The writing of the well-meaning Soviet hacks in residence at Yalta and
Riga was merely bad, having long since lost touch with reality in its ideological
compliance. That of the exiles and refugees on the sixth floor of the Gorki Institute
is anathema to the young Albanian. The writing moves from satiric realism to
nightmarish surrealism as Kadare imagines a writer's hell in which language has
dried up like water in a desert, leaving him gasping for words. In this powerful
evocation of linguistic death Kadare expresses his fear of loss of identity as a writer
in Albanian. In the confrontation with those writers from Eastern Europe who have
sacrificed their ethno-linguistic identity, Kadare discovers the depth of his sense of
Albanianness. It is a Herderian expression of the existential significance of language
as an individual and a national identity-marker. The Gorki Institute is a vision of
what he would become were he to identify as a Soviet writer. Kadare moves among
these tortured souls, but, like Dante, is not one of them.

The socialist writers on the sixth floor, who have renounced their native
languages, and the denouncers, the apparatchiks, the liars and the sycophants, along
with his friend, Stulpanz, who has 'not yet' renounced his native language and
culture, represent what he might have become: a Soviet party hack, an apparatchik,
or a soul in limbo, separated from home and alone in the Soviet Union. The writers
of socialist-realist utopias in Riga bore the young Kadare, the apparatchiks lining
up to denounce Pasternak appal him, and the group vomiting sessions on the fourth
floor disgust him. But it is the refugees and exiles who have renounced their native
tongues who arouse his contempt.

In 1958, before the break, it was by no means unthinkable that the young writer
would seek to realize his ambitions and broaden his horizons by remaining in the
cosmopolitan Soviet capital. In 1961 a book of his poems was published in Moscow
as part of a series dedicated to young communist writers edited by the critic, David
Samoïlov.[122] Had the break not occurred, he might have been able to realize both
his personal ambitions and his commitment to Albanian literature, commuting
between Moscow and Tirana. But looking back from the mid-1970s, he recognizes
that the compromises involved in remaining in Moscow were too great. In 1960 of
course, Kadare did not know what was in store for him in isolationist Albania and
was too young seriously to consider exile in the Soviet Union. He had little choice
other than to return to his homeland.

> Assez-moi, me dis-je. Je me bouchai les oreilles de mes mains et, marchant,
> ainsi, me frayant difficilement un chemin parmi eux, finis par atteindre ma

chambre. Je me jetai à plat ventre sur mon lit sans ôter mes mains de mes oreilles. Qu'est-ce que ce pays et pourquoi est-ce que je me trouve ici? me demandai-je. (*Le Crépuscule* 131)

Leave me, I said. I held my hands over my ears and, walking on like that, I made my way through them with difficulty, finally reaching the door to my room. I threw myself flat onto my bed without shifting my hands from my ears. What is this country, and why am I here, I asked myself.

Language is a core value in his existence as a writer. Unlike the Quprili family in *The Palace of Dreams*, Kadare will not sacrifice his language to 'the gods of the steppe'.

The Pasternak Affair

At the Gorki Institute Kadare learns what it means to be a Soviet writer. He studies the works of the European tradition, of decadent modernism and bourgeois subjectivism, and comes to understand the dynamics of writing as a social and political act. As a member of the Albanian *Aufbaugeneration*, the generation which grew up with the establishment of communism and the construction of the post-war nation, Kadare is something of an outsider in the Soviet environment, where communism was already a way of life. His poetry shows signs of Western modernism and bohemian rebelliousness and he must habituate himself early to self-criticism (108), the ritual of confession and self-exculpation for those suspected of heterodoxy. In classes Kadare is criticized for bourgeois formalism, and he is censured for the subject of a planned novel about the general of a 'dead army':

Comme nous entrions, le professeur s'approcha de moi et me sourit froidement.
'Votre sujet était merveilleux, me dit elle.
— Quel sujet? Fis-je, presque effrayé; je ne connais aucun sujet'.
Elle continuait de sourire.
'Une armée vivante commandée par les fantômes d'un général et d'un prêtre morts, poursuivit-elle. C'est une trouvaille fantastique.
— Non, ce n'est pas exact, murmurai-je, bien que je n'eusse guère envie de lui fournir des éclaircissements; c'est plutôt le contraire. Il s'agit d'une armée morte commandée par un général et un prêtre vivants.
— Ah oui?' fit-elle, et elle pencha la tête alors que je pensais: quand donc lui ai-je raconté cela? Je ne me souvenais de rien.
'Encore mieux, reprit-elle. Je trouve que c'est encore plus beau. Avez-vous appris l'affaire Pasternak?
Oui'. (*Le Crépuscule* 139–40)

As we entered, the professor approached me and smiled coldly.
'Your subject was marvellous', she said, and continued to smile.
'A living army commanded by the ghosts of a dead general and a military chaplain', she continued. It's a wonderful idea.
'No, that's not quite right', I murmured, although I didn't really want to have to provide clarification; 'it's the opposite, actually. It's about a dead army commanded by a living general and chaplain'.
'Oh, yes?' she said and leaned her head to the side as I thought to myself: 'when did I tell her that?' I didn't remember anything.

'Even better', she replied. 'I find it an even more attractive idea. Have you heard of the Pasternak affair?'

'Yes'.

He has been warned. The implication that his story has become known through word of mouth is not lost on him. This is part of the dynamics of writing in a closed society and belongs to his ongoing education. At the Institute Kadare discovers several hundred pages of a *samizdat* novel.[123] It is Pasternak's *Dr Zhivago*, newly published in the West, which is now circulating in *samizdat* form. Half-way between waking and sleeping, Kadare overhears on the radio the first news of Pasternak's denunciation:

> 'Docteur, docteur, soulagez-moi! Je me sens très mal . . . Ah! Docteur Jivago, docteur Jivago . . . [. . .] C'était une voix bizarre, qui, après deux ou trois secondes, sembla s'éclaircir et secouer les brouillards sonores qui l'avaient accompagnée jusque dans ma conscience à moitié endormie'. (*Le Crépuscule* 132–33)

> Doctor, doctor, ease my pain! I feel bad . . . Oh, Doctor Zhivago, Doctor Zhivago . . . [. . .] It was a strange voice which, after two or three seconds seemed to lighten up and shake off the fogginess of sound which had accompanied it in my half-sleeping state.

Boris Pasternak's love story set during the Russian Revolution became a *cause célèbre* in the Cold War when the author was awarded the Nobel Prize for Literature in 1958. Pasternak finished *Dr Zhivago* in 1955 and offered it to the Moscow literary journal *Novy Mir* in the following year. It was rejected on the basis that it misrepresented the revolution and the structure and leadership of Soviet society. In 1957 an Italian translation appeared with Feltrinelli, and by 1958 the novel was circulating in various languages in the West. It was not so much the foreign publication which caused trouble for Pasternak. The authorities had let the Italian publication of *Dr Zhivago* pass without comment since the text remained well beyond the reach of Soviet citizens. The Nobel Prize, however, could scarcely be kept from the Soviet people or ignored by the Party. Kadare's comrade, the Greek partisan, poet, and exile Petros Antéos, refers to Pasternak as one of the phantoms in the battle against Stalin and explains the dialectics of Soviet cultural policy to the young Albanian:

> 'Il y a trois ans que le Docteur Jivago a été publié en Occident et ceux-là n'en parlent pas. Maintenant qu'il a décroché le prix Nobel, ils sont contraints de prendre position. [. . .] Ils vont peut-être le déporter'. (*Le Crépuscule* 142)

> 'It's three years since *Dr Zhivago* was published in the West and they didn't talk about it then. Now that he's picked up the Nobel Prize, they have to take a position. [. . .] Maybe they'll want to deport him'.

Pasternak was a member of the pre-revolutionary bourgeoisie whose early symbolist poetry placed him at the forefront of European modernism. Individuals, not history or the proletariat, are at the centre of his humanist world-view. History separates people and causes anguish in Pasternak's novel. However as Antéos points out, it was not the theme of *Dr Zhivago* that had suddenly rendered Pasternak dangerous. The Nobel Prize directed toward Pasternak the internal political tensions arising from Khrushchev's post-Stalinism. It was imperative for Khrushchev that Pasternak identify in terms of the post-Stalinist Soviet Union and reject the award from the West. At this stage, following the critique of Stalin when he could not afford to be seen to be losing control of the ideological sphere, Khrushchev could not allow any suggestion that Western acclaim of the writer could be seen to influence Soviet affairs. Hence the attack on the ageing and unwell writer was relentless.

> Avec une lucidité acérée comme la pointe d'un poignard, je voyais toute l'horreur de cette machine gigantesque qui fonctionnait maintenant à plein rendement. Être le cible, être pris dans son tourbillon! Je m'imaginais la tête mythologique slave qui gonflait ses joues horribles dans la steppe. La propagande soviétique avait commencé à lui ressembler. Quelques années plus tôt, cette tête avait soulevé un ouragan de poussière contre Staline, et maintenant, qui sait pourquoi, elle le faisait souffler contre ses propres zélateurs. Être objet de ses attaques! pensai-je à nouveau. Être pris dans les engrenages de ce mécanisme effroyable! (*Le Crépuscule* 150)

> With a lucidity as sharp as the point of a rapier, I saw all the horror of that gigantic machinery which was operating at the height of its performance. To be the target, to be caught up in its whirlwind! I imagined to myself the mythological Slavic head on the steppes puffing out its hideous cheeks. Soviet propaganda had begun to gather that force again. Some years earlier that head had raised a massive dust-storm against Stalin, and now, who knew why, it was blowing against its own champions. To be the object of those attacks! I thought again. To be pulled into the workings of that terrible mechanism!

As the ritual of denunciation and harassment takes place, Kadare watches and learns from the events that he would see repeated in Albania in respect of *The Winter of Great Solitude* and *The Palace of Dreams*. The creative intelligentsia behaves in a class fashion, manipulated from above and replicating the processes of harassment throughout their ranks.

The process against Pasternak takes its course. Denunciations by leading figures adorn the front pages of the *Literaturnaya Gazeta*. After the media harassment the formal proceedings begin. At plenary sessions and hearings the leading figures of the Union of Writers line up to speak against Pasternak, and petitions are sent to the regime demanding his expulsion from Russia. The posturing of Ladontchikov, an apparatchik and 'hero of Soviet positivity' whose only honesty of feeling is to be found in his anti-Semitism, fills Kadare with a sense of revulsion and cynicism. Figures such as Yevtushenko and Kuznetsov, who had allowed their liberal ideas to be instrumentalized in the anti-Stalinist thaw, now see themselves potentially isolated, excluded from the nomenklatura, and their privileges endangered unless they too denounce Pasternak's counter-revolutionary humanism. At the Gorki Institute the rhetoric and grandstanding is imitated by the students. In fact their education lies in internalizing the rituals of denunciation and auto-critique, not merely in learning the craft of socialist realism.

The counter figure to these Soviet writers is the Greek refugee, Petros Antéos, who spent the years after the defeat of the communists in the Greek civil war in Kadare's home town of Gjirokastra before finding refuge in Moscow. Antéos represents a narrative link to Kadare's past, both to the period of war documented in *Chronicle in Stone* and to the immediate post-war era. Antéos and the memory of the Greek partisans who had been treated at the hospital in Gjirokastra bring a level of reference to the privations and difficulties of the war years, as a contrast to the milieu of the nomenklatura and the failed bureaucrats of the Gorki Institute. In this moribund and inauthentic communist environment, Antéos represents 'l'ancien esprit épique de la révolution' (*Le Crépuscule* 100, 'the old epic spirit of the revolution'). He has maintained the link between word and deed, albeit as his pseudonym suggests, in darkest exile from his native land (*Le Crépuscule* 101). Kadare cannot understand how those who spoke out against Stalin at the height of the criticism of the personality cult can now support Khrushchev in the attack on Pasternak. It is the 'ancient Greek' Antéos, who disabuses the young writer of any illusions about the 'positive heroes' of communist arts and letters. Soviet politics has moved beyond such simple ideological identifications and Antéos explains how denunciation and political opportunism function in the post-Stalinist political environment. Looking back over this affair from the vantage point of the mid-1970s when he was writing *Twilight*, Kadare must have become aware of the ambiguities of Pasternak's position. Pasternak's international reputation was both a protective force and a point of weakness for the writer in 1958, a time of political and ideological sensitivity. After the publication of *The General* in France in 1970, Kadare, like Pasternak, had some protection from the more extreme forms of molestation, but it also rendered him a political target.

Death to Life: The Writer's Calling

Kadare's girlfriend Lida considers writers a suspect group, best when they are dead, since in life they confuse the boundaries between art and reality (at this point he has led her to believe that he is merely a translator for the cinema):

> Je lui dis en riant que je trouvais étonnant qu'elle éprouvât si peu de sympathie pour les écrivains, et précisément là, dans leur fief. Elle eut un haussement d'épaules, pui m'expliqua qu'en réalité elle aimait beaucoup la littérature, et les écrivains . . . morts; quant aux vivants, peut-être parce qu'elle en avait connu deux ou trois, peut-être aussi à cause de son amie, elle ne les aimait pas. . . Je me dis: encore les morts et les vivants sur le même cheval, comme dans la ballade de Constantin et Doruntine. (*Le Crépuscule* 66–67)

> Smiling I said to her that I was amazed at her lack of sympathy with writers, especially there, on their own territory. She shrugged her shoulders and explained that in fact she loved literature and . . . dead writers. As for living ones, perhaps because she had known two or three, or perhaps because of her friend, she didn't like them. . . . I said to myself: once again the dead and the living on the same horse, just as in the ballad of Constantine and Doruntine.

Appalled by the vomiting session, Lida rejects the young man when she realizes that he too is a writer. Later she writes to him, expressing her pity for him as a writer involved in this bizarre world of dishonesty and inauthenticity.[124] Disgusted with his metier, Kadare experiences a wave of self-contempt and hatred for his fellow-writers.

Je lui dis que moi aussi, si je ne m'enfuyais pas au plus tôt, je vomirais comme eux, et non seulement dans les couloirs, mais aussi des fenêtres sur les têtes des passants sur les taxis, du sixième étage, des tours du Kremlin, de . . . de . . . (*Le Crépuscule* 122)

I told her that if I didn't escape quickly enough, I too would vomit from the sixth floor like them, not just in the corridors, but from the windows, onto the roofs, the passers-by, the taxis, the Kremlin towers, the . . . the . . .

The encounter with Lida brings home to him that he is first and foremost a writer, and hence a part of that bizarre limbo between life and death, between reality and art, truth and illusion. He tells Stulpanz that as far as Lida is concerned he is dead:

'Téléphone-lui un soir et dis-lui que je suis parti, ou que je suis devenu fou, ou bien . . . attends, dis-lui, plutôt que je suis mort! Tu m'entends? Dis-lui que j'ai péri dans une catastrophe aérienne!' (*Le Crépuscule* 123)

'Ring her one evening and tell her that I have left, or that I've gone mad, or even . . . no, wait, tell her that I'm dead! Do you hear me? Tell her that I perished in an air catastrophe!'

Her response to him is a form of confirmation:

Voilà! Elle préférait les morts aux vivants. Et ses mots de consolation n'étaient pas vains. (*Le Crépuscule* 158)

There! She preferred the dead to the living. And her words of consolation were not in vain.

To be a writer means to accept metaphorical death. At this point the news breaks of Khrushchev's rift with Hoxha. Politics intervenes in the story of the education of the communist writer. Kadare, along with the rest of his generation of future intellectuals, technocrats, and functionaries, must discontinue his studies and return to Albania. In the already tense atmosphere another crisis occurs. Smallpox has broken out, and the capital is put under quarantine. Kadare prepares to leave the Soviet Union and sees Lida for the last time at the entry of the metro station, Novoslobodskaya:

Elle devait avoir l'impression de parler avec un fantôme. [. . .] Le temps d'aller seller mon cheval, songeai-je. La froide dalle de marbre muée en cheval. Je l'attendis comme d'habitude à l'ancienne bouche du métro Novoslobodskaïa. [. . .] A deux ou trois reprises j'eus l'impression qu'elle jetait un regard furtif sur mes cheveux comme pour y découvrir des traces de la terre du tombeau. J'avais bien fait de ne raconter la légende de Constantin et Doruntin [. . .] Nous chevauchions confusément les vitres des devantures dans le demi-jour, just comme dans la légende la vivante et le mort sur le même cheval. J'avais de la fièvre. L'effet du vaccin, sûrement. [. . .] Je sentis s'accentuer la pression de sa main sur mon bras. Geste de compassion? Désir de s'assurer qu'il y avait un vrai bras à l'intérieur de ma manche et non l'os dur, desséché, d'un squelette? (*Le Crépuscule* 211–14)

She must have had the impression that I was a ghost. [. . .] It was time to saddle my horse, I thought. For the cold gravestone to turn into a horse. I waited for her as usual at the old exit of the metro station, Novoslobodskaya. [. . .] Repeatedly I had the impression that she was looking furtively at my hair, as if to see whether there were any traces of soil from the grave. I had done well to tell her the story of Constantine and Doruntine [. . .] We seemed to be astride the shop windows in the half-light, just as in the legend the living and the dead are astride the one horse. I had a fever. The effect of the vaccine, for sure. [. . .] I felt the pressure of her hand on my arm. A gesture of pity? Did she want to assure herself that there was a real arm in my sleeve, and not the dry bones of a skeleton?

Albanians have been prohibited from all further contact with Soviet citizens. Kadare realizes that the relationship must end. The separation is cast metaphorically in terms of the legend of Constantine and Doruntine as the sick poet meets his lover one last time before returning to the grave.

Qu'avais-je fait! Une bouffée de chaleur envahit mes tempes, enveloppa mon front. [. . .] Mon esprit était confus et, si elle m'avait demandé: 'Pourquoi as-tu de la terre sur tes cheveux?' je ne m'en serais pas étonné. C'est une promesse que je lui ai faite, me répétais-je; je lui ai donné ma parole l'été passé, et même beaucoup plus tôt, il y a mille ans. (Le Crépuscule 214–15)

What had I done! My temples were flushed, my forehead hot. My spirit was confused and, if she had asked me: 'why do you have earth in your hair?', I would not have been surprised. It's a promise that I made to her, I said to myself; I had given her my word last summer, earlier, in fact, a thousand years ago.

Constantine and Doruntine

Kadare relates the legend of Constantine and Doruntine to his girlfriend at the beginning of the novel and it reappears at the end as the story of the *besa*, or pledge, of a man's duty to his word and his honour. In the ancient Balkan legend Constantine is the youngest of nine brothers and one sister, Doruntine. Against her mother's wishes Doruntine has been married out to a Bohemian nobleman; however, Constantine has promised that he will return Doruntine to her mother should anything happen to their family. Shortly after Doruntine's marriage, the nine brothers go to war and all die, including Constantine. Kneeling before his grave, the mother rebukes her last-born for having failed to fulfil his pledge. That night Constantine emerges from his crypt to seek out his sister in Bohemia and restore her to her mother before returning to his cold place of rest.

The legend of Constantine and Doruntine appears in various forms in the Balkans. A popular Greek version, the 'Song of the Dead Brother', focuses on Constantine's rescue of his sister, Areti ('virtue'). Other versions are to be found among the Serbs and the Arbërësh-speaking Albanian communities in southern Italy who trace their origins back to the time of Scanderbeg.[125] According to Robert Elsie, the story is known 'wherever Albanian is spoken'.[126] In different contexts Kadare focuses on different aspects of the myth. In *Invitation to the Writer's Studio* he describes his 'writer's workshop' as a type of junk-yard of bits and pieces of literary machinery, waiting to be put together into working pieces of literature.[127] The symbolic importance of the Constantine story lies in the idea of passage from one world to another. The figure of Constantine fulfils many functions in Kadare's stories: as the dutiful son, the honourable warrior, the bearer of a *besa* or pledge, the faithful brother rescuing his abandoned sister, Doruntine, the gothic revenant arisen from the tomb, the taboo-breaker, crossing from one world to the other. He is the visitor from the other world — of death, history, and dream — who, like the ghost of Hamlet's father, troubles the conscience of the living.[128] The death of Constantine is the death of literature. Constantine's role in Kadare's twilit world of death and life is ambiguous. He is a visitor from the other side whose role is to bring truth (reality) into accord with words. His promise, pledge or *besa*, to bring back Doruntine predicates his return from the nether world — not vice versa. Constantine is thus an image of the poet and of the profoundly binding relationship between poetry and life for the Albanian writer. Constantine is the Albanian hero and symbol of an Albania whose existence is the result of the word, the conduit and the substance of Albanian culture. For this reason the theme of the oral versus the printed is of such importance to Kadare. For the oral is the living, breathing Albanianness which has been submerged beneath the ice of foreign occupation and domination, existing in the printed words of ancient documents, songs, and poems.

This legend becomes the basis for Kadare's sense of his Albanian identity, the original, unchangeable existence which is his by virtue of language and birth, and to which he is bound to return. To compromise this identity is to break a pledge and must result in the existential inauthenticity which he witnesses at the Gorki Institute. When the break with the Soviet Union occurs and the students are sent home, the Constantine legend moves to the forefront of Kadare's consciousness as the defining trope of his identity and the basis for his self-understanding in writing. The word precedes and determines reality in the legend. Constantine is an image of the writer whose existence is predicated on the word. Constantine's *besa* is the writer's act of honouring the word by returning it to life. As an Albanian, Kadare is pledged to his Albanianness, not to the inauthentic supranationalism of Soviet dogma; as a writer he is pledged to literary truth, not the falsehoods of the communist hacks.

Until the break with the Soviet Union, the writer's understanding of art has been of a truthfulness to life which he has seen betrayed by the Soviet writers, with their stories of positive heroes and heroines, their renditions of life under communism as a new pastoral, and their personal bad faith (*Le Crépuscule* 52, 151). In this environment, Kadare's promise to himself is that he, like Pasternak, will remain true to writing, against the dogma of socialist realism and the politics of literature in the Soviet Union. With the break in relations between the Soviet Union and Albania, Kadare adds a further level of complexity to his articulation of the legend of Constantine. At the end of *Twilight* it becomes clear to the young writer that the bedrock of his existence is his Albanianness. However, he imagines this return in terms of Constantine's return to the grave after having brought Doruntine home. Echoing Hamlet's 'undiscovr'd country from whose bourn/No traveller returns', he imagines Lida as Doruntine in the final words of the novel, 'attendant vainement que je revienne de cette région d'où personne n'est jamais revenu' (*Le Crépuscule* 217, 'waiting in vain for me to return from that place from which no-one has ever returned'). Elsewhere Kadare refers to the proximity of the Acheron and the Styx to the town of his birth, Gjirokastra. He can only remain true to the pledge of his ethnic identity by returning to the Albania of the dictatorship, imagined as the realm of death. The return from Moscow to Albania is imagined as Constantine's return to the grave after fulfilling his *besa* to redeem Doruntine. She, typically in Kadare's work, as an image of existential authenticity and the truth of life, is a lover, symbol of that which is most precious and alive to the young man.

The set of opposing values by which the modern European mind has conceptualized the relationships between reality and aesthetics is reversed in terms of its priorities: life/death = reality/imagination = experience/art = history/eternity = motion/stasis. From now on art, death, the imagination, eternity, and stasis constitute Kadare's primary existential sphere. This reversal of the metaphoric oppositions of life and death, reality and art, will remain with Kadare for the rest of his writing life. Inasmuch as he *lives* in Albania, he does so through his writing, existing metaphorically on the border of life and death and drawing vital energies not from the present of the dictatorship but from language and the national past. Constantine is the guiding spirit of Kadare's work. He is the revenant from the land of the dead, fulfilling his word to bring his sister Doruntine home, and returning to the grave after completion of his mission. Unlike Stulpanz, whose link to his native language is less deeply imbedded, Kadare has his language, which will henceforth be his lifeline to reality and the world of human normality. Like Constantine, he will return to Albania but he will keep his pledge to life through literature. In order to retain language he will sacrifice life. The relationship of life and death will become reversed as Kadare descends into the nether world of Albanian reality, quarantining the realm of human normality to the hypothetical imaginative sphere of art. The theme of the inversion of art and life and of life and death remains a constant in Kadare's later work, emerging in the form of the ancient Albanian legend of Constantine and Doruntine and in the imagery of the Albanian border as the dividing line between life and death, upper and nether worlds. Doruntine figures as an image of Albania abducted and abandoned in various of Kadare's works. In the 1979 novel *Doruntine* she is that which is missing and whose recovery will restore life and meaning to the community; in *The Shadow* she is the distant, desirable, and ethereal Silvain Doré, who no longer recognizes her origins but is the agent of the narrator's redemption to life. The figure of Constantine, alive in death and dead in life, with an outstanding promise to remain true to life (to return a banished and displaced Albania to itself), will remain central to Kadare's literary identity.

The end of his Russian love affair marks the passing from youth to maturity and the beginning of Kadare's life as a writer. At this point the young man recognizes that he cannot both write and participate in ordinary life. He must commit himself entirely to the writer's existence. Kadare cannot pretend to be a normal person like Lida, who inhabits an uncomplicated everyday Soviet life-world of family, study, and work. Nor can he identify with his peers at the Institute, who have betrayed reality with their writing. The dictatorial environment is as poisonous as the formalin in which the metaphorical bodies of the ageing Soviet writers are embalmed. He cannot deny the writer in himself and the only alternative is the compromised and inauthentic life of the party hack. The modernist trope of the existential loneliness of the artist is refunctioned in the Albanian political environment as a statement of the impossibility of human normality and of the inversion of relationships between reality and art, and life and death in the dictatorship. As he would write much later, from the vantage point of post-communism:

> Tout [. . .] se transmue dans l'esprit de l'écrivain. Tout ce qu'il a connu en ce monde est broyé dans les meules de son atelier afin de fabriquer cette farine particulière dont ses œuvres son pétries. Dans cette farine, tous — lui-même le premier — se trouvent brassés, sacrifiés. Indistinctement, inexorablement, il se fond avec les autres: héros, saints, prostituées, brigands, presidents, épileptiques, homosexuels, gardes des sceaux, syphilitiques, privilégiés ou miserables. Au prix de ce sacrifice, il s'est, comme nombre de souverains, arrogé le pouvoir de juger [. . .]. (*Invitation* 101)

> Everything [. . .] mutates in the writer's mind. All that he knows in this world is crushed by the mill-stones in his studio in order to make that particular flour from which his works are kneaded. Everyone, first and foremost himself, is thrown in, sacrificed to that mixture. He becomes a part of the foundation along with all the others: heroes, saints, prostitutes, robbers, presidents, epileptics, homosexuals, custodians of the seal, syphilitics, the privileged and the wretched. At the cost of that sacrifice he assumes the right to judge [. . .]

November 1960 is the date of his metaphorical death, the date from which he operates as a voice from the nether world of the dictatorship. The year 1960 put an end to the possibility of the 'Quprili solution', the compromise that the ancient Albanian-Ottoman dynasty makes with the 'United Ottoman States' (U.O.S.) in *The Palace of Dreams*. This type of arrangement of ethno-national identity and Soviet power ended for Albanians in 1960. It lasted until 1989 for most of the other Eastern European nationalities. *Twilight* marks Kadare's literary recognition of the consequences of the break, namely that the Soviet paradigm for self-realization of the Albanian socialist writer has ended. As he and Stulpanz put it into rhyme while sitting over coffee in Moscow:

> Que peut-on faire d'autre sous une dictature,
> Si ce n'est l'amour et de la littérature?
> L'un et l'autre faits, prends un pieu,
> Creuse ta tombe et au monde dis adieu.[129]

> What can you do under a dictatorship
> Other than make love and literature?
> Having done the one, do the other, then turn in,
> Dig your grave and bid the world goodbye. (*Invitation* 104)

Kadare's narratives of his childhood and early adulthood in *Chronicle in Stone* and *Twilight of the Steppe-Gods* are driven by the need to come to terms with his identity as a writer, an individual, and an Albanian under the dictatorship. The personal history of *Chronicle* is the means by which he begins to reconnect past and present, establishing a mode of subjective authenticity which is intrinsically opposed to socialist realism. The spirit of the Soviet Union is evoked in the image of the 'gods of the steppe' as a desiccating, killing force blowing the life out of everything in its path: 'Ils parlaient leurs langues à moitié mortes et les mots sifflaient comme une tempête de sable, desséches par le soleil implacable du désert' (*Le Crépuscule* 74, 'they spoke their half-dead tongues and the words whistled like a sandstorm, dried out by the unrelenting desert sun'). This image expresses the aridity of the dictatorial environments of Eastern Europe, of the Ottoman Empire and Asia Minor and of China reflected into fiction. The dictatorial environment is symbolized above all in the image of the decapitated head, the headless body, the turban of the Ottoman grave-stone, and the bodyless head of the idol on the dusty steppes: 'L'échafaud sur lequel jadis on coupait les têtes se dressait encore là, à quelque distance de ses murs, comme une lune à l'écart de l'horizon' (*Le Crépuscule* 75; 'the scaffold on which they used to cut off heads still stands there, a short distance from the walls, like a moon standing out on the horizon').

Neither Enver Hoxha nor the Albanian socialist regime is mentioned in *Twilight*, but by the mid-1970s Kadare had experienced the perversions of creativity under totalitarianism. The degradation of the Soviet writers, the harassment of Pasternak, and the decline of Fadeyev,[130] Mayakowsky, and others into depression, alcoholism, and suicide prepare him for the life of the writer in Albania, where the situation was worse than in the Soviet Union under Khrushchev. On his return, he writes, he gave up poetry as his primary form of expression in the hostile Albanian writing environment. Prose writing offered a compromise between words and power.[131]

Eternal Albania: *The Three-Arched Bridge*, 1978

On New Year's Eve, 31 December 1975 Kadare's father died. Kadare had just returned to Tirana from the Myzeqe to celebrate the New Year. In the brief descriptions in the autobiographical works the writer's father emerges as a man of decency, worried about his son's future under this regime of which he scarcely approved. The death made Kadare aware of the effect his writer's existence was having on those close to him. The death of a parent brings home, too, the realization of one's own mortality. Kadare was about to turn forty and was tiring of the nerve-wracking battle of wits with the regime.

> Il fallut cette mort pour qu'entre l'État et moi s'établisse un pacte tacite: je n'écrirais plus de romans. De son côté, l'État me laisserait tranquille.[132]

> That death was necessary for the State and myself tacitly to establish a pact: I would write no more novels. For its part, the State would leave me in peace.

Moreover, the generation of the fathers, the wartime partisans and the overseers of post-war reconstruction, was beginning to pass on. In October 1973 Enver Hoxha celebrated his sixty-fifth birthday. But only hours before the lavish reception was to begin he was struck down by a cardiac arrest. A heavy smoker with diabetes, he too was entering the last phase of his life.[133] The passing of the Chinese leader Mao Tse-tung in 1976 reminded those who had lived through the previous two decades of the suffering and the losses caused by the Cultural Revolution.

And now with the Chinese alliance finally ended, Albania would go it alone in world communism. Death and loss appeared to be the companions of the Albanian isolation, which reached its peak in 1978. In the cold of the Myzeqe Kadare imagined Albania itself as an orphan, with neither the dictator nor the writer still alive, 'séparée, isolée, dans une autre époque [. . .], comme une orpheline [. . .] à la merci du destin' ('separated, isolated, in another era [. . .] like an orphan [. . .] at the mercy of fate'.)[134] In the Myzeqe Kadare observed the full extent of the regime's desecration of Albanian traditions and history. Churches were destroyed, crosses ripped down, and communist slogans scratched into the stonework.

> L'Albanie se désagrégeait. Nul besoin d'être très clairvoyant pour comprendre que le communisme, après l'avoir jetée bas, la vidait de sa substance. [. . .] L'Albanie se défaisait sous nos yeux. (*Le Poids* 400–01)

> Albania was disintegrating. You didn't need to be a clairvoyant in order to understand that communism, having thrown the country to the ground, was now emptying it of its substance. [. . .] Albania was coming undone before our very eyes.

This Albania demanded his attention. In the wake of the failure of the pedagogical exercise of the 'corrective mask' and entering middle age amidst the reminders of mortality and the losses of the cultural revolution, Kadare sought a deeper engagement with the national identity that had provided him with such strength over the previous decades and in which, he claims, he found an alternative to the Albania of the present.

History is the key to the novels of the 1970s. In *The Castle* (1970), *The Niche of Shame* (1976), *The Secular Chronicle of the Hankonis* (1976), *Broken April* (1978), *The Three-Arched Bridge* (1978), *Doruntine* (1979), even *The File on H* (1982), and *The Palace of Dreams* (1981), Kadare brings together literary allegory with the historical novel in a body of works depicting his country's past from the perspective of the present. Kadare's development of the genre of the historical novel under communism is one of his greatest achievements. As the title of his 1976 collection of poems implies, *Koha (Time)*, history and the passage of personal/individual and communal/national time became a dominant theme as the writer entered his forties. These works from the late 1970s are among Kadare's most popular.

Questions of leadership, cultural influence, and patterns of domination and control figure large in these works. Based on Martin Barletius's Latin narrative of the *Siege of Shkodra*, *The Castle* takes as its theme the Albanian defence against the Turkish occupation.[135] Shkodra fell to Sultan Mehmet II in 1478, almost a century after the Battle of Kosovo. The Ottoman siege of an Albanian fortress is viewed through the eyes of a tired and demoralized Turkish leader some time in the mid-fifteenth century, after Tamerlane's assaults on the eastern edges of the Empire pushed the Ottomans to overcome the last sites of Balkan resistance. *The Niche of Shame* (called 'The Head's Journey' at this stage) was finished after *The Twilight of the Steppe-Gods*. Kadare tells the story of Ali Pasha of Tepelena, the solitary Albanian warlord who carved a dominion from Ottoman Rumelia for thirty-three years from the last decade of the eighteenth century. Like Hoxha, he was a ruthless leader who used domestic brutality and strategic alliances (in Ali Pasha's case with France and Britain, in Hoxha's with China) against the imperial power. Without the alibi of the 'corrective mask', the ambiguity of the figure of the Albanian leader predominates. The image of the Albanian patriot and freedom fighter, offered as a bribe for political change in *The Great Winter*, pales beside the despot and assassin of *The Niche of Shame*.

In *Broken April* Kadare evokes the intensity of the Kanun as the common law of the Albanians, overriding the enjoinments of religion and imperial powers. In light of the failure of religion and communism, the Kanun appears as the only force to provide a binding set of beliefs powerful enough to underpin a national culture. In *Broken April* and some of his later works and essays, Kadare seeks to validate aspects of the ancient canon of Albanian traditional justice. In light of the communist disregard for the rule of law, the Kanun has an open, popular, democratic and liberating aspect, despite the brutality of some of its punishments and conventions. 'Son principe fondamental est l'"égalité du sang", autrement dit, l'"égalité des hommes" ('Its fundamental principle is the "equality of blood", meaning, "the equality of men"').[136] Kadare is not suggesting some sort of return to this code which is, as he is the first to comment, valid for men only, since women have no status in its 'democratic' purview. Nevertheless it is the only chthonic Albanian body of law applying across geographical and religious borders and hence the possible basis for a national renewal. Since the communists tried to put an end to Kanun, Kadare's evocation of it in these works is highly provocative.

> Il faut avoir vécu sous la dictature communiste, avoir éprouvé ce qu'on appelle 'la justice inspirée de la lutte de classe', avoir eu connaissance des tortures, des exécutions sommaires, de l'extermination de familles entières par suite de la condamnation d'un seul de leurs membres, pour comprendre l'espace de liberté contenu dans l'ancien Coutumier et la nostalgie avec laquelle il était invoqué par les Albanais.[137]

> You had to have lived under the communist dictatorship, to have felt what was called 'justice arising from class conflict', to have known of the tortures, the summary executions, the extermination of whole families in the wake of the condemnation of one of their members, in order to understand the type of liberty contained in the ancient Kanon and the longing with which Albanians remembered it.

Late the following year *Doruntine* appeared, a striking retelling of the ancient story of the return of the Albanian girl to her homeland, motivated partly by the ongoing troubles in Kosovo. In all of these works Kadare evoked 'another Albania, eternal, magical, opposed to the sterility and aridity of communist Albania'.[138] Kadare's unique style of historical writing is nowhere better exemplified than in *The Three-Arched Bridge,* in which the early formative events of Albanian history are presented as the 'concrete pre-history of the present' in Lukács's terms.[139] From 1976 until 1978 he worked on this novel, 'like a monk in the depths of his monastery',[140] to restore the icon. In *The Three-Arched Bridge*, as in *Doruntine*, he evokes the 'eternal Albania' which is the inspiration behind so many of his works from *The General of the Dead Army* onwards, and which surfaces in the minds and imaginations of protagonists such as Mark-Alem in *The Palace of Dreams* and even Besnik Struga in *Winter of Great Solitude*. The Albania of *The Three-Arched Bridge*, he writes,

> n'était pas sans lien avec l'actuelle, la tragique, dans laquelle je vivais. Ainsi, les pierres dont est construit ce pont medieval sont d'époque [. . .] alors que l'angoisse et la terreur, elles, sont de l'ère communiste.[141]

> was not unrelated to the tragic everyday in which I lived. And so, the stones which the bridge is constructed from are of the medieval era [. . .] while the anguish and the terror are of the communist era.

FIG. 19 (above): The ageing and ailing Enver Hoxha in 1978, at the time of *The Concert.*
(Source: *40 Years of Socialist Albania*, Tirana: 8 Nëntori Publishing House, 1984.)

FIG. 20 (below): Looking across towards Montenegro from the Rozafat citadel in Shkodra.
(Photo: Peter Morgan.)

He saw himself as both writing a novel and recreating the Albania of his imagination, a different, 'phantom' Albania which would act as a challenge to and defiance of the present.

> Cette autre Albanie devait notamment constituer un défi à l'Albanie réelle, l'Albanie communiste, morne et aride. Elle serait un spectre, un éternel remords de conscience, mais aussi, envers et contre tout, un espoir de résurrection.[142]

> That other Albania had chiefly to constitute a defiance to the real Albania, the arid and gloomy Albania of communism. It would be a phantom, an eternal source of remorse, but also, and in spite of everything, a hope of resurrection.

In a well-known and often-quoted speech from the mid 1960s, Enver Hoxha likened the builders of the new socialist infrastructure and industrial plants to the stonemasons sacrificed 'in our beautiful legends about the building of bridges and castles'.[143] For Hoxha legends such as the ancient story of human sacrifice in the building of the Rozafat castle at Shkodra provided the foundations for modern literature. In this legend three brothers, stonemasons working on the castle of Shkodra, are told that they must pledge to sacrifice the first of their wives who arrives with food at the worksite the following morning. Otherwise, the walls of the castle will continue to collapse. The older two brothers break their word, warning their wives to stay at home, but the younger keeps his vow or *besa*, and to his horror his wife appears at the building site, unaware of the cruel fate in store for her. This foundation legend of modern Albania becomes something much more ambiguous for Kadare.

> Dans ce récit, j'ai principalement traité du vieux thème du sacrifice. Cela a été l'un des thèmes fondamentaux de la propagande communiste: le sacrifice au nom de l'avenir! Il justifiait tout: la pauvreté, l'ennui, et surtout l'oppression. Là, j'ai décrit un sacrifice qui n'était en fait qu'un meurtre prémédité, par consequent un crime.[144]

> In this story I mainly dealt with the ancient theme of sacrifice. That was one of the fundamental themes of communist propaganda: sacrifice for the sake of the future! It justified everything: poverty, boredom, and especially oppression. There, I described a sacrifice which was nothing other than a premeditated murder, and thus a crime.

History and the Albanian Nation

Kadare's novel takes the form of a chronicle written by the Catholic monk Gjon Ukcama written in the year 1377, just over a decade before the Battle of Kosovo and at the time of the early Ottoman incursions into Albania. The story concerns the building of a bridge in a fictional north-eastern Albanian setting, probably in the area of Mirdita or Puka. An unknown traveller suffers an epilepic fit on the banks of the fictive river *Ujana e Keqe* ('Wicked Waters'), and a vagrant fortune-teller prophesies that this is a sign for a bridge to be built. Shortly afterward a mysterious foreign deputation arrives at the town to propose the building of a bridge. They appear to be in the pay of rich business interests of unknown provenance, whose interest in crossing the river at this point suggests that the bridge will have wider strategic importance in a time of change. Gjon Ukcama is summoned to translate for his lord, Count Stres of the Gjikas, but struggles to understand the curious multilingual babble of the foreigners. They offer the count a profitable deal on the rights to construct the bridge. Count Stres, preoccupied with the illness of his daughter and in debt as the result of a conflict with the Duke of Tepelena, agrees, although he is already under contract to the owners of 'Boats and Rafts' for the fording of the river at this point. (Ten years earlier, in 1367, all of the rafts and ferries throughout Arberia were bought up by a single entity called 'Boats and Rafts'.) The building of the bridge commences and is surrounded by rumour, suspicion, and uncertainty as mysterious damage occurs overnight during the building. A man is apprehended and immured under bizarre and murderous circumstances in the bridge's central pylon. The monk, Gjon Ukcama, wants to set the truth straight about this appalling episode in the construction of this first stone bridge in his homeland.

'Boats and Rafts' is rooted in Albanian tradition and history since Roman times. The company's dealings with the local counts and princes are based on contracts which have been honoured on both sides for centuries and they have been 'reliable down to the last penny'. However, these operations still take place within a feudal framework and the foundations for this proto-capitalism are weak. The contract between the owner of 'Boats and Rafts' and Count Stres is historically credible within the feudal framework of a lord who needs money to pay off debts arising from military conflict and to attend to his sick daughter's needs. The ambiguous power relationship between feudal and early capitalist interests is reflected in the relative weakness of the company's bank in Dürres to force the count to honour his agreement with 'Boats and Rafts' in this pre-national environment. The princes must be paid off, bribed, or otherwise cajoled into allowing bridges to be built; the people are wary and must be convinced; and cultural identifications and practices must be changed. The raftsmen who have been plying travellers across the rivers for centuries will lose their livelihood. The new structure is seen as an affront to the spirit of the waters. People are distrustful of the demonic machinery used to build the bridge; religion and superstition come into play on all sides as the bridge-builders stage visitations and prophecies and the owners of 'Boats and Rafts' stage counter-strategies.

The builders of bridges represent a new force of modernity altogether. The owner is not a lord, but a rich bourgeois who has bought up mines and the old imperial roads. They are surveyors and engineers, who measure and quantify carefully, remaining impervious to the folk customs and beliefs of the local populace. The threats of the old woman, Ajkuna, for whom the bridge remains the work of the devil, elicit no response from the foreign engineer and master-builder. For him the bridge is the symbol of the coming new order.

> Selon des signes qu'il avait observés depuis quelque temps déjà, dans cette partie de l'Europe avaient commencé à se dessiner vaguement, très vaguement, les contours d'un ordre nouveau qui devait faire avancer le monde de plusieurs siècles. [. . .] Tout ce mouvement, disait-il n'était rien d'autre qu'un signe à la fois de vie et de mort, le signe de la naissance d'un monde nouveau et de la mort de l'ancien. (*Le Pont* 85)[145]

> According to signs that he had been studying for some time, the lineaments of a
> new order that would carry the world many centuries forward had faintly, ever
> so faintly, begun to appear in this part of Europe. [. . .] And all this movement,
> he said, was a sign simultaneously of life and death, of the birth of a new world
> and the death of the old. (*Bridge* 101)

The town is a backwater in central Albania, but it lies on the Via Egnatia, the
ancient road which passed from Rome through Dürres or Apollonia and across
Albania on the way to Constantinople. With the increases in trade from the
caravans passing through Arberia to Macedonia and beyond, and with the growing
interest of various powers in the harbour at Orikum, new forces are coming into
play. Money is to be made from the construction of roads throughout the peninsula,
in which bridges rather than ferries provide reliable passage in all weathers for larger
and larger numbers of travellers. Bitumen mines used by the Romans but long since
abandoned, have suddenly become valuable again for war and road building, and
bitumen is sold everywhere, 'aux Turcs et aux Byzantins, comme aux comtes et
aux ducs d'Arberie, incitant les deux camps à se déchirer' (*Le Pont* 25; 'to the Turks
and Byzantium on the one hand, and to all the counts and dukes of Arberia on the
other, fomenting quarrels on both sides', *The Bridge* 23).

This is an era of transition, in which the old structures are no longer dominant
and in which the new is just beginning to take shape. The Byzantine Empire is in its
final years. The death of the powerful Serb king Stefan Dushan in 1355 has created
the conditions for an independent Albania,[146] but the Albanian lords are divided by
religion and foreign interest and are fighting among themselves. The Ottomans are
already entrenched in the eastern Balkans and about to occupy Greece, Albania,
and Serbia. Western Europe is weakened by plague and the Hundred Years War,
and the papacy is divided between Rome and Avignon. The ambitions of the newly
minted feudal barons and counts of Albania were exemplified in the move of the
Norman governor of the Serb principality of Zeta, who assumed the title of Balsha
I and formed an independent Albanian state with Skutari as its capital between 1366
and 1421. Other strong clans or rulers also existed with ambitions of extending their
power: the Topias, Dukagjins and Kastriotis, the southern Muzakis and others.
However, the Balkans lie on the edge of various spheres of influence. The Crusaders
under Frederick Barbarossa, the Knights Templars, the St John's Knights, and the
Teutonic Order have passed through the country, using the ancient Via Egnatia to
reach Jerusalem. Remnants of Norman influence are still to be felt in names such as
the 'Inn of the Two Roberts' (visited during the First Crusade by Robert Guiscard,
Count of Normandy and Robert, Count of Flanders). Venetian, Ragusan, and
other foreign interests are supporting the infighting of the Albanian leaders in order
to keep the country divided. Mercenaries, including Turkish battalions, have been
involved, opening the way for the later Ottoman expansion.

At the annual hunting party of Count Stres, a countess from the northern Balsha
clan mentions anxiety over the Orikum (ancient Vlora) naval base, which has again
become a source of conflict. The reasons are not given, but it is noted that one
fork in the newly revived road from Rome to Constantinople leads to the military
base at the town. Orikum is partly under the jurisdiction of the Byzantines and

partly under the Albanian Komnenis. On the basis of ancient legal documents, Aranit Komneni attacked and claimed full possession of the base. The Byzantine rulers, anxious to appease the Albanians at a time of dwindling power, have agreed to an intermarriage to maintain part ownership but are nevertheless forced by the Ottomans to cede their share. Aranit Komneni seeks to form a coalition of Albanian princes to protect this most important Adriatic port but dies without support from the Albanian lords. His son-in-law Balsha II uses Komneni's death to claim Orikum for the new principality of Albania — also without support from the Albanian lords. As the novel draws to a close we learn that the situation at Orikum is about to come to a head with the occupation of the Komneni lands by Balsha II and the likelihood of war with the Ottoman Turks.

Kadare goes to considerable lengths to paint an Arberia emerging from Byzantine influence, on the verge of proto-national identity but about to be plunged into servitude under the Ottomans. His Arberia lies on the cusp between medieval and early modern development. Speaking to a fellow-monk returning to Rome from Constantinople Gjon Ukcama describes the new national identity of his fellow-countrymen in terms of popular consciousness as *'shqiptarë'* (Shkipetars or Albanians). Unlike the Serbs and the Bulgarians, the Albanians did not experience the formation of a proto-national political core identity. Responsibility for this failure lies not only with the foreign powers, but also with the Albanian feudal lords. 'Au cours des cent dernières années, les querelles entre les princes et seigneurs albanais ont été désespérément fréquentes' (*Le Pont* 40; 'quarrels among the Albanian princes and lords have been hopelessly frequent for the last hundred years', *Bridge* 43), writes Gjon Ukcama, alluding to the political developments which represented the beginnings of a feudal consolidation that would fail to come to fruition in the creation of a single kingdom or proto-national structure.

> Les princes du nord, les Balsha [. . .] sont rarement en bons termes avec les fiers Topia, dont la maison est prétendante au trône de toute l'Albanie. Les Balsha n'ont pas eu de bons rapports non plus avec les comtes de la Myzeqe, les Muzaka [. . .] De même, les Muzaka ont été en conflit quasi perpétuel avec le puissant prince de Vlorë, Aranit Comnène, bien que les deux parties se soient alliées aux empereurs de Byzance, et cela à la différence des Dukagjin, des Balsha et des Topia, qui n'ont noué d'alliances au-dehors qu'avec la maison royale de France. Les Muzaka ne se sont pas bien entendus non plus avec les Kastriote [. . .] (*Le Pont* 40)

> The Balsha family, princes of the north [. . .] could seldom agree with the proud Topia family, who have pretension to the throne of all Arberia. Nor have the Balshas been on good terms with the counts of Myzeqe, the Muzakas [. . .] Yet the Muzakas likewise have been in almost continual animosity with Aranit Komneni, the powerful prince of Vlorë, even though both families are allied by marriage to the emperors of Byzantium, in contrast to the Dukaghins, Balshas, and Topias, who have forged their marriage alliances abroad, exclusively with the French royal family. Nor have the Muzakas been on good terms with the Kastriotis [. . .] (*Bridge* 43–44)

Marriages with foreigners have not been any more successful, he writes, neither the liaison of the Topias with the French house of Anjou, nor that of the Komnenis with the Byzantine royal family. Of course, a principality such as French Anjou had been involved in the same sorts of political processes in the ninth century as these Albanian lands in the fourteenth.

> Les seigneurs de l'Arberie ont pensé pouvoir éteindre toutes ces querelles par des alliances. Mais, comme je l'ai dit, les alliances jetées sur cette mer déchaînée ne furent que quelques rares arcs-en-ciel, aussitôt engloutis par le gouffre. (*Le Pont* 41)

> The lords of Arberia imagined they could settle these quarrels by marriages. But as I mentioned, the alliances thrown across this stormy sea have been merely like rainbows straining to climb a few degrees above the abyss. (*Bridge* 44)

Like the Byzantines, the leading Albanian clans, the Topias, Balshas, Muzakas, Komnenis, Dukagjins, Kastriotis and others, called upon the services of Turkish mercenaries to help fight their battles, introducing these Eastern warriors to the peninsula.

> Il y a quelques temps, j'ai eu l'occasion de voir un de leurs détachements, qui, après avoir participé au conflit entre les habitants de Ohri et les Balsha, regagnait sa base. C'était une unité de mercenaires, de ceux qui se battent pour un temps et une solde fixés par contrat. Depuis plusieurs années, les princes albanais, à l'exemple de tous les princes des Balkans et des empereurs de Byzance eux-mêmes, faisaient appel à des détachements turcs pour les utiliser dans leurs querelles. C'est sous cette forme qu'ils sont apparus dans les régions balkaniques. (*Le Pont* 44)

> Some time ago, I happened to see one of their military units on its homeward journey after taking part in the dispute between the barons of Ohri and the Muzakas. It was a body of mercenaries who had fought for a fixed period for a fee, under a contract. The Albanian princes, like those elsewhere in the Balkans, and the Byzantine emperors themselves, have for some years been calling on Turkish units for use in their squabbles among themselves. This was how they first appeared in the Balkan lands. (*Bridge* 46–47)

Not only are impoverished or debt-ridden lords selling land and hiring Turkish mercenaries, they are also entering into marriage contracts and even adopting the language of the Turks. The new expression, 'Balkan', has become adopted throughout the peninsula, undermining the existing proto-national boundaries and identities.

> 'Aujourd'hui, nos deux langues, l'albanais et le grec, sont toutes deux menacées par la langue turque comme par un sombre nuage'. [. . .] 'La langue turque avec son fameux suffixe "lik", repris-je doucement un moment après alors que nos regards se perdaient l'un dans l'autre, pèse sur nous comme une terrible massue'. (*Le Pont* 61–62)

> 'Now the Ottoman language is casting its shadow over both our languages Greek and Albanian, like a black cloud'. [. . .] 'The language of the East is drawing nearer', I repeated after a while. [. . .] 'With its "-luk" suffix', I went on slowly. 'Like some dreadful hammer blow'. (*Bridge* 70–71)

In this period in the second half of the fourteenth century, exactly six hundred years before the time of writing, there was, as Kadare's monk laments, a lost opportunity for the Albanians to work together rather than sabotaging their own interests through infighting and through the use of Turkish mercenaries.[147]

The three-arched bridge belongs to Kadare's literary geography, inventoried in *The Invitation to the Writer's Studio* as 'un seul pont: celui aux trois arches, d'où irradie toujours le malheur' (*Invitation* 246, 'a single bridge, with three arches, from which misfortune irradiates'). That the bridge is symbolic of the land of Albania is already implied in the structure, its arches representing the three eras of foreign occupation — Roman, Byzantine, and Ottoman.[148] The bridge is an image of modernization and progress in a land over and through which historical forces have passed for centuries, but in which they did not coalesce or consolidate. Feudal fragmentation, primitive social conditions, and above all the position on the edges, between Byzantium and Rome, are responsible. The bridge represents both progress and unfreedom. Ideally it enables traffic and communication; in reality it becomes an avenue of imperialism, war and murder:

> Au fond, c'était l'exécution d'un meurtre qui planait depuis longtemps dans l'air. Nous étions tous éclaboussés par le sang qui en avait jailli, et les cris d'horreur qu'il aurait dû susciter étaient déjà consumés. Le long duel des aquatiques avec les terrestres s'était terminé par la victoire de ces derniers. 'Ne cherchez pas à nous nuire, car vous trouverez la mort'. C'était ce cri qui montait de la première arche du pont. (*Le Pont* 102)

> This was only the final act of a murder that had been in the wind for a long time. Its spurts of blood had already spattered us all, and its screams had died away long ago. The long duel between the men of the water and the men of the land had concluded with the victory of the latter. 'Do not try to harm us again, or you will be killed'. That was the cry that came from the first arch of the bridge. (*Bridge* 123)

That first, Roman, arch of the bridge represents the beginning of the history of imperial conquest and the shape of things to come for the Albanians. The conflict between 'Boats and Rafts' and the bridge-builders thus acquires ideological and cultural connotations as well as associations of freedom and unfreedom. For the Albanian townspeople, 'le monstre des eaux, "Bacs et Radeaux", nourrissait une hostilité féroce à l'égard du fauve terrestre qui construisait des routes et des ponts' (*Le Pont* 23, 'the demon of the waters, in the person of 'Boats and Rafts', was in bitter enmity with the demon of the land, who built roads and bridges', *Bridge* 21). The popular superstition has parabolic connotations, and Gjon Ukcama too refers to the conflict between land and water (*Le Pont* 117, *Bridge* 142). The bridge is referred to as a 'bât' (48, 'pack-saddle'), and as 'le premier malheur jeté brutalement sur le libre esprit des eaux' (*Le Pont* 23, 'the first misfortune inflicted on the free spirit of the waters', *Bridge* 21). At the same time, it is associated with the forces which cure Count Stres's daughter of her mysterious illness. Gjon Ukcama is reminded of a story told to him by a Dutch monk from Africa about the battle to the death between the tiger of the land and the crocodile of the water in which the former will be victorious (*Le Pont* 24, *Bridge* 22). The battle has an elemental ferocity reminiscent of Kadare's parable of the battle to the death of the writer and the dictator in *Albanian Spring*.

The conflict of the bridge and the waters is to be found in the earlier *Chronicle in Stone*, in which the young narrator viewed the battle between the swollen river and the stone bridge of Gjirokastra as a particularly Albanian version of the opposition of nature and civilization. In that earlier story, the child, by no means sympathetic to the forces of nature, observes the temporary truce symbolized in the rainbow. Kadare's bridge, standing in defiance of nature, is a very different image of progress, modernization, and civilization in a hostile natural environment from Ivo Andrić's more famous structure at Visegrad. In Andrić's parable the bridge is man's attempt to right the destruction caused by the devil in scratching God's newly-made and smooth world.[149] For Kadare the bridge is an imposition of man-made order over nature. It represents the constraint of civilization over nature, of dogma over truth, and of political structure over innate national identity in Kadare's romantic nationalism. We might even infer that in Kadare's mythology 'eternal Albania' ceased in 1367 with the first steps into modernity, symbolized in the monopoly of 'Boats and Rafts' over the fordable sites of the river. Albanian development stopped at this point, and everything since has been an imposition and a constraint from outside.

With this story of bridge-building, modernization, and sacrifice we find ourselves in familiar Kadarean territory. Here we have in a nutshell the dilemma of modernization, Kadare's ambivalence towards Albanian communism expressed as a parable of Balkan history: on the one hand the promise of modernity;[150] on the other, constraint, force, and obligation, using all of the means of a dictatorship to ensure compliance to a foreign system and set of values among an impoverished and traditional people. The figures of the folklorist and the master-builder represent the two sides of the argument for modernization that Kadare, and with him a host of Central and Eastern European intellectuals, came to recognize as the antinomies of communist modernization, an extreme version of the European syndrome of progress and loss familiar since Rousseau. For many of these intellectuals, blinded by the possibilities of accelerated progress, the sacrifices were valid or at least justifiable. Soon the confidence behind these judgements waned, and the contours of the conflict between freedom and constraint became increasingly clear in the communist environment. The antinomies of modernization and loss, which have been central to Kadare's work since *The City without Signs*, underpin *The Three-Arched Bridge*.

Sacrifice and Loss

As the bridge is being built a new threat emerges. Damage is found on the central pillar. The people believe that the demons of the river are fighting back. A collector of folktales turns up and gleans from the monk details of the Rozafat legend. He leaves and the monk suspects him of having been in the pay of the bridge-builders. Sure enough, soon afterwards bards arrive singing a changed version of the legend. The new immurement story is not about three brothers building a castle wall, but about masons building a bridge, which is destroyed at night by the spirits of the waters.

'Que vienne quelqu'un qui consente à se sacrifier aux pieds du pont, chantaient les rhapsodes. Qu'il se sacrifie pour le bien des miliers de voyageurs qui passeraient sur ce pont en hiver et en été, sous la pluie et dans la tempête, allant vers la joie ou le malheur, infinie multitude humaine qui défilerait dans les siècles à venir'. (*Le Pont* 88)

'Let someone come who is willing to be sacrificed in the piers of the bridge, the bards sang. Let him be a sacrifice for the sake of the thousands and thousands of travellers who will cross that bridge winter and summer, in rain and storm, journeying toward their joy or to their misfortune, hordes of people down the centuries to come'. (*The Bridge* 104–05)

Talk of sacrifice becomes self-perpetuating. 'La ballade, c'était clair, ne présageiait que du sang' (*Le Pont* 88, 'clearly the ballad portended nothing but blood', *Bridge* 105), 'on parlait de ce sacrifice propitiatoire le plus naturellement du monde (*Le Pont* 91, 'It became a most simple and natural thing to talk about a sacrifice', *Bridge* 110). The only question is who will offer himself and under what conditions?

Tout cela me faisait l'effet d'un rêve étrange. C'étaient des choses dont nous n'avions jamais entendu parler, une sorte de mort à devis, à cachets et à taux d'intérêt. J'en avais parfois le vertige et je n'y comprenais rien. [. . .] Cette affaire du tarif pour le sacrifice venait tout embrouiller.

To me this all resembled a bizarre dream. This was something we had never heard of before, a kind of death with accounts, seals, and percentages. It made me dizzy sometimes and I didn't understand anything of it. [. . .] This business of calculated sacrifice confused me completely. (112★)

The only surprising thing about the inevitable victim, Murrash Zenebisha, is his ordinariness. 'Il était difficile de trouver parmi les hommes du commun quelqu'un de moins singulier que lui' (*Le Pont* 95, 'it would have been difficult to find anyone more commonplace than he', *Bridge* 114). By the time Gjon Ukcama hears of the event, the body has been walled up in the stonework, leaving only his shoulders and head visible. Suspicions, gossip, rumour abound, but the monk becomes convinced that Murrash was caught in the act of sabotage and murdered by the bridge-builders. The monk had been privy to discussions between the Count and the bridge-builders about the sabotage:

Assurément, le sort de Murrash Zenebishe avait été fixé alors. Les terrestres avaient découvert que les aquatiques payaient quelqu'un pour démolir la nuit une partie du pont. Cet homme était le modeste Murrash Zenebishe. Par trois fois il avait accompli sa besogne de démolition sans se faire pincer. La quatrième, on l'avait pris sur le fait et on l'avait tué. (*Le Pont* 101)

Murrash Zenebisha's fate had been sealed on that day. The road builders had found out that the water people were paying someone to damage the bridge at night. This person was the ordinary Murrash Zenebisha. He had done his job three times without being caught. The fourth time they had caught him red-handed and killed him. (*Bridge* 122★)

The new ballads reflect the bridge-builders' interest in creating a myth of human sacrifice which will legitimize and sanctify the structure and warn against further sabotage. They encourage the belief that Murrash was immured alive, bringing this contemporary matter into line with the hyperbole of legend. As Gjon Ukcama writes, 'Le crime n'avait qu'un mobile: répandre la terreur (*Le Pont* 104, 'The crime had only one purpose — to inspire terror', *Bridge* 124). Murrash is cynically instrumentalized as a symbolic sacrificial victim immured in the central column of the bridge. The story is surrounded by untruths. In the unravelling of the crime in this peculiar detective story, questions of responsibility, guilt, and compliance are every bit as complex as those of sacrifice, loss, and gain. Kadare emphasizes three different views of the sacrifice through the mouthpieces of the monk, the folklore collector and the master-mason responsible for the planning and construction of the bridge. Gjon Ukcama reads the legend as a metaphoric statement of the collective consciousness of the nature of self-sacrifice in constructive human labour.

> La légende avait pour base l'idée que tout travail, ou toute grande action, nécessite un sacrifice [. . .]. Ce qui était nouveau et particulier dans la ballade de notre peuple, c'était que le sacrifice ne se rattachait pas à une entreprise de guerre, à une expédition, ou même à un rite réligieux, mais à une simple construction. [. . .] Je voulais dire aussi que les gouttes de sang de la légende n'étaient en réalité que des ruisseaux de sueur, mais que la sueur humaine est, notoirement, de condition servile comparée au sang, qu'elle est anonyme et que, de ce fait, personne n'a composé de chant ou de ballade en son honneur. [. . .] Il va de soi qu'en versant sa sueur, chacun sacrifie quelque chose de soi-même, et le plus jeune des frères sacrifia son bonheur. (*Le Pont* 81–82)

> The true kernel of the legend was the idea that all labour, and every major task, requires some kind of sacrifice [. . .]. What was new, and peculiar to the ballad of our people, was that the sacrifice was not connected with the outbreak of war or some march, nor even a religious rite, but concerned a wall, a simple work of construction. [. . .] I wanted to say that in truth the drops of blood in the legend were nothing but streams of sweat. But we know that sweat is a kind of humble nameless servant in comparison with blood, and therefore nobody has devoted songs and ballads to it. [. . .] alongside his sweat every man sacrifices something of himself, like the youngest brother, who sacrificed his own happiness. (*Bridge* 96–97★)

For the monk the legend of Rozafat is a metaphor of progress and sacrifice. He renders the barbarity of human sacrifice harmless in the legend by interpreting it as a metaphor of the individual's self-sacrifice for the collective. In this enlightened version of the myth, sweat becomes blood, symbol of the organized, collective giving up of individual freedoms, the loss without which civilization or progress is impossible. The violence is a literary device rather than a reflection of reality. The folklorist collects information about the sacrifice in order to manipulate it into a version of the popular Rozafat legend for the use of his masters, the bridge-builders. His cynicism in manipulating the story of the humble, nameless servant, the everyday Albanian worker, appals the monk. Whereas the latter tries to understand the complexity of the human situation, the ambiguity of sacrifice and progress, the folklore collector reduces the story to a set of hypotheses which can be manipulated to the advantage of the bridge-builders and presented as progress. For the master-builder, the bridge is indicative of the appearance of the new order of things. The construction is nothing other than 'un signe à la fois de vie et de mort, le signe de la naissance d'un monde nouveau et de la mort de l'ancien' (*Le Pont* 85, 'a sign of life and death, of the birth of a new world and the death of the old', *Bridge* 101). This bridge, he argues, is at least functional and useful, as against those other bridges built by the capitalists, the 'ponts-cadavres' (*Le Pont* 85, 'corpse-bridges', *Bridge* 101) designed purely for the pleasure of the leisured classes. The bridge over the *Ujana e Keqe* 'même s'il doit être arrosé de sang, est mille fois plus utile qu'eux, (*Le Pont* 86, 'even if washed in blood, is a thousand times nobler than those', *Bridge* 102). Hence for him too, the immurement becomes a part of the mythology of change and progress: unfortunate, but necessary, and hence not worth lingering over. His is the voice of the technocrat wedded to progress.

The monk alone recognizes the moral ambiguities concealed in the high words of the modernizing project. Through his eyes we see the ways in which the bridge and the sacrifice are understood, manipulated, and used.

> J'eus subitement une envie folle de le saisir par le col de sa pèlerine, de le coller au pilier du pont et de lui crier en pleine figure: 'cet ordre nouveau dont tu me parlais un jour, cet ordre à vous, de banques, et d'intérêts, qui devrait soi-disant faire progresser le monde d'un millénaire, est baigné de sang à ses fondements tout comme l'ordre barbare d'antan'. (*Le Pont* 108)

> I suddenly felt a crazy desire to seize him by the collar of his cape, pin him against the bridge pier, and shout in his face: 'That new world you told me about the other day, that new order with its banks and percentages, which is supposed to carry the world a thousand years forward, it is founded on blood just like the barbarism of earlier times'. (*Bridge* 129*)

As he announced at the outset of his chronicle, his aim is to represent events as objectively as possible, in view of the fact that 'on continue de répandre à son sujet des légendes et des rumeurs non fondées, maintenant donc que sa construction est achevée' (*Le Pont* 7, 'people continue to spread legends and baseless rumours about it, now that it has been finished', *Bridge* 1*).

Soon even Murrash's fate becomes ordinary. People become used to the sight of the body in the bridge pier and his family have begun to quarrel over the money. At first the people are unwilling to use the bridge. But a stray wolf, and then some sheep cross over. Later a convoy arrives carrying pitch for the naval base at Orikum. War is brewing. Balsha II, the leader of northern Albanian principality, has deployed troops over the Komneni lands on the death of Aranit Komneni, and the Byzantines have ceded their share of the Orikum base to the Ottomans. In the final pages a skirmish breaks out on the bridge between Turkish scouts and local sentries, heralding the bloodshed to come. The novel finishes with Gjon Ukcama's apocalyptic vision of the Ottoman invasion of Albania and attack on Europe:

> Mon regard se voila et, de même que j'avais distingué alors la tache de sang déteint sur le cou de Murrash Zenebishe, ainsi, j'eus l'impression que sous ce bain de lune je voyais des plaines entières inondées de sang et de montagnes réduites en cendres. Je voyais les hordes turques qui rabotaient le monde pour y étendre l'espace islamique. Je voyais les feux et leurs cendres, et les restes calcinés des hommes et des chroniques. [. . .] Cette nuit qui s'approche sera longue. (*Le Pont* 144)

> My eyes darkened, and just as I had seen that pale patch of blood under Murrash Zenebisha's neck, so it seemed to me that now, under that moonlight, I saw whole plains awash with blood, and mountain ranges burned to ash. I saw Turkish hordes flattening the world to spread the realm of Islam. I saw the fires and the ash and the scorched remains of men and their chronicles. [. . .] That coming night would be long. (*Bridge* 183★)

The sacrifice preoccupies the monk to the point where he feels the bridge closing in over him, suffocating him. Faced with the lifeless plaster mask of Murrash, he is terrified by the vision of his own fate. 'Ses yeux semblaient me dire: "nous deux, ô moine, nous sommes proches l'un de l'autre"' (*Le Pont* 145, '"We two are very close, monk", his eyes seemed to say', *Bridge* 184). The sense of identity as victims is strong, and the monk returns to complete his chronicle before the arrival of the invaders.

> Je pensais que je devais rentrer chez moi au plus tôt pour terminer ma chronique. Rentrer au plus tôt parce que les temps étaient troublés, que bientôt tomberait peut-être la longue nuit et qu'alors quiconque écrirait des chroniques pourrait le payer de sa tête. Cette chronique, tout comme le pont, demanderait peut-être un sacrifice, et qui pourrait être la victime, sinon moi [. . .]. (*Le Pont* 145)

> I felt I should return home as soon as I could to complete my chronicle. To return as soon as possible, because the times were troubled, and soon the long night would fall, and whoever is writing chronicles may pay with his head. This chronicle, like the bridge itself, may demand a sacrifice, and that sacrifice can be none other than myself [. . .]. (184)

Historical Allegory and Double Coding

Viewed from one angle Kadare's text appears to be historical, a representation of the Balkan edge of the transitional world of fourteenth-century Europe; viewed from another angle it is shot through with references to the post-war communist Albania. Kadare double-codes his text, running it simultaneously along historical and allegorical tracks. Much of the story can indeed be interpreted in terms acceptable to the regime. The theme of the Orikum base located on the Pasha Limani inlet, for example, must be read as a reference to the break with the Soviet Union in 1961 in which the question of Soviet access to the Vlora naval base played a central role. The romantic nationalism of the bridge as symbol, the presentation of Albania as the victim of imperialist powers, the threat of the Ottomans and the references to industrial sabotage echoing accusations made at the time of the Soviet and the Chinese withdrawals, can all be read allegorically as references to the writer's present. The bitumen and tar which are so important to trade and conflict, as Alexandre Zotos has pointed out, can also be seen to allude to oil and the first global oil crisis of 1973.[151] Above all Murrash Zenebisha is the archetypal worker sacrificed to capitalism. These aspects of the story could certainly be used by the regime in the service of its own xenophobic and isolationist Albanianism — but only by being taken out of the context of the novel as a whole.

Nowhere is the difficulty of Kadare's stance clearer than in *The Three-Arched Bridge*, where so much of the story can be interpreted in terms acceptable to the regime. It is not surprising that this writer, who refused to find creative outlet in modernist internalization, absurdism, or other forms of literary opposition within the dictatorship, but who continued to engage with Albanian reality in his writing, should find himself mirroring the concerns of the regime. The interests of the writer and of the dictator intersected particularly over the issue of the spiritual leadership of the nation. However, Enver Hoxha had also demanded that historical fiction leave the Albanian reader in no doubt as to the truth of history.

> The emphasis laid on the values of the past of our people should not create even the slightest confusion in the minds of the people of our time of socialism. It is our duty to cleanse the treasures of our national culture of their bad aspects, and these treasures should serve the socialist order we are building.[152]

Yet in *The Three-Arched Bridge* Kadare seems to have made it his goal to contradict the supreme leader's injunction to represent history with clarity as a single truth. Ambiguity is its keynote. There are too many jagged edges for orthodox Enverist interpretations to sit easily with this novel.

In 1971, according to Jacques, there were only fourteen Catholic priests still alive in Albania, twelve in labour camps or prisons and two in hiding. In the following year the regime caused international outrage with its execution of a Roman Catholic priest, Shtjefen Kurti.[153] In December 1973 the eighty-year-old Orthodox Archbishop Damian Konessi died after six years of imprisonment. As part of the regime's battle against religion the official newspaper *Bashkimi* published in July 1973 an article calling for 'folk intelligence' to be situated in every village in order to provide a base 'for working against religious survivals'.[154] In the following year the three remaining Catholic bishops were sentenced to prison for conducting religious services in private. In mid-1975 the survival of religious customs was denounced in *Zëri i Popullit* and at the end of the year *Bashkimi* included a further attack. In the aftermath of the prohibition of religion in 1968, Enver Hoxha substituted a politically sterilized form of Albanianness as the national cult. In 1960 the Albanian Institute of Folklore was founded and was active in researching, publishing, and popularizing Albanian national material. The Institute for the Preservation of the Monuments of Culture had been founded in 1965, presenting the regime as the legitimate heir of Albania's heroic past. After the mid-1970s even churches, monasteries, and other religious monuments were preserved. In 1971 the first national conference for folklore studies took place and in 1978 a major folk festival was held in Gjirokastra. Unlike most of the official celebrations, this one caught the people's imagination and appears to have been a genuine success. The event was turned into a five-yearly celebration of Albanian identity. However, while the architecture and the art were celebrated, the religious belief inspiring them was condemned. As Champseix writes, the Albanian leaders literally made a *tabula rasa* of the past.

> The majority of mosques, the baths and bazaars, which were overly reminiscent of the orient, the villas and certain boulevards in Shkodra and Tirana, built by the Italian invaders, were razed and replaced by brick buildings, often without render, since the available cement was used for the construction of bunkers.[155]

However, Hoxha's romantic nationalist reading of the nation's past ended with the Ottomans.[156] After that came the disastrous monarchy of Prince Wied, the short-lived experiment in democracy and the Zog period, all of which could be read as a prelude to the war and the glorious history of partisan national liberation. Hoxha's regime, that is, made a radical break in history between this instrumentalized romantic-nationalist past and the national communism that was introduced in 1945. The new constitution of 1976 ratified this model of history in confirming Albania as the world's one and only true communist state.[157]

Kadare shared with the regime a highly valorized, Herderian, and romantic reading of his nation's history. There is, indeed, a strained tone in works such as *The Autobiography of the People in Verse* (especially in the early 1980s when the situation in Kosovo flared up again). Hoxha may even have been influenced by Kadare's reading of the nation's history in poems such as 'What are these mountains thinking about?'. However there are crucial differences between the writer's and the regime's representations of Albanian history. The exploitation of Albanian nationalism that underpinned Hoxha's communism represented a provocation to the writer, who had come to view himself as a spokesman for a deeper and more profound sense of national identity than that propagated by the regime. Kadare's romantic nationalism does not end with the Ottomans. On the contrary, his history is continuous and repetitive into the present. This is the most destabilizing aspect of his engagement with the regime. He reveals the extent to which the Hoxha regime is a repetition, not a supersession of the past. Thus the apocalyptic vision of the coming of the Ottomans at the end of *The Three-Arched Bridge* can also be read as the symbolic recurrence of an ever more profound force of unfreedom taking control over Albania. The wave of unfreedom from the East, the spirit of the steppe, that essentially Kadarean vision of the cultural and political sterility of communism, is symbolized in the apocalyptic Ottoman invasion in the last pages of the novel. This spirit of Eastern European Marxism-Leninism, or Stalinism, as imported by the Albanian regime, is itself a repetition of that history which saw the Topias and others at the time of Gjon Ukcama importing Turkish mercenaries to fight their internal battles.

Whereas the regime's history insisted on unity of voice, Kadare's history does not. Above all, his *Catholic* monk is rational and questioning, not dogmatic, and his popular national consciousness is located in the people, not in the leadership, which is characterized throughout as divided, self-interested, clannish, and partial. Kadare's reading implies patterns and repetitions in his country's history, in particular between foreign invasion and national isolation, where the advent of Marxism-Leninism is tacitly identified with the former category, as the entry into the country of an alien dogma anathema to Albanian identity, tradition, and customs. The comments of the folklorist and the builder, the monk, and the lesser characters on the building of the bridge and the sacrifice of Murrash Zenebisha, reflect Kadare's awareness of the extent to which history is controlled, manipulated, and reworked in the interest of different groups. Whoever has control of the story, as the monk all too clearly recognizes, has control of history and the people. At a time of transition of generations and leaders, after the depredations of the cultural revolution and the constitutionalization of communist atheism, Kadare reflects on the themes of historical change, modernization, sacrifice, and loss. From Gjon Ukcama's narrative perspective, Enver Hoxha's isolationist reading of Albania's interests in 1977 can certainly be interpreted as a form of Albanian nationalism. But it can equally validly be interpreted as yet another variation in the eternal manipulation of national history, yet another spin on the legend of Albania, in order for the regime to stay in power and for the sacrifice of the Albanian everyman to continue. Against those for whom Kadare's work is a literary simulacrum of Hoxha's nationalist-communist ideology, perhaps the strongest argument is that of narrative voice and self-referentiality. The voice of the sceptical monk in 1377 is that of the author in 1977. It is not the voice of the holders of power — of Count Stres, of 'Boats and Rafts', or of the bridge-builders. This Catholic narrator aims to present history as chronicle, not dogma. From the facts, and interpreting the multiple voices of self-interest, he aims to chronicle the truth.

In the face of the threat facing his land in 1377, Gjon Ukcama, the sceptical and enlightened monk is terrified. The self-referentiality that would become more pronounced in Kadare's late work under the regime makes itself felt here as the monk's objectivity gives way in the face of death and the extinction of his writing. The dichotomy of the engaged and the disengaged writer breaks down as the essential function of writing, the truth of the witness, is endangered. This theme of the last pages of the novel would increasingly concern Kadare over the next six years, until the death of Hoxha. His packaging of the message of the dead writer in the 1984 novel, *The Shadow*, with its powerfully self-referential theme, is an indication of the seriousness with which he viewed the threat to his existence. In this *roman à clef* the author's death is the key to the unlocking of the manuscript from its secret vault, allowing his voice to continue to speak to the living world. The metafiction of *The Shadow* ensures that like Constantine he will be heard from beyond the grave.

The Albanian 'vicious circle of despotism and deference'[158] is about to repeat itself with Uncle Enver as the one and only patriarch in a nation entirely cut off from the rest of the world. The syndrome of extremes of foreign occupation or nationalist isolation is being played out again in 1977 as it had been in 1948 and 1961. Gjon Ukcama's reflections echo down the generations to warn his countrymen six hundred years later of the apocalypse of unfreedom about to break over their land. As Albania was entering its period of most extreme isolation under the communist regime, this warning can hardly be construed as nothing more than a historical condemnation of the Ottomans or a patriotic call against a threatening outside world. In works such as *The Three-Arched Bridge*, Kadare implies a multi-layered and sceptical reading of history and the present, alert to the possibilities of misrepresentation, manipulation, and misuse.

The vision of a free Albania which is nothing more than the consciousness of the people of being Albanian, survives at the end of the novel in the voice of the monk, but its survival is by no means assured. This last representative of reason and Western scepticism may be sacrificed, immured into silence, leaving only the dogma, only the one truth of the regime's Albania. Is it really so unthinkable to interpret Gjon Ukcama's fear of silence as a warning against the ongoing supremacy of the Albanian Party of Labour at this time of closure?

The Critique of Kadare's Albanianism

Critics of Kadare since the 1970s have observed with bitterness the writer's astuteness in responding to the signs of ideological change and elaborating on them in his work. In the late 1980s the refugee Albanian-American, Arshi Pipa, coined the pejorative term 'double game' for Kadare's literary strategies in a critique which was taken up by various commentators in the West.[159] Pipa referred to *The Three-Arched Bridge* as having been 'written for a foreign audience':

> The government liked it because it seconded government propaganda that pre-socialist Albania was a tribal society with Zog as a soap opera king, a situation which the Communist Party revolutionized, making Albania an exemplary modern country without vendetta and other endemic plagues, and with the blessings of Albanian socialism.[160]

Pipa set the tone for later critics by referring to the author's relationship with Enver Hoxha as a 'gentlemen's agreement' marking a 'memorable stage in the history of the unholy alliance between dictatorial power and literary talent'.[161]

In a television interview in 1991, moderator Bernard Rapp introduced Kadare to French audiences as a potential Nobel prize winner.[162] However, the suggestion unleashed decades of pent-up suspicion of the author. The San Francisco-based journalist Steven Schwarz recycled politically and ethnically biased accusations about Kadare during the 1990s, despite withering criticism by specialists such as Noel Malcolm. In 1993 Hans Joachim Hoppe published a short critical account of Kadare, in which the writer is identified as a patriot but 'not the dissident which he himself and others want to make of him'. Kadare's occasionally critical views of the regime were nothing more than 'slips' ('Ausrutscher'), writes Hoppe, who concludes that while many view Kadare as an important voice of reform, the truth is filtering through 'that Kadare was an active part of the totalitarian system'.[163]

In post-communist Albania, too, members of the younger generation of intellectuals, such as Fatos Lubonja and others, represented Kadare as one of the 'grey wolves' of the communist intelligentsia, who 'dipped their paws in flour before entering the house of democracy'.[164] Kadare's critics write that 'the main aim of all Albanian literary and cultural activity in general, guided and paid for by the Party of Labour, was to educate the new man in what [. . .] we have called the national-communist spirit'.[165] Kadare, like Agolli and others, they contend, promoted the regime's 'historical grandiosity, fear of foreigners, isolation conceived as resistance to the enemy, the sacrifice of the individual for the sake of the collective, and the exaltation of socialist successes'.[166] The works of Kadare and the other members of the *grey zone*[167] are thus 'an integral part of [. . .] the "*black zone*" of the regime itself'.[168] For Lubonja, Kadare is a 'pilot fish' who latched onto the sharks of the regime and swam with them.[169] He is accused of exalting Hoxha's communist ideology into cultural and literary myth, and linking 'Hoxha's old totalitarian ideology to nationalist and ethnic principles' with the 'provincial taste [. . .] of an

FIG. 21 (above): The mosaic from the National Historical Museum, completed in 1981 and depicting the unity of ancient Illyrians, Albanian nationalists and communist partisans. (Photo: Peter Morgan.)

FIG. 22 (below): The citadel at Kruja, site of Scanderbeg's resistance against the Ottomans, and setting for Kadare's *The Castle*, rebuilt in the late 1970s as a national museum. (Photo: Peter Morgan.)

amateur local historian, who, to cover up the misery of the present, imagines a glorious mythical past'. He too, they write, was 'part of the old regime'.[170]

The critique of Kadare was given wide coverage by Noel Malcolm in an influential article in the *New York Review of Books* in 1997.[171] Since the fall of Albanian communism in 1990, wrote Malcolm, Kadare had come under attack for having been 'a beneficiary and active supporter' of Enver Hoxha's Stalinist regime. Malcolm criticized Kadare for the 'plaintive and insistent' tone of the post-communist works, suggesting that the writer's revisions are motivated by a 'sense of unwilled complicity' in the Albanian dictatorship and finding in them worrying 'omissions and mystifications'. Reviewing *The Three-Arched Bridge*, which had just been translated into English, Malcolm referred generally to Kadare's strategy of survival under the regime. Malcolm reiterates Pipa's criticism that Kadare conceals any critical moments behind a 'mass of officially approved references to capitalism, foreign oppressors, the Soviet Union'.[172] In assembling an '"official" structure of symbolic references [. . .] strong enough to satisfy the censors', he writes, Kadare built 'a structure solid enough to serve the purposes of his enemy'. *The Three-Arched Bridge* presents 'Albania as the victim of historic processes (the development of capitalism) and foreign enemies (the Ottoman Turks)'.[173] The immurement of Murrash Zenebisha is an allegory of the history of capitalism achieved through the exploitation of the workers. The references to the Orikum naval base in the *Three-Arched Bridge*, for example, are a 'transparent reference to Hoxha's confrontation with the Soviet Union' over the Pasha Limani base. This is the Enverist interpretation, which rendered the novel acceptable to the regime. However, Malcolm also cites Hoxha's well-known speech on the arts and literature from 1965 to support Kadare's claim to Alain Bosquet that the text does indeed contain a critical moment.[174] 'Sacrifice', Kadare writes in the interview with Bosquet, 'was a central theme of communist propaganda: people were exhorted to sacrifice themselves for the country, for the Party, for Enver Hoxha'. Kadare's aim, Malcolm summarizes, 'was to show that such sacrifice is nothing more than a crime, a cynical murder'. It is scarcely thinkable, he writes, that readers in the Albania of 1978 will convert the overt references to the capitalist bridge-builders into critical references to communism. We are able to read this novel as a critique, he writes, only because Kadare 'from his post-Communist, Parisian vantage point', has told us of his dissident intentions. Malcolm ends with scepticism regarding Kadare's stance. 'One might say that his message was immured in the book, buried under a great weight of stone'.[175] Malcolm recognizes Kadare's literary merit, but he concludes his piece reiterating that Kadare remained 'an employee of the Palace of Nightmares that was Enver Hoxha's Albania'.[176] Malcolm's review was written before Maks Velo's discovery of the 'Red Pashas' manuscript or Shaban Sinani's publication of the regime's files on Kadare, and is coloured by his objections to Kadare's 'self-promoting' and 'defensive' autobiographical works of the 1990s. 'There is something just a little too tidy about Kadare's post-1990 explanations of his work'.[177] However, it was not necessary for an attentive reader to make the connection to Enver Hoxha's 1965 speech in order to link the themes and symbols of unfreedom in the novel with the situation in contemporary Albania. Enver Hoxha's obsessive and self-serving rhetoric of sacrifice for the nation was notorious, just as were his warnings against plots and conspiracies. Kadare had reflected the regime's use of the language of political intimidation and terror as early as 1965 in *The Monster*. In the decade between Hoxha's speech at the 15th Plenum and the writing of *The Three-Arched Bridge*, Kadare had many opportunities to hear political rhetoric of this kind. The calls to sacrifice, like the promotion of fear from outside, were the lifeblood of the regime, heard and seen on a daily basis in its slogans and propaganda.

Kadare's texts are Aesopian in the extreme, having had to operate with the logic of contradiction rather than of irony in order to exist at all. *The Three-Arched Bridge* offers the possibility of multiple, even opposed, readings. This strategy was necessitated by the extremity of the regime's control over dogma and truth in the late 1970s, arguably the period in which dissent was least possible. Kadare had little choice other than to occupy the so-called 'grey zone' of the intelligentsia who submitted to the regime in order to survive. He long ago (in *The Twilight of the Steppe-Gods*) documented his decision to return to Albania for the sake of his language and culture. It is all too easy to judge him from Malcolm's 'post-communist, Parisian vantage point'. We must try to understand from the inside, not from Paris in 1997 but from Tirana in 1977. Kadare spoke for an Albania that remained inviolable for political ends.

Eternal Albania

What remains, then, of Kadare's 'eternal Albania' in this novel? The first version ends with the approaching apocalypse and the monk's hope that his chronicle will somehow survive for succeeding generations. In the later version, produced after the fall of the regime in the 1990s, Kadare extrapolates from the bridge to the rainbow, the iconic progenitor of all bridges.

> Brusquement me vint l'idée que l'arc-en-ciel devait être la première configuration d'un pont et que le ciel, depuis une éternité, avait suggéré cette image à l'esprit humain. [. . .] l'intention divine avait été pure. Tandis que le pont, lui, bien qu'il prétendit la matérialiser, avait eu pour préalable la mort. (*Le Pont, Œuvres* 1:521)

> Suddenly it flashed into my mind that nothing other than a rainbow must have been the first sketch for a bridge, and the sky had for a long time been planting this primordial form in people's minds. [. . .] The divine model had been pure. But here, although the bridge pretended to embody this idea, it had death at its foundations. (151)

The rainbow has no supportive arches. It is the prototype image of Gjon Ukcama's free Arberia, Kadare's 'eternal Albania'. Like writing itself, it defies the regime by never being able to be simply subsumed into it. It remains untouchable. This Albania belongs in the realm of the ideal, the ahistorical, and the mythical. It cannot be reduced to any one phase or aspect. Kadare's 'eternal and bewitching' Albania is thus an imaginative idea rather than a reality and hence is unable to be used to an end. It lives in its people, its culture, and its language. For Kadare, the falsity of the regime's Albanianism lies not in the nature of the myth of Albania, but in the use of that myth to support the politics of the present and to propagate a single reading of history.

> L'arc-en-ciel, sa préfiguration, peut-être aussi son âme que, grâce au Ciel, nul ne savait encore construire et encore moins enchainer [. . .] (*Le Pont, Œuvres* 1:525)

> A rainbow, the bridge's model and perhaps its inspiration, is something that, thank God, nobody yet knows how to build, and still less to chain in fetters [. . .] (157)

This fully worked-out symbol of the bridge as 'eternal Albania' is implicit in the earlier version, although at that stage Kadare would not qualify his monk's historical chronicle with such an image of hope. Nevertheless, from *The City without Signs* onwards, the image of an eternal and incorruptible Albania shimmers in the background. The idea of 'eternal Albania' had grown steadily in importance in the writer's work. It is increasingly tangible in *The General of the Dead Army*, the second version of *The Great Winter* in particular, and the autobiographical novels, *Chronicle in Stone* and *The Twilight of the Steppe-Gods*. In *The Palace of Dreams*, Kadare's next major work after *The Three-Arched Bridge*, eternal Albania will be powerfully evoked in the songs of the Bosnian rhapsodists who carry their message of Albanian identity to the heart of the empire of unfreedom, breaking into the consciousness even of the pallid bureaucrat, Marc-Alem.

The Concert 1978–1981

The Concert takes as its theme the Chinese alliance with Albania and its gradual decline into mutual suspicion and hostility. While it shares themes with *The Great Winter*, using the break with China as a point of reflection on the state of Albania, and introducing some of the same characters, such as the writer and authorial alter ego, Skender Bermema, the novel is very different in tone.[178] The plot focuses on the broad interactions of the Chinese and the Albanians in the final years of the alliance. The structure of the novel is ambitious in attempting to bring the historical events of the Albanian-Chinese relationship over the years from 1971 to 1978 into the space of a few months during the fictive year of 1971, writes Eric Faye. The action begins in autumn 1971, when the Americans were preparing Nixon's trip to Peking (end of February 1972), and makes reference to the death of Chou En-lai (January 1976) and of Mao (September 1976), the arrest of Jiang Qing (October 1976), the arrest of the Chinese aide in Tirana, and the departure of approximately 500 Chinese co-workers from Albania (July 1978).[179] The Chinese events of the novel take place under the omniscient and malevolent eye of a mythically drawn Mao Tse-tung, secreted in a mountain fastness and exercising total control over his realms. At the celebratory concert with which the work ends, Kadare evokes the climate of political opacity and inscrutability of the mid-1970s, projecting onto the Chinese much of what he observed in Tirana. With his acute sense of political machinations, Kadare unwittingly foreshadowed in the events surrounding the death of Mao Tse-tung's second-in-command, Lin Biao, Enver Hoxha's destruction of his own deputy, Mehmet Shehu, in 1981.

The Chinese presence is evoked at a time when it was politically safe to represent the ex-ally negatively. However, even here, as in *The Great Winter*, the message is ambiguous. Inasmuch as Mao Tse-tung represents oppressive political power and the spirit of unfreedom, he is a reflection of all dictatorships, including the Albanian. This is one of the keys to Kadare's 'double game' of compromise and critique. Here too Kadare's insight into the psychology of the dictator proved prophetic. While the representation of the Chinese is stereotypically negative and led to charges of racism, the critique is directed primarily toward the figure of Mao Tse-tung and the *habitus* of the Chinese as symbolic of the deformations of life under a dictatorship.[180]

The fate of *The Concert* is indicative of the curious situation of inner censorship, official critique, and authorization for publication in Albania. The novel was accorded, at the manuscript stage, the first prize in a national competition celebrating the foundation of the Party, but several months later Kadare was informed that the Central Committee had prohibited its publication.[181] This was unusual, since generally prohibitions were brought down after publication. (It was submitted for publication under the title *Cold Blood* in 1981.) The situation reflects Kadare's relationship to the regime. He was universally recognized as a writer without an equal in his country; at the same time he was often far too risky to allow into print. It must be remembered that there was no official pre-publication censorship, which put enormous pressure on the managing editor, as well as the writer, to make sure that a published text was politically safe before it was put into print. In his review of the manuscript, Dritëro Agolli, President of the Union of Writers, wrote that *The Concert*, along with *The Great Winter*, aimed to create 'an epic of Albanian life at the time of the imperialist-revisionist blockade when the Albanian people were fighting for progress and socialism'.[182] While this might be the goal of the novel, however, Agolli recognized that the satirical edge cuts two ways, writing that *The Concert* is 'nothing other than a satire which makes fun of communism, its principles and ideas', written from the point of view of a European 'liberal for a foreign (French) audience rather than for his own people', using the camouflage of the Chinese to speak about Albania.[183] The Central Committee concluded that the work was 'anti-socialist, riddled with attacks against the Party and the figure of Comrade Enver Hoxha, sarcastic, racist and of an artistically mediocre quality'.[184] *The Concert* was proscribed for the following seven years, appearing only in 1988.

The Concert marks a further stage in Kadare's relations with the regime after the stand-off of the mid-1970s. He had broken the unspoken commandment since *The Great Winter* not to write any further novels (meaning, evidently, larger-scale works about contemporary Albanian life) and yet the ongoing translation and authorization of works such as this for publication in France represented a tacit acceptance by the regime of Kadare's international significance. The kudos of supporting a writer of international stature, the income from royalties (which were channelled back to the regime) and, most importantly, Hoxha's ongoing concern to be seen as a patron of the arts played an important role. Of course the French publications were inaccessible to anyone in Albania and Kadare's reputation in France and elsewhere was known only by hearsay to most Albanians.

In 1978 authorization was given for the revised edition of *The Great Winter* to be reissued in Albania and translated into French by Jusuf Vrioni for eventual publication with Hachette in Paris. It was a stroke of good fortune, for Kadare's name was fading from memory in France and he had received no invitations from his most important contacts in the West for several years. During this period he undertook trips overseas on official business, to the Soviet Union, China, Vietnam, and elsewhere. While international travel was impossible for the vast majority of Albanians, for members of the nomenklatura such as Kadare, the authorization of a passport and of participation in ambassadorial and other delegations also represented a form of control. He, like his colleagues, was not free to refuse the privilege but he was obliged to toe the official line. Failure to do so would result in pressure back home and the deeper effect of this participation was the internalization of their beholdenness to the regime for a privileged position that came at a great cost. Of course, his family remained at home in Albania as hostages should he behave inappropriately while away, or fail to return.

Conclusion

At the beginning of the 1970s Kadare looked inward to himself, his origins, and his adult identity in the autobiographical work *Chronicle in Stone*. Later, in *The Twilight of the Steppe-Gods*, he revisited his experiences as a student in Moscow. The revision of his origins and his identity as a writer laid the basis for the works of his mature period, in which he grapples with the fundamental questions of his existence: the possibility of survival as a writer in the environment of communist modernization; the battle for the existence of the other, 'eternal' Albania which comes to exist in a parallel world to the communist present; and the search for the origins of the present in the historical novels dealing with the end of the Byzantine era, the arrival of the Ottomans, and the chaotic beginnings of Albanian modernity in the year 1912–13 and under the Zog regime. In *The Great Winter* Kadare tried his most audacious literary ploy, namely to offer the lure of a 'corrective mask' to the dictator, to flatter him to change. It failed, but the process of writing led to an engagement with Hoxha which was no longer displaced or projected into allegory, symbolism, or historical costume. After *The Great Winter* Kadare was no longer in doubt about the nature of the dictator or the dictatorship. In his masterpiece, *The Palace of Dreams*, completed as the dictator was sliding into illness and dementia in the early 1980s, Kadare would bring the themes of his mature period together in a work which marks the culmination of his career and the end of the Hoxha era. With the death of the dictator in 1985, Kadare's work enters a new, penultimate phase coinciding with the first transition of power in communist Albania, in which the dictator and his nemesis and alter ego, the writer, enter into their final battle. In these five years before the collapse of the regime, Kadare would confront the dictator head-on in a series of works in which the dictator appears as the principle of closure, order, death, and control and the writer his foil, nemesis, and alter ego, spokesman for an Albania of hope, of coming to terms with the past, and of opening to the future.

Notes to Chapter 3

1. Kadaré/Bosquet, pp. 8–10; Kadaré, *Le Poids*, pp. 323–33.
2. Kadaré/Bosquet, p. 45.
3. Ismail Kadaré, 'Préface', in Bashkim Shehu, *L'Automne de la peur*, trans. by Isabelle Joudrain-Musa (Paris: Fayard, 1993), pp. 7–31 (pp. 24–25).
4. Kadaré in Shehu, *L'Automne*, p. 17.
5. Kadaré, *Le Poids*, pp. 532–33.
6. 'Hier sitze ich, forme Menschen nach meinem Bilde'. Johann Wolfgang Goethe, 'Prometheus' (1774), in *Sämtliche Werke* (Zürich: Artemis, 1950), I, 320–21.
7. Johann Wolfgang Goethe, *Aus meinem Leben: Dichtung und Wahrheit*, in *Sämtliche Werke* (Zurich: Artemis, 1950), X, 698–99.
8. Hoxha, 'Literature and the Arts', p. 855.
9. Hoxha, 'Literature and the Arts', p. 855.
10. Kadaré, 'Prométhée', *Œuvres*, I, 63. All further French references are indicated in brackets after the text. Translations are my own.
11. The expression derives from a popular 1930s song in the Soviet Union, which captured the mood of the times and came to be called the *Suicide Tango*. Nikita Mikhalkov's film of the same name links the mood of nostalgic disillusionment to those 'burnt by the sun' of Stalin and the Revolution.
12. Kadaré, *Le Poids*, pp. 354, 383.
13. Ismail Kadare, 'Train Timetables', trans. by Robert Elsie, in Elsie, *An Elusive Eagle Soars*, p. 84.
14. The chronology of these works is not entirely clear. Kadare tells Denis Fernandez-Récatala that he wrote them both in the immediate wake of *Winter of Great Solitude*, before he had submitted the manuscript of that novel to Ramiz Alia, and that he pre-dated them, in order to cover his tracks. However, it may be that he completed them after carrying out the preliminary archival research for the epic novel, and before finishing the manuscript. In *Le Poids* he writes that both *The Castle* and *Chronicle* were finished by 1970, i.e. before *Winter of Great Solitude* (p. 327). *The Castle* appeared at the end of 1970 or the beginning of 1971, and *Chronicle in Stone* was published in 1971. In fact, as Arshi Pipa has shown, *Chronicle in Stone* had its origins in the sequence of twelve scenes from the writer's childhood, published in *Nëntori* in 1964 as *The Southern City*, and revised and extended in 1967. The manuscript of *Winter of Great Solitude* was finished in (late) 1972. Kadaré and Fernandez-Récatala, *Temps barbares*, pp. 73–75; Pipa, 'Subversion vs. Conformism', p. 52.
15. Pipa, 'Subversion vs. Conformism', p. 52.
16. Ismail Kadaré, *Chronique de la ville de pierre*, trans. by Jusuf Vrioni (Paris: Hachette, 1973), p. 7. All further French references are indicated in brackets after the text.
17. Ismail Kadare, *Chronicle in Stone*, trans. from the Albanian (New York: New Amsterdam 1987), p. 11. The unnamed translator was the émigré Albanian philologist, Arshi Pipa. All further English references will be indicated in brackets after the text. In places where Pipa's translation lacks accuracy I have adopted the corrections of David Bellos in Ismail Kadare, *Chronicle in Stone* (Edinburgh: Cannongate, 2007). An asterisk (*) identifies modified translations.
18. Fischer, *Albania at War*, p. 189.
19. The relationship of the past in the historical novel to the present for Lukács 'does not consist in alluding to contemporary events [. . .] but in bringing the past to life as the prehistory of the present, in giving poetic life to those historical, social and human forces which [. . .] have made our present-day life what it is and as we experience it.' Georg Lukács, *The Historical Novel*, trans. by Hannah and Stanley Mitchell (London: Merlin Press, 1962), p. 53.
20. Sinani, p. 128.
21. Kadaré/Bosquet, p. 103.
22. Kadaré/Bosquet, p. 65.
23. Kadare writes that the Sigurimi was the 'magic key' to the regime and that it was controlled by Nexhmije Hoxha, Hysni Kapo, and Kadri Hazbiu, Minister of the Interior. Kapo and Hazbiu would both fall foul of the dictator and die under questionable circumstances. Kadaré, *Le Poids*, pp. 311, 328.

24. Kadaré, *Le Poids*, p. 318.

25. Kadaré, *Le Poids*, p. 318.

26. Kadaré, *Le Poids*, p. 335; Kadaré/Bosquet, pp. 40–42.

27. Kadaré/Bosquet, pp. 44–45.

28. Kadaré/Bosquet, p. 71.

29. Ismail Kadaré, *L'Hiver de la grande solitude*, trans. by Jusuf Vrioni (Paris: Fayard, 1978, 1999), p. 496. Translation is my own.

30. Dashnor Mamaqi, '"Une sorte d'angoisse existentialiste": Demande de censure de *L'Hiver de la grande solitude*, par le comité central du Parti', in Sinani, p. 54.

31. Kadaré, *Le Poids*, p. 338.

32. Kadaré, *Le Poids*, p. 360.

33. Kapo was to die in Paris of unknown causes at the age of sixty-four in September 1979, and Shehu committed suicide under suspicious circumstances in December 1981.

34. In November 1970 Mao sent his first invitation indirectly through the Romanians who had good relations with both China and the United States; after much diplomatic activity, including a secret visit by Henry Kissinger in July 1971, the meeting between Mao and Nixon took place in February 1972. Chang and Halliday, pp. 703–09.

35. Power resided in the networks of clans as well as in political and other allegiances. According to Jean-Paul Champseix, about twelve clans wielded power under the watchful eye of the dictator. Champseix, 'Itinéraire d'une œuvre inespérée', p. 39; cf. also Miranda Vickers, and James Pettifer, *The Albanian Question: Igniting the Balkans* (London: I. B. Tauris, 2005), pp. 12, 28, 33.

36. Kadaré and Fernandez-Récatala, *Temps barbares*, p. 80. According to Kadare the average first print run in Albania was 30,000 copies, after which additional printings would reach 60,000–100,000 copies. Hence, he claims, his work was well known throughout Albania under the dictatorship. Cf. Kadaré/Faye, *Entretiens*, p. 79; Paul de Sinety, 'Entretien avec Claude Durand', *L'Oeil de Boeuf*, 20 (May 2000), 29–34 (p. 33).

37. Kadaré, *Le Poids*, p. 365.

38. Denunciations in the form of letters to the newspaper were a normal strategy of the regime, satirized in the suggestion in *The Palace of Dreams*, that certain dreams are 'planted' in order to discredit or damage individuals and groups.

39. Kadaré, *Le Poids*, pp. 553–54; Kadaré/Faye, *Entretiens*, pp. 42–43.

40. Sinani, pp. 53–56.

41. Sinani, p. 66.

42. Sinani, pp. 54–55. Cf. Tönnes, pp. 200–02, on Albanian youth.

43. Sinani, pp. 53–56.

44. Sinani, pp. 57–64.

45. Sinani, pp. 62.

46. Sinani, pp. 101–02.

47. Ismail Kadaré, *Le grand hiver*, trans. by Jusuf Vrioni (Paris: Fayard, 1978), p. 552. All further French references are indicated in brackets after the text. Translations are my own.

48. On the term, '*tourdjuman*', which Kadare used from the original transcripts, cf. Ismail Kadaré and Denis Fernandez-Récatala, *Les quatre interprètes* (Paris: Editions Stock, 2003), pp. 13–15.

49. Sinani, pp. 101–04.

50. Cf. 'Wir töteten nie ohne Grund' ('We didn't kill without reason'), Interview with Nexhmije Hoxha, *Der Spiegel*, no. 15 (5 April, 2004), pp. 135–36.

51. Kadaré, *Le Poids*, p. 383.

52. Kadaré, *Le Poids*, p. 374.

53. Koço Bihiku, *Histoire de la littérature albanaise* (Tirana: Editions '8 Nëntori', 1980), p. 222.

54. The 1999 paperback edition of *L'Hiver de la grande solitude* is, with minor differences, the same version as that printed in *Œuvres*, VII. This is thus essentially the same as the first version of the novel. The main additions that Kadare made for the second edition in 1978 are suppressed. Kadare writes that passages were inserted into the second (1978) version, 'qui laissent penser que le people fait bloc derrière ses dirigeants', ('which encourage the reader to think that the people rise up in support of their leaders'). These insertions were deleted for the 1999 paperback edition 'qui, grosso modo, constitue un retour à la version originelle', ('which, more or less, constitutes

a return to the original version'). Ismail Kadaré, *L'hiver de la grande solitude* (Paris: Fayard, 1999), rear cover.

55. Schreiber, p. 114.

56. Champseix and Champseix, *L'Albanie ou la logique du désespoir*, p. 202.

57. Kadare repeats himself from *Le Poids* p. 318: 'C'est au *Grand Hiver*, indépendamment des tracas qu'il me causa, que je dus non seulement mon salut, mais les quatre cinquièmes de mon œuvre'. 'I owe not only my health, but four-fifths of my work to *The Great Winter*, regardless of the trouble it caused me'.

58. Tönnes, p. 199.

59. Cf. Harry Hodgkinson, *Skanderbeg* (London: I. B. Tauris/Centre for Albanian Studies, 1999), p. 219.

60. Schreiber, pp. 189–90; cf. Hall, p. 37.

61. Prifti, *Remote Albania*, p. 20.

62. Jacques, pp. 494–95.

63. Prifti, *Remote Albania*, p. 172.

64. Jusuf Vrioni notes that Albanians were able to watch Bertolucci's controversial film of 1972, *The Last Tango in Paris*, screened on Yugoslav television, before it was shown publicly in Italy. Of course by this time the viewing was more clandestine, but it still occurred. Vrioni, p. 255.

65. Tönnes, p. 201.

66. Tönnes, p. 201: 'Only through drastic intervention of the state was it possible to set limits to youth vagrancy in Albania. At the beginning of the seventies groups of hippies and rockers, influenced by Italian television, acted provocatively, wearing their hair long and dressing in jeans, behaving badly, pushing and shoving in public transport and shops, responding to objections to their behaviour with crude expressions or by setting their transistor radios to Western pop-music channels and turning the volume up to full.' (my translation)

67. Tönnes, p. 201.

68. Tönnes, pp. 201–03.

69. Prifti, *Remote Albania*, pp. 172–73.

70. Kadaré, *Le Poids*, p. 370.

71. Jacques, pp. 494–95.

72. Prifti, *Remote Albania*, pp. 138–39.

73. Pearson, III, 631–32; Tönnes, p. 204.

74. Cf. Jacques, p. 493; Tönnes, pp. 203–18.

75. Prifti, *Remote Albania*, pp. 219–20.

76. Prifti, *Remote Albania*, p. 221.

77. Jacques, p. 491.

78. 'Les Pachas rouges', trans. by Jean-Paul Champseix. Unpubl. manuscript provided by the translator.

79. 'The Red Pashas', trans. by Robert Elsie. Accessed from the web. 'Albanian authors in translation', http://www.albanianliterature.com/authors3/AA3–15poetry.html (as at October 01, 2007).

80. Sinani, p. 71.

81. Velo, p. 60; Agolli's full speech is reprinted in Velo, pp. 58–69, and the record of the Central Committee meeting is to be found in Sinani, pp. 74–86.

82. Sinani, p. 92. Kadare's full self-criticism is reprinted in Sinani, pp. 92–95.

83. Sinani, pp. 92–94.

84. Shehu, *L'Automne de la peur*, preface by Ismail Kadaré. Cf. Sinani, pp. 96–97; Kadaré, *Le Poids*, pp. 423–25.

85. Kadaré, *Invitation*, pp. 258–59.

86. Kadaré, *Le Poids*, p. 382.

87. Kadaré/Bosquet, pp. 68–69.

88. Velo, p. 10. Velo's documentation of the 'Red Pashas' affair was published in Albania in 2002 and in France in 2004.

89. In the wake of the rediscovery of 'The Red Pashas', Sinani sifted the archives in order to reconstitute the 'Kadare file', bringing together from diverse sources the regime's documentation of Kadare's literary and other activities. Not surprisingly, the resulting file was vast. Many

archives and other sources of information were excluded in order to keep the project under control, and *The Kadare File* was published in Albania in 2004, a volume of over 1,000 pages and the result of five years' work. Sinani, pp. 21–31.

90. Kadaré/Courtois, *La Vérité*, p. 203.
91. Kadaré/Courtois, *La Vérité*, p. 163.
92. Kadaré/Courtois, *La Vérité*, pp. 163, 200.
93. Velo, pp. 8–9.
94. Velo, pp. 166–67.
95. Velo, p. 169; cf. Kadaré/Bosquet, pp. 104–05.
96. Kadare cites the case of Bashkim Shehu, in Velo, pp. 175–78.
97. Kadaré/Bosquet, p. 104.
98. Kadaré, *Le Poids*, p. 354.
99. Kadaré/Bosquet, p. 75.
100. Kadaré, *Invitation*, pp. 243–50.
101. Kadaré/Bosquet, p. 152.
102. Kadaré, *Invitation*, p. 273.
103. Kadaré/Courtois, *La Vérité*, pp. 170–71.
104. Kadaré/Courtois, *La Vérité*, pp. 170–72.
105. Cf. Kadaré, *Invitation*, pp. 141–45; Kadaré, *Le Poids*, pp. 298–301, *Printemps albanais* 59–60, *Albanian Spring* 61–62, Kadaré/Faye, *Entretiens*, p. 98.
106. Kadaré/Courtois, *La Vérité*, p. 157.
107. Kadaré/Courtois, *La Vérité*, pp. 171–72.
108. Quoted in Rama, p. 108.
109. Kadaré/Courtois, *La Vérité*, p. 159.
110. Quoted in Sinani, p. 58: '[Kadaré] a tenu compte d'une bonne partie des blâmes et a opéré des changements parfois perceptibles dans certains points névralgiques de l'œuvre. Certains faiblesses, carences, phrases équivoques, ont été évitées'.
111. In this sense the processes of censorship and creativity in the Eastern European communist states were comparable to those which developed in earlier enlightened absolutist state structures. Cf. Reinhard Koselleck, *Kritik und Krise: Eine Studie zur Pathogenese der bürgerlichen Welt* (Frankfurt a.M.: Suhrkamp, 1976), pp. 49–60 and passim.
112. Kadaré, *Le Poids*, pp. 431–32.
113. Kadaré, *Le Poids*, p. 297.
114. Cf. Helena Kadare's comments regarding the attempts of Ismail to recover the manuscript of *The Niche of Shame* from the editor of the Naïm Frashëri publishing house, Thanas Leci, at the time of the 'Red Pashas' affair, Velo, p. 102.
115. This information was given to me in a meeting with Fatos Lubonja in Tirana on 30 June 2003. In fact his death sentence was commuted to fifteen years' imprisonment, which was subsequently augmented by a further ten years; he was released in 1990. Cf. Fatos Lubonja, 'Courage and the Terror of Death', *Social Research*, 71 (2004), 117–34; *The Second Sentence*, trans. by John Hodgson (New York: Arcade, 1999).
116. Kadaré, *Le Poids*, pp. 388, 398, 536: 'En 1975 [. . .] je vivais en semi-relégation à Fier'. 'In 1975 [. . .] I lived in semi-relegation in Fier'.
117. Kadaré, *Le Poids*, p. 392.
118. Kadaré, *Le Poids*, p. 405. After the fall of the regime, Hoxha's home in Gjirokastra was damaged and subsequently rebuilt as a museum; the Kadare house is currently (2008) under reconstruction.
119. Ismail Kadaré, *Le Crépuscule des dieux de la steppe*, trans. by Jusuf Vrioni (Paris: Gallimard, 1996). All further French references are indicated in brackets after the text. Translations are my own.
120. Paustovsky was nominated for a Nobel Prize for Literature in 1965, but the award went to Mikhail Sholokhov, a figure considered more loyal to the Soviet regime. In the following year along with over 125 intellectuals Paustovsky co-signed a letter to the 23rd Party Congress appealing against re-Stalinization.
121. According to Kadare in November 2004, this friend from the Moscow days returned to Greece and was still living in Athens.

122. Kadare's early poems were of a modernist and subjectivist cast and would, Samoïlov felt, be censured. As a friendly mentor he advised Kadare privately not to publish some of these works, in order to save himself trouble with the authorities. In his preface to the volume he protected himself from blame as editor, and defended the young poet's talent while mildly condemning the signs of Western experimentalism. Personal comment by Ismail Kadare, 6 November 2004.

123. 'Samizdat' means literally 'self-published' and refers to prohibited literature that was copied and distributed clandestinely.

124. Kadare reproduces various documents from his ex-girlfriends in Moscow, on whom the figure of Lida and her letter are based, in Kadaré, Invitation, pp. 102–04.

125. 'Tragoudi tou nekrou adelfou', in Dimotika Tragoudia, eklogai apo ta tragoudia tou Ellinikou laou, ed. by N. L. Politou (Athens: Ekdoseis dionysos, 1975), pp. 138–40; Giuseppe Schirò, Storia della Letteratura Albanese (Milan: Nuova Accademia Editrice, n.d. [1959]), pp. 25–26.

126. Elsie, A Dictionary of Albanian Religion, p. 74.

127. Kadaré, Invitation, pp. 33–68; Kadaré/Faye, Entretiens, pp. 15–16.

128. Eric Faye, 'Introduction', in Ismail Kadaré, Qui a ramené Doruntine?, Œuvres , I, 247.

129. Kadare learned later that Stulpanz committed suicide in Latvia in 1989. Kadaré/Bosquet, caption to photograph of Kadare and Stulpanz following p. 96.

130. Aleksandr Fadeyev (1901–56), who had fought in the Revolution, had been a communist writer since the 1920s. His novel The Young Guard (1945) was criticized as insufficiently pro-communist. He was demoted in the Union of Soviet Writers, suffered depression and alcoholism, and committed suicide.

131. Kadaré, Invitation, pp. 168–69.

132. Kadaré, Le Poids, p. 404.

133. Schreiber, pp. 204–05.

134. Kadaré/Bosquet, p. 62.

135. Kadaré/Bosquet, p. 91.

136. Kadaré/Bosquet, pp. 107.

137. Kadaré/Bosquet, pp. 106–07.

138. Kadaré/Bosquet, p. 62.

139. Lukács, The Historical Novel, p. 53.

140. Kadaré, Le Poids, p. 405.

141. Kadaré/Bosquet, p. 62.

142. Kadaré/Bosquet, p. 99.

143. Hoxha, 'Literature and the Arts', p. 837.

144. Kadaré/Bosquet, p. 62.

145. Ismail Kadaré, Le Pont aux trois arches, trans. by Jusuf Vrioni (Paris: Fayard, 1981). English quotations are from Ismail Kadare, The Three-Arched Bridge, trans. from the Albanian by John Hodgson (New York: Vintage, 1998). Hodgson writes that his translation is based 'on an unpublished Albanian manuscript by Ismail Kadare'. The version used by Hodgson for the English translation is the same as that published in Œuvres, I, in 1993. This latter version is dated 'Tirana 1976–1978' (Œuvres, I, 543), implying that it is the original version published under the dictatorship. The main differences are in the development of existing themes and motifs, with the exception of the analogy of the bridge with the rainbow, which appears to be a product of the revisions from the early 1990s. Where necessary I have amended the translation to reflect the original 1978 version of the novel (marked with an asterisk). All further references are indicated in brackets after the text.

146. Sugar, p. 20.

147. Alain Ducellier, 'Genesis and Failure of the Albanian State in the Fourteenth and Fifteenth Centuries', in L'Albanie entre Byzance et Venise, Xe-XVe siècles (London: Variorum Reprints, 1987), chapter 12, pp. 3–22; Jacques, pp. 156–97.

148. Charles Haroche, 'Gespräch mit Ismail Kadare', Sinn und Form, 42 (1990), 706–14 (p. 711). My translation.

149. 'When Allah the Merciful and Compassionate first created this world, the earth was smooth and even as a finely engraved plate. That displeased the devil who envied man this gift of God. And

while the earth was still just as it had come from God's hands, damp and soft as unbaked clay, he stole up and scratched the face of God's earth with his nails as much and as deeply as he could. Therefore [. . .] deep rivers and ravines were formed which divided one district from another and kept men apart, preventing them from travelling on that earth that God had given them as a garden for their food and their support. and Allah felt pity when he saw what the Accursed One had done, but was not able to return to the task which the devil had spoiled with his nails, so he sent his angels to help men and make things easier for them. When the angels saw how unfortunate men could not pass those abysses and ravines to finish the work they had to do, but tormented themselves and looked in vain and shouted from one side to the other, they spread their wings above those places and men were able to cross. So men learned from the angels of God how to build bridges, and therefore after fountains, the greatest blessing is to build a bridge and the greatest sin to interfere with it, for every bridge [. . .] has its guardian angel who cares for it and maintains it as long as God has ordained that it should stand.' Ivo Andrić, *The Bridge over the Drina*, trans. by Lovett F. Edwards (London: Harvill Press, 1995), pp. 208–09.

150. The modernizing achievements of the socialist regime are summarized by Kristo Frasheri: 'The liquidation in 1946 of the latifundia, the elimination within twelve years of illiteracy, the construction of secondary schools in every region, the foundation of several universities during the fifties, the complete attachment of the whole country to the electricity grid by 1972, the establishment of social security, retirement pensions, and guaranteed invalid benefits, the opening of numerous hospitals, polyclinics, maternity wards and pharmacies even in inaccessible mountain areas, the existence of free medical treatment, the elimination of malaria and syphilis, the development of the arts and sport, the improvement of land as a result of draining of marshy areas, construction of industrial complexes and railroads — all things which the backward Albania of the pre-war era did not know.' 'À l'assaut du pouvoir', in *Albanie Utopie: Huis clos dans les Balkans*, ed. by Sonia Combe and Ivalyo Ditchev (Paris: Éditions Autrement, 1996), pp. 42–52 (pp. 51–52); my translation.

151. Alexandre Zotos, *De Scanderbeg à Ismaïl Kadaré: Propos d'histoire et de littérature albanaises* (Saint-Etienne: Publications de l'Université de Saint-Etienne, 1971), p. 61. Cf. Edith Lhomel, 'Le défi de l'autarcie économique', in *Albanie Utopie: Huis clos dans les Balkans*, ed. by Sonia Combe and Ivalyo Ditchev (Paris: Éditions Autrement, 1996), pp. 68–77 (p. 71).

152. Hoxha, 'Literature and the Arts', p. 842.

153. Jacques, p. 495; Rama, p. 52.

154. Cited in Jacques, p. 496.

155. Jean-Paul Champseix, 'Fétiches staliniens: tentative d'inventaire', in *Albanie Utopie: Huis clos dans les Balkans*, ed. by Sonia Combe and Ivalyo Ditchev (Paris: Éditions Autrement, 1996), pp. 150–58 (p. 155).

156. Fatos T. Lubonja, 'A Critical Spirit, editorial' (1995), in *Përpjekja/Endeavour: Writing from Albania's Critical Quarterly*, ed. by Fatos T. Lubonja and John Hodgson, trans. by John Hodgson (Tirana: Botime Përpjekja, 1997), pp. 19–25 (pp. 20–21): 'The period from the beginning of the history of the Albanian people down to the declaration of independence remained largely the stuff of legend, mystification, and panegyric, and retained the spirit of the romanticism of the national renaissance, even though the communists claimed to inherit a doctrine that was very critical of the past'.

157. Cf. Piro Misha, 'Invention of a Nationalism: Myth and Amnesia', *Albanian Identities: Myth and History*, ed. by Stephanie Schwandner-Sievers and Bernd J. Fischer (Bloomington: Indiana University Press, 2002), pp. 33–48 (pp. 47–48).

158. Lubonja, 'A Critical Spirit', p. 27.

159. Pipa, 'Subversion vs. Conformism', p. 77. 'In olden days kings learned about the negative sentiments of their subjects through the mouths of their fools. In our days and in totalitarian countries that role has devolved on talented heretical writers specializing in doublespeak'. Arshi Pipa, *Contemporary Albanian Literature*, East European Monographs 305 (Boulder: East European Monographs dist. by Columbia University Press, 1991), p. 67.

160. Pipa, *Contemporary Albanian Literature*, p. 93.

161. Pipa, 'Subversion vs. Conformism', p. 77. Pipa, himself a victim of and exile from Hoxha's regime, was involved in an ongoing feud with Kadare over the linkage in this article of

the writer to the rumour of the dictator's homosexuality. Kadare considered Pipa to have endangered his life. Cf. Robert Elsie, 'Modern Albanian Authors in Translation', http://www.albanianliterature.net/authors3/AA3–25.html, for Pipa's biography. In *The Weight of the Cross* Kadare recounts the sequence of events (pp. 534–35) and in *Invitation to the Writer's Studio* refers bitterly to Pipa's acts of 'denunciation' (pp. 260–61).

162. Bernard Rapp, *Caractères: Engagement* (= Caracteres no. 25), Interview with Ismail Kadare (*Printemps albanais*), Marie Gautheron (*L'honneur*), Gilles Plazy (editor/biographer of Vercors), Bernhard-Henri Lévy (*Les aventures de la liberté*), Antenne 2, 1991.

163. Hans-Joachim Hoppe, 'Ismail Kadaré: ein regimetreuer Dissident?', *Osteuropa*, 43 (1993), pp. 988–91.

164. Lubonja, 'Albanian Culture and Pilot Fish', p. 37.

165. Lubonja, 'Albanian Culture and Pilot Fish', p. 36.

166. Lubonja, 'Albanian Culture and Pilot Fish', p. 36.

167. 'This zone was made up of writers, artists, academics, teachers, and directors of schools, in short "salaried graduates", who, in order to survive and to some extent to profit, conformed to the regime, submitted, and kowtowed before it'. Lubonja, 'Albanian Culture and Pilot Fish', p. 35.

168. Lubonja, 'Albanian Culture and Pilot Fish', p. 36.

169. Lubonja, 'Albanian Culture and Pilot Fish', pp. 39–40.

170. Costantino Marco, 'Nationalism and Art' (1995), in *Përpjekja/Endeavour: Writing from Albania's Critical Quarterly*, ed. by Fatos T. Lubonja and John Hodgson, trans. by John Hodgson (Tirana: Botime Përpjekja, 1997), pp. 41–44 (pp. 42–43, 44).

171. Noel Malcolm, 'In the Palace of Nightmares', review of *The Three-Arched Bridge*, *The New York Review of Books*, vol. 44, no. 17 (November 6, 1997), pp. 21–24. Cf. also the interchange with Ismail Kadare in vol. 45, no. 1 (January 15, 1998), pp. 59–60, and Steven Schwartz's comments in vol. 45, no. 6 (April 9, 1998), p. 80.

172. Malcolm, p. 22. 'Now we understand why *Chronicle in Stone* was a "difficult chronicle", the main difficulty consisting in concealing a subversive message in the folds and creases of an ambiguous and at times cryptic language which even a critical reader would find difficult to grasp.' Pipa, 'Subversion vs. Conformism', p. 64.

173. Malcolm, p. 22.

174. Kadaré/Bosquet, pp. 62, 99.

175. Malcolm, p. 22.

176. Malcolm, p. 23.

177. Malcolm, p. 22.

178. Despite the differences, Kadare chose to present the two novels as related and sequential, if not a sequence, in volumes VII and VIII of his *Œuvres* under the joint title of *Le Temps des querelles* (*The Time of Conflicts*).

179. Faye, 'Introduction' to *Œuvres*, VIII, 14–15.

180. Dritëro Agolli makes this accusation in his 1983 critique of the manuscript, *Le Sang froid* (*The Concert*), reprinted in Sinani, pp. 118, 119.

181. Kadaré, *Le Poids*, p. 432.

182. Sinani, pp. 112, 126.

183. Sinani, pp. 112, 116, 126.

184. Faye, 'Introduction' to *Œuvres*, VIII, 12.

CHAPTER 4

Kadare's Final Political Vision at the End of the Regime

Kosovo and the Shehu Affair, Early 1980s

The death of the Yugoslav leader, Josip Broz Tito, in May 1980 ushered in an era of uncertainty in Yugoslavia which would end with the fall of communism and the emergence of the nationalist leader Slobodan Milosevic at the end of the decade. In the year following Tito's death conflict broke out in Kosovo. Kosovar Albanian students at the University of Pristina demanded autonomy from Serbia as a seventh Yugoslav republic, not just an 'autonomous region' as created by Tito in 1945. The Yugoslav regime acted ruthlessly and brutally, killing and incarcerating large numbers of Kosovar Albanians, despite official claims to the contrary.[1] Kadare heard the news outside Albania. He was in Rome for a couple of days at the beginning of April and heard on his way home of the massacre that had taken place on 31 March 1981, 'l'un des plus sauvages perpétrés sur notre continent depuis la Second Guerre mondiale' (*Le Poids* 414; 'one of the most savage [massacres] carried out on our continent since the Second World War'). Conflict between Albanians and Serbs in Kosovo would continue to escalate throughout the 1980s as the Serbian backlash against perceived inequalities of the Tito years gained momentum.

Kosovo was an embarrassment for Hoxha's regime. Since the end of the war Hoxha had desisted from making claims for Kosovo from the Yugoslavs, knowing that he could neither afford nor win any resulting conflict. It was also well-known that the Kosovar Albanians considered themselves better off under Tito than their ethnic brethren south of the Accursed Mountains.[2] After the Soviet-led invasion of Czechoslovakia in 1968, too, Hoxha was wary of upsetting the fragile stand-off between Albania and Yugoslavia and providing the Soviet Union with a pretext to increase its presence in the eastern Mediterranean and/or to invade the Balkans. After the fall in July 1966 of the Yugoslav functionary, Ranković, whom Hoxha particularly loathed, and in response to the Soviet invasion of Czechoslovakia, some attempts were made at rapprochement over the Kosovo issue. Relations with Romania were also kept on a stable level, despite Nicolae Ceaușescu's softening of stance toward the West. Nationalist Albanian demonstrations had occurred in Kosovo in 1968, but were not allowed to upset the Balkan balance at this precarious time. Despite the rhetoric of ideological difference, trade between Albania and Yugoslavia continued uninterrupted, and full diplomatic relations were re-established between the two countries in 1971. Prifti considers the Soviet suppression of the Prague Spring to have been the primary reason for Hoxha's ongoing silence on the Kosovo issue.[3]

For Ismail Kadare, who was privy to inside information about Hoxha and whose responses to the Kosovo issue were fuelled by a powerful nationalism, the situation of 1981 was one of national shame. The silence of the international community, particularly of Europe, appalled him; the initial silence of Tirana left him incensed and outraged.

> Ce silence était deux fois, trois fois, cent fois plus honteux que celui de l'Europe. Et d'autant plus insupportable. Ce n'est qu'au bout de neuf jours que les journaux albanais publièrent enfin un article contre les massacres serbes. Que s'était-il passé durant ces neuf jours? Quelles tractations avaient été menées dans le dos du Kosovo? Cela faisait combien de fois que la trahison se répétait, comme en 1941, en 1943, en 1947, en 1960, en 1975 . . .? Quel en était le prix? De quoi avait-on menacé Enver Hoxha? Que lui avait-on proposé en échange de l'abandon répété du Kosovo? Quels dossiers allaient disparaître à Brioni, quelles lettres, quels récits, quelles photographies? (*Le Poids* 414–15)

> That silence [i.e. of the regime] was twice, three, one hundred times more disgraceful than that of Europe. And all the more unbearable. It wasn't until nine days later that the Albanian newspapers finally published an article against the Serb massacres. What had been happening during those nine days? What negotiations had been carried out on Kosovo's back? How many times had the betrayal been repeated since 1941, 1943, 1947, 1960, 1975 . . .? And what was the price of betrayal? What had Enver Hoxha been threatened with? What had been offered in exchange for the repeated abandonment of Kosovo? Which files would disappear on Brioni, which letters, which stories and photographs?

For Kadare the roots of the modern Kosovo problem were to be found in the history of the partisan networks in the last years of the war. On 8 November 1941 the two future dictators, Hoxha and Tito, committed the first of a series of criminal acts in subordinating Kosovo to their respective domestic interests.

> Cela faisait un tiers de siècle, depuis ce sombre jour du 8 novembre 1941, que les deux dictatures serbe et albanaise flirtaient dans le dos du Kosoo. Le Kosovo était leur commun crime, la chaîne qui les liait l'une à l'autre. [. . .] Plus les Albanais du Kosovo étaient écrasés par les communistes serbes, plus il était facile aux communistes albanais de détourner l'attention de la terreur qui régnait en Albanie. Et vice-versa: la sauvagerie de la dictatur albanaise profitait pour les mêmes raisons aux Serbes. Les deux dictatures étaient renforcées par leur commune barbarie. (*Le Poids* 415)

> It was a third of a century since that gloomy day of 8 November 1941, when the two dictatorships, the Serb and the Albanian, flirted with each other on the back of Kosovo. Kosovo was their crime in common, the chain which linked them to each other. [. . .] The more the Kosovar Albanians were crushed by the Serb communists, the easier it was for the Albanian communists to deflect attention away from the terror which reigned in Albania. And vice versa. The savagery of the Albanian dictatorship could be used for the same ends by the Serbs. The two dictatorships were reinforced by their common barbarism.

Kosovo was a scapegoat for the Albanian as well as the Yugoslav regime. The internal domestic pressures arising from the mismanagement of the country could be projected outwards onto the Serbs as the instigators of ethnic injustice towards Albanians in Kosovo. Likewise for the Serbs, Montenegrins, and Macedonians in Yugoslavia, the Kosovar Albanians, despite their autonomy, were ethnic (non-Slav) and religious (largely Muslim) outsiders, whose occupation of the core locations of Serbian Orthodox identity remained an open wound even during the years of Titoite iron control of ethnic tensions in the federation.

However, there was a further sinister component to Kadare's suspicion of Enver Hoxha's role in the betrayal of Kosovo. Kadare was convinced that important members of the Yugoslav leadership were aware of what he calls the 'supreme rumour' of Enver Hoxha's homosexuality and were in possession of material that could be used against him.[4] The Yugoslav and Albanian communists were closely connected via the clandestine networks of the inter-war period and as a result of the partisan collaboration during the war. Any mention of Hoxha's homosexual escapades in France and Belgium had been ruthlessly quashed in Albania. The possibility of blackmail was a further reason for Hoxha's special interest in breaking all ties with Yugoslavia as soon as the Albanian communist party had taken control of the country, and in having the pro-Yugoslav faction of the party arrested and executed as soon as possible on charges of treason. The machismo of the partisan culture, the prudery and hypocrisy of the communist regimes and Hoxha's paranoia regarding the Yugoslavs rendered this a potent threat. Kadare was fascinated by Hoxha's dandyism, and his repeated references to the 'supreme rumour' reflect his preoccupation with these aspects of Hoxha's personality. The rumour was linked to Kadare by the Albanian-American refugee Arshi Pipa in the late 1980s in a discussion of *Chronicle in Stone* in which a link is suggested between the references to homosexuality in the novel, and the figure of Hoxha. This created an extremely dangerous situation for the writer at a time when the sick and paranoid dictator's moods and actions had become even more volatile and unpredictable.[5] Kadare suggests that the Yugoslav government had threatened Hoxha with exposure in order to silence him on the subject of Kosovo.

The ethnic unrest in Kosovo deepened Kadare's involvement with questions of ethnicity. In 1975 he had written a study of Albanian epic song traditions in the *Autobiography of the People in Verse*, developing material that he would use in *The Great Winter*, *The Palace of Dreams*, and for the preface to the *Songbook of Albanian Epic*. *Doruntine*, written in late 1979, foreshadows his interest in the question of Kosovar-Albanian identity. *The Marriage Procession Turned to Ice* was written in 1981 and, with its clear references to the Kosovo crisis, was banned before publication. The other work from this year, *The File on H.*, also has strong associations with northern Albania and Kosovo, where the traditions of epic poetry had remained strong. *The File on H.* was published in two editions of the literary journal *Nëntori* in 1982, but was prohibited from publication in book form until the late 1980s. In Ankara in 1979 Kadare met the Balkan anthropologist Albert Lord, who told him about Milman Parry's research into the traditions of oral poetry in the 1930s in Yugoslavia. *The File on H.*, one of Kadare's best-loved novels, re-enacts the visit of two Irish-American anthropologists to the north of Albania in the 1930s in search

FIG. 23 (above): Ismail Kadare with the German writer, Heinrich Böll at the time of *The Palace of Dreams* in 1981. (Photo: Private collection of Ismail Kadare.)

FIG. 24 (below): Enver Hoxha meeting artists in the Tirana Art Gallery, December 24, 1981, only a week after the death of Mehmet Shehu and shortly before the storm was about to break over *The Palace of Dreams*. (Source: *40 Years of Socialist Albania*, Tirana: 8 Nëntori Publishing House, 1984.)

of the descendents of Homer to record their epic songs. They are treated with awe and suspicion as foreigners and for attempting to imprison the free poetry of the land in their tape-recorders. In fact, however, the opposite occurs as the Americans themselves are affected, and one of them begins unconsciously to mimic the behaviour of the traditional rhapsodists by the end of the novel. The power of the Albanian song is such as to pare away gradually the ephemera of modern life, keeping only the essentials, much as happens in the final chapters of the revised version of *The Great Winter*. Modern machinery is no match for the eternal verities of the epic.

Kadare refers to this novel as dealing with the 'Slav invasion' and the critic Arshi Pipa criticizes the nationalist intent of *The File on H.*, in particular Kadare's presentation of the origins of the rhapsodies in the Albanian highlands, when, he writes, they were known to have originated in Bosnia and from there travelled to Kosovo and Northern Albania.

> In its anti-Yugoslav hysteria [. . .] Albanian Stalinism appropriated the nationalistic thesis that South Slavs borrowed the rhapsodies in question from the Albanians, going so far in this direction as to claim as an Albanian Milos Obilic, the Serbian hero of the battle of Kosova. Kadare's novel upholds the official thesis.[6]

However, this novel, like *The Three-Arched Bridge*, while defending Albanian traditions and culture, reads neither as a confirmation of state policy nor as an attack on the Serbs as a people. The comedy of the plot and the deference to the songs of the highlanders renders it one of Kadare's most readable and accessible works. There is no sabre-rattling and even the representation of the urban and rural Albanians is marked by an ironic and self-deprecating humour. In the context of Balkan politics, especially as the decade drew to a close, Kadare remained committed to non-violence despite the occasional shrill tones of his patriotism in works such as *The Autobiography of the People in Verse*.

In this already tense period another crisis occurred. On 26 April 1980, Mehmet Shehu was relieved of duties as Minister of Defence and succeeded by Kadri Hazbiu, ex-Minister of the Interior. On 17 December Shehu was found shot dead in suspicious circumstances. Shehu was one of the original partisans who marched with Hoxha through the streets of Tirana after the German withdrawal, and who had established a reputation as a ruthless, hard-line Stalinist in the regime. Hoxha made a public announcement that Shehu had committed suicide after having been exposed as an enemy counter-agent. One of Shehu's sons committed suicide, his widow, Fiqret was removed from her post as secretary in charge of ideology on the Central Committee and imprisoned and interrogated along with Shehu's other sons. There had earlier also been a scandal over the planned marriage of Shehu's second son to the daughter of a 'class enemy', a dangerous move for anyone, let alone a member of the ruling elite. Tirana was awash with fear and rumour. A period of renewed political terror, dubbed by Bashkim Shehu the 'autumn of fear', descended over the country as Mehmet Shehu's 'accomplices' were named and purged.[7] Kadare suspected that the ageing and paranoid dictator had become suspicious of his long-time comrade and wanted to remove him as he had done with so many powerful figures over the past four decades. Kadare does not doubt that Yugoslav agents were at work and that messages were passing back and forth between the two regimes. Far from being an agent, however, Mehmet Shehu was hated by the Yugoslavs for his role in blocking Tito's planned Balkan federation. The Yugoslavs had an interest in destabilizing Albanian internal affairs in order to take the focus away from Kosovo, and had sent secret messages aimed at Shehu.

> L'histoire découvrira un jour le traget suivi par le message serbe, et sa destination. Comme en 1943, comme en 1945, comme en 1947, ce message atterrissait toujours chez quelqu'un de précis. Le glas sonnait surtout pour ceux que le tyran albanais, pour diverses raisons, considérait d'un mauvais œil. Lorsque le message slave concordait avec les souhaits du tryan (c'était le plus souvent le cas), rien ne pouvait plus sauver la victime. (*Le Poids* 418)

> One day history will uncover the route taken by the Serb message, and its destination. As in 1943, in 1945 and 1947, this message would always land at the door of a specific person. It sounded the death knell especially for those whom the Albanian tyrant, for whatever reason, was suspicious of. When the Slav message corresponded with the wishes of the tyrant (as was more often than not the case), nothing would save the victim.

Shehu's third son, Bashkim, was a young writer who had sent his work to Kadare for comment. Kadare knew him to be a fierce critic of the regime, protected so far by his family's status. He was close enough to Kadare to have read the manuscript of *The Concert*.[8] Shortly before his father's death he had visited Kadare with information regarding conversations that had taken place between his father and Enver Hoxha regarding the writer. After Shehu's death and the imprisonment of Bashkim, Kadare feared that information that had passed between him and Bashkim would be extorted from the young man. Kadare was terrified that any comments he may have made to Bashkim about Hoxha's sexuality and the issue of Kosovo might be extracted under interrogation or torture.[9] Such an admission would have warranted the death sentence. (While this information was sought under duress, according to Bashkim, it was not given.) A day before Mehmet Shehu's funeral service writers and artists were invited to an art showing at which Enver Hoxha was to be present. Kadare was not invited. Familiar with the rituals of exclusion and denunciation, he guessed that something was afoot, that he was in danger, and that it had to do with the death of the Prime Minister and the imprisonment of Bashkim. According to a letter which Bashkim sent to Kadare after his release from prison in 1991, he had indeed been interrogated about Kadare as a 'dangerous enemy of the people' over that week by senior members of the regime, including the then Minister for the Interior, Rexhep Kolli.[10]

Bashkim Shehu would write up his memories of this affair in *L'automne de la peur*, which was published in French in 1993. In his preface to Shehu's work Kadare confirms much of this material and adds further details regarding the relationships between Hoxha and the Yugoslav security apparatus. The Yugoslav archive, he writes, houses thousands of documents from the period 1941–48 on the activities of the Albanian partisans and other communists.[11] After the 1981 massacres, the Yugoslavs tried to blackmail Hoxha into silence by publishing part of a denunciation of Hoxha by Naku Spiru to the Comintern. Realizing that Hoxha would have to protest the situation in 1981, the Yugoslavs demanded in turn that Hoxha purge Shehu for treason:

> La déstabilisation de l'Albanie était en fait la seule issue permettant à la Yougoslavie d'étouffer le Kossovo. Et c'est bien ce qui se produisit: traumatisée comme elle ne l'avait jamais été par le limogeage du premier ministre et la vague de terreur de cet hiver-là, l'Albanie oublia le Kossovo. D'autre part — et c'est l'essentiel -, lorsqu'ils apprirent que le pays sur lequel ils avaient trente années durant fondé leurs espoirs était gouverné par un agent serbe, les Albanais du Kossovo trovèrent cela plus cruel que d'être massacrés par les Serbes.[12]

> The destabilization of Albania was the only outcome which would permit Yugoslavia to stifle Kosovo. And that's exactly what happened. Traumatized as never before by the dismissal of the prime minister and the wave of terror of that winter, Albania forgot Kosovo. On the other side of the border — and this is the crux of the matter — the Albanians of Kosovo discovered that the country on which they had based their hopes for the past thirty years was governed by a Serb agent. This seemed crueller to them even than the Serb massacres.

At the time Kadare was worried that he would become involved in the wave of repressions that were sure to follow as Shehu's 'accomplices' in the plot to assassinate the dictator were identified and brought to justice. The Central Committee was in the process of reviewing *The Concert*. In this work Kadare had portrayed Mao Tse-tung as a shadowy and sinister tyrant responsible for the aeroplane crash in late 1971 that would kill his second-in-command Lin Biao and his family on their flight to Hong Kong after the failed assassination attempt on the leader. The death of Lin Biao had taken place only eight years before the manuscript of *The Concert* was completed in 1979, and less than two years before the death of Mehmet Shehu. It was all far too close for comfort.

This was the era of the passing of the partisan generation, foreseen by Kadare with the death of his own father, and heralding a critical period of transition. Hoxha was obsessed with purging Albania of impure elements before his own demise. Adil Çarçani succeeded Shehu as Premier and Hoxha's new favourite, Ramiz Alia, replaced Haxhi Lleshi as chief ideologist and President. In November 1982 the Soviet General Secretary Leonid Brezhnev died after a period of senescence and the last of the old guard, Andropov and Chernenko, would follow in quick succession. The ascent of Gorbachev would herald a new era and bring Soviet communism to an end. The next generation of Albanian leaders, Hekuran Isai, the new Minister for the Interior, Haxhi Lleshi, Adil Çarçani, and other members of the Central Committee, were desperately seeking preferment. The one remaining powerful member of the old guard was Kadri Hazbiu. (Hysni Kapo had died of unknown causes in France in 1979.) Hazbiu had been Minister of the Interior since the early days of the 'division of power' in 1954. At that time Hoxha had given up the Prime Ministership in order to focus power in the role of General Secretary. Mehmet Shehu, the former Minister of the Interior became Prime Minister and Shehu's brother-in-law Kadri Hazbiu, became Minister of the Interior and Director of the Sigurimi. After Shehu was dispatched, it was Hazbiu's turn. In September 1982 a group of commandos, made up of Albanian exiles led by Xhevdet Mustafa and equipped to provoke a coup, made a secret landing on the Albanian coast. Hoxha was forewarned by British double agents, and the commandos were killed or taken prisoner as they landed. The regime presented the scenario as a 'plot' by right-wing Albanians in exile with inside collaborators to overthrow the government. But the commando raid seemed too conveniently timed. Details of the affair remained unclear, with suspicion directed at King Zog's son, the exiled Leka, as the organizer. Leka denied all knowledge of the raid, although it was known that he had been planning some sort of coup and was found to have a cache of weapons on his South African property. However, the dim-witted Leka had been fantasizing about staging an armed coup and restoring the monarchy since his childhood. The other possibility suggested by various commentators was that the raid was staged by the regime 'to explain the elimination of an internal opposition group'.[13] The coup, the 'plot', and the subsequent purge in autumn 1983 brought down the Minister for Foreign Affairs, the Minister for Health, and various high-ranking officials, along with the prize, Hazbiu, who 'committed suicide' late, but nevertheless according to plan.[14] The rumour that his tongue had been cut out to stop him talking was probably more a reflection of the fears of some and the relief of others than of the truth. In passages reminiscent of the bizarre and morbid dream-world of *The Shadow*, Kadare imagines the supreme leader's revenge fantasies of betrayal and destruction which would transform Tirana into a nightmare world as he planned Hazbiu's suicide after the long years of political intimacy. To add a note of black farce to events, the production of the film version of *The General of the Dead Army*, due to begin in mid 1982, became caught up in the events. In June the actor Michel Piccoli arrived in Tirana as the first of the Italian crew under director Luciano Tovoli to star alongside Marcello Mastroianni. However, in the environment of paranoid fear of foreign agents, the regime withdrew authorization at this already advanced stage of planning, causing a debacle with the arriving film crew. The film was subsequently completed in the following year in Italy using Italian-Albanian settings with Marcello Mastroianni in the role of the general and Michel Piccoli playing the chaplain.

'The Darkest Phase': *The Palace of Dreams, 1981–1982*

It was into this environment in 1981 that Kadare lobbed his most incendiary piece of writing, *The Palace of Dreams*. In fact the first two chapters were included in a collection of stories and reportages under the title *L'Emblème de jadis* in 1979 and the complete novel was published in book form two years later at the end of 1981 shortly before the Shehu affair took place.

Quoting Heraclitus, that 'those who sleep are alone, those awake are with others', Kadare uses the collective sleep of the peoples of the Empire in *The Palace of Dreams* as a satire on and metaphor for existence under the dictatorship.[15] Like the other great political novels of the twentieth century, Koestler's *Darkness at Noon*, or Orwell's *1984*, it is 'world literature', transcending local and national boundaries to speak directly to an international audience. At one level it is, like *1984*, a satire on totalitarianism. Like Orwell's Ministry of Truth, the Palace is a powerful state institution in control of the mass unconsciousness of the Empire. At another level it is an analysis of the ways in which power functions within dictatorial regimes. However, Kadare's novel is more than a satire on the types of control typical of the communist dictatorships. Alongside the political satire runs a second, intricately coded theme of ethnic identity at a time of change in power-relationships in the Empire. In passages reminiscent of the terror evoked in Kafka's *The Trial and The Castle*, Kadare creates a modern parable, haunted by the theme of Albanian ethnic identity in the form of ancient bardic songs. This novel represents tensions between ethno-national and imperial identity for an individual and a dynasty whose fate is bound up in both national and supranational politics. Kadare's protagonist, Mark-Alem, is a complex figure, the object of both pity and scorn, who embraces spiritual death before Albanian identity. Mark-Alem is Kadare's most powerful expression of the inauthenticity of an existence bereft of ethnic identity. He is a particularly Albanian version of the Central European 'man without qualities', a figure of contempt as an individual even as power and prestige are thrust upon him.

The Palace of Dreams is set in the 'United Ottoman States' ('U.O.S'.), an imagined Ottoman Empire late in the last century.[16] The original motif of the Palace is to be found in Kadare's earlier work, *The Niche of Shame*, in which the *Yildis Sarrail* and the idea of the control of dreams is mentioned in passing.[17] The Palace is a vast state organization dedicated to the interpretation of the dreams of the subjects throughout the length and breadth of the Empire. All dreams are recorded, scrutinized for signs of impending social and political unrest, interpreted and classified. On the basis of the interpretations, policy is formulated by the Sultan and his ministers, and the administration of the Empire is carried out. The most significant dreams are classified as Master-Dreams and carry great weight in the decision-making processes. However, there are also indications that dreams are planted for political purposes, to destabilize the regime or to denounce powerful political players. At the beginning of the novel, Kadare's protagonist, Mark-Alem Quprili, has just commenced working at the Palace of Dreams, first in selection and later providing interpretations of potential Master-Dreams. The plot depends on the tension between Mark-Alem's function as an officer of the Sultan, and his position as the youngest son of the Quprilis, an Albanian Ottoman dynasty at a time of political unrest. Warned by his uncle, the Vizier, of the politically sensitive nature of his work at the Palace, Mark-Alem nevertheless fails to identify a crucial Master-Dream, planted by the family's enemies, which will ultimately bring about the downfall of his family. At the same time he discovers in himself a sympathy with the ethnic nationalism of his rebellious uncle, Kurt, and a longing to reclaim his Albanian roots, after listening to a version of the family's epic sung by foreign bards in contravention of the wishes of the Sultan. His uncle, whose Austrian connections also imply an element of foreign interference at a time when the Slavs and the Habsburgs are competing for influence over the Balkan peninsula, brings about the denouement of the story through his acts. The Vizier is toppled and the family disgraced, but strangely all is not lost, as Mark-Alem finds himself promoted to more and more powerful positions in the Palace. The novel ends with Mark-

Alem torn between his sense of Albanian ethnicity and his blossoming career as a high-ranking functionary of the Sultan's Empire.

The setting in late nineteenth-century Istanbul bears resemblance to nothing so much as Moscow, Belgrade, Tirana, or any of the Eastern-bloc capitals in the last decades of the socialist era. Indeed the description of the mosque, the bank, and the clock-tower in the opening pages is strikingly reminiscent of the area around Scanderbeg Square in central Tirana.[18] Various powerful dynasties are jockeying for influence around the Sultan in Istanbul, and in distant provinces subject peoples are becoming restive. While at one level the historical allegory can be read as a blatant reference to Tirana politics with its 'sultan', its clan loyalties and power plays among the factions, at another level the novel is an allegory of South-Eastern Europe caught in the conflict between ethnicity and imperialism. A key to Kadare's vision lies in the recognition that these structures of power and oppression replicate themselves from the minor and local level of the regional Party to that of the regime and beyond to the level of the nation, the (Balkan) regional and the Soviet bloc. Power is wielded through the politics of inducement, intrusion, and terror, and ethnic identity exists as the repressed substratum of the 'individual' and 'social imaginary'.

Kadare provokes and challenges on several fronts in this novel. The historical allegory scarcely disguises the political satire; the evocation of Albanianness is controversial in the context of Hoxha's particular form of communist nationalism, and the characterization of the protagonist penetrates to the heart of Kadare's existential critique of the dictatorship. Moreover, the writer refers obliquely to Albanian and Balkan history and culture and to relatively little-known Albanian and Bosnian epic traditions in order to represent the conflicts between ethnicity and political power.

The Quprili Family and the Palace of Dreams

Mark-Alem is the pampered and protected scion of a ruling caste family of Albanian origins. For generations the Quprili family have served the Sultan as viziers, government officials and bureaucrats of the Empire. The name Quprili, which Mark-Alem inherits through his mother's line, is a translation of the Albanian word *Ura*, meaning 'bridge'. (The Serb word meaning 'bridge', *ćuprija*, used by Andrić, for example, also derives from the Turkish 'köprü'.) In the Quprili family chronicle the (presumably Turkish) root is transliterated in various forms as *qyprija*, or *kurpija*. Despite pressure from the Sultan to use the more acceptable Ottoman transliteration, *Köprülü*, the family has retained the traditional Albanian spelling, *Quprili*. (This also raises indirectly the question of when and why the Quprilis adopted the Turkish rather than the Albanian root word in their name.) Only in the Larousse encyclopaedia entry have they compromised by allowing the Turkish form to be used. The name itself refers back to the family's original association with 'un pont à trois arches situé en Albanie centrale, édifié à l'époque où les Albanais étaient encore chrétiens, et dans les fondations duquel on avait emmuré un homme' ('a bridge with three arches in central Albania, constructed in the days when the Albanians were still Christians and built with a man walled up in its foundations').[19]

After the bridge was finished, one of the builders and founding ancestor of the family adopted after his first name, *Gjon*, the name of *Ura* (bridge) 'en même temps que la marque du crime qui y demeurait attaché' (*Le Palais* 9, 'together with the stigma of murder attached to it', *Palace* 9).

Albanians played important roles in the Ottoman ruling classes from the sixteenth century onwards. Kadare makes use of a prominent Albanian clan, the Köprülüs. The Larousse entry cited by Kadare in the novel identifies Mehmed (Meth) Pasha Köprülü (1575–1661), Grand Vizier under Sultan Mehmed I who came from a village in Albania to found a dynasty of grand viziers, prime-ministers, admirals and generals, ministers and high-ranking officials in the Ottoman Empire.[20] This Albanian family was notable too for its activity in the defence and the expansion of the Ottoman Empire, providing generations of leaders in the Ottoman expansion north-westwards and quelling national rebellions in the Balkans, northern Africa, and elsewhere. The historical importance of the family, however, ends in the early eighteenth century.

The novel begins on Mark-Alem's first day of work at *Tabir Sarrail* or Palace of Dreams. The Palace was originally the *Yildis Sarrail*, dedicated to producing astrological interpretations and counselling the Sultan, but it has has been modernized in recent times, and the collection and interpretation of the dreams of the empire reorganized along scientific lines. All dreams are recorded and scrutinized for signs of impending social and political unrest:

> L'idée qu'a eue le Souverain de créer le Tabir total repose sur le fait qu'Allah lance un rêve annonciateur à la surface du globe avec la même désinvolture qu'Il lâche un éclair, dessine un arc-en-ciel ou rapproche subitement de nous une comète qu'Il va tirer d'on ne sait quelles profondeurs mysérieuses de l'Univers. Il lance donc un signal sur cette terre, sans se soucier du lieu où il va tomber, car, lointain comme Il est, Il ne peut s'occuper de ce genre de détail. [. . .] l'explication de ce rêve, tombé comme une étincelle perdue dans le cerveau d'un des millions d'individus endormis, peut aider à prévenir le malheur du pays et de son Souverain, à éviter la guerre ou la peste, voire engendrer des idées nouvelles. [. . .] Tout ce qui est trouble et néfaste, ou qui le sera dans quelques années ou quelques siècles, apparaît d'abord dans les rêves des hommes. Toute passion ou idée malfaisante, tout fléau ou crime, toute rébellion ou catastrophe projette nécessairement son ombre longtemps avant de se manifester dans la vie réelle. (*Le Palais* 22–23)

> The idea behind the Sovereign's creation of the *Tabir* is that Allah looses a forewarning dream on the world as casually as He unleashes a flash of lightning or draws a rainbow or suddenly sends a comet close to us, drawn from the mysterious depths of the Universe. He dispatches a signal to the earth without bothering about where it will land; He is too far away to be concerned with such details. [. . .] the interpretation of that dream, fallen like a stray spark into the brain of one out of millions of sleepers, may help to save the country or its Sovereign from disaster; may help to avert war or plague or to create new ideas. [. . .] All that is murky and harmful, or that will become so in a few years or centuries, makes its first appearance in men's dreams. Every passion or wicked thought, every affliction or crime, every rebellion or catastrophe necessarily casts its shadow long before it manifests itself in real life. (*Palace* 19–20)

FIG. 25 (above): The minaret of the mosque of Ethem Bey, and the clock-tower in central Tirana, mentioned in the opening pages of *The Palace of Dreams*. The ministry buildings to the right were built by King Zog in the 1930s with Italian support. (Photo: Peter Morgan.)

FIG. 26 (centre): The General Committee headquarters in Tirana, possible model for the Tabir Sarrail or *The Palace of Dreams*. (Photo: Peter Morgan.)

FIG. 27 (left): The single-stringed *lahuta*, used to accompany recitations of Albanian epic and song. (Photo: Peter Morgan.)

The hierarchy of the Palace of Dreams extends from the Copying rooms and Archives below, to the offices of Selection and Interpretation above. Mark-Alem is soon promoted from his first position where he selects dreams for further attention, to providing interpretations of potential Master-Dreams, the most significant of the thousands of dreams which flow in each week from throughout the Empire. 'N'oublie pas que le chemin vers les cimes du Tabir Sarrail passe par l'Interprétation', (*Le Palais* 86, 'The road to the heights in the Tabir Sarrail passes through Interpretation', *Palace* 69), Mark-Alem is told shortly after his promotion, and later his uncle confirms that 'quiconque a la haute main sur le Palais des Rêves détient les clés de l'Etat', (*Le Palais* 141, 'whoever controls the Palace of Dreams controls the keys of the State', *Palace* 113).[21] A fairy-tale lends popular appeal to the institution of totalitarian control. 'Depuis longtemps courait une légende d'après laquelle un pauvre hère de quelque sous-préfecture ignorée avait, grâce à son rêve, sauvé l'Etat d'une affreuse calamité', (*Le Palais* 48, 'There was a time-honoured legend about some poor wretch who lived in a forgotten byway and whose dream saved the State from a terrible calamity', *Palace* 39). As a reward he is offered one of the Sultan's nieces in marriage. However, the reality is different: the dreamer of the 'Master-Dream' is subjected to interrogation, torture, and death in the state's relentless pursuit of control.

> Ce devait être là le véritable but de son incarcération: il fallait lui faire oublier son rêve. Cet interrogatoire harassant, jour et nuit, l'interminable procès-verbal, la quête de prétendues précisions sur une de ces visions qui, par nature, ne peuvent jamais être précises, jusqu'à ce que le rêve se désagrège et finisse par se dissoudre irrémédiablement dans la mémoire de son auteur: Autant dire un lavage de cerveau, pensa Mark-Alem. [. . .] Apparemment, il s'agissait de brasillements d'idées subversives que l'Etat, pour un motif ou un autre, se devait d'isoler, tout comme on isole le microbe de la peste jusqu'à ce qu'il soit neutralisé. (*Le Palais* 104)

> That must be the real object of his incarceration: to *make* him forget it. That wearing interrogation night and day, that interminable report, the pretence of seeking precise details about something that by its very nature cannot be definite — all this, continued until the dream begins to disintegrate and finally disappears completely from the dreamer's memory, could only be called brain-washing, thought Mark-Alem. [. . .] It must be a question of flushing out subversive ideas which for some reason or other the State needed to isolate, as one isolates a plague virus in order to be able to neutralise it. (*Palace* 83–84)

The Quprili Dream and the Quprili Epic

Mark-Alem's powerful family is responsible for his placement. However, from the beginning he is unsure of himself. The administration and the functions of the organization are opaque. The process of selection and assignment of duties is mysterious, as is the rationale for his accelerated promotions. Mark-Alem's family is powerful, but their relations with the Palace and with the Sultan himself have been strained, even adversarial in the past. In the first weeks of his employment, Mark-Alem's uncle, the Vizier, warns him that the bureaucracy of the Tabir is corrupt and that dreams are planted by those in power in order to damage their enemies. The Quprili family has been the object of such attacks:

> 'Certains', poursuivit le Vizir, 'pensent que le monde des angoisses et des rêves, bref, votre monde à vous, est celui qui dirige ce monde-ci. Moi, j'estime que c'est de ce monde-ci que tout est dirigé. Que c'est en fin de compte celui-ci qui choisit et les rêves, et les angoisses, et les délires qu'il convient de faire remonter à la surface, comme un seau remonte l'eau du fond d'un puits. Tu vois ce que je veux dire? C'est ce monde-ci qui, dans ce gouffre, choisit ce qui l'intéresse. [. . .] On dit que, parfois, le Maître-Rêve est fabriqué de toutes pièces', lâcha-t-il doucement. 'T'es tu jamais figuré une chose pareille?' Mark-Alem était glacé d'effroi. Fabriqué, le Maître-Rêve? Jamais il n'aurait imaginé qu'un esprit humain osât concevoir pareille horreur, et encore moins ordonner à sa bouche de la formuler explicitement. (*Le Palais* 145)

> 'Some people', the Vizier went on, 'think it's the world of anxieties and dreams — your world, in short — that governs this one. I myself think it's from this world that everything is governed. I think it's this world that chooses the dreams and anxieties and imaginings that ought to be brought to the surface, as a bucket draws water from a well. Do you see what I mean? It's this world that selects what it wants from the abyss. [. . .] They say the Master-Dream is sometimes a complete fabrication', he whispered. 'Has that ever occurred to you?' Mark-Alem went cold with fright. A fabrication? The Master-Dream? He could never have imagined a human mind daring to think such a thing, let alone say it in so many words. (*Palace* 116–17)

Mark-Alem approaches his new job with a sense of foreboding and unwillingness to know or do anything more than necessary to avoid attracting attention to himself. He carries out his tasks in a state of anxiety, fearing that he will make a mistake and miss a vital clue, or will show himself too knowledgeable and hence suspect to his superiors. When warned by his uncle, the Vizier and Foreign Minister to the Sultan, of the machinations and intrigues behind the scenes in the Palace, his response is to plead for rescue: 'Mark-Alem éprouvait l'irrépressible envie de se jeter aux pieds du Vizir et de l'implorer: "Fais-moi quitter cet endroit-là, mon oncle, sauve-moi!"' (*Le Palais* 146, 'Mark-Alem had an almost irresistible desire to fling himself at the Vizier's feet and implore him: "Get me out of there, uncle! save me!"', *Palace* 117).

Shortly after commencing at the *Tabir*, Mark-Alem's attention is taken by the dream of a local fruit-seller:

> Un terrain abandonné au pied d'un pont; une espèce de terrain vague, de ceux où l'on jette les détritus. Parmi les ordures, la poussière, les éclats de lavabos brisés, un vieil instrument de musique à l'aspect insolite, qui jouait tout seul dans cette étendue déserte, et un taureau, apparemment mis en furie par ces sons, qui mugissait au pied du pont . . . (*Le Palais* 55)

> A piece of waste land by a bridge, the sort of vacant lot where people throw rubbish. Amongst all the trash and dust and bits of broken washbasin, a curious musical instrument playing all by itself, except for a bull that seems to be maddened by the sound and is standing by the bridge and bellowing . . . (*Palace* 45*)

In fear of making a wrong move after initially considering it unworthy of further analysis, Mark-Alem classifies the dream at the last minute as of possible interest, to be passed on to the selection and interpretation hierarchy. Later, after he has been promoted to Interpretation, Mark-Alem comes across this dream again and is still puzzled by it, despite his uncle's warning.

> Le pont, n'était-il pas lié à son tour à leur propre patronyme? . . . Peut-être quelque sombre présage?. . . Il relut de nouveau le texte et sa respiration se fit plus légère: le taureau ne se ruait nullement contre le pont. Il tournait en rond dans le terrain vague, sans plus. Rêve creux, se dit-il. (*Le Palais* 111)

> Wasn't the bridge connected with his family's own name? . . . Perhaps this was some sinister omen?. . . He re-read the text and began to breathe more freely again: the bull wasn't really attacking the bridge at all. It was just rushing around the piece of waste ground. It's a dream without any meaning, he thought'. (*Palace* 89)

Ironically, he recognizes that the dream could be of significance, if the bull were attacking the bridge — but it is not. In his literal-mindedness he misses the clue — or does not want to face what it might mean. The *lahuta*, the single-stringed instrument of the Albanians, provides an unmistakeable clue. With its *lahuta*, the bridge, and the raging bull, this dream turns out to be of great importance, signifying to the powers-that-be in the Palace of Dreams a threat from the Quprilis.

Mark-Alem's responses to his family, his career, and his place of employment have been marked from the beginning by timidity, anxiety and awe, fear and intimidation. His obtuseness comes about from his desire not to know, which has its roots in his family history. For centuries the family has experienced glory and misfortune. From his earliest childhood he remembers the crises and tragedies of the family as individual members were catapulted into favour and the highest offices or fell to disgrace, imprisonment, and execution, and his mother's main aim since his father's death has been to protect her only son from this destiny.

Kadare's dreams are masterpieces of parody. With their powerful imagery and surreal logic, they are interpretable in manifold ways — politically or otherwise. Mark-Alem never realizes this, and hence does not learn the central lesson that his uncle is trying to teach him, namely that he must be on guard against any dream which specifically points towards the Quprilis, because it will most probably have been planted in a political manoeuvre to unseat the family. This dream, whether planted by enemies of the family or dreamt by a provincial from the western — Albanian — provinces of the Empire, alerts the Sultan to a threat from the Quprilis. Mark-Alem fails to recognize the significance of the three-arched bridge and to intercept the dream before it brings his family into danger.[22]

It is not only the symbol of the *lahuta* and the three-arched bridge that links this particular dream to the Quprili family. The Quprilis are a family of assimilated Ottomans, for whom power and prestige long ago took priority over ethnicity. Themes of ethnicity are present but dormant in the historical associations with the bridge, with Christianity, conversion, and assimilation into the Turkish Empire. The main symbol of Quprili power and identity is an epic poem in which the legendary deeds of the family have been preserved since the time of the Turkish occupation of the Balkans. For centuries the Quprilis have celebrated their power and influence in the Empire by inviting Bosnian bards to visit the capital and recite a heroic song glorifying the deeds of this Muslim family in the Serb language, accompanied on the single-stringed Serb *gusla*.[23] This private annual celebration has been a source of contention between the Quprilis and the Sultan. It is said that the Sultan is jealous of their cultural eminence when he himself can command nothing more profound than the eulogies of court poets. Like the spelling of the name 'Quprili' (rather than the Turkish 'Köprülü') the epic represents a provocation. It indicates the degree of Quprili power, prestige, and pedigree as a prominent Muslim family in the context of the interest groups and political factions around the Sultan. (The Quprilis are implied to be involved in a power-faction against the 'powerful Sheikh-al-Islam' faction, which is close to the *Tabir Sarrail*).

Mark-Alem's memories of this ritual go back to his earliest childhood when he was frightened by its bloody images and lugubrious tone.

> Au début, il avait imaginé l'*epos* (on l'appelait également ainsi) comme quelque chose de long, créature intermédiaire entre l'hydre et le serpent, vivant au loin dans quelque montagne enneigée et dont le corps, comme celui des monstres fabuleux, renfermait le sort de sa famille. (*Le Palais* 72)

> At first he'd imagined the *epos*, as they called it, as a long thin animal, midway between a hydra and a snake, which lived far away in some snowy mountains, and which, like a beast of fable, carried within its body the fate of the family. (*Palace* 58)

But even as a child he was puzzled by the epic.

> En fait, Mark-Alem s'expliquait mal comment les Quprili pouvaient vivre et tenir le haut du pavé dans la capitale impériale alors qu'au loin, à l'intérieur des étranges Balkans, dans la province nommée Bosnie, on chantait une geste à eux mal à consacrée. Et son esprit avait encore plus de mal à concevoir que cette geste fût chantée non pas dans le pays natal des Quprili, en Albanie, mais en Bosnie, et, de surcroît, qu'elle n'existât pas dans leur langue maternelle, l'albanais, mais en serbe. (*Le Palais* 73)

> He couldn't quite see how it was that the Quprilis lived and lorded it in the imperial capital, while people recited an epic about them in a faraway province called Bosnia in the middle of the Balkans. And he had even more difficulty in understanding why it was sung in Bosnia and not in Albania, where the Quprilis originally came from? And above all why it did not exist in their mother tongue, Albanian, but in Serbian? (*Palace* 58–59*)

These questions lead us to the heart of *The Palace of Dreams*: to the complex ethnic, religious, cultural, and political implications of the Quprili epic. For it turns out that there *is* an Albanian version of the epic. The family knows of its existence, but chooses to ignore it. In that version, stemming from their own ethnic homeland, their role is *not* celebrated.

At a family dinner Mark-Alem's uncle Kurt announces that he has invited rhapsodists from Albania to attend the family celebrations and recite the Albanian version of the epic. Kurt is a very different type from his serious, career-minded siblings:

> Blond, les yeux clairs, les moustaches roussâtres, et avec ce nom germano-albanais de Kurt, celui-ci passait pour la rose sauvage du clan des Quprili. A

la différence des ses frères, il ne s'était jamais fixé à quelque poste important
[. . .] Célibataire endurci, il montait à cheval en compagnie du fils du consul
d'Autriche [. . .] (*Le Palais* 62)

He had fair hair, and with his light-coloured eyes, reddish moustache and
half-German, half-Albanian name, Kurt, he was regarded as the wild rose of
the Quprili tribe. Unlike his brothers he had never stuck to any important job.
[. . .] He was a confirmed bachelor, went riding with the Austrian consul's son
[. . .] (*Palace* 50)

According to Kurt, the Austrian ambassador considers the Bosnian epic to be on a
par with the great German epic, the *Nibelungenlied*, and the Albanian version to be
even superior. The Quprilis, he says, are the only great family left in Europe who
are the subject of an epic, but 'c'est à peine si vous y prêtez attention!' (*Le Palais*
72, 'you scarcely deign to notice it', *Palace* 58). Kurt's brothers are surprised and
concerned at the invitation and its likely consequences. And they are nonplussed as
to why Kurt has invited the Albanian rhapsodists, when their song, unlike that of
the Bosnians, does not feature the Quprili family. In response, Kurt pretends to be
merely curious, echoing Mark-Alem's question:

Ces jours-là, je n'ai cessé de me reposer la question qui fut si souvent formulée
dans notre maison. Pourquoi les Slaves ont-ils composé une geste en notre
honneur, alors que nos compatriotes albanais dans leur épopée, se taisent à notre
sujet. (*Le Palais* 74)

For days I've been pondering the question we've all asked so often: Why have
the Slavs composed an epic in our honour, while our compatriots the Albanians
don't mention us in *their* epic? (*Palace* 59)

The tensions between the uncles in various official posts in the Empire and the
dilettante intellectual, Kurt, with his Germanic name and Austrian connections,
manifest themselves in the following discussion. While Mark-Alem is typically
confused about the epic and his family's importance and involvement with it, his
uncles are not. Kurt may be naive or disingenuous, but for his brother, the issue
is clear: The Austrians are using Kurt and the Quprili epic to involve themselves
in affairs of state. The novel draws on late nineteenth-century Ottoman history
in presenting Austria and Russia as the two neighbouring powers interested in
undermining Ottoman unity by appealing to national groups at the fringes and
the centre of the Empire. Later, the external power-framework of this crisis will
become clearer, as the Russians move to side with the Sultan after the influence of
the Quprilis and, with them, the Austrians is broken. However, there is more to the
theme of national and ethnic identity than merely an allegory of changing power
blocs in the Empire.

The Albanians and the Ottoman Empire

What follows is a long discussion of the Turkish occupation of Albania, the family's
role in the Empire, and the ambivalence of the Albanians towards the Quprilis. For
the assimilated Ottoman members of the family, the Turks brought with them not
slavery, but the freedom to share in the Empire:

'Je n'oublie pas une réflexion que m'a faite un jour un Juif: Quand les Turcs se ruaient sur vous en brandissant leurs lances et leurs sabres, vous autres Albanais avez pensé à juste titre qu'ils venaient vous conquérir, alors qu'en fait ils vous apportaient en présent tout un Empire!' (*Le Palais* 75)

'I remember what a Jew said to me one day: When the Turks rushed at you brandishing spears and sabres you Albanians thought they'd come to conquer you, but in fact they were bringing you a whole Empire as a present!' (*Palace* 60)

The Ottoman Turks brought to the Albanians the wide open spaces that they lacked in their tiny, mountainous country. Without the Ottoman conquest, the Quprilis, for example, would have remained holed up in their mountain fastnesses. Hence, for these imperial Ottomans, Albanian independence would represent a backward step.

Ils conquerront un jour leur vraie indépendance, mais ils perdront toutes ces vastes possibilités, reprit le cousin. Ils perdront cet espace immense où ils pouvaient voler comme le vent, ils se renfermeront sur leur territoire étroit, leurs ailes seront entravées dans leurs movements et ils irons battre d'une montagne à l'autre comme ces oiseaux qui ne peuvent suffisamment prendre leur essor; ils s'étioleront, se ramolliront et se diront en fin de compte: Qu'avons-nous gagné à cela? (*Le Palais* 76–77)

'One day they'll win real independence, but then they'll lose all those other possibilities,' continued the cousin. 'They'll lose the vast space in which they could fly like the wind, and be shut up in their own small territory. Their wings will be clipped, and they'll flap clumsily from one mountain to another until they're exhausted. Then they'll ask themselves, 'What did we gain by it?' (*Palace* 61–62).

The metaphor of the eagle underpins the argument with an image of ethnicity: Albanians, *shqiptare* or 'sons of eagles', are caged animals in the modern world unless they can break out of their tiny land.[24] This discussion explains the ambiguous position of the Quprilis vis-à-vis their erstwhile countrymen. This family has used the structures of the Empire to move out of and beyond their tiny country. The Albanians resent the Quprilis for having preferred Ottoman assimilation over ethnic identity. While they have refused to yield to the Ottoman expectation of complete assimilation (by spelling their name 'Köprülü'), their adoption at some stage in the past of the Turkish, rather than Albanian root ('*ura*'), is indicative of their status. The question arises whether it is possible to be both Albanian and free in this sense of being able to unfold one's potentialities in the wider world. In their ethnic provincialism the Albanians fail to see what the Quprilis have achieved for Albania, namely the opening up of opportunities and spaces for the people, cramped in their tiny mountainous land.

'C'est un très ancien malentendu entre notre famille et les Albanais. Ils ont du mal à se faire aux dimensions impériales de notre famille, ou plutôt, c'est quelque chose qui ne leur paraît pas essentiel. Ils ne font guère cas de ce qu'ont accompli et continuent d'accomplir les Quprili pour l'ensemble de l'Empire dont l'Albanie n'est qu'une petite partie. Ce qui les intéresse, c'est seulement ce que nous avons fait pour cette petite partie-là, pour l'Albanie'. (*Le Palais* 74)

'It's an ancient misunderstanding between our family and the Albanians. They can't get used to our imperial dimension, or rather they don't think it's of any consequence. They care little for what the Quprilis have done and continue to do for the Empire as a whole, of which Albania is just a small part. All that matters to them is what we've done for that small part, for Albania'. (*Palace* 60*)

For these members of an Ottoman Albanian family the Empire is a means of advancement, self-fulfilment, and widening of options and opportunities. At the same time, their proximity to the centre of power involves them in responsibility for the political acts of the Empire, such as the oppression of individuals and of peoples, including their own. One of the cousins points out that their integration into the Empire brought violence and bloodshed, and Kurt concurs: 'Partager le pouvoir, cela veut dire avant tout partager les crimes!' (*Le Palais* 76, 'Sharing power means sharing crimes', *Palace* 61). Implicit in this discussion has been the question of the balance in the family between Ottoman political and Albanian ethnic identity. This issue becomes explicit when one of the brothers makes a slip of the tongue:

'De toute façon, ce sont les Turcs qui nous ont donné nos véritables dimensions', enchaîna le cousin. 'Et nous les en avons maudits'.
    'Non, pas nous. Eux!' intervint le gouverneur.
    'Oui, pardon: eux, les Albanais de là-bas'.
    Il s'installa un silence tendu [. . .] (*Le Palais* 76)

'Anyhow, it's the Turks who helped us to reach our true stature', said the cousin. 'And we just cursed them for it'.
    'Not <u>us</u> — <u>them</u>!' said the governor.
    'Sorry — yes . . . <u>Them</u>. The Albanians back home in Albania'.
    A tense silence followed [. . .] (*Palace* 61)[25]

The point here is the self-identification of the cousin. He unconsciously identifies himself as an Albanian with the Albanians in Albania. The governor, the most senior of the brothers (the Vizier is not present), is at pains to avoid any false or dangerous identifications. He corrects his brother to distinguish the Quprilis as 'we', the cosmopolitan Ottoman Quprilis in the capital, not 'them', the Albanians 'back home'. Any dynastic identification with the Albanians at this tense point in history must be kept well under control. They are an Ottoman family of ethnic Albanian descent. The distinction of the political from the ethnic is of utmost importance at this point.

For the Albanians in Albania, ethnic identity is not compatible with the role in the Empire to which they are subjected; for the Quprilis, Albanian identity can include an imperial dimension which enables them to exist at the centre of political power. The family shares this sense of ethnic identity and, until this point, have not questioned it. Their Albanian identity is not inimical to the Empire. They are, after all, a family of converts to Ottoman Islam who have benefited greatly from the Empire. Some identify more strongly with it than others. Any overt allegiance to Albania, understood as something more than a point of historical origin and now a group of remote provinces of the Empire, is — or was — unthinkable. Now, however, Kurt has used the family epic to raise the question of ethnic as opposed to imperial identity. Realizing the danger of this line of thinking, his brothers warn him that such thoughts must not be allowed outside the walls of the family home. The family must present themselves publicly as Ottoman Muslims for whom Albanianness represents a secondary identity. The Bosnian epic, around which this discussion revolves, both symbolizes the family's Ottoman power and preserves the memory of its Albanian origins.

We never discover whether Kurt is a bored rich playboy flirting with adventure and manipulated by the Austrians (whose involvement in Balkan politics in Montenegro and Bosnia would lead to the outbreak of the the First World War), or whether his contacts with them signal something more dangerous for his family, namely that he has become a renegade, an ethnic nationalist, hoping to liberate his homeland with the help of the Austrians. He certainly appears to have an agenda :

> 'N'empêche que pour le moment, ils font silence sur nous', objecta Kurt.
> 'Un jour, ils nous comprendront', fit le frère aîné.
> 'Nous aussi, nous devons les écouter'.
> 'Mais s'ils se taisent, comme tu viens de le rappeler?'
> 'Ecoutons leur silence', dit Kurt. [. . .] 'nous figurons dans l'épopée slave'.
> 'Cela ne suffit-il pas? [. . .] Tu as toi-même dit que nous sommes la seule famille en Europe et peut-être même à être célébrée par un peuple dans une chanson de geste. Cela ne te paraît-il pas assez? Tu voudrais peut-être que nous le soyons par deux peuples?'
> 'Tu me demandes si cela ne me suffit pas', fit Kurt, 'et moi, je te réponds: Non!' (*Le Palais* 78–79)

> 'Anyhow', said Kurt, 'for the moment they don't say anything about us'.
> 'One day they'll understand us', said the governor.
> 'We ought to listen to them too'.
> 'But you just said they don't say anything'.
> 'Then we should listen to their silence', said Kurt. [. . .] 'we *are* in the Slav epic'.
> 'Isn't that enough? [. . .] You said yourself that we're the only family in Europe and perhaps in the world that's celebrated in a national epic. Don't you think that's sufficient? Do you want us to be celebrated by *two* nations?'
> 'You ask if that isn't enough for me', said Kurt. 'My answer is no!' (*Palace* 62–63)

The Albanian epic, unlike that of the Bosnians, does *not* celebrate the heroic deeds of the Quprilis. Kurt's advice to his brothers to listen to the silence of the Albanian epic on the subject of their family is indicative of his changing attitudes. He interprets it as a critical silence. For all its Ottoman prestige, the family has lost its links with the spirit of the Albanian homeland. In this discussion Kurt reveals to the others how uneasily their Albanianness sits with their Ottoman identity: on the one hand they are powerful members of an Empire which oppresses other national and ethnic groups, and on the other hand they themselves are members of one of these oppressed groups. The story of the origins of the family, of the three-arched bridge with its sacrificial victim from before the Turkish occupation, when the Albanians were still Christians, symbolizes this problematic double identity. Ironically, it is Mark-Alem, the pallid and characterless employee of the Palace of Dreams, who will respond powerfully to the call of Albanian ethnicity in the music of the *lahuta*.

The Epic Songs of Albania and Bosnia and the Question of Identity

The two epics introduce questions relating to the ethnic identities of Albanians, Bosnians, and Serbs in parts of Albania and the former Yugoslavia, in particular Kosovo. The Albanians are predominantly Muslim, having converted to Islam from Christianity in the past. They speak a non-Slav language and trace their cultural roots back to ancient times. The Bosnians are Muslim Slavs whose language is extremely close to Serbian and whose religious identity was forged during the period of the Ottoman occupation. The Serbs, Orthodox Christian Slavs, key aspects of whose identity were born of the opposition to Ottoman rule in the Balkans and in particular in Kosovo, also play a role in the ethnic configuration of the novel. All three groups composed epic songs using similar themes over the period of the Ottoman occupation.[26]

Up until the point where the Albanian version of the epic is introduced, the discussion revolves around factions and political power in relation to the Ottoman Sultan, rather than around questions of ethnic identity. With the theme of the Albanian versus the Bosnian epic, however, the matter becomes more complex. In order to understand the significance of the Albanian epic, we must delve further into the history of the heroic songs of Albania and Bosnia.

In the early 1970s, while revising *The Great Winter* to include the epic motifs of the ending, Kadare researched the songs of his homeland and wrote his first long analysis and vindication of the ancient Albanian origins of these works of the national consciousness, *Autobiography of the People in Verse*.[27] In this work he drew on the researches of the Austrian anthropologist, Maximilian Lambertz (1882–1963), as well as the works of the earlier poet and nationalist, Italian-Albanian poet, Jeronim de Rada (1814–1903).[28] Shortly after *The Palace of Dreams* appeared, Kadare drew on this material for the foreword to a collection Albanian ballads and short epic poems translated into French under the auspices of the Albanian Academy of the Sciences. In this short piece in particular he refers to the material worked into the fiction of the *Palace of Dreams*. The Albanian epics were born under the 'cold sun' of the Albanian mountains, he writes. Their origins lie in Illyrian antiquity, but they were suppressed in 'the long night of the Turko-Islamic occupation and by the fierce chauvinist passions of neighbouring lands'.[29] He bases his argument on the similarity of theme with earlier Greek legends, in particular those of Orestes, Circe, and Odysseus, and refers to an 'Illyro-Albano-Greek' tradition not shared by South Slav mythology.[30] Kadare compares the Albanian folk poems in importance with the *Nibelungenlied*, the *Chanson de Roland*, and *Le Cid* in a long passage which is used almost verbatim in the novel.[31] This material allows us to explicate the crucial differences between the two epics as represented in the novel. The most important of these is the Orestes theme, which Kadare mentions in his preface to the *Chansonnier épique albanais*. Kurt translates parts of the Albanian epic for the son of the Austrian consul who notes the similarity with the story of Orestes. Lambertz considers Zuk an Orestes figure specific to the songs of northern Albania.[32]

> 'C'est le preux Zuk, aveuglé traîtreusement par sa mère et l'amant de celle-ci, qui erre par les monts enneigés sur sa monture également aveugle'. 'Aveuglé par

sa mère! Mon Dieu!' s'exclama l'Autrichien. 'Mais cela évoque L'Orestie! Das ist [sic] die Orestiaden!' (*Le Palais* 189)

'This is the knight, Zuk, treacherously blinded by his mother and her lover, who wanders over snowy mountains on his blinded steed'. 'Blinded by his mother! My God!' exclaimed the Austrian. 'But it's like the *Oresteia! Das ist* [sic] *die Orestiaden!*' (*Palace* 152–53)

Another motif which helps us to identify this material more closely is the figure of 'Çuperli', or 'Çypri' in the original epics. Lambertz links the figure of 'Çuperli', or 'Çypri', a vizier in the Ottoman government to the historical Köprülü family, the model for Kadare's Quprilis. Çuperli is treated as a figure of contempt in Albanian epic. He is the dupe to whom a rebellious daughter is married off, when she rejects the pashas or viziers chosen by her father, and has eyes only for her Albanian hero.[33] Skendi also refers to the Köprülü family in his discussion of Milman Parry's (at that time unpublished) collection of Serbo-Croation oral poetry, where a minor character by the name of 'Cuprili' (Tchouprilitch or 'Tschuprili' in its Serb transliteration) appears.[34] While the Quprili family is not mentioned in this particular Albanian epic in the novel, the figure of Çuperli is a stock figure in this body of songs.[35] For the Albanian bards the Quprilis are not the stuff of heroic legend, but on the contrary play minor comic roles as Ottoman sycophants and dupes. When the Albanian rhapsodists arrive for the recitation, they do indeed appear to hold the Quprili family in contempt:

Plûtot que le mépris, leurs yeux semblaient exprimer le refus d'accueillir tout ce qui leur était proposé, le renvoyant en bloc. Les valets servirent aux rhapsodes du raki [. . .] mais les Albanais se bornèrent à les effleurer des lèvres. (*Le Palais* 185)

Their bright eyes seemed to express not so much scorn as complete rejection of anything that might be offered them. The footmen had served them raki [. . .] but the Albanians merely touched them with their lips. (*Palace* 150)

The theme of human sacrifice, live interment, or life-in-death, also occurs in the epic. The Albanians sing a version of the 'Ballad of the Three-Arched Bridge', also hitherto known only to the Quprilis in its Bosniak (i.e. Slav) form, although it deals with the origins of their family fortune (*Le Palais* 187, *Palace* 151). The motif of the buried warrior, taunted by his live enemy to come out to battle, occurs in the Mujo and Halil cycle and is evoked in the epic which Kurt struggles to translate for his audience. The material used, then, for the Albanian epic in the novel is based on this body of songs from central and northern Albania, in particular the 'Mujo and Halil' cycle, where the story of Zuk and other motifs such as the figure of Çuperli, and live interment are to be found.

It has not yet been determined whether the songs of this part of the Balkans have their origins in Albanian folk-epic from the pre-Christian and Christian eras, which was then overlaid with Islamic culture after the Ottoman conversions, as Lambertz and Kadare argue, or whether they are originally Christian Slav material which had penetrated the folk culture of the Albanians and had been subjected to Islamic influences, as has been suggested in more recent research. Stavro Skendi demonstrates the complexity of the problem by comparing Bosnian Muslim, Albanian Muslim, and other South Slav versions of material going back to the battles with the Turks in the fourteenth century and earlier. Through analysis of the terms used for the different ethnic, religious and cultural groups within and in the liminal areas of the Ottoman Empire, Skendi describes the Bosnian and Albanian self-identifications as differing in terms of the emphasis on religion versus ethnicity: 'The difference between the struggles of the two peoples is that those of the Bosnians were totally religious, those of the Albanians were primarily ethnical'. The term '*shkja*' which figures in the Mujo-Halil cycle 'means both Slav and Christian Slav, but primarily the former'. Regardless of the origins of this material, that is, Skendi demonstrates that religion has receded as the single primary identifier in the northern Albanian songs over the period since the conversion of these tribes to Islam, in favour of a cultural identification in terms of both religion and ethnicity. In the Bosnian works religion remains paramount: '[the Albanian songs] do not have the strong Moslem colour of the Bosnian songs. The Bosnians were fanatical. In their songs they do not know of a higher aim than to fight for the *din* (Moslem faith) and the Sultan'.[36] Skendi relates this to the different interests underlying Bosnian and Albanian Islam. In Albania, he writes,

> Islam had been embraced primarily as a means to tax relief and the protection of the Turkish state, whereas in Bosnia it was a much more deeply religious conversion. As a result of this, the Turkish-Moslem element is attenuated in the northern Albanian songs: 'True, the *kaur-s* (the infidel — Christians) in the Albanian songs are the enemies of the heroes of Jutbina. [. . .] But we do not meet them very often, for the *Shkje* [the neighbouring Slavs-PM] take their place'.[37]

The Balkan epics do not of course use modern categories of nationality, and they pre-date modern national boundaries of Bosnia, Albania, Montenegro, Serbia, and Slav Macedonia. They take place in parts of modern Albania, Kosovo, Krajina and Bosnia, and feature the threshold territories between Christian and Muslim occupation. Social units are the clan, the tribe and the people, and after the Ottoman invasions and conversions of numbers of Balkan peoples to Islam, religious differences override most others, so that the major categories are not, for example, Albanian (*Shqip*) or Serb, but Turk (meaning Ottoman Muslim, not Turk) and *Kaurr, gjaur* (i.e. *giaour*, Christian).[38] For the Christian Slav, according to Lambertz, the opposition Slav/Albanian corresponded simply to that of Christian/Turk. The use of the Turkish and Albanian languages identified the Muslim, whether ethnic Albanian or Ottoman Turk.[39] However, the identification of religion with nationality of the Balkan Muslims by the Christian Slavs was a simplification of more complex ethnic and cultural issues. Among the Muslims themselves differences existed between 'Albanian' and 'Slav' — in this case 'Bosnian' — and these differences were becoming exacerbated in the era of decline of the Ottoman Empire and growth of Balkan nationalisms.

These epics are also linked to the Battle of Kosovo, the main foundation myth for the national and ethnic identities of the Albanians, Bosnians, and Serbs: Mark-Alem 'avait souvent entendu parler chez lui de cette tragique bataille' (*Le Palais* 160, 'had often heard his family speak of the tragic battle', *Palace* 130) of 1389 'contre tous les Balkans', (*Le Palais* 160, 'against all the Balkans', *Palace* 129). The Battle of Kosovo, in which Prince Lazar died, was commemorated by the Serbs in particular as the end of the medieval Serbian kingdom, after which the Ottoman period of subjection began.[40] However, this battle was a Balkan event in which a coalition of Serbs, Bosnians, Albanians, and others opposed the invading Ottomans. The Bosnian, Albanian, and other Slav versions of these events were to be coloured over time by differing religious, cultural, and ethnic interests and by the extraordinary complications of Balkan history.[41]

We are now in a position to answer Mark-Alem's question why the epic is sung in Bosnia and not in Albania, and why in Serbian, not Albanian. Sung in the Serb language, and glorifying the deeds of the Albanian Muslim Quprili family, the Quprili epic is identified with those Albanians and Slavs (Bosnians) who converted to Islam in the wake of the Ottoman conquest of the western Balkans after the Battles of Savra (near Berat in modern Albania, 1385) and Kosovo Polje (1389), and some of whom founded powerful dynasties within the Ottoman Empire. Hence the Bosnian Slav epic identifies the family primarily as Ottoman and Muslim, and only secondarily as Albanian in a cultural context where this latter ethnic identification has little importance, since the significant identifications are between Turk (i.e. Muslim, including converts regardless of racial or ethnic identity) and Christian. In this version of the epic, the religion and culture of western Balkan converts to Islam is the point of convergence. For the Bosnian Serbs, Muslims like the Albanians, the epic is a celebration of the origins of their Ottoman identity. The socio-religious culture of Ottoman civilisation overrides ethnicity as the primary identifying factor.

The Albanian epic, with its omission of the Quprilis, other than as minor figures of ridicule, and its celebration of both religion and ethnicity, with the latter moving strongly upward in the hierarchy of core values, has developed differently from the Bosnian version in line with the differences between Albanian and Bosnian Islam noted by Skendi above. Where the Bosnians were primarily Muslims, Albanian Islam was much less deeply rooted, and ethnic identifications had begun to displace religious identifications, particularly in the northern Albanian cycles of Mujo and Halil on which Kadare bases his fiction. The Albanian epic, that is, in which the Quprilis do not appear, has a primarily ethnic (Albanian Muslim) focus, whereas the Bosnian Slav version, in which the family does figure, is primarily Ottoman Muslim in focus. The Bosnian song is about Muslims versus Christians, whereas the Albanian version is primarily about Albanians versus Turks and Slavs. The one is determined by religious difference where the other expresses ethnic identity in the process of consolidation.

The theme of the two epics thus raises complex ethnic and political questions. For Kadare, following Lambertz, the song of the Albanian rhapsodists belongs to a prior, authentic tradition, against which the Bosnian Slav version is an adoption and retelling by a different people who arrived later on the Balkan peninsula.[42] Likewise Kurt, the Albanian nationalist, identifies the Albanian version of the epic as the authentic one. It is Islamic and Albanian, but hearkens back to a pre-

Islamic, pre-Christian tradition. The Bosnian version, on the other hand, has been overlaid by Slav language and customs as well as Ottoman Islamic elements. There is thus a three-way conflict between Kurt, the Quprili family, and the Sultan: Kurt represents an Albanian ethnic nationalism which is Islamic, but is also strongly aware of its pre-Islamic roots; his brothers and the Vizier represent the family's political compromise with the Ottoman Empire as Ottoman Muslims ('Balkan' rather than 'Albanian' converts to Ottoman culture and religion); and the Sultan represents the Empire, a long-standing force of occupation of the Balkans with a foreign religion and culture, an imperial capital far from the Albanian periphery, and an interest in maintaining religious and cultural order throughout the Balkans — not merely in Albania. The Quprilis with their Bosnian Slav epic appear to have betrayed Albania on several fronts: they have risen to prominence as heroes of the Ottoman occupation of the Balkans, fighting where necessary against Albanian secessionists as well as against Serbs and others, and they have adopted an epic in the Serb, as opposed to the Albanian, language at this time of national awakening. The latter, Albanian, version is dangerous for the family of Ottoman converts.

Folk Epic and the Albanian National Awakening

Having established the significance of the epics, we can take our argument a step further by linking this material to the fictional and historical context, namely the era of resurgence of the Balkan nations at the end of the nineteenth century. Toward the end we hear that 'La guerre contre la Russie venait de s'achever. La Grèce s'était détachée de l'Empire, le reste des Balkans était en effervescence' (*Le Palais* 233, 'the war against Russia was just over. Greece had left the Empire, and the rest of the Balkans was in turmoil', *Palace* 188). The war against the Russians can only be the Russo-Turkish war of mid 1877, formally ending with the Treaty of San Stefano, signed in January 1878. As a result of the agreements of the Congress of Berlin in 1878, the Ottoman Empire retained power over Albania, Macedonia and the eastern part of Thrace including the capital, Istanbul. Romania, Serbia, and Montenegro had been declared independent, and it was far from inconceivable that the Ottomans would lose control over the remaining Balkan possessions. Mark-Alem's first file of dreams for sorting is dated 19 October. On the day in which he reviews the fateful dream of the *lahuta* and the bridge, he reads another dream dated 18 December — presumably of the year 1877. The fictive period of the novel thus begins in the winter of 1877/78 and ends in the spring of 1878. Kadare has located the novel at the end of the '*Tanzimat*' or 'reorganization' period of the Ottoman Empire (1839–70) dominated by the Westernizing and modernizing Turkish Ottoman grand vizier Ali Pasha (Mehmed Emin). However, the description of the 'U.O.S.' (United Ottoman States) in the novel implies a much more profound level of political reorganization than actually occurred during this period. By this time a powerful Albanian national movement had taken shape partly in response to the Ottoman failure to protect the interests of this largely Muslim subject nation after the Treaty of San Stefano, in which Albanian-inhabited territory was assigned to Serbia, Montenegro, and the Bulgarian provinces.[43] The uniqueness of the Albanian situation lay in the fact that a large part of the Albanian elite (as represented by the Quprili family in the novel) was integrated into Ottoman state and military structures. This was not the case among the Serbs or Bulgarians, and it hampered the attempts of Albanian nationalists to forge a state identity around which Albanian cultural identity could crystallize.

In summer 1878 a conference of Albanian nationalists was held and permanent headquarters established in Prizren. The Ottoman government was willing to support this organization as long as the representatives identified as Ottomans (i.e. Muslims) rather than Albanians (i.e. ethnic nationalists regardless of religion). The situation oscillated between hard-line nationalists seeking Albanian unification and autonomy and the use of Albanian language in education and government, and those willing to compromise with semi-autonomy from central Ottoman government. In early 1881 the Ottoman armies were brought in to defeat the nationalist resistance and restore centralized authority. Even after this national insurrection, however, the Ottomans continued to regard the Albanians as closely linked to them on the basis of religion and tradition, in comparison to the Serbs, Croats, and other Balkan Christian national and ethnic groups. Nevertheless, the seeds of Albanian political nationalism had been sown.[44]

The Albanian uprising followed the pattern of Herderian nationalism, basing itself on language and folk-culture and led by intellectuals who collected, selected, and moulded this material in line with national aspirations. During this period Albanian epic and heroic songs were used to propagate the idea that what bound the Albanians together was 'common blood, language, customs, and common aspirations', which led Albanians to love their country and countrymen, even if they belonged to other religions.[45] This latter point is important, since it indicates a shift towards a primary ethnic identification in terms of Albanianness understood as a link with Albania through 'blood', language, and culture, and away from primary allegiances in terms of religion and/or Ottoman identity. The glorification of Scanderbeg as the national hero of the Albanians epitomizes this shift from religion to ethnicity. The Moslem Albanians ignored the fact that Scanderbeg was a Christian fighting against the Ottomans. What mattered was that he was an ethnic Albanian who had fought for the liberation of the country. 'He was made a symbol of unification and became a national hero'.[46]

For the Albanians experiencing a national awakening on the western perimeter of Kadare's crumbling Empire, this powerful family with its Bosnian epic is scarcely a subject for national glorification. Ethnic and quasi-national identity is, or has become, the central issue. For them the Quprilis are turncoats whose feats are likely to be seen as betrayal of the national cause, rather than as the embodiment of Albanian heroic values. We are dealing here with a novel set at the time of growth of Albanian nationalism in the wake of the other Balkan nationalist movements, when the new nations were seeking ancient pedigrees in language, myth, and folk poetry. The imagery of burial alive which appears at important points in the novel, in the foundation myth of the Quprili family and again in the Albanian ballad described at the climax of the political intrigue, suggests that the issue here is the revival of Albanian identity in the 1870s after a long period of suppression and repression by a powerful occupying force.

The friction between the Sultan and the Quprili family over the Bosnian epic revolves around questions of factional power and politics in the capital. Kurt's brothers warn that any sign of interest in the Albanian epic could be interpreted by the Sultan as a political manoeuvre in the context of the unrest in Albania and with the Austrians sitting in the western wings of the Empire. They are concerned that the family's Albanian origins might be used against it in this period of imperial instability. The Albanian epic in fact, however, introduces a deeper level of threat and danger to the family. It signals a turn within the family towards ethnic rather than political identifications, with their ethnic homeland rather than with their political masters. And it introduces a new factor into the power-politics of the Empire, one of which the brothers are only dimly aware, namely the issue of ethnic nationalism, ultimately of separatism. The Bosnian epic, representing the converted peoples of the Balkans who had identified primarily with their Ottoman masters, is displaced in favour of the Albanian epic, in which 'blood' and the ethnic homeland are given primacy over dynastic and Ottoman identity.

Moreover, the Austrians have an interest in Kurt's new-found ethnicity. Kurt's alliance with the Austrian ambassador is seen by the Sultan to indicate a destabilizing and subversive activity on the western periphery of the Empire, against which he, the Sultan, moves eastwards towards rapprochement with Russia in order to secure his regions against Habsburg intervention. This reflects the alliances and strategic positionings that were occurring in the east and west of the Ottoman Empire in the last decades of the nineteenth century. In this period of political tension the Quprili family's interest in the Albanian version of the epic signals a shift in balance. This non-Slav version is politically loaded towards the Habsburgs on the western border of the Empire, who support the non-Slav peoples of the U.O.S., whereas the Russians support the Slav peoples and favour the Bosnian (i.e. Slav) version of the epic:

> Il ne s'agit pas ici seulement de poésies ou de chants [. . .] C'est une affair on ne peut plus complexe Tout cela a trait à des implantations et à des transferts de populations dans les Balkans, aux rapports entre les populations slaves et non slaves, tels que les Albanais; bref, cela concerne directement la carte des Balkans. [. . .] L'Autriche soutient les peuples non slaves; quant au petit père le Tsar, comme les Slaves appellent l'empereur russe, il intervient au contraire en permanence auprès de notre Sultan sur les conditions faites aux populations de sa race. [. . .] Et cette geste a trait précisément aux rapports entre les peuples des Balkans. (*Le Palais* 207)

> This is not just a matter of poetry and song, [. . .] In fact it's an exceedingly complex business, to do with settlements and transfers of population in the Balkans, and the relations between Slav peoples and non-Slav peoples, like the Albanians. In short, it directly concerns the whole map of the Balkans. [. . .] Austria supports the non-Slav peoples, whereas the Slavs' 'little father', the Tsar, is always on at our Sultan about the way the people of his race are treated. [. . .] This epic deals precisely with the relations between the peoples of the Balkans. (*Palace* 167)

It is indicative of the political state of the Empire that the Sultan is moved to seek Russian support against the threat of the Habsburgs at a time when Panslavism was becoming a powerful force.[47] For the Ottomans religion remained paramount above ethnicity and language. Among the Orthodox peoples of the Balkans, religion remained a strong linking factor, especially in opposition to the Ottomans. For the Albanians who were predominantly Muslim by the end of the eighteenth century, as for the other Balkan ethnic groups, ethnicity, 'blood', and native language were moving to the fore in determining group identity by the late nineteenth century. However, for the Albanian (and Bosnian) Muslims, religion remained a strong link to the Ottomans which was absent in the Christian ethnic and national movements. The Quprilis are caught among these changing political, national, and ethnic signifiers in the late Ottoman Empire. In the context of dismemberment of the Empire and creation of ethnic nation states, the Quprili family would be acceptable in neither camp: neither that of the Turkish majority, nor that of the newly liberated Albanians.

The Soul of the Nation

Surprisingly perhaps, given his passivity and lack of character, Mark-Alem is strongly aware of his Albanian heritage. On the morning of his first day of work he goes into the library and peruses the family history stretching back to the building of the three-arched bridge in central Albania. We are told that he was 'très attaché à ses origines albanaises, [et] enregistrait mechaniquement tout ce qui pouvait se dire sur ce pays' (*Le Palais* 50, 'Mark-Alem set great store by his Albanian origins and automatically registered anything that concerned Albania', *Palace* 41). Early in the novel an opposition is established between the life of the bureaucrat imprisoned in gloomy rooms along endless dimly lit corridors behind the high walls of the *Tabir Sarrail* and the world of snow, rain, and springtime blossoms which is associated with the Albania on whose soil Mark-Alem has never set foot, but whose name promises escape, freedom, and fulfilment.

> Soudain, il redressa la tête. Il avait l'impression qu'on le hélait de très loin au moyen de quelque signal étrange, très faible, presque plaintif, semblable à un appel au secours ou à un sanglot. Qu'est-ce? Se demanda-t-il. Cette question eut tôt fait d'envahir tout son être. Sans qu'il s'expliquât pourqoui, ses yeux se portèrent alors vers les grandes fenêtres. C'était la première fois qu'il les contemplait. Derrière leurs carreaux, élément familier mais désormais lointain, la pluie tombait, mêlé de fins flocons de neige. Les flocons tourbillonnaient, hagards, dans cette matinée elle aussi lointaine, comme appartenant à une autre vie d'où lui avait peut-être envoyé cet ultime signal. (*Le Palais* 43)

> Suddenly he looked up. He felt as if someone were hailing him from a long way away, sending out some strange, faint, doleful signal like a call for help or a sob. What is it? he wondered. The question soon absorbed him absolutely. Without knowing why, he looked at the high windows. It was the first time he'd done so. Beyond the window panes the rain, so familiar but now so distant, mingled as it fell with delicate flakes of snow. The flakes eddied wildly in the morning light, now distant too — so far away it seemed to belong to another life, another world from which perhaps that ultimate signal had been sent out to him. (*Palace* 35–36)

This longing for freedom is evoked throughout the novel and is set in contrast to the environment of the *Tabir Sarrail*. Later it is explicitly related to Mark-Alem's sense of ethnic identity, to the '*lahuta* in his breast'. Hence when Kurt introduces the topic of the Albanian epic and evokes the romanticism of lost homeland, he finds an avid, if naive, audience in his nephew. Mark-Alem is eager to hear the hitherto unknown Albanian version of the epic, in the hope that it will arouse the sense of solemnity and profundity which he misses in the familiar Serb version. He is initially disappointed that the instrument, the *lahuta*, is a simple single-stringed instrument no different from the Serb *gusla*, not the weighty, majestic, and imposing instrument he had imagined as necessary to accompany the solemn subject matter. The music begins as a long lament redolent of death and eternity. But then a transformation occurs.

> Mark-Alem ne pouvait détacher les yeux de la fine corde solitaire tendue au-dessus de la caisse de résonance. C'était cette corde qui sécrétait la complainte, et la caisse, en dessous, la répercutait en l'amplifiant dans des proportions effrayantes. Soudain, il eut la révélation que cette cage creuse était la poitrine contenant l'âme de la nation à laquelle il appartenait. C'est de là que montait, vibrante, la complainte séculaire. Il en avait déjà entendu des fragments, mais ce n'était qu'aujourd'hui qu'il lui était donné de l'entendre dans son intégralité. Ce creux de la *lahuta*, il le sentait à présent dans sa propre poitrine. [. . .] Il se sentit brusquement une irrépressible envie de jeter aux orties son demi-prénom asiatique d'Alem et d'apparaître sous un nouveau, l'un de ceux que portaient les gens de sa terre natale: Gjon, Gjergj ou Gjorg. Mark-Gjon Ura, Mark-Gjergj Ura, Mark-Gjorg Ura. . ., se répétait-il comme s'il s'évertuait à s'habituer à son demi-prénom de substitution chaque fois qu'il entendait prononcer le mot *Ura*, le seul qu'il comprît parmi les paroles du rhapsode. (*Le Palais* 187)

> Mark-Alem couldn't take his eyes off the slender, solitary string stretched across the sounding box. It was the string that secreted the lament; the box amplified it to terrifying proportions. Suddenly it was revealed to Mark-Alem that this hollow cage was the breast containing the soul of the nation to which he belonged. It was from there that arose the vibrant age-old lament. He'd already heard fragments of it; only today would he be permitted to hear the whole. He now felt the hollow of the *lahuta* inside his own breast. [. . .] Mark-Alem suddenly felt an almost irresistible desire to discard 'Alem', the Asian half of his first name, and appear with a new one, one used by the people of his native land: Gjon, Gjergj or Gjorg. Mark-Gjon, Mark-Gergj Ura, Mark-Gjorg Ura, he repeated as if trying to get used to his new half-name, every time he heard the word '*Ura*', the only one of the rhapsodist's words he could understand. (*Palace* 151–52)[48]

At this point Mark-Alem undergoes an epiphanic experience, finding in the music of the *lahuta* the powerful expression of a hitherto unarticulated desire for freedom felt as ethnic belonging. Just as at the beginning the name in the ancient chronicle arouses his sense of kinship, he now feels the pull of his origins in the story and its music. This is highly ironic, of course, since the *gusla* and the *lahuta* are basically the same instrument with different names — the latter sharing its etymological root with the word *lute*, and the former having a Slavic derivation. The Slav epic which he has known since childhood as played on the *gusla* has not had this effect on him.

At the height of the recital of the Albanian rhapsodists, the Sultan strikes. Troops arrive to disperse the guests. Kurt is arrested, later to be executed, the Albanian rhapsodists are assassinated, the Vizier is publicly humiliated, and a punitive expedition is sent to Albania. The older brothers' dinner-table fears are realized. At the same time as his past, undefined sense of ethnic Albanian identity and solidarity is given a focus, Mark-Alem sees his family ruined and himself put in danger. His private fantasy of freedom, ethnicity, and self-determination is enacted before him as a scenario of humiliation, political intrigue, and murder. Moreover, he is also involved by association. The morning after the catastrophe, he returns to work to find that rumours are flying about the state of emergency, about the power-contest between the Quprilis and the Sultan, and about possible ramifications for the Palace and its staff. He waits for some dreadful fate to befall him, and discovers that the dream which he had twice held in his hands, and had been tempted to discard, was indeed the Master-Dream which alerted the Sultan to Kurt's activities. With its three-arched bridge, the *lahuta* playing in isolation, the raging bull, and the desolate plot of land it pointed to the Quprilis, indicating their Albanian ethnic identity, suggesting their potential involvement in subversive political activity in far-off homelands, and identifying them as a dangerous force close to the seat of power.[49] The presence of the Albanian rhapsodists was seen to have validated this interpretation of the dream, and the Sultan acted, as Mark-Alem witnessed the previous night, to forestall any dangerous political developments. Mark-Alem hears that a group of officials is being sent to the Balkans to eliminate the Albanian epic, which is regarded as the cause of the trouble.

At the *Tabir Sarrail* in the days following the blow against the Quprilis, gossip and anxiety are rife, but little happens. It is rumoured that the Sultan has sent back the Master-Dream, rejecting it, or rejecting the interpretation of it. Mark-Alem fears that he will be punished, but then, some days later, further political ructions occur as soldiers are seen swarming through the courtyards of the Palace. Watching from a window above, Mark-Alem thinks of the family carriages with the letter 'Q' on their doors rushing back and forward across the city, and it is whispered throughout the halls of the Palace that the Quprilis have retaliated. Just how this has occurred is not clear.

> Un affrontement, un échange de coups aussi terribles que sourds s'est produit dans les profondeurs, les soubassements de l'Etat. Nous n'en avons ressenti que les ébranlements en surface, comme pour un tremblement de terre à l'hypocentre très, très profond. C'est donc dans le courant de la nuit que s'est produit ce heurt redoutable entre les deux groupes rivaux, ou, si tu préfères, entre les forces qui se contrebalancent au sein de l'Etat. [. . .] nous-mêmes qui sommes içi, où ce mystère prend sa source, n'en savons pas davantage. (*Le Palais* 215–16)

> Some confrontation, some secret and terrible exchange of blows has taken place in the darkest depths of the State. We've felt only the surface repercussions, as you do in an earthquake with a very deep hypocentre. So, as I was saying, during the night a terrible clash took place between the two rival groups, the two forces that counterbalance one another within the State. [. . .] even we, who're at the very source of the mystery, are still in the dark. (*Palace*, 174)

It is implied that the Quprilis have powerful mining interests in distant provinces and that they have used these to strike back at the Sultan. But the nature of the conflict is never clarified.

The Employee of the Palace of Dreams

The original Albanian title of the novel, *Nëpunësi i pallatit të ëndrrave* or 'The Official' or 'Employee of the Palace of Dreams', places emphasis on the figure of Mark-Alem rather than on the Palace. Mark-Alem's influential uncles brought about his appointment in the first place, but their role after that is not clear, and it is implied that Mark-Alem's presence in the Palace is desired by the powers that be for some sinister purpose ('Tu nous conviens', *Le Palais* 53, 85; 'You suit us', *Palace* 43, 68). His rapid rise through the hierarchy is never explained.

Being related to the Quprilis through his mother, Mark-Alem does not share their name. He has been a naive, passive, and timid participant both in his family's political affairs and at work in the Palace of Dreams. Soon after the Vizier is toppled, Mark-Alem is unexpectedly promoted. And with his promotion a certain change comes about: he becomes important, taciturn, and unapproachable, identifying 'de plus en plus avec cette catégorie d'individus que, depuis toujours, il portait le moins dans son cœur: les hauts fonctionnaires' (*Le Palais* 220, 'more and more with the sort of people he'd always liked least: the senior civil servants', *Palace* 178).

In the meantime Kurt is summarily executed. Mark-Alem still expects the fall-out from the coup against his family to affect him, but again he is promoted, this time to the position of First Assistant Director of the Palace of Dreams. In his new position he returns to the Archives and reads through the Master-Dreams of the past months, from those dreamt on the eve of the Battle of Kosovo to the fateful Master-Dream that had led his uncle to the grave and raised him, Mark-Alem, to be a director of the *Tabir*. The city greengrocer who had the dream has been interrogated and, like his predecessor, whom Mark-Alem had seen carried out in a coffin earlier that year, disappears shortly afterward. With that, the coup seems over. Mark-Alem 'n'était pas parvenu à élucider l'énigme de cette nuit-là, le coup porté aux Quprili, suivi de leur riposte', (*Le Palais* 228, 'never succeeded in clearing up the mystery of that night, with the attack on the Quprilis followed by their counter-attack', *Palace* 184). Nor is his position ever clarified for the reader. It is unclear whether his promotion to the position of Acting Director General of the *Tabir Sarrail* is the result of his family's powerful counter-attack against the Sultan, or whether more insidious forces are at work. For while the family was instrumental in placing Mark-Alem in the Palace of Dreams to begin with, the Vizier makes it clear that the upper echelons of the Palace are powerfully against the Quprilis. But on the other hand, important changes have taken place in the leadership of the Palace, with Mark-Alem himself set to take over full control from his ailing Director General in the wake of the coup and the counter-attack. Mark-Alem now belongs among the most powerful of officials, responsible for the sleep and dreams of the whole Empire.

Mark-Alem is not a rebel like Kurt. Characterless and insipid, he is slow on the uptake but surprisingly accessible to the habitus of power once he finds himself in charge. After some months in his job he begins to prefer the environment of the Palace to the dreary and mundane world outside. By the end of the novel he has accustomed himself to the gestures of the powerful without having shown any comparable increase in understanding the way power has worked to further his interests. He is truly an employee of the Palace of Dreams, an apparatchik who has acceded to power. Like figures from Kadare's own environment, such as his friend and nemesis Dritëro Agolli, Mark-Alem will be the perfect tool of those who wield power because he is the instrument of his own humiliation.[50] For if Mark-Alem represents the resurrection of the Quprili family fortunes in the Ottoman state, he does so under a very different mantle to his forebears. The political power represented in the figure of the Vizier has been dashed and will take time to reassert itself. The ethnic nationalism represented by Kurt has been dealt a body blow. Mark-Alem is deeply traumatized by the events surrounding Kurt's execution and his own involvement in the affair. He sees the result of political positioning, he recognizes his own role in the power-struggles, and most importantly he learns how dangerous his ethnic longings can be. By the end of the novel Mark-Alem will have internalized the structure of his own humiliation in repressing his desire for self-identity and projecting the frustration of his desires into an image of death and transfiguration.

For centuries power has changed hands as a result of intrigues, machinations, coups, and palace revolts among factions of the ruling class around the court of the Sultan, but no structural change has taken place. In this closed bureaucratic state-structure power is exercised from above, and the individual, such as Mark-Alem, born into a ruling caste must internalize the rules of appropriation of power — including its gestures and habitus. In order to do so, he must become 'characterless', a 'man without qualities', since he must be ready to follow the dictates of power regardless of personality and personal allegiances. In the works of Kafka, in particular *The Trial* and *The Castle*, we see the middle-man, the individual who is sandwiched between the holders of power and those without power; in Orwell's *1984*, likewise, we see in Winston Smith the middle-man as intellectual and member of the lower state apparatus, whose attempt to maintain a personality is at odds with his position in the power-structure of the state. Mark-Alem is born into the ruling caste of the Quprilis. He is a born 'man without qualities' who discovers in himself a 'quality' — his sense of Albanian ethnic identity. As a consequence he is faced with the existential choice in this closed society, either to become a rebel like Kurt, or to accede to the structures of power which infiltrate his innermost being, and to submit the sense of identity expressed in his dream of ethnicity to the demands of the state. Even given his privileged position he has little choice, and Kadare demonstrates in him the deformation of human character which takes place as a result of the suppression of individual dreams and longings in the service of total social control.

Repression and the Perpetuation of Ethnic Identity

In the meantime Spring has come around. Mark-Alem, now twenty-eight, arrives home one evening to find his uncles discussing his betrothal.[51] Life has resumed its course. Returning to the family chronicle with which the novel began, Mark-Alem thinks back to the image of the falling snow in his ethnic homeland, which has been the touchstone for his desire for freedom and personal integrity:

> De son côté, l'Albanie [. . .] pareille à une foide et lointaine constellation, elle se voilait, de plus en plus distante de lui, et il se demanda s'il avait seulement conscience de ce qu'elle renfermait [. . .] Il resta ainsi un moment, dubitatif, tandis que sa plume s'alourdissait dans sa main, jusqu'à ce que, s'étant abaissée, elle se posât sur le papier et, au lieu du mot Albanie, inscrivît: *Là-bas.* Il contempla cette locution qui s'était substituée au nom de sa patrie et en ressentit subitement le poids que sa conscience, sur l'instant, qualifia de *tristesse quprilienne*, expression qui ne se rencontrait dans aucune langue au monde mais qui eût mérité d'être introduite en toutes. (*Le Palais* 233)

> As for Albania [. . .] it grew more and more distant and dim, like some far cold constellation, and he wondered if he really knew anything about what went on there. He sat there uncertainly, his pen growing heavy in his hand, until finally it rested on the paper and instead of writing 'Albania' wrote: *There.* He gazed at the expression that had substituted itself for the name of his homeland, and suddenly felt oppressed by what he immediately thought of as 'Quprilian sadness'. It was a term unknown to any other language in the world, though it ought to be incorporated in them all. (*Palace* 188–89)

Mark-Alem has learned his lesson: Albania, the romantic homeland, has become the undefined 'there'. Suppression of identity leads to 'Quprilian sadness', the sense of loss felt by this dynasty which has traded ethnic identity for political power. 'Quprilian sadness' is represented in this novel as having recurred throughout the history of the family's collaboration with the Ottoman Empire. It is linked with the theme of betrayal of Albania symbolized in the blood on the bridge, the immurement of the sacrificial victim, and in the family's name-change first to the Albanian *Ura* and then to the Ottoman-Albanian *Quprili*.

> *Là-bas, maintenant, il doit avoir neigé. . .* Il n'ajouta rien d'autre [. . .] il songea à ce lointain bisaïeul prénommé Gjon qui, plusieurs siècles auparavant, par un jour d'hiver, travaillait à la construction d'un pont et, avec ce pont même, avait édifié son nom. Dans ce patronyme, comme un message secret, était prédit le destin que connaîtraient les Quprili génération après génération. Pour que le pont tienne bon, à ses pieds avait été sacrifié un homme. Tant de temps avait beau s'être écoulé depuis lors, les traces du sang versé persistaient encore jusqu'à eux. Pour que tiennent bon les Quprili . . . (*Le Palais* 233–34)

> *It must have been snowing there. . .* Then he stopped writing, [. . .] he thought of the distant ancestor called Gjon who on a winter's day several centuries before had built a bridge and at the same time edified his name. The patronymic bore within it, like a secret message, the destiny of the Quprilis for generation after generation. And so that the bridge might endure, a man was sacrificed in its building, walled up in its foundations. And although so much time had gone by since, the traces of his blood had come down to the present generation. So that the Quprilis might endure . . . (*Palace* 188–89)

The destiny of the Quprilis is symbolized in the bridge. They are identified in terms of their split identity: as Albanian, originally Christian, on the eastern fringe of Europe, the creators of the three-arched bridge symbolizing the land of Albania itself on the one hand, and as Ottoman, converted Muslims, at the centre of the Empire, having betrayed their ethnic origins in this environment where ethnicity is either dangerous ('Albania') or repressed ('there').[52] The immured man symbolizes the repression of ethnic identity in this family who created a bridge to pass through central Albania and thereby opened up their land to the Empire — and the Empire to themselves. (The bull of the Master-Dream is, of course, the opposite of immurement. It is the earthy, animal roar of primal identification.)

After all that has happened, Mark-Alem reflects nostalgically on his desire to throw off the 'Islamic half-shield' of Ottoman identity superimposed over the original language, religion, and culture of the Albanians, and resume his ethnic identity, understood as his original, 'native' identity after all these centuries. But in the end, of course, he does not. We can only smile at the incongruity as this pampered only son remembers 'ces noms d'autrefois qui attiraient le danger et étaient marqués par la fatalité' (Le Palais 234, 'those ancient names which attracted danger and were marked by fate', Palace 189). Mark-Alem still toys with the idea of reclaiming his life and becoming a hero, but deep down he has known all along that he could never become another Kurt.[53] It is hard to imagine him following his heart and turning his back on the Quprili traditions of power and prestige. The romantic nostalgia of his dreams is in direct proportion to the unlikelihood of his ever realizing them.

The novel ends with a powerful evocation of the coming of spring:

> Quelque chose, là, derrière la vitre, l'appelait avec insistance. [. . .] Les amandiers sont en fleur, se dit-il avec émotion. [. . .] Là, derrière, à deux pas, il le savait, il y avait le renouveau de la vie, les nuages à présent tiédis, les cigognes et l'amour, tout ce qu'il avait feint d'ignorer de crainte d'être arraché à l'emprise du Palais des Rêves. (Le Palais 235)

> Something beyond the window was calling him insistently. [. . .] The almond trees are in bloom, he thought. [. . .] There, a few paces away, was life reviving, warmer clouds, storks, love — all the things he'd been pretending to ignore for fear of being wrested from the grasp of the Palace of Dreams. (Palace 190)

Mark-Alem retains the Islamic 'shield' of his double-barrelled name and suppresses the siren-call of his ethnic homeland, 'the *lahuta* in his breast', to become another colourless, faceless official of the Empire. He has remained in the service of the Sultan: fear, power, and prestige have overridden ethnic identity and the desire for freedom which it expresses.

> Malgré toutes ces pensées qui lui venaient à l'esprit, il n'éloigna pas son visage de la vitre. Je commanderais bien dès maintenant un rameau d'amandier en fleur au graveur pour ma tombe, songea-t-il. De la paume de la main, il balaya la buée sur la vitre, mais la vision qui s'offrait à lui ne devint pas plus nette pour autant, les images se réfractaient, s'irisaient. Alors il se rendit compte que ses yeux étaient voilés de larmes. (Le Palais 235–36)

> But despite these thoughts he didn't take his face away from the window. I'll order the sculptor right away to carve a branch of flowering almond on my tombstone, he thought. He wiped the mist off the window with his hand, but what he saw outside was still no clearer: everything was distorted and iridescent. Then he realized his eyes were full of tears. (Palace 190)

His tears on the last page manifest the famous 'Quprilian sadness', the melancholy arising from repression of desire, the killing of this life-force explicitly associated in the novel with ethnic identity. In his vision of a tombstone of flowering almond we can see the vicarious romanticism of a successful young man who has never lived, and is now about to be consigned to a life of constriction and routine. Mark-Alem's nostalgia for a life of heroic action is safely circumscribed by the window of his Director's carriage. His life-choice has been made for him in the power-structures of the Sultan, his family and the Palace of Dreams. Kadare's hero has a position of power at the centre of the Empire yet he remains a victim of structures beyond his control. This is perhaps the most devastating aspect of Kadare's satire: his hero is part of the innermost circle of the Empire. He holds a post of supreme importance, but like Kafka's heroes, the most damning images of rootless individuality and uncomprehending existence in modernity, he is completely alienated. Moreover, this powerful bureaucrat is the instrument of his own repression. In his Director's carriage, Mark-Alem imagines one last time what he most desires: death, martyrdom, and spiritual life in his ethnic Albanian homeland. Spring can only be captured for ever in cold bronze and the blooming almond trees promise more in the relief of death than they do in the new life around him. The final image of springtime is undercut by these associations with death. Mark-Alem's life as an official of the Palace of Dreams has taken place in an environment of winter and spiritual death and he realizes that the wind of winter can return at any time:

> Il avait le sentiment que s'il se tapissait là, tout au fond, c'était justement pour se protéger, et qu'au moment où, cédant à l'attrait de la vie, il abandonnerait ce refuge, au moment donc de la trahison, l'enchantement prendrait fin et qu'alors précisément, par une fin d'après-midi comme celle-ci, le vent ayant tourné pour les Quprili, on viendrait l'emmener, comme on avait fait pour Kurt, peut-être avec plus de ménagements, pour le conduire là d'où l'on ne revient plus. (*Le Palais* 235)

> He felt that if he was crouching there it was to protect himself, and that if ever, some late afternoon like this, he gave in to the call of life and left his refuge, the spell would be broken: the wind would turn against the Quprilis and the men would come for him as they'd come for Kurt, and take him, perhaps a little less unceremoniously, to the place from which there is no returning. (*Palace* 190)

Meanwhile, ironically, all Albania has fallen 'prey to insomnia' (178): it is 1878 and the 'National Awakening' is well under way as the Albanians translate their dreams of national autonomy into reality.

Mark-Alem does not succumb to the pull of his Albanian origins to become a champion of ethnic identity and national separatism like his uncle Kurt. Nevertheless the struggle between ethnicity and empire is powerfully evoked in the novel as a contest imbibed by each generation from history, environment, and family tradition and internalized as the desire for an identity drawing on a powerful repository of stories and music, myths and images and promising an identity which is more than the individual. The blood of that first sacrificial victim to the bridge, which was to enable the Quprilis to leave their mountainous homeland, reappears in the myth for each generation, a reminder of the origins and the sacrifice which they made in becoming Ottoman Albanians.[54] Mark-Alem's Albania of the imagination is born of his family's history, memories, and stories. It taps a deeper and wider sense of being, a timeless, 'oceanic' collectivity, which is a measure of the shallowness and narrowness of his life-world. Its most powerful image in this work, even if tinged with irony, is that of the Albanian rhapsodists' age-old lament. This is a very different version of Albanianness from that which the regime manipulated and instrumentalized in the service of communist state patriotism.

In Mark-Alem's imagination Albania represents escape from the grim world of the Palace of Dreams. This dream of ethnic liberation and self-fulfilment is captured, submitted to interrogation, killed before his eyes, and held up as a trophy to the politics of dictatorial, centralized power. With the assassination of the rhapsodists we would, perhaps, expect Mark-Alem to be thoroughly disabused of this dream of ethnic self-identification. But, strangely, it lives on, resurfacing at the end as a desire for death and self-sacrifice and manifesting all of the negativity and morbidity (*thanatos*) of the Quprili epic. In its appeal to an imagined community — based on the ethnic identification of family, tradition, culture, and homeland — Mark-Alem's dream links him to something which is missing from his life-world: a sense of community, no matter how romantic in inspiration, morbid in expression, or impossible in reality. For Mark-Alem ethnic identity is imbued with the spirit of freedom. But that spirit is deformed over the course of the novel into a dream of death, an expression of *thanatos*. Finally we are left with an image of the polarization of instrumentalized power and romanticized ethnicity. The assimilated bureaucrat, Mark-Alem, has internalized the structure of instrumentalized power alongside its opposite, the romantic dream of imagined community. Mark-Alem betrays himself by internalizing the polarized structure of control and romanticism. In him the Empire has found its ideal subject.

In Kadare's hands the Palace becomes an allegory of the ways in which Central and Eastern European communist dictatorships functioned during the post-war era: the murky power-structures, the instrumentalization of myth and legend in the service of ideology, the creation of a ruling class or *nomenklatura*, the bureaucratization of human relationships and the insecurity, anxiety, and fear which this gives rise to, the ostentatious display of order and stability in a situation in which power-structures no longer have a rational base, where change occurs as the result of 'seismic' eruptions among factions, where civil society as a binding and mediating force is absent, and where the individual is a cipher in the algebra of power. For Maks Velo this novel defines the aims of dictatorship as absolute surveillance: 'The surveillance of the human brain. Not of the waking state. But of the sleeping brain. Absolute surveillance'.[55]

While his literary forebears are Orwell and Kafka, and his fictional institution of the Palace of Dreams owes something of its conception to the Ministry of Truth and the Castle, Kadare's surreal image of dictatorial control is far from derivative. In linking contemporary Eastern European literature with the tradition of the European political novel, Kadare deepens the understanding of the mechanisms of psychological intimidation of *1984*, and introduces the theme of ethnic identity into the Eastern European political novel. In the context of the Eastern European novel, the stylistic link with Kafka makes a politically loaded statement of creative-aesthetic association, just as the echoes of Orwell imply an identification with the Western European anti-Stalinist political novel. Where Western European political writers such as Orwell revealed the oppositions between individual desire and dictatorship, Kadare goes beyond this in identifying ethnic identity on the individual as well as the group level as the primary threat to dictatorships at the end of the twentieth century.

The issue of Kosovo cannot be separated from the evocation of ethnic identity in *The Palace of Dreams*. The time of writing and the inclusion of historical and oneiric motifs (in references to the Battle of Kosovo and in Mark-Alem's tour through the dream archives in which the Empire's dreams of Kosovo are stored) explicitly relate to Kosovo and its history. A folder in the Archives of the Palace is dedicated to the dreams of the first Battle of Kosovo and hold the seven hundred or so dreams 'fait la veille du jour fatal' (*Le Palais* 160, 'dreamed on the eve of the fateful day', *The Palace*), including the Master-Dream prophesying the bloody ending to the battle, in which the whole Balkan army was wiped out. Even now, after five centuries, the Archive assistant tells Mark-Alem, the Balkan peoples often dream of the battle. The dilemma of the Quprilis, caught between nascent Albanian nationalism and their traditional role as functionaries of the Empire, has relevance to those ethnic Albanians from Kosovo who had also identified with the ideology of Yugoslav communism with its centre in Belgrade. For the Albanian rhapsodists, the Quprili family have sold out not only to the Ottomans but also to the Slavs in identifying with a Balkan Slav culture. They have thus betrayed the primacy and authenticity of Albanian language and culture. The references to Kosovo and the 1389 Battle of Kosovo in the novel indicate Kadare's awareness of the simmering issue of ethnic identity within the Yugoslav state and of the potential tensions that will arise should Yugoslavia openly espouse a politics of ethnicity (whether Slav or national) over the cosmopolitanism of communist dogma. In the context of the hostilities after 1988 Kadare referred to his repeated attempts over previous decades to present Albanian as an 'Illyrian-Balkan' culture pre-dating Slav influence, and reiterated his fears of Serb expansionism.[56] As he was speaking in 1990, in the wake of the events in Kosovo in 1988 and cognizant of the threat of Serb expansionism in the post-communist environment, Kadare's fears and warnings were not unfounded. *The Palace of Dreams* integrates the ethnic question into the political novel of socialist Eastern Europe. At the same time Kadare provides a critical framework for this dream of 'the captive mind' (Milosz). For while ethnicity can express itself as a liberating component of identity, in the figures of Kurt and the Albanian rhapsodists it turns into a fundamentalist version of utopia.

The Official Response to 'The Palace of Dreams', 1982

Unsurprisingly, *The Palace of Dreams* created an uproar in Tirana in the wake of its publication in late 1981. Kadare wrote the final chapters in the early winter months of that year, and so could defend himself from charges that the Sultan's jealousy and the toppling of the powerful Quprili family in the novel alluded to the Shehu affair. But of course every one realized that it mattered little that he imagined these events before they happened. His vision was precise, audacious, and compelling. The book was proscribed immediately after publication, at the beginning of 1982, for including allusions against the communist regime. Twenty thousand copies had been printed, almost all of which were bought by libraries, according to Maks Velo, and hence would have disappeared when the novel was banned.[57] Some copies would have made their way into private hands to be circulated among the avid readers that Hoxha had, ironically, created with the literacy programme that was central to the regime's break with past traditions.

'Je priai Dieu que cette œuvre ne vînt pas à tomber entre leurs mains, surtout entre *les siennes!*' (*Le Poids* 434, 'I prayed to God that this work would not fall into their hands, in particular into his hands'), writes Kadare. But how could the novel *not* fall into *their* hands, or even *his*? A novel written by Albania's one indisputably famous writer, in which a coup takes place against the state, at the height of the hysteria over the death of Shehu? Admittedly, Kadare had published the opening sections in 1979 in a collection of short pieces entitled *Emblem of that Time*. However, these two early chapters scarcely enable the reader to guess what would come. As the novel was withdrawn censure rained down on Kadare from all sides. He cites the comment of a political prisoner of the time: 'With a book like this, either the author should be here with us, or the regime no longer has any bite'.[58] Not only did the opening pages of the novel locate it unmistakably in Scanderbeg Square, central Tirana, but the satire of the workings of the *Tabir Sarrail* were an open allusion to the Ministry of the Interior with its basement Archives, its machinations, and above all the idea of the Master-Dream, the ubiquitous plot against the state, the product of *agents-provocateurs*, the class enemy, and bourgeois revisionists. And the conflict between the Quprilis and the Sultan mirrors the politics of the centre, between various clans and cliques, most recently the Shehus, and the dictator.

A plenary meeting of the Party was convened by Ramiz Alia, the new second-in-command and successor to the supreme leader. It took place over two days in March 1982 in the concert hall of the Palace of Culture in Tirana, was chaired by the President of the Union of Writers and Artists, Dritëro Agolli, and stage-managed, according to Kadare, by Nexhmije Hoxha, his most powerful enemy and member of the old guard after the deaths of Shehu and Hazbiu. Agolli read the official report on the novel. He was an old friend of Kadare, who played a double game under the dictatorship and, as was revealed by Shaban Sinani, profoundly compromised himself in informing on his long-time friend and colleague.[59] There was a general understanding that self-criticisms were demanded of the writers by the Party and were carried out in ritual fashion behind the closed doors of the Union of Writers, although punishments could still be substantial. Over four hundred people attended the plenum planned for Kadare's humiliation in 1982.[60] Large open plenums such as this were very serious affairs. They were less predictable than the smaller affairs at the Union of Writers, and were more likely to escalate into affairs of state with major consequences. Albania at this time was still very much like the Soviet Union in 1937.[61]

According to Élisabeth and Jean-Paul Champseix, the criticism of Kadare focused on three main points: his use of historical settings in order to avoid representing the construction of socialism (with the exception of *The Great Winter* and *The Concert*); the survival of 'religious and reactionary' elements in his subjectivist use of myth; and finally his elitism and intellectualism, which distanced him from the people and were calculated to please the capitalist world with negative allusions to socialist Albania.[62] In his self-criticism Kadare accepted the points regarding the 'disproportion between actual and historical themes' in his works. But his literary practice, he asserted, was based on the need for a realism which reflected the actualities of Albanian life. He took the lead 'from Hoxha's saying that 'the times demand the enlargement of the thematic range [. . .] in order that the great tableau of socialist realism be completed by writers and artists', not through 'schematism, but real life, not poverty, but richness, not narrowness, but breadth'.[63] He criticized slavish adherence to the principles of socialist realism as a capitulation to Soviet cultural hegemony and cited the memoirs of the supreme leader himself as worthy models for imitation and guides to the practice of contemporary realism in the communist environment. In his summation Ramiz Alia pronounced the threat that would resurface almost verbatim in Kadare's next novel, the gloomy and sinister *The Shadow:* 'Le peuple et le Parti vous hissent sur l'Olympe, mais si vous ne leur êtes pas fidèle, ils vous précipitent dans l'abîme', ('the people and the Party raise you to the heights of Olympus, but if you do not remain true to them, they will hurl you into the abyss').[64] It seemed that Kadare's time had finally come, and his enemies were celebrating publicly.

The events surrounding this plenum, repeating in a major key the events of 1975, give us greater insight into the nature of the relationship between the writer and the regime even at this late stage. In an interview in November 2001 Nexhmije Hoxha accused Kadare retrospectively of insincerity, commenting with surprise that he had failed to learn from his first plenary self-criticism in relation to 'The Red Pashas' in 1975, and hence had to be subjected to the 1982 plenum, at which the same criticisms and justifications were repeated.[65] Her belief that this process was necessary and salutary for both writer and country appeared genuine, as did her belief, expressed with neither regret nor guilt in an interview with the German magazine *Der Spiegel*, that those who insisted on acting against the interests of the Party had to be eliminated. Her comments make clear the extent to which Kadare was operating within a known system of behaviours, values, and rituals. Certainly, it was a potentially dangerous, even fatal, environment for the writer. However, it was an environment of fundamentalism, single meanings, and absence of irony, which a writer such as Kadare, gifted, self-confident, and adept in the workings of the Party, could manipulate. He might well not come out unscathed, but it was unlikely he would suffer the draconian penalties meted out to those who protested more clumsily. In the wake of the plenum an urgent meeting of the Union of Writers was called and a delegate of the Central Committee addressed them briefly regarding Kadare's novel. The matter was closed, the aim of the Party achieved, and all further discussion of the novel in the media and elsewhere prohibited.

> Ce livre devait être oublié, comme s'il n'avait jamais vu le jour, lui-même pareil
> à un rêve. L'encerclement bourgeoiso-révisionniste de l'Albanie se faisait plus

menaçant que jamais; tous les écrivains devaient se mobiliser comme un seul homme autour du Parti et du camarade Enver (*Le Poids* 455)

The book should be forgotten, as if it had never seen the light of day, just like a dream. The bourgeois-revisionist ring around Albania was more threatening than ever; all writers were to rally as one around the Party and Comrade Enver Hoxha.

Kadare escaped with a warning. He, and, no doubt, his enemies in the Party, were stunned. For him there was no shadow of a doubt that the dictator stood behind this message, and it exemplifies Hoxha's malign genius to have intervened to protect the writer from potentially serious punishment (by consigning the work to oblivion) and thereby deepen the hatred of those colleagues who had been celebrating Kadare's fall the previous day with songs of victory in a Tirana restaurant. As a friend remarked to him after the plenum, he was freer than ever: he had been denounced in an open plenum as hostile to the regime, and yet the regime now seemed afraid to touch him.[66] Nevertheless the possible consequences were not lost on Kadare.

Ma liquidation éventuelle ou ma simple condamnation, mon emprisonnement ou l'impossibilité de me jeter en prison, la recherche d'autres solutions, la possibilité ou l'impossibilité de trouver, etc. — autant de questions qui non seulement m'obsédaient depuis longtemps, mais tarabustaient aussi beaucoup de gens en Albanie (*Le Poids* 460)

Would they get rid of me, finally, or just condemn me, imprison me or accept that they couldn't throw me into prison, would they look for other solutions, would they find them or were none to be found? These were the questions which preoccupied me and many other people in Albania for a long time.

While he seemed to have become untouchable by the regime, his very success was dangerous. From this period he thought that he might be quietly removed, that the whole machinery of the Party which he manipulated so well might simply be sidelined by a well-placed bullet or a car-accident. Support from France became more important than ever in maintaining Kadare's profile internationally in the wake of *The Palace of Dreams* and in the unstable environment of the years from 1982 until the death of Hoxha in 1985. Prominent figures such as Claude Durand and Michel Piccoli realized that the possibility of a shift to more sinister means of dealing with the writer must be loudly and clearly recognized in the West. At the instigation of his friends in French publishing and the arts, the *Quotidien de Paris* devoted a series of five articles to Kadare in 1983, and a prominent Parisian bookshop, the Librairie Lamartine opposite the Albanian Embassy, dedicated a showcase window to photographs of the writer and copies of his works. Inside Albania *The Great Winter* was his lifeline. The main thread holding him safe was the dictator's recognition that if Kadare disappeared, then the novel in which he himself featured as an Albanian hero would also have to disappear. This was at a time when the ageing dictator was increasingly concerned to preserve his literary existence. Hoxha's *Years of Childhood*, which invited comparison with Kadare's *Chronicle in Stone*, had appeared and envoys were sent out to France and elsewhere seeking (unsuccessfully) publication by a respected Western press, including Kadare's own publisher, Fayard. Any individual or group which moved against Kadare was also on dangerous ground in second-guessing Hoxha's desires or intentions.

> Il y a beau temps qu'ils vivent sous la dictature et ils ont appris à bien connaître certaines de ses lois. Ainsi, ils comprennent fort bien qu'il n'est aucune force au monde qui puisse vous protéger contre la colère de Zeus, si ce n'est Zeus lui-même. (*Le Poids* 461)

> It's a long time that they [the various figures around Hoxha] have been living under a dictatorship and they have come to know its laws well. And so they understand well that there is no force in the world which can protect you against the wrath of Zeus, unless it is Zeus himself.

Zeus, however, was old, frail, and beginning to suffer from the long-term effects of diabetes. He would lose a leg to the disease and began to suffer longer and more serious bouts of senility and paranoia. As if to verify Kadare's recognition of the potential new state of play, a threat suddenly appeared from nowhere in the form of thugs, orchestrated by the Sigurimi to harass the writer and his family, shouting abuse and throwing stones through the windows of his flat in central Tirana. An acquaintance from the police department would later warn him not to complain to the police of threats to his safety. The situation would have been organized by the Sigurimi precisely in order to create a file on him, which would be brought out in case of his death to show that he had long been harassed by anti-social elements (*Le Poids* 521). Kadare was interviewed — in a prison — by a magistrate, regarding the public denunciations of a woman who was set up by the Sigurimi to shout accusations outside his apartment. In this environment of active and passive harassment, he was unexpectedly given permission in spring 1983 to travel to France for the premiere of Tovoli's film of *The General of the Dead Army*, which was completed in Italy after the debacle of the Albanian project. While he was in Paris his wife was advised that a charge had been laid against him and that he would be arraigned on his return. Elisabeth and Jean-Paul Champseix surmise that the authorization to travel and the trumped-up charge were part of a scheme organized by Kadare's enemies in the upper echelons of the regime to frighten him into seeking exile in France. This would have enabled the regime to label him a traitor and agent of French interests at a time when the 'escape of traitors' had become an important element of the regime's scenarios of plots and internal threats. It was probably the only way of manipulating Hoxha against him.[67]

Resilience or Exile, 1982–85

At this point in 1982 and 1983, the darkest years of the dictatorship, we must broach the topic of Kadare's resilience. The situation in which he found himself was extraordinary. Kadare was living in a dictatorship in which the harassment, interrogation, torture, and even assassination of dissidents was common. And yet he produced works which were provocative and potentially seditious. He appears to have suffered greatly from the strain of writing, unable either to rein in his imagination or refrain from publicizing his work in the volatile and politically explosive environments of the 1970s and 1980s. He describes the machinations of the Party factions, the intimacies, hatreds, and daily familiarities of the tiny Tirana nomenklatura. He made enemies among the old guard, including Nexhmije Hoxha, and in the Sigurimi in a country where a word out of place could bring about imprisonment, physical harm, and death. Like many others he was sent to Berat in 1967 in the wake of the cultural revolution, but worked as a journalist and writer there and appears to have been free to return to Tirana. While the events surrounding the production of *The Great Winter* and 'The Red Pashas' were dangerous, he succeeded in creating a protective shield from the dictator's vanity and survived the scandal of his attack on the Party bureaucracy. The belief that he could take on the dictator, offering him a 'corrective mask' in the late 1960s and early 1970s, becoming a mentor to power, although rebuffed, was not brutally punished. He was censured and feared the worst, yet was sent into internal exile under relatively anodyne conditions. By the end of 1975 he was on his way back to Tirana and an unspoken truce appears to have been put in place. He was known to Enver and Nexhmije Hoxha and was on first-name terms with members of the highest echelons of the regime. With the exception of the dictator and his wife, anyone could be toppled, as so many had already. But Kadare survived. His work was prohibited and he was subjected to harrowing procedures of official criticism, chastisement, and censorship. But he was spared drastic forms of punishment, such as incarceration in prison or labour camps, even the second time around after *The Palace of Dreams*. And he not only survived unscathed but appeared untouchable. The acclaim he received from his French and worldwide public was used as the basis of accusations of counter-revolutionary behaviour and even espionage on behalf of Western powers. The French translations were authorized in Albania, and the royalties flowed into state coffers. Kadare was refused publication rights, was harassed for provocative works such as 'The Red Pashas', and was forbidden to write novels, but he continued to write and publish 'narratives' which are indistinguishable from his longer novels. He was suspected of being an enemy agent, but travelled extensively on government business, even enjoying the privilege of unaccompanied periods of travel to France, the place where he was most at home in the West. The dictator spread a protective wing over the poet and withdrew into retentive silence at those points where Kadare was most under fire from Nexhmije and the left wing of the Party.

These contradictions have fuelled the suspicions that Kadare was somehow complicit with the regime. One of the striking aspects of Kadare's personality, identifiable from an early age, is his extraordinary belief in his ability as a writer, along with the self-confidence, even arrogance, which came of this. This confidence supported him through the terrible years of the dictatorship. Already as an adolescent he wrote poems which were at odds with the requirements of socialism, and he called on his inner resources to withstand the criticisms and the threats which his writing provoked even at this early stage. From the 1970s until Hoxha's death, Kadare pursued his writer's existence as the 'other' of the dictator, his shadow and nemesis, the voice of 'eternal Albania'. Both Enver Hoxha and Kadare knew that without the writer the dictator would be no different from his brutal colleagues throughout Eastern Europe.

Hoxha was an intelligent and complex narcissist, capable of extraordinary ruthlessness, although uninterested in carrying out acts of violence himself (like the Builder in *The Monster*). He was a handsome, Westernized dandy who read widely in European literature, idealized France, and could exude charm. He viewed himself as the creator of a new Albania in his own image. He recognized that Kadare was without a peer in Albania and, a would-be writer himself, was both intimidated and provoked by Kadare. To have Kadare entirely humiliated, obliterated, or killed would have been an admission of defeat for Hoxha, an admission that he could not compete with this genius of Albanian letters whose name might overshadow his own. He had to keep Kadare alive and even protect him from becoming modern Albania's first great martyred writer. Of course, other goals were achieved by his protection of Kadare, including the factionalization of the creative nomenklatura, who came to hate the nation's leading writer for the invisible force-field that protected him. The deep arrogance of the creative spirit is thus the saving grace of the writer under threat who knows that come what may, his work will survive him and will bestow an immortality denied to others. In retrospect such sentiments may seem romantic or self-indulgent; however, history has revealed their truthfulness. That invisible presence which carried Kadare through the darkest years of the dictatorship was the peace of mind, depth of purpose, and sense of identity which came of his 'second chronology' as a writer. It was a quality for which lesser talents, such as Agolli and the rising new star of Albanian writing, K. Kosta, hated him.[68]

By 1982 Hoxha was sick, demented, and physically waning. As the dictator's health deteriorated so too did the conditions of Kadare's safety. By the early 1980s he genuinely feared for his life. In spite of his resilience, the affair of *The Palace of Dreams*, the nightly presence of the thugs outside his apartment, and the fear that old scores would be settled in the period of transition as the dictator lay dying took their toll on the writer, leading him to reconsider seeking exile in France. The main hold that the communist regimes maintained over their *Reisekader*, the members of the upper nomenklatura who were permitted to travel to the West, was the threat to their families should they fail to return. Kadare and his wife Helena discussed the consequences of his remaining in France. It would have meant potential imprisonment or worse for his family. At no time was the ambiguity of life and death clearer to him than in 1983 when faced with this decision. His life as a husband and father in the land of his birth, and his life as a writer in the underworld of communist Albania, were diametrically opposed. His thoughts on life and death, writing and dictatorship, France and Albania find expression in the opening pages of *The Shadow* where the theme of Constantine's release from the tomb is reiterated in the flight to France as a flight to life.

A passport for international travel was a curious thing in socialist Albania. Highly sought after, it could signal the resurrection into public life of a disgraced official, enabling the family members, friends, and colleagues of that person to hope that their chances would improve now that the stain of association was erased. It could also indicate that certain compromises had been made, certain services rendered, denunciations or accusations supported in the chain of misfortune that the regime depended on for its power. It was also one of the dictator's sadistic strategies to give the potential victim a false sense of security, as was the case with the second son of Mehmet Shehu, granted a passport to travel to Sweden at exactly the moment his father was killed and his family arrested.[69]

During the trip to France Kadare was allowed to contact and visit friends without the accompaniment of his chaperone. He discussed the possibilities of seeking refuge, as the regime intended. He returned to Albania, but the threats continued. His exclusion from a planned French colloquium on the Albanian novel, and the politicking that was going on in relationship to the second of the five-yearly folk-festivals held in Gjirokastra alerted him to the ongoing existence of plots and designs against his well-being among his enemies in the regime. But again the authorization came through for his passport and again the writer discussed with his wife during walks outside their bugged apartment the scenario and the consequences of his failure to return. Recognizing his vulnerability in the environment of morbidity and potential change of leadership at this time, Kadare secreted some of his recent manuscripts and smuggled them out of the country to France where they would remain in a bank-vault should anything happen to him:[70] the novels, *The Shadow*, with its powerful depiction of a demented ruler and of the divided self of the writer in a dictatorship, and *Agamemnon's Daughter*, paralleling the tragic fate of the Shehu dynasty with that of the Ancient Greek Atreides; the short story, 'A Bird Flying South'; and five short poems, 'The Novel-Killer', 'That Winter', 'Easter Sunday', 'The Grave', and 'The Safe'.[71] Again his French friends and colleagues organized a powerful statement of support. This time it was the well-known and respected literary commentator Bernard Pivot who remarked pointedly in the popular and influential French magazine *Lire*, 'It's Kadare himself whom we want to see on French television, not his decapitated head'.[72] Again a period of tense calm ensued. The thugs disappeared from outside his apartment as the 'Orwellian year' of 1984 began. During this time Kadare maintained his prodigious output of stories and short novels, including 'The Bearer of Bad Tidings' (1983), 'The Blinding Order' and 'The Morgue' (1984), *Clair de lune*, 'The Bringer of Dreams', 'Abolition of the Profession of Curser', and 'Death of a Russian Woman' (1985), and the novel of Albanian independence, *The Black Year* (1985).

The Black Year traces the fortunes of a group of soldiers whose primary loyalty is to their country, but who are unable to tell even in which direction they must go to defend it, or, in fact, what they are defending it from. The confusion of 1912/13 is the theme. Albania gained its independence in 1913, only to be turned into a monarchy with a minor German prince (Wied) and then thrown into a further decade of uncertainty with the First World War. The reign of Zog, which Kadare has latterly reviewed in more positive terms,[73] is represented as an interregnum in which Italian influence gained the upper hand, leading to the catastrophes of the 1930s and the occupation by Count Ciano, the Greek counter-offensives against the Italians, and the German occupation in the final years of the Second World War. The descent of the communist partisans into the towns in early 1945 marked the end of the period of chaos that had begun in 1913. *The Black Year* recapitulates the tragic interruptions of Albanian political development, themes which Kadare had developed earlier in *The Three-Arched Bridge*, *The Castle*, and *The Niche of Shame*.

Failed political development, the catastrophic choices forced on the Albanians by the great powers, and the internal incompetence which compounded the disasters of the year of liberation, leading to the following forty years of domestic mismanagement and foreign intervention, are the subject of this novel, one of Kadare's best. Written in 1985, it did not appear until in 1987.

Apologia pro vita sua: The Shadow, 1984–1986

It is in *The Shadow*, however, that Kadare best captures the 'climat de mysticisme' of Tirana during Hoxha's final years (*Le Poids* 487). The mixture of rumour, suspicion, paranoia, and uncertainty that pervaded the capital at this time was felt elsewhere in the dying years of European communism. In the Soviet Union, too, a bizarre atmosphere of morbidity prevailed as the empire declined into bankruptcy and stagnation under an ageing and corrupt nomenklatura with Brezhnev at its head. In the German Democratic Republic writers such as Wolfgang Hilbig and Hans Joachim Schädlich were exploring a post-Kafkan world in which the contours of power take precedence over the realism of everyday life and where nothing is as it seems. In Peter Nadás's *Book of Memories* as in Andreï Makine's *Le Testament français*, the rhythms of the past make themselves heard again after the decades of communism. *The Shadow* is a novel about the deformations of life under a dictatorial regime, in particular the deformations of intellectual life and creativity. 'Tous servaient Enver Hoxha. Lui seul ne rapportait à personne. Il rapportait à son ego, à son ombre dictatoriale. Cette ombre qui s'étendait sur tout le pays' ('Everyone served Enver Hoxha. Only he alone did not report to anyone above. I reported to his ego, to his dictatorial shadow').[74] A deeply introspective work, it brings together the private and personal with the public and political in imagery which is at once deeply intimate and politically significant. This novel brings one of Kadare's greatest gifts, his ability to show the interrelationships of these two spheres, typically kept so separate in Western European literature, to bear on the milieu closest to himself, namely the creative and artistic nomenklatura.

The Metafictional Contextualization

According to Claude Durand, Kadare did not believe that he would live to see the end of the regime at the time of writing of *The Shadow*.[75] The manuscript was finished in 1986 and hidden in his apartment until 1987 when he smuggled it to France under the title of *The Three K's*, a translation from the German of the left-liberal novelist Siegfried Lenz. The names had been rendered German throughout and the location switched from Paris to Vienna, but as Kadare notes, the disguise was thin, and was designed primarily for the inspectors at the airport, should his hand-luggage be searched.[76] In Paris the manuscript was consigned to the safety of a bank vault by Claude Durand, editor of the major French publishing house, Fayard, with the authorization to reopen it when he thought it appropriate. The subtext of the agreement was, however, that the novel should not be published until after Kadare's death, as Kadare notes in his interview with Alain Bosquet: 'mon contrat avec lui était clair: le roman ne devait être publié qu'après ma mort' ('my contract with him was clear: the novel should only be published after my death').[77]

In this work Kadare turned his attention to his own divided consciousness under the dictatorship. The narrator is a privileged but untalented member of the artistic nomenklatura who secretly loathes the Party and who lives for his trips to France. His friend, a gifted writer, held at a certain distance by the Party as a result of the brilliance and the independence of his work, plays an important role as a narrative alter ego. Both reflect aspects of Kadare's existence. The narrator's trips to France are imagined as temporary flights to life from the grim underworld of death that Kadare had associated with communism at least since finishing *The Great Winter*. The ancient ballad of Constantine and Doruntine is refunctioned into the modern setting of Tirana and France in the final year of the dictator's death, and the evocation of the demented fantasies of the supreme leader, whom Kadare had observed so closely for the duration of his life, gives this otherwise complex and difficult work of introspection a powerful political impetus.

Several aspects of the narration render *The Shadow* difficult, particularly for those unfamiliar with Kadare's life and context. The environment of the halls of power in Tirana during the dictator's last years is murky and opaque. The narrative interest is divided between the two nameless protagonists and narrative alter egos, the cinéaste-narrator and his friend the disgraced writer. These two figures can be seen to characterize the Albanian bureaucrat and the creative writer respectively, but both are also alter egos of the writer. Throughout this analysis these two figures will be referred to as the *narrator* and the *writer* for the sake of clarity. The *narrator's* one completed film screenplay is an adaptation of an earlier novel by the *writer*. A third difficulty derives from Kadare's use of the leitmotif of the medieval Albanian legend of Constantine and Doruntine as form of *mise en abyme*. A further aspect, perhaps, is the inwardness of the text, very different in its personal reference to more identifiably autobiographical works, such as *Chronicle in Stone* or *The Twilight of the Steppe-Gods*. *The Shadow* marks a clear development in Kadare's writing, demonstrating the writer's extraordinary literary inventiveness, and introducing aspects of the late style that would be carried through into works of the post-communist era, such as *Spiritus*, *The Life, Game and Death of Lul Mazrek*, and *Accident*.

The predication of the novel's appearance on the death of the author (i.e. the understanding with Claude Durand) brings the contemporary political situation into the ambit of the novel, inviting the reader to consider the specificities of dictatorship, intimidation, and physical peril in order to comprehend its bizarre plot. We must read the novel in terms of this retrospective contextualizing which functions as a metafictive device, obliging us to read *The Shadow* as a posthumous work, the final testament of a writer whose death occurs at the behest of the dictator. The time-setting of the novel is the *narrator's* present in around 1984. Rumours abound of the blindness, senility, and imminent death of the Supreme Guide, the unnamed dictator, around whose body the various factions are gathering, led by his hawkish wife. The metafiction of the author's death consigns the fiction to history, bringing about closure and implying a perspective on the ending which would otherwise be lacking, namely as the *final* reckoning of the author, Kadare, with the dictatorship of Enver Hoxha. It presages one of Kadare's main themes of the late 1980s, the conflict between the writer and the dictator as an endgame of power and imagination in the post-war history of Eastern European socialism.

The Narrator and the Writer

Kadare's *narrator* is a self-confessed 'failed' screenwriter employed in the Foreign Affairs department of the State Film Studios in Tirana. He travels frequently to France in order to finalize cultural exchange agreements between the Albanian and French governments regarding the showcasing of Albanian films. The *narrator* is well-connected to the Party via an uncle who is a communist stalwart with powerful contacts. On his trips to the French capital the *narrator* has made contact with various figures in cinema, theatre, and cultural circles, in particular a young actress, Sylvaine Doré, with whom he has an affair. A second figure enters the story as an alter ego of Kadare himself: a writer who befriended the *narrator* while both were studying in Moscow. After their return to Albania their paths diverge as a result of individual talent and political forces. The *writer* has been harassed by the regime and has been limited in his contacts with the West. The one more or less successful work of the scriptwriter-*narrator* is based on a story by the *writer* about his last weeks in Moscow before being repatriated by the Albanian regime in 1960.

The *narrator* is neither a party stalwart nor a dissident. He is a typical member of the nomenklatura, the bureaucratic intelligentsia of the socialist state. He is ordinary in every respect, other than that he benefits from the travel privileges that come with his job as cultural ambassador. He hates the regime, but does not dare step out of line; he dreams of escape to France, but does not pursue the possibility of seeking exile. He is a scriptwriter, but has never seen his scripts turned into film. A descendant of Kafka's Central European protagonists, he is an Albanian everyman of the bureaucratic-administrative class, caught among a welter of opposing and irrational forces. He typifies the inauthenticity of everyday life in Albania under the regime, the sense that 'life is elsewhere' (Kundera) and that the reality of the socialist *Alltag* ('everyday life') obstructs human living. The *narrator* is not represented as culpable, but as having so far been incapable of extraordinary behaviour. If the *narrator*'s defining characteristic is his lack of talent and his inability to realize his dreams, his friend the *writer* is defined by his talent to the point that his writing takes precedence over his life. Like Kadare, he has written an autobiographical novel in which his Moscow experiences are imagined in terms of an ancient Albanian literary motif. Kadare brings into *The Shadow* a large amount of material from his 1976 novel *The Twilight of the Steppe-Gods*. In order to understand this self-reflexivity in *The Shadow* we must return briefly to that earlier autobiographical work.

Mise en abyme of Twilight of the Steppe-Gods

In *The Twilight of the Steppe-Gods* Kadare retells his experiences at the Gorki Institute in Moscow leading to his repatriation in late 1960 as a result of the break between Albania and the Soviet Union. Here he witnessed at first hand the Pasternak affair and learned what it meant to be a writer in a communist regime. However, the young writer from Gjirokastra also experienced Russian civilization and the life of a major Eastern European metropolis and modern capital of a world power. Forced to abandon his Muscovite girlfriend, a medical student named Lydia Snieguina, and recognizing that the return will result in a dramatic curtailment of his intellectual freedom, Kadare is repatriated to his tiny, Stalinist homeland at the end of *The Twilight of the Steppe-Gods*. The Albania to which he returns is imagined as a realm of the dead:

> En m'éloignant, je l'imaginai, debout sur le boulevard Tverskoï, le visage tourné vers les grilles sombres du jardin de l'Institut, attendant vainement que je revienne de cette région d'où personne n'est jamais revenu. (*Le Crépuscule* 217–18)

> As I left, I imagined her standing on the Boulevard Tverskoi, her face turned towards the darkened grill of the Institute garden, waiting in vain for me to return from that region from which no one has ever returned.

The theme of return to a nether world is associated with a motif which deepens and complicates the associations of return for the young Albanian. During his last days with Lydia, Kadare's autobiographical narrator imagines himself as the dead Constantine, who has given his pledge to see his lover before returning to the grave:

> 'Je t'avais donné ma parole'. Il ne me restait plus maintenant qu'à secouer la terre de mes cheveux. 'Je t'avais donné ma parole, répétai-je, en approchant ma tête de ses cheveux, depuis longtemps, depuis l'époque des grandes ballades'. Elle me regarda fixement, comme si je délirais. Je fus tenté de lui dire: 'Tu ne comprends pas cela, toi, tu as d'autres ballades et d'autres divinités'. [. . .] 'Mais tu brûles! Me dit Lida. Tu aurais dû rester chez toi'. Elle avait raison, je n'aurais pas dû sortir. Mais j'avais donné ma parole. C'était la faute de cette ancienne légende. (*Le Crépuscule* 215–16)

> 'I gave you my word'. Nothing remained for me but to shake the earth from my hair' I have given you my word', I repeated, 'for a long time, since the time of the great ballads'. She looked at me intently, as if I were delirious. I was tempted to say to her: 'You wouldn't understand that, you have other ballads and other gods'. 'But you're burning!' Lydia said to me. You should have stayed at home. She was right, I shouldn't have come out. But I had given my word. It was the fault of that ancient legend.

In *The Twilight of the Steppe-Gods* the Constantine theme is associated primarily with the pledge or *besa*, the tribal and early feudal statement of personal honour in Albanian culture. In Kadare's mythology this pledge symbolizes the facticity of ethno-national identity and belonging. The novel ends with the young writer's pledge to return to Albania rather than to consider alternatives of exile. The pledge is thus situated at the beginning of Kadare's adult self-consciousness, underwriting his existence as an Albanian intellectual and writer after his return from Moscow in 1960. It gives expression to Kadare's recognition and acceptance of ethnic identity as the primary formative and motive force in his existence as a writer, and it expresses a Herderian sense of the relationship of language and culture.

In *The Shadow* the figure of the *writer*, based on Kadare, and the identification with the legendary Constantine is taken a step further. The complex narrative structure of reduplication in *The Shadow* can be illustrated as a double *mise en abyme* in which the current text recursively reiterates material from the earlier text, *The Twilight of the Steppe-Gods*, which in turn is based on Kadare's life. In each of these reduplications the figure of Constantine gains in symbolic importance. At the risk of simplification we can represent the *mise en abyme* schematically as follows:

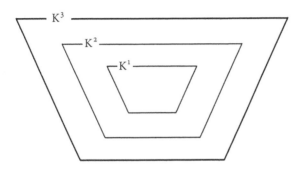

Constantine the Albanian Hero

In their first rendezvous over dinner, the Frenchwoman Sylvaine and the *narrator* of *The Shadow* discuss his screenplay, which is based on the *writer*'s story of his return to Albania.

> 'J'ai beaucoup aimé', reprit-elle. [. . .] 'Mais surtout le passage où le personnage principal — c'est-à-dire toi — se sépare de cette jeune fille russe à la porte de l'Institut et la sensation d'être mort. [. . .] Mais cette histoire ne t'est pas arrivée à toi, n'est-ce pas? Je crois que tu m'as dit qu'il s'agissait de quelqu'un d'autre, d'un de tes camarades de l'Institut Dostoïevsky, si je ne me trompe'. 'De l'Institut Gorki'. 'Oui, c'est ça'. 'En fait, cette histoire n'est pas non plus la sienne. Elle date d'au moins mille ans!' 'C'est vrai', acquiesça Sylvaine. 'C'est ce qui ressort clairement du scénario . . . L'histoire du frère mort qui sort de sa tombe pour ramener sa soeur mariée d'une contrée lointaine. C'est une ancienne légende, n'est-ce pas?' (*L'Ombre* 44)[78]

> 'I especially liked the passage where the main character — that's you — leaves the Russian girl at the gate of the Institute and the sense of being dead. [. . .] But that story didn't happen to you, did it? I think you said that it was about someone else, one of your friends at the Dostoyevsky Institute, if I'm not mistaken'. ' — The Gorki Institute'. ' — Yes, that's it'. ' — In fact that story isn't his either. It's at least a thousand years old'. 'That's true', Sylvaine agreed. 'That comes out clearly in the script . . . The story of the dead brother who rises from his grave in order to bring his married sister back home from a distant land. It's an old legend, isn't it?'

The Constantine story is identified as an ancient legend which somehow has a life of its own, reappearing down the centuries to affect the lives of the *writer* and the *narrator*. 'Peut-être s'agit-il d'une histoire . . . comment dire . . . contagieuse. En l'entendant, on a l'impression de pouvoir la vivre soi-même', remarks the *narrator*, 'j'ai eu l'impression qu'une part de son récit m'était arrivée, à moi ..'. (*L'Ombre* 44, 'Perhaps it's about a . . . how would you say it . . . an infectious story. In hearing it, one has the impression of experiencing it oneself . . . I had the impression that a part of his story had happened to me').

The infectious history which taints those who come into contact with it is the history of Albania:

> Il était naturel que nous autres, jeunes Albanais qui étudiions alors à l'étranger, éprouvions tous une certaine affinité avec le Konstantin de la légende. Notre pays se coupait de plus en plus du reste du monde et nous nous sentions comme exclus de cette autre vie. Nous rentrions l'un après l'autre pour nous enfermer en quelque sorte dans une tombe. (*L'Ombre* 45)

> It was only natural that we others, young Albanians still studying in foreign countries, should feel a certain affinity with the Constantine of the legend. Our country cut itself off more and more from the rest of the world and we felt excluded from that other life. We returned, one after another, as if to the grave.

The story of Constantine gathers up the later stories into itself, becoming the trope of an Albanian experience which links the three figures as one:

> 'La seule différance tenait à ce qu'à l'histoire macabre de Konstantin était accollé un fragment de vie contemporaine, la séparation de mon ami d'avec sa compagne, une étudiante en médecine de Moscou . . . Plus tard, peut-être, dans un autre café dans un autre pays, on raconterait à nouveau cette histoire, sauf que, cette fois, sur la croupe de cheval de Konstantin mort, nous serions là toute une petite bande: mon ami, moi-même, la Moscovite Lydia Snieguine, la Parisienne Sylvaine Doré'. (*L'Ombre* 46)

> 'The only difference was that a piece of contemporary life was tied up in the macabre story of Constantine, the separation of my friend from his companion, a student of medicine in Moscow . . . Later, perhaps, in another cafe in another country, the story will be retold, except that this time we will all be there on the back of Constantine's horse, the Muscovite, Lydia Snieguina, the Parisienne Sylvaine Doré'.

The epidemic from which Albania must save itself through the repatriation of its foreign students and the establishment of closed borders is the revisionism of the Khrushchev years. It is both war and plague: an aggressive enemy from outside and an insidious disease within the host body. Kadare's ambiguity is deliberate: the Albanian government fears those influences from outside, which, once carried within its borders, will continue to develop and spread from body to body. The object of fear, that is, originates from inside as well as from outside. The forces which killed Constantine and his brothers are the same: pestilence and war, a motif of destruction which occurs throughout Kadare's work. The image of infection is thus an expression of fear of sameness. The closure of borders is a preventative measure aiming to stop the spread of something originating from outside. However once present in the protected community, it will spread. The conditions exist within the closed community as well as outside for the spread of the disease and of the dissatisfaction with Stalinism, of which disease is a metaphor. The ambiguity of the metaphor lies in the implication that the politics of Albanian closure is based on the recognition of sameness. The external differences between nations are belied by the sameness of human beings in relation to questions of identity and sexual attraction.

The predominant metaphor for this mixture of desire and fear, here as elsewhere in
the literature of ethno-national identity, is sexual desire versus the fear of sexually
transmitted disease. This sense of the dual nature of belonging — the pledge of
belonging versus the drive towards otherness — is ubiquitous in Kadare's work and
it represents something much deeper in Albanian national consciousness than the
political divide of the post-war era between the regime and its opponents.

Doruntine: Sister and Lover, Self and Other

For the *narrator* the story of Constantine is about the pledge to return to the realm
of death. Yet there is a further motif in the *writer's* retelling of the story. He refers
to a second version in which the incestuous attraction between brother and sister
underlies the motivation of departure and return. In this version the driving force of
the story is neither the pledge nor the achievement of the impossible, but the incest
motif and the social ramifications of exogamy and endogamy. Doruntine is sent
away at Constantine's behest as a means of averting the possibility of the incestuous
relationship. He is the youngest of nine brothers and the fate of the family seems
unthreatened by the departure of the sister. However, when the brothers are
suddenly wiped out by war and pestilence, only the female side of the clan remains:
the ageing mother at home and Doruntine far away in Bohemia.

Doruntine's marriage to a Slav nobleman, the destruction of the male side of
the clan, and the redemption of Doruntine by Constantine are powerfully evoked.
In the pre-feudal environment of this legend, issues of exogamy and endogamy
were central to the identity and survival of the clan.[79] On the one hand, the sister,
Doruntine, must be sent away in a symbolic statement of the necessity of marrying
out in order to avoid inbreeding; on the other hand, her loss is felt as a weakening
of the family.[80] Against the maintenance of language, customs, and ethnic identity,
exogamy is both threatening and necessary. It introduces the foreign, the other,
the unknown, and the potentially dangerous into the group, and it leads to the
weakening and dissipation of the group through marrying out, strengthening
potential rivals and enemies. The maintenance of ethnic identity and the fear of
deracination, dispersion, and loss of cultural coherence belongs anthropologically to
the feudal past for most of Western Europe, but remains a powerful theme of ethno-
national consciousness in parts of Central and Eastern Europe and in particular
in the Balkan lands. In its Albanian form it reflects the mentality of a clan-based
culture, in which the problematic opposition of self and other is expressed in terms
of marriage and incest taboos which determine the make-up of the group and its
relationships to the outside world. This early legend of incest, to which Kadare
elsewhere refers as the Albanian equivalent of the Oedipus story, gives expression
to fears of internal as well as external forces which could undermine the social
structure of the early Albanians.[81]

The figure of Doruntine represents both the necessity of exogamy, of preserving
the clan through the marrying out of daughters and sisters, and the fear of loss of
identity and assimilation to the 'other'. Constantine's pledge to redeem his sister
is the compromise on which the resolution of the conflict between the demands
of the exogamous and the endogamous is based. The departure of Doruntine to

marriage and of the nine sons to war represents the primacy of the exogamous and the turn outwards to the world; the return of Doruntine and the death of the sons represents the ascendancy of the counter-principle of endogamy and turning inwards. The relationship of Constantine and Doruntine thus consists of the two opposed movements of separation and redemption, giving expression to the ambivalence in the relationship of brother and sister, man and lover, self and other in this legend. The promise of the redemption of the sister at the point of social crisis is the price for the move outward to the world.

The Frenchwoman Sylvaine Doré in *The Shadow* embodies everything that the Albanian men in the novel imagine a sophisticated Parisian woman to be, but her name is a reminder of her origins. For she is both the lover and the long-lost sister, now a European, fully assimilated to her French identity, and with no memory of her earlier existence, which is preserved in her name only. As lover and sister she represents desire and fear. She is both the late twentieth-century European and the desired and feared incestuous object, symbol of Albanian isolation; the modern European individual and the image of a pre-feudal ethno-racial identity which has been preserved as a cultural value through the centuries of foreign and imperial domination of the Balkan peninsula. If the *narrator*, and the *writer*, as Constantine, are bound by their pledge to return to the country of their ethnic origins, Sylvaine Doré, the Doruntine of this novel, is the figure of the sister who has assimilated a European identity so thoroughly that she has forgotten her legendary roots in the home country, and hence is an image of cultural loss. She represents an extreme version of Mark Alem's alienation in *The Palace of Dreams*.

In the story of Constantine and Doruntine Kadare finds the cultural archetype of his nation's complex identifications of the endogamous and the exogamous, the lawful and the unlawful, of the identity-giving factors of self and other. The theme of the pledge to overcome death encapsulates the sense of fragility of Albanian identity, caught between the demands of self and other, of the opposition of similarity and difference which, in the nation's history, was so fraught with loss and destruction. The exogamous movement outwards towards the other represents loss (death of the brothers, abandonment of the sister), the endogamous movement inwards to the self represents closure (incest between brother and sister).

The point of the *mise en abyme* in *The Shadow* is to recapitulate this leitmotiv from Kadare's life and works and to show the extent of these identifications in the contemporary Albanians' encounter with Europe. Albanianness rests on a deeply felt sense of ambivalence towards the world outside. On the one hand, it is the object of intense fantasies of escape, fulfilment, and redemption (expressed in powerful sexual imagery in the novel); on the other hand, the world represents fear of loss of self, deracination, and fragmentation of the bases of group identity for the *narrator* and the *writer*, Kadare's representatives of the contemporary Albanian nomenklatura in this work. Using the literary technique of the *mise en abyme*, Kadare links the contemporary problematics of dissidence and existential authenticity under the dictatorship to historical patterns of Albanian culture and individual existence.

The Relationship between the Writer and the Narrator

The figures of the *writer* and the *narrator* shadow each other throughout the novel. The *writer* is introduced in relation to the screenplay which the *narrator* has given to Sylvaine to read:

> Je lui dis que c'était une histoire que m'avait contée un ami quand nous étudiions ensemble à Moscou, lui à l'Institut Gorki de Littérature, moi dans une académie de cinéma . . . (*L'Ombre* 36)

> I told her that it was a story which a friend had told me when we were studying together in Moscow, he at the Gorki Institute of Literature and I at an academy for cinema.

The two had met before leaving Tirana. Both had applied for scholarships to study in Moscow. The *writer* is at first rejected, ostensibly on account of tubercular shadows on his x-rays, a diagnosis which turns out to be mistaken once the checks on his personal record have been completed. The closeness of the two young men is expressed in an image of physical identity as they search their x-rays unsuccessfully for the signs of difference which have resulted in the rejection of the *writer*:

> Nous y cherchâmes la petite tache qui avait été cause de son échec, mais les ombres de nos cages thoraciques sur les deux radios paraissaient si identiques qu'après nous être repassé les clichés à plusieurs reprises, nous finîmes par les confondre et eûmes l'impression de nous trouver, cent ans après, devant une fosse commune, à rechercher nos propres ossements. (*L'Ombre* 62)

> We looked there for the small spot which had caused the hold-up for him, but the shades of our thoracic cavities on the two x-rays looked so identical that after we had passed the negatives back and forward a few times, we got them mixed up in the end and felt as though we had found ourselves one hundred years later in front of a common grave, looking for our own bones.

While the *narrator* and the *writer* share the same experiences of youth, love, and education in Moscow, their paths diverge after their repatriation. Both realize that their task as creative intellectuals will be difficult in their homeland, where cinematic works are subjected to even greater control than literature.

Hoping that his screenplay with its memories of their youth in Moscow will bring them together again, and wanting to tell his old friend about Sylvaine, the *narrator* is upset at the *writer's* cold and aggressive response:

> Je m'étais senti offensé comme je l'avais rarement été et j'avais attendu impatiemment le moment de le quitter pour ne plus avoir à affronter ce regard méprisant qui paraissait dire: tu me casses les pieds avec tes Russes ou tes Suissesses, toutes tes Lydia Snieguine et tes Doruntine, et tes rues Monsieur-le-Prince dont je ne veux même plus entendre prononcer le nom. . . (*L'Ombre* 84)

> I felt offended as rarely before, and I waited impatiently for the moment when I could leave and no longer have to put up with that contemptuous look which seemed to be saying: you're a pain in the neck with your Lydia Snieguinas and your Doruntines, your rues Monsieur-le-Prince. I never want to hear their names again . . .

He wants to respond in kind: 'Tu as eu un certain succès et tu crois avoir déjà accédé à l'Olympe, mais gare à la dégringolade!' (*L'Ombre* 85, 'You've had a certain success and you think you've reached the top of Olympus, but pride comes before a fall!'). But he desists. Later he discovers that the *writer* is about to be placed under sanctions on account of his most recent novel. Kadare draws explicitly on his experiences of reprisal and harassment after the publication of *The Palace of Dreams*. Listening to the official debate about his friend's new novel on the radio, the *narrator* hears the same expressions as he himself had been tempted to use: 'Le peuple te hisse sur l'Olympe et le peuple t'en fait redescendre' (*L'Ombre* 85, 'The people raise you to the heights of Olympus and the people will bring you down'). These words echo those used by Ramiz Alia in the formal proceedings against Kadare, discussed above.[82] The *narrator*'s inner complicity with the regime is complete. Not only has he kept his distance from his friend out of fear of the consequences of too close a relationship, but he has replicated the response of the hated regime:

> J'avais pour la première fois du remords. Il me semblait que, ce jour-là, j'avais attiré le malheur sur sa tête en le maudissant. (*L'Ombre* 85)

> For the first time I felt regret. I felt that I had brought misfortune down upon him by cursing him on that day.

The *writer* reappears as a dreamlike figure clutching refugee forms and a copy of the x-rays from their youth, and makes a bizarre final appearance in Paris as a delegate of the Writer's Union on the eve of the dictator's death. The point is reiterated that these two figures are images of each other and that it is only the *writer*'s gift which separates them. At the same time they share fundamental elements of identity with their Albanian archetype, Constantine:

> En ce monde, la plupart des êtres ne font que rejouer la même pièce. Seuls changent leur regard, leur chevelure, leur stature, comme les perruques que troquent les acteurs avant de retourner en scène interpreter un rôle qu'ils ont maintes et maintes fois répété. Sylvaine et moi ne faisions que revivre ce qui était advenu à mon copain de Moscou, cette nuit-là, dans la neige qui tombait près des grilles de l'Institut Gorki, le visage blafard, sans doute effrayé par les phares des taxis et les fanfares du socialisme, était apparu le médiéval Konstantin. Nous avions beau faire, nous ne pouvions pas ne pas répondre à son appel, nous ne pouvions rejeter notre identification au Cavalier: les rênes, l'itinéraire, tout le reste était depuis longtemps en place. (*L'Ombre* 227)

> In this world most human beings just replay the same story. Only their looks, their hair-dos, and their height are changed, like the wigs that actors swap before returning to the stage to interpret a role which they have played over and over. Sylvaine and I did nothing other than relive that which had happened to my friend from Moscow, on that night when, in the falling snow close to the gates of the Gorki Institute, our faces pale, startled, no doubt, by the headlights of the taxis and the fanfares of socialism, the medieval figure of Constantine appeared. Whatever we did, we could not but respond to his call, we could not repudiate our identification with the knight: the horse, the journey, all the rest had been in place for a long time.

Through the *mise en abyme* Kadare identifies the archetypal elements in the identities of the *narrator* and the *writer*. Through the fiction of the screenplay he shows how the *narrator* attempts, but fails, to emulate the *writer*'s creativity. The points of similarity and difference are clearly demarcated between the two figures. If the main theme of this novel is the perversion of the Albanian life-world and its distorted relationship to the normality of modern life in the French capital as seen through the eyes of the *narrator*, the secondary theme, reflected through the figure of the *writer*, based on Kadare himself, is the necessary perversion of art in an inauthentic life-world (i.e. the transformation of his novel into the second-rate screenplay).

In the final pages the *narrator* and the *writer* are seen cringing in the rear of their respective taxis-cum-carriages in a nightmarish trip through Paris. Each represents a compromise and a failure of a different kind. The *narrator* has failed to bring together his two realities of Albania and France in order to live an authentic life. Hating the regime and the life it enforces in his home country, he has compromised, survived, and thrived as a bureaucrat. However he cannot escape the Albanianness which takes him back home each time, and he does not seek refuge in France. While the *narrator* is a weak character — a typical Kadarean protagonist — his return to his homeland is not motivated by his privileged position, nor is it determined by factors such as family responsibility or the inertia of habit and routine. Underlying his debilitating and inauthentic existence between Albania and France is a deeper truth for Kadare, namely of his Albanianness. Like Mark-Alem in *The Palace of Dreams*, he is deeply and unchangeably Albanian. Yet authentic existence is rendered inaccessible to him by the pseudo-Albanian reality of the dictatorship. The two sides of his existence, Albania and France, reality and imagination, exist in a false existential opposition. He, the everyday Albanian 'new man', is unable to draw on his ethno-national identity and as a result his life swings between two poles of inauthenticity.

If the *narrator* lacks creativity, the *writer* represents the embattled realm of the imagination in the dictatorship. We see him through the eyes of his erstwhile friend and ungifted colleague as withdrawn, arrogant, and hostile. He is not represented as the dissident-cum-hero. His unpopularity with the regime is due to works such as the novel on which the *narrator*'s screenplay is based (*The Twilight of the Steppe-Gods*) and a recent novel which has led to formal arraignment (*The Palace of Dreams*). In both of these works he challenges the regime's image of Albania rather than the ideology of socialism. Against the *narrator*, whose text is defined by confusion of the inner and the outer worlds, the *writer* is revealed as a figure who has not mixed the worlds of imagination and reality, France and Albania. In the final image he stays faithful to Albania, both turning his back on the inauthenticity of life under the dictatorship and remaining impervious to the seductions of Paris. For the Albanian intellectual, the encounter with Paris can lead in only one of two directions: either to a betrayal of his past and exile to the West, or to a renewed and cognizant embrace of the Albanian prison as the true place of his existential identity. In this final image, the *writer* is blinded. Blindness in Kadare's works is a symbol of living in the past and of refusal to live in the present. The blind rhapsodists and old women of Kadare's world live in the past; the hodja in *Chronicle in Stone* blinds himself rather than witness the arrival of communism. The image is ambivalent. Like the Irish-American anthropologist, Bill, in *The File on H.*[83] the *writer* is becoming a rhapsodist, entering the 'second chronology' of those for whom present time is secondary to the national *longue durée* preserved in Albanian language and song. He has renounced the Western environment in order to remain an Albanian. However, this choice also involves a compromise. He is torn between the demands of the dictatorship and those of his Albanian identity symbolized in the figure of Constantine, the eternal Albanian. In the figure of the *writer* Kadare clearly reprises aspects of his own development since the 1970s.

Dissidence and Inauthentic Life

The *narrator* lives in a double world, slipping from one level of consciousness to another. On the boulevards of Paris he is suddenly transported by the sight of black limousines to the guns and barbed wire of Albania's borders:

> Sur les quais, je distinguai au loin quelques corps gisant sur le macadam. Des segments de barbelés frontaliers se tortillaient à leurs côtés et des mares de sang maculaient la chaussée. On n'avait aucun mal à deviner que c'était un lambeau de temps en provenance directe d'Albanie, de la rive pierreuse du lac de Pogradec. De la côte de Saranda, aussi. (*L'Ombre* 186–87)

> On the quays I could make out a long way off some bodies lying on the asphalt. Some twisted bits of barbed wire stretched alongside them and pools of blood stained the street. There was no difficulty in guessing that it was a shred of time straight from Albania, from the pebbly shore of Lake Pogradec. From the coast of Saranda too.

Transported to Lake Pogradec or the beach of Saranda he relives the experiences of border barbarism which were essential to the maintenance of terror in Albania. The deep structures of Albanian experience impinge on modern consciousness, shaping it and rendering the unfamiliar familiar:

> Ce n'était plus seulement l'inversion des clairs et des foncés, comme sur une radio. [. . .] C'était pire. Il y avait là, comme je l'avais décelé quelques jours auparavant, une sorte de vice fondamental. Toutes les pièces du métier à tisser le temps présentaient quelque anomalie. Roulés en boule, comme recroquevillés par la paralysie ou la polio, certains jours commenaient le soir et finissaient à l'aube. [. . .] le plus terrible, malgré tout, demeurait la marche du temps. Désormais, j'étais persuadé qu'il se mouvait à reculons, comme un crabe. [. . .] A un moment donné, je me demandai si j'étais encore de ce monde et si les mots, tout comme les poils de barbe sur le visage d'un mort, ne continuaient pas à pousser en pure perte, absurdement. (*L'Ombre* 206–07)

> It wasn't just the inversion of light and dark, as on an x-ray. [. . .] It was worse. [. . .] There was, as I had disclosed several days before, a sort of fundamental defect. The loom of time was damaged and its fabric flawed. Rolled into a ball, as if twisted by paralysis or polio, some days began in the evening and finished at dawn. [. . .] Even worse was the way time flowed. I was convinced that it was moving backwards, like a crab. [. . .] At one moment I wondered whether I was still of this world and whether the words were continuing to flow from my mouth absurdly and uselessly, like the beard of a dead man.

In these images we can identify the origins of the *narrator*'s traumatized consciousness. The Albanian history of repression and oppression is imagined not as a progression over time but as an eternal presence in parallel worlds. In his drunken and nightmarish sorties through the city, the *narrator* experiences France as a dream world in which past and present, East and West, are superimposed in a phantasmagoria of images of the forces of history, culture, and politics which determine his life.

The *narrator* imagines himself warming slowly to life on entering France, and on returning to Albania he feels his body temperature drop and his vital energies diminish. Kadare used this powerful image to describe his own feelings of emergence and descent on leaving and re-entering Albania. As he enters Michel Piccoli's Parisian apartment he feels the last of the clumps of earth and pieces of gravel dropping from his hair and shoulders.[84] Yet even this powerful metaphor of the relationship of life and death fails as the *narrator* loses his ability to correlate the two spheres of his existence. He finds himself incapable of reconciling the two worlds, and remains caught in a half-way world between reality and imagination, mapping the horrors of Albania onto Paris, just as he and his friends had projected their imaginings of Paris onto their Albanian reality.

Throughout the text sexual attraction symbolizes the connection between Albania and the West. The *narrator*'s friends back home expect lurid descriptions of his exploits in Paris with sexy French women. In France he is overcome by performance anxiety, failing to reach orgasm with his classy Parisian lover, Madame V. and, until the end, with Sylvaine. Consummation of the sexual act becomes a persistent image of the problematical relationship between Albania and the West. Finally, dogged by impotence and terror, the *narrator* warms to life to the point where he can experience sex with Sylvaine as an excruciating act of transmission and connection. As the sperm separates itself from his gelid body, becoming warm in the process and lodging in her womb, the *narrator* experiences the agony of the escape from death to life:

> La chute fut terrifiante; je sentis les sanglots de l'espèce opposer une ultime résistance à la consanguinité, et le fouet cruel de la volonté, et le péché, et la terreur de châtiment. [. . .] J'avais l'impression d'entendre des aboiements se rapprocher. J'aurais voulu lui rendre ses caresses, mais je ne pouvais rien faire d'autre que me protéger le visage de mes avant-bras contre la morsure des chiens.
>
> Cela dura longtemps. Le temps restait comme suspendu, jusqu'à ce que je sentisse une douleur inhumaine me parcourir l'épine dorsale à l'instant où mon sperme se détachait enfin de moi et, tel quel, encore gelé, charriant l'épouvante, comme les blocs de glace flottant dans les ténèbres là où se séparent les confins des mondes, pénétrait dans les profondeurs de son ventre. (*L'Ombre* 251–52)

> The fall was terrifying; I felt nature putting up a final resistance to consanguinity. I felt the cruel whip of desire, I felt sin and the fear of punishment. [. . .] I thought I could hear the baying of hounds heading towards me. I would have returned her caresses, but all I could do was use my arms to protect my face from the ravening animals.
>
> It lasted a long time. Time seemed suspended. Finally I felt an inhuman pain run down my spine just as my sperm finally separated itself from me and, still frozen, carrying its terror with it, like blocks of ice floating in the darkness where the edges of the worlds break away from each other, it penetrated to the depths of her womb.

He has achieved sexual union with Doruntine, thereby breaking both the incest taboo and the pledge to return. In a state of apocalyptic trepidation he expects to be dragged down again into the Albanian nether world:

> Mon propre tourment suffit à m'anéantir! [. . .] J'ai péché avec ma sœur. [. . .] Je me demandai à nouveau si nous n'étions pas le même être scindé par hasard et dont les deux moitiés cherchaient enfin à se rejoindre. Le taxi glissait dans le noir; les yeux mi-clos, j'attendais la chute. Ce que j'avais fait me paraissait de plus en plus abominable. Ce n'était pas seulement l'inceste. L'inceste en soi n'avait été que le premier tabou que j'avais transgressé, mainfestation superficielle d'un mal plus profond. J'avais violé un autre pacte beaucoup plus important. J'étais venu ici à certaines conditions. J'étais un mort qui devait s'en tenir à la forme qui lui avait été concédée. Ma nationalité le voulait ainsi. Mes frontières et mon destin aussi. (*L'Ombre* 254)

> My suffering was enough to destroy me! [. . .] I had sinned with my sister [. . .] I asked myself again whether we weren't perhaps the same being separated by chance, whose two halves were seeking to rejoin each other. The taxi slid through the dark; my eyes half-closed, I waited for the fall. What I had done seemed to me more and more abominable. It wasn't just incest. Incest was just the first taboo which I had broken, the surface manifestation of a deeper evil. I had broken another, much more important pact. I had come here under certain conditions. I was a dead body which had to keep the form granted to it. My nationality wanted it thus. My frontiers and my destiny also.

But the power of those forces that tortured him in the night and that appear to him without warning in the daylight of Paris seems to have been broken. As the lift takes him up to his hotel room on the way to the airport in the final paragraphs, he experiences a sense of ecstatic redemption. The transmission of the message of Albanianness, symbolized in the sexual act with Sylvaine, leads to a fantasy of personal and national redemption.

> Puis, comme l'ascenseur s'élevait, engloutissant les étages, premier, deuxième, dans un fracas de chaînes brisées, de portes et de grilles arrachées, de nouveaux aboiements de chiens, de coup de marteau enfonçant des clous dans des croix, parmi les barbelés qui m'écorchaient, m'ensanglantaient sans parvenir pour autant à me faire rebrousser chemin, je me rendis compte que s'était produit l'incroyable: j'avais franchi la frontière et étais resté en vie.
>   À présent, ce n'était plus l'ascenseur qui m'élevait, mais un hymne antique, et après moi en montaient des milliers et des milliers d'autres, toutes les nobles et graves générations d'Albanais laissant derrière elles la glaciation de la mort au milieu des carillons, des alléluia et de l'annonce: 'Albanie est ressuscitée, amen!' (*L'Ombre* 258)

> The elevator ascended, devouring the floors, the first, the second, amidst the din of breaking chains, of gates and grills being torn off their hinges, of baying dogs, of hammer blows driving nails into the cross. Barbs flayed my skin, leaving me bleeding but not turning me back. And then I realized that the unbelievable had happened: I had broken through the border and had survived. Now it was no longer the elevator which lifted me up, but an ancient hymn, and after me thousands and thousands of others rose up on it as well, all the noble and solemn generations of Albanians leaving behind the iciness of death amidst bells and alleluias: 'Albania is risen, amen!'

In these final paragraphs Kadare's prose is at its most ambiguous. The world of psychotic self-fulfilment that flashes through the narrative, intruding dream onto reality, appears to have triumphed in an insanity born of the *narrator*'s inability to integrate the inner and the outer worlds. In this ending, liberation to the West is revealed as the fantasy of a dying man. If this redemption can be seen as release from the dictatorship, then the ending is positive; if, however, as seems more likely, the redemption is the psychosis of a figure who is incapable of bringing together imagination and reality, the Paris of his dreams with the death-in-life in Albania, the ending is as gloomy as that of Kadare's model, Kafka's *The Trial*. It confirms Albanian existence as schizoid, operating between two mutually exclusive spheres of imagination and reality, death and life, which remain incapable of resolution and which must lead, sooner or later, to tragedy. Where the authorial figure of the *writer* has achieved connection and clarity through his identification with Constantine in his novel, the *narrator* does not seem to. His experience is marked by confusion, inauthenticity, and madness as he fails to reconcile the oppositions of East and West, past and present, Albania and France. He remains a victim of the dictatorship, a figure whose experience of everyday life as the gloomy, subterranean inauthenticity in his native land is incapable of preparing him for the experience of everyday life in a contemporary Western environment. Kadare's novel is thus a testament to contemporary Albanian reality which disallows life as normality. Like so many heroes of earlier Central and Eastern European literature, Kadare's *narrator* is a victim not of political oppression, but of the dislocation of imagination and reality in the dictatorship. This is the tragedy of everyday life under the regime.

The critique of the inauthenticity of life under the regime, rather than of the regime itself, is the key to *The Shadow*. Kadare does not use the *mise en abyme* to collapse past and present into the mythological time of the legend. On the contrary, he sets up the legend as a mythical and timeless standard of Albanian being against which the deformations of the present can be judged. Constantine's achievement of the impossible, of making the transition from death to life and back again, symbolizes both the necessity and the impossibility of overcoming Albanian identity in order to live. This is an extremely negative assessment from a writer whose fame rests partly on his powerful evocations of his nation's identity. However, we must see it in the context of both the continuum of Kadare's work and the metafiction of the author's death. Kadare's representation of communist Albania since his repatriation from Moscow has been uniformly negative. In *The City without Signs*, *The General of the Dead Army*, and *The Great Winter* the communist present is grey and wintry, characterized by the rain and fog that the dictator hated.[85] For Kadare the Albania of the dictatorship is inauthentic, and the art born of the dictatorship is damaged by its provenance. In returning to his native country, rather than going into exile, he chose a life in which his art would of necessity be compromised:[86]

> Naturellement, comme toute œuvre d'art née dans la violence, celle-ci pâtissait de toutes les déficiences, mutilations, défigurations liées à la monstruosité de l'époque. [. . .] Qu'il s'agît d'une œuvre gravement abimé, c'était évident. Elle avait été principalement déformée par la pression de la tyrannie. (*Le Poids* 540–41)

> Naturally, like every work of art born amidst violence, this one suffered from all of the deficiencies, mutilations, and distortions which were the result of this monstrous era. [. . .] We are clearly dealing here with a body of work that is seriously deformed. It was the pressure of the tyranny which caused this damage.

In the context of the imminent death of the dictator and the battle for supremacy of the various factions in the Party, Kadare wrote a novel whose reading depends on the outcome of history. Should he, the author, be killed in the struggles for power and reprisal, the archetypal fate of Constantine will have been reconfirmed with his interment, and the message of Albanianness will not be passed on to the world other than as a message from the grave passed on by his friend and literary executor, Claude Durand. Kadare's death will signify the failure of resolution of the Albanian life-in-death and Albanian history will continue its gloomy subterranean existence. Should he survive the regime however, the novel will await a different outcome. After the short period of office of Hoxha's successor, Ramiz Alia, this is what happened with the revolution of 1990/91, in which the negative paradigm was finally broken and a period of change commenced. The publication of the novel in 1994 marked Kadare's dissolution of the metafiction, releasing the novel from its grave-existence in the bank-vault into the life-world of Albania after the dictatorship.

Death of the Dictator, 1985

After the first months of 1984 Enver Hoxha withdrew from public view on the pretext of completing his memoirs. It was clear that he was sick and incapable of maintaining his public role. Ramiz Alia ran the affairs of state, watched hawkishly by Nexhmije. The conservative Bavarian state premier, Franz Josef Strauß, visited Tirana at this time, offering loans and investment in an important overture from the West. He was rebuffed on the basis that Albania no longer (since the new constitution in 1976) dealt with capitalist concepts such as international monetary loans. The chances are, however, that in this crucial era of transition, nothing was about to be changed, no matter how dire the economic need of the people.[87]

Hoxha made his last public appearance on 28 November 1984 for the celebration of Albanian National Day.

> La mine lugubre, comme s'il avait déjà passé contrat avec la mort, contrairement à tous les usages du communisme, il ne faisait rien pour dissimuler sa morosité. (Le Poids 542)

> With the grim expression of someone who had already entered into an agreement with death, against the usual communist custom, he did nothing to hide his despondency.

Hoxha's 'Salute to the People', according to his biographer Thomas Schreiber, was a lyrical evocation of his achievements in the light of the glorious history and rich literary traditions of the Albanian people:

> Chaque pouce du sol albanais est à la fois chantier de construction et de création, école et barricade infranchissable pour l'ennemi et en même temps une estrade

où nos gens, les créateurs de tous les biens dont nous jouissons, chantent à la gloire du Parti, du peuple, de la liberté et du socialisme.[88]

Today every inch of Albanian soil is the scene of construction and of creation; it is a school, it is an insurmountable barricade to her enemies; it is a stage on which our people, creators of all of our benefits, sing the praise of the Party, of their life, of freedom, and of socialism.[89]

However, notes Schreiber, even this last address to his people was full of warnings against the 'enemy within'.[90] This was four months before his death. Unlike many of the communist leaders, Hoxha never adopted the iconography of immortality in his ubiquitous appearances on signboards and the screen. He was represented in the different stages of his life, ageing, and even sick, as he got older. (After his death, according to Jean-Paul Champseix, he even appeared as a 'chubby angel in the corners of posters'.[91]) Advanced diabetes robbed him of a limb and then of his sanity. In a state of advanced dementia he spent his final days and nights tormented by the bloodied ghosts of his past. 'Sombrant dans le démence, amputé d'une jambe, hurlant toute la nuit, terrifié par les ombres qu'il croyait voir défiler dans sa chambre, le dictateur vivait ses derniers jours' (*Le Poids* 547, 'Sinking into dementia, one leg amputated, screaming throughout the night, terrified of the shades which he believed were passing through his room, the dictator lived out his last days'). On the night of 10/11 April Enver Hoxha died, aged 76. Ramiz Alia was elected by the Central Committee to succeed Hoxha as First Secretary although Nexhmije, Kadare's Lady Macbeth of Tirana, kept a steely grasp on the reins of power.[92] The death was announced the next morning. At the funeral on 15 April, Alia signalled to Albania and the world that Hoxha's political line would continue with no deviations. No changes in domestic or foreign policy should be expected. At this dangerous point of transition the regime clove to rigid orthodoxy in order to maintain stability. But what had Enverism achieved? After over forty-five years in power, writes Jacques, the regime of Enver Hoxha still ruled over the poorest nation in Europe.

With the highest birth-rate in Europe they had the lowest per capita income. Instead of the much vaunted 'dictatorship of the proletariat', only 4% of the population held membership in the ruling Communist party. Their industrial plants were becoming antiquated. Spare parts were not available. Bureaucratic control was top-heavy. Labour unions were forbidden. The peasant on a collectivized farm produced much less than he would on his own little plot. State food shops usually had long queues waiting, but shelves were often bare. People were not free to change their job or their residence or to visit another country. They were not free to choose their own employment or profession, to drive an automobile instead of a bicycle or to run for public office. They were not free to subscribe to a foreign magazine or newspaper, to voice disagreement with party policy or to practice the religion of their choice. Then, they were quite isolated from both East and West; they were quite alone.[93]

On the evening of the dictator's death, 10 April, Kadare's enemies in the Union of Writers, the Politburo, and Central Committee conspired one last time to arraign the writer. The short novel *Clair de lune*, critical of Albanian society, but hardly as explosive in its implications as other works, underwent the process of formal critique by the Party. A girl in a modern factory is subjected to humiliation, bullying, and sexual harassment in this exposé of the narrowness and malice of contemporary Albanian society. Civic culture feeds on frustration, suspicion, and hatred. The idealized communist solidarity of *The Wedding*, for example, is conspicuously absent.

As he was opening the hastily organized sitting to denounce the work, the President of the Union of Writers, Dritëro Agolli, along with other members of the Central Committee, already knew that Hoxha had passed away.[94] Kadare immediately sensed the influence of Nexhmije.

> Au début de 1985, poussé peut-être par le diable, ou comme quelqu'un qui, une lanterne à la main, explore les ténèbres de son jardin pour vérifier si le danger s'est éloignee, je publiai ma nouvelle *Clair de lune*. La réaction fut instantanée. Visiblement, l'épouse du tyran s'était d'ores et déjà emparée des rênes. On sentait là son style, son étroitesse d'ésprit, cette animosité rancuneuse qui, à la différence de celle de son mari, était marquée chez elle d'impatience. (*Le Poids* 546)

> At the beginning of 1985, moved by the devil, perhaps, or like someone who explores the dark at the bottom of his garden with a lantern in his hand to see if the danger has disappeared, I published my novella, *Clair de lune*. The reaction was instantaneous. Clearly the wife of the dictator had already seized the reins. You could recognize her style, the narrowness of spirit, the spiteful animosity which, unlike that of her husband, was characterized by impatience.

In this gesture Kadare reads the panicked obsession with remaining true to the Party line, with maintaining continuity and control in the crucial period of the dictator's death, and indeed the days and months following Hoxha's death were marked by a hysterical need to pledge ongoing allegiance to the dictator's memory and legacy.[95]

Kadare ends *The Weight of the Cross* with a curious but entirely appropriate image of the dead Hoxha, not as the senile paranoiac screaming with fear, nor as the ruthless dictator at the height of his power, but as the young dandy of 1941 crossing the path of one of the delegates at the first meeting of the Albanian Communist Party. There is none of the anger that might be expected, nor the aggression that is expressed in the later documentation of the regime's fall, *Albanian Spring*. Owing something perhaps to Bulgakov, this image reveals the writer's fascination with the similarities and contradictions in his lifelong nemesis and guardian.

> Son visage était pâle, mais serein et beau. On eût dit que, libéré de ses démons, il avait fini par remettre le masque dont on lui avait naguère fait don. [. . .] L'air angélique, alors âgé de trente-trois ans, l'âge du Christ à sa résurrection, vêtu à la dernière mode, arborant une chaîne de montre à son gousset et une canne de dandy qu'il faisait tournoyer entre ses doigts, il avait surgi devant le délégué comme le diable dans les contes anciens. *Quo vadis, Satanas . . .* (*Le Poids* 549)[96]

> His face was pale, but calm and beautiful. One might have said that, freed of his demons, he ended up redonning the mask that had not long ago been given to him. [. . .] With an angelic expression, thirty-three years old, the age of Christ at his resurrection, clothed in the latest fashions, sporting a watch-chain from

his fob and turning a dandy's cane in his hand, he suddenly appeared before the delegate like the devil in an old story. *Quo vadis, Satanas . . .*

For Kadare there are deep links between the writer and the dictator. Hoxha was for so long his alter ego and his nemesis. Kadare imagined Hoxha as the megalomaniac artist whose visions of a new Albania are narcissistic fantasies. He was Zeus to the writer's Prometheus, the man of power versus the man of imagination. Creator of modern Albania, father to the nation and bloodied tyrant, he was the man who brought unity to this land divided over millennia. He gained its independence and then sacrificed it to his dream of absolute control. The one could merge into the other. Kadare was fascinated by the dialectic of power and imagination in the Hoxha story and the interdependence of the writer and the dictator was long since apparent to him.

> Ma situation était plus ou moins similaire à celle qu'on rencontre dans les mythes anciens, quand, entre père et fils, entre le créateur et sa créature, s'est établi un rapport tragique, autrement dit quand l'un est voué à supprimer l'autre. (*Le Poids* 463)

> My situation was more or less similar to that of the ancient myths, in which a tragic relationship develops between father and son, between the creator and his creature, when the one devotes himself to the elimination of the other.

The year 1985 saw momentous changes, despite the attempts of the regime to pretend that all would continue as before. In the Soviet Union Mikhail Gorbachev, the sorcerer's apprentice, took power as General Secretary, announcing a raft of changes to render socialism open, flexible, and effective. But having cast the spell of freedom, he was unable to rescind it. Constitutional change, reform of parliament, restructuring of the bureaucracy, nuclear disarmament, rapprochement with the West, and withdrawal from Afghanistan followed, leaving the other communist regimes bewildered and increasingly out of touch. In Albania an atmosphere of pious mourning and steely control set in as Ramiz Alia and Nexhmije attempted to maintain stability. In fact Enver had done much of their work for them, having compelled an already politically docile populace through the use of terror and impoverishment to accept complete control, and eliminating those figures most likely to have created instability from within the ranks of the Party.[97]

The Wrong Side of History: *Aeschylus or the Great Loser*, 1985

Kadare's first major literary-intellectual essay, *Aeschylus or the Great Loser*, has its origins in this period of stand-off with 'the monster', Kadare's ongoing metaphor for the regime.[98] The first version, *Aeschylus or the Eternal Loser*, was published as the preface to an edition of the works of Aeschylus in early 1985. Hoxha had not yet died, but the signs of imminent death were clear to those on the inside, at least. In 1988 Kadare revised and augmented the text and changed the name to *Aeschylus or the Great Loser*; the revised version was published with Fayard as an independent paperback in 1995 and in volume eleven of *Œuvres* in 2002. Sensing change, Kadare begins the first of his long literary-intellectual essays, in which he develops his understanding of the role of the writer in Albanian culture. In the context of the possibility of change, he presents a detailed, discursive rendition of his conception of Albanian culture. In this reading, Albania is a Balkan and European entity, linked at its origins with ancient Greece and unrelated to the Ottoman, Soviet, and Slavic civilizations which subsequently threatened it. The essay is a powerful counter-interpretation of the past and the future of Albania, to that of the regime after the death of its only real leader. Gathering together themes and arguments about Albanian identity which he had developed since the early 1960s, Kadare presents a reading of his country's culture which differs significantly from the official Albanianism of the regime.

The Common Cultural Origins of Albania and Greece

For Kadare a nation's identity is to be found in its language and literature. Literature represents national memory and the base level of literature is remembrance. Whether oral, where remembering was the single function, or written, where it has been overlaid with other functions, literature is primarily remembering. Without remembrance a community or a nation cannot move forward. However, a literature and, with it, a nation, can be lost. This is what almost happened to Albania. Even dominant cultures lose huge amounts of their culture and history, as the loss of most of ancient Greek drama demonstrates. Small cultures are much more exposed to loss, and hence to the forgetfulness of the world. What hope was there for Albania after half a millennium of Ottoman occupation and a further half-century of global isolation under the communists?

As we have seen in relation to *The Palace of Dreams*, Kadare posits an original 'Illyro-Albano-Greek' civilization of the Balkan peninsula, which pre-dated the Slav migrations of the following millennium, and found expression above all in the epic songs of the Homeric tradition.[99] This civilization was shared from the Ionian islands to the plains of Kosovo and across to Thrace, and from the Accursed Mountains throughout the peninsula to mainland Greece, the Peloponnese peninsula, and beyond to the islands of the eastern Mediterranean, to Ionia and Anatolia. It was a living tradition of oral literature throughout these lands, a form of expression which accompanied life through change and adaptation, incorporating and deleting, adding and modifying the collected body of human experiences.

This living literature represented memory. For Greek civilization the war in Troy became the primal collective deed which tormented a people and generated the possibility of great literature through the discovery of tragedy. Literature — and the nation — was born of the recognition of the misuse of power and the loss of national innocence.

> Tout comme quelqu'un qui, subitement, se rappelle un méfait commis dans sa jeunesse, qu'il croyait avoir oublié, de même le people grec, arrivé à maturité, sentit se réveiller en lui le remords d'un crime perpétré dans son jeune âge. Huit cents ans plus tôt, il avait étouffé dans son sommeil un autre people, les Troyens. [. . .] Il devint la nourriture essentielle de la littérature grecque antique (*Eschyle* 15–16)[100]

> Like someone who suddenly remembers a misdemeanour committed in his youth, which he thought he had long since forgotten, the Greek people, having

come to maturity, felt remorse for a crime committed at a young age. Eight
hundred years earlier it had extinguished another people, the Trojans. [. . .] This
deed became the source of ancient Greek literature.

The pre-literate, oral epic represented a civilization that died in Greece with
Aeschylus and the birth of drama. The new, modern form of literature was fixed,
written down, and preserved. The end of the Homeric tradition in Greece was
a product of, and charted the development of, new forms of human culture
and society. The origins of Greek development can be traced back to the small
historical window in history between the Persian Wars and the fall of Periclean
Athens, during which time the oral, pre-historical culture of myth and Homeric
rhapsody made the crucial step forward to the modern literary form of the tragedy
and to the creation of a civic state. The exigencies of the city-state in the period
of Athenian florescence between the Persian Wars and the end of the Periclean era
determined the new literature. For Kadare, Aeschylus is the figure who forged the
transitional path from the oral legacy of Homeric Greek to the written forms of
modern literature.

The living, moving, and changing medium of the epic was lost, but new forms
of determinacy were gained. In Aeschylean drama, the unitary song fragmented
into separate voices. The totality was lost, but the differentiation of the chorus
and the protagonists emerged. In *The Persians*, Aeschylus splits the voices, putting
the enemy onto the Greek stage. For the first time the point of view of the other
is represented, and right is distinguished from ethnicity. Literary objectivity or
irony enables the audience-members to remove themselves from their personal and
communal attachments and view questions in terms of ethics and morality as well
as ethnicity and identity. In representing the Persians on the Greek stage, Aeschylus
discovered a new dialectic between literature and the community. In educating the
Greeks to supersede simple identifications Aeschylus, for Kadare, is a patriot and
a nation-builder of a higher order. However, the rulers of Athens objected to the
representation of the Persians as a potentially destabilizing and seditious moment.

In the process of development of literary representation, drawing on the rich
fund of legends from the area, Aeschylus sketched out the basic themes of political
literature for Greek, and implicitly, Albanian, culture. *The Persians* introduces right
and rights into the language of the state against the laws of belonging, power,
and control. Drama accompanied the political and social development of Athens,
commenting on it and relating it to the broader concerns of human life. For the first
time we can speak of an aesthetic education, or *paideia*. In the *Prometheus* trilogy, of
which only the first play, *Prometheus in Chains*, survives, Aeschylus gives expression
to another archetypal theme of European political literature, the ancient political
myth of the 'new man'. The play is about a conflict between the gods regarding
the destiny of humanity. At stake is the survival of humanity or its annihilation
in favour of a new race (*Eschyle* 88–89). The wish to change humanity, to replace
existing people with the 'new man' of utopian dreams and despotic control, has been
the aim of the worst tyrannies of human history. Aeschylus' love of humanity is
translated into Prometheus' action to save that humanity despite its weaknesses and
against the despotic wishes of the god (*Eschyle* 90). Aeschylus thus uses the figure of

FIG. 28 (above): The ruins of Butrint near Saranda, remnants of the ancient Greek-Illyrian civilisation, referred to in the Aeschylus essay. (Photo: Peter Morgan.)

FIG. 29 (below): The amphitheatre of Butrint, referred to at the beginning of *The Great Winter*. (Photo: Peter Morgan.)

Prometheus, saviour of mankind, to justify the ways of *man* to *god*, 'speaking truth to power' for the first time. Prometheus in this version is the Titan who conspired to save mankind from Zeus' disillusionment. Taking pity on humanity, he rebels against the calamity that his gift of divination allows him to foresee and that Zeus has planned for his first creation. The gift of fire is Prometheus' defiant act of compassion and belief in the possibilities of human development, in opposition to the supreme leader's apocalyptic disappointment, absolute control, and sweeping intentions of total change. Prometheus is condemned for having stolen the celestial file, but in fact his 'dossier' is based on the much broader crime of 'amour envers le genre humain' (*Eschyle* 91). His gifts to mankind, that 'crowd of benighted shadows', include memory, writing, thinking. 'Ainsi, tout en symbolisant la révolte et le martyre éternels, la figure de Prométhée incarne-t-elle aussi le progrès, le génie du travail, de la civilisation et de la libre pensée créatrice' (*Eschyle* 92, 'Thus, in symbolizing rebellion and eternal martyrdom, the figure of Prometheus also embodies progress, the spirit of work, of civilization and of free, creative thought'). Prometheus is thus the archetypal modern rebel, who not only dared to defy the gods, but who condemned Zeus as a tyrant and predicted his fall. Giving mankind fire, he enabled existing, evolutionary (historical) humanity to evade the fate that Zeus intended, namely annihilation and replacement with a 'new man', ideal, unchanging, and uncorrupted by history or the desire for self-determination. The old humanity, beloved by Prometheus, is the evolutionary (as opposed to the revolutionary) human being. Kadare's explication of the Prometheus myth is, of course, a late version of his own increasingly defiant advocation of Albanian history and tradition against the modernizing sweep of the socialist agenda.

The implicit critique of the regime's reduction of Albanian history to a past stage, preceding and superseded by the revolutionary history of the new Albania and the new man, which we identified in the analysis of *The Three-Arched Bridge*, is presented in the Aeschylus essay immediately after the death of 'Zeus', in the form of a literary-cultural thesis. In the two lost continuations of Prometheus' story, we know that the Titan finishes by obtaining Zeus' pardon in exchange for his revelation of the nature of Zeus' fall; and in the third part of the trilogy Prometheus reclaims his place on Olympus and becomes the god of artisans, ceramics, and creativity. In the 1990s, as part of his ongoing engagement with and debunking of the regime after its fall, Kadare wrote a continuation of the Prometheus story in his only drama, *Bad Season on Olympus*. Of all of Kadare's literary-political themes, that of the relationship between Zeus and Prometheus proved the most flexible and constructive in the writer's commentary on his relationship to the dictator and the regime. In this later play, the reinstatement of Prometheus represents a rapprochement between power and imagination, politics and art, after the stand-off of the preceding half century.

Whereas the *Prometheus* plays are concerned with the dialectic between power and humanity, the *Oresteia* gives expression to an even more basic conflict in ancient Balkan cultures, between matriarchy and patriarchy, the personal and the social in the structuration of human society. The ancient law of the Furies, based on individual vengeance, is in decline and the new law of the Greek city-state, of Athena and Apollo, based on a legal code, is becoming predominant. Where *Prometheus* is about power and human life, the *Oresteia* is about justice and vengeance. Aeschylus tackles a fundamental question of the urban-civil society of the Greeks, asking whether matriarchy or patriarchy, endogamy or exogamy, vengeance (vendetta) or justice (law) should be the foundation of human society.

> L'un des thèmes principaux de l'œuvre est celui de la primauté reconnue à l'ascendance paternelle ou à l'ascendance maternelle. [. . .] Ce débat est l'un des points fondamentaux sur lesquels ont été édifiés tous les codes juridiques anciens et récents, et il a suscité, dans l'histoire de l'humanité, des drames anonymes sans nombre. (*Eschyle* 102)

> One of the principal themes of the work is that of the primacy accorded to paternal or maternal ancestry. [. . .] This conflict is one of the foundations on which ancient as well as modern juridical codes are built and it has given rise to innumerable anonymous dramas in the history of humanity.

In the environment of the Greek city-state Aeschylus found himself obliged to engage with political power in ways which involved new demands on and new dangers to literature. The written word, the individuation of voice, the introduction of moral conscience and plurality of perspective over and against the single voice of communal identity, represented a threat to political power which the writer had to negotiate. His position became precarious. Literature now existed — potentially — in opposition to power. It was a threat to and threatened by power. The writer could be forced into exile, the written word could be extinguished, and the text could disappear as a result of political censorship or the movements of history. Kadare had explored these themes as early as 1965 in the figure of the fictive Trojan poet Thremoh in *The Monster*. Censorship had become one of the determinants of writing. Politics was intervening in literature, manipulating and perverting life. Kadare imagines his embittered poet fleeing to the shores of Illyria or even further, in order to escape his country. But exile, whether self-imposed or under compulsion, is no solution to the writer in conflict with his political masters. 'Il porterait la Grèce et la Grèce le porterait' (*Eschyle* 185, 'He would carry Greece and Greece would carry him').

And yet in this environment, too, Aeschylus shows a spirit of creative compromise. Far from being simply a dissident, he seeks to find an agreement with power. 'Une lecture attentive des Perses révèle bien vite le désir d'Eschyle de composer une pièce que les autorités pussent accepter. Le souci du compromis y est apparent' (*Eschyle* 71, 'A close reading of *The Persians* soon reveals Aeschylus' desire to write a play which the authorities could accept. There is a clear concern for compromise'). Despite his representation of a plurality of voices, Aeschylus is not simply the voice of defiance against political authority. Why, asks Kadare, was the poet willing to submit to the 'regard glacé du fonctionnaire qu'il avail en face de lui' (*Eschyle* 72, 'the icy glare of the official standing opposite him?'). Was it through fear for his safety? No, writes Kadare. It was because the great writer recognized the legitimacy of the state's concerns. The Greek state was obliged to protect itself from the dissolution that could arise as a result of the free play of the literary imagination in the political context of the threat from the Persians. The writer also had to represent the national interest, and the state had to limit the writer who acted too strongly against its interests in this situation.

> Les tragiques grecs furent les premiers à prendre conscience du péril d'une interprétation abusive de la liberté. Les interventions de la censure, la partialité des jurys ou des stratèges étaient naturellement gênantes, mais une liberté sans limites, laissant l'esprit vaguer a sa guise, se serait sans doute révélee encore plus néfaste pour l'art. Elle aurait engendré une mollesse, un relâchement, une dispersion qui eussent rendu consécutivement impossibles la pression, la tension si indispensables au façonnage de l'oeuvre d'art. (*Eschyle* 79–80)

> The Greek tragedians were the first to take to heart the danger of an interpretation which was damaging to liberty. The interventions of censorship, the partiality of juries or of strategists were naturally a hindrance, but freedom without limits, leaving the spirit to roam unhindered, would have turned out to be even more damaging to art. It would have bred a softness, a slackening, a thinning out which would have rendered impossible the tension and the pressure so necessary to the creation of a work of art.

Aeschylus, like Kadare, was also a guardian of the state as the structure in which the Greek nation lived, regardless of its current regime. It is this concern for the role of the writer as nation-builder and as custodian of the ethnic community which is so compelling in Kadare's analysis. In the fifth century BC, Greece reached the evolutionary point where the rich anarchy of competing forces indicated a society in a state of ferment and change which must find a structure, or exhaust itself in the internecine struggles foreshadowed in Aeschylus' *The Seven against Thebes*. The Greek city-states remained fragmented even while under duress from foreign forces (in, for example, *The Seven against Thebes*). This disunity is reflected culturally in the contradictory and conflicting fragments of Greek myth and history. Cultural unity, and the possibility of political unity, were brought about through the creation of Greek tragedy as the unified cosmos of the nation. Without the consolidating genius of tragedy, the anarchic cultural wealth of the Greeks would have exhausted itself, to become a conflicting and competing mass of cultural directions.

Kadare compares the Persians in Greece to the Ottomans in the Balkans, but reference to the Soviets in the early 1960s in Albania, and to all imperialist or colonialist forces, is implicit in the argument. As the moral conscience and creative legislator of the people, the poet must also protect the nation-state from external as well as internal destructive forces:

> Eschyle n'oublie pas de rappeler que la Grèce subissait l'attaque d'un Etat tyrannique, arriéré à tous égards, qui, s'il venait à la soumettre, éteindrait à jamais la lumière et la démocratie à laquelle sa culture et sa civilisation avaient donné le jour. (*Eschyle* 74)

> Aeschylus doesn't forget that Greece was subjected to the attacks of a tyrannical state, backward in all respects, which, if it managed to conquer Greece, would have extinguished forever the light and the democracy which Greek culture and civilization brought to the light of day.

Aeschylus represents the point of transition from orality to a literacy in Greek culture, a dangerous point, since it involved abandoning the old mode of transmission, which depended on human memory and moving to the new mode of writing as the means of committing to words the dramatic narrative. The danger of this new literature, for Kadare, was its fragility. War, invasion, occupation, or cultural decrepitude could lead to irretrievable loss. Of the sealed stone epics of the fictive Trojan poet Thremoh in *The Monster* only half a line remains, discovered in the sand of the Tartar steppes, after the destruction of Troy and the disappearance of the Hittite civilization which provided the exiled Trojan with temporary refuge. For Kadare, Aeschylus is both the originator and the 'great loser' of ancient Greek literature, because he too suffered this fate. Of his seventy estimated plays, only seven remain, because the Emperor Hadrian centuries later called for an anthology of the best Greek dramas. Even Aeschylus survived only through the intervention of one man who decided that a selection of his plays must be preserved through the 'froid mirroir latin' (*Eschyle* 166) for the edification of Imperial Rome.

The drama of Aeschylus was played out in the amphitheatres of Apollonia and Butrint (near modern-day Saranda) as well as in Athens and Delphi. Aeschylus' themes link the cultures of the Balkans as an original cultural neighbourhood. However, the paths of the Greek and the Albanian world began to separate and diverge. The bedrock of the oral epic, which was common to both and to the European literary tradition, became obsolete in Greek literature with the new political and social developments. By the time of the Roman Empire Greek literature had made the transition to world literature, de-contextualized as classical high culture in Rome and for the succeeding centuries in the European Renaissance.

Albania's original twin, Greece, survived to become a modern linguistic and cultural entity whereas Albania did not. Albania did not have its Aeschylus. Its oral epic continued as a living literature, to be sure, but was threatened with diminution and loss. Like a wild flower it bloomed on the margins of European civilization. But its time of florescence passed and it became dry and fossilized. Albania's heroic song did not make the transition to a literary culture until over two millennia later, when the national awakening took place. But by that time, the heroic literature of antiquity had been fragmented, deformed, and mutilated by centuries of regression, cultural servitude, dilution, and subjection.

> Tel fut le sort qui échut dans une certaine mesure au gros de l'épopée albanaise, qui, n'ayant pas eu la chance d'être consignée par écrit au moment opportun, parvint jusqu'au xxe siècle gravement mutilé, parfois jusqu'à l'irréparable. (*Eschyle* 79)

> This was by and large the fate which befell Albanian epic. Not having been consigned to writing at the right moment in its history, Albanian epic reached the twentieth century seriously damaged, in some cases irreparably.

The image of the lost moment in the creation of cultural unity is the key to Kadare's Albanian identity. The metaphors of frozenness, stagnation, and morbidity, which are repeatedly invoked in relation to Albania in Kadare's work, point to this state of cultural arrestation as the fundamental problem of Albanian identity. Against this, the particular political problems of the present, even of the socialist regime, are a symptom rather than a cause.

Aeschylus is thus not only poet but judge of the nation and the affairs of men, conscious of moral as well as ethnic responsibility. It is this confluence of (social and individual) conscience with narrative which gives a new depth to Greek tragedy in Aeschylus. He is no longer a naive bard, but has become the modern writer whose role is active and engaged on behalf of the nation and humanity. Thus there are two forces at work within the great national work of art: the force of national responsibility, of unity in a cultural, linguistic and even political sense, and the force of human responsibility, of unity in the broader battle between civilization and barbarism. The two fundamental questions of Kadare's own literary life, of belonging and judging, of ethnicity and right, are thus formulated by way of the figure of Aeschylus. These are the forces which determine Kadare's writing and which are the key to his work.

Albanian Traditional Culture and the Links to Europe

In the remnants of Albanian culture Kadare finds the archetypal forms of the Greek myths and legends. In the Kanun are to be found the petrified remains of the Homeric social code based on vengeance, vendetta, and *besa*, the core values of the warrior society. Here, matriarchy, the 'law of blood', remains stronger than the legal codes of the patriarchal state, which did not eventuate in Albania. In the marriage and funeral rituals of the Kanun are fossilized the ancient tragic world-view of the original Balkan civilization. The Kanun, from being the living accompaniment of a developing culture, became the remnant of an ancient codification of laws and right. Kadare's view of the Kanun, expressed in a passage which is strongly reminiscent of the deserter's idyll in *The General*, is strongly equivocal.

> Des tintements de sonnailles et des aboiements de chiens de berger, des bruits de moulin, de forge, des débats, des parties de chasse, des cérémonies nuptiales, etc., sont interrompus par l'intervention brutale de la mort et de la violence: meurtres, atrocités, enlèvements, outrages à la table de l'hôte, violations de l'hospitalité, vendettas se perpétuant de génération en génération, justification de la reprise du sang, puis dénonciation de la même pratique, jugement par le jury des anciens, cérémonies mortuaires, tombeaux etc. (*Eschyle* 113–14)

> The tinkling of the bells, the barking of the shepherds' dogs, the sounds of the mill, of the forge, of discussions, of hunting parties and of marriage ceremonies, etc. are interrupted by the brutal sounds of death and violence: murders, atrocities, abductions, outrages at the table of the host, violations of hospitality, vendettas lasting for generations, defence of the taking of blood, followed by denunciations of the same practice, judgment by juries of elders, death ceremonies, tombs, etc.

Comparable to other primitive European legal codes in its origins, this traditional Albanian code of law represents for Kadare the legalistic spirit, the aspiration of the nation for order and structure. However, it became rigid during Albania's lost years. 'Véritable encyclopédie de la grandeur et de la déraison, il est tout aussi logique qu'illogique, tragique que grotesque' (*Eschyle* 113, 'A true encyclopaedia of greatness and of unreason, it is as logical as it is illogical, as tragic as it is grotesque').

Devoid of the literary-narrative spirit, that evolving and humanizing life-force against the dead letter of the law, the Kanun remains Albania's only code of law and the nation, but, like the epic songs which chronicle the nation's history and identity, it has been damaged by history.

Just as the stagnation of the late Roman and post-imperial era was coming to an end with the developments on the peninsula of the fourteenth century, the Ottoman invasion occurred, closing the nation off from its European roots for a further five hundred years. Albanian socialism, promising a break with the spirit of Eastern unfreedom in 1961, succumbed to its own form of self-disenfranchisement, cutting itself off and leaving only the writer to remember the moribund links with European civilization. For Kadare, the modern Albanian writer inherited a stagnant literary, cultural, and national identity. After the long Middle Ages under the Ottomans, modernity arrived in the form of ethnic nationalism, and modernization came about in the form of a brutal Stalinism masquerading as nationalist communism. Ethno-national identity has survived the history of oppression, brutalization, and marginalization from the mainstream of Europe, but the forms it has taken are damaged and sterile.

Kadare is not just interested in literary history. Aeschylus is a version of Kadare himself in this essay in which the writer's gratitude to the European tradition, maintained throughout the years of the dictatorship and throughout the centuries of national oppression, takes the form of a willing identification with the great writer of the Greek transition from oral to written culture. As was the case with Milan Kundera, Czeslaw Milosz, and other members of the Central and Eastern European literary intelligentsia, Kadare's sense of socio-political exclusion from Europe heightened his appreciation of the values of European literature and civilization.[101] Unlike these writers of Central Europe, however, the Balkan writer does not have access to a European heritage of the Renaissance and Enlightenment. Kadare is obliged to dig much deeper into history to find the European origins of the Albanians. The bond with the Greeks was broken a long time in the past, but the shared original 'Graeco-Illyrian' culture was the foundation stone of Europe.

The fear of annihilation and the threat of loss of group identity, which was expressed in terms of such desperation in the final pages of The Three-Arched Bridge and in The Shadow, is allayed by the hope of rediscovery of, and reconnection with, Europe. Gjon Ukcama's chronicle may not be lost. The manuscript of the novel may not be condemned to oblivion in a bank-vault. The Albanian epic may survive the transformation into the modern novel, and Albania might be saved. The signs of hope that change is possible, that all is not lost, are palpable during the second half of the 1980s. Nothing would change after the death of Enver, the Party declared, but figures such as Kadare knew also that nothing would ever be the same.

Conscious of his obligations to both the nation and to humanity, bridging the millennia-old break between Illyro-Albanian culture and the new age in which rapprochement with Europe might again be possible, Kadare 'is' Aeschylus. The modern Albanian writer begins the long process of transition, seeking to retrace his and his nation's path to modernity amid the conflicting demands of individual, ethnic, and state identity. The novel, that essentially European form with its origins in the Homeric epic, which speaks of 'the relativity and ambiguity of things human' and is incompatible with the 'one single Truth' of the totalitarian universe, survived the Hoxha era.[102] Kadare's reading of ancient history and culture may be questionable, amounting more to an allegory of the national culture than a history of ancient Greek literature, but with its intuition of the passing of an era, and its anticipation of the writer's need to prepare the ground for the nation's cultural and political future developments, *Aeschylus or the Great Loser* is an imaginative, courageous, and magisterial work.

In his next major work, *Agamemnon's Daughter* (1986), Kadare finds in the ancient Greek legends of the house of Tantalus the excesses of power, ruthlessness, and brutality to match the story of the Shehu dynasty.[103]

> La maison aux trois portes des Atrides devint à mes yeux la demeure symbole de tout dirigeant communiste. Dans tous les pays de l'Est existaient de pareilles résidences. Mais celle du Premier ministre albanais Shehu, où, dans la nuit du 17 décembre 1981, fut perpétré le meurtre affreux [. . .] fut peut-être la plus ressemblante au palais d'Agamemnon.[104]

> The three-portalled door of the Atreids became in my eyes the symbolic dwelling of every communist leader. These same residences existed in every country of the East. But that of the Albanian Prime Minister, Mehmet Shehu, where on the night of 17 December 1981 the terrible murder was perpetrated [. . .] was perhaps the closest to the palace of Agamemnon.

In Iphigenia's fate we find the archetypal European story of the sacrifice of human innocence for political advantage. The betrayal of a daughter by her father, and the chain of violence and crimes that follows in the house of Agamemnon, reveals the ultimate inseparability of the political and the private realms. This account of the perversions of power becomes another version of the story of the sacrifice of Albania by her leaders. And yet, with its roots in the common history of Greece and Albania, it is also a European story. During the post-communist period, the writer would build on this early work of transition with the sequel, *The Successor* (2002–03). In the new millennium, studies of Dante and Shakespeare would follow in the writer's ongoing explication of the Europeanness of his nation.[105]

Signs of Change, Late 1980s

As early as 1987 signs of political change began to emerge. The war with Greece (never formally ended after 1945) was officially ended. The previous year the railway link between Shkodra and Titograd was opened and transport links with Switzerland, Hungary, Romania, Greece, Trieste, and Yugoslavia were increased. However, we should not underestimate the ongoing ruthlessness of the regime, nor the seething hatreds and deep fears which forty years of brutal governance had engendered. Socialism was not yet finished, and Albania had already demonstrated the extent to which, even in the Eastern bloc, national differences could be maintained. Even in 1987 the Albanians did not experience the post-totalitarianism that had given a softer image to the Soviet Union and its allies. In 1988 Kadare became a member of the Institut de France, a high honour which would continue to protect him from the regime, if not from his enemies in the Sigurimi and elsewhere.

In the following year Eastern European communism collapsed as a result of its own internal contradictions. The Chinese crackdown on the student demonstrations which took place between April and June 1989 was both a warning and an inspiration to the increasingly open dissident movements in the GDR and elsewhere. On the one hand it still seemed possible that another crackdown would take place in Eastern Europe, as had happened in Prague twenty years before. On the other, however, Mikhail Gorbachev promised to bring change to Soviet socialism. The events in China gave the Eastern European leaders the opportunity to demonstrate that their socialism was different from the Maoist version and that they would not repeat the mistakes of 1968. At the Fortieth Anniversary celebrations of the GDR on 5 October 1989, the East German leader, Erich Honecker, himself a member of the old guard of wartime communists, looked forward with anticipation to another century of socialism behind the 'anti-fascist protection wall'. Immediately afterwards, General Secretary Gorbachev warned the uncomprehending Honecker that 'life punishes those who come too late' and the genie was let loose in the GDR. Gorbachev's words were interpreted as an indication that the Soviet Union would no longer shore up those regimes which were incapable of change. The Wall came down in Berlin and the regime of Central and Eastern Europe fell in a series of 'velvet' revolutions marked by euphoric, non-violent change. In South-Eastern Europe things did not go so easily. Romania erupted into civil violence as the long-term thugs and hirelings of the Ceauşescu regime emerged to carry out reprisals. When Nicolae and Elena Ceauşescu were taken hostage and executed on Christmas Day 1989, the video images flew around the globe. They struck the regime in Albania with lightning force.[106]

Ismail Kadare was nominated in 1989 (by Nexhmije Hoxha) for the position of Vice-President of the Albanian Democratic Front. This was a long-standing broad-based organization for cultural, professional, and political groups, chaired until December 1990 by Nexhmije, which had succeeded the National Liberation Front in 1945, and had the nominal function of providing a popular channel for the expression of political views and for mass political education. Its main task was to reinforce the relationship between the Party and the people and to popularize and implement the policies of the Albanian Party of Labour. The 'reformers' in the regime hoped to avoid bloodshed while appearing to initiate change. However, the presence of figures such as Nexhmije in the leadership roles rendered this body suspect as anything other than a cover for the preservation of power among the elite.

At this time, images of intellectuals-turned-political-spokesmen, such as Vaclav Havel and various figures from the new political groupings of Eastern Europe, New Forum, Solidarity, and Civic Forum, were dominating news broadcasts as they were elected to the positions of political power they had looked forward to for so long. Timothy Garton Ash would coin the term 'refolution' for 'a mixture of reform and revolution, with more of a revolutionary push from below in Poland and more of pre-emptive reform from above in Hungary'.[107] Kadare accepted the nomination. At this point rejection of the role was no more an option for Kadare than nomination to the Party had been in 1970 or to the People's Assembly in 1972. He cannot be expected to have foreseen the future at this point. Moreover, he may well have believed that this was the best way of managing change without the civic breakdown that was taking place in Romania. It was a badly advised move, taken under duress in a moment which seemed to call for action. The Democratic Front, with its newspaper *Bashkimi*, may have seemed at the time to be the appropriate body for the transition to democracy, but ultimately it, like the whole structure of the regime, was discredited.

Kadare recognized his mistake. In his musings on the figure of Prometheus in *Albanian Spring*, Kadare allows us to intuit the logic of this political decision, and to consider for ourselves the level of development of his political insight.

> Prométhée n'a jamais été un héros du sacrifice inutile; c'est au contraire le héros de l'intelligence, de la raison éclairée. C'est grâce à cette raison, et non par une obstination aveugle, qu'il a remporté son combat et sauvé l'humanité. Les concessions mutuelles entre Zeus et Prométhée, la tolérance, le dialogue constituent l'essence du mythe. [. . .] Plus fidèlement qu'aucun autre, ce mythe porte témoignage des souffrances par lesquelles a dû passer l'humanité à travers terreurs, chaînes et destructions, pour accéder à l'Olympe, donc au Parlement, et y envoyer enfin son premier député. Depuis lors, au sein de ce Parlement, on a cessé de n'entendre qu'une voix, celle de Zeus. (*Printemps albanais* 136)

> Prometheus was never the hero of useless sacrifice; on the contrary, he is the hero of intelligence and reason. Indeed, it was through reason, not blind obstinacy, that Prometheus won his victory and saved humankind. And mutual concessions between Zeus and Prometheus, tolerance and dialogue, are the essence of his myth. [. . .] More faithfully than any other, this myth testifies to the sufferings that humanity has borne — terror, chains, destruction — to reach Olympus (i.e. Parliament) and to send their first deputy to it. Since then, in the halls of Parliament, people have ceased to hear only a single voice, the voice of Zeus. (*Albanian Spring* 132)

In this environment in late 1989 and 1990 Kadare took a strong stand in favour of change. Fearing the outbreak of civil war, he sought a meeting with Ramiz Alia to discuss human rights, the general levels of poverty, Tirana's abandonment of Kosovo, and the brutality of the Sigurimi. In *Albanian Spring* he would reproach Alia for his failure to take action.[108] His introduction to the novel *The Knives*, by Neshat Tozaj, high-ranking functionary of the Ministry of the Interior, was written in 1989 as an attempt to explicate the workings of the Securitate to a people for whom all mention of such a topic was taboo.[109] The point of Kadare's article is to emphasize the extent to which the Sigurimi had become a form of mafia, a group whose *raison d'être* was no longer a product of political categories such as class or dogma, but an ethos of shared self-interest. Groups such as this, wrote Kadare, perhaps with an eye on the Romanian situation where the Sigurimi staged a violent counter-revolution, had become networks in and for themselves, abusing privileges, and abusing the dogma of communism in order to maintain themselves. They were made up of opportunists and sadists. Tozaj, writes Kadare, 'se révolte et dénonce les pratiques douteuses de ceux qui, censés être les serviteurs du peuple, se conduisent en maîtres' ('revolts against, and denounces the dubious practices of those who were supposed to be the servants of the people, but who conduct themselves like their masters').[110] Kadare appealed to the sense of equality entrenched in Kanun, the Albanians' ancient code of law, which preceded the French Revolution and the Declaration of the Rights of Man by centuries. Here, as in his literary-intellectual essays, Kadare takes pains to link European traditions of modern democracy to Albanian tradition for a people about to take on political self-determination after decades of political infantilism. This line of argument would become more dominant in his thinking during the 1990s, finding expression later in *Albanian Spring*:

> Rattaché à la tradition démocratique, l'Albanie l'était foncièrement. Elle était le seul pays balkanique qui, au sein de l'Empire ottoman, était régi par son ancien Code coutumier, dont certains principes de base, comme l'égalité devant la loi ou le respect de l'individu (mâle), élevés au niveau d'un culte, avaient appris à ce peuple à vivre dans une sorte de démocratie par ailleurs primitive et tragique. (*Printemps albanais*, 37)

> Albania has deep roots in the democratic tradition. She was the only Balkan country that, while in the bosom of the Ottoman Empire, was governed by her own ancient Code, in which certain basic principles, like equality before the law and respect for the individual (male), raised to the level of a cult, taught people to live in a kind of democracy — one as primitive as it was tragic. (*Albanian Spring* 39–40)

His long essay on the work of the great Albanian poet, Migjeni, 'The Eruption of Migjeni into Albanian Literature', building on themes from *Aeschylus or the Great Loser* of the difficulty of the poet in the Albanian environment, was also completed in 1990. In March of that same year the editor of *Zëri i Rinisë* and long-time friend of Kadare, Remzi Lani, interviewed the writer on a range of political topics. Kadare nailed his colours clearly to the wall: 'Les dogmes ne doivent pas entraver le bien-être, les libertés et la démocratie' ('Dogmas must not impede the well-being and the freedoms of democracy'), he told Lani. Kadare reiterated his critique of the Sigurimi and divided the educational and cultural sectors of the current regime into two groups, one of which was reform-minded, 'agile of mind and with a sturdy vision of the future', and the other of which was opposed to change of any sort and must be 'booted out of power'.[111] As a result of this interview he was accused of aping Vaclav Havel by his detractors.[112] His actions were undertaken in the hope of minimizing the disruption of the inevitable upheavals. Kadare was not so naive as to assume that power would pass easily or smoothly through a transitional coalition of democrats to a popularly elected democracy.

In summer 1990 the first open anti-government demonstrations took place. The regime began to make moves designed, at least, to lend a semblance of democracy. At the Plenum of the new Central Committee in July 1990, the Democratic Party, the first legal opposition, was allowed. The constitutional ban on foreign capital and credit was revoked in order to lift living standards, and the Enverite policy of isolation was ended as the government indicated its intention of opening diplomatic relations with the two arch-enemies, the United States and the (soon to be defunct) Soviet Union.

On 25 October 1990, during the 'time of dark forces' when the Sigurimi and other groups were battling for power as the regime teetered on the verge of collapse, Kadare left his homeland for the safety of France. After an initial hope for a peaceful transition to democracy and political openness, he recognized that compromised figures and factions from the regime were staying in power by changing their political colours. The democratic reforms in Albania had not gone far enough and political power remained in the hands of the Tirana ruling class.

> Je m'étais dit que dès lors qu'un régime totalitaire accepte de cohabiter avec une littérature véritable, c'est le premier signe montrant qu'il accepte de s'amender (de s'humaniser). Par mon œuvre, j'avais répandu cette illusion dans le peuple albanais et parmi des milliers de lecteurs partout dans le monde. Je comprenais maintenant que, même s'il y avait quelque chose d'authentique dans ce rêve, l'illusion restait bel et bien une illusion. Pour la transformer en réalité concrète, elle avait besoin d'une impulsion, d'une dimension nouvelle. Se serait mon ABSENCE. (*Printemps albanais* 56)

> I had told myself that the day the totalitarian state agreed to live with a genuine literature would be the first real sign of reform, of the regime's attempt to humanize itself. Through my work, I've held this dream up to the Albanian people and to thousands of readers around the world. Now I understood that, although there is something authentic in the dream, the illusion was no more than an illusion. To make it a reality there had to be some new impulse, a new dimension. That impulse would be my *absence*. (*Albanian Spring* 58–59)

However, there was good reason to suspect that he felt unsafe in the transitional environment where old scores could be settled in a context of upheaval and change. He had never lacked enemies. He was hated by the Sigurimi, by factions in the Union of Writers and by Nexhmije Hoxha and her associates as well as by parties outside Albania, and criminal groups with shadowy links to the regime. Rumour had it that a 'black list' had been compiled with Kadare at its head.[113] Moreover, he now understood the danger of being drawn into compromising associations. This was a time when it was essential that he continue to speak with his own voice, even, if necessary, from a position outside Albania. He realized that his name could be used as an imprimatur in an environment in which democratic government would finally come about.[114]

In December 1990 student protests escalated throughout the country. Multiparty elections took place in March the following year. The Albanian Party of Labour, now a political party in the multiparty environment, won, owing to its control of the media and the ignorance and conservatism of the rural population in particular. Ramiz Alia, the Previous Chairman of the Presidium of the Popular Assembly, was installed as the new President. However when Hoxha's massive statue in central Tirana was toppled on 20 February 1991, it was clear that the regime's chances of staying in power were over. It took a further general strike in April, before a transitional 'government of national salvation' was set up. The nation was in a state of crisis, with food riots occurring and large numbers of people fleeing the country. At the elections of March 1992 the Democratic Party won a landslide victory, installing Sali Berisha as President. Kadare returned to Albania on 6 May 1992, after the March elections appeared to indicate that the country's political situation had stabilized. Nevertheless, the country continued to suffer food shortages and riots. A massive Italian aid programme was undertaken in order to stop the haemorrhaging of economic refugees. The election of Albania to the Council of Europe in 1995 offered hope. Political fragmentation and infighting continued and economic and social chaos dogged the country in the mid-1990s as its population became the victim of international pyramid investment schemes after having bankrupted itself in communism.

Conclusion

Enver Hoxha aimed to bring national fervour to Stalinism in order to strengthen dogma with the emotional and ritual qualities of a secular system of belief and identification. For Hoxha at the high point of his political and cultural isolationism, everything had to be home-grown. 'Genuine culture', he maintained, 'cannot be truly so if it is not part of the blood and flesh of the people who create it and use it, if it is not conceived in their history, life, struggle and interests'.[115] However, Hoxha's patriotism was a far cry from the liberationist politics of ethnic identity which had begun to flourish elsewhere in the communist bloc as well as globally. As we have seen in the analysis of *The Three-Arched Bridge*, this state nationalism was not based on a popular sense of democratic self-identification, tradition, and shared consciousness.[116] Only those aspects of Albanian culture which suited the regime's political vision were granted legitimacy. Core components of Albanian culture (religion, historical consciousness, and ethnic customs) were rigidly controlled and, where necessary, suppressed.[117] In *Albanian Spring*, Kadare refers to *The Palace of Dreams* as the novel which launched the most ferocious attack on the dictatorship.[118] In recognizing ethnicity to be both a deeply embedded and politically instrumentalized aspect of Albanian identity, *The Palace of Dreams* is as much an assault on Hoxha's state nationalism as it is a satire on totalitarian aspirations to complete control, or a veiled attack on Ottoman, Soviet, or Serb imperialism. In this novel, Istanbul, Moscow, Belgrade, and Tirana are all seats of totalitarian power in conflict with the ethnic self-determination of peoples. After *The Palace of Dreams* there was no going back. In this work, more than any other, Kadare marshals the forces of literary satire and of ethnic identification to attack the regime. Here too, moreover, he deepens his implicit critique of the regime's Albanianism. In contrast to the official national celebrations of the regime, Mark-Alem's ethnicity is deeply felt and personal. In compromising his sense of ethnic identity, Mark-Alem stems the wellsprings of his being and embarks on a life of inauthenticity as an official of the Ottoman Empire.

The focus on the inauthenticity of life under the regime provides the key to Kadare's work from *The Palace of Dreams* onward. Kadare continually seeks to peel back the layers in order to find an authentic core to Albanian existence. He finds this, in *The Shadow* as throughout his works of the 1970s and 1980s, in the Christian Albania of the Byzantine Middle Ages, in the period immediately preceding the Ottoman invasions. At this time the core cultural documents of the Albanians, the epics descended from the ancient culture of the Homeric songs, reached their highest level of development. Throughout his work Kadare has suggested the existence of an alternative Albania to that of the regime, intimating that the historical roots of his nation can give birth to different versions of Albanian identity from those of the Albanian Party of Labour. In the figure of Constantine in *The Shadow* and elsewhere Kadare finds an authenticity of existence which is Albanian and which can be pitted against Hoxha's 'new man' and the inauthenticity of life under the regime. It is a symbol of the profound ambivalences in Albanian culture towards self and other, the nation and the world, which for Kadare determine Albanian identity. In this diagnosis the dictatorship is a symptom rather than a cause.

In the *Aeschylus* essay Kadare develops his imaginative evocations of Albanian identity into a programmatic literary history of the southern Balkans, the original Greek and Illyrian civilization of Homeric antiquity. Sensing the imminent death of the dictator and realizing that nothing would be the same, no matter how controlled the transition to the new leader, Kadare set about consolidating his alternative vision of Albania. Like *The Shadow*, *Aeschylus* is already a work of transition. Enver Hoxha's death did not, of course, signal the end of the dictatorship, and in 1985 the regime seemed as strong as ever. However, the force of Hoxha's personality was such that his death represented a major point of transition: not, of course, to democracy and the end of the dictatorship, but certainly to a changed regime. It took another four years for those in and close to power to realize that even Albanian socialism would have to change. Enver Hoxha had left behind a much less charismatic, powerful, and ruthless figure than himself in the 'frail' Ramiz Alia. As a member of the Politburo and, since 1982 as second-in-command, Alia was a long-term collaborator in the crimes of the dictatorship. The formidable Nexhmije was still firmly in control in the background, and an ambitious younger generation was lining up for power. However, figures such as the new Minister for the Interior, Hekuran Isai, were of a different cast from Mehmet Shehu and Kadri Hazbiu. Whether they would be able to maintain the rule of steel, even if they wanted to, was open to debate. In November 1986, at the 9th Congress of the Albanian Party of Labour, Ramiz Alia was re-elected and the new Central Committee reaffirmed its commitment to the ideals of Enver Hoxha.

Drawing on the emotional and spiritual foresight of the artist, Kadare sensed that nothing would be the same again. And, in anticipation of new directions, he set about creating the intellectual and spiritual environment for a new and more profound reattachment of Albania to its European heritage. The broadening of the European Union, in particular the foreshadowed inclusion of countries from the former socialist Eastern Europe, would strengthen the writer's resolve to work towards the restitution of Albania's European cultural heritage during the 1990s. Whereas earlier the use of Greek myths such as that of Prometheus represented a provocation to the communist government's atheism and nationalism, now it gained an added significance. The detailed study of the common roots and the shared themes of Albanian and Greek culture contributed to the writer's vision of a new and committed rapprochement with Europe. No longer hindered by his early belief in the necessity of communism as a modernizing force, or by the later resentment at the failure of Europe to have acted to save Albania from the East, Kadare established Albania's European credentials and his European voice in the essay on Aeschylus.

Postscript: After Socialism

The early 1990s were a period of transition in which Kadare experienced bitterness and hostility from both inside and outside Albania.

> On a beaucoup disserté sur le courage en dictature; c'est un domaine où on ne s'est pas montré avare de leçons. Cette morale, on la faisait depuis les cafés de Paris ou de Vienne, ce qui était sans doute confortable. [. . .] D'autres, des compatriotes à toi, te font aussi la morale. Mais ceux-là le font bien plus tard, quand la dictature commence à s'assouplir, oubliant que ce sont eux qui avaient rempli les salles de meeting pour chanter sa gloire. Se marteler après coup la poitrine, quand la dictature a perdu ses dents, jouer à qui mieux mieux les dissidents pour afficher son courage, se targuer d'avoir été le premier à émettre une critique, d'être allé le plus loin dans la dénonciation, s'accuser réciproquement, se couvrir mutuellement de boue, se calomnier, etc., ce n'est là qu'un mince aperçu du misérable charivari postdictatorial dans un certain nombre de pays de l'Est. Au milieu de cette cacophonie, il n'est pas rare que les authentiques opposants à la dictature, eux qui, des années durant, ont miné ses fondations, restent à l'écart, relégués dans l'oubli. (*Printemps albanais* 179–80)

> Much has been said about courage under dictatorship; the matter is one about which people have not been chary with their advice. Moralizing has been popular in the cafés of Paris and Vienna, and is no doubt a comfort. [. . .] Others, one's compatriots, also lecture you. But they do it too late, when the dictatorship begins to soften, and they forget that they were the people who once filled the public halls to sing its glory. To beat one's breast after the fact, when the dictatorship has lost its teeth, playing at dissidence to show one's courage, to pride oneself on having been the first to express criticism, to have gone furthest in denouncing this or that, to accuse one another, to throw mud at one another, to beat oneself, etc. is all a tiny sample of the post-dictatorial uproar in a number of East European countries. In all that cacophony, it often happens that the real opponents of dictatorship, those who for long years had been mining its foundations, are thrust aside and forgotten. (*Albanian Spring* 173)

His period of adjustment was short. As a writer he had always occupied a 'second chronology', a *longue durée* determined by the rhythms of European literature, not the short term of a life. Unlike many of his colleagues in Eastern Europe, he continued to write. *Invitation to the Writer's Studio* accompanied *Albanian Spring* and was followed by *The Weight of the Cross* in a line of works explaining to his compatriots and the world his activities as a writer and as an eminent figure of Albanian culture and society. In 1993 he completed the second part of *The Pyramid*, begun in 1988, achieving in the figure of the young Pharaoh a subtle portrait of the dictator as modernizer and tyrant, whose monument is built solely with the purpose of depleting the energies and imaginations of his people and thereby keeping them under control. Although Kadare began work on this novel in 1988, the same year as the regime undertook to construct the huge pyramid-shaped museum to Enver Hoxha and his works, he wrote several poems in the 1960s foreshadowing this theme, and the symbolism of the ancient Middle Eastern despotism occurs frequently throughout his oeuvre. In 1993, too, he began the artistic revision of his works for the comprehensive dual language (Albanian and French) publication of his *Œuvres* by the French publisher Fayard, under the brilliant leadership of Claude Durand. He maintained his residence in Paris, moving back and forward between Albania and France during the 1990s and into the new millennium. *Spiritus* (1995) began a series of post-communist novels including *Spring Flowers, Spring Frost* (2000), *The Life, Game and Death of Lul Mazrek* (2002), *The Successor* (2003), and *Accident* (2008) in which episodes from the history of the regime are evoked in bizarre and surreal environments reminiscent of *The Shadow*. His most recent novel, *One Dinner too Many* (*Le Dîner de trop*, 2009) harks back to the days of the German occupation of Gjirokastra in a parable of occupation and betrayal. In 1996 the French government recognized Kadare's services by making him a member of the highly prestigious Académie Française. The ongoing problems of Kosovo demanded his attention in *Three Elegies for Kosovo* (Tirana, Paris, March 1997–March 1998). The war in 1999 took Kadare to Kosovo and resulted in the documentation *This Mourning was Necessary to Find Ourselves (Journal of the War in Kosovo)*. Now into his eighth decade he continues his prodigious output of new material, exploring and revealing the secrets and the perversions of the 'captive mind' (Milosz) under the Albanian dictatorship. These works of the transition and of post-communism lie beyond our scope in this study of Kadare and the regime of Enver Hoxha. Their time will come when Kadare's work after the fall of the dictatorship, during the post-communist period, and in the period of re-inclusion into Europe can be assessed as a whole.

Notes to Chapter 4

1. Cf. Pearson, III, 640–41. A comprehensive and reliable discussion of this matter is to be found in Noel Malcolm, *Kosovo: A Short History* (New York: Harper Collins, 1999), pp. 314–56.
2. Cf. Malcolm, *Kosovo*, p. 337.
3. Prifti, *Remote Albania*, pp. 32–33.
4. Kadaré, *Le Poids*, pp. 311–12, 343, 531–36, 557.
5. Pipa's article 'Subversion vs. Conformism' first appeared in the journal *Telos* in 1987. On the basis of internal evidence, Kadare dates its original composition back to 1983 or 1984 at the latest. Cf. *Le Poids*, pp. 534–35 and fn. 19, p. 557.
6. Pipa, *Contemporary Albanian Literature*, p. 94.
7. Jacques, p. 512.
8. Kadaré, *Le Poids*, p. 443.
9. Kadaré, *Le Poids*, pp. 420–30.
10. Kadaré, *Le Poids*, p. 555.
11. Kadaré in Shehu, *L'Automne*, p. 25.
12. Kadaré in Shehu, *L'Automne*, pp. 26–27.
13. Pearson, III, 642, citing a range of British newspapers, 25–26 September 1982.
14. Kadaré/Bosquet, pp. 72–73; Kadaré, *Le Poids*, p. 485.
15. Frédéric Mitterrand and Thérèse Lombard, *Du côté de chez Fred*: Interview with Ismail Kadare (Paris. Antenne 2, 1990), minute 39.
16. Kadare is using the period of the 'Tanzimat' reforms, the era of 'reorganization' of the Ottoman Empire (1839–70) dominated by the Westernizing and modernizing Turkish Ottoman grand vizier Ali Pasha (Mehmed Emin). However, the description of the 'U.O.S'. in the novel implies a much more profound level of political reorganization than actually occurred during this period.
17. Kadare, 'The Art of Fiction', 216.
18. Kadaré, *Le Poids*, p. 410.
19. Ismaïl Kadaré, *Le Palais des rêves*, trans. by Jusuf Vrioni (Paris: Fayard, 1990), p. 9; Ismail Kadare, *The Palace of Dreams*, trans. by from the French of Jusuf Vrioni by Barbara Bray (London: Harvill, 1993), p. 9. All further references in brackets after the text are to these editions.

Occasional changes to the published translation, marked with an asterisk (*), are made for the sake of accuracy.

20. A long entry on the Köprülü family is to be found in the *Larousse du XXe Siècle en 6 Volumes* (Paris: Librairie Larousse, 1931), IV, 257. Later editions of the *Larousse Encyclopaedic Dictionary* include shortened versions of the article. According to Sugar, the Köprülü family were associated with reform movements within the Empire, notably after 1650 when they attempted to reverse the decline that had set in after the reign of Süleyman I. Sugar, pp. 14, 319. See also Jelavich, *History of the Balkans*, I, 81; Maximilian Lambertz, 'Die Volksepik der Albaner', *Wissenschaftliche Zeitschrift der Karl Marx Universität* (Leipzig), 4 (1954–55), 243–89 and 439–70 (p. 270); Skendi, *The Albanian National Awakening*, p. 21; and Stanford J. Shaw, *History of the Ottoman Empire and Modern Turkey*, 2 vols. (Cambridge: Cambridge University Press, 1976–1977), I, 206–13.

21. Kadare writes that the Sigurimi, under the control of Nexhmije, Kapo, and Hazbiu, was the 'magic key' to the regime, *Le Poids*, pp. 311, 328.

22. Mark-Alem's failure can perhaps be better understood in context. While this dream has particularly obvious symbolism, most of the dreams he is given are extremely suggestive, and could be interpreted to indicate ethnic unrest or changing power-relations in the Empire.

23. The identification of languages in the novel is potentially confusing. Kadare's characters use the term 'Serb' for the language of the epic from Bosnia. Contemporary usage might prefer the term 'Bosniak', for this Slav language spoken by the Bosnian Muslims, but virtually identical to Serbian.

24. Since the sixteenth century Albanians have called their language *Shqipe*, their country *Shqipëria*, and themselves *Shqiptarë*. It was earlier believed that these names derive from the word '*shqipe*' meaning 'eagle', 'Albania' thus translating as 'land of the eagle'. More recent research has indicated that the name derives from the word *shqiptoj*, meaning 'to speak intelligibly'. William B. Bland, *Albania*, World Bibliographical Series, vol. 94 (Oxford: Clio Press, 1988), p. xvii. The text here suggests the Albanian self-identification as 'sons of eagles' in their mountainous homeland.

25. Barbara Bray's English translation of Jusuf Vrioni's French is unclear, as a result of the confusion of the French conjunctive and disjunctive pronouns (underlined).

26. Cf. Norris, *Islam in the Balkans*, pp. 138–60.

27. Ismail Kadaré, *Autobiographie du peuple en vers* (Tirana: Edition '8 Nëntori', 1988). First published in Albanian in 1971.

28. Pipa in particular is critical of Kadare's use of De Rada's theses in relation to the Northern Albanian rhapsodies', Pipa, *Contemporary Albanian Literature*, p. 94.

29. Ismaïl Kadaré, 'Foreword' to *Chansonnier Epique Albanais*, ed. by Qemal Haxhihasani, Luka Kolë, Alfred Uçi, and Misto Treska, version française, trans. and ed. Kolë Luka (Tirana: Academie des Sciences de la RPS D'Albanie, Institut de Culture Populaire, 1983), pp. 7–10.

30. Kadaré/Haxhihasani, p. 9.

31. Cp. Kadaré/Haxhihasani, pp. 7–8 and *Le Palais des rêves*, p. 78. Cf. also Kadaré, *Autobiographie du peuple en vers*, pp. 14–16 and passim.

32. Lambertz, 'Die Volksepik der Albaner', p. 248.

33. 'This Çuperli, also Çupri, is an actual historical figure. He is a member of the Köprülü family. [. . .] They saved and revived the Ottoman Empire in the 17th century. Mohammed Köprülü created internal order and left to his son a ready army [. . .] In Serbian songs he is called 'Cuprili' [. . .] after the 'Köprü' (bridge) of his town of birth.' Lambertz, 'Die Volksepik der Albaner', p. 270; my translation.

34. Stavro Skendi, *Albanian and South Slav Oral Epic Poetry*, Memoirs of the American Folklore Society, vol. 44 (Philadelphia: American Folklore Society 1954, New York: Kraus Reprint Co., 1969), pp. 60–61; cf. also Milman Parry, and Albert Bates Lord, eds, *Serbocroatian Heroic Songs* (Belgrade and Cambridge, Mass.: Serbian Academy of Sciences and Harvard University Press, 1954), p. 206.

35. Kadare mentions the 'Tchouprilitch' family as faithful to the Ottomans in *Autobiographie*, p. 122.

36. Skendi, *Albanian and South Slav Oral Epic Poetry*, p. 125.

37. Skendi *Albanian and South Slav Oral Epic Poetry*, pp. 126–27; see also Norris, *Islam in the Balkans*, pp. 157f. on the relationships between Albanian and Bosnian epic traditions.

38. Lambertz, 'Die Volksepik der Albaner', p. 267.

39. Lambertz, 'Die Volksepik der Albaner', p. 255.

40. Jelavich, *History of the Balkans*, I, 31.

41. Stefanaq Pollo and Arben Puto, with the collaboration of Kristo Frasheri and Skënder Anamali, *The History of Albania from its Origins to the Present Day* (London: Routledge and Kegan Paul, 1981), p. 57; Lambertz, 'Die Volksepik der Albaner', pp. 270f.

42. Kadaré/Haxhihasani, p. 9.

43. Cf. Jelavich, *The Ottoman Empire the Great Powers Question*, pp. 111–16; Jelavich, *History of the Balkans*, I, 361, 363–64; Skendi, *The Albanian National Awakening*, pp. 31–110.

44. Jelavich, *History of the Balkans*, I, 365 and II, 84–89.

45. Skendi, *The Albanian National Awakening*, pp. 121–22.

46. Skendi, *The Albanian National Awakening*, p. 123.

47. Cf. Jelavich, *History of the Balkans*, I, 353.

48. The name Gjergj or Djerz in particular occurs in Albanian and Bosnian epic respectively: 'The famous hero, Gerz-Iljas, is also mentioned in the long account [. . .] of the fighting in the Bosnian borderland in the years 1479 to 1480'. Norris, *Islam in the Balkans*, p. 159.

49. In *The General of the Dead Army*, the image of the raging bull is associated with Albanian vendetta (*General* 134–35), and hence in *The Palace of Dreams* with the powerful Albanian family in Istanbul.

50. Kadare and Agolli were both from Gjirokastra, were close in age, and both studied in Russia at the same time. After their return, they were friends. Agolli went on to become a successful writer, President of the Union of Writers, and member of the Central Committee. Agolli officiated at several meetings of censure and criticism of Kadare, but also confided in him in private and shared many points of view critical of the regime. Kadare refused to condemn outright his ex-friend and colleague when it was revealed that Agolli had denounced and informed on Kadare to the regime. Aspects of Agolli might be identifiable in figures such as the narrator in Kadare's late novel, *The Shadow*. Sinani, pp. 188–93.

51. The surreal way in which life goes on after the crisis reflects the workings of the regime, in which a close member of the innermost circle, isolated and purged, would be removed from sight and from documentary evidence overnight.

52. Kadare uses the image of the bridge with three arches as a symbol of Albania, in particular in *The Three-Arched Bridge*. Each arch stands for a long period of the country's foreign occupation: Roman, Byzantine, Turkish.

53. 'Mark-Alem aurait rêvé de l'imiter, mais il s'en sentait bien incapable'. *Palais* 62, 'Mark-Alem might have thought of imitating him, but he knew he was incapable of it', *Palace* 50.

54. This image of the bridge has archetypal significance in the pre-Slavic Greek and 'Illyrian' folklore of the Balkan peninsula. See Georgios A. Megas, *Die Ballade von der Arta-Brücke: Eine vergleichende Untersuchung* (Thessaloniki: Institute for Balkan Studies, 1976), passim, and Ardian Klosi, *Mythologie am Werk: Kazantzakis, Andrić, Kadare: Eine vergleichende Untersuchung am besonderen Beispiel des Bauopfermotivs*, Slavische Beiträge 277 (Munich: Verlag Otto Sagner, 1991), passim.

55. Velo, p. 147.

56. 'The Albanians are, along with the Greeks, the oldest Balkan nation. One has to understand, that this nation, which has survived the tyranny of three empires — the Roman, the Byzantine, and the Ottoman — rejects the chauvinism of the Serbs. This Serbian chauvinism is the chauvinism of newcomers. It is full of inferiority complexes and morbid jealousies. It attempts the impossible: to force the Albanians to forget their culture, their history, and their freedom. [. . .] I wanted to remind Balkan, and in particular Serbian, writers that no people can have a peaceful conscience when it oppresses another people.' Quoted in Haroche, pp. 711–13; my translation.

57. Velo, p. 153.

58. Kadaré/Bosquet, p. 70; Velo, p. 171, confirms this statement.

59. Documentation of Agolli's behaviour and Kadare's response are to be found in Sinani, pp. 105–08, 188–95.

60. Velo, p. 153; Kadaré/Courtois, 'La Vérité', p. 156.

61. Kadaré/Bosquet, p. 71.
62. Champseix and Champseix, *L'Albanie ou la logique du désespoir,* p. 207.
63. Quoted from Pipa, 'Subversion vs. Conformism', p. 74.
64. Kadaré, *Le Poids,* p. 451; cf. also p. 520.
65. Kadaré/Courtois, *La Vérité,* p. 149; cf. also Velo, p. 11.
66. Kadaré, *Le Poids,* p. 459.
67. Cf. Champseix and Champseix, pp. 208–09; Kadaré, *Le Poids,* pp. 514–27, 556 (endnote 14).
68. Kosta would subsequently fall foul of the regime and be purged from his position in 1985 as a result of a damning indictment of his story 'The Three who . . .' as hostile to the regime.
69. Kadaré, *Le Poids,* p. 506.
70. Claude Durand, 'Note de l'éditeur', preface to Ismail Kadaré, *La Fille d'Agamemnon* (Paris: Fayard, 2003), pp. 7–9.
71. *La Fille d'Agamemnon,* 'L'Envol du migrateur,' 'La Romanicide', 'Cet Hiver', 'Dimanche de pâques', 'La Tombe', 'Le Coffre-Fort'. Kadaré/Bosquet, pp. 51–52; Eric Faye, 'Introduction', in Ismail Kadaré, *Œuvres,* x, 17–18.
72. Kadaré, *Le Poids,* p. 529. Cf. Champseix and Champseix, p. 209; Kadaré/Courtois, *La Vérité,* pp. 168–69.
73. Personal communication during an interview with Ismail Kadare, held on 6 November 2004, in Paris.
74. Velo, p. 146.
75. Durand, p. 8.
76. Kadaré/Bosquet, p. 83.
77. Kadaré/Bosquet, p. 52. Durand, p. 8, confirms that this included 'accidental' death in Albania.
78. Ismail Kadaré, *L'Ombre,* trans. by Jusuf Vrioni (Paris: Fayard, 1994). All further French references are indicated in brackets after the text. Translations are my own.
79. Claude Lévi-Strauss, *The Elementary Structures of Kinship,* rev. edn (London: Eyre & Spottiswoode, 1969), pp. 12–25, 42–51; Robin Fox, *Kinship and Marriage: An Anthropological Perspective* (Harmondsworth: Penguin, 1967), pp. 54–76; Ian Whitaker, 'Familial Roles in the Extended Patrilineal Kin-Group in Northern Albania', in *Mediterranean Family Structures,* ed. by J. G. Peristiany (Cambridge: Cambridge University Press, 1976), pp. 195–204.
80. Cf. M'raihi, pp. 116–18.
81. Ismail Kadaré, *Eschyle ou le grand perdant* (Paris: Fayard, 1995), pp. 120–21.
82. 'Le peuple et le Parti vous hissent sur l'Olympe, mais si vous ne leur êtes pas fidèle, ils vous précipitent dans l'abîme', *Le Poids,* p. 451. Cf. 'The Response to *The Palace of Dreams,* 1982' above.
83. The well-meaning but naive Irish-American ethnologist, Bill, begins to metamorphose into an Albanian bard as he enters into the culture that he has been researching and recording. At that point he begins to go blind and to register the material that he has been collecting not as an objective observer, but as the mouthpiece for the myths of Albanian history, life, and death.
84. Kadaré, *Le Poids,* pp. 503–04.
85. According to Kadare, who had it from one of Hoxha's physicians, the dictator was morbidly depressed by rain and fog, *Le Poids,* p. 458. On the theme of fog and mist in Kadare, see Edmond Jouve, 'Ismail Kadaré et ses paysages intérieurs', in *Ismaïl Kadaré, Gardien de Mémoire,* ed. by Jacques Augarde, Simone Dreyfus, and Edmond Jouve (Paris: Sepeg International, 1993), pp. 147–72 (pp. 153–58); Kadaré and de Rapper, *L'Albanie entre la légende et l'histoire,* p. 49.
86. Kadaré, *Invitation,* pp. 145–47.
87. 'Wir töteten nie ohne Grund' ('We didn't kill without reason'), Interview with Nexhmije Hoxha, *Der Spiegel,* no. 15 (5 April, 2004), pp. 135–36.
88. Schreiber, pp. 244–45.
89. Enver Hoxha, *Selected Works,* vi: *July 1980–December 1984* (Tirana: 8 Nëntori Publishing House, 1987), p. 832.
90. Schreiber, p. 245.
91. Cf. Champseix, 'Fétiches staliniens', p. 151.
92. In 1987 Kadare wrote a poem entitled 'Lady Macbeth's Soap', Velo, p. 154.
93. Jacques, p. 644.

94. Kadaré, *Invitation*, p. 256.

95. Kadaré, *Le Poids*, pp. 557–58, fn. 20.

96. In his interview with Denis Fernandez-Récatala, Kadare refers to the dead Hoxha as a 'séducteur italien [. . .] un *latin lover* de Cinecitta', *Les quatre interprètes*, p. 85.

97. 'Of the 14 members of the Central Committee, elected when the Party of Labour of Albania was founded as the Albanian Communist Party in 1941, Hoxha was the only one still alive; 14 of the 31 members of the Central Committee elected in 1944 had been 'liquidated' and only nine remained in office; of the original 109 members of the National Assembly, 17 had been shot, 15 had been imprisoned, two had committed suicide, and only 29 were still politically active.' Pearson, III, 573.

98. Kadaré, *Le Poids*, p. 530.

99. Pipa challenges Kadare on this theory of the origins of Albanian epic song. According to Pipa this culture originated in (Slav) Bosnia, and from there travelled to Kosovo and northern Albania, where it was modified considerably in accordance with the northerners' psychology and traditional mores. 'In its anti-Yugoslav hysteria dating from Albania's break with Yugoslavia, Albanian Stalinism appropriated the nationalistic thesis that South Slavs borrowed the rhapsodies in question from the Albanians, going so far in this direction as to claim as an Albanian Milos Obilic, the Serbian hero of the battle of Kosova. Kadare's novel upholds the official thesis. Two Irish folklorists travel to Northern Albania to collect the rhapsodies in question. The conclusion of their study is that the rhapsodies are remnants of a medieval poem which disintegrated during the centuries-long Ottoman occupation, a thesis likewise maintained (but with regard to Southern Albanian folk songs) by the Italo-Albanian poet De Rada. Kadare appropriates De Rada's thesis, applying it to the Northern Albanian rhapsodies.' Pipa, *Contemporary Albanian Literature*, p. 94.

100. Ismail Kadaré, *Eschyle ou le grand perdant*, rev. and exp. edn, trans. by Jusuf Vrioni (Paris: Fayard 1988). While Kadare revised and added material for this edition, the substance is largely unchanged from the original version, *Eschyle ou l'eternel perdant*, of 1985.

101. Milan Kundera, 'The Tragedy of Central Europe', *The New York Review of Books*, 26 April 1984, pp. 33–39, repr. in *From Stalinism to Pluralism: A Documentary History of Eastern Europe since 1945*, ed. Gale Stokes (New York : Oxford University Press, 1991), pp. 216–23.

102. 'As a model of this Western world, grounded in the relativity and ambiguity of things human, the novel is incompatible with the totalitarian universe. This incompatibility is deeper than the one that separates a dissident from an apparatchik, or a human rights campaigner from a torturer, because it is not only political or moral but *ontological*. By which I mean: the world of one single Truth and the relative, ambiguous world of the novel are moulded of entirely different substances. Totalitarian Truth excludes relativity, doubt, questioning; it can never accommodate what I would call *the spirit of the novel*.' Milan Kundera, *The Art of the Novel* (London: Faber and Faber, 1986), pp. 13–14.

103. Cf. Kadaré/Bosquet, p. 119.

104. Kadaré/Bosquet, p. 143.

105. Ismail Kadaré, *Dante, l'incontournable, ou Brève histoire de l'Albanie avec Dante Alighieri*, trans. by Tedi Papavrami (Paris: Fayard, 2006); Ismaïl Kadaré, *Hamlet, ou le prince impossible*, trans. by Artan Kotro (Paris: Fayard, 2007).

106. Champseix and Champseix, *L'Albanie ou la logique du désespoir*, p. 213.

107. Timothy Garton Ash, *In Europe's Name: Germany and the Divided Continent* (London: Vintage, 1993), p. 344.

108. Kadare gives details of this meeting in *Printemps albanais*, pp. 23–33; *Albanian Spring*, pp. 26–34. Cf. Champseix and Champseix, *L'Albanie ou la logique du désespoir*, p. 214.

109. Ismaïl Kadaré, preface to Neshat Tozaj, *Les Couteaux* (Paris: Denoël, 1989), pp. 9–15. Tozaj's novel was originally published in *Drita*, 15 October 1989.

110. Kadaré, 'Preface' to *Les Couteaux*, p. 12.

111. Quoted in Jacques, pp. 598–99.

112. *Printemps albanais*, pp 62–63, *Albanian Spring*, p. 64; cf. Champseix and Champseix, *L'Albanie ou la logique du désespoir*, p. 214.

113. Champseix and Champseix, *L'Albanie ou la logique du désespoir*, p. 214.

306   Kadare's Final Political Vision

114. See Kadare's letter to the President of the People's Socialist Republic of Albania, 23 October 1990, *Printemps albanais*, pp. 109–10, *Albanian Spring*, pp. 108–09.
115. Vickers and Pettifer, *The Albanian Question*, pp. 118–19.
116. Elsie, 'Evolution and Revolution', p. 258.
117. Elsie, 'Evolution and Revolution', p. 259; Kadaré, *Printemps albanais*, p. 125, *Albanian Spring*, p. 122; Arshi Pipa, 'The Adventure of Albania's Young Turks', *Telos*, 92 (1992), 99–106 (p. 99).
118. Kadaré, *Printemps albanais*, p. 7, *Albanian Spring*, p. 8.

CONCLUSION

For the Western left, Kadare's greatest fault was his failure to speak out against the regime. They wanted a Solzhenitsyn, or a Havel, a heroic dissident in the post-totalitarian mould. However, it was impossible to be a dissident in the post-1968 mode in Albania. Hoxha's dictatorship was Stalinist to the last and all signs of opposition or dissent were dealt with ruthlessly. Opposition could only exist outside the country. Kadare did not and could not fit the 'post-totalitarian' model of the Eastern European dissident.[1] Ironically Kadare was also unpalatable to the Maoist-dominated French left during the 1960s and early 1970s. He was, after all, a figure of dissent in the only European Maoist state, and hence an uncomfortable reminder of the realities of this political system for the Parisian revolutionaries.

In his recent study of European intellectuals in times of crisis, Ralf Dahrendorf enters a plea for what he calls the Erasmian mode. Dahrendorf's Erasmian intellectual is characterized primarily by the refusal to be seduced by the grand projects of modernity, whether of the left or the right. His point is that there are alternatives to heroic dissidence, and that the Erasmian virtues of intellectual (as opposed to political or activist) engagement, commitment to reason, self-determination, and refusal to be seduced by ideology have a place in our assessment of the twentieth-century intellectuals. Not heroic dissidence, which often meant unsupportable physical suffering or death, but truthfulness to self, is one of the core values of Dahrendorf's Erasmian intellectual, even if accompanied by a measure of outward conformity.

> It is not easy for intellectuals to survive in dictatorships. And yet there are public intellectuals, Erasmians, who have managed to survive, albeit with unavoidable but excusable limitations. Conformity, whether through occasional acts or by regularly turning a blind eye is just one of several ways.[2]

It is not easy for intellectuals to survive in dictatorships. And yet there are public intellectuals, Erasmians, who have managed to survive, albeit with unavoidable but excusable limitations. Conformity to the regime, whether through occasional acts or by regularly turning a blind eye, is just one of several ways.

Dahrendorf identifies 'inner emigration', cleared of its associations with Nazi Germany, as a type of behaviour 'compatible with the Erasmian virtues'.[3] He identifies the need for an alternative to the language of idealistic heroism (or compromised cowardice) in speaking of the situation of the dissident intellectuals in the totalitarian environments.[4] While not fully an Erasmian in Dahrendorf's sense, Ismail Kadare chose to compromise in order to continue living and writing in Albania, without adopting the suicidal role of the heroic outsider on the one hand, and without supporting the dictatorship on the other. The refusal to succumb to the inner censor is a manifestation of Kadare's Erasmian qualities in the particular situation of the Albanian dictatorship. This refusal contradicted the everyday normality of Kadare's life as a member of the creative elite. It reveals Kadare to be a figure whose 'second chronology', or inner exile in the world of literary creativity, was a form of opposition to the dictatorship and everything it stood for.

In Kadare's terms, literature and dictatorship are completely opposed to each other as mutually exclusive realms of human being.

> La dictature et la littérature véritable ne peuvent cohabiter que d'une façon: en se dévorant nuit et jour l'une l'autre. L'écrivain est l'ennemi naturel de la dictature. [. . .] La dictature et la littérature ne peuvent être figurées que comme deux bêtes fauves qui se prennent en permanence à la gorge. Bien qu'elles aient des griffes différentes, l'une comme l'autre provoquent également des blessures, différentes elles aussi. Les blessures qu'essuie l'écrivain peuvent paraître affreuses, car immédiates. Tandis que celles qu'il cause, lui, à la dictature, sont des blessures à retardement, mais de celles qui ne guérissent jamais. (*Printemps albanais*, p. 6)

> Dictatorship and literature coexist in only one way: they devour each other day and night. A writer is the natural enemy of dictatorship. [. . .] Dictatorship and literature can only exist together like two wild beasts that have each other by the throat. Their claws are different, and they each inflict different kinds of wounds. The wounds sustained by the writer may appear terrible because they are so immediate. But those the writer inflicts on the dictatorship have a delayed effect. They are the sort that never heal. (*Albanian Spring* 8, my trans.)

His is not the heroic dissidence of the GDR dissident Jürgen Fuchs, for example, which expressed itself in dogged refusal to be bowed by the mechanisms of intimidation, and which resulted in imprisonment, physical and psychological injury, and death. However, it is a form of bearing witness, of refusal to be silenced, and of the maintenance, from within, of belief in the possibility of an alternative to the megalomania of the dictatorship. Many twentieth-century European intellectuals were seduced by the promises of modernization in its various forms. Those honest enough to confront reality rather than dogma faced a long journey of engagement and confrontation with the disappointments and betrayals of the modernizing project. Some chose heroic opposition, others chose subtler forms of defiance. Kadare belonged to the latter group. He never referred to himself as a dissident. He was a writer who tried to produce 'une littérature normale dans un pays anormal' ('normal literature in an abnormal country').[5] His literary praxis was a form of opposition inasmuch as he steadfastly refused to surrender his language and identity or to be forced into exile.[6] He expressed defiance through the representation of the impossibility of everyday life under communism and through the evocation of an 'eternal Albania' which was more ancient, more durable, and more decent than the new Albania of Enver Hoxha. However, he also paid dearly in personal terms for his refusal to succumb to the dictatorship. In his late work *The Shadow*, he appears embittered and obsessed, a remnant of an early talent deformed by the spirit of refusal. And in the final pages of *The Weight of the Cross*, he looks back over a body of work deeply damaged by its environment. Like all art born amidst violence, he writes, his work suffered the 'deficiences, mutilations, and defigurations' of the epoch. Nevertheless, the refusal to participate in the rosy lies of socialism, which hid a deep hatred of humanity, was enough to render his works a 'funeral lament' amidst the sterile festivities of socialism. That, he writes, was his 'greatest defiance'.[7]

★ ★ ★ ★ ★

In the European imagination since Shakespeare, Albania has been the place of wild barbaric customs and romantic adventures. Byron's 'rugged nurse of savage men' excited generations of European romantics, Karl May's adventures 'Among the Shkipetars' fired the German imagination, and the redoubtable Briton, Edith Durham, campaigned for her wild Albanian highlanders in the last days of the Ottoman Empire. The Albanian memoirs of the British agents of the Second World War, Julian Amery and David Smiley, read more like nineteenth-century romance than records of modern warfare. It is hardly surprising that in 2007 the children's author J. K. Rowling chose the forests of Albania in which to hide Harry Potter's nemesis, the arch-villain Voldemort.[8] Culture is conservative and the images of a medieval, wild, or romantic Albania still loom large in the Western imagination despite the twentieth-century history of national liberation, communist dictatorship, and democratization. In describing Kadare as a Balkan bard and progeny of Homer, Professor John Carey, chairman of the International Man-Booker committee, contributed to the well-meaning but romantic simplification of the writer and his land.[9]

However, it is time for a change. With an eye on the European Union in the 2006 essay, 'The European Identity of the Albanians', Kadare reiterated the need for Albania to be reincluded into Europe. Having been excluded twice already, in the late fourteenth century and in 1944, it would be a catastrophe if Albania were excluded from Europe a third time.[10] History is at fault, he writes in *The Weight of the Cross*, but so is the ignorance and the arrogance of Europe and the West, 'la connaissance extrêmement partielle, pour ne pas dire l'ignorance de cette nation par le reste du monde' ('the extremely patchy knowledge, not to say the ignorance about this nation, among the rest of the world').[11] It is time for the world to listen to Kadare and to see Albania through the mirror of his work as a modern nation poised to re-enter European life.

Notes to the Conclusion

1. Kadare uses the term 'post-dictatorial' to express the difference between Albanian Stalinism and the environment of dissidents such as Havel and Solzhenitsyn: *Printemps albanais*, pp. 62–63; *Albanian Spring* p. 64. Structural changes and developments within Eastern European totalitarian states especially after the death of Stalin are analysed by Hannah Arendt, *The Origins of Totalitarianism* and Vaclav Havel, 'The Power of the Powerless', in *Open Letters: Selected Prose 1965–1990*, sel. and ed. by Paul Wilson (London: Faber and Faber, 1991), pp. 125–214. On post-totalitarianism, see Heller, *Das Alltagsleben*, pp. 7–23, 24–31.

2. Ralf Dahrendorf, *Versuchungen der Unfreiheit: Die Intellektuellen in Zeiten der Prüfung* (Munich: Beck, 2006), p. 112 (*Temptations of Unfreedom: The Intellectuals in Times of Trial*, my translation).

3. Dahrendorf, p. 112.

4. Dahrendorf, pp. 150–51.

5. Kadaré/Courtois, 'La Vérité', p. 196.

6. Kadaré/Bosquet, pp. 37–39.

7. Kadaré, *Le Poids*, p. 541.

8. Lord Byron, 'Childe Harold's Pilgrimage', Canto 2, *The Major Works*, pp. 67–73; Karl May, *Durch das Land der Skipetaren* (Stuttgart: Fackelverlag, 1962); Edith M. Durham, *High Albania* (1909; London: Phoenix Press, 2000), *The Burden of the Balkans* (London: Thomas Nelson and Sons, n.d.); Julian Amery, *Sons of the Eagle: A Study in Guerilla War* (London: Macmillan, 1948); David Smiley, *Albanian Assignment* (London: Chatto & Windus, 1984); J. K. Rowling, *Harry Potter and the Deathly Hallows* (London: Bloomsbury, 2007).

9. John Carey, *The Guardian*, Friday, 3 June 2005, http://www.guardian.co.uk/uk/2005/jun/03/world.books, echoing Eric Faye, 'Introduction aux *Œuvres* d'Ismail Kadaré', *Oeuvres*, I, 18.

10. Kadaré/Bosquet, p. 202: 'Je suis originaire d'un pays européen qui a été exclu de l'Europe à deux reprises. La première fois, au XVe siècle, lorsqu'il est tombé sous l'occupation ottomane en même temps que le reste des Balkans. La seconde fois, en 1944, quand il est tombé sous la dictature communiste. Manquer l'Europe une troisième fois serait catastrophique pour l'Albanie.' 'I am a native of a European country which has been excluded from Europe twice over. The first time, in the fifteenth century, when it fell under Ottoman occupation along with the rest of the Balkans. The second time in 1944, when it fell under the communist dictatorship. To miss Europe a third time would be catastrophic for Albania.'

11. Kadaré, *Le Poids*, pp. 540–41.

CHRONOLOGY

Historical details were compiled with reference to a broad range of works listed in the Bibliography, particularly Jacques and Pearson

1908   Enver Hoxha born.

1912/13   Albanian Independence

1923   Enver Hoxha enters the French school in Gjirokastra.

1927   Enver Hoxha enters the French school in Korça as a scholarship student.

1928   Ahmed Zog proclaims himself king of Albania.

1930   Enver Hoxha at the university of Montpellier.

1933–34   Enver Hoxha in Paris.

1934–36   Enver Hoxha works for the Albanian consulate in Brussels.

1936   Ismail **Kadare** born 28 January, in Gjirokastra.

1937   Enver Hoxha teaches at the French school in Korça.

1939   6–7 April: Italians attack Albania. 28 November: Hoxha heads an illegal demonstration on the anniversary of independence, leaves Korça to run a café in Tirana.

1940   October: Mussolini attacks Greece. King Zog exiled.

1941   Consolidation of communist resistance in Albania with Yugoslav support.

1942   16 September: Supreme Committee for National Liberation, dominated by the communists. Formation of Balli Kombëtar. Hoxha enlists Yugoslav Communist Party help to establish the Albanian resistance. August: First issue of *Zëri i Popullit*.

1943   March: 1st National Conference of the Albanian Communist Party. Enver Hoxha in charge of political affairs, Mehmet Shehu of military and strategic affairs. May: Formation of the fourth collaborationist regime; 25 July: Fall of Mussolini; 8 September: Italian capitulation. National accord agreed to between communists and republicans (Balli Kombëtar). The Yugoslav communists condemn the accord, Hoxha backs down, and betrays his envoy to the Balli Kombëtar (Ymer Dishnica). Civil war between communists and non-communists begins.

1944   Spring: liberation of Korça by the communists under Shehu. Anti-communist alliance of the northern clan chiefs and the Republican Front. 28 May: Hoxha named commander-in-chief of the National Liberation Army. 9 October: Churchill and Stalin meet in Moscow to discuss the fate of the Balkans and omit Albania. 22 October: Hoxha is designated President, Minister of Defence and of Foreign Affairs. 17 November: German *Wehrmacht* withdraws from Tirana. 29 November: Hoxha's Provisional Democratic Government moves into Tirana.

1945   Spring: communists are in charge throughout Albania; mass arrests of 'war criminals', anti-communists, and 'collaborators'. August: 1st Congress of the Democratic Front. September: Tito recognizes Kosovo as an 'autonomous region' in Yugoslavia. October: Union of Albanian Writers established. First phase of land reform.

1946   Stalin supports Tito as tutor to Hoxha and protector of communist Albania. October: Corfu incident with Great Britain.

1947   May: work begins on the Albania's first railway, linking Durrës with Peqin and Tirana. 16 July: Hoxha is received by Stalin in Moscow. November: conflict between Koçi Xoxe (pro-Yugoslav) and Naku Spiru (Albanian nationalist); Hoxha supports both, Spiru discovers this, feels betrayed, and commits suicide. Stalin encourages Yugoslavia to 'swallow' Albania, criticizes Hoxha for nationalism, and is tacitly willing to see him toppled.

1948   14 February: At the 8th Plenum, Koçi Xoxe (pro-Yugoslav) holds Hoxha responsible for the wrong path that the Party has taken; Hoxha undertakes self-criticism for infraction of the Party line and for prejudice against relations with Yugoslavia. Shehu is accused of anti-Yugoslav activity and is excluded from the Central Committee. Stalin discovers Yugoslavian federalist intentions in the Balkans; beginning of break between Soviet Union and Yugoslavia. 28 June: Tito is accused of revisionism and of national chauvinism by Stalin. Hoxha uses the Stalin–Tito break to undermine the pro-Yugoslav faction; 1 July: all treaties, accords, etc. with Yugoslavia are declared null and void and all mention of Tito in schools etc is censored. 11th Plenum of the Central Committee: Hoxha denounces the Yugoslav faction and rehabilitates Naku Spiru as a victim of the Titoists. Consolidation of power of Hoxha and Shehu. November: 1st Congress of the Communist Party of Albania. New constitution and new name, Party of Labour of Albania (PLA). Policy of industrial development, along five-year plans with state controlled development of every phase of Albanian life. Shehu takes over as Minister for the Interior and Head of the Sigurimi (till 1954). Enforced co-operation leading to full nationalization of land (by 1967).

1949   11 June: execution of Koçi Xoxe as 'Titoist and revisionist'. 23 November: Hoxha visits Moscow to request financial aid.

1950   28 May: PLA wins elections with 98% majority.

1951   19 February: explosion of a bomb in front of the Soviet Legation, 'Jakova Affair', leading to arrests, terror, and executions, particularly within the Party and the Central Committee. May: Hoxha and Shehu in Moscow.

1952   April: 2nd Congress of the Party of Labour of Albania. First radio station established in Tirana. Writer's Union adopts the new standardized (Tosk) language. Universal elementary education compulsory through to grade 8. October: Hoxha and Shehu attend 19th Congress of the Soviet Communist Party.

1953   March: death of Stalin. 1st Five-Year Plan (1951–55) with program of industrialization. October: 14th Plenum of the Board of the Writers' Union. Post-Stalinist thaw begins in Soviet Union: Pomerantsev's 'On Sincerity in Literature' published in *Novy Mir*. December: 2nd Albanian Writers' Congress. **Kadare** enrols at the Institute of Philological Studies in Tirana (this becomes the Faculty of Letters when the University of Tirana is established in 1958); publishes his first collection of poems, *Youthful Inspiration: Lyrics*.

1954   Mehmet Shehu replaces Hoxha as Prime Minister; Hoxha remains head of the Party. Shehu's brother-in-law Kadri Hazbiu, becomes Minister of the Interior and Director of the Sigurimi. The journal *Nëntori* (*November*) becomes the official organ of the Writer's Union. Albanian Writers' Union seeks a 'middle way' rather than adopt socialist realism as official literary style. Ehrenburg's *The Thaw* published in the Soviet Union.

1955   May: Albania enters the Warsaw Treaty Organization. Pasternak completes the manuscript of *Dr. Zhivago*. **Kadare**, 'Lost Memories'.

1956	14–25 February: 20th Congress of the Communist Party of the Soviet Union. 14 February: Khrushchev's 'Secret Speech' and denunciation of Stalin; doctrine of co-existence with capitalism; promotion of pro-Khrushchev members to Central Committee and high party offices. 25 May: 3rd Congress of the PLA. Hoxha gains full control over the party; refusal to rehabilitate Xoxe represents the first public defiance of Moscow; trial and execution of critics and 'Titoist agents' Liri Gega and Dalli Ndreu. Hoxha witnesses Budapest uprising on the way back from a trip to China (for the 8th Congress of the Chinese Communist Party) and North Korea. 2nd Five-year Plan (1956–60). Dudintsev publishes *Not by Bread Alone* in Soviet Union.
1957	16 May: 1st Congress of the Albanian Writers and Artists. Merger of the Albanian Union of Writers with the Union of Albanian Artists to form the League of Albanian Writers and Artists (LAWA) with a membership of 150. Pasternak's *Dr Zhivago* published in Italy. Khrushchev signals the end of the thaw. **Kadare** publishes second book of poems, *Dreams*.
1958	Pasternak awarded the Nobel Prize, but refuses it after threats of expulsion from Russia. August: **Kadare** enters the Maxim Gorki Institute for World Literature, Moscow; *The Princess Argjiro*.
1959	January: Hoxha visits East Germany and Czechoslovakia. 25 May: Khrushchev visits Albania, suggests nuclear-free Balkans. May: 3rd Congress of Soviet Writers. October–November: hostility between China and Soviet Union. **Kadare** in Riga (summer); finishes *The City without Signs*.
1960	30 May: Death of Pasternak. June: Hoxha does not attend the gathering of East European leaders in Bucharest, or join Khrushchev at the UN General Assembly in New York in September. Break between Peking and Moscow. Deterioration of Albanian relations with Soviet Union. Deputy Prime Minister Abdyl Këllëzi visits China and concludes a technical assistance agreement with the Chinese government. 10 November: Moscow conference opens; 16 November: Hoxha supports Stalin against the revisionists. Pro-Soviet Liri Belishova jailed. **Kadare**: returns to Albania in October; 'A stroll through the cafes', published in *Zëri i Rinisë*.
1961	January: Last attempt by Soviet Union to smooth relations with Albania; 13–20 February: 4th Congress of the Albanian Party of Labour. Hoxha uncovers an 'American–Greek–Yugoslav plot' to overthrow the regime. May: Trial and execution of alleged anti-government conspirators, including the Commander-in-Chief of the Albanian Navy, Admiral Teme Sejko. 1 September: Soviet termination of Soviet–Albanian cultural agreement of 1952. October: 22nd Congress of the Soviet Union: Khrushchev excommunicates Albania; November: withdrawal of Soviet Ambassador; 11 December: TASS announces the final break of the Soviet Union with Albania. Beginning of the 3rd Five-Year Plan (1961–65). Death of King Zog in exile. **Kadare** finishes 'On the Edge of the Airport'; publishes *My Age: Poems*, 'The Nude', and 'The Emperor'. Collection of poems, *Lyrika* published in Moscow translated, and with a preface by David Samöilov.
1962	China is Albania's premier trading partner. Alexander Solzhenitsyn, *A Day in the Life of Ivan Denisovich*. **Kadare**: first trip outside the Eastern bloc, to Finland. Marriage to Helena. *The General of the Dead Army* published in two issues of *Zëri i Rinisë*; 'Days of Drink' written.
1963	**Kadare**: Novel version of *General of the Dead Army* published.

1964   January: state visit by Chou En-lai. Enver Hoxha warns against the survival of bourgeois elements and 'moral corruption'. 15 October: Khrushchev steps down, Brezhnev takes over as General Secretary. **Kadare**, 'On a Lost Train in the Winter Night', Fourth poetry collection, 'What are these mountains thinking about?'.

1965   March: Albania not invited to the international conference of communist parties in Moscow; Hoxha denounces the meeting as 'factional, separatist, and revisionist'. 20 April: *Zëri i popullit* accuses the Soviets of collaborating with imperialists to share the domination of the world. October: 15th plenum of the Party of Labour. Hoxha calls for 'socialist realism tinged with cultural nationalism'. **Kadare**: *The Monster* appears in a literary journal, is criticized and banned.

1966   February: Sinyavsky and Daniel trial and imprisonment in Soviet Union; protests of Moscow writers. March: China and Albania boycott the 23rd Congress of the Communist Party of the Soviet Union. April: Mehmet Shehu leads delegation to Beijing and in June Chou En-lai pays a return visit. Beginning of Albanian Cultural Revolution. November: 5th Congress of the Party of Labour. Fourth Five-year Plan (1966–70). **Kadare**: spends time in Berat, 1966–68.

1967   7 February: Hoxha launches the Albanian cultural revolution. 5th Congress of the Party of Labour: Hoxha announces that the period since the 4th Congress (1961) as the most difficult in the party's history, but claims significant increases in investment and output during the 3rd Five-Year plan (1961–65). November: private commerce prohibited; abolition of religion and of lawyers. **Kadare**: *The Southern City*, 'The Song', 'Prometheus', early version of *The Wedding*, entitled *The Drum-Skin* printed in *Nëntori*. Revised second version of *The General of the Dead Army* appears. Autumn: visits Hanoi (Vietnam) and China with writers' deputation.

1968   January: 500th anniversary of Scanderbeg; unveiling of monument in Scanderbeg Square. September: Albania withdraws from the Warsaw Treaty Organization, condemns Soviet occupation of Czechoslovakia. **Kadare**: *The Wedding* published in book form, 'Winter Season at the Cafe Riviera', 'She to whom Misfortune Occurs', *Solar Motifs: Poems*.

1969   Albania receives (Soviet-made) arms from China, in response to the presence of the Soviet fleet in the Mediterranean and the Warsaw Pact occupation of Czechoslovakia; missile bases are built with Chinese aid to defend the two main ports and the island of Sazan in the Pasha Limani inlet. Albanian separatist demonstrations in the Yugoslav autonomous province of Kosovo-Metohija. Individual income tax is abolished. June: 8th Plenum of the Central Committee. **Kadare**, 'That Something of Anna might Continue to Live', *The Castle*.

1970   Hoxha continues his stance against the 'two imperialist great powers', the USA and the Soviet Union. China grants a long-term, interest-free loan of one-fifth of Albania's annual revenue for the construction of thirty major industrial plants during the 5th Five-Year plan (1971–75). Hoxha begins to expand diplomatic, commercial, and cultural ties with Western Europe and Third World countries (until beginning of 1973 when a new freeze begins). **Kadare**: becomes 'Deputy' for Tirana in the Popular Assembly. *The General of the Dead Army* is published in France. First visit to Paris.

1971   Diplomatic ties resumed with Greece. Improvement in diplomatic relations with Yugoslavia. November: 6th Albanian Party of Labour conference; no Chinese delegation attends. 5th Five-Year Plan (1971–75). **Kadare**: visits Denmark and Sweden; autumn: spends a period in France. Completes *Autobiography of the People in Verse*, *Chronicle in Stone*. Begins *Winter of Great Solitude*. Revision of *The General of the Dead Army*.

1972   21 February: visit of Richard Nixon and official detente between USA and China. Execution of Roman Catholic priest, Fr. Stefan Kurti as a Vatican spy. 1st National Conference of the Albanian Institute of Folklore. Foundation of the Albanian Academy of Sciences. **Kadare** joins the Party. October: travels to Kosovo. Finishes *Winter of Great Solitude*.

1973   Purge of liberal party officials including Todi Lubonja and many leading figures of the Albanian Writers' Union (at the 4th Plenary Session of the Central committee on 26–28 June). Hoxha attacks behaviour and dress of young people. Willy Brandt (FRG) initiates 'Ostpolitik'. **Kadare**: *Winter of Great Solitude* is criticized.

1974   June: 4th Plenum; 18 June: Colonel-General Beqir Balluku purged. **Kadare**: 'The Red Pashas' sent to *Drita* and disappears (October). *November of a Capital* appears; begins *The Niche of Shame*.

1975   Continuing purges of conspirators and others in the regime. 6th Five-Year Plan (1975–80). **Kadare**: 24 October, self-criticism and condemnation to manual work in the Myzeqe; prohibition of novels. 31 December: death of Kadare's father.

1976   New constitution adopted. People's Socialist Republic of Albania becomes the official name of the country; the Party of Labour is the sole directing political power, and the First Secretary of the Central Committee is Commander-in-Chief of the Armed Forces as well as Chairman of the Defence Council. Abolition of private property, equal rights for both sexes, abolition of taxation of citizens, and elimination of religious foundations and formal declaration that the practice of religion is illegal. April: Discovery of revisionist plot aimed at sabotaging the Sino-Albanian friendship. September: death of Mao Tse-tung; moderates take control in China. October/November: 7th Party Congress: Hoxha announces less reliance on China in future; purges in the wake of discovery of a new plot among pro-Soviet senior officials. 6th Five-Year Plan (1976–80). **Kadare**: *The Niche of Shame*, *Twilight of the Steppe-Gods*, *Secular Chronicle of the Hankonis* completed; sixth poetry collection: *Time: Poems*.

1977   July: *Zëri i Popullit* castigates the 'three-worlds' theory invoked by Chinese leaders to justify better relations with the USA and the West. Hoxha is dissatisfied with shrinking Chinese aid. Purge of pro-Chinese officials. **Kadare**: *The Three-Arched Bridge* finished; publication of *The Great Winter* (2nd version).

1978   24 June: Albania supports North Vietnam (against China and Cambodia); 7 July: China ends aid to Albania; July: end of commercial ties; diplomatic ties are retained but all Chinese workers leave by August. Albanian students repatriated from China. Albania improves ties with Yugoslavia, which has become Albania's leading trading partner. October: first national folk festival, in Gjirokastra. *Kadare*: Publication in a single volume of *The Niche of Shame*, *The Three-Arched Bridge*, *The Twilight of the Steppe-Gods*. Publication in France of the first version of *Winter of Great Solitude*.

1979   Commemoration of 100th anniversary of Stalin's birth. September: death of Hysni Kapo, third-ranking member of the regime. **Kadare**: *Doruntine* finished.

1980   26 April: Mehmet Shehu relieved of duties as Minister of Defence, succeeded by Kadri Hazbiu (ex-Minister of the Interior). **Kadare**: *Doruntine* and *Broken April* published in a collection; *On the Songs of the Warriors* appears. Seventh collection of poems, *Smiles on the World*.

1981   March–May: Demonstrations in Kosovo; November: 8th Congress of the Albanian Party of Labour. 7th Five-Year Plan (1981–85). Shehu purged. 17 December: death of Shehu. **Kadare**: *The Palace of Dreams* published in book form and censured (September–November). The *Concert* submitted for publication under the title *Cold Blood*, wins a national literary prize, but is proscribed. Begins work on *The File on H.* and *The Marriage Procession Turned to Ice*.

1982   Adil Çarçani succeeds Mehmet Shehu as Premier. Ramiz Alia is made chief ideologist. Italian film crew arrives in Albania to begin *The General of the Dead Army*. 25–26 September: armed coup. November: death of Leonid Brezhnev. **Kadare**: denunciation of *The Palace of Dreams* and self-criticism at an open plenum of the Union of Writers (March). *The File on H* appears in *Nëntori*.

1983   Executions of 'spies' for Yugoslavia, the Soviet Union, and the USA, death of Kadri Hazbiu. **Kadare**: considers exile in France. Finishes *The Wedding Procession turned to Ice*, 'The Bearer of Bad Tidings'.

1984   Hoxha retreats into the background, to 'complete his memoirs'. Ramiz Alia runs affairs of state. **Kadare**: 'The Blinding Order', 'The Morgue'.

1985   10–11 April: Death of Enver Hoxha, aged 76; 13 April: Ramiz Alia elected by Central Committee as First Secretary of the Party. **Kadare**: *Clair de lune, Aeschylus or the Eternal Loser*, 'The Bringer of Dreams', 'Abolition of the Profession of Curser', 'Death of a Russian Woman', *The Black Year*. *The Black Year* is published in a collection with *The Wedding Procession Turned to Ice*.

1986   November: 9th Congress of the Albanian Party of Labour, reaffirmation of the ideals of Enver Hoxha. Ramiz Alia is re-elected and the new Central Committee chosen; the new thirteen-member Politburo elected. Opening of Shkoder–Titograd railway link. 8th Five-Year Plan (1986–90). **Kadare**: finishes *The Shadow, Agamemnon's Daughter, A Bird Flying South*, 'The Time of Love', 'The Great Book'.

1987   Signs of emergence from diplomatic isolation. **Kadare**: 'Good-Bye to Evil', 'Ballad on the Death of J.G.'.

1988   **Kadare** nominated to the Institut de France. *The Concert* appears; the first part of *The Pyramid*, 'Night of the Sphinx', 'The Hair-Do' written. *Aeschylus or the Great Loser* is published. Kadare appears on the French television interview series *Apostrophes*, hosted by Bernard Pivot.

1989   **Kadare** is nominated Vice-President of the Democratic Front. Writes the Preface to Tozaj's *The Knives*.

1990   Mid-year: first anti-government demonstrations. July: 11th Central Committee plenum results in cosmetic changes to the regime. December: Student protests escalate; multiparty elections scheduled for early 1991; the Albanian Democratic Party, the first legal opposition, is founded. Government indicates willingness to open diplomatic relations with the two arch-enemies, USA and Soviet Union. The communist conservatives regain the upper hand in Tirana. **Kadare**: revises *November of a Capital* to remove pro-Hoxha material; 25 October: leaves Albania and requests political refuge in France. The essay, 'The Eruption of Migjeni in Albanian Literature', 'Subterranean Passages', 'Before the Bath', *Invitation to the Writer's Studio* written; *The Pyramid* finished and published in *Nëntori*; December: *Albanian Spring* and *Conversations with Eric Faye* .

1991   February: Hoxha's statue is toppled. April: general strike and fall of the regime.

Government 'of national salvation' established. Albanian Party of Labour renamed Socialist Party of Albania. Food riots and exodus of refugees to Italy and Greece. June: 10th Congress of the PLA. **Kadare**: 'The Bringer of Dreams', 'Cousin of Angels', *The Weight of the Cross*.

1992   22 March: victory of the Albanian Democratic Party; 9 April: Sali Berisha becomes first post-war democratically elected president. 'Operation Pelican', Italian humanitarian aid programme. 6 May: **Kadare** returns to Albania after the election. *The Pyramid* appears.

1993   Ramiz Alia and Fatos Nano tried and convicted to prison sentences; Pope John Paul II visits in April, the first papal visit since 1464. **Kadare**: 'The Great Wall of China'. Fayard *Œuvres* edition commences in Albanian and French.

1994   **Kadare**: 'The Church of Saint-Sophia', *Dialogue with Alain Bosquet*.

1995   Albania is elected 36th member of the Council of Europe. Privatization and lowering of foreign debt. **Kadare**: 'The Eagle', 'The Theft of Royal Sleep'.

1996   26 May: Third post-communist parliamentary elections: Democratic Party gains control; USA gives $100 million aid. **Kadare**: becomes member of the Académie Française. Writes *Bad Season on Olympus*, *Spiritus*, 'Men's Beauty Contest in the Accursed Mountains'.

1997   February: collapse of the pyramid investment schemes; state of emergency, social dissolution, vigilante groups, and criminal gangs. Resignation of Democratic Party and national reconciliation government established. **Kadare**: *Time of Silver*.

1998   Imprisonment of corrupt members of Berisha's government on charges of crimes against humanity during 1997 unrest. 28 November: first post-communist constitution signed into law. Outbreaks of violence between Kosovo Liberation Army (UCK) and Serbian police and army. **Kadare**: *Three Elegies for Kosovo*.

1999   War in Kosovo; arrival of NATO troops in Kosovo. Albanian Kosovar refugees stream into Albania. Dispersal of criminal gangs. **Kadare**: *This Mourning was Necessary to Find Ourselves* (*Journal of the War in Kosovo*), 'Art as Sin'.

2000   European and US aid packages stabilize the economy. President Rexhep Meidani travels to Kosovo, stresses the importance of a Europe of regions versus a 'Greater Albania'. **Kadare**: 'Knight of the Falcon', 'History of the Albanian Writers' Union Reflected in a Woman's Mirror', *Spring Flowers, Spring Frost*.

2001   Ethnic conflict between Albania and Macedonia; June and July: Socialist Party gains an absolute majority in fourth democratic general elections.

2002   **Kadare**: *Life, Game and Death of Lul Mazrek*.

2003   **Kadare**: *The Successor*.

2004   **Kadare**: *A Climate of Madness*.

2005   **Kadare**: Shaban Sinani publishes *The Kadare File*; Kadare receives the inaugural International Man-Booker prize for Literature; *Dante, the Irremediable, or Brief History of Albania with Dante Alighieri*.

2006   **Kadare**: 'The European Identity of the Albanians'; *Hamlet, the Impossible Prince*.

2008   Independence of Kosovo. **Kadare**: *Accident*.

2009   **Kadare**: *One Dinner Too Many*.

BIBLIOGRAPHY

Works by Ismail Kadare

Agamemnon's Daughter, trans. from the French by David Bellos (Edinburgh: Canongate, 2007)

Albanian Spring: The Anatomy of Tyranny, trans. from the French by Emile Capouya (London: Saqi Books, 1995)

Albanie: Visage des Balkans, Écrits de lumière. Photographies de Pjetër, Kel et Gegë Marubi, trans. by Jusuf Vrioni, and Emmanuelle Zbynovsky (Paris: Arthaud, 1995)

Autobiographie du peuple en vers, trans. by Edmond Tupja and Pashuk Matia (Tirana: Editions '8 Nëntori', 1981)

Broken April, no trans. identified (London: Harvill, 1991)

Chronicle in Stone, trans. from the Albanian by Arshi Pipa, ed. by David Bellos (Edinburgh: Canongate, 2007)

Chronicle in Stone, trans. from the Albanian by Arshi Pipa (New York: New Amsterdam Books, 1987)

Chronik in Stein (Salzburg: Residenz Verlag, 1988)

Chronique de la ville de pierre, trans. by Jusuf Vrioni (Paris: Hachette, 1973)

Clair de lune, trans. by Jusuf Vrioni (Paris: Fayard, 1993)

Dante, l'incontournable, ou Brève histoire de l'Albanie avec Dante Alighieri, trans. by Tedi Papavrami (Paris: Fayard, 2006)

Das verflixte Jahr, trans. by Joachim Röhm (Zurich: Amman Verlag, 2005)

Der große Winter, no trans. identified [Giuseppe de Siati] (Kiel: Neuer Malik Verlag, 1987)

Der Schandkasten, trans. by Joachim Röhm (Salzburg: Residenz Verlag, 1990)

Der General der toten Armee, trans. Joachim Röhm (Frankfurt a.M.: Fischer, 2006)

Der zerrissene April, trans. by. Joachim Röhm (Zurich: Amman Verlag, 2001)

Dialogue avec Alain Bosquet, trans. by Jusuf Vrioni (Paris: Fayard, 1995)

Die Festung, trans. by Giuseppe de Siati (Kiel: Neuer Malik Verlag, 1988)

Die Schleierkarawane-Erzählungen, trans. by Oda Buchholz and Wilfried Fiedler (Kiel: Neuer Malik Verlag, 1989)

Doruntinas Heimkehr, trans. by. Joachim Röhm (Salzburg: Residenz Verlag, 1992)

Doruntine, trans. from the French by Jon Rothschild (Lanham, MD: New Amsterdam Books, 1988)

Entretiens avec Éric Faye en lisant en écrivant (Paris: José Corti, 1991)

Eschyle ou le grand perdant, trans. by Jusuf Vrioni and Alexandre Zotos (Paris: Fayard, 1988, 1995)

'Foreword', *Chansonnier Epique Albanais*, ed. by Qemal Haxhihasani, Luka Kolë, Alfred Uçi, Misto Treska, trans. by Kolë Luka (Tirana: Academie des Sciences de la RPS D'Albanie, Institut de Culture Populaire, 1983), 7–10

Froides fleurs d'avril, trans. by Jusuf Vrioni (Paris: Fayard, 2000)

Gjirokastër: La ville de pierre, trans. by Edmond Tupja, photographies d'Etienne Revault (Paris: Editions Michalon, 1997)

Hamlet, ou le prince impossible, trans. by Artan Kotro (Paris: Fayard, 2007)

Il a fallu ce deuil pour se retrouver: Journal de la guerre du Kosovo, trans. by Jusuf Vrioni (Paris: Fayard, 2000)

Invitation à l'atélier de l'écrivain, suivi de *Le poids de la croix*, trans. by Jusuf Vrioni (Paris: Fayard, 1991)

Invitation à un concert offiel, et autres récits, trans. by Jusuf Vrioni (Paris: Fayard, 1985)

Konzert am Ende des Winters, trans. by Joachim Röhm (Frankfurt a.M.: dtv, 1995)

La Fille d'Agamemnon, trans. by Tedi Papavrami (Paris: Fayard, 2003)

La Grande Muraille, suivi de *Le Firman aveugle*, trans. by Jusuf Vrioni (Paris: Fayard, 1993)

L'Aigle, trans. by Jusuf Vrioni (Paris: Fayard, 1996)

La Légende des Légendes (Paris: Flammarion, 1995)

La Niche de la honte, trans. by Jusuf Vrioni (Paris: Fayard, 1984)

L'Année noir, suivi de *Le Cortège de la noce s'est figé dans la glace*, trans. by Jusuf Vrioni and Alexandre Zotos (Paris: Fayard, 1987)

'La Vérité des souterrains', interview with Stéphane Courtois, in *Le Dossier Kadaré*, ed. by Shaban Sinani, trans. by Tedi Papavrami (Paris: Odile Jacob, 2006), 141–205

La Ville sans enseignes, trans. by Jusuf Vrioni (Paris: Fayard, 1996)

Le Concert, trans. by Jusuf Vrioni (Paris: Fayard, 1989)

Le Concours de beauté masculine (Paris: Stock, 1998)

Le Crépuscule des dieux de la steppe, trans. by Jusuf Vrioni (Paris: Fayard, 1981)

Le Dîner de trop (Paris: Fayard, 2009)

Le Firman aveugle, trans. by Jusuf Vrioni (Paris: Stock, 1997)

Le Firman aveugle et autres romans courts, trans. by Jusuf Vrioni and Alexandre Zotos (Paris: Fayard, 2007)

Le Général de l'armée morte, trans. by Jusuf Vrioni (Paris: Albin Michel, 1970)

Le Grand hiver, trans. by Jusuf Vrioni (Paris: Fayard, 1978)

Le Monstre, trans. by Jusuf Vrioni (Paris: Fayard, 1991)

'L'entretien d'Ismaïl Kadaré et d'Alain Bosquet', preface to Alain Bosquet, *Les Trente premières années* (Paris: Bernard Grasset, 1993)

L'Envol du migrateur: trois microromanes, trans. by Tedi Papavrami (Paris: Fayard, 2001)

Le Palais des rêves, trans. by Jusuf Vrioni (Paris: Fayard, 1990)

Le Pont aux trois arches, trans. by Jusuf Vrioni (Paris: Fayard, 1981)

Les Adieux du mal, trans. by Jusuf Vrioni (Paris: Stock, 1996)

'Les Couteaux, un roman marquant de la littérature albanaise', preface to Nexhat Tosaj (Tozaj), *Les Couteaux*, trans. by Loïc Chauvin (Paris: Denoël 1989), 9–15. First publ. *Drita*, 15 (October, 1989)

Les Tambours de la pluie, trans. by Jusuf Vrioni (Paris: Fayard, 1985)

Le Successeur, trans. by Tedi Papavrami (Paris: Fayard, 2003)

L'Hiver de la grande solitude, trans. by Jusuf Vrioni (Paris: Fayard, 1999)

'L'Irruption de Migjeni dans la littérature albanaise', Migjeni, *Chroniques d'une ville du Nord et autres proses*, trans. by Jusuf Vrioni (Paris: Fayard, 1990), 9–121

L'Ombre, trans. by Jusuf Vrioni (Paris: Fayard, 1994)

Lyrica (Moscow: Izdatelstvo Inostranoj Literaturi, 1961)

Mauvaise saison sur l'Olympe: Tragédie de Prométhée et d'un groupe de divinités en quatorze tableaux, trans. by Jusuf Vrioni (Paris: Fayard, 1998)

Novembre d'un capital, trans. by Jusuf Vrioni (Paris: Fayard, 1997)

Œuvres, ed. Erik Faye, 12 vols (Paris: Fayard, 1993–2004)

Poèmes 1957–1997 (Paris: Fayard, 1997)

Poèmes 1958–1988 (Paris: Fayard, 1989)

'Préface', Bashkim Shehu, *L'Automne de la peur*, trans. by Isabelle Joudrain-Musa (Paris: Fayard, 1993), 7–31

Printemps albanais: Chronique, lettres, réflexions, trans. by Michel Métais (Paris: Fayard, 1991)

Qui a ramené Doruntine, trans. by Jusuf Vrioni (Paris: Fayard, 1986)

Recits d'outre temps (Paris: Stock, 1995)

Spiritus: roman avec chaos, révélation, vestiges, trans. by Jusuf Vrioni (Paris: Fayard, 1996)

Spiritus, trans. by Joahim Röhm (Zurich: Amman, 2007)

Spring Flowers, Spring Frost, trans. from the French of Jusuf Vrioni by David Bellos (London: Harvill, 2002)

'Statement on Going into Exile, and Interview', *East European Reporter,* 4 (1990), 45

'Sur quelques-uns de mes livres', interview with Shusha Guppy, *L'Oeil de Boeuf,* 20 (May 2000), 69–71

'The Art of Fiction', interview with Shusha Guppy, *Paris Review,* 147 (1998), 194–217

The Castle, trans. by Pavil Qesku (Honolulu: University Press of the Pacific, 2002)

The Concert, trans. from the French of Jusuf Vrioni by Barbara Bray (London: Collins/ Harvill, 1994)

The File on H, trans. from the French by David Bellos (London: Harvill, 1997)

The General of the Dead Army, trans. from the French by Derek Coltman (London: Harvill, 1998)

The Palace of Dreams, trans. from the French of Jusuf Vrioni by Barbara Bray (London: Collins/Harvill, 1993)

The Pyramid, trans. from the French of Jusuf Vrioni by David Bellos in consultation with the author (New York: Vintage, 1998)

The Successor, trans. from the French of Tedi Papavrami by David Bellos (Edinburgh: Canongate, 2006)

The Three-Arched Bridge, trans. from the Albanian by John Hodgson (New York: Vintage, 1997)

The Wedding, trans. from the Albanian by Ali Cungu (Tirana: The 'Naim Frashëri' Publishing House, 1968)

Three Elegies for Kosovo, trans. Peter Constantine (London: Harvill, 2000)

Trois chantes funèbres pour le Kosovo, trans. by Jusuf Vrioni (Paris: Fayard, 1998)

'*Un climat de folie*' suivi de '*La Morgue*' et '*Jours de beuverie*', trans. by Tedi Papavrami (Paris: Fayard, 2005)

Vie, jeu et mort de Lul Mazrek, trans. Tedi Papavrami (Paris: Fayard, 2002)

(and Denis Fernandez-Récatala), *Les quatre interprètes* (Paris: Editions Stock, 2003)

(and Denis Fernandez-Récatala), *Temps barbares: De l'Albanie au Kosovo. Entretiens* (Paris: L'Archipel, 1999)

(and Gilles de Rapper), *L'Albanie entre la légende et l'histoire* (Arles: Actes Sud, 2004)

(and Noel Malcolm), '"In the Palace of Nightmares": An Exchange', *New York Review of Books,* 45.1 (January 15, 1998), 59–60

General Bibliography

AGOLLI, DRITËRO, *Splendeur et décadence du camarade Zulo* (Paris: Gallimard, 1990)

ALBINI, MARIA BRANDON, 'Poèmes chevaleresques des Albanais de Calabre', *Calabre* (Paris: B. Arthaud, 1957)

ALDCROFT, DEREK H., *Europe's Third World: The European Periphery in the Interwar Years* (Aldershot, Hants: Ashgate, 2006)

ALEXEYEVA, LUDMILLA, and PAUL GOLDBERG, *The Thaw Generation: Coming of Age in the Post-Stalin Era* (Boston: Little, Brown and Company, 1990)

AMERY, JULIAN, *Sons of the Eagle: A Study in Guerilla War* (London: Macmillan, 1948)

ARNASON, JOHANN P., 'Communism and Modernity', *Daedalus,* 129 (2000), 61–90

AUDOIR, JACQUES, and DAVID TEBOUL, *Ismail Kadaré* (Paris: Coproduction France 3, Tanguera Films, Klan TV, 1999)

AUGARDE, JACQUES, SIMONE DREYFUS, and EDMOND JOUVE, eds, *Ismaïl Kadaré, Gardien de*

Mémoire, Actes du 2e. colloque international francophone du Canton de Payrac organisé par l'Association des écrivains de langue française (A.D.E.L.F.) à Payrac (Lot) du 11 au 13 septembre 1992 (Paris: Sepeg International, 1993)

AUSTIN, ROBERT C., 'Greater Albania: The Albanian State and the Question of Kosovo, 1912–2001', in *Ideologies and National Identities: the Case of Twentieth-Century Southeastern Europe*, ed. by John R. Lampe, and Mark Mazower (Budapest: CEU Press, 2004), 235–53

BARTL, PETER, *Die albanischen Muslime zur Zeit der nationalen Unabhängigkeitsbewegung (1878–1912)*, Albanische Forschungen 8 (Wiesbaden: Otto Harrassowitz, 1968)

BELLOS, DAVID, 'The Englishing of Ismail Kadare: Notes of a Retranslator', *The Complete Review: A Literary Saloon and Site of Review*, 6.2 (May, 2005), http://www.complete-review.com/quarterly/vol6/issue2/ bellos.htm

BENINCASA, RINO, *Enver Hoxha, der Pharao des Sozialismus und der Söhne des albanischen Adlers* (Lengwil: PrismaPoint, 1995)

BIBÓ, ISTVÁN, *Die Misere der osteuropäischen Kleinstaaterei*, trans. by Béla Rásky (Frankfurt a.M.: Verlag neue Kritik, 1992)

——*Misère des petits états d'Europe de l'est* (Paris: Albin Michel, 1993)

BIHIKU, KOÇO, *Histoire de la littérature albanaise* (Tirana: Editions '8 Nëntori', 1980)

BISLIMI, MUZAFER. 'Balkan Peoples about Scanderbeg and his Uprising against the Ottoman Empire', *Acta Studia Albanica*, 1 (2005), 93–100

BLAND, WILLIAM B., *Albania*, World Bibliographical Series, vol. 94 (Oxford: Clio Press, 1988)

BORKENAU, FRANZ, *European Communism* (London: Faber & Faber, 1953)

BRIAN, JOSEPH D., 'Some Ancient Shared Metaphors in the Balkans', *Acta Studia Albanica*, 2 (2005), 43–46

BROWN, DEMING, *Soviet Russian Literature since Stalin* (Cambridge: Cambridge University Press, 1978)

BROWN, L. CARL., ed., *Imperial Legacy: The Ottoman Imprint on the Balkans and the Middle East* (New York: Columbia University Press, 1996)

BYRON, JANET, 'Albanian Folklore and History in the Fiction of Ismail Kadare: A Review of Two French Translations', *World Literature Today*, 58 (1984), 40–42

——'Albanian Nationalism and Socialism in the Fiction of Ismail Kadare', *World Literature Today*, 53 (1979), 614–16

BYRON, LORD [GEORGE GORDON], *The Major Works*, ed. by Jerome J. McGann (Oxford: Oxford University Press, 2000)

CABEJ, EQREM, *Sitten und Bräuche der Albaner*, Südost-Forschungen 25 (Munich, 1966)

CANAPE, MARIE-PAULE, 'L'Islam et la question des nationalités en Yougoslavie', *Radicalismes islamiques*, vol. 2, ed. by O. Carré and P. Dumont (Paris: L'Harmattan, 1986)

CASTELLAN, GEORGES, *L'Albanie* (Paris: PUF, 1980)

CHAMPSEIX, ÉLISABETH, and JEAN-PAUL CHAMPSEIX, *57 Boulevard Staline: Chroniques albanaises* (Paris: Éditions la Découverte, 1990)

——*L'Albanie ou la logique du désespoir* (Paris: Éditions la Découverte, 1992)

CHAMPSEIX, JEAN-PAUL, 'Communisme et tradition: un syncrétisme dévastateur', in Combe and Ditchev, eds, 53–61

——'Fétiches staliniens: tentative d'inventaire', in Combe and Ditchev, eds, 150–58

——'Itinéraire d'une œuvre inespérée', *L'Oeil de Boeuf*, 20 (May 2000), 39–48

——'Nouvelles albanaises', in Combe and Ditchev, eds, 176–90

CHRISTOFFERSON, MICHAEL SCOTT, *French Intellectuals against the Left: The Antitotalitarian Moment of the 1970s* (New York: Berghahn Books, 2004)

CLARK, KATERINA, *The Soviet Novel: History as Ritual*, 3rd edn (Bloomington: Indiana University Press, 2000)

CLAYER, NATHALIE, ed., *Religion et nation chez les Albanais, XIX–XXe siècles* (Istanbul: Isis, 2002)

COHEN, SHARI J., *Politics without a Past: The Absence of History in Postcommunist Nationalism* (Durham: Duke University Press, 1999)

COMBE, SONIA, 'Les victimes', in Combe and Ditchev, eds, 98–108

——AND IVALYO DITCHEV, EDS, *Albanie Utopie: Huis clos dans les Balkans* (Paris: Éditions Autrement, 1996)

CONQUEST, ROBERT, ed., *The Politics of Ideas in the USSR* (London: The Bodley Head, 1967)

COON, CARLETON S., *The Mountains of Giants: A Racial and Cultural Study of the North Albanian Mountain Ghegs*, Papers of the Peabody Museum of American Archaeology and Ethnology, vol. 3, no. 3 (Cambridge, Mass., 1950)

COSTA, NICOLAS J., *Albania: A European Enigma*, East European Monographs 413 (Boulder: East European Monographs; New York: dist. Columbia University Press, 1995)

COURTOIS, STÉPHANE, NICOLAS WERTH, JEAN-LOUIS PANNÉ ET AL., *Le livre noir du communisme: Crimes, terreur et répression* (Paris: Robert Laffont, 1997)

CUSACK, DYMPHNA, *Illyria Reborn* (London: Heinemann, 1966)

DAHRENDORF, RALF, *Versuchungen der Unfreiheit: Die Intellektuellen in Zeiten der Prüfung* (Munich: Beck, 2006)

DE WAAL, CLARISSA, *Albania Today: A Portrait of Post-Communist Turbulence* (London: I. B. Tauris, 2007)

DITCHEV, IVAYLO, 'D'Oncle Enver à Oncle Sam: les ruines de l'utopie', in Combe and Ditchev, eds, 28–39

DIUK, NADIA, and ADRIAN KARATNYCKY, *New Nations Rising: The Fall of the Soviets and the Challenge of Independence* (New York: John Wiley and Sons, 1993)

DJILAS, MILOVAN, *Conversations with Stalin* (London: Hart-Davis, 1962)

—— *The New Class* (London: Unwin Books, 1957)

DJUKIC, MIODRAG, *Anti-Yugoslav Pretensions of Enver Hoxha* (Belgrade: Tanjug News Agency, 1984)

DOJA, ALBERT, 'A Political History of Bektashism in Albania', *Totalitarian Movements and Political Religions*, 7 (2006), 83–107

DOMINIAN, LEON, *The Language Frontiers of Europe* (n.p.: Henry Holt and Company, 1917)

DRAPER, STARK, 'The Conceptualization of an Albanian Nation', *Ethnic and Racial Studies*, 20 (1997), 123–44

DUCELLIER, ALAIN, *L'Albanie entre Byzance et Venise, Xe–XVe siècles* (London: Variorum Reprints, 1987)

DURAND, CLAUDE, 'Note de l'éditeur', preface to Ismail Kadaré, *La Fille d'Agamemnon* (Paris: Fayard, 2003), 7–9

DURHAM, M. EDITH, *Albania and the Albanians: Selected Articles and Letters, 1903–1944*, ed. by Bejtullah Destani (London: I. B. Tauris, 2004)

—— *The Burden of the Balkans* (London: Thomas Nelson and Sons, n.d.)

—— *High Albania* (London: Phoenix Press, 2000)

EISENSTADT, S(amuel) N., 'The Breakdown of Communist Regimes and the Vicissitudes of Modernity', *Daedalus*, 121 (1992), 21–41

—— 'Multiple Modernities', *Daedalus*, 129 (2000), 1–29

—— *Tradition, Change and Modernity* (Malabar, Florida: Robert E. Krieger, 1983)

ELSIE, ROBERT, *A Dictionary of Albanian Religion, Mythology, and Folk Culture* (New York: New York University Press, 2001)

—— 'Albanian Literary History: A Communist Primer', in *History of the Literary Cultures of East-Central Europe: Junctures and Disjunctures in the 19th and 20th centuries*, ed. by Marcel Cornis-Pope and John Neubauer, 3 vols. (Amsterdam and Philadelphia: John Benjamins Publishing Co. 2004), III, 409–11

——'Altes und Neues zur Erforschung der albanischen Volksepik', http://www.kakanien. ac.at/beitr/fallstudie/RElsie1, 1–12–07

——*Dictionary of Albanian Literature* (Westport, Conn.: Greenwood Press, 1986)

——*Early Albania: A Reader of Historical Texts, 11th-17th centuries*, Balkanologische Veröffentlichungen, Bd. 39 (Wiesbaden: Otto Harrassowitz, 2003)

——'Enver Hoxha's Dictatorship Stifles Albanian Theater', in Cornis-Pope and Neubauer, III, 231–34

——'Evolution and Revolution in Modern Albanian Literature', *World Literature Today*, 65 (1991), 256–63

——*History of Albanian Literature*, 2 vols. (Boulder: Social Science Monographs; New York: Columbia University Press, 1995)

——'The Hybrid Soil of the Balkans: A Topography of Albanian Literature, in Cornis-Pope and Neubauer, II, 283–301

——'The National Role of the Albanian Literary Journals', in Cornis-Pope and Neubauer, III, 92–94

——'The Rediscovery of Folk Literature in Albania', in Cornis-Pope and Neubauer, III, 335–38

——'Rezeption albanischer Literatur im deutschen Sprachraum', *Aspekte der Albanologie*, Akten des Kongresses 'Stand und Aufgaben der Albanologie heute' 3–5 Oktober 1988, Universität zu Köln, ed. by Walter Breu, Rolk Ködderitzsch, and Hans-Jürgen Sasse, Balkanologische Veröffentlichungen, Bd. 18 (Wiesbaden: Harrassowitz, 1991)

——*Studies in Modern Albanian Literature and Culture* (Boulder: East European Monographs; New York: Columbia University Press, 1996)

——, ed., *Albanian Folktales and Legends* (Tirana: Shtëpia botuese 'Naim Frashëri', 1994)

——, ED. and TRANS., *An Elusive Eagle Soars: Anthology of Modern Albanian Poetry* (London and Boston: Forest Books, 1993)

ENTWISTLE, WILLIAM J., *European Balladry* (Oxford: Clarendon Press, 1939)

ERDEM, HAKAN, '"Perfidious Albanians" and "Zealous Governors": Ottomans, Albanians, and Turks in the Greek War of Independence', in *Ottoman Rule and the Balkans, 1760–1850: Conflict, Transformation, Adaptation*, Proceedings of an international conference held in Rthymno, Greece, 13–14 December 2003, ed. by Antonis Anastasopoulos and Elias Kolovos (Rethymno: University of Crete, 2007), 213–42

FAVEYRIAL, JEAN-CLAUDE, *Histoire de l'Albanie* (Peje: Dukagjini, 2001)

FAYE, ÉRIC, *Ismail Kadaré: Prométhée porte-feu* (Paris: Jose Corti, 1991)

——'Ismail Kadaré: Sphinx en hiver', in Combe and Ditchev, eds, 124–37

——'Souvenirs d'une autre Europe: Rencontres avec Ismail Kadaré à Tirana, avril 1990', *L'Oeuil de Bœuf*, 20 (May 2000), 19–28

——, ed., *Ismaïl Kadaré: Entretiens avec Eric Faye en lisant en écrivant* (Paris: Jose Corti, 1991)

FEHÉR, FERENC, 'The Social Character of Khrushchev's Regime', in *Eastern Left, Western Left: Totalitarianism, Freedom and Democracy*, ed. by Ferenc Fehér and Ágnes Heller (London: Polity, 1987), 77–103

FEHÉR, FERENC, ÀGNES HELLER, and GYÖRGY MARKUS, *Dictatorship over Needs* (Oxford: Basil Blackwell, 1983)

FIGES, ORLANDO, *Natasha's Dance: A Cultural History of Russia* (London: Penguin Books, 2003)

FISCHER, BERND J., *Albania at War 1939–1945* (West Lafayette: Purdue University Press, 1999)

——*King Zog and the Struggle for Stability in Albania* (Boulder: Westview Press, 1984)

FISHTA, GJERGJ, *The Highland Lute (Lahuta e Malcis): The Albanian National Epic*, trans. by Robert Elsie and Janice Mathie-Heck (London: I. B. Tauris/Centre for Albanian Studies, 2005)

FORTSON, BENJAMIN W., *Indo-European Language and Culture: An Introduction* (Oxford: Blackwell, 2004)

FOWKES, BEN, *The Disintegration of the Soviet Union: A Study in the Rise and Triumph of Nationalism* (New York: St. Martin's Press, 1997)

FRASHERI, KRISTO, 'À l'assaut du pouvoir', in Combe and Ditchev, eds, 42–52

GARTON ASH, TIMOTHY, *In Europe's Name: Germany and the Divided Continent* (London: Vintage, 1993)

GASHI, DARDAN, 'The House as a Popular Symbol of the Albanians', in Lubonja and Hodgson, eds, 113–18

GELLNER, ERNEST, *Nationalism* (London: Weidenfeld & Nicolson, 1997)

——*Nations and Nationalism* (Oxford: Blackwell, 1983)

GOETZ-STANKIEWICZ, MARKETA, ed., *Good-bye, Samizdat: Twenty Years of Czechoslovak Underground Writing* (Evanston, Il.: Northwestern University Press, 1992)

GREENE, MOLLY, 'The Ottoman Experience', *Daedalus*, 134 (2005), 88–99

GRIFFITH, WILLIAM, *Albania and the Sino-Soviet Rift* (Cambridge, Mass.: MIT Press, 1963)

GUT, CHRISTIAN, 'La vendetta dans le 'Kanun', in Combe and Ditchev, eds, 62–67

GUY, NICOLA C., 'Fixing the Frontiers? Ethnography, Power Politics and the Delimitation of Albania, 1912 to 1914', *Studies in Ethnicity and Nationalism*, 5 (2005), 27–49

HADAJ, GËZIM, 'Composantes stylistiques du '*Général de l'Armée morte*' d'Ismaïl Kadaré', *Les Lettres Albanaises*, 11 (1988), 201–08

HADJI-RISTIC, PETAR, 'Shaking Albania's Torpor: Young People Feel Betrayed by Leading Writer's Departure', *Index on Censorship*, 20 (1991), 10–11

HALL, DEREK, *Albania and the Albanians* (London: Pinter Reference, 1994)

HAROCHE, CHARLES, 'Gespräch mit Ismail Kadare', *Sinn und Form*, 42 (1990), 706–14

HAWKSWORTH, CELIA, MURIEL HEPPELL, and HARRY NORRIS, eds, *Religious Quest and National Identity in the Balkans* (Basingstoke: Palgrave, 2001)

HEINICH, NATHALIE, 'Les dimensions du territoire dans un roman d'Ismaïl Kadaré', *Sociologie et sociétés*, 34 (2002), 207–18

HELLER, AGNES, *Das Alltagsleben: Versuch einer Erklärung der individuellen Reproduktion*, ed. by Hans Joas (Frankfurt a.M.: Suhrkamp, 1978)

HOBHOUSE, JOHN [THE RIGHT HON. LORD BROUGHTON, G.C.B.], *Travels in Albania and Other Provinces of Turkey in 1809 and 1810*, 2 vols. (London: John Murray, 1855)

HOBSBAWM, ERIC JOHN, *Nations and Nationalism since 1780: Programme, Myth, Reality* (Cambridge: Cambridge University Press, 1990)

HOBSBAWM, ERIC JOHN, and TERENCE RANGER, *The Invention of Tradition* (Cambridge: Cambridge University Press, 1983)

HODGKINSON, HARRY, *Skanderbeg* (London: I. B. Taurus/Centre for Albanian Studies, 1999)

HOPPE, HANS-JOACHIM, 'Ismail Kadaré — ein regimetreuer Dissident? Porträt eines albanischen Schriftstellers', *Osteuropa*, 43 (1993), 988–91

HOSKING, GEOFFREY, *Beyond Socialist Realism: Soviet Fiction since Ivan Denisovich* (London: Grenada Publishing, 1980)

——'The Twentieth Century: In Search of New Ways, 1953–80', in *The Cambridge History of Russian Literature*, rev. edn, ed. by Charles A. Moser (Cambridge: Cambridge University Press, 1992), 520–94

HOXHA, ENVER, *The Artful Albanian: Memoirs of Enver Hoxha*, ed. Jon Halliday (London: Chatto & Windus, 1986)

——'The Further Revolutionization of the Party and the State', speech delivered at the joint meeting of the basic party organizations of the Kërraba coal mine, the 'Enver' plant, the 'Wilhelm Pieck' agricultural cooperative, the army detachment No. 5009 and the University of Tirana, 6 February 1957, *Selected Works*, IV (Tirana: Nëntori Publishing House, 1982), 209–21

—— *The Khrushchevites: Memoirs* (Tirana: S Nentori Publishing House, 1980)

—— 'Literature and the Arts Should Serve to Temper People with Class Consciousness for the Construction of Socialism', closing speech delivered at the 15th Plenum of the CC of the PLA, 26 October 1965, *Selected Works*, III: *1960–1965* (Tirana: Nëntori Publishing House, 1980), 832–59

—— *Reflections on China*, 2 vols. (Tirana: Nentori Publishing House, 1979)

—— *Reflections on the Middle East* (Tirana: Nentori Publishing House, 1984)

—— *Selected Works*, I: *1941–1948* (Tirana: Nentori Publishing House, 1974)

—— *Selected Works*, II: *1948–1960* (Tirana: Nentori Publishing House, 1975)

—— *Selected Works*, III: *1960–1965* (Tirana: Nentori Publishing House, 1980)

—— *Selected Works*, IV: *1966–1975* (Tirana: Nentori Publishing House, 1982)

—— *Selected Works*, V: *1976–1980* (Tirana: Nentori Publishing House, 1985)

—— *Selected Works*, VI: *1980–1984* (Tirana: Nentori Publishing House, 1987)

—— *The Titoites* (Tirana: Nentori Publishing House, 1982)

—— *With Stalin* (Tirana: Nentori Publishing House, 1979)

HUPCHICK, DENNIS, *Culture and History in Eastern Europe* (New York: St. Martin's Press, 1994)

JACQUES, EDWIN E., *The Albanians: An Ethnic History from Prehistoric Times to the Present* (Jefferson, N.C.: McFarland & Co., 1995)

JAMES, C. VAUGHAN, *Soviet Socialist Realism: Origins and Theory* (London: Macmillan, 1973)

JANDOT, GABRIEL, *L'Albanie d'Enver Hoxha, 1944–1985* (Paris: L'Harmattan, 1994)

JELAVICH, BARBARA, *History of the Balkans*, I: *Eighteenth and Nineteenth Centuries*; II: *Twentieth Century* (Cambridge: Cambridge University Press, 1983)

—— *The Ottoman Empire, the Great Powers, and the Straits Question 1870–1887* (Bloomingon: Indiana University Press, 1973)

—— *The Establishment of the Balkan National States, 1804–1920* (Seattle: University of Washington Press, 1977)

JONES, POLLY, 'From Stalinism to Post-Stalinism: De-Mythologising Stalin, 1953–56', *Totalitarian Movements and Political Religions*, 4 (2003), 127–48

JOUVE, EDMOND, 'Ismail Kadaré et ses paysages intérieurs', in *Ismaïl Kadaré, Gardien de Mémoire*, ed. Jacques Augarde, Simone Dreyfus, and Edmond Jouve (Paris: Sepeg International, 1993), 147–72

JOWITT, KEN, *New World Disorder: The Leninist Extinction* (Berkeley: University of California Press, 1992)

—— *Revolutionary Breakthroughs and National Development: The Case of Romania 1944–1965* (Berkeley: University of California Press, 1971)

JUNG, CHANG, and JON HALLIDAY, *Mao: The Unknown Story* (London: Vintage, 2006)

KAMUSELLA, TOMASZ D. I., 'Language as an Instrument of Nationalism in Central Europe', *Nations and Nationalism*, 7 (2001), 235–51

Kanun, Der: Das albanische Gewohnheitsrecht nach dem sogenannten Kanun des Lekë Dukagjini, kodifiziert von Shtjefën Gjeçovi, trans. by Marie Amelie Freiin von Godin, ed. by Robert Elsie (Pejë: Dukagjini Publishing, 2001)

KARPAT, KEMAL H., 'Millets and Nationality: The Roots of the Incongruity of Nation and State in the Post-Ottoman Era', in *Christians and Jews in the Ottoman Empire: The Functioning of a Plural Society*, I: *The Central Lands*, ed. by Benjamin Braude and Bernard Lewis (New York: Holmes & Meier, 1982), 141–70

KEEP, JOHN, 'Redefining Stalinism: Recent Western Views of Stalin's Russia: Social and Cultural Aspects', *Totalitarian Movements and Political Religions*, 4 (2003), 149–66

KLOSI, ARDIAN, 'Kadare's Politics of Literature', *Albanica*, 2 (1991), 163–66

KLOSI, ARDIAN, 'La littérature albanaise après 1945', in *Prosateurs et Poètes d'Albanie et du Kosovo*, ed. by Christiane Montéco, and Alexandre Zotos, *La main de singe* 17 (1995), 106–14

——*Mythologie am Werk: Kazantzakis, Andrić, Kadare: Eine vergleichende Untersuchung am besonderen Beispiel des Bauopfermotivs*, Slavische Beiträge 277 (Munich: Verlag Otto Sagner, 1991)

KOLA, PAULIN, *The Search for Greater Albania* (London: Hurst, 2003)

KONRÁD, GYÖRGY, and IVÁN SZELÉNYI, *Die Intelligenz auf dem Weg zur Klassenmacht* (Frankfurt a.M.: Suhrkamp, 1978)

KORNAI, JÁNOS, *The Socialist System: The Political Economy of Communism* (Princeton: Princeton University Press 1992)

KORT, MICHAEL, *The Soviet Colossus: A History of the USSR*, 2nd edn (London: Routledge, 1992)

KUZMIC, TATIANA, 'Childe Harold's Pilgrimage in the Balkans', *Comparative Critical Studies*, 4 (2007), 51–65

LALLEMANT, PHILIPPE dir. *La Marche du Siècle: Edgar Morin: Un Homme curieux de son temps*, Round-table interview with Ismail Kadare et al. (Paris: Fr3/France Inter, 1991)

LAMBERTZ, MAXIMILIAN, *Albanische Märchen und andere Texte zur albanischen Volkskunde*, Schriften der Balkankommission, Linguistische Abteilung 12 (Vienna: Wiener Akademie der Sprachwissenschaft, 1922)

——'Die Volksepik der Albaner', *Wissenschaftliche Zeitschrift der Karl Marx Universität, Leipzig*, vol. 4 (1954–55), 243–89 and 439–70

—— *Volkspoesie der Albaner: Eine einführende Studie, Zur Kunde der Balkanhalbinsel* (Sarajevo: n.p., n.d)

LAMPE, JOHN R., and MARK MAZOWER, *Ideologies and National Identities: The Case of Twentieth-Century Southeastern Europe*, Budapest: Central European University Press, 2004)

LHOMEL, ÉDITH, 'Le défi de l'autarcie économique', in Combe and Ditchev, eds, 68–77

LLOSHI, XHEVAT, 'Albania', *Handbuch der Südosteuropa-Linguistik*, ed. by Uwe Hinrichs (Wiesbaden: Harrassowitz Verlag, 1999), 277–99

LOEWENSTEIN KARL E., 'Ideology and Ritual: How Stalinist Rituals Shaped the Thaw in the USSR, 1953–4', *Totalitarian Movements and Political Religions*, 8 (2007), 93–114

LOSEFF, LEV, *On the Beneficence of Censorship: Aesopian Language in Modern Russian Literature*, Arbeiten und Texte zur Slavistik (Schuylkill Haven, PA: Hermitage, 1985)

LUBONJA, FATOS T., 'Albanian Culture and Pilot Fish, editorial', in Lubonja and Hodgson, eds, eds, 33–40

——'Between the Glory of a Virtual World and the Misery of a Real World', in *Albanian Identities: Myth and History*, ed. by Stephanie Schwandner-Sievers and Bernd J. Fischer (Bloomington: Indiana University Press, 2002), 91–103

——'Courage and the Terror of Death', *Social Research*, 71 (2004), 117–34

——'Kadare's Work too must be Judged in the Light of the Truth', in Lubonja and Hodgson, eds, 49–53

——'Pyramids of Slime, editorial', in Lubonja and Hodgson, eds, 83–92

LUBONJA, FATOS T., and JOHN HODGSON, eds, *Perpjekja/Endeavour: Writing From Albania's Critical Quarterly* (Tirana: Botime Përpjekja, 1997)

LUKÁCS, GEORG, *The Historical Novel*, trans. by Hannah and Stanley Mitchell (London: Merlin Press, 1962)

LUKÁCS, GEORG, *Solzhenitsyn*, trans. by William David Graf (London: Merlin Press, 1970)

M'RAIHI, MARIAM, *Ismaïl Kadaré: ou l'inspiration prométhéenne* (Paris: L'Harmattan, 2004)

McCAULEY, MARY, *Soviet Politics 1917–1991* (Oxford: Oxford University Press, 1992)

McDERMOTT, KEVIN, 'Archives, Power and the "Cultural Turn": Reflections on Stalin and Stalinism', *Totalitarian Movements and Political Religions*, 5 (2004), 5–24

MALCOLM, NOEL, 'Crypto-Christianity and Religious Amphibianism in the Ottoman Balkans: The Case of Kosovo', in *Religious Quest and National Identity in the Balkans*, ed. by Celia Hawksworth, Muriel Heppell, and Harry Norris (Basingstoke: Palgrave, 2001), 91–109

——'In the Palace of Nightmares', *New York Review of Books*, 44.17 (6 November 1997), 21–24

——*Kosovo: A Short History* (New York: Harper Collins, 1999)

MARCO, COSTANTINO, 'Nationalism and Art' (1995), in Lubonja and Hodgson, eds, 41–44

MARMULLAKU, RAMADAN, *Albania and the Albanians* (London: C. Hurst, 1975)

MATARD-BONUCCI, MARIE-ANNE, and PIERRE MILZA, *L'Homme Nouveau dans l'Europe fasciste, 1922–1945: entre dictature et totalitarisme* (Paris: Fayard, 2004)

MATTHEWS, RONALD, *Sons of the Eagle: Wanderings in Albania* (London: Methuen & Co., 1937)

MEDVEDEV, ROY A., and ZHORES A. MEDVEDEV, *Khrushchev: The Years in Power* (Oxford: Oxford University Press, 1977)

MEGAS, GEORGIOS A., *Die Ballade von der Arta-Brücke: Eine vergleichende Untersuchung* (Thessaloniki: Institute for Balkan Studies, 1976)

MÉTAIS, MICHEL, ED. and TRANS., *Ismaïl Kadaré et la nouvelle poésie albanaise* (Paris: Pierre Jean Oswald, 1973)

MIGJENI [MILLOSH GJERGJ NIKOLLA], *Chroniques d'une ville du nord* (Paris: Fayard, 1990)

——*Free Verse*, trans. by Robert Elsie (Pejë: Kukaghini Publishing House, 2001)

MISHA, PIRO, 'Invention of a Nationalism: Myth and Amnesia', in *Albanian Identities: Myth and History*, ed. by Stephanie Schwandner-Sievers and Bernd J. Fischer (Bloomington: Indiana University Press, 2002), 33–48

MITCHELL, ANNE-MARIE, *Ismail Kadaré: Le rhapsode albanais* (Marseille: Le temps parallèle, 1990)

MITTERRAND, FRÉDÉRIC, and THÉRÈSE LOMBARD, *Du côté de chez Fred*, Interview with Ismail Kadare (Paris: Antenne 2, 1990)

MORGAN, PETER, 'Ancient Names . . . Marked by Fate: Ethnicity and The "Man without Qualities"', in Ismail Kadare's *Palace of Dreams, The European Legacy*, 7 (2002), 45–60, repr. in *Contemporary Literary Criticism*, cxc, ed. Tom Burns and Jeffrey W. Hunter (Detroit: Thomson Gale, 2004), pp. 141–51

——'Between Albanian Identity and Imperial Politics: Ismail Kadare's *The Palace of Dreams*', *The Modern Language Review*, 97 (2002), 365–79, repr. in *Contemporary Literary Criticism*, cxc, ed. by Tom Burns and Jeffrey W. Hunter (Detroit: Thomson Gale, 2004), pp. 152–62

——'Ismail Kadare: Modern Homer or Albanian Dissident?', *World Literature Today*, 80 (September–October 2006), 7–11

MOSELEY, RAY, *Mussolini's Shadow: The Double Life of Count Galeazzo Ciano* (New Haven: Yale University Press, 1999)

MOSER, CHARLES A., ed., *The Cambridge History of Russian Literature*, rev. edn (Cambridge: Cambridge University Press, 1992)

MUSTAFAJ, BESNIK, *Albanien: Zwischen Verbrechen und Schein*, trans. by Joachim Röhm (Frankfurt a.M.: Frankfurter Verlagsanstalt, 1997)

NANDRIS, JOHN, 'Prolegomenon to Religion in the Balkans', in *Religious Quest and National Identity in the Balkans*, ed. by Celia Hawksworth, Muriel Heppell, and Harry Norris (Basingstoke: Palgrave, 2001), pp. 19–36

NORRIS, H[ARRY] T[HIRWALL], *Islam in the Balkans: Religion and Society between Europe and the Arab World* (London: Hurst & Company, 1993)

——*Popular Sufism in Eastern Europe: Sufi Brotherhoods and the Dialogue with Christianity and 'Heterodoxy'* (London: Routledge, 2006)

NORTON, JOHN, 'The Bektashis in the Balkans', in *Religious Quest and National Identity in the Balkans*, ed. by Celia Hawksworth, Muriel Heppell, and Harry Norris (Basingstoke: Palgrave, 2001), 168–99

O'DONNELL, JAMES S., *A Coming of Age: Albania under Enver Hoxha* (Boulder: Eastern European Monographs; New York, Columbia University Press, 1999)

PANO, NICHOLAS C., 'Albania: The Last Bastion of Stalinism', in *East Central Europe: Yesterday, Today, Tomorrow*, ed. by Milorad M. Drachkovitch (Stanford: Hoover Institution, 1982), 187–218

—— 'The Albanian Cultural Revolution', *Problems of Communism*, 23 (1974), 44–57

PAPLEKA, NDOC, 'Paralleles Balkaniques du Mythe d'Œdipe', *Acta Studia Albanica*, 1 (2005), 115–28

PARRY, MILMAN, and ALBERT BATES LORD, eds and trans., *Serbocroatian Heroic Songs* (Belgrade and Cambridge, Mass.: Serbian Academy of Sciences and Harvard University Press, 1954)

PASTERNAK, EVGENY, *Boris Pasternak: The Tragic Years 1930–60*, trans. Michael Duncan (London: Collins Harvill, 1991)

PEARSON, OWEN, *Albania in the 20th Century*, I: *Albania and King Zog: 1900–1939*; II: *Albania in Occupation and War: 1939–1945*; vol. III: *Albania in Dictatorship and Democracy: 1945–1999* (London: I. B. Tauris/Centre for Albanian Studies, 2006)

PIPA, ARSHI, 'The Adventure of Albania's Young Turks', *Telos*, 92 (1992), 99–106

—— *Albanian Stalinism: Ideo-Political Aspects*, East European Monographs 187 (Boulder: East European Monographs; New York: Columbia University Press, 1990)

—— 'Concerning a Novel on the Albanian State Security Agency', *Albanica*, 2 (1991), 156–62

—— 'Conformisme et subversion: Le double jeu de Kadare', *Autre Europe*, 24.5 (1992), 138–51

—— *Contemporary Albanian Literature*, East European Monographs 305 (Boulder: East European Monographs; New York: Columbia University Press, 1991)

—— 'The Political Culture of Hoxha's Albania', in *The Stalinist Legacy: Its Impact on Twentieth-Century World Politics*, ed. by Tariq Ali (London: Penguin, 1984), 435–64

—— *The Politics of Language in Socialist Albania*, East European Monographs 271 (Boulder: East European Monographs; New York: Columbia University Press, 1989)

—— 'Subversion vs. Conformism: The Kadare Phenomenon', *Telos*, 73 (1987), 47–77

POGGIOLINI, ILARIA, 'Translating Memories of War and Co-Belligerancy into Politics: The Italian Post-War Experience', in *Memory and Power in Post-War Europe: Studies in the Presence of the Past*, ed. by Jan-Werner Müller (Cambridge: Cambridge University Press, 2002), 223–43

POLLO, STEFANAQ, and ARBEN PUTO, with the collaboration of KRISTO FRASHERI and SKËNDER ANAMALI, *The History of Albania from its Origins to the Present Day* (London: Routledge and Kegan Paul, 1981)

PRIFTI, PETER R., *Land of Albanians: A Crossroads of Pain and Pride* (Tirane: Horizont, 2002)

—— *Remote Albania: The Politics of Isolation* (Tirana: Onufri, 1999)

—— *Socialist Albania since 1944: Domestic and Foreign Developments* (Cambridge, Mass.: MIT Press, 1978)

QOSJA, REXHEP, 'A Critical Spirit or Critical Exemplars', in Lubonja and Hodgson, eds, 31–32

RAMA, EDI, 'The Vote against the Constitution', in Lubonja and Hodgson, eds, 72–75

RAMA, LUAN, *Le long chemin sous le tunnel de Platon* (Paris: Edition du Petit Véhicule, 1999)

RANCE, DIDIER, *Albanie: Ils ont voulu tuer dieu: La persecution contre l'Église catholique, 1944–1991* (Paris: Aide à l'Église en Détresse, n.d.)

RAPP, BERNARD, *Caractères: Engagement* (Caracteres no. 25), Interview with Ismail Kadare (*Printemps Albanais*), Marie Gautheron (*L'honneur*), Gilles Plazy, (editor/biographer of Vercors), Bernhard-Henri Lévy (*Les aventures de la liberté*) (Paris: France Antenne 2, 1991)

RAPPER, GILLES DE, 'Espace et religion: Chrétiens et musulmans en Albanie du Sud', *Etudes balkaniques*, Cahiers Pierre Belon, 9 (2002), 17–39

ROSELLI, ALESSANDRO, *Italia e Albania: relazioni finanziarie nel ventennio fascista* (Bologna: Il Mulino, 1986)

——and M. KASER, *Italy and Albania: Financial Relations in the Fascist Period* (London: I. B. Tauris, 2006)

ROTHSCHILD, JOSEPH, *East Central Europe between the Two World Wars* (Seattle: University of Washington Press, 1974)

RUSS, WOLFGANG, *Der Entwicklungsweg Albaniens: Ein Beitrag zum Konzept autozentrierter Entwicklung* (Meisenheim: A. Haim, 1979)

SAKO, ZIHNI, *The Albanian Entombment and the other common Balkan Different Versions: Questions of the Albanian Folklore* (Tirana, n.d.), 155–65

SAMOÏLOV, DAVID SAMIOULOVITCH, *Pour Mémoire* (Paris: Fayard, 1997)

SCHIRÒ, GIUSEPPE, 'Die Literatur im heutigen Albanien', *Wissenschafttlicher Dienst Südosteuropa*, VI, 5/6 (May–June 1957), 90–91

——*Storia della Letteratura Albanese* (Milan: Nuova Accademia Editrice, [1959])

SCHNYTZER, ADI, 'The Socialist People's Republic of Albania', *The New Communist Third World*, ed. by Peter Wiles (New York: St. Martin's Press, 1982)

SCHREIBER, THOMAS, *Enver Hodja: Le sultan rouge* (Paris: J.-C. Lattès, 1994)

SCHWANDNER-SIEVERS, STEPHANIE, ' "The Enactment of 'Tradition' ": Albanian Constructions of Identity, Violence and Power in Times of Crisis', in *Anthropology of Violence and Conflict*, ed. by Bettina E. Schmidt and Ingo W. Schröder (London: Routledge, 2001), 97–120

SCHWANDNER-SIEVERS, STEPHANIE, and BERND J. FISCHER, EDS, *Albanian Identities: Myth and History* (Bloomington: Indiana University Press, 2002)

SEGEL, HAROLD B., *The Columbia Guide to the Literatures of Eastern Europe since 1945* (New York: Columbia University Press, 2002)

SHAW, STANFORD J., *History of the Ottoman Empire and Modern Turkey*, 2 vols. (Cambridge: Cambridge University Press, 1976–77)

SHEHU, BASHKIM, *L'Automne de la peur*, trans. by Isabelle Joudrain-Musa (Paris: Fayard, 1993)

——'La Cité interdite', in Combe and Ditchev, 159–66

——'Criticism as Rational Judgement and Angry Strokes of the Pen', in Lubonja and Hodgson, eds, 45–48

ŠIKLOVÁ, JIŘINA, 'The "Gray Zone" and the Future of Dissent in Czechoslovakia', in Goetz-Stankiewicz, Marketa, ed., *Good-bye, Samizdat: Twenty Years of Czechoslovak Underground Writing* (Evanston, Il.: Northwestern University Press, 1992), 181–93

SIL, RUDRA, and MARC MORJÉ HOWARD, 'Introduction: Ken Jowitt's Universe', in *World Order after Leninism: Essays in Honour of Ken Jowitt*, ed. Vladimir Tismaneanu, Marc Morjé Howard, and Rudra Sil (Seattle: University of Washington Press, 2006), 3–18

SINANI, SHABAN, *Le Dossier Kadaré*, suivi de *La Vérité des souterrains, Ismaïl Kadaré avec Stéphane Courtois*, trans. by Tedi Papavrami (Paris: Odile Jacob. 2006)

SINETY, PAUL DE, 'Entretien avec Claude Durand', *L'Oeil de Boeuf*, 20 (May 2000), 29–34

——and JEAN-LUC TINGAUD, 'Entretien avec Ismail Kadare', *L'Oeil de Boeuf*, 20 (May 2000), 7–16

SKENDI, STAVRO, *Albania* (London: Atlantic Press, 1957)

——*Albanian and South Slav Oral Epic Poetry*, Memoirs of the American Folklore Society 44 (Philadelphia: American Folklore Society, 1954; New York: Kraus Reprint Co., 1969)

——*The Albanian National Awakening, 1878–1912* (Princeton, NJ: Princeton University Press, 1967)

——'The Millet System and its Contribution to the Blurring of Orthodox National Identity in Albania', *Christians and Jews in the Ottoman Empire: The Functioning of a Plural Society*, I: *The Central Lands*, ed. by Benjamin Braude and Bernard Lewis (New York: Holmes & Meier, 1982), 243–57

——*Skenderbeg and Albanian National Consciousness*, Südost-Forschungen 27 (Munich: Oldenbourg, 1968)

SMILEY, DAVID, *Albanian Assignment* (London: Chatto & Windus, 1984)

SMITH, ANTHONY D., *The Ethnic Origins of Nations* (Oxford: Blackwell, 1986)

——*National Identity* (London: Penguin, 1991)

SMITH, GRAHAM, ed., *The Nationalities Question in the Soviet Union* (London: Longman, 1990)

SOULÉ, VÉRONIQUE, 'Envoyée spéciale au Pays des Aigles', in Combe and Ditchev, 191–98

STAVRIANOS, L. S., 'Antecedents to the Balkan Revolutions of the Nineteenth Century', *Journal of Modern History*, 29 (1957), 335–48

SUGAR, PETER F., *Southeastern Europe under Ottoman rule, 1354–1804* (Seattle: University of Washington Press, 1977)

SUGARMAN, JANE C., 'Imagining the Homeland: Poetry, Songs, and the Discourses of Albanian Nationalism', *Ethnomusicology*, 43 (1999), 419–58

SUNY, RONALD GRIGOR, *The Revenge of the Past: Nationalism, Revolution and the Collapse of the Soviet Union* (Stanford: Stanford University Press, 1993)

SVIRSKI, GRIGORI, *Écrivains de la liberté: La résistance littéraire en Union Soviétique depuis la guerre*, trans. by Daria Olivier (Paris: Gallimard, 1981)

SWAYZE, HAROLD, *Political Control of Literature in the USSR, 1946–1959* (Cambridge: Harvard University Press, 1962)

SWIRE, JOSEPH, *Albania: The Rise of a Kingdom* (London: Williams & Norgate, 1929)

SZÜCS, JENÖ, *Die drei historischen Regionen Europas* (Frankfurt a.M.: Verlag Neue Kritik, 1994)

TERPAN, FABIENNE, *Ismail Kadaré* (Paris: Edition universitaires, 1992)

TERRAS, VICTOR, 'The Twentieth Century: The Era of Socialist Realism, 1925–1953', in *The Cambridge History of Russian Literature*, ed. by Charles A. Moser, rev. edn (Cambridge: Cambridge University Press, 1992), 458–519

TILMAN, H. W., *When Men and Mountains Meet* (Cambridge: Cambridge University Press, 1946)

TISMANEANU, VLADIMIR, 'Lenin's Century: Bolshevism, Marxism, and the Russian Tradition', in *World Order after Leninism: Essays in Honour of Ken Jowitt*, ed. by Vladimir Tismaneanu, Marc Morjé Howard, and Rudra Sil (Seattle: University of Washington Press, 2006), 19–33

TODOROVA, M. N., *Balkan Identities: Nation and Memory* (New York: New York University Press. 2004)

TOMES, J., *King Zog of Albania: Europe's Self-Made Muslim King* (New York: New York University Press, 2004)

TÖNNES, BERNHARD, *Sonderfall Albanien: Enver Hoxhas 'eigener Weg' und die historischen Ursprünge seiner Ideologie*, Untersuchungen zur Gegenwartskunde Südosteuropas 16 (Munich: Oldenbourg, 1980)

TUPJA, EDMOND, 'Le 'divorce politique', in Combe and Ditchev, 138–47

TVARDOVSKY, ALEXANDER, *Tyorkin and the Stovemakers*, trans. Anthony Rudolf (Cheadle, Cheshire: Carcanet Press, 1974)

VELO, MAX, *Le Commerce des jours: Nouvelles albanaises*, preface by Ismail Kadaré (Vijon: Lampsaque, 1998)

——*La Disparition des 'Pachas rouges' d'Ismail Kadaré: Enquête sur un 'crime littéraire'*, trans. by Tedi Papavrami (Paris: Fayard, 2004)

VICKERS, MIRANDA, *The Albanians: A Modern History* (London: I. B. Tauris, 1999)

VICKERS, MIRANDA, and JAMES PETTIFER, *Albania: From Anarchy to a Balkan Identity* (London: Hurst, 1997)

——*The Albanian Question: Igniting the Balkans* (London: I. B. Tauris, 2005)

VOSLENSKY, MICHAEL S., *Nomenklatura: Die herrschende Klasse der Sowjetunion in Geschichte und Gegenwart*, foreword by Milovan Djilas (München: Nymphenburger, 1987)

VRIONI, JUSUF, *Mondes Effacés: Souvenirs d'un Européen* (Paris: Jean-Claude Lattès. 2001)

WHITAKER, IAN, 'Familial Roles in the Extended Patrilineal Kin-Group in Northern Albania', in *Mediterranean Family Structures*, ed. by J. G. Peristiany (Cambridge: Cambridge University Press, 1976), 195–203

—— 'Tribal Structure and National Politics in Albania, 1910–1950', in *History and Social Anthropology*, ed. by I. M. Lewis, A.S.A. Monographs 7 (London: Tavistock, 1968), 253–93

WHITBY, MICHAEL, 'The Late Roman Army and the Defence of the Balkans', in *The Transition to Late Antiquity: On the Danube and Beyond*, ed. by. A. G. Poulter (Oxford: Oxford University Press, 2007), 135–61

WHITE, ANNE, 'Kosovo, Ethnic identity and "Border Crossings" in the *The File on H* and other novels by Ismail Kadare', in *Border Crossings: Mapping Identities in Modern Europe*, ed. by Peter Wagstaff (Berne: Peter Lang, 2004), 23–53

WILKES, JOHN, *The Illyrians* (Oxford: Blackwell, 1992)

WINNIFRITH, TOM. J., *Badlands–Borderlands: A History of Southern Albania/Northern Epirus* (London: Duckworth. 2003)

——, ed., *Perspectives on Albania* (London: Macmillan, 1992)

WITTROCK, BJÖRN, 'Modernity: One, None, or Many? European Origins and Modernity as a Global Condition', *Daedalus*, 129 (2000), 31–60

XANTHAKOU, MARGARITA, 'Le voyage du frère mort ou le mariage qui tue', *Etudes rurales*, 1997/98, 153–89

ZIMMERMANN, ZORA DEVRNJA, 'Moral Vision in the Serbian Folk Epic: The Foundation Sacrifice of Skadar', *Slavic and East European Journal*, 23 (1979), 317–80

ZOTOS, ALEXANDRE, *De Scanderbeg à Ismaïl Kadaré: Propos d'histoire et de littérature albanaises* (Saint-Etienne: Publications de l'Université de Saint-Etienne, 1997)

INDEX

The English titles of Kadare's works are used throughout;
see pp. xi-xiii for corresponding French and Albanian titles.
References to illustrations are italicized.